ONIONS ARE MY HUSBAND

ONIONS ARE MY HUSBAND

Survival and Accumulation by West African Market Women

GRACIA CLARK

THE UNIVERSITY OF CHICAGO PRESS
Chicago and London

Gracia Clark is assistant professor
of anthropology at Indiana University.

The University of Chicago Press, Chicago 60637
The University of Chicago Press, Ltd., London

Printed in the United States of America

03 02 01 00 99 98 97 96 95 94 1 2 3 4 5

ISBN: 0–226–10779–5 (cloth)
0–226–10780–9 (paper)

Library of Congress Cataloging-in-Publication Data

Clark, Gracia.
Onions are my husband: Survival and accumulation by West African market women / Gracia Clark.
p. cm.
Includes bibliographical references (p. 431) and index.
1. Women merchants—Ghana—Kumasi. 2. Markets—Ghana—Kumasi. 3. Women, Ashanti—Ghana—Kumasi—Economic conditions. 4. Kumasi (Ghana)—Commerce. I. Title.
HD6072.2.G43C57 1994
331.4'8138118'09667—dc20 94-1907
CIP

This book is printed on acid-free paper.

CONTENTS

List of Illustrations vii

List of Tables ix

Preface xi

1 Stepping into the Market 1

2 The Regional Web 34

3 Persistent Transformation 73

4 Buying and Selling 126

5 Control of Resources 172

6 "We Know Ourselves" 216

7 Queens of Negotiation 248

8 Multiple Identities 283

9 Home and Husband 330

10 The Market under Attack 372

11 Surviving the Peace 402

Appendix: Survey Methodology 427

References 431

Index 455

ILLUSTRATIONS

Photos

Galleries following pages 16, 145, 234, and 272

Figures

8.1 Age Distribution 293
8.2 Traders' Age Distribution Compared to City and Region 294

Maps

1.1 Ghana 4
1.2 Kumasi Central Market (plan) 10
2.1 Road Traffic Flow in Ghana, 1969 40
2.2 Ghana: Vegetation Zones with Some Important Markets 49
2.3 Kumasi: Old Market Extension Proposed in 1914 64
2.4 Kumasi: Central Market and Smaller Markets, 1967 65
3.1 Ghana: Ethnic Groups 84
3.2 Bowdich's City Plan of Kumasi, 1817 112
3.3 Kumasi: Market at Conquest, 1900 113

TABLES

2.1 Source of Goods Sold by Male and Female Traders 38
4.1 Processing of Goods 153
4.2 Stall Type 157
5.1 Traders Giving or Taking Credit 176
5.2 Source of Present Trading Capital 182
5.3 Source of Access to Current Trading Location 183
5.4 Learning Trading Skills 190
5.5 Division of Labor among Partners 194
5.6 Who Becomes Partner 199
6.1 Traders with Regular Clients 233
7.1 Commodity Leadership 255
8.1 Sex Ratios: Women to Men by Type of Commodity 286
8.2 Capital Reported Required to Trade at Current Level 288
8.3 Regional Background of Traders 289
8.4 Trading versus Craft Production by Hometown and Gender 296
8.5 Father's Occupation 300
8.6 Mother's Occupation 300
8.7 Trading and Kin Relationships 301
8.8 Parental Education 306
8.9 Traders' Education 306
8.10 Level of Education Attained by Traders 306
8.11 Work Changes 312
8.12 Work Prior to Marriage 313
8.13 Previous Work 313
8.14 Childhood Work 313
8.15 Proposed Use of Windfall Capital 315
9.1 Cooking 355
9.2 Care of Young Children 358
9.3 Traders' Performance and Delegation of Domestic Tasks 364
9.4 Age and Domestic Work 369
9.5 Wives' Domestic Work 369

PREFACE

Interpreting any book depends heavily on knowledge or assumptions about its conditions of production and the author's background, so I will narrate here something of the diverse persons and agendas that first set my feet on the path to Kumasi Central Market. Theoretical discussions of "situated knowledge," pioneered by Donna Haraway and Sandra Harding, now give high priority to specifics of the author's positionality and location as key aspects of any piece of intellectual work. Patricia Hill Collins further encourages writers to "use their own concrete position as situated knower" (1990, 17) by validating concrete experience and connection as the basis for knowledge claims in Black feminist thought.

The preliminary phrases with which authors once acknowledged the support and advice of friends and mentors provided readers with rather haphazard clues to their intellectual and social locations. This same location within the book still seems appropriate for discussing more explicitly (to the extent of my self-awareness) my own personal and intellectual history, the interests and circumstances that led me to do this research, the theoretical and political concerns that informed it, and my relationships with market traders. The information and interpretations presented throughout this book came through the specific window created by these relationships, based primarily on what traders told and showed me, shaped by our mutual preconceptions and experiences. Since I discuss the actual process of fieldwork in more detail in chapter 1, my aim here is to honor these influences as they shaped and nourished my research agenda.

As an economic anthropologist, it is perhaps predictable that I feel strongly my economic relations to Kumasi Central Market traders, as well as emotional and intellectual links. I have built my professional life as an academic and a development consultant around the same market that sustains its traders in a very different way. Part of the sense of obligation and loyalty I feel toward them and their market stems from an awareness of this debt for supporting my family. Another part arises from the affection that has grown through years of personal interaction: sympathy, support, and advice. These were mutual on some occasions, although it is surely more difficult for me to imagine my life without them than vice versa. This commitment, based on shared life experience and effort, has something in common with a long-term friendship or marriage, in that the circumstances I relate here, those that initiated the relationship, were influential in shaping it and perhaps are interesting for the reader but they no longer completely define or validate it. I would do many things differently now, but I would rather accept than disavow the detours, idiosyncracies, and pieces of luck that so characterize ethnographic fieldwork.

In College

My first interest in West African markets was as the best example I could find of a flourishing contemporary marketplace system. Undergraduate historical research on medieval Flanders led directly to my unorthodox introduction to anthropology and African studies through a seminar on peasant markets taught by Carol Smith at Stanford in 1972. I was investigating commercial and labor relations in Flanders' high-volume wool cloth industry between the twelfth and fourteenth centuries, a time when chronic political upheavals which were forging the French and English nations and aborting the Flemish one included what was then called a worker-peasant alliance. The success and failure of successive revolts and invasions clearly depended on shifts in market locations and trading institutions for wool, cloth, and grain for urban workers. In Smith's class we discussed substantivist and geographical central place theories of power in market trading systems in light of her own recent fieldwork in Guatemala, my fellow students' research results or intentions, and classic anthologies of case studies from Africa and Latin America. This initiation predisposed me to conceptualize the social organization of markets in terms of spatial systems and historical change in relation to technological changes and state formation processes.

Ethnographic research attracted me as I came up against the starker limitations of archival research. The archives of all three major Flemish cloth towns had been completely destroyed; if not leveled in the First World War they had burnt in the Second. The immediacy of interviewing live people was irresistible, simply asking them what I wanted to know. Fieldwork presents its own stark limitations, negotiated in a continuous wrestling with one's own preconceptions and ignorances in framing questions and with others' assumptions and suspicions in eliciting answers. But this struggle looked enjoyable and rewarding (especially through Smith's contagious example) compared with facing a more implacable adversary in the systematic construction and destruction of the historical record.

Some of my current research questions also date from this medieval research. Dismaying encounters with pages of execution lists, the final relics of the most innovative and democratic Flemish independence movement, underlined both the attractions and dangers of economic and political positions of autonomy, marginality, separatism, and incorporation. These issues arose again in a related project, a short article about the communities of autonomous single women called *beguines*, numerous in Flanders and elsewhere in Northern Europe during the same centuries. They negotiated within bourgeois guild and Catholic monastic institutions for a social space that included access to restricted male-dominated guild occupations and to voluntary religious activism, but these same privileges eventually attracted hostility from the Church and the urban population. I had been gratified and encouraged by the enthusiastic response to this apparently esoteric case among feminists who found it relevant to their current strategic decisions about separatism and work.

Washington, DC

My interest in the shifting gendered structure of employment expanded through both this academic work, completed in Washington, DC, and nonacademic work experiences there. For several of the same years, I did construction work through a union apprenticeship, participating in affirmative action negotiations at a time when federal contracts brought some protections and expanded options for blacks and women. Experiencing the daily dynamics of a recently all-male, recently integrated occupation gave me a vivid perception of the social construction of the gender and racial identification of particular jobs and highlighted the limits of individualist, egalitarian reforms. At the same historical moment that black and female workers gained entry to the skilled trades, deskilling and de-unionization steadily undermined our job security, upward mobility, technical autonomy, and hours and conditions of work.

Choosing this nontraditional work drew me into deeper involvement with the Washington, DC, feminist community in the mid-1970s. I was fortunate to have first encountered feminism at a time and place where the presence of active, articulate Black feminists had an unmistakable influence on theory and practice. The overlapping conflicts then raging between black and white women, between middle-class and working-class women, and between academics and activists, while perhaps most explosive within the lesbian community, also reached a broader feminist audience in Washington, DC. White feminists too often responded with paralysis to these diverse and heated critiques of the unquestioning extension of Marxist, liberal, or radical feminist principles to the circumstances of Black women and men, but at least the experience did inoculate us against naive assumptions of sisterhood. To borrow Audre Lorde's phrase, "It was a while before we came to realize that our place was the very house of difference rather than the security of any one particular difference" (1984, 226). Sheer persistence in refusing to ignore each other did lead to some innovative coalition work, for example in the DC Rape Crisis Center, which nourished my hope that acknowledging difference would lead away from paralysis to positive cooperation and insightful new ways of working on issues. Similar confrontations across the country were triggering an explosion of theoretical and artistic creativity that confirmed this optimism. We attended traveling poetry/story readings then that raised funds for the eventual publication of collections now deployed as classics—*This Bridge Called My Back* and *Home Girls.*

Debates over separatist and integrationist organizational strategies, among feminists and nonfeminists, actually encouraged me to make more definite plans for anthropological research. Questions about autonomy and marginality that had intrigued me in my medieval research, perhaps for personal reasons, were clearly active issues whose current strategists were looking for comparative examples. Were racially mixed feminist organizations or coalitions possible, or a waste of energy? To what degree should or could separatism be advocated, logically or ethically, by either black nationalists or radical feminists? Was feminist separatism racist in devaluing the community solidarity many black women considered essential protection against genocide? What degree of autonomy did women need to establish from socialist, Marxist, nationalist, liberal, or Christian movements and analyses to qualify as feminists or to accomplish significant change? What were the tradeoffs, and under what circumstances did each choice become advantageous? I found myself in later years resurrecting my thoughts on these issues to join in analogous debates on women and development projects and on academic "mainstreaming."

I can identify several other issues brought home to me then from black and racially mixed feminist organizations that remained central in formulating my eventual research in Kumasi. Those who had been subjected to white, middle-class organizing or research efforts strongly felt as an insult the use of pre-established frameworks (whether socialist, feminist, or mainstream) to name the central issues and questions of their own lives. They demanded that priorities for action or study be formulated according to the strategic and life priorities of the people directly involved, after work with them had begun. This process required a sequence of positive acts, first identifying their major concerns by asking them and watching how they spent their time, and then following these concerns up in discussions and in the allocation of research time and other resources.

Theoretical schema formulated in a distant academic setting for professional advancement were as dubious, by these lights, as political schema conforming to the experience of white, middle-class activists. Theory was respected as a tool, to inform strategic choices by evaluating the extent and nature of power present or accessible in a given situation. Black feminists like The Combahee River Collective (1981 [1977]) were quite willing to appropriate elements of theory from single-issue analyses of race, class, or gender, but by definition none of these could address their whole situation. Their call for an eclectic approach—a theoretical "by any means necessary"—linked eclecticism to taking multiple linked identities and oppressions as the norm rather than as the exceptional case.

The relevance of these local debates to my eventual research was reinforced by similar points that Third World women leaders and academics were making at international conferences. Friends attending these conferences returned with reports of these responses and *Quest* received and published some when I co-edited a special issue on international feminism (El Sadaawi, Mernissi and Vajrathon 1978). Like local Black feminists I had heard in person, African scholars and activists criticized externally-rooted researchers and analysts for their romantic universalization of sisterhood and for their limited, preset agenda of issues. Both of these rigidities assumed a continuing domination of Western feminists and their models that objectified African women and assigned them a passive position as victims of sexism (Awe 1977; Okeyo 1981; Savane 1982).

This suspicion of universalist models carried over into my subsequent research agenda, leaving it deeply marked by the resulting eclecticism and particularism. The prominent attention anthropology gave to cultural difference confirmed my interest in anthropology, but the relationship between universal and context-specific modes of explanation was presented as oppositional then, although it is more often seen as dialectical now. Theoretical writers such as Sherry Ortner and Michelle Rosaldo, who sought general explanations of phenomena like gender subordination, tended to explain away variations. Those who found variations most significant, such as Carol MacCormack and Marilyn Strathern, argued against generalization and sought explanations in terms of the local context. Debates over the universal applicability of dichotomies between public and private or nature and culture influenced my decision to study in England rather than in the United States. Because of my experiences in Washington, DC, I respected writers who used theory to interpret specific sets of circumstances, rather than using local settings to explore new theories.

During those same years in the mid-1970s, another point raised in coalitions and mixed groups also soaked in deeply. Black feminists in Washington, DC, did not see why they should be interested in working with white women for its own sake, based on the intangible benefit from interracial contact itself or from increasing the white women's understanding of racism. Although destructive interactions would not be tolerated, the quality of the interaction was even less of a goal in itself for them, either in terms of its political correctness or its emotional nuances. Black activists often categorized self-reflective talk and writing by white feminists as self-indulgent, even though writers like Gloria Anzaldua had already begun to demonstrate the political potential of introspection. White women joining them should bring some definite skill, knowledge, or resource not often readily available to them, one that bore a recognizable relation to their own stated high-priority goals. Internalizations of these critiques later intensified my hesitations about more introspective ethnographic modes, in which analyzing the ethnographic encounter itself is a primary focus of the research.

I came closest to holding such a useful skill, or at least useful knowledge, through my comparative and analytic training in marketplace systems, which offered grounds for imagining a practical contribution through research. This is one of several reasons my research placed considerable emphasis on the technical aspects of trading, such as bargaining, credit, and seasonality. Choosing a tightly focused topic, so clearly in the public domain, also seemed more respectful and realistic. It did not force me to inquire into intimate values and incidents that people might not wish to discuss at the onset of our relationship. I had even more ambivalence about expecting to interpret material on such subjects as an outsider, after only a year or two in the field. I later found an echo of this attitude in the "respectful distance" Ong endorsed (Ong 1988). Serious ethical and epistemological critiques by U.S. and overseas participants had already undermined research presuming the right to ask and the right to define. The privileging of expert, exterior understanding, either in setting the terms and the value of the encounter or in the realm of meaning, was particularly problematic when analysts asserted "real" meanings not perceptible to the subjects themselves. I felt I could speak more legitimately of what I had seen and what people had told me about relatively concrete, simple events and behavior in an area that was conceptually familiar to me—the marketplace system.

Research Training

With my bias against generalization, intensive case studies held the most attraction for me. Many were by British social anthropologists, who still considered this their core ethnographic project while untangling themselves from the more confining aspects of structural-functionalism. I was fortunate to meet Dorothy Remy, a professor at the University of the District of Columbia familiar with both English and U.S. anthropological studies of West African women and trade as part of her own work on Nigerian women. She was kind enough to suggest and discuss readings, notably by British materialist feminists who satisfied my historian's thirst for detailed context by producing the kind of "careful, politically focussed, local analysis" Mohanty later endorsed in Mies (Mohanty 1988; Mies 1982). As di Leonardo remarked of them recently, "amassing this economic and institutional knowledge . . . is a far cry from plunging into Nisa's first-person narrative," but it was a genre I could more easily defend (di Leonardo 1991, 14).

Further reading did reassure me that my central analytic questions about autonomy and integration were implicated in a variety of strategic decisions facing African women. African and other non-Western feminists argued about the benefits of gender parallelism, some echoing U.S. cultural feminists in praising the precolonial dual hierarchies of West African societies and goddesses (Jain 1978; Steady 1981). Women and development experts debated the benefits of separate women's projects compared with mainstreaming women within larger projects. Dependency theorists also reconsidered integration arguments when they assessed the desirability and feasibility of different degrees of de-linking or separation from the world system, using complex analyses of Tanzania, India, and China. Radicals of both sexes debated the applicability of Marxist or modernization models of economic and political change to their societies and the strategic benefits or pitfalls of allying with international organizations that endorsed them. Early writers on the informal sector also asked whether its partial exclusion from the formal national and international circuits signaled its autonomy or its marginality.

As I followed up on these thematic interests, they began to steer me energetically toward West Africa. In order to assess both the strengths and weaknesses of relations rooted in market trade, I needed to choose a market network with a significant degree of autonomy, not a vestigial institution catering mainly to the tourist, the gourmet, or the destitute. In those locations where formal shops (state or private) heavily dominate other forms of distribution, marketplace traders are confined so narrowly to a few leftover or rejected lines of goods and segments of demand that spatial and other gross aspects of the market system cannot reflect its internal dynamics very accurately. My bloody medieval examples had dispelled any utopic visions that a local system could operate outside or encapsulated within the constraints of the international economic system, but I needed to find traders with visible room to maneuver.

West African markets were reported to be among the most dynamic contemporary marketplace systems, expanding rather than withering away under long contact with capitalism. The relatively skeletal formal sector there, restricted partly because of their own vigor, clearly left market traders with considerable economic autonomy. The apparent personal independence and forcefulness of market women in the West African forest zone featured prominently in detailed studies and casual references alike, even to the point of stereotype. A predominantly female workplace had a strong appeal after several years in all-male workplaces and raised interesting issues about gender and work. I hoped to distinguish those strengths and weaknesses in market women's position which were linked to the predominance of women in the occupation from those linked to its separation from or connection to other economic sectors.

As I began to read more anthropology, two books early evoked the response that "I could do that." Niara Sudarkasa's study (1973) of Yoruba women traders in Nigeria demonstrated that integrating the range of occupational, economic, and domestic issues that fascinated me could be accomplished without glossing over the diversity of traders' life situations. Polly Hill's study (1963) of migrant cocoa farmers in Ghana gave me a vivid sense of field interaction, with her meticulously respectful interviews with farmers and discussions with them of their investment histories and strategies. I hoped to combine Sudarkasa's insights into the interactions between household responsibilities and commerce with Hill's concern for the conscious dynamics of local economic processes. I was intrigued to discover in graduate school that both Hill and Sudarkasa had actually worked in Kumasi Central Market briefly after these larger studies.

For several reasons, the idea of studying Kumasi Central Market came up early. The matrilineal organization of the dominant Asante ethnic group promised an interesting contrast to patrilineal market women such as the Yoruba, whose commercial organization seemed very similar. The geographical coverage of major market studies was uneven, with the Yoruba exceptionally well covered by Sudarkasa, Remy, Trager, and others. In Ghana, early market studies had stayed near the coast, with Robertson and Sanjek working in Accra (the capital), Quinn and Gladwin in Cape Coast, and Schwimmer in Suhum. In the coastal capital, the disproportionate influence of governmental and international institutions might also distort local commercial dynamics. Kumasi, the second largest city and much farther inland, was likely to present a broader range of commercial relations and a more balanced geographical hinterland than Accra, another coastal city, or a very small town.

Ghanaian market women's commercial activities had immediate relevance to an active policy debate (all too actively justifying violent repression) and yet had received relatively little extended study from either outsiders or Ghanaians. Early articles on Kumasi by Hill and Sudarkasa and recent work by Schildkrout analyzed immigrant groups and the commodities they traded rather than the local Asante population which predominated in the market. As I came to understand more clearly the importance of Kumasi as Ghana's transportation hub and largest single market, the minimal research done there seemed a shocking blank on the economic map, although fortunate for me. Economic decisions were clearly being made without basic general information on Kumasi Central Market that should have been highly useful for economic planning, although I cannot say it has in fact been used much.

Diffidence about ethnographic authority encouraged me to plan a specialized study of market relations rather than aiming to understand the total lives of traders in any definitive way. Household, kinship, and marriage relations are presented here primarily as they affect trading or as traders brought them up. Many aspects of Asante culture are hardly touched on, such as religion, music, proverbs and other oral literature, even though some traders were very active in them. Fortunately, there was an excellent, longstanding and continuing scholarly record on Akan arts, society, and history, to which Ghanaians as well as Westerners have contributed fully. This removed the pressure for blanket coverage during my thesis research and enables me still to draw on much more broadly founded conclusions by these others than any lone researcher could reach.

I decided to study at Cambridge partly because this scholarship was readily available there, since a number of faculty had worked in Ghana. Although circumstances prevented me from studying with Polly Hill, I worked closely with Esther Goody, briefly with Jack Goody and Meyer Fortes, and also with Carol MacCormack, recently returned from Sierra Leone. Their commitment to thickly contextualized ethnography and their deep knowledge of West African contexts nourish my enthusiasm for detail and sustained me through a rapid introduction to general theory and analysis in social anthropology. I absorbed as much as I could digest of the Ghanaian and other West African materials in Cambridge libraries, alongside massive chunks of general anthropological literature for my "conversion" degree. Close ties between Cambridge and Ghana brought another benefit when I met Ghanaian scholars studying there. Professor Nelson and Alice Addo, Professor Kofi and Comfort Asomaning and Emmanuel Addo were kind enough to teach me the rudiments of Twi and talk about Ghana, which helped ease my transition immensely. The academic community there also helped me gain financial support for my thesis work from the then Ministry of Overseas Development's Economic Research Programme.

I was fortunate also to receive an early orientation to women's issues from the viewpoint of Ghanaian as well as European researchers. The National Council for Women and Development had scheduled a conference on Women and Development in Ghana soon after my arrival in the capital, so I was able to extend my stay there for a couple of weeks in order to attend it. Speakers gave general overviews of the status of women and identified issues of special concern or neglect. Memorable papers by Elizabeth Ardayfio on Shai traders, by Katherine Church (now Abu) on Asante women in Mampong, and by Stella Dzidzienyo on Accra maidservants had an immediate influence on my work.

In Kumasi

My first contacts in Kumasi were with local professionals, who introduced me to Central Market traders who were relatives and friends. Nii Tsui Alabi, a friend of my parents, welcomed me to a teacher training college which became my first base of operations. Patience Konadu, the Twi teacher there, gave me language lessons and my Asante name, Konadu. The Rev. and Mrs. Victor Acquah-Harrison graciously opened their home to me for several months while I was searching for permanent accommodation. At the University of Science and Technology in Kumasi, Professor Martha Tamakloe was particularly generous with advice and encouragement.

My reception in the market was courteous, if puzzled. Mr. Alabi took me to greet the senior market leader first, to explain the purpose of my research and what I would like to do with traders. After consulting with the other leaders, she gave me permission to sit with her and other traders, observing and asking questions about their business affairs. Although I also went to introduce myself to the Market Manager and to other city officials, her endorsement was the critical one that allowed me to work undisturbed in the market and which encouraged traders to cooperate by calming their fears that I was some new kind of police informer about price control violations. After formal introductions, I gradually established relationships with individual traders, including several of the market leaders, by spending time with them day after day. They reacted with various combinations of warmth and acerbity to this blatantly incompetent visitor; both reactions were equally valuable for learning about the market, as I discuss later.

My determination not to disrupt traders' business dealings and cause them to lose income I could not replace meant that most of my learning took place through observation, participation, and short remarks in between transactions. My knowledge accumulated over time, through what Bettina Aptheker calls "the dailiness of women's lives." Extended narratives or topical discussions were difficult to maintain in the market, as we were constantly interrupted by customers. The pace of work was even more hectic at home, as mothers raced to feed, bathe, and nurture their children before nightfall. Although as individuals many market women are highly articulate and vocal, many of their stories "were not told, they were enacted" (Aptheker 1989, 41). This lack of direct explanation turned out to be typical of how Asante children acquire trading skills; they are brought to market young and expected to show good sense in understanding what they see.

As I went through my fieldnotes one more time, while revising this book, I realized that these practical constraints combined with acute political tensions to shape my research agenda in a direction that was partly unconscious at the time. Price controls, import controls, and other official regulations put traders in constant fear of arrest and confiscation of their goods. The national government had outlawed many of their standard trading practices and made others illegal retroactively at short notice. Taping interviews or bargaining sessions in the market, already problematic because of the noise level, was out of the question since traders knew they could be readily identified by their voices. Traders stopped wondering if I were a police agent after a few months of testing my harmless idiot persona, but I still might reveal damaging information out of ignorance. Although in fact police and military personnel showed no particular interest in me, my reticence about pushing for personal detail probably contributed to the surprisingly full cooperation they gave me under such sensitive conditions.

Traders' security and confidentiality concerns were reflected in refusals and deflections of questions which I internalized, and which continued to shape my research directions significantly. My written notes reproduce the literal absence of taped "voices" in certain ways. Chronic harassment of individual traders and massive crackdowns every few months made me concerned that my notes might at some point be confiscated and used to incriminate my closest associates. I kept roughly verbatim accounts of what traders said, but avoided the circumstantial details or the combination of home and market identifying markers that would have made attributions easy by others. These accounts yield an oddly depersonalized account of comments and opinions that were generated by a host of deeply personal interactions. Deregulation of trade since 1985 and reduced political tensions make it feasible now to plan to redress this balance through life history research before long.

Direct influence by traders on my research agenda is a more complex issue, because their own priorities were so diverse. One market leader was interested in concrete benefits I might bring to traders by arguing their case to the government or attracting foreign assistance for market projects. Her expressed concerns confirmed my own interest in addressing policy issues directly in my writings and later employment. She had little sympathy with participant observation and wondered aloud why I was staying so long, seeming to consider it a sign of inefficiency. She remarked approvingly years later of an academic colleague who had arrived for a two-week social assessment, "written everything down," and left.

Satisfying this important collaborator would have displeased another market leader, who was more reserved and suspicious at first. Years later, she praised the humility I had shown by sitting down quietly beside them for long periods of time, explaining that another person who would have just come up and asked a lot of questions would have been told less. Emphasis on the quality of our personal interaction was expressed in positive terms by another close associate, who remarked how unusual it had been to have a white person living and eating together with her and talking like an ordinary person. Others had shown an equal emphasis on interactional issues in their criticisms, for example, when I did not meet their standards of formal manners, industriousness, or proper eating habits. Although I responded to these explicit and tacit concerns in my immediate behavior, I incorporated them less into my research priorities because of my recent contradictory experiences in Washington, DC.

Beyond their immediate security concerns, traders were more coherent in their disinterests than their interests. Their apparent indifference to the contents of my thesis or book was striking. I never heard anyone ask whether or how an incident or story would appear, suggest how to write about it, or even ask for something to remain "off the record." I can hardly imagine that they trusted my personal discretion so much, since they hid what they occasionally felt needed hiding effectively enough. They showed the same lack of concern about a television program a British crew made about them, in which I was not involved (Granada Television International 1983). Even avid television watchers expressed no resentment that they had never seen the final product. I still intend to get their reaction to the book and the video, if possible, but perhaps they felt they had enough control over what was said and seen.

Market women also seemed to find the situation of a woman studying women much less problematic than I did, fresh from the battles over sisterhood in the U.S. feminist movement. When I began to explain that I was studying Asante culture, several traders jumped ahead with remarks that of course I was coming to the market because that was where the women worked. Those who discussed U.S. marriage ages and joint bank accounts with me also discussed bridewealth systems with women neighbors from other West African countries. While they never forgot our national and racial differences, they often universalized about me, assuming I shared their goals and ignoring evidence to the contrary as my unfortunate miscalculations. My continued childlessness after finishing my degree, for example, was treated with delicate sympathy for a personal tragedy, only too common to overeducated women. My female-oriented social life was especially respectable for the young married woman I was then. Friendships remain so sex-segregated for Asantes that cross-gender research would be more difficult here.

Subsequent research was facilitated and shaped by institutional support that gave me access to broader sources of information as well as funding. Additional perspectives from outside the circle of market traders raised penetrating new questions about commercial issues after I finished my initial research. During a two-year consultancy for the International Labour Office in Ghana, from 1982 to 1984, I was able to talk with village women producers in six regions about their own problems with the trading system. A four-month consultancy in New York with UNIFEM put me in touch with experts on a broad range of food issues affecting women, especially agriculture. Their accounts reported many rural women from different parts of Africa analyzing their own production and marketing problems. The University of Wisconsin and the Wenner-Gren Foundation provided helpful funds for further library research. The Center for Afro-American and African Studies at the University of Michigan generously provided research assistants for many years, and the Office of the Vice President for Research there funded my return to Ghana in 1989–90 to collaborate with Takyiwaa Manuh on a study of structural adjustment policies.

Members of the Women's Caucus of the African Studies Association, the Society for Economic Anthropology, and the University of Michigan Women's Studies Program and Feminist Anthropology Group were invaluable in resocializing me into U.S. academic life after thirteen years away. These and many other colleagues continued to provide advice and encouragement throughout the preparation of this book. We shared so many discussions of issues central to it that I hesitate to single out individuals. I am particularly grateful to those who read draft chapters—Maxwell Owusu, Lillian Trager, Karen Hansen, Claire Robertson, Janet MacGaffey, Florence Babb, Kristen Mann, and Ruth Behar. If I could have successfully incorporated all of their suggestions, this would be a masterpiece.

1 STEPPING INTO THE MARKET

As travelers to Kumasi, Ghana, reach the heart of the city, they pass or enter the central Kejetia traffic circle and truck parking lot, and the congestion and excitement of Kumasi Central Market swings into view. Its commanding visual presence announces both the dynamism and unruliness of the economy of the city, Ghana's second largest. It spreads a living carpet of energetic, even desperate commercial initiative down a broad wedge of valley land, overflowing the original rows of stalls, built inside a sharp bend in the railway line, into adjacent streets and open areas. Tables, stalls, and storefronts display a dizzying range of commodities, from local foodstuffs, services, and crafts through imports and locally manufactured goods, including all items regularly bought by local residents.

Its size and complexity make Kumasi Central Market an appropriate symbol of the power of the city and of the market women identified with it. The importance of its traders' economic relations only confirms its impressive appearance. Most interregional trade for local consumption in imports, manufactures, and local foodstuffs passes through its wholesale yards. Its daily trading population, estimated at fifteen to twenty thousand, makes it the largest single market in Ghana, perhaps the largest in West Africa. Like other marketplaces in southern Ghana and the forested regions of other West African countries, this market population is predominantly female (70 percent) and dominated organizationally by groups of women who trade each major local food crop. A comparable degree of dominance by one ethnic group, the Asante (65 percent), reflects Kumasi's role as the capital of the still influential Asante confederacy and the Ashanti Region, which replaced it as a territorial unit.[1]

1. The Asante are a culturally and politically distinctive subgroup of the matrilineal Akan peoples, who number about two-thirds of the Ghanaian population. Throughout this book I will use the spelling Asante to refer to the cultural group and the spelling Ashanti to refer to the administrative and geographical region. Asante is the more accurate phonetic spelling of the word for them in Twi, their language, which was transcribed as Ashanti or Ashantee in early European accounts. The spelling Ashanti, adopted by the British colonial authorities, remains a common spelling in public media and the official spelling for the region in legal documents and records. I find it useful to have two distinct terms available, since they overlap considerably but by no means entirely. The Asante became an independent political unit in 1701 and developed distinctive cultural and linguistic features along with strong loyalty to their chiefly hierarchy, which continue to the present.

A search for the "typical" trader would be defeated by the very range of enterprises included, which is a characteristic feature of a major market. Its traders number some of the largest wholesale magnates in the region and some of the poorest strolling hawkers, living hand-to-mouth. At one entrance, the wealthy rice and sugar dealer leans on dozens of burlap bags, making her long-distance telephone call, while a hawker passes selling cooked rice by the spoonful from a pot on her head. At another entrance, dozens of tomato vendors each squat with a single basket near others who stand on tall stacks of wooden tomato crates unloaded from semi-articulated trucks.

Formal classification of enterprises along scales of modernity, competitiveness, capitalist orientation, legality, or size does not say enough about this diversity either. The contrasts are certainly there, but in surprising juxtapositions. In the bustling local foodstuffs sections, streams of yams, tomatoes, and mounds of dough pass in public, businesslike transactions from trucks in wholesale yards to rows of open-walled stalls on the carts and headloads of carriers, without the benefit of written accounts. Lines of stalls with half-closed shutters, opened only to friends of friends, create a secretive atmosphere in the cloth section reminiscent of Middle Eastern bazaars, despite its industrial product. One young man, wearing mirror sunglasses, sells cigarettes and chewing gum along the railway line, while his neighbor sits on a blanket spread with the bones and amulets of "Northern medicine." A small storefront inside the market shows counters and shelves stocked with modern pharmaceuticals, and paid employees provide written receipts. Another small storefront drugstore on a downtown street uses unpaid family labor and sells packaged herbal medicines alongside modern drugs.

This study aims to embrace rather than sidestep this diversity. Flex-

---

At the nineteenth-century height of its power, the Asante *oman* or polity incorporated parts of adjacent regions in addition to their original territory in present-day Ashanti Region, especially large sections of present-day Brong-Ahafo Region. Many Asantes live outside Ashanti Region, especially in Brong-Ahafo Region, and many non-Asantes live inside Ashanti Region, in both rural and urban locations, including Kumasi. The plural form in Twi is *Asantefo,* but the English format plural Asantes is commonly used in Ghanaian English language publications, so I have adopted it here. The parallel transcription of Kumasi would be Kumase, which was also spelled Kumasi or Koumassee in early accounts. I have used the Kumasi spelling here since it is the most common in Ghanaian English-language publications and since both refer to the city. For simplicity of printing and reading, this book does not use phonetic characters in transcribing Twi words and phrases. Many printed materials in Ghana do likewise for the same reason, including some printed in Twi. I hope that the limited linguistic content of this book is enough to excuse this compromise.

ibility and variation are exactly what gives the marketplace system its continuing ability to link other commercial and noncommercial sectors, since the relationships between them constantly shift. Instead of aiming to explain away variations between traders and over time, or reduce them by dismissing all but a few significant variables, the intention here is to identify the key social forces which generate, maintain, and continue to reshape this diversity. Some of these come from within the marketplace itself, while others arise from its links with household, community, and international-level processes that necessarily create contradictory interests and pressures inside the marketplace and in individual traders as they struggle to survive and to accumulate wealth. It is these very contradictions that constantly renew and transform the full range of trading relations, including their constraints.

The size and central economic position of Kumasi Central Market makes it an important arena for the playing out of struggles between big and small traders, between men and women, between North and South, between ethnic groups, between city, small town, and village, and between imports, exports, and local products. As the leading market in the second largest and most centrally located city in Ghana, its traders mediate urban/rural and farmer/importer/consumer relations for the whole region (see map 1.1). Interest continues to grow in policy circles on the role of traders in famines and in food security generally (Ravallion 1987; Sen 1981). It also plays a key role in gender relations, housing the most powerful positions available regionally within the marketplace system, a major employment sector for women. The trading strategies displayed within this market therefore test the limits of resources women can draw on to accumulate capital, showing the dynamics of success and of stagnation. As an extreme rather than a typical case of both economic and gender contradictions, Kumasi Central Market is an apt location for studying both in their fullest manifestations.

Through many centuries of trading in this part of West Africa, identities based on gender, on Asante citizenship in relation to coastal polities and non-Akan savannah peoples to the north, and on the town of Kumasi in relation to other towns and marketplaces have been constructed through constant interaction. To a considerable extent, other identities have been exercised here in terms of control or exclusion from specific kinds of trading because of the historic importance of commerce and production for sale. Trading positions controlled in the name of these identities might be defined by geographic location, by commodity, or by distributive function, but usually by some combination. Specific positions, such as access to key towns or functions, have

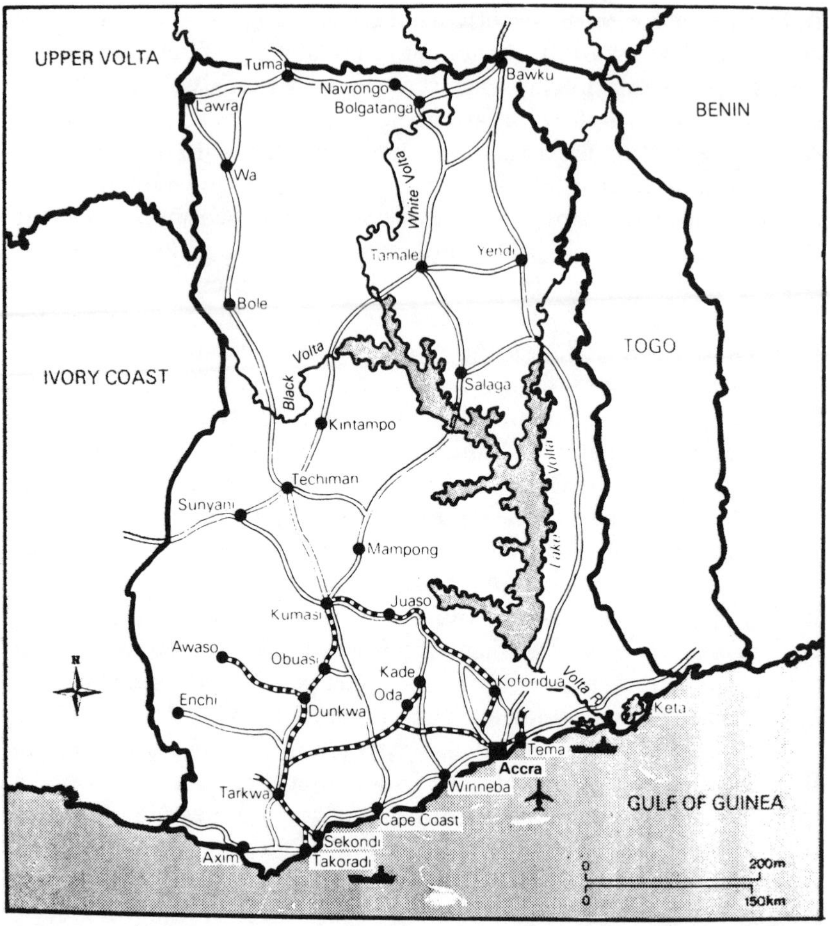

Map 1.1 Ghana (Source: Maps on File. Copyright © by Martin Greenwald Associates. Reprinted with permission by Facts On File, Inc., New York)

been significant targets and assets in both historical and contemporary contests over the relative power of social groups and social categories based on gender, ethnicity, nationality, and shifting elite membership qualifications, which might include chiefly connections, education, or political loyalty at any given time.

My intention in beginning this research was to assess the capacity of market women to engage in effective social action and the contribution of their market relations to that effectiveness (whether as trader groups or individually in their families and communities). How valuable was trading to traders in their other struggles, and how important were their other resources for their trading? When I encountered incidents during fieldwork and historical trends that gave traders occasion to defend their interests or adapt to new pressures, I responded by reshaping my methodologies and exploring new topics in order to incorporate the actions they were undertaking. A rapid series of political crises drew my attention to traders' relations with the national government, openly hostile during the 1979 "housecleaning" campaign against corruption and price inflation. Direct physical and verbal attacks on market women traders, repeated before and after several changes of regime, made it clear that political connections had a major and immediate impact on the daily decisions and economic survival chances of the traders before my eyes.

The succession of political and economic crises during the decade of my research provided painfully excellent conditions for verifying the exact extent of traders' social and economic resources, since these were tested to the very limits. The changes of government, price control raids, and currency exchange exercise, which took place during the first research period, provided unusual opportunities for direct observation of the events and secondary effects of such crises and traders' responses. Otherwise sensitive and controversial topics could be introduced naturally in the context of commiseration, when I seemed to receive more candid reportage and comment than when I had not experienced the events. For this reason, I gladly interrupted my organized program of research during acute crises or government interventions to note and discuss traders' current actions.

Such frequent and intense attacks highlighted both the strengths and weaknesses of the traders' position. On the one hand, substantial economic and social resources had enabled traders to survive decades of recurrent official hostility. Events during the research period showed that they could weather short periods of surprising adversity and quickly resume their original social relations. Some impressionistic published accounts had implied that market women, particularly in Ghana, enjoyed a virtually untouchable position (Little 1973). Far from being invulnerable, Kumasi market women suffered severe losses from the attacks I witnessed and showed only a limited capacity to defend their interests, in groups or individually. Their social relations with kin, producers, and public institutions, among others, produced no open and few effective allies in those times of crisis, leaving them vulnerable to continued attack and compounded damage. Their rapid collective rebound after such attacks demonstrated a lack of alternatives more than a lack of damage.

I also found unexpected drama in the historical record, which led me to devote more attention to it. The tension and hostility evoked by traders' gender and wealth surprised me partly because scholarly accounts of West African market women had often portrayed the markets as a supposedly timeless, "traditional" female occupational sector, which should therefore have been well accepted and integrated with Asante cultural norms. In life histories and oral histories collected toward the end of my stay, however, I gathered eyewitness accounts of relatively recent shifts in the gender and ethnic domination of trading positions. Current gender and economic stratification patterns in the market reflected contemporary power balances which were still hotly contested, not stable precolonial traditions.

Further investigation of historical and archival materials confirmed these stories and clarified longer-term historical trends. Asante men had moved out of market trading in many commodities now considered stereotypical for women around 1910, shortly after colonial conquest, and had moved into cocoa farming, which then brought them higher incomes and better upward mobility prospects. Asante women and Northern men had expanded aggressively into the space they had left. The British colonial government had also set the precedent for price control during both World Wars and used market traders as a scapegoat for worsening terms of trade. As economic problems deepened after independence, successive national governments returned to those arguments and resorted to increasingly severe measures with increasing popular support. Making sense of such historical retreats and advances into specific market positions and disputes over regulations and resources that affect access to them requires, first, an understanding of the marketplace system, since the value commercial positions can have for individuals or for social groups as a platform for future action depends on their relation to other parts of the marketplace system.

The Market Mosaic

One way to begin understanding Kumasi Central Market, an exceptionally complex location, is to consider it as a mosaic of distinguishable subsystems assembled but only partly integrated into a single common system. Divisions within it are defined by commodity, by geographical location, and by commercial technique (such as unit of sale). These boundary markers turn out to be relevant to a wide range of trading practices and demographic variables, even while they cross-cut each other. Each market location attracts a characteristic set of buyers and sellers by the kind of transactions it offers, although some shift their character on a daily or weekly cycle. Traders themselves need to break the market into manageable subunits as badly as analysts do, not in order to stay within these divisional boundaries but in order to maneuver effectively between them. An elderly yam trader who sells both wholesale and retail does each more expeditiously because she does them in different market locations, where buyers go for that purpose, and need only move her person to signal her strategy change. The spatial and functional categories introduced here are those used as major points of reference by traders in locating social actors and relations, and these will form the basis for further description and analysis in the following chapters.

The Lines

Many market locations are identified by a commodity name, testifying to the central importance of shared commodity ties in organizing the traders within them as well as to the visual impact of these solid ranks of repetitive displays on customers and traders from other locations. Commodity-specialized retail sections dominate the market's central core of close-packed lines of stalls within an encircling wall with locked gates and serve as landmarks within it. Directions given to me, other visitors, or children sent on errands referred to locations by the name of the commodity followed by *dwa* (market), *apata* (shed or stall), or "line" in Ghanaian English: for example, as *bayere dwom* (in the yam market), *djenne apatem* (in the onion shed), and "provisions line." Any single commodity or set of commodities sold in sufficient volume in the market, such as tomatoes or grains with beans, has one of these concentrated retail areas. The easy price comparisons and substantial quantities of goods available there make these locations attractive both to consumers and to buyers for resale, despite their congestion.

These specialized retail areas particularly attract buyers and sellers handling slightly larger transactions than the usual daily family meal, such as small retailers who buy in sub-wholesale amounts and wealthy consumers who feed a large household well. For example, one woman who cooks boiled yam with *kontommere* leaf stew (similar to collard greens) daily to sell for breakfast buys her greens and ten or twenty yams daily in the specialized retail areas for greens and yams. She explained to me how with more capital she could increase her income without expanding her business. "If I had enough money to buy a hundred yams at once, I could buy them once a week. Then I could buy in the wholesale yard at a lower price, where they only sell yams by the hundred. But if I had that much money, I would be selling something else." Hawking cooked food is equally notorious for its low entry capital and low income. She buys her small daily supplies of peppers, fish, and onions at stalls located conveniently on her way in or out of the market.

The rows of seemingly identical displays in the retail lines provide vital price and supply information for the careful shopper or the professional buyer. For some commodities, the retail lines are the primary type of sales location; considering which kind of commodities these are underlines the specific information services they furnish. Craftsmen and sellers of major items like cooking pots and lanterns concentrate almost entirely in such recognized specialist locations. It can be hard to sell such items elsewhere, because buyers rarely make such purchases on impulse but go out looking for a selection of models to compare. One former scarf seller had inherited her stall and a flourishing business from her mother, but felt she had no choice but to switch to selling canned goods when other stalls in that area changed over. "When people want to buy a scarf they go to the scarf line," she said with a shrug.

The identification of some commodities with minority ethnic sellers names a few market sections. Fante women so dominate trade in smoked fish from the coast that the smoked fish section is called *Fante dwom* (Fante market). Even non-Fante fish traders, who mainly sell smoked fish from local lakes or northern rivers, use this phrase to describe their stalls or buying locations. On the opposite edge of the market, an area where men from the French-speaking countries north of Ghana sell shoes and other items is called the "French line." Asante men and women also make and sell shoes, but in another part of the market called the *mpaboa apatam* or shoe stalls.

The Yards

The wholesale yard or *bode* (plural, *mbode*) represents quite another type of visually distinct location specialized by commodity. Each of the local foodstuffs sold in the highest volume has a wholesale yard along the outer edge of the market, where trucks can squeeze in to unload. The small numbers of traders dwarfed by huge piles of goods there contrast sharply with the surrounding open retail areas, where swarms of small-scale traders dwarf the goods they display. Wholesale traders use stacks of boxes, bags, or baskets to keep squatting retailers and passing traffic from encroaching on their territory.

The *mbode* are set up to move large amounts of goods quickly, unloaded each morning from solid ranks of massive trucks. Specialist traders who spend most of their time on the road bring in goods by the truckload, even if several have joined together to fill a whole truck. I use the English word traveler for these traders, since the yam traders use it in their written group membership records and the Twi term *nkwansufo* translates rather awkwardly as "on the road people." In oranges and some other commodities, individual farmers also commonly harvest their crops in quantity and bring a truckload to the commodity yard. Kumasi-based wholesale traders do most of the actual selling in the yards, either on commission or on a profit basis. Such a wholesaler stays in the yard daily to receive goods from one traveler after another, disposing of each truckload to a cluster of buyers. She has exclusive, if brittle, relationships with some of these travelers, and with some buyers, and knows many more by sight.

Several types of buyers frequent the wholesale yards; anyone can enter and make a purchase if they are willing to buy in the appropriate wholesale quantity: one hundred yams, a standard wooden crate of tomatoes, or a secondhand Cocoa Marketing Board burlap sack packed with oranges or greens. Consumers only occasionally buy wholesale, for example, if a wealthy householder plans a big party around Christmas. Retail traders from the Kumasi Central Market and from Kumasi neighborhood and streetside markets buy perishable items daily. Traders from small towns with good road access to Kumasi will also buy here, bypassing nearer secondary centers. Highly valued customers include market wholesalers from other cities and agents or employees who make regular purchases for schools, prisons, barracks, and large restaurants. These bulk buyers need a location where they can almost always find five or ten hundreds without delay. Traders use the English terms "suppliers" or "contractors" for those who purchase for institutions, or the hybrid word *supplyfo.* Processors such as distillers, bakers, and poultry farmers also buy their raw materials from the *mbode* in bulk, but at longer intervals.

The *mbode* have tight organizational, spatial, and functional links to the concentrated retail areas. The order of yams, tomatoes, onions, and fish yards along the southern edge of the market roughly corresponds to the arrangement of their specialized retail areas inside the market walls (see map 1.2). Plantain and orange wholesalers unload near the garbage dump or *bola,* all too often needing to dump off large quantities of spoiled produce. The dump gives its name to their yards, and its expansion and contraction shifts their exact locations with the vagaries of garbage pickup. For oranges, consumed mainly as a juice snack, street hawkers are the most important steady buyers. The wholesale yard stands at one end of a specialized retail area where these low-capital regulars replenish their stocks daily or more often. For mi-

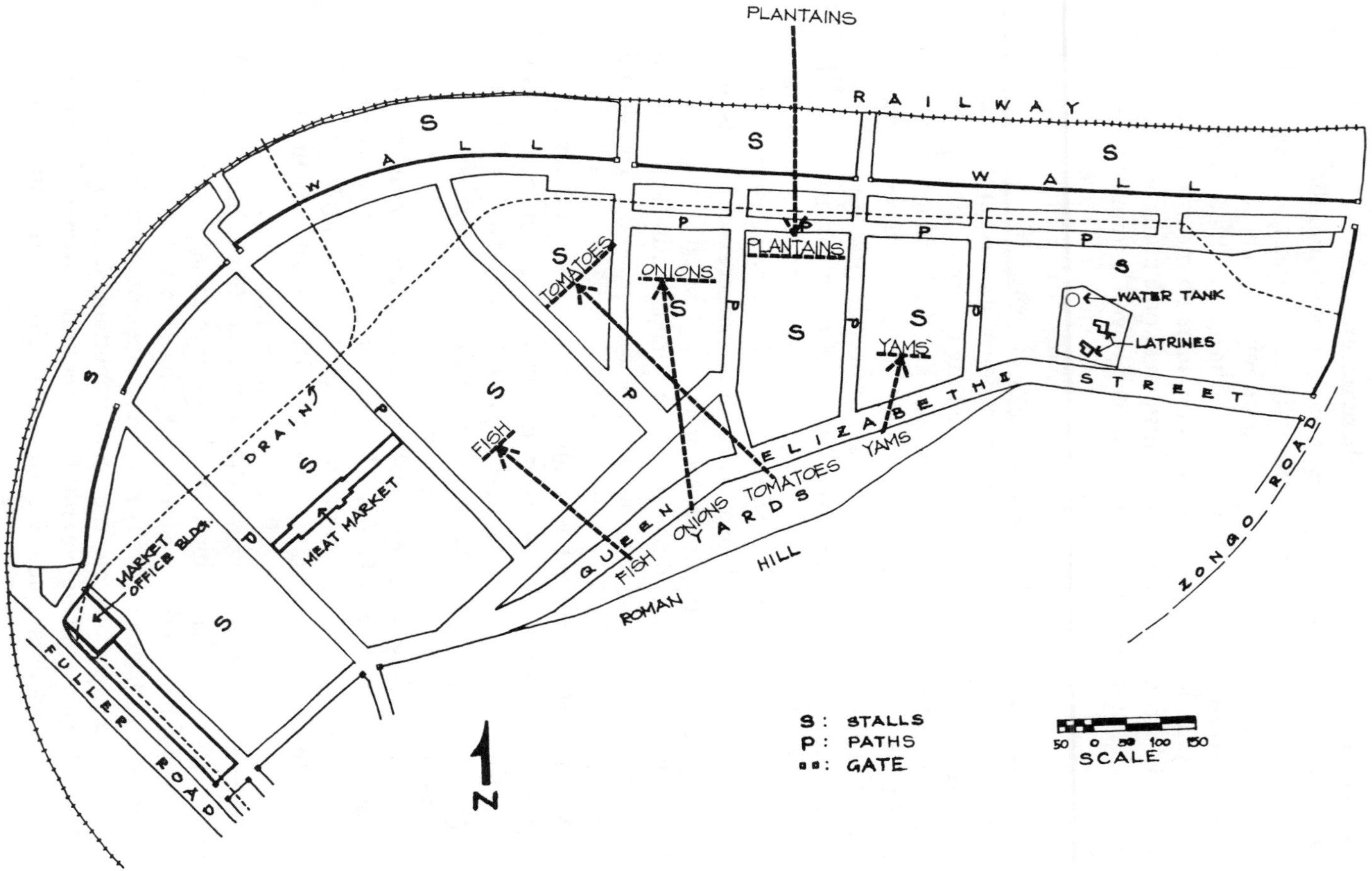

Map 1.2 Kumasi Central Market

nor commodities with lesser total volume, any wholesaling done takes place within the specialized retail area, from the stalls of the larger retailers.

Mixed Retail Areas

In large open areas around the edges of the market, beside and between the wholesale yards, traders dealing in different goods intermingle. Sellers of garden eggs, avocados, tomatoes, and salt sit side by side, and the same trader might display all four. Mixed commodity areas take their names from physical features of their locations, for example, *bola su,* "on the garbage heap," and "railways" along the tracks. Most mixed areas do specialize more broadly by commodity category. The *bola* and railways areas feature staple foodstuffs and inexpensive craft products, while the area facing Kejetia Roundabout, called "seventeen" for reasons I could never discover, offers a mixed range of canned foods (here invariably called "provisions"), drugs, chemicals, rubber sandals, and other manufactured goods.

At first glance, these mixed retail areas seem to duplicate the function of the specialized retail areas, which offer the same commodities in equally small lots. In fact, the mixed commodity areas cater to a specific demand for rapid shopping. Buyers in a hurry can make their daily purchases within a few yards' radius and avoid plunging into the crowded market. Mixed retail areas serve the same purpose as neighborhood or village markets, for people living or working near Kumasi Central Market. Shoppers in full-time employment usually patronize these fringe areas or actual neighborhood markets for convenience, as do young children afraid of the press of crowds in the Central Market core. Even some hawkers and traders who buy for resale in very small quantities for lack of capital, perhaps several times a day, also buy in the mixed retail area to reduce the time they take off from actual sales.

Specialized and mixed retail areas nonetheless overlap considerably in the kinds of buyers and sellers who use them, competing directly for both supply and demand. Some thrifty women shopping for their families prided themselves on taking the time to visit the specialized retail areas and compare relative prices and quantities carefully. Others disputed the virtue of this strategy, insisting they saved money by buying in the fringe areas, where traders have lower overhead costs without monthly rents or roofs. Many traders told me they sold in mixed retail areas not from preference, but because they could not find or afford a space in the crowded market core.

The visual jumble of the mixed retail areas echoes their diverse commercial relations in comparison with the ordered affairs of retailers in the specialized commodity areas, who almost invariably buy in their wholesale yard, if one exists, and belong to the traders' group based there. Market neighbors who run visually identical retail operations may have radically different supply relations in mixed areas. Some travel to village periodic markets in the early morning to collect produce directly from farmers, retailing some and selling some to Kumasi market neighbors. Another trader sitting next to them, showing a similar assortment of goods, lives in a nearby village and sells her own and her neighbors' garden produce, returning home from Kumasi each night. Some do buy daily in the wholesale yards or the specialized retail areas within Kumasi Central Market. Others are "lorry-chasers," rising early each morning to run after incoming passenger trucks in the Kejetia "lorry park" or truck loading and unloading yard, buying from villagers arriving at dawn with produce.[2] Small-scale traders stocking a variety of imports and manufactures can buy directly from "briefcase businessmen" who will deliver modest amounts of smuggled or diverted goods to the market stall. Kumasi factories and shops also sell limited amounts of manufactured items directly to small-scale traders, on legal and illegal terms, as well as supply wholesalers inside and outside the market, from whom retailers buy in turn. Considering these varied sources of supply, the remarkable similarity in the amount and quality of goods traders in mixed retail areas display from their small tables, chairs, and baskets testifies to regularities in the customers they vie for and the constraints that keep them out of other parts of the market.

Mobile Traders

Hawkers or ambulatory traders are a conspicuous part of the Central Market scene, attracted by the large numbers of traders and shoppers accessible there. They load goods into a basin, box, or headtray to circulate through the market aisles and the surrounding streets. Some sell services rather than goods, such as shining shoes, mending clothes, and sharpening knives. Thousands more buy in the market and then circulate throughout the residential and office districts of the city.

The minimal overhead of hawking makes it the last refuge or the first toehold of the most impoverished traders. Many comfortably established traders from poor families told me of beginning as young

2. The institution of the Ghanaian lorry park is so different from a United States truck stop, though derived from a British word "lorry" equivalent to the United States "truck," that I will retain the phrase lorry park throughout this book. Lines of passengers await departure for various destinations in vehicles ranging from rebuilt small trucks to vans and sparkling buses. Porters and hawkers swarm around them, and stalls offer snacks, meals and general merchandise. Distinctions be-

children by hawking a few items given or loaned by a relative or neighbor and building up a respectable capital for market trade through long hours, persistence, and self-denial. Market-based retailers of oranges, peanuts, bread, ice water, and other snacks introduced eight- or twelve-year-old hawkers to me as steady customers who bought on credit based on their record for reliability. Several traders bankrupted by confiscations or illness took up cooked-food hawking, if they had the strength for it, as a way to recoup a minimum capital. Hawkers completely without capital resources work on commission or as assistants to individual retailers. One tomato retailer sent her young niece out to hawk one or two full headtrays during slow periods of the day, after the girl had helped in the stall during the morning rush hour. The aunt also sold to several independent hawkers, from the market environs and elsewhere in town.

Mobile traders do not move through commercial space at random, but establish relations with particular locations in several ways. Hawkers develop a steady clientele, important for business expansion, by following a regular daily route. One teenager selling smoked fish made the rounds of the cloth and provisions stalls, where traders were reluctant to leave their stalls unattended for their daily shopping. Another older woman made huge pots of rice and stew at home and carried it to market. She had arranged to sit and sell from a couple of different stalls for a few hours each day, where nearby traders counted on her clean and tasty lunches. In the late afternoon, crowds of exhausted hawkers invade the wholesale yards and mixed retail areas, as the regular occupants pack up shop, to rest and to catch workers and stall-based traders heading home.

Relations in Time

Movements through time are an important means by which this single market accommodates a range of commercial activity more commonly distributed over several separate locations. One of the first ways I began tracking relations between the different sections of the market just discussed was by visually monitoring temporal cycles in trading activity. As I did so, I found that traders themselves used visual inspection as a primary means of monitoring daily and seasonal fluctuations in supply, demand, quality, and individual behavior.

---

tween passenger and freight service are blurred, since travellers' baggage often includes goods they intend to sell. Traders with moderate amounts of goods, for example, six cocoa bags of corn, haggle for space on passenger or mixed vehicles. In smaller towns, traders hire trucks for full loads in these same lorry parks, but in Kumasi this is usually done in the wholesale yards.

The daily cycle in Kumasi Central Market is dominated by the peak period for consumer retail shopping, between eleven and two o'clock. Wholesale yards peak an hour or two earlier than this retail peak, since retailers restock in preparation for their busiest period. Prices for highly perishable goods peak most sharply. Traders cannot easily hold stocks over to the following day, so they reduce prices heavily in the late afternoon. Consumers need to purchase tomatoes and other vegetables daily, so they expect to find fresh supplies daily. Buying begins even earlier in the fringe areas, at dawn. In the lorry parks at Kejetia and on the north side of the market, villagers from farming areas alight with bundles of vegetables they sell on the spot. Retailers and wholesalers from the Central Market and nearby neighborhood markets buy the entire stocks of these villagers, who want to return immediately for a day's farming. These lorry-chasers acquire enough for each day's supplies by buying from several such villagers. Some thrifty shoppers also rise early to take advantage of the low prices villagers offer there. Some market traders who rarely bought at Kejetia would still pass by on their way in to check the size of the lorry-chasers' piles, as part of estimating overall supply conditions for the day. By nine o'clock these lorry-park sales have dropped off. Villagers arriving now intend to retail their goods personally throughout the day, joining the local retailers in setting up tables in the open mixed retail areas. Snack sellers move in to dominate the fringe areas for an hour or two, to feed departing villagers, arriving traders, and other commuters getting on and off their lorries.

The next surge occurs in the wholesale yards, also on the market edges, between nine and ten o'clock. Sellers begin unloading their goods there soon after dawn. The market gates open at six, just before dawn, allowing access to those yards inside the gates. In the yam and tomato yards, the commodity group leader starts each day's trading with a formal announcement between eight and eight-thirty. Plantain and cassava traders at yards located outside the gates can sell as soon as their goods arrive, but they wait to start bargaining until a reasonable number of buyers has assembled. How early buyers show up depends on expected scarcity and so serves as a visual index to scarcity. Retailers from this or smaller Kumasi markets bargain intensely, aiming to complete their target purchases by nine or ten. They need time to deliver and arrange their stall displays before the midday retail rush begins around ten. Travelers bringing local foodstuffs to Kumasi make strenuous efforts to coordinate their arrival with this wholesale rush and its peak prices by reaching Kumasi in the early morning.

Wholesale yards maintain a lower rate of sales until two or three in the afternoon, when they virtually close down. Buyers from out of town or contractors for institutions, who do not face retailers' time pressures, continue buying later in the morning. Some Kumasi Central Market retailers return to restock several times in the course of the day, but in smaller quantities. Buying in several installments enables traders in very perishable items to estimate their total needs more exactly. Other retailers simply lack the capital to buy enough goods at once. These retailers also stop buying in the early afternoon to make sure of clearing their stocks before going home. A good indication of the current balance between supply and demand for a local food crop is how soon the wholesale yard empties, either of stocks or buyers.

The number of retail buyers and sellers peaks at noon along with sales volume. Each trader aims to be on duty with as many assistants as possible and her goods sorted and priced during the rush hours from ten to two. Retailers who delay in buying their supplies have trouble bringing them to their stalls, since aisles in popular sections like the tomato and smoked fish lines become so crowded that even shoppers can barely pass. Hawkers avoid being caught or slowed down in this traffic jam, where they would lose time and money. They abandon the core areas and cluster at entrances and exits, serving shoppers daunted by the sight of the central crush.

After one or two o'clock, the pressure eases. Traders can take time to eat and do their own shopping. Hawkers pass through to offer them meals, daily food purchases, and personal items like headscarves. Traders with young assistants send them off with headtrays to sell leftover goods in the market and adjoining streets, or they will send them off with baskets and instructions to do the daily shopping. Other retailers leave the assistant or a neighbor to watch the stall while they go off to eat or shop.

Institutional buyers prefer to visit the specialized retail areas in the afternoon. Peak crowds interfere with the careful bargaining and inspection needed for these large purchases and with their transport out. Traders who have succeeded in attracting this kind of valuable customer must make sure to be on hand throughout the afternoon. Some ordinary consumers prefer late shopping for the same reasons, or for bargain hunting. Nervous retailers begin to lower their prices to move perishable items more quickly, and because the best goods went early and the second-best have deteriorated further under the noonday sun.

By the late afternoon, after three o'clock, the market shows signs of winding down. Retailers prepare to go home; those without someone to cook for them at home leave soon after three. Tomatoes and other perishables drop sharply in price, since they will have little value the next day. Traders in the open areas or without permanent stalls reduce even nonperishable goods, since storage or transport home can mean considerable expense. The wholesale yards have emptied, but refill with scores of squatters, many of them hawkers resting after a day's walking. As traders flood out of the market gates, a few new arrivals set up alongside the exit paths, through the just-deserted open areas. They sell cooking oil and charcoal, often bought on the way home because they are messy to carry and store.

This daily interweaving of both complementary and competitive trading activities is accomplished through continual negotiation, testing, and insistence. Individual stallholders are frequently approached with proposals for using their space during specific hours or initiate such arrangements themselves. For example, one oil seller who sublet tables around her kiosk to pepper sellers sought out charcoal sellers to re-rent the same area for a few late afternoon hours, after the pepper sellers had packed up their tables. Illicit encroachment was also common. The tomato elders complained regularly during 1979 to the Market Manager, a city official, about the daily infiltration of their wholesale yard by squatting vegetable retailers as tomato wholesalers disposed of their stocks. The tomato group leader would occasionally go out to harangue these squatters and try to chase them away.

Seasonal variations in supply trigger openly recognized reorganization of market space. One of the first duties of the cassava leader mentioned by her group members was "she shows us where to unload our goods." As supplies expand, this involves diplomatically appropriating more territory from adjacent yards and retailers. The boundaries of the tomato wholesale yard shrink slowly to the benefit of neighboring yam and fish yards as the dry season advances and tomato supplies dwindle. Retail space allotments also expand and contract sharply with the seasonal ebb and flow of supplies. The specialized retail areas for plantains, cassava, and oranges lie outside the market core, in areas without permanently built stalls. Their boundaries and appearance both change as their traders disperse or switch to shelling corn in the off season. The snail market, tucked into a crowded central location, stands partly empty in the dry season because only a few traders bother to sell dried snails and few customers would seek anything else there.

Changes unfolding in a longer-term, historical time frame are also reflected fairly promptly in spatial reallocations. The explosion of secondhand clothes sellers in the 1980s took over territory from vendors of new clothing and other scarce imports. Likewise, during low points of printed cloth availability and legality, the highly desirable,

The orange line

Bargaining at the tomato line

Young men selling sewing notions to save for a welding machine

Selling local craft products for cooking and cleaning

Panorama of Kumasi Central Market, 1979

centrally located stalls in the cloth section were loaned or rented to sellers of cosmetics, baby clothes, and other less vulnerable items.

State-sponsored demolitions in 1979 and again in 1982 of substantial sections of stalls and open retail areas outside the market walls were a particularly open form of dispute over land use and the commercial identity of specific locations. City officials had registered and collected rents from these occupants, and some officials had reportedly argued for restricting the scope of the demolitions. Still, national goals like civic beautification, traffic control, and promised monumental construction projects could be invoked to justify reclaiming the space when tighter control of commercial processes was desired.

My Market Entrance

The understanding of market processes and of traders as persons on which I base this book is inevitably framed by the mutual interaction which gave me access to the market. Although this initial participant observation was supplemented by archival and comparative research and discussions with Ghanaians from other cities, markets, and farms over fifteen years, it laid the mental framework through which later information was interpreted. Through thousands of daily incidents and comments, traders gradually wore down my ignorance and created something more useful to both of us, still a highly partial comprehension. Observation of events in the market and conversations about actions and people I saw eventually enabled me to participate in market and home routines and travel with traders on buying trips. Systematic interviews and a formal sample survey complemented these interactive methods by locating my experiences and friends within the marketplace as a whole.

The visual introduction that opens this chapter echoes my own first weeks in the market, when visual observation was one of my main sources of orientation. It remained an important habit throughout my research precisely because traders themselves absorbed and passed on so much information in this way. After greeting and explaining my plans to the senior market leader, queen of the yam traders, and the Market Manager, a city employee, I began my mornings in the market with a small number of traders, including relatives or friends of my Twi teacher and other faculty at a local teacher training college and some yam traders introduced to me by the yam queen. High Asante standards of hospitality (as well as my novelty value as a "European" visitor) virtually guaranteed me an exchange of greetings and a brief chat, all I could manage in Twi to begin with. I observed bargaining and other trading procedures in the main different types of location found in the Central Market, including the daily rhythm of business. I asked simple questions about the identity of their customers and the source of their goods, learning terminology for categories of people and relationships through everyday incidents. I accompanied these early contacts to their buying locations and homes and started observations and conversations in other sections through shopping, passing by traders' stalls regularly and exchanging greetings.

The start of fieldwork is exhilarating, but also frustrating. I could understand only part of what I saw and heard, and my first research assistant turned out to be unreliable. But this slow start helped me to signal clearly my willingness to let traders take the lead, informing my research agenda by indicating what I should do or say and, consequently, what I should learn. The pride and self-possession so notable among Asantes, not overly impressed with European culture, meant that they did not hesitate to correct my mistakes in behavior or lines of questioning. Instead of simply refusing to talk to me when I entered an unfamiliar part of the market, traders would tell me to go explain myself to the appropriate commodity leader first, or they would take me to her. When a big truckload arrived, they would quickly shoo me away or give me the baby to hold. This was a fast way to learn commercial and social etiquette and what activities interfered with taking care of customers. I learned a great deal about cooking practices and values from their trenchant critiques of my daily market basket. As I discussed in the preface, their preoccupation with survival and accumulation became the primary focus of my work.

This relatively passive early period also turned out to be a valuable investment because it established my reputation as a safe, trustworthy (or at least harmless) visitor before I took up sensitive topics. Because of the extensive use of undercover informants by police in price control enforcement, traders needed to see for themselves that no arrests or other disasters followed their talking to me. At first I was confined to fairly innocuous subjects by my lack of Twi skill. I had picked up enough knowledge of current political tensions from Ghanaian friends in Cambridge to show a studied disinterest in prices or regulated commodities unless an incident happened in front of me. I only learned to discuss these subjects in Twi by learning how traders talked about them, so I could approach them in a nonthreatening way and in the context of a personal relationship. Their continuing concern with confidentiality still steered me away from recording detailed personal accounts they could imagine officials confiscating and using to identify them. My apparent reputation as a genial loafer, just sharp enough to keep my mouth shut on embarrassing secrets, proved a useful one the next year, when fears and tensions rose along with enforcement of price regulations at the very time I was preparing for a sample survey of the whole market. Although few of the over six hundred interviewed knew me personally, only one feared that I was a government spy.

During the first few months, I learned the interactional skills and acquired the sponsorship of individuals that I needed to work at full speed. One of the middle-aged traders I often sat with noticed when the heat or crowds began to overwhelm me and found me quiet, dark corners and cool drinks. Learning the cycles of snacks and slack periods, I learned how to spend whole days in the market without overtiring myself or my various hosts. As my conversational ability expanded, the sheer novelty of seeing a white woman in the market also gradually wore off. I could now have extended conversations with a trader without subjecting her to the disruption of bystanders who blocked foot traffic by staring at me or who laughed and clapped when I began to speak Twi. Friends at the local university introduced me to an excellent new research assistant, Esi Munkoh, a recent middle school graduate whose linguistic skills and good judgment went far beyond reliability. She translated interviews as necessary, while continuing to teach me Twi and advise me on Asante etiquette and proper behavior.

My new friends realized I was serious about moving out of my respectable minister's family house, which they considered highly appropriate for a young foreign visitor, when I started sharing with them the various real-estate scams and inflated rents I was being offered and felt forced to consider. Shocked, they found me very nearly what I was looking for within a few weeks, despite the tight housing situation. I rented a single room in a "passenger" or rental house within walking distance of the market, where several traders' families also rented rooms or suites and the landlord himself had interesting business ventures. The veranda and courtyard here were my first window onto the integration of trading operations and home life and enabled market traders to visit me comfortably. These neighbors became some of my closest associates, and our informal discussions included sensitive and difficult family issues.

One of the indications of my developing relationship with traders was my increasing social age. The raucous applause that greeted my halting Twi sentences at first mystified me. Asantes seemed otherwise rather blasé about Europeans, and Kumasi residents could effectively insult one who made too much fuss as *nkraaseni*—a villager. Then I noticed the same reaction in miniature to a toddler waving her diapered bottom in an attempt to dance. Like her, I cheerfully kept on trying, and gradually proved myself teachable. Other unnerving responses also made sense later in comparison to interactions with children. One elderly women trader continually startled me by interjecting comments on the theme of "My husband! You will bring me cloth!" into my peaceful conversations with her middle-aged daughter at their stall. I had classified this as a rather bizarre case of the much-remarked honorary male status given women ethnographers, but very similar joking aimed at male toddlers and preschoolers was a popular pastime, proposing marriage and kin relations considered hilarious because of the boy's age and incomprehension. The same old woman gradually became one of my best sources of instruction, comment and companionship, and developed an especially close relationship with my research assistant, Esi. Toward the end of my stay, she even refused my pretext for a gift of money, but accepted with some indication of affection to share a pound of sugar I had managed to find, precious in its scarcity.

During my first stay in Kumasi, from 1978 to 1980, I gradually progressed through adolescence. As I learned the basic rudiments of commercial practice and social etiquette, I began to be more useful and less dangerous, no longer requiring constant supervision. I began to be entrusted with tasks appropriate to a five-year-old—watching the stall against theft or playing with the baby. Then I was promoted to eight- or nine-year-old status, capable of making ordinary retail sales and purchases and carrying complex messages. I could attend meetings and join traders on trips, since I knew enough to keep quiet when appropriate and keep myself out of trouble. When I was looking for a room, a number of thirteen- to sixteen-year-old girls declared me their best friend and tried to arrange for me to rent in their houses, but they lost interest as I aged. I was now allowed to "mind the stall," and my mistakes in bargaining elicited clearer instructions and more extensive discussions on the subtler distinctions between categories of customers and bargaining assumptions. As a teenager, it was appropriate to initiate me into more complex discussions of trading strategy and current events. My husband's visit also helped to establish me as a functional young woman. By the time I left, I estimate that I had reached about age twenty (at age 27), rough equality with Esi at a mature nineteen. My low but growing knowledge and skill in language and social interaction could be judged much more accurately and consistently by Asante women than my biological age, of which estimates ranged from sixteen to fifty.

Traders understood my basic project of learning about their work and culture through familiar models of travel and study they would explain to me. They mentioned friends and family members who had migrated to different parts of Ghana, Europe, and America, to get ahead but also just to "travel and see." Several reminisced about their own travels or said they would also like to travel to Britain or the United States to see how people lived and did business there. How I could get paid for this was more mysterious to them. When I compared my thesis to a book, some concluded I would get paid a substantial amount of money for publishing this book, like best-selling authors they had heard about. Several traders concluded that I was learning to sell things so that I could set up my own business, as women followed a friend to market before switching commodities. Perhaps I would start trading in the United States on my return, argued one who persisted in this belief. She had heard from returned migrants that yams, for example, were scarce and expensive there, so the potential profits seemed obvious. But then why was I spending so much time with tomato traders, when tomatoes were cheaper in the United States?

My current student role was also familiar to those who had relatives or children at college or had met students from the local university, some of whom did research locally for their undergraduate theses. Besides being confirmed by me, this schoolgirl status accounted well for my privileged family background, currently limited resources, social immaturity, contraception, and predictable middle-class future. I could hardly aspire to full adulthood with no job, no car, no house, and no dependents except my research assistant, who moved in with me after a family quarrel. As I acquired these signs of social maturity, I gradually caught up with my chronological age on subsequent visits. When I spent two years in Ghana later, working for the United Nations, driving a car and renting a house in Accra, my trader friends remarked that I had at last become "tough" or *kakraka;* they said that I had been *ketewa,* or small, before. Although I am rather tall, I could hope that they referred to some gain in my maturity and determination as well as weight. I had often heard the words *kakraka* and "tough" used to describe or compliment mature market women, frequently spoken together, with a gesture of flexed arms and clenched fists in front of the navel, and a broad smile of satisfaction. When I asked if particular women were "tough," those who looked young, frail, or undernourished did not qualify, despite their mental tenacity. Any simply large woman who was not both energetic and assertive was labeled "mmere" or soft. I never heard a man described as *kakraka* or "tough," just as I have never heard a woman called "burly" in the United States. On my last visit, yam traders carefully asked my age and, hearing that I had turned forty, sat me with the elders at a market new yam ceremony.

The transition to a second phase of research in 1978 was marked by more systematic interviews. I decided to interview all of the male and female commodity leaders I could locate, in order to check how widely distributed were the trading practices and relations I was encountering. These interviews also gave the market leaders an opportunity to ask questions about my research and to see for themselves which subjects I asked about. Then I asked to interview several other traders in each commodity group, selected from the categories of variation they had used. These interviews confirmed the leaders' accounts and furnished details on less familiar trading practices, including short life or work histories for information on career choices and obsolete trading practices as well as the commercial history of the market. This process also uncovered sections or commodities that had no leaders or groups, where I did additional interviews.

Questions about transactions and events as they took place turned out to be more productive than formal interviewing. Only market leaders and elders accepted requests for formal interviews comfortably, as being part of the official duties which might interrupt their trading at any time, like dispute settlement. Ordinary traders responded to questions on general practices with formal, idealized rules that might have little direct connection to what they actually did. For example, one trader stated firmly that she never gave goods on credit, but she was extending credit to most of her buyers several months later because market conditions required it. "If I didn't give credit, no one would buy from me." Many times traders avoided abstract discussions, showing discomfort by changing the subject or making short, impatient responses, even when we knew each other much better. They would comment at length on individual cases, including general pronouncements then about what ought or ought not to be done.

About the same time, I began to accompany buyers and travelers on their trips to supply areas or linked markets, soliciting consent from a range of traders in important perishable and nonperishable commodities from both nearby and distant producing areas. Acute shortages of gasoline and vehicles made finding transportation very difficult and time consuming. Often we traveled out sitting seven to a row in passenger trucks heaped with baskets, sacks, and suitcases, after exchanging home-town gossip with the driver. Traveling as traders did was an important way of seeing how their cajoling, threats, and inside tips managed to get their bulky and perishable goods back to Kumasi. Long, tense negotiations with drivers over freight charges and when repairs would be finished ended with two or three of us crammed into the front seat or perched in the back of a freight truck racing back to Kumasi late at night. These transport delays made a systematic regional analysis of the whole hinterland impractical; more than once we had to wait several days to return, or spend the night on the ground in lorry parks to be first in line. I eventually visited several nearby and more distant village periodic markets at different seasons and the main regional periodic markets in contact with Kumasi: Techiman, Ejura, Accra, Mankessim, Tamale, and Bolgatanga.

When this second phase of looking at a wide range of commodity groups and trading roles was virtually complete, I tightened my focus again for concentrated work with a more limited number of commodity groups and individual enterprises. I followed the yam, orange, and onion leaders for days, observing and discussing their actions in dispute settlement, commercial regulation, and funeral observance. Sitting with individual traders, I could observe their interactions with customers and creditors with more understanding, discussing their strategies as these unfolded in current decision making and bargaining.

As I got to know these traders better, I gathered more systematic information on their domestic arrangements and the problems and preferences I could now discuss more freely, in the market and at home. I made efforts to go home with traders, who occupied a wide range of commercial positions, to meet their children and neighbors. Although these visits provided valuable insights, I found that women worked at a more frantic and unbroken pace once they reached home to get the family fed and bathed before nightfall. Extended conversations, even about home life, were in fact more possible and less disruptive at work. The home visit sample was more idiosyncratic than my market contacts, since it depended more heavily on the warmth of our relationship and how hard it was to reach the trader's home by public transportation.

I was also concerned that what I learned about domestic strategies might be dismissed in academic contexts because my contacts were primarily with traders, although trading was the largest single occupation for urban women in Ghanaian cities. They had been treated as exotic and titillating oddities, for example by Little (1973), in accounts that acknowledged their large numbers. I therefore sought out discussions and observations with nontraders met outside the market or in traders' houses, to check whether they had markedly different domestic practices than market women or expressed different preferences or value judgments about these choices, but found no obvious distinctions between traders and other women with similar income levels. After ten months in Kumasi, as I began to identify and understand the more common trading and domestic relations in these open-ended interviews, I organized a sample survey of the Central Market to check the frequency and distribution of these strategies. This delayed timing made it possible to use concepts and terms (in Twi) already familiar to traders, and habitually used by them, and to group questions to follow their logical flow of thought from one topic to the next, making their responses easier, faster, and more accurate. When asked a question, the trader often answered the next two or three in the series, and many volunteered further details or anecdotes, which the interviewers had space to record. Details of the survey procedures are discussed in the Appendix.

Interviews with market leaders and representative traders had uncovered some unsuspected radical changes in the gender and ethnic configuration of the regional marketplace system during the twentieth century. During the last few months of this first eighteen-month research period, I followed up on these leads by searching through archival materials in the Asantehene's Record Office and the National Archives in Kumasi. I checked and amplified this information through oral history interviews with elderly traders, market leaders, palace officials, and longtime Kumasi residents. I collected more archival material at the National Archives in Accra for several weeks, mainly from colonial records that passed the fifty-year confidentiality standard. Finally, on my way back to the United States, I visited comparable urban markets in Ivory Coast, Togo, Benin, and Nigeria to check the typicality of the market configurations in Accra and Kumasi and to suggest possible historical factors that had generated such a large single market in Kumasi.

Further periods of research made it possible to track new historical changes in trading conditions in Kumasi Central Market. I took a job as a rural sociologist with an appropriate technology project, administered by the International Labor Office (a United Nations affiliate) and requested by the National Council for Women and Development, from 1982 to 1984. I was eager for the chance to return to Ghana and to apply my interviewing skills and knowledge of the marketing system to support a locally based organization and technology. My work with women's producer groups took me to different regions of Ghana and provided contacts with rural food processors and farmers, whose perspectives on trading practices complemented my previous work. I had been identified with Kumasi traders by the farmers and small-town residents I encountered when I accompanied traders on buying and selling trips or hometown visits. Now I was visiting small-scale processors who sold both raw and processed local foodstuffs to urban and small-town traders. I heard their complaints about the adequacy of their trading relations, with market traders and government agencies, and conversely learned what aspects of the system they considered more or less satisfactory. Despite acute gasoline shortages and intermittent restrictions on travel by foreigners, I also managed to visit Kumasi on weekends to monitor market conditions and to check on the situation of individual traders during the extreme food shortages of 1983–84 and the somewhat better harvest year of 1984. This famine sparked an interest in food security and food systems that matured through my next consultancy: preparing a background paper on Women in African Food Systems for UNIFEM (the United Nations Development Fund for Women, based in New York). This surveyed women's participation across the continent in farming, fishing, and processing, as well as trading, to identify and recommend priority interventions for the Special Session on the African Food Crisis. It required a massive literature review that placed what I knew about Kumasi traders within wider regional trends in agricultural and commercial policy and degenerating food security, forming a link with my interest in the history of Ghanaian commercial policy. It also directed my attention to structural adjustment policies, the currently dominant development paradigm.

I eventually returned to Ghana to gather information on the specific implementation policies and impact of its Structural Adjustment Programme, often held up as an example of success to other African countries. This sharp reversal of commercial and other economic policies began in Ghana in 1985, so that substantial effects were visible in December 1989 and January 1990, my most recent research period. I spent four weeks in Kumasi interviewing traders and market leaders about changes in market conditions and their personal circumstances, especially the lives and enterprises of traders I knew from my dissertation research. I also revisited several villages from the appropriate technology project for an update on rural conditions of production and distribution under the new policies. Reflecting on these conversations and experiences defined my central analytic focus in this book on the human issues of survival and accumulation. Accumulation was a vital goal of trading, enthusiastically discussed and pursued by most of the traders I knew, although not reached with great success by many. It was also a central issue in the political debates around trading; the allegation that traders accumulate disproportionate wealth through predatory practices was a cornerstone of the arguments used to justify attempts to destroy their power. Survival seemed at times as elusive a goal as capital accumulation. Surviving enforcement episodes and seasonal fluctuations with family members alive and capital intact was a treasured goal, not a certainty, and that uncertainty shaped many commercial decisions. The famine of 1983–84 did not threaten me personally, as a privileged United Nations employee with special import privileges, but many of the market traders I knew suffered and lost weight dramatically. I can never again talk about "mere" survival; the capacity to survive such events was a major demonstration of power and autonomy on the part of some traders and failure on the part of others. The analysis of African food security priorities made me realize how sharply this survival issue confronts the continent as a whole. Traders' actions not only helped their families to survive but affected, for better or worse, the survival capacity of their communities and nations.

Theoretical Windows

Assessing market women's capacity for social action combined assessing how valuable the market was to traders in their other struggles and how valuable other resources were to them as traders. I needed a theoretical framework that could integrate the full range of resources and strategies they integrated, identifying their most significant aspects and suggesting how they fit together without necessarily privileging one or another in an absolute way. The specific relations that Kumasi women traders drew upon to accumulate or to survive included family and ethnic relations, international and regional relations, and national politics, as well as marketplace relations. I wanted to talk about these relations together without suppressing the distinctive historical experience of each and without implying that I was leaving the women behind as women by talking about concerns of theirs not simply defined by gender. Their multiple identities as women, Africans, traders, Ghanaians, *Asantefo, Kumasifo,* etc. did not just have effects on each other, but each was only experienced in a form that incorporated the others. This mutual construction process involved as much contradiction as reinforcement, and traders themselves constantly used one identity as leverage upon another. Each identity group was deeply differentiated by the same processes of mutual implication that generated them and empowered them for effective social action and eventual historical transformation.

In searching for a theoretical framework hospitable to this multifaceted analysis, I found myself drawn back to the Black American feminists who had impressed me so strongly before I decided to go to Kumasi. Black feminists are among those who have engaged with particular seriousness in the theoretical problem of integrating multiple forms of oppression that are neither homogenous nor historically stable because these form their own basis for social action. They take the heterogeneity and overlap of social categories as an expectation, rather than a messy exception. That there is more than one way to be a woman does not make it impossible to act as a woman, since there is also more than one way to be an Asante, a trader, a Ghanaian, or any other category one might substitute, since all are constructed by such a process. People generally do act on the basis of conflicting multiple identities, explicitly or implicitly, so it is precisely this kind of action that maintains and transforms what we can see of society. In the later 1970s, a resurgence of Black feminist theoretical innovation began that built on a review of earlier generations of writers. One pioneering statement called for the analysis of race, class, and gender through combining insights from single-issue analyses of each (Combahee River Collective 1981 [1977]; see also Smith and Smith 1981; Hull, Scott, and Smith 1982). Smith's formulation of interlocking systems of oppression allows explicitly for multiple systems that reinforce, compound, and compensate for each other as easily as they conflict (Smith 1983). This seems to correspond to the experience of race, class, and gender by many black women more closely than de Lauretis's more neutral concept of "multiple conflicting identities" (de Lauretis 1986). It accommodates social action more directly because it allows more explicitly for expressions of domination or resistance in institutional and material forms that do not necessarily rely on individual or group identities.

Calls for critical appropriation of useful segments of theory from diverse single-system frameworks have also arisen from a number of white authors concerned with questions of public policy and social action. Sacks pays substantial attention to analyses by minority and working-class women in surveying and integrating frameworks used for race, gender, and class analysis (Sacks 1989). Nader presents a spirited defense of eclecticism for public interest ethnography addressing social problems in the United States, in which "the questions were driving the methods," rather than "subordinated to a school of thought or an intellectual style" (Nader 1988, 155).

In a recent synthesis, Patricia Hill Collins develops a matrix model incorporating interlocking axes of domination and individual, group, and systemic levels of domination, which she calls a matrix of domination (Collins 1990, 225). She discusses the matrix in terms of race, class, and gender, but the model could easily be expanded to accommodate additional axes, such as ethnicity. Like Smith, she argues that multiple oppressions are interlocking rather than simply additive. For example, the fact that gender and race intensify each other's impact in wage discrimination but interfere with each other in community organizing does not make them weaker categories, but makes each more effective as a system of domination, becoming an important characteristic of each system. She also ends by proposing an organized eclecticism drawn from more specialized analyses. For Collins, this takes the form of a permanent dialogue, which she values over falsely universalistic accounts, between specific standpoints which each generate partial perspectives and different situated and subjugated knowledges (Collins 1990, 235). The geometry of Collins's matrix model creates both strengths and limitations, which her own highly nuanced discussion of Black women and the Black community reveals in the same book. The matrix can be visualized as stacks and rows of boxes that position each personal or collective standpoint with respect to all of her three dimensions at once, so that no category can be internally homogenous. It allows for both negative oppressive power and positive sustaining power exerted by different systems or by the same system on one person, so that there are very few pure victims or oppressors. But the various standpoints still sit within defined boxes rather than sliding around; her model presents the three systems as relatively distinct social forces operating on each person. Her historical account of Black churches goes further to show the subtler dynamics of mutual redefinition of her individual, community, and system levels as well as race, class, and gender markers (Collins 1990, 223). This model of sophisticated handling of the dynamics of accommodation and protection I apply more directly than her formal matrix model in my own treatment of the somewhat different but equally interlocking systems of domination operating in Ghana.

Such deeply contextualized accounts of gender construction do require plowing through a considerable mound of detail on local kinship structures, state policies and political-economic processes, as di Leonardo complains (1991, 14). African and Asian feminist anthropologists have criticized Western feminist anthropologists for their unwillingness to make this investment of time and effort instead of plunging into the illusory intimacy of first-person narratives and universalizing psychologies (Ong 1988; Amadiume 1987). Recent detailed historical studies of complex, multidimensional transformations of gendered economies in Africa have confirmed that the effort is fruitful. Guyer pieces together precolonial and colonial stages of agricultural transformation in Cameroon to show the importance of changing gender relations in establishing colonial political and ecological relations as well as new norms of kinship and marriage (Guyer 1984). Muntemba and Parpart make the same point about industrial urbanization in Southern Africa (Muntemba 1982; Parpart 1986). Vaughan studied a colonial Malawi famine where overlapping systems of gender, ethnic, racial, and political relations interacted to determine the extent and distribution of suffering (Vaughan 1987).

Neither race, class, nor gender models can be projected unproblematically from Europe and the United States onto Africa, but each speaks to analogous relations in the Ghanaian context. The global system of black/white relations definitely has its direct impact on marketplace transactions, although this differs significantly from the impact in a settler colony such as Kenya or a slave colony such as the United States. Interethnic relations between Asantes and their northern and southern neighbors take on some of the same flavor from the history of Asante imperial expansion and slavery. Gender holds a very different but still powerful meaning for Asantes, implicated through matriliny in the division of family financial and domestic responsibility. Western European gender models also influence some Ghanaians strongly through church, school, government, and business. Class categories of bourgeois and proletariat, originating in Western Europe, likewise have a very restricted although privileged scope here, but their constituent principles of access to land, labor, and capital have wider significance. Commercial actors struggle to establish privileged access to social assets specific to trading—geographical and spatial location, information and customers, as well as capital. Each of these arenas of contest has its expertise, so players and analysts alike must try to balance awareness of its unique dynamics and the multipositionality of each actor.

Constructing the Book

The most immediate expression in this book of the dialogic synthesis Collins holds up as a goal is the repeated shifts of theoretical perspective from chapter to chapter. In order to deal adequately with either gender, ethnic, or commercial relations, for example, I need to invoke the analytic frameworks that respond to their specific historical dynamics. Kumasi Central Market traders rely a great deal on the power of their central position in the city and the region, so the insights drawn by Smith, Skinner, and others from economic geography are needed to interpret the power built into their geographic position. Political economy approaches place traders accurately within broader trends in world history and nationalist political alliances, including, but not limited to, debates over modes of production. Economic analyses have much to say about the particulars of trading practices such as bargaining, credit, and clientship. To understand traders' positions in ethnic and family relations, debates over lineage and household units, chiefship and domestic labor become relevant. Each chapter incorporates arguments and methods from a particular assortment of these frameworks, as its subject requires.

In reflecting on the combination and recombination of these different strands in successive chapters, I find a theatrical metaphor fitting. The cast of characters includes not only different theoretical approaches, but material from different research methods. Statistical, technical, geographical, ethnological, and socialist characters (among others) walk on and off the stage to participate in particular scenes where they have something to say or do. Visual, archival, anecdotal, and interview materials each contribute within episodes that feature one or another. The multivocal dialogue that results takes place between my own diverse internal voices, none of whom represent traders' voices directly but many of whom report what they heard traders say.

The book divides into four consecutive parts, according to the broad or narrow focus of their chapters. The first part features the marketplace system as a heterogenous whole, setting Kumasi Central Market in its commercial context visually, spatially, and historically. The second part drops down to the smaller units of individuals and enterprises within the market, describing their behaviors and intentions and their internal dynamics. The third part concerns middle-level organization within the market, including informal networks and formal commodity groups. The fourth part shows how these small units and the marketplace system itself are imbedded in broader regional and national processes of state and class formation and the renegotiation of gender, lineage, and ethnicity. Chapter 1 has offered a visual and interactional introduction. Chapter 2 explains the regional network of markets in other cities, towns, and villages that link Kumasi to farming and consuming areas across the country. It draws heavily on the regional analysis pioneered by Skinner and Smith, as later elaborated with reference to world systems theory (Smith 1972 and 1984a; Skinner 1964–65a, 1965b, 1985). The central location of Kumasi privileges it within specific urban/rural relations that not only advantage Kumasi traders but stratify them within Kumasi Central Market according to their differential access to these relations. Chapter 3 considers the historical process through which contemporary market institutions and relations have been constructed. The long history of international and local trading in this part of West Africa presents both substantial continuities with the past and a series of dramatic transformations in trading patterns. Looking at these past changes through the lens of political economy identifies key resources, actors, and trends that help explain current change processes.

Chapters 4 and 5 delve deeply into the technical aspects of trading in Kumasi Central Market—the way individuals and enterprises carry out their routine transactions. In these daily processes, never quite repeating themselves, the multidimensional relations of power are manifested in the market context. The balances of power according to gender, ethnicity, and wealth are also contested at this level, primarily through these daily processes, in the continual see-saw of seasonal and individual variation. Chapter 4 outlines the conventional procedures traders need to manipulate, and chapter 5 outlines the resources, both material and cultural, needed to manipulate those procedures successfully. Comparisons with detailed trading studies in other locations are important here to assess the implications of variations achieved, abandoned, or attempted. Policy interventions generally aim to address such operational constraints and needs.

Chapters 6 and 7 look at the organizational structures and practices through which traders manage these resources. The first considers vertical and horizontal principles of organization within the Kumasi market that involve traders as individual network builders and as group members. Chapter 7 focuses on the leaders of formal commodity groups, who negotiate publicly on behalf of traders. Both theories and comparative cases that consider principles of group formation, dispute settlement, leadership, and stratification are incorporated here.

The next three chapters broaden the focus again to include the wider context of ethnic, community, national, and gender identities in which market women participate. Chapter 8 considers the population from which Kumasi Central Market traders are drawn, to establish the multiple identities on which they can draw for resources supporting their trading position, or which can undermine that position. Chapter 9 examines in detail the family position of Asante women, the predominant trading group, as their families both provide and demand valuable resources from them. Theoretical discussions of domestic labor and gender are brought to bear on material from the many other ethnographers of Asante who analyze kinship and marriage, as well as the material gathered in the course of this study.

Chapter 10 considers the ambiguous relations between market traders and various parts of the state apparatus, which have protected them, depended on them, and preyed on them in shifting configurations. The book returns to a focus on international levels of political economy in order to look at international as well as local pressures to which the government still continues to respond under structural adjustment. In chapter 11, the different strands of subordination and power are woven together in a provisional assessment of current directions of historical movement and the potential they contain for traders' social action within them.

Building Bridges

Traders' capacity for social action is no hypothetical construct; they constantly demonstrate it as they defend their interests and accomplish their goals. Social action encompasses both their daily routines and the dramatic confrontations and transformations in which they take part, because these are strongly linked levels of action. A trader's success in daily bargaining, in wooing customers, in putting food on the table by buying and cooking it, and in ensuring cooperation and respect from her fellow traders builds the social resources she then employs in avoiding marriage, expanding her position against other kinds of traders, resisting government regulations, surviving government attacks, and participating in national politics. The strategies they enact in the realms of commerce, politics, and domestic life respond to chronic pressures and emergencies that reflect the interlocking systems of domination out of which they must build lives for themselves, their families, and their fellow citizens.

A significant resource for Kumasi traders consists of the favored position of their market within the marketplace system and their personal commercial positions in relation to this regional dominance. Worldwide, women rarely dominate an occupation or a location offering such a valuable economic base. In West Africa, marketplaces remain the major institution for the sale of consumer goods and remain relatively self-managing within broad economic and political constraints. Although Ghanaian markets have been in steady direct contact with European capitalism since before it was fully capitalist, they stubbornly refuse to wither away as predicted (Bohannon and Dalton 1962). Markets handle the majority of local transactions, and trading provides incomes ranging from the highest to the lowest. Kumasi Central Market combines service to local consumers in a large city with dominance of interregional trade in imports and farm produce to build firm linkages with other sectors. Power relations between other economic and political sectors are to a large extent enacted through pricing or other processes taking place within the market.

Asante market women in Kumasi Central Market provide an unusually clear window on the intersection of multiple systems of domination because they have significant autonomy to maneuver within more than one. Most market traders are self-employed, and collegial relations encourage the formation of cohesive groups. Kumasi Central

Market may be no paradise for women, but market trading under these circumstances, in combination with certain features of Asante culture, does provide significant sources of strength on which these women can build. In the market, Asante women have considerable control over their hours and conditions of work, within economic constraints, so the forms these take can reflect the demands made by their responsibilities at home. Conversely, Asante cultural norms give them considerable control over their own domestic arrangements. They can legitimately exercise a wide range of options in marital, residence, and labor-use patterns to accommodate the demands of market trading. Whether this balancing act resembles harmonious orchestration or frantic juggling, in the experience of traders it holds the key to daily survival and successful accumulation.

2 THE REGIONAL WEB

Among the most important power dynamics operating within Kumasi Central Market are those rooted in its dominance of the regional marketplace system. As an institution on a regional and national scale, this market draws power from other systems of domination enacted on the same regional and national stage. Struggles for control of access to key supply areas and transfer points within the region, including Kumasi itself, are inextricably linked to contests over racial, chiefly, ethnic and gender dominance. These social categories have jockeyed for position, in large part, by negotiating and fighting for control of commercial position. Historical trends in migration, urban/rural, international, and gender relations have altered the significance of specific commercial positions, whether defined geographically or functionally, without decreasing the intensity of conflict and negotiation over control of trade. Understanding the current interrelation between location, role, and identity within the marketplace system, in the light of this history, therefore takes an essential step toward interpreting the commercial resentments and goals so central to broader nationalist contests over race, gender, and economic development.

The city has been a point of contact since before colonial times with international corporations and interests with enormous power. Restrictions on African participation in commerce never reached the extremes found, for example, in South Africa, but Kumasi market traders did experience exclusion and repression in their interactions with the state and state-sponsored commerce. At the same time, market traders also participated in that domination by profiting from the urban domination of rural districts that went along with it. Even the smallest retailer still gains some advantage from her location in this bustling commercial center, and the largest wholesalers could not operate on that scale elsewhere.

The intense demand for selling space within Kumasi Central Market gives a visible indication of the power access to it can offer. Its traders are a privileged minority in one sense, compared with hawkers and roadside traders and with traders from less powerful markets in suburban neighborhoods, villages, and small towns. Rights to stalls within the market precincts constitute valuable working assets for these individuals and their families, rights which can be unofficially bought, leased, borrowed, and inherited. Less prestigious locations in the adjacent open areas and lorry parks also gain value because of their proximity to the Central Market, drawing high traffic that promises a better chance at a livelihood. The value of these positions derives in turn from the strength of this market's position within the regional and national marketplace system, which arises and shifts with its historically specific relations to farmers, industrialists, corporations, and other regional economic institutions, including the state as an economic actor.

Divisions within the marketplace itself are rooted in differential placement with respect to these external relations. Contact with relatively influential suppliers and customers, or with relatively exploitable ones, lays a particular basis for stability and accumulation. Even within an enterprise or a network of customers, one is placed to take more advantage of these connections than others. Hierarchies within the market both reflect this differential access and represent the success or failure of strategies to improve access. Outside leverage or dependency creates divergent loyalties among traders, tracing the outlines of conflicts of interest or potential cleavages under pressure. At the same time, the economic strength all traders draw on to some degree from their primary market creates a strong interest in promoting and preserving that market when it is under attack by outsiders.

This geographical solidarity could cut both ways; a range of political actions against urban market women also drew heavily on their geographical identification. To traders and producers in the surrounding villages and small towns, Kumasi Central Market looms like a spider in her web. Traders based in Kumasi and market conditions there do dominate commercial connections throughout Ashanti and Brong-Ahafo Regions and make most commercial links across those regions between Northern and coastal cities. Economic and moral tensions between urban and rural areas and between the North and South of Ghana, although rooted in wide-ranging political and social conflicts, are focused to a considerable degree on the person of the Kumasi trader who moves between them.

The Power of Location

Geography emerges prominently in everyday commercial identity and practice as well as during dramatic confrontations. Traders' identification with named locations corresponds directly to the commercial roles they practice and perceive as options, confirming the validity of using location as a conceptual boundary for analytic purposes. The correspondence between location and role is by no means one-to-one. Patterns of division of labor remain extremely diverse and vary between and within commodity categories, but locational identification is never trivial.

Exposure to central place analysis had predisposed me to take note of the regional geography of trading, but the conspicuous appearance of place-names and geographical identities in Kumasi market conversations confirmed this interest early in my research. Location was treated as an important characteristic of both people and goods. When I asked traders to identify the suppliers and buyers visiting their stalls with the simple question, "Who is this?" they most often chose to mention the person's primary trading location first, "She is from Obuasi," rather than her name, ethnic group, commercial role, family, or other known identifier. This title also represented her value to the trader; those receiving the warmest welcome were the trader's link to a location especially important for her commodity as a supply or distribution area.

Goods also gained in value because of their geographical identity. Retailers crying out their wares featured the name of the district of origin (Sehwi plantain, or Axim cassava) in order to attract customers. Longstanding local specializations apparently help maintain consumer acceptance through districts' reputations for consistent quality as well as reasonable price. I noticed that quieter traders often discussed the origin of their goods with customers during bargaining, but also with competitors and neighbors, suggesting that this was considered an important piece of information but no secret. I soon began consistently asking traders, "where is this from?" and found that they readily answered and almost always knew, even when they had purchased the goods themselves from intermediaries in Kumasi.

Traders seemed to act within a conscious framework that was conceptually organized as a regional spatial network linking Kumasi Central Market and other Ghanaian markets and nonmarket locations on which they depend directly or indirectly for supplies and buyers or consumers. Traders renting stalls in Kumasi Central Market have mainly indirect links with other trading locations, buying through intermediaries traveling to and from those locations rather than traveling to buy goods there themselves. But even traders who never buy or sell outside it understand that they gain an important kind of power from its centrality in the regional market hierarchy. The regional dominance of Kumasi Central Market was instrumental in its growth to its present complexity and size, from which they benefit directly.

The market survey confirmed my observations that Kumasi Central Market traders holding stalls rarely bought or sold in other locations themselves. Those sampled bought most of their goods in Kumasi, including those goods produced within the surrounding Ashanti Region or in Accra, locations readily accessible by a one-day buying trip (see table 2.1). This is even more true of women traders than men; even more of them buy in Kumasi and within the Central Market itself, although a small number do buy in stores located elsewhere. Only a few of the traders surveyed buy directly from factories, farms, or homes. Intermediaries bring the goods to their stalls, to market or wholesale yards, or to city stores. Most stall traders apparently cannot spare the time or gather the information needed for regular outside buying and also maintain a successful market stall operation.

These regional connections penetrate the market itself, creating cleavages and stratifications based on differential access or participation in these relations of domination. Traders who deal personally with suppliers and buyers from other locations have more leverage than those who operate entirely within the market. Wholesalers in imported foods, subordinate links in a hierarchy topped by monopolistic international firms, can control their retail customers more tightly through credit and opportunities to buy scarce goods than those who wholesale local food crops, linking mainly poor farmers to mainly poor urban consumers. Individual traders and categories of traders are better placed than others to exercise or benefit from these relations because they have better transport access and capital strength, the same factors that underpin dominance of one location over another. Tracing the effective geographical and functional limits of Kumasi Central Market's regional control therefore also indicates limits to individual traders' capacity to control the conditions of their own work and survival. Traders constantly press against these limits in using their ability to accumulate within the larger regional economic formation, through the same transactions that constitute their commercial routine. Farmers and smaller traders push back just as energetically to reinforce these limits on their central dominance, while those in superordinate locations (factories, ports, import houses) try to further limit city traders' dangerous autonomy.

The critical role of location in anchoring power within marketplace systems meant that some of the earliest acknowledgment of stratification and most sophisticated analyses of control in peasant markets within ethnographic work on markets drew heavily on central place theory developed by economic geographers (Christaller 1966). Skinner's pioneering work on Chinese market towns discusses the relation between their spatial organization and the key role designated for them in the social and bureaucratic hierarchy (Skinner 1964, 1965a,

Table 2.1 Source of Goods Sold by Male and Female Traders

A. Where Purchased
Percentage of Commodities Bought There*

Region	Men	Women	Both
Kumasi	70.2	80.5	77.4
Accra	20.0	9.1	12.4
Abroad	2.6	.2	1.0
Ashanti Region	3.6	4.4	4.2
Northern Region	.5	2.0	1.5
Other Ghana	3.1	3.8	3.5

B. Where Produced
Percentage of Commodities Produced There*

Region	Men	Women	Both
Kumasi	31.3	22.3	25.0
Accra	35.4	22.0	26.1
Abroad	19.0	14.2	15.6
Ashanti Region	6.7	17.2	14.0
Northern Region	4.6	8.0	6.9
Other Ghana	3.0	16.4	12.3

C. Type of Buying Location
Percentage of Commodities Bought There*

Location	Men	Women	Both
Own Stall	6.2	7.1	6.7
Market	29.4	55.8	47.8
Wholesale Yard	18.0	15.8	16.5
Store	27.8	14.2	18.3
Factory	8.8	2.4	4.4
Other	9.8	4.7	6.3

* Up to four separate goods recorded per trader (average 1.4)
SOURCE: 1979 Kumasi Central Market Survey

1965b). He also noted a connection between the dendritic (rootlike) pattern of markets in marginal areas and the greater economic and political dependence of the smaller markets on the largest town at one end, toward more central areas. More mature, balanced systems covered a region more completely with a honeycomb pattern that connected each smaller market to several larger centers. In mountainous areas, dendritic networks persisted due to transport difficulties, while the honeycomb network filled in more easily in China's floodplains.

Smith built on this framework for a more detailed, hands-on analysis of Western Guatemalan markets that demonstrated from the outset how relations between places illuminate relations between persons. The locational arrangement of markets corresponded to the ethnic hierarchy between Indios, Ladinos, and Spanish, and the social relations of resistance (Smith 1972, 1975, 1984a). She contrasts the dendritic system of Ladino-dominated markets along motor roads with the more balanced, multicentric honeycomb network of Indio-dominated markets in villages connected by paths. She continues to explore the implications of geographical distinctions for both commercial and community stratification, as Skinner continued to consider more contemporary market transformations in China (Skinner 1985).

Several studies of West African trading networks also employ a geographical and historical approach and confirm its usefulness for explaining the power structures implied in contrasting trading patterns. A discussion of the precolonial Dahomeyan market system figured prominently in Polanyi's development of the ideal type of the port of trade, which emphasizes the geographical as well as organizational confinement of trade within an official dendritic pattern (Polanyi 1957). Schwimmer pays close attention to the historical development of spatial networks and their social implications in a fascinating study of Suhum, then a newly settled district and market town between Kumasi and Accra (Schwimmer 1976). He documents a shift from a dendritic to a honeycomb pattern as the area became fully settled. Contrasts between distinctive commodity patterns reveal even more precisely the relation between kinds of power and the geographical configuration of trading relations. Trager found diversity within a Yoruba market system, in the distance to supplies and dispersal of supplies, which corresponded to variations in commercial practices between and within commodities (Trager 1976, 1981a).

Variation between commodities in the spatial pattern of their effective marketplace network is also marked within the Kumasi hinterland. In that sense, the overall regional marketplace network centered

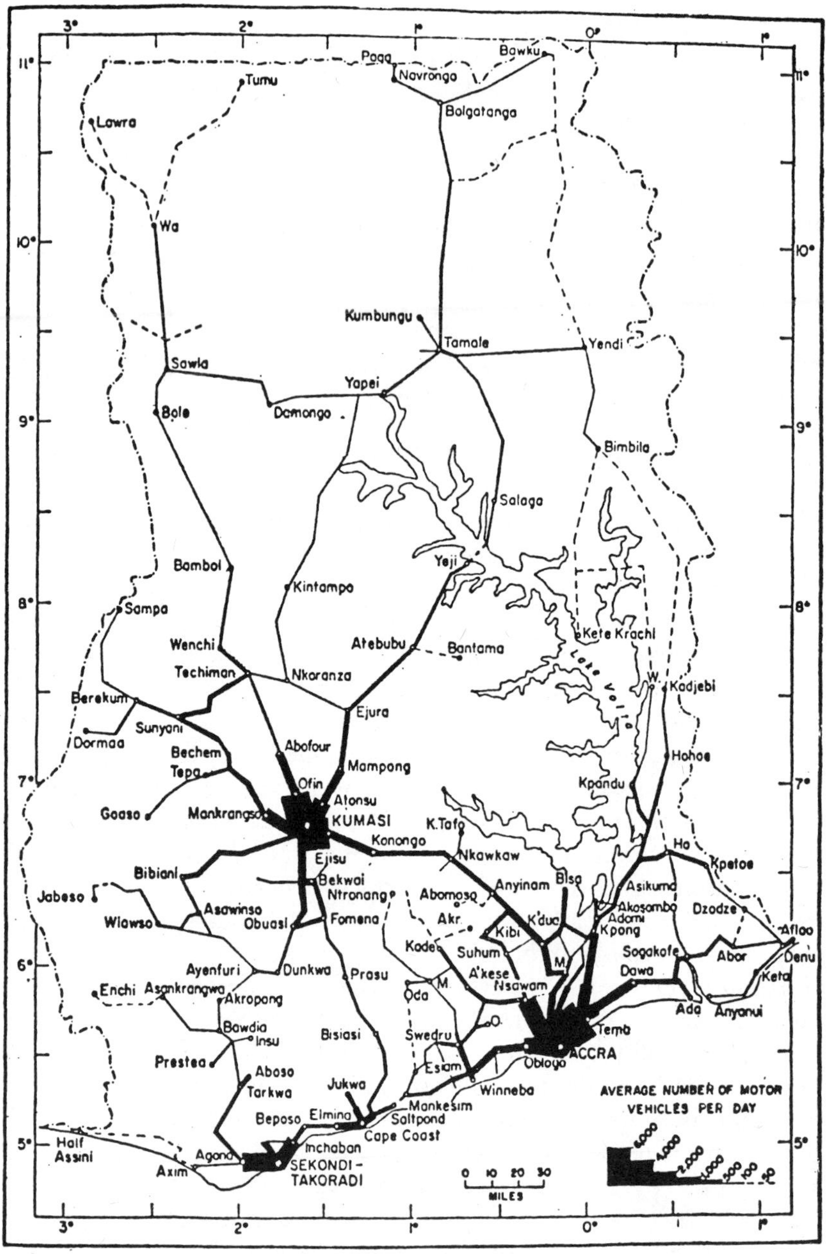

Map 2.1 Road Traffic Flow in Ghana, 1969 (Source: Road Traffic Census, 1969, PWD, Accra)

on Kumasi Central Market can be conceived as the overlap or accumulation in layers of these more selective networks. For each commodity sold there, specific districts which produce commercial surpluses are known to Kumasi Central Market traders and referred to by the name of a central market town. These local crop specializations take advantage of relevant climate and soil conditions which foster both good yields and valuable differences in harvest timing. Traders habitually buy major farm crops from a series of widely spaced supply areas in succession in order to minimize the annual period of short supply. For example, yams mature earlier in districts only slightly north of Kumasi, in adjacent Brong-Ahafo Region, and traders plan on visiting their suppliers there first for the new yams. When supplies in those towns are exhausted each year, the traders move on to yam growing districts in the Northern Region, where rains and harvests come later. Traders spoke of moving from Techiman to Kintampo, Ejisu, Ejura, Yeiji, Salaga, and Tamale through the season, although not every trader included each of these districts (see map 2.1).

The supply network for some farm crops is both far-flung and discontinuous; there may be several significantly different ones for one commodity. For example, tomatoes come from Akumadan and other towns within Ashanti Region and the adjacent Brong-Ahafo Region in the rainy season. When nearby supplies literally dry up, traders pack up and move north to Bolgatanga to buy at seasonal markets in towns accessible to irrigation projects in the most distant Upper Region. Tomatoes from intermediate distances are fewer and go to feed the intervening regional capital at Tamale. Major supplies of plantains come both from the immediate ring of feeder markets less than fifty miles from Kumasi and from new cocoa farms in western Sehwi near the Ivory Coast border.

The geography of each network defines categories of traders whose specific trading relations and division of labor correspond quite directly with their relation to different locations. Each functioning network sustains a chain of intermediaries who each control or staff a particular geographical segment, long or short. When an individual moves from one place to another along this chain, for example to follow her husband to a new job, to compensate for seasonal shortages in the first location, or to take up an inherited market stall, she must switch her work to distributive tasks that match her new location. This tight fit between location and commercial relations justifies choosing location as a convenient and meaningful conceptual boundary between categories of traders.

Women on the Road

One specialized set of traders are called *nkwansofo,* people on the road, because their role is to shuttle constantly back and forth. I refer to them as travelers and encountered them in the market when they delivered goods to the Kumasi wholesale yards. They seemed to have little to do there after unloading and sat on benches or in nearby sheds, eating and keeping a suspicious but exhausted eye on the wholesaler selling their goods. Those I interviewed brought goods regularly to Kumasi Central Market, but did not maintain stalls there or in other markets. A traveler's work takes place outside and between markets, buying directly from farmers in commercial farming districts and in distant markets. As the pattern of seasonal abundance shifted, a traveler might start buying a different commodity or move along to the next of an annual rota of supply locations. When asked who travelers were, their Kumasi buyers would identify them first with the supply area they currently served, but next with their primary residential base (important for debt collection). Travelers with a Kumasi residential base compete with others based primarily in the supply areas, who are not necessarily members of Kumasi Central Market commodity groups, although some are. Most of the minority of male travelers who sold foodstuffs in which female traders predominated had rural bases, where their social bonds with male farmers compensated for their lack of similar bonds with fellow traders.

Specialization among traders stimulates as well as depends on specialization among farmers and farm districts. Specialist travelers who buy at the farmgate appear in marketing networks for crops in which supply is concentrated locally, at a distance from demand (Trager 1981a). Such fields will be large enough to attract full-time specialist travelers only when this crop is a major cash crop for both the location and the individual farmer involved. Traders cannot justify the investment in travel and information-gathering needed to include a location in their regular rota when only a few farmers regularly sell large amounts, so farmers find it easier to sell what their neighbors already plant. Large amounts are easiest for the traveler to obtain when the farmer disposes of all or most of his or her crop in a single transaction. This presumes that the entire yield can be harvested at one time, as with root crops such as yams or cassava. Vegetables like tomatoes or garden eggs, a small, yellow variety of eggplant, must be plucked and sold every few days throughout the bearing season. In less specialized farming areas, or for crops requiring repeated harvests, travelers buy in village markets and from house to house.

Since travelers are constantly en route, they can also divert their supplies to alternative selling locations when they wish. Those I met did so less regularly than they rotated to new buying locations, but they made sure to maintain their effective capacity to sell in several markets. Farm buyers who routinely bring their goods to Kumasi Central Market also follow price levels at large markets on the road to their supply areas. Occasionally, they break their usual journey to buy or sell in them and renew personal contacts. One middle-aged yam traveler bought yams in the rich farming region just past Ejura, a regional periodic market, but I saw her regularly bringing them straight to her regular customers in Kumasi Central Market from the farmgate. When I began to visit her at home and monitor her travel schedule, I learned that she not only kept a sharp eye on supplies and prices in Ejura as she was passing through, but frequented the Ejura station at Kejetia lorry park to question visitors from there about what they had seen and heard. She even made special day trips to check Ejura market personally and confer with her contacts there. Ejura-based wholesalers sold to local and Kumasi institutional buyers and to market women from coastal cities who bypassed Kumasi. She explained that if prices were high enough, she was always ready to sell there instead of paying freight all the way to Kumasi. Buying supplies there was rarely worthwhile, precisely because strong demand kept prices up.

Village Periodic Markets

These irregular detours were not enough to change that yam trader's identification as a Kumasi traveler. Those who spend their work days mainly in other markets constitute a different set of traders called *dwadifo,* or marketers, not *nkwansofo.* They travel and return each day to one of the markets within the ring of village periodic markets that are in daily commuting distance of Kumasi, a ring which extends to a fifty-mile radius on a reliable road. Their Kumasi customers did not always know which markets each woman frequented; they would say she went to the villages, lumped as a single commercial arena.

Village markets meet weekly throughout southern Ghana (van Appeldoorn 1972). Each Kumasi-based marketer has a set weekly schedule of village markets she attends, leaving at dawn and returning in early afternoon to sell in Kumasi Central Market. These may be in adjacent villages or in opposite directions from Kumasi, since each trip is self-contained. Adjacent villages meet on different days of the week to avoid competing directly for the same clientele, as in many parts of the world. This also allows farmers to visit several accessible villages in their market "ring" if they wish to sell more often or compare prices, but neither farmers nor traders can attend more than one per day.

Village periodic markets have quite a different daily rhythm than Kumasi Central Market, interlocking as they do with its rhythms and those of farming based on the transport constraints of their patrons. They start later, at nine or ten in the morning, because many farmers walk in from surrounding hamlets. The outside buyers also rise early to ride in on trucks from Kumasi or other towns. The market also closes earlier than an urban market, around three o'clock in the afternoon, because the farmers need to reach home before dark. Bulking buyers start loading their goods for Kumasi even earlier, shortly after noon. They said it could be difficult to dispose of their goods if they returned in the late afternoon when most retailers there have stopped buying.

Auntie Comfort, a trader I accompanied to these markets, traveled with a friend of hers to a different village market each day of the week except Sunday and Thursday. They met at dawn at an abandoned gas station across from Kumasi Central Market to join a busload of traders going to their market, including two Northern women. The driver of this bus was from Auntie Comfort's hometown in Ashanti; she takes the same bus every day to a different market, but not including their hometown. Personalized relations with farmers in each of her regular markets were clearly a high business priority for her. She constantly asked after villagers' relatives and neighbors, whether or not they had sold her something. Her companion was learning some Northern languages in order to befriend the many Northern migrants who had settled in Ashanti villages as cocoa farm caretakers. The bus from Kumasi included women of Northern origin, and a wealthy, elderly Northern woman living in the village bulked palm oil on an even larger scale.

Unlike travelers at the farmgate, who specialize firmly by commodity, these village market buyers must be prepared to purchase a range of the commodities commonly sold near Kumasi. Auntie Comfort preferred to buy palm nuts and palm oil, which she sold to her mother in Kumasi Central Market. She said that her profits in these items were more reliable because she kept the most accurate information on their price and quality levels. She usually bought more of these than anything else, but sometimes high local prices made her main items completely unprofitable, so she bought other things to avoid wasting the trip. I also saw her buying small quantities of miscellaneous herbs and vegetables, explaining to me that they seemed plentiful and cheap, or that her usual palm nut suppliers had brought some to sell and expected her to accept them as a convenience.

The favorable transport position of these nearby villages makes it practical for marketers to collect highly perishable produce from less specialized producers. They buy in the odd lots and container sizes brought in by their local suppliers, bulking or making up the standard container sizes that serve as wholesale units for resale in Kumasi. The damp climate and soil conditions near Kumasi favor production of surpluses of cocoyam leaves, palm nuts, fresh cassava, plantain, peppers, okra, and spices. Marketers also buy palm oils and other farm products processed for easier storage and transport in quantity from the more remote farms or in villages between market days. Sudarkasa (1973) and Trager (1976) give detailed accounts of closely comparable foodstuff bulking markets in Western Nigeria.

In slightly more distant areas, Kumasi-based traders frequent the village markets only seasonally, when they offer abundant supplies of a local specialty not suitable for farmgate buying. I accompanied one garden-egg trader to her home district in Axim during the off season, when she visited farmers' homes in several adjacent villages to cajole small amounts of produce out of them rather than stopping at one or more of the local markets she patronized during the rainy season. She spent more time retailing in the off-season and operated more like a traveler in the harvest season, although her level of health also affected her ability to keep up a heavy travel schedule during the period I knew her best. Traders buying tomatoes in districts in Ashanti or Brong-Ahafo Regions that specialize in tomatoes patronize daily or biweekly markets in small towns at seasons when large quantities are available. One trader from near Techiman explained that outside tomato traders stopped visiting her local market during the dry season, leaving the small amount of hand-irrigated production to be sold to locally based traders visiting farmers at home. During the rainy season harvest, she also bought her tomatoes in the local market and resold in the Kumasi *bode.* Only high off-season prices for tomatoes and garden eggs and local hometown connections justify these traders' willingness to purchase at homes in small amounts and still make the trip back to Kumasi.

Ashanti village and small-town markets frequently boast of permanent cement stalls built decades ago as revenue sources for local government treasuries. These typically have tin roofs and half walls with generous spaces for traffic and open areas. Bulking buyers sometimes used stalls, but more often occupied an open corner or stacked their purchases along the roadside. Sellers approach them to bargain and then move off, perhaps adding their goods to the growing pile of foodstuffs, baskets, and oil tins at the trader's feet. In several village markets I visited, the cement stalls stood empty or partly occupied while retail traders crowded the open space with mats or temporary tables, paying lower rents or daily fees only. Only some traders in the more valuable items, such as dried fish and cloth, were willing to pay higher rent for cleaner, more solid facilities.

Marketplace typologies frequently designate bulking as a characteristic feature of one type of marketplace or location. Thompson and Huies (1968) assign agricultural produce bulking to urban "bazaar" markets, as opposed to rural "peasant" markets, on a cross-cultural basis. In Ghana and Nigeria, bulking takes place mainly in rural periodic markets that have little else in common with urban bazaars, but which also sell consumer goods to villagers (Trager 1981a). Smith (1975) distinguishes rural bulking markets, dominated by town buyers, from other village markets that serve local consumer needs. In the Philippines, small-town shops outside of the marketplace system bulk much of the agricultural produce (Davis 1973).

Typologies proposing a set correspondence between geographical location and function not only lack general applicability, but miss those factors which actually explain why specific functions, relations, or economic institutions are located where they are. Classical central place theory accommodates the mere fact of heterogeneity within a given marketplace neatly enough, since higher-level (bigger) centers by definition include the functions of lower-level centers. In their detailed expositions, the most geographically oriented authors seem to assume separate personnel for higher- and lower-order functions (Skinner 1964; Hodder and Ukwu 1969). The generative model used classifies centers by how many central place functions they provide, assuming an additive, directional hierarchy of both functions and centers. The bulking section of village periodic markets may be the part most important to Kumasi Central Market traders, but not to local residents. In those village markets I visited, urban marketers took over a designated area at the back of a market or outside of its walls, a much smaller area than the retail section where villagers buy their needs. A different set of traders, also called *dwadifo,* take manufactured goods or foodstuffs from other regions from Kumasi to their own weekly rota of markets. I met traders who sold salt, cookware, and secondhand clothing in the nearby village markets and lived in Kumasi; a few even owned or shared stalls in Kumasi Central Market. These traveling retailers are more often based in a rural town, returning to Kumasi weekly or monthly to renew their supplies from a wide area of the Ashanti, Brong-Ahafo, and Northern Regions. I met them when I took longer trips to these more distant towns with traveling farmgate buyers who would use one as a temporary base when we visited the local weekly market.

These retail services are vital because many farmers in the Kumasi hinterland depend on market purchases to maintain a balanced diet. Vegetables from other parts of Ghana are brought in to supplement inadequate local supplies in farming districts that specialize heavily in a single crop and in most districts during the dry season. These include dried onions and other vegetables, beans, and irrigated tomatoes, but also fresh plantain and other staples. The significant proportion of Northerners farming in the Ashanti and Brong Ahafo Regions creates a demand for Northern foodstuffs in rural markets there. For these "local foodstuffs" from other parts of Ghana, prices are higher in villages than in Kumasi.

Even subsistence farmers count on buying smoked fish, salt, kerosene, and used clothing at their local market. The damp forest zone is chronically short of protein foods, since many domestic animals do not thrive there and stocks of indigenous game and snails are becoming exhausted. The less-expensive varieties of smoked fish always take up a large section in village markets. Canned fish and other consumer imports and manufactures are carried as supplies and incomes permit. Secondhand clothing expanded into a major section of village markets between 1978 and 1990. The meager handful of stalls displaying this exotica in 1978 had taken over one-quarter to one-half of the marketplace surface in those markets revisited in 1990, when few farmers could afford more prestigious new clothing or cloth.

Small towns and villages also support a noticeable number of cooked food sellers on market days, local residents who cater to buyers and sellers alike. Farmers who may have walked long distances to market need fortification for the trip home, as do returning Kumasi traders and transport workers. Sellers of snack foods and light meals can also be found daily not only in the nearly deserted marketplace, but also at the roadside and along paths leading to the fields. Local farmers buy prepared foods surprisingly often before and after the long trip to their farms. Only a small section of a village market retails locally grown raw foodstuffs to the tiny nonfarming population (such as schoolteachers) or to farmers who have stayed at home temporarily. This set of traders usually remains in the village or town marketplace on nonmarket days, along with a few cooked-food sellers who offer a treat or a fast bite, creating the appearance of a tiny urban neighborhood or street-corner market.

Regional Periodic Markets

A few periodic markets perform regional bulking and transfer functions for goods which pass between the major ecological zones—the coast, the forest, and the savannah (see map 2.2). At Ejura and Techiman in Brong-Ahafo Region, north of Kumasi, Kumasi traders gather weekly with those traders from the Northern and Upper Regions. I accompanied Kumasi-based traders on several buying trips, and each time I saw others I knew. Kumasi traders buy yams, grains, and beans in both of these regional markets in addition to buying in the north and from northern traders in Kumasi. Southern traders also bring forest produce and manufactured goods to sell there to northern wholesale and retail traders who need not come as far south as Kumasi. Some yam travelers from the coastal cities of Accra and Takoradi purchased their bulk yams at Ejura and Techiman markets instead of at the Kumasi wholesale yard. Both regional centers also bulk yams and agricultural produce from their own rich local hinterlands and supply the periodic and daily consumption needs of town residents. To a lesser degree, Kumasi traders also patronize Mankessim, just inland from the coast, for bulk supplies of kenkey and smoked fish produced on the Fante coast. The closer, larger demand from Accra apparently draws in all the vegetable foodstuffs bulked there.

These weekly regional markets offer wholesale services similar to those found in the Kumasi Central Market *mbode* (their commodity-specific locations are also called *mbode*), but instead of serving primarily retailers and consumers from the same market or town, they serve primarily distant cities and rural districts. Their physical facilities have the same simple style as periodic markets in other towns of their size but cover a much larger surface area. Their market "day" has also expanded to fill the preceding and following days as well in order to accommodate more visiting traders. The full transition to an urban daily market seems arrested because of the lack of the stabilizing force of substantial local consumer demand. Their size and prosperity depends much more on long-distance traders (based locally or not) and on interregional linkages, which leaves them much more vulnerable to transport or production changes that may encourage traders to bypass them or transfer to other routes. For example, the regional position of the Ejura market, straddling the Great North Road to Tamale, was strong

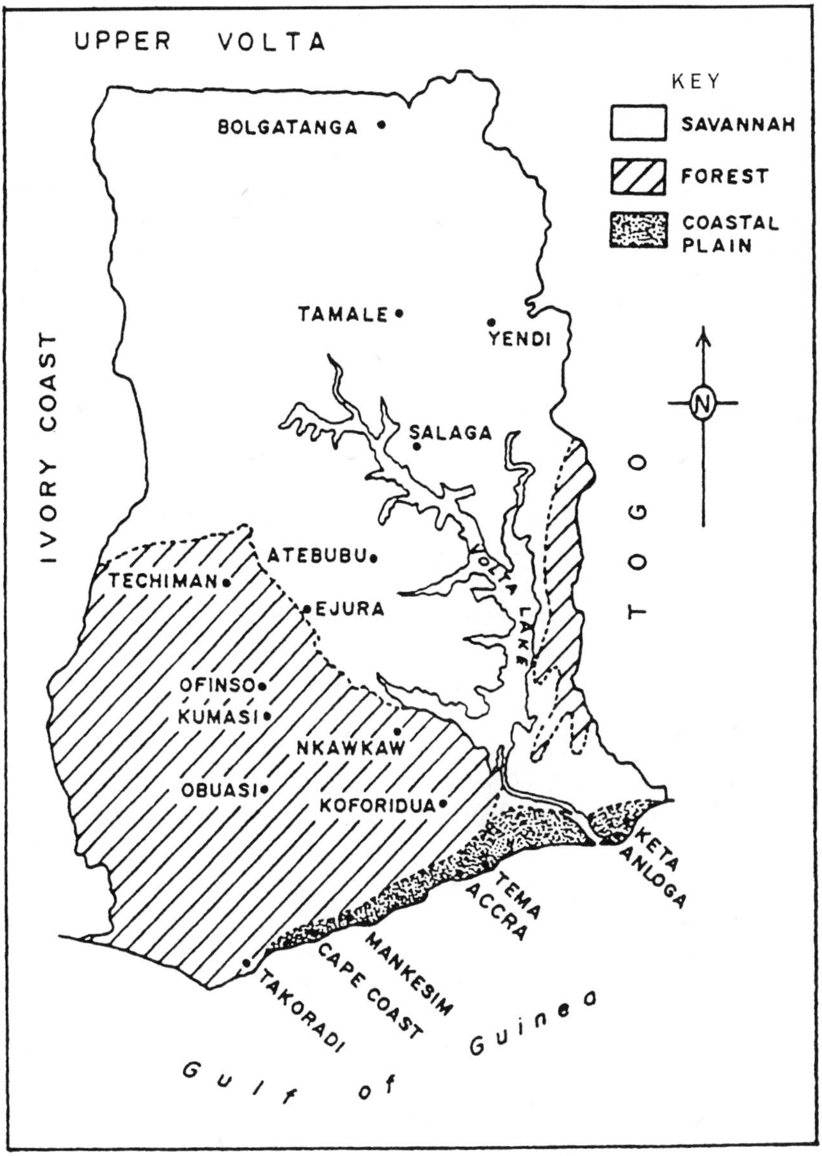

Map 2.2 Ghana: Vegetation Zones with Some Important Markets

as long as the ferry crossing the Volta was reliable enough that traders could count on arriving from the north on market day.

The existence of these regional markets places an important limit on the control Kumasi-based traders exercise over this interregional transfer trade by providing alternative transfer points. I encountered no specialist travelers who shuttled between Kumasi Central Market and these regional periodic markets, although my Kumasi friends pointed out some who did so from the coastal cities. Rather, these markets substituted for or competed with the traveling role in supplying Kumasi or points south and north. Kumasi yam traders who bought in bulk at Techiman were either larger retailers or institutional contractors who would otherwise buy supplies travelers brought in to Kumasi wholesalers.

Kumasi Central Market retailers in northern specialties (for example, beans, peanuts, and shea butter) with enough capital to buy in at least the largest wholesale unit were most likely to buy in Techiman. Would-be travelers could not easily buy these directly from northern farmers because small surpluses were sold by scattered women and farmers throughout the north rather than from large commercial fields, as for yams. Local northern traders buying in village or town markets collected together bulk units for transport to Techiman or to Kumasi for sale to other Northern men who sold wholesale in Kumasi storefronts. One peanut trader who bought in Techiman explained that Kumasi wholesalers' prices were high enough to make her trip worthwhile every week or two.

Periodic markets linked to Kumasi Central Market did not have a controlling influence over its traders and barely affected its weekly rhythm. The Friday regional wholesale market at Techiman is an important national supply point for grains and beans, but hardly ripples the surface of price and availability levels in this market. Wholesale prices for these items do fall slightly when the weekly supplies from Techiman arrive, but resale transactions most often take place outside the Central Market in the nearby storefronts. Many market retailers can store enough to buy consistently at the lower price, so retail prices remain steady.

Only one weekly periodic market takes place within Kumasi Central Market, a small Monday market for Asante waist beads where craftswomen and traders from the villages which specialize in this craft display their wares aggressively. Kumasi residents and buyers for resale rarely patronize the few full-time bead stalls, who sell at double the Monday price. In 1979, this weekly event took over a plantain shed inside the market walls for the day, but it had been exiled to the marginal "French line" by 1989. During the same interval, the handmade glass beads were increasingly displaced by lighter, cheaper plastic beads in similar patterns.

Weekly market cycles in Kumasi Central Market are best understood in relation to urban consumption patterns, which makes Saturday by far the busiest day of the week. Traders display extra stocks and raise prices according to demand. Workers buy extra food for a more elaborate Sunday meal. They also time major purchases like cloth or hardware for Saturday, when they have more time to compare prices and styles. Wholesale volume paradoxically drops on Saturday. Travelers seldom plan to arrive then, because any mishap would delay them until Sunday, when most wholesale yards are closed. Retailers take care to reduce stocks that will deteriorate further over Sunday. The few traders who sell tomatoes and other perishable vegetables on Sundays charge extra for their foregone holiday and low expected volume. On Mondays, volume slightly exceeds other weekdays because shoppers and traders renew their supplies after Sunday. Buying rises again slightly on Fridays, when shrewd shoppers avoid Saturday's higher prices.

This Saturday pattern contrasts with the "market day" pattern of strong weekly or biweekly peaks shown by wholesale vegetable markets in other West African cities, like Accra's Malata market, where volume expands and prices drop markedly on Wednesdays and Saturdays. This locally generated cycle suggests a heavy weight to fundamentally local bases of commercial power here. The dominant group of sellers in Kumasi Central Market are its resident wholesalers, and the dominant group of buyers are retailers from within the market, who ultimately face local consumers directly. In Techiman, long-distance traders and, in Accra, suburban retail market traders dictate a periodicity that suits their different needs.

The Center of the City

A second basis of locational power for Kumasi Central Market traders rests in the dominance it enjoys over smaller Kumasi marketplaces. If the regional periodic markets undercut Kumasi Central Market's absolute control of its hinterland, no other market challenges its monopoly of the advantages of location within Kumasi itself. I systematically asked for additional buying and selling locations when talking to stallholders, their suppliers and buyers, and market leaders. Usually the locations mentioned turned out to be in another part of Kumasi Central Market, across the street or down the block.

The size and complexity of Kumasi Central Market are unusual partly because it engrosses central place functions more commonly divided between several markets in a city of such size. Commodities, services, and enterprise types, which in other cities occupy several distinct markets, group in and around Kumasi's disproportionately large Central Market. In Accra, four or five markets of roughly equal size divide wholesale functions for specific commodities between them. Specialized periodic markets on the edge of town handle bulk produce for Cotonou in the Republic of Benin and Ibadan in Nigeria, cities of roughly comparable size to Kumasi. Farmers' markets, where villagers sell their own produce directly to consumers, are also missing from Kumasi, although reported in smaller towns (Gore 1978). The urban night markets of Western Nigeria, specialized on temporal principles, have no parallel here (Sudarkasa 1973).

A spatial structure of markets articulates with relations of physical accessibility, competition, information and auxiliary services that have strong implications for trading relations and, consequently, for the expansion potential of the market traders' enterprises. Access to central locations is essential to commercial success for reasons of efficiency for traders and convenience for customers. The magnet of a dynamic commercial core in large cities like Kumasi increases the attractiveness of the city center. Studies of illegal street hawkers and markets in India, Hong Kong, and Washington, DC, show that the same high foot traffic that motivates the efforts of store owners and other formal commercial interests to move traders away from their doors keeps the traders returning to central business districts, where they make attractive incomes despite constant harassment, confiscations, and arrest (Lessinger 1988; J. Smart 1988; Spalter-Roth 1988). McGee's study of Hong Kong traders (McGee 1973) and Sariri's study of traders in Chandigarh, India, (Sariri 1979) discuss how important relations linked to location are for the commercial survival of market and nonmarket traders relocated or excluded by zoning and market planning policies. Wholesaling for some commodities in Kumasi takes place outside the Central Market complex, but not in other markets. Major stores in the nearby commercial district operate wholesale outlets for imported and manufactured goods, although some wholesalers also operate from the specialized retail section of the Central Market called the "provisions line." Storefront traders in streets adjoining the market handle most of the wholesale trade in grain and beans. Wholesale yards for secondhand clothes and charcoal have overrun a disused petrol station across the street from the northern edge of the market. All of these other wholesale districts cluster around the Central Market, intensifying its economic centrality. Such overflow locations are visually and functionally extensions of the Central Market complex, if not conceptually or organizationally. The practical advantages of contiguity include easy transport and information access, as traders and goods circulate continually between them. Separation carries its own advantages, however, allowing traders to avoid accountability to market groups and allowing a larger degree of privacy or concealment in the storefront facilities than in market stalls.

In Kumasi, the only major commodities whose primary wholesale locations are geographically distant from the Central Market moved as a result of government action. Cattle sales were transferred when a new slaughterhouse was built on the periphery. The State Fishing Corporation frozen fish outlet was located at the model Asafo market in a promotional effort undermined by erratic supplies. In 1979, kola traders relocated under pressure to an underused neighborhood market a few blocks away from the Central Market. Some "French line" traders followed them temporarily after the demolition of this section.

Supplementary wholesale yards do open in other markets for a seasonally or locally limited clientele. The Bantama and Asafo neighborhood markets have smaller wholesaling locations for oranges, yams, and plantains that serve retailers within these large markets and in the near neighborhoods. These reach substantial volumes during the peak harvest season, when available supply overflows the capacity of the Central Market *mbode,* but their volume is not sufficient to displace the Central Market *mbode* as primary in size or price influence. Supplementary wholesale yards for tomatoes and a few other perishables also spring up in Kejetia lorry park, across the street from the Central Market, during the harvest season.

Only Asafo and Bantama Markets, with some autonomous wholesale activity, show the potential for developing into rival or complementary wholesale markets following the multicentric pattern more common in large West African cities such as Accra, Kano, or Cotonou. Asafo Market has its own lorry station in the rear, and its traders can buy supplies of several agricultural commodities directly from disembarking villagers. High-volume imports and manufactures traders there buy from stores or producers rather than through Kumasi Central Market. The State Fishing Corporation outlet for frozen fish is located there. Bantama Market is also much larger than other neighborhood markets and has independent unloading points for plantains, oranges, and other Southern produce. Each has embryonic wholesale yards in a few commodities for its own retailers but does not appear to provide wholesale services for other markets at present.

Other Kumasi neighborhood markets remain commercially dependent on Kumasi Central Market because of its wholesale functions. Traders from these markets buy in the wholesale or concentrated retail areas of Kumasi Central Market alongside buyers from mixed retail areas and nearby village markets and on much the same terms. They are a valued category of customers because they buy regularly in wholesale units or large retail quantities. Depending on their commodity and distance from the Central Market, they buy daily or weekly, opening their stalls when they return.

Although neighborhood markets in residential areas of Kumasi do not challenge the dominance of the Central Market, they compete directly with its mixed retail areas in appearance and function. Like traders in mixed retail areas, these traders display the vegetables and starchy staples bought daily by most urban Ghanaians along with inexpensive manufactured items. They offer the convenience of buying all of the items usually needed without wading through a congested aisle or standing in line for public transport downtown. Craft workers and cooked-food sellers work from market stalls or nearby streets. In return for low rent and accessibility, neighborhood enterprises settle for poor physical facilities; smaller markets in Kumasi lack permanent or enclosed stalls and cement paving. Only Asafo Market, built as a model market during the Nkrumah period, has elaborate buildings.

Diffuse sales outside the precincts of recognized city markets, by hawkers, streetside sellers and house sellers, did not bypass this structure of dominance because their supply channels ran straight through it. I talked to these sellers on the street, as well as in front of their market suppliers, about their perceived alternatives for buying strategies. They preferred to come to Kumasi Central Market for supplies or raw materials rather than neighborhood markets, whose higher prices would handicap them in competition with other hawkers. They compete for retail customers with market-based traders but also complement their activities. Consumers bound to the home workshop or by dependent care rely on nearby or passing traders for their daily supplies. They handle the same range of commodities as neighborhood markets or Central Market mixed retail areas, but with more emphasis on cooked food. Fruit, snack, and meal sellers find a large part of their potential customers in residential areas and near workplaces.

Nonmarketplace trade complements market trade in terms of employment as well as consumer demand. Small children, poor personal health, and norms of wifely seclusion acknowledged by most Muslims to some degree keep some women at or near their homes temporarily or permanently. They can still earn an independent income, although usually smaller than in market trade. Within the individual life cycle, nonmarket options keep both former and potential market traders employed so they can maintain or develop trading skills and capital levels. Low capital forces some people who might prefer or aspire to a marketplace business to trade part-time or from rent-free locations. Many current traders mentioned saving up their starting capital through hawking or other nonmarketplace work. Market traders' own lifestyles contribute to the specialized convenience demand that such nonmarketplace sellers satisfy. Relations with sellers of cooked food and soup ingredients in their own neighborhoods play an essential part in many traders' domestic arrangements. Small children who could not brave the hazards of Central Market shopping can run errands to nearby stands for the essential tomato or onion, bridging a labor gap in some households. Cooked-food sellers provide reliable meals for children left home alone and a safety net when a woman is delayed in the market or on the road, or taken ill suddenly. Hawkers and roadside chop bar restaurants cater to women traders on the road (women at noon, others at night) as well as to single people and all-male households, giving them an extra degree of flexibility.

Retail sales in the city as a whole were effectively dominated by Kumasi Central Market's full-time retailers because most retail channels passed through them sooner or later. Their commanding position in the distribution chain between farmer or importer and urban consumer contributed an important element to the appearance of power in the hands of the market woman. Arguments that market women deliberately intensified inflation assumed that their monopolistic actions prevented consumers from buying directly from farmers and stores at lower prices (Clark 1988). Similar accusations in Peru also led to repression of traders and unsuccessful promotion of direct sales by farmers (Babb 1989). While these formulations paint too extreme a picture, the actual degree of independent access farmers, consumers, and other traders can exercise does establish a significant parameter for the power of traders in a particular market.

Farmers sold surprisingly little of their own produce directly to urban consumers in Kumasi, contradicting not only the common stereotype of the farmer/trader in idealized descriptions of Ghanaian market women, but also the verbal designation of several fringe areas of Kumasi Central Market as the villagers' market, or *nkraasefuodwom*. These are mixed commodity areas where traders sell small amounts of goods spread on the ground or small tables, without even flimsy stalls, near lorry stations where passenger trucks arrive from nearby villages. Its name, location, and minimal facilities correspond to a market near the lorry park in Koforidua, a much smaller Ghanaian town not far from Kumasi, where villagers actually did most of the selling (Gore 1978). Upon spending time in the Kumasi Central Market villagers' markets, however, I discovered that most of the traders there are Kumasi residents who buy in small amounts either from villagers arriving on the trucks and buses or from Kumasi Central Market wholesale yards.

Those few traders I found who lived in a village were not selling primarily their own produce, but produce bought from village neighbors to make up sufficient stocks to make the trip to Kumasi worthwhile. As a daily occupation, this is only viable from an extremely restricted set of villages close enough to Kumasi so that the daily trip in and back leaves them enough time for a full day's retailing. These villages can contribute only a minor portion of Kumasi's food, the more so since villages so near the city often have very little good farmland left. Villagers traveling to Kumasi for family visits or business may bring some produce along for sale to finance the trip, but they usually sell the whole lot to a Kumasi-based trader in the lorry park on arrival. Farmers interviewed in both nearby and distant villages expressed no interest in selling their own produce in Kumasi and, in fact, resented when lack of buyers made this trip necessary.

Even though few farmers exercise the option of direct sales, these open market areas retain a hidden economic importance because they preserve the option of direct access between farmers and Kumasi Central Market consumers. Kumasi Central Market wholesale traders cannot exploit their position unduly, either in price or other terms, because they do not control access absolutely. These areas play an active role in price formation despite their comparatively small size and volume. Both farmers and retailers do monitor prices inside and outside the wholesale yards, which will be discussed in a later chapter. Kumasi traders' accounts of their own casual entry into rights to specific squatting locations there and in the Kejetia lorry park market indicate no social barriers that would keep villagers out, so it seems that more farmers could sell in or near Kumasi Central Market if they wished. Attempted market distortions by the government did cause these alternative sites to grow rapidly in a matter of days in 1979.

Villagers most often appear in Kumasi Central Market as buyers. Farmers from all over Ashanti and Brong-Ahafo Regions will travel to Kumasi to make major, infrequent purchases such as cloth, cooking utensils, fertilizer, or building materials. When they come to Kumasi on business or for these major purchases, they will also take the opportunity to buy other goods they might otherwise buy at a nearby market town. I had opportunities to hear village residents planning their trips to Kumasi on buses, in lorry parks, and on visits to rural producers. Their expected shopping habits, if not their commercial acumen, tallied closely with Kumasi traders' reports. An unusually large number of villagers come in just before Christmas to buy their gifts, and they have a perceptible influence on trading stocks and practices. Their expected presence contributes to the high price levels at that time. The farmer takes advantage of the lower prices and larger selection found in Kumasi, while the trader takes advantage of the farmers' lack of price information and bargaining skill.

Factory Linkages at Home and Abroad

Buying relations link market women to the most powerful as well as the least powerful categories of actors in their national economy. If Kumasi Central Market traders as a whole clearly dominate traders in smaller marketplaces or on the street, they are just as clearly subordinate in their relations to another set of sales locations. Traders in imported and manufactured goods buy their supplies from factories, small shops, and large import firms and from individuals with connections to these. Although many of these transactions were illegal for the first five years of my research, traders allowed me to accompany them on the rounds of their contacts at flour mills, warehouses, and back alleys and to discuss more of their successful and unsuccessful attempts to locate supplies. Kumasi Central Market stallholders buy these items most often from factories and commercial outlets in Kumasi but outside the Central Market. Some traders made direct resale arrangements with small local producers of baby clothes, shoes, and other inexpensive items. Individuals bring relatively small amounts of goods into the Central Market in suitcases as samples, for traders to see and order. Before 1984, these were mainly smuggled or diverted goods, but by 1990 they included legally acquired supplies. After trade liberalization in 1984, retailers buying in smaller quantities (a dozen, rather than a hundred) could also buy supplies in local shops and through legal middlemen.

The geographical framework of imports and manufactures distribution differs sharply from that of local foodstuffs and is weighted sharply toward the coast. Kumasi has branches of all the larger import firms and a number of factories producing consumer goods, but these outlets are concentrated outside Kumasi, in the Accra-Tema area. The resulting dendritic pattern, with Kumasi firmly subordinated to Accra and in turn firmly subordinating its northern neighbors, is associated with deeper stratification in trade and between communities in comparative studies (Smith 1975). Local foodstuffs distribution shows a more balanced, honeycomb pattern including more alternative channels and giving Kumasi a much more favorable position between Accra and the North.

Unlike traders in foodstuffs, the high-volume wholesalers in factory-made goods frequently travel themselves to buy supplies in other towns and occasionally to other countries. For example, Kumasi Central Market traders regularly visited the palm oil processing plant near Takoradi and the flour mills and State Fishing Corporation at Tema in 1979. They also circulated to shops and branches of import firms in Accra to compensate for irregular supplies in Kumasi. All the women I met who operated in these circuits had a partner or trusted assistant to remain in Kumasi and manage sales in their absence, since the length of time it might take them to locate and take delivery of goods was so unpredictable. By 1989, better transport and fewer regulations made such trips easier, while more reliable supplies in Kumasi made them less necessary. For cloth and other fashionable goods, lower prices and a better choice of goods in the Accra-Tema area still justified regular trips by Kumasi-based retailers.

During the late seventies, the distribution of imports and manufactures had to accommodate very unsettled economic conditions which seriously disrupted the operations of factories, import firms, and shops. The large legal import firms, such as Ghana National Trading Corporation, Paterson Zochonis, and Kingsway, offered irregular and unpredictable supplies of goods which could not satisfy consumer demand or keep traders in business for either the long or short run. Local factories operated intermittently or under capacity. Illegal supplies were actually steadier and a necessity for those traders still working. Historical evidence suggests such disruption was frequent in preceding years; it was repeated in the years between 1981 and 1983. Shortages and irregular legal supplies determined distribution patterns throughout the seventies and early eighties.

Purchasing supplies from legal sources (not always legally) required skillful manipulation of the system of allocations and chits. Traders obtain legal wholesale supplies from the large importing firms at special locations in Kumasi called yards or warehouses, which the firms keep separate from their retail department stores and technical stores. When price controls were in effect, before 1984, these large firms sold very little on a walk-in basis or in amounts suitable to small retailers, such as one carton of evaporated milk. The bulk of their wholesale transactions were in larger quantities, solicited by repeated visits to the offices of the firm. Traders and institutional buyers received chits, or written notes, from high officials of the firm authorizing them to purchase a given amount.

Some institutions and cooperatives were assigned regular monthly allocations of imports, although actually receiving them also required frequent visits. Ghanaian factories also legally supplied goods through an allocation system in which individuals registered by name on a list of approved wholesalers to receive a set amount of goods each week or month. They had to collect and pay for their allocations promptly to stay eligible, although machinery breakdowns or raw materials shortages made the production timetable irregular. Many factories also honored chits from management, further reducing the supplies available for allocation.

Given the grossly unsatisfied consumer demand, competition between traders centered on getting an allocation or a chit rather than on efficient sales. Smaller traders depended on diverted and smuggled supplies from illegal intermediaries, also based in Kumasi but outside Kumasi Central Market. Few of them had the connections needed to obtain substantial legal or illegal supplies from retail outlets and smaller shops. Sometimes these transactions took place on or near factory or store premises in Kumasi, but from persons of influence who resold their allocation almost immediately. Both legal and illegal channels required personal connections and constant personal availability to circulate between possible buying locations and pay immediately for goods. Public legal sales of confiscated consumer goods during 1979 at controlled prices favored urban residents, but did not help Kumasi traders much, since active traders had little effective access to them. Access depended first on speedy information about when goods would become available and then on the willingness or capacity to stand for hours, sometimes days, in the long lines that promised popular items like soap, rice, or sugar.

Under these conditions, traders and consumers based in villages or small towns were even less likely to gain access to imports and manufactures. Obtaining legal allocations and illegal chits both involved spending so much time in the city that only urban residents realistically had much chance of buying from large import firms and factories, or even from the top layers of intermediaries. The resulting intensified dendritic hierarchy in the national network made Kumasi traders more dependent on ultimate sources in Accra and Tema, but it made more remote traders even more dependent on sources in Kumasi.

The only mitigation of price and supply differentials came in rural locations near the nation's borders, through their favored access to smuggled supplies. Zaire presents a more extreme case of this paradox: the capital offers commercial benefits from access to the bureaucratic elite and the remote border districts offer the benefit of distance from the same controlling elite (MacGaffey 1987; 1991). Both situations can generate windfall profits.

If traders had difficulty buying from the formal sector in the late seventies and early eighties, reverse linkages where stores or factories bought from market traders were extremely rare. Stores stock mainly imported and manufactured goods supplied by factories or government agencies. Those that stock vegetables, baked goods, or craft products apparently contract directly with large-scale producers. In contrast to situations like the Philippines, where Davis reported stores buying up vegetables from traders as well as supplying manufactures to traders, no Kumasi trader reported supplying stores for resale or raw materials for factories (Davis 1973).

Food processing factories existed in several regions in Ghana but did not buy their supplies through marketplace channels or use contractors. They could not pay current market prices because official price controls regulated their final sales prices at levels too low to recoup such costs. Many that depended on local raw materials suspended operations during periods when price controls were enforced strictly, for months or years. Before and after price controls were in effect, these factories had attempted to buy directly from farmers, though with mixed success. I was able to discuss factory buying with farmers raising irrigated tomatoes in the Upper Region, where the government had sensibly located a tomato cannery, and with coconut and palm oil processors in villages working with raw materials they could or legally should have sold to government agencies for local oil mills or export. According to them, the problems lay as much in rigid or unreliable buying procedures as in price. This will be discussed in more detail later in connection with other state purchasing efforts.

An important exception was the successful supply through marketplace channels of local foodstuffs for institutional catering facilities at factory canteens, prisons, schools, and other institutions and restaurants. They employ or contract with buyers who visit Kumasi Central Market wholesale yards regularly to supplement official allocations of staples with market purchases. Traders in other towns and cities reported similar patronage by local institutions, but some contractors from more distant small towns appeared as regular customers in Kumasi or the regional periodic markets because they were willing to travel in order to buy their less perishable items at lower prices. The location of many such institutions in and near Kumasi, a major regional capital, gives traders in its Central Market better access to these outlets than traders in small towns have, although such outlets are fewer than in Accra and Tema.

Struggles for Position

Control of geographical positions within the trading system has been hotly and repeatedly contested over the centuries in this part of West Africa precisely because so much economic power is linked to geography. Traders have negotiated and fought for access to particular markets, supply areas, and commercial roles as members of ethnic groups and polities whose identities were largely constituted in terms of these commercial assets. Meanwhile, these historical transfers of trading roles between racial, ethnic, and gender groups, along with transport and other technological changes, altered the power implications of controlling the contested positions. Commercial positions taken over by a group subordinated in some other arena tended to become weaker, while otherwise stronger groups strengthened the positions they already controlled.

Asante market women in Kumasi inherit a regional and international trading network where there has been substantial historical continuity in their identities as women, as marketplace traders, and as Asantes. The trading roles open to them as Kumasi residents and as women have expanded and intensified during the course of this century, within the lifetimes of the oldest traders I interviewed. Asante trading territory extended farther, but lost its exclusivity as members of other ethnic and racial groups gained freer passage into and through it. The same colonial-era forces that generated those expansions simultaneously subordinated market trade more firmly to overseas interests, and trends have continued in this direction during the last ten years. National intervention in market trading has been substantially reduced as a result of tighter control by international policymakers. Direct confrontations have ceased between the archetypically male military authorities and the archetypically female market traders, but male infiltration of the ranks of market traders has accelerated as structural shifts in the economy impoverish more men.

The central position of Kumasi and the Asante people, compared with neighboring rivals, has remained remarkably consistent over several centuries despite dramatic reconfigurations of trade—a testimonial to their strenuous and effective efforts. The Asantes emerged as an identifiable political unit in the seventeenth century when Akans moved into the forest to control gold mining areas and trade routes linking the ancient caravan routes across the Sahara to the European shipping routes pioneered by Portuguese explorers in the late fifteenth century. The Asante capital, Kumasi, lies about halfway between the coastal fort towns and the Northern savannah towns. Asante diplomacy and warfare first focused on defeating and absorbing their former overlords to the south to maintain free access to the coast. Then attention turned to its northern borders, turning the chiefs of Brong, Gonja, and Kete Krachi into subjects or tributaries (Arhin 1975; Maier 1983). Close relations with its "home port" of Elmina were threatened several times in the early 1800s by blockades or sieges by the British and Fante. The Asantes at first attempted to send more of their trade east via Accra and west via loyal ports around Takoradi. When the hostile British took over Elmina from the Dutch in 1868, the Asante army invaded it twice, in 1870 and 1874 (Wilks 1975). To the north of Asante, repeated unrest in the subjugated Brong chiefdom of Gyaman shifted trade west from its capital, Bonduku, to Salaga, and later to a new market at Kintampo when Salaga rebelled (Arhin 1971).

Negotiations and regulations concerning commercial practices preoccupied Asante, Fante, and the other Akan polities as persistently as physical control over trade routes. Coastal chiefs took care to renew and enforce regulations mandating use of their citizens with chiefly credentials as trading intermediaries by both Europeans and foreign Africans. The Asante government managed international trade even more tightly through an elaborate system of border controls that kept trade inside the boundaries of Asante in local hands, partly for military security (Arhin 1971, 210; Wilks 1975, 703). Regulations and loans kept much of the most profitable trade in the hands of men with chiefly connections or sponsorship, concentrating power within that system in the political capital, Kumasi. Commoners and women had greater access to the considerable trade supplying coastal and inland cities with craft products and foodstuffs, which extended to other West African ports. Salt, smoked and dried fish, smoked game and snails, palm oil, shea butter, kola, and handwoven cloth were traded long distances. Women did join these caravans, but more visibly dominated local retail markets, selling fresh vegetables from farms near the towns, cooked food, and inexpensive imports (De Marees 1985 [1602]). Geographical patterns of trade thus reflected but also reinforced broader patterns of stratification.

Trading nations could monopolize the benefits of a location indirectly, through negotiating privileged access to specific trading roles there. As the balance of power on the coast shifted increasingly toward Europeans after about 1750, each European nation began imposing more favorable trading regulations in the fort towns it controlled. Restrictions were enforced with greater success against African traders doing business with Europeans from other countries or with European interlopers from the dominant country who lacked royal licenses. The British consolidated their formal administrative and commercial control over the Gold Coast gradually after 1830. The scheduled steamship service begun in 1852 made more feasible direct control of local officials and private employees by their superiors remaining in Europe. In 1874, the British army repulsed the Asante invasion and sacked Kumasi, establishing direct governmental control of the whole coast in 1875. By the end of the century, a few large British firms had consolidated control of the commercial linkage to Britain, driving out of business most of the larger African and mulatto traders and bankrupting or buying out the independent Europeans based on the coast (Hopkins 1973, 199; Howard 1978, 184). To avoid direct rule, the Asante government tried to negotiate independent concessions with British business interests for trading, mining, and railway development in 1892 and 1894. The British occupied Kumasi in 1896 to install a Resident, canceled these agreements, and effectively prevented further independent negotiations by exiling the Asantehene (Wilks 1975, 655). When the Resident openly declared permanent sovereignty in 1900, the resulting armed rebellion turned defeat into conquest.

British colonial authorities were as obsessed with their citizens' commercial access as the Asante chiefs had been. They immediately gave European firms official planning support, allocating sites for their future Kumasi branches as the town rebuilt after the 1900 siege. They revoked chiefly privileges, intending to break the Asante monopoly on north-south trade. Coastal Fantes and northerners assured of free access to Asante produce and consumers at first swelled the size of Techiman, Ejura, and other regional markets within Asante territory. After a few years of peace, these neighboring groups immigrated in large numbers to Kumasi and became a significant commercial presence in its market.

British city planning policies worked to the advantage of Kumasi's Central Market traders by holding down trade at other city locations. Streetside traders and ambulant hawkers could evade taxes and sanitary regulations more easily than traders with fixed stalls. The first location assigned in the center of the Adum commercial and residential district was soon painfully congested (see map 2.3). The largest vacant piece of land near the city center lay along a river bottom, already hastily drained for the railway which was conveniently located across from the main city lorry park (see map 2.4) (NAK8). Anticipating a quick return from market revenues, the Kumasi local government issued bonds

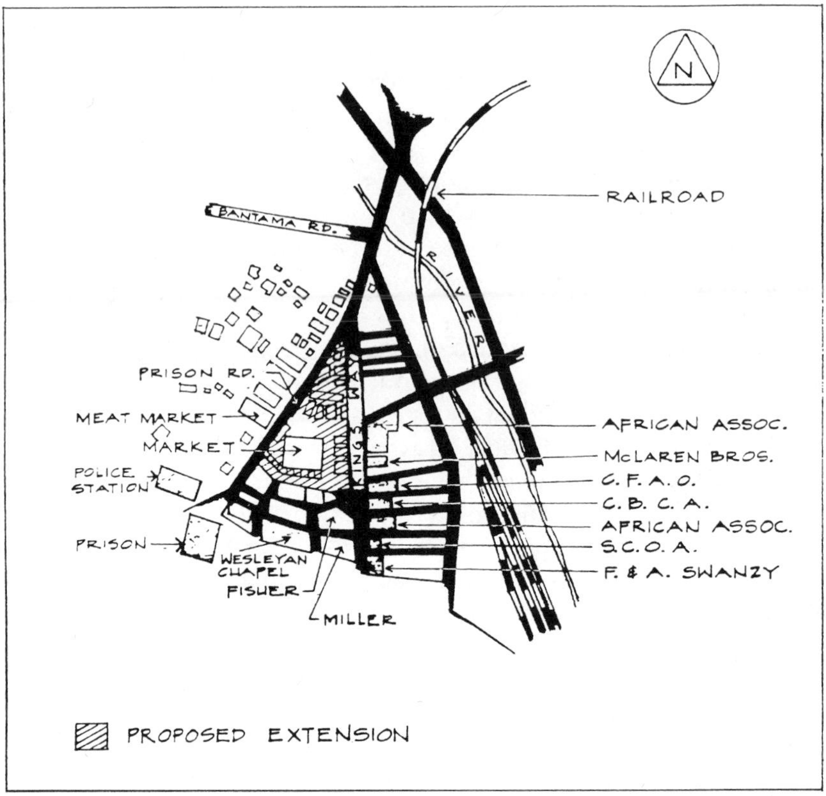

Map 2.3 Kumasi: Old Market Extension Proposed in 1914

in 1924 and erected the first sheds within a year (NAK1). New market sections continued to open at a steady pace until the outbreak of the Second World War, eagerly filled or even constructed by established and aspirant traders. European officials argued for eliminating hawkers altogether, while African representatives defended their useful services to the community and won authorization for neighborhood markets (NAK9). Governments through the 1990s continued to invoke financial and sanitary arguments in repressing street trading, but also turned those arguments against market traders themselves.

Transport Cycles

The layout and condition of national and regional transportation networks has been an important determinant of the strength of Kumasi's position within the national central-place system through

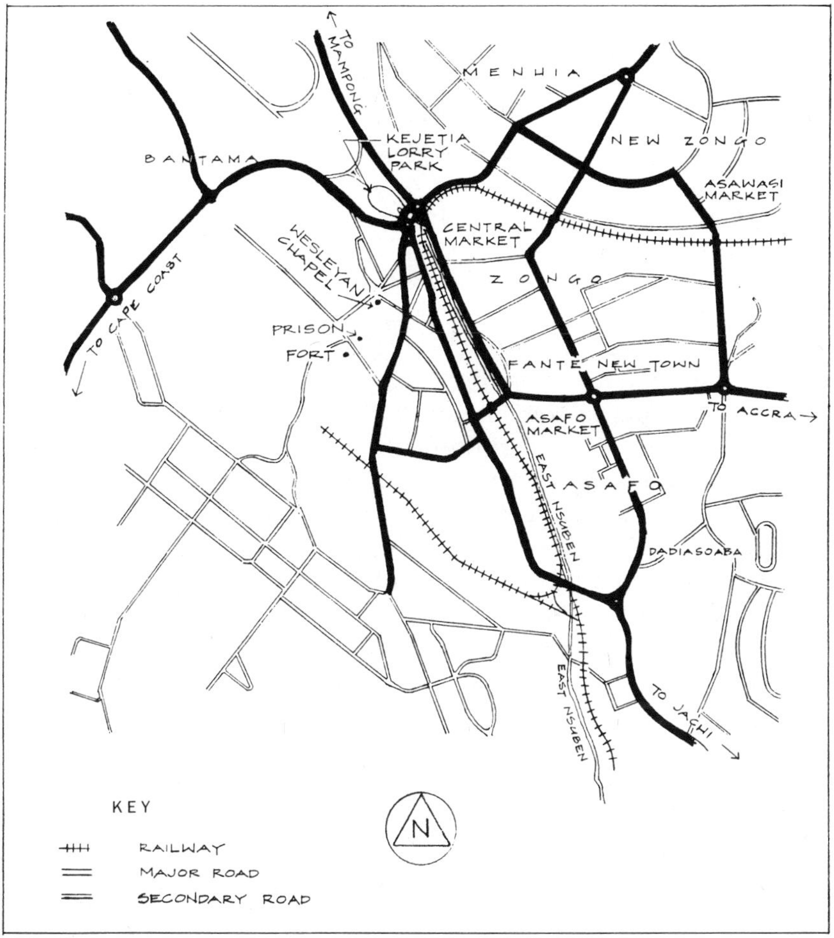

Map 2.4 Kumasi: Central Market and Smaller Markets, 1967

cycles of expansion, degeneration, and revival. New forms of transportation transformed the basis of physical access to and from Kumasi. The colonial authorities may have pushed through the rail to Kumasi to ensure military access, but they also ensured that consumer goods for the Ashanti Region and farther north would be loaded onto trucks there. The network of roads designed to feed cocoa and other exports to the railhead directed the movement of foodstuffs through Kumasi on the way to the coastal cities, including the colonial capital of Accra (see map 2.1). Kumasi itself could tap fresh food supplies by road from a new ring of village periodic markets, many of which continue supplying it today. Less perishable staples could now arrive reliably from virgin farmlands north and west of central Ashanti, and grain and livestock come directly from across the Volta, tying these distant regions more tightly to Kumasi as an economic center than ever before. The population of Kumasi expanded rapidly along with its volume of marketplace trade.

The expansion of railways and roads in the early twentieth century, continuing after independence in 1954, cemented the dominance of Kumasi traders over an expanding hinterland no longer limited by chiefly political administration. Accelerating deterioration in these transport infrastructures from the 1960s through the mid-1980s forced Kumasi traders to relinquish direct access to some locations and revert to gathering supplies from intermediaries in district and interregional periodic markets. This decentralizing trend preserved commercial institutions more open to rural producers and traders, but it also entrenched Kumasi's intermediary position between the coast and the North.

Overall deterioration in road quality and the number and condition of vehicles on the roads, compounded by gasoline and oil shortages, retarded further commercial unification and rationalization. The scarcity of transport created the need for special knowledge of road conditions and transport personnel that reinforced the position of intermediate markets, since traders from coastal cities could not expect to pick up transport on their own past Kumasi. Intermediaries based in Kumasi or regional markets had more leverage with drivers they hired frequently and had convenient access to larger transport yards. Farmers and rural traders from supply areas had extreme difficulty in convincing drivers to risk their trucks on dubious roads to collect their loads. The network of alternative connections to adjacent district capitals fell into disuse, and many villages fell off the transport map entirely.

The addition of transport search and waiting time to actual riding time kept the radius from which villagers could commute to Kumasi easily or Kumasi-based traders could visit weekly markets small. In some ways, this froze the intensification of the central place system at 1930 or 1950 levels. Schwimmer documents dramatic configurational change in a newly settled area near Suhum, between Kumasi and Accra (Schwimmer 1976). Admittedly, the area around Kumasi had already been densely settled and commercialized for many decades before colonial conquest, let alone independence. Still, the rapid postwar intensification of commercial production within Ashanti might logically have generated market realignments around fewer centers, if transport could have responded to demand.

Even major trunk roads deteriorated under financial pressure during the 1970s, eventually undermining Kumasi's national commercial position when direct contact with several other regional capitals virtually ceased. Before the 1960s, traffic from both Cape Coast and Takoradi could reach Kumasi by going directly north on separate trunk roads. Passenger buses going north from Takoradi passed through Cape Coast and Kumasi by 1979, and the road via Tarkwa saw little traffic due to disrepair. Public and private carriers stopped traveling the road to Cape Coast in 1979 and 1980, as it crumbled off the hillsides, severing Kumasi's shortest route to the sea. By 1983 both Takoradi and Cape Coast busses took a route passing near Accra (see map 1.1). Kumasi's Fante smoked-fish traders with family suppliers there had to send their goods through Accra at greater expense, and Cape Coast buyers began to purchase in Accra.

The late-1980s road rehabilitation concentrated trade geographically because it restored only one North-South route. The Great North Road through Yeiji to Tamale became uneconomical when low water levels and lack of repairs disrupted ferry service across the Volta. Diversion of commercial traffic to the longer western route, recently repaved, reinforces the commercial position of Techiman, located on that road. All coastal traffic is still forced to pass through Accra, intensifying Accra's primacy over Kumasi. The long overdue extension of the coastal road westward to Abidjan further encourages traffic through Accra. The Ghanaian central-place network now presents a dendritic more than a balanced honeycomb pattern, which comparative studies associate with more rigid commercial hierarchies and higher levels of rural dependence (Smith 1975).

Limited road and rail rehabilitation in the later 1980s under the Structural Adjustment Program expanded the effective long-distance reach of Kumasi traders beyond Techiman, but it also did the same for coastal and Northern traders moving into and through Ashanti Region. When transport improves, Kumasi traders use it to extend their range into more distant supply regions and to bypass local periodic markets in rural districts within their hinterland. During the same periods, easier transport undermines their local dominance from another direction, by facilitating efforts by traders from coastal cities (especially Accra) to bypass Kumasi and buy directly from rural or small-town sources within its hinterland and further north. Northern and small-town Asante traders also travel south more easily through Kumasi to the Accra-Tema region to buy imports and local manufactures directly.

By 1989 some of these predictable effects could be perceived. Transport conditions had improved dramatically after deregulation of fares, fuel, and parts imports; the increase in functional vehicles and fuel had brought more frequent service even on smaller roads on nonmarket days. Some of the village periodic markets nearest Kumasi were already shrinking. Villagers could more easily travel to Kumasi for sales or purchases, and traders were starting to buy at the farmgate. Long-distance traders were also extending their routes; one had reactivated contacts dating back several decades, when she had been based in Northern Brong-Ahafo. Kumasi traders reported regular buying and selling trips as far north as Wa. Accra traders were reported to be bypassing Kumasi and trading directly in Techiman and Tamale markets. Such trips had not been unheard-of earlier, but now seemed to involve more commodities and new personnel. With liberalization of imports trading, traders from farther north and smaller towns could also bypass Kumasi more easily to buy in Accra and Tema.

Control over Space

The relationship between power and location within marketplace systems is strengthened, not weakened, by its variability over history, for different commodities and at each geographical scale from global to a single marketplace. Typologies which imply a one-to-one correspondence between location and trading function or personnel impoverish the contribution more dynamic analyses can make to understanding the workings of contingencies and constraints. The spatial distribution of trading roles and practices mediates between power and location through the activities of traders who strategically manipulate these links. Some categories of traders are defined by their exclusive rights to one location, others precisely by their relation to more than one location. Travelers gain power by linking locations, but their relations at each end need to be different, since these must be conditioned by other dominant relations affecting the regional or local position of that supply area or wholesale yard.

These relations between power and location reveal more information about the geographical structure of power when problematized as the matter to be explained, rather than presented as the answer. More static approaches externalize historical change by passing over the constant fluidity and intense contestation of the connection between location, personnel, and function. Heterogeneity within locations illuminates the dynamics of variability that construct this historical change. Negotiability and flexibility in who does what and where, however confusing to the analyst, create the structural resilience that enables marketplace systems to persist over the long and short terms. A known trader, trading relation, or function can move to a different place or time, or even stop temporarily without compromising its identity or accepted form and behavioral content. For example, a wholesale yard can move or shut down temporarily with minimal disruption to its core members and resume full operation quickly. The wholesalers, their commodity, and the relations between them persist when the primary wholesale yard moves from town to city or melts into a multipurpose marketplace site during the off season. Important trading institutions, like landlord clientship, or commodities, like dried fish, have been transferred across gender or ethnic lines rather permanently and rapidly without loss of vigor or sophistication. A market can incorporate a much wider range of commercial and productive relations than could stay together in the long run if held strictly in any one pattern of articulation.

The regional system makes a relevant backdrop to Kumasi Central Market both because some individual traders move about within it and because far more traders are touched by economic connections to it through intermediary traders. At the regional level, the marketplace system links traders at village, regional, and urban markets into a reasonably coherent network that also knits together nonmarket locations such as farming districts, factories, and stores. Its own still larger frame, at the global and national levels, includes international corporations and agencies, foreign governments, and diverse national government agents and agencies, whose connections will be discussed at length in a later chapter. Geographical proximity is a significant index to power in these networks, but not the only factor involved. Transport facilities, regulations, and unofficial connections contribute to structural closeness and distance and are as hotly contested as physical access.

Parallel factors emerge in locational power struggles at smaller geographical scales between markets within a single city or inside a single marketplace. Access to space within a city is negotiated in terms of property rights and urban land use planning. Traders from other markets, shop owners, and other commercial actors jockey for privileged status and state support through debates on licensing, zoning, and taxation. Within Kumasi Central Market, gaining access to favored sales locations plays a key role in establishing legitimate access to central wholesale networks and customer pools and the information needed to use access profitably.

At each geographical scale, power attaches to locations that give access to bulk supplies. On the regional level, easier access to import firms and factories gives urban areas an intractable basis for dominance over rural areas, which some urban residents can then turn to commercial advantage. Produce bulking plays a key role in many marketplace systems in enacting rural/urban power relations and in establishing food security for urban populations and food-deficit districts or households. The geographical placement of bulking needs to be analyzed, not taken for granted, as one of the aspects of the bulking relation that contributes to constructing historically contingent rural/urban and interregional relations. Climate, soil, and transport advantages make certain rural Ghanaian farm districts primary sources of certain staple food crops. Traders can effectively control access to steady bulk quantities, at least for key seasons for specific commodities, by controlling those geographical links. Inside the city of Kumasi, those key bulk and long-distance supplies pass through the Central Market wholesale yards. Spatial and institutional proximity to those yards gives Central Market retailers a significant advantage over traders from other markets.

Transport plays a very significant role in specifying the benefits of location. Road and rail networks reconfirmed Kumasi's centrality at a juncture when political developments consciously undermined it, but these advantages are not just established once and for all. For example, petrol and spare parts shortages exaggerated the advantage Kumasi Central Market retailers enjoyed because their competitors from other markets had to search long for taxis and vans, but their head porters were unaffected. The heavy foot traffic privileges retailers in specialized commodity lines, but the resulting congestion drives other customers away. Spatially concentrated customer pools attract many hawkers to the market aisles and downtown streets, but congestion provokes hostility from store merchants and public officials. Continuing street clearance campaigns still aim to preserve "free access" or priority access to through traffic and store displays.

Tracing the establishment, evasion, and loss of control of locations involves following a concrete trading relation or task through a shifting network of physical locations and of ethnic, class, and gender identifications. These trajectories direct attention to the political, cultural, and economic conditions that shape the overall marketplace configuration. Zoning and licensing policies confront specific technical and cultural features that determine economies of transport and space use, perishability, accessibility to specific buyer groups, and availability of supporting services. These pressures can frustrate enforcement with all the force of survival imperatives at the enterprise or community levels, but they can also make traders vanish rapidly when their generating conditions shift (Sariri 1979; McGee 1973).

The constant need for adjustment between subsystems within the marketplace system creates commercial units whose centers remain more stable than their boundaries. The internal structure and the core membership of the subunit are built around its characteristic defining relation, which may be a trading task, an institutional pattern, a kind of source area, etc. Specialized retail areas, for example, contain those retailers firmly linked to the wholesale yards and their associated commodity groups, although some individuals may also obtain supplies from the lorry park or other retailers. Those defining relations link the subunit to its main trading partners and are affected most directly by shifting power balances between them. Changes in other factors affecting boundary maintenance and recruitment, such as layoffs or a credit squeeze, trigger transfers of marginal personnel but only gradual structural change in the subsystem itself.

These transfers permit radical adaptation to rapid economic and policy fluctuations without reducing the wide repertoire of trading relations readily available for future use. Problems such as transport and physical vulnerability to attack can quickly rearrange the locations of specific traders and transactions, but less quickly change how they expect to do business. Viable or dormant alternative distribution locations and relations help ensure an appropriate response to unpredictable future changes and also provide checks and balances against abuse by controllers of the currently dominant channels. More complete or successful control would require preventing subordinates from evading the channels controlled, increasing the rigidity of that segment of the marketplace system and reducing the overall strength of the system. This kind of flexibility is a key to the survival of both marketplace institutions and individual traders in the extremely fluid commercial environment of contemporary Ghana.

The current diversity of trading subsystems at the local and regional levels reflects all the historical complexity of these generating processes. Layers of somewhat distinct trading institutions accumulated from those established during earlier historical periods; these continued operating in vestigial form during the expansive 1950s and were reactivated as political and infrastructural conditions deteriorated and economic disintegration became apparent by the 1970s. The several trading networks associated with each commodity also accumulate, joining together to support market institutions and personnel none could keep going by itself. Each layer carries its history of racial, ethnic, class, and gender assignment and of contests in which those groups or categories tried to enlist the support of the state. Historical trends reveal the relationship between locational and commercial power through a complex, interlocking series of struggles never finally resolved, but each feeding into subsequent struggles that invoke the same or different identities. Questions about this interlocking process itself address the crosscutting ties in which particular actors participate as both dominant and subordinant in different respects. What kind of leverage does commercial position give, in terms of traders' ability to promote their national, ethnic, and gender interests? When and under what circumstances do gender, ethnic, and national struggles turn to control of commercial space as a key issue, both symbolic and material? The dynamics of reproduction and change of the economic hierarchy unfold as diverse categories and groups manage to enshrine their old advantages within new contexts and to deploy their new strengths to dismantle old constraints.

3 PERSISTENT TRANSFORMATIONS

The long succession of radical and dramatic changes in the racial, political, ethnic, and gender boundaries within the marketplace system of present-day Ghana locates Kumasi Central Market traders within a history where innovation and conservatism are equally hard-won. The recurrent questions—who will buy and sell what, where, and how—had no automatic answers, traditional or modern. Past efforts by specific groups of traders to defend and expand their commercial positions and by farmers and importers to undermine or restrict traders' positions have given each group the material and ideological resources they draw on in their current conflicts. This chapter presents considerable detail about these long trajectories of commercial change because the implications of recent and contemporary changes in trading roles and the effectiveness of recent strategies must later be assessed in this context. When traders and others act to influence the future directions of change, how these actions continue or diverge from the overall trend of similar successful and unsuccessful actions indicates how likely they are to reinforce or turn around current directions.

The multiplicity of possible directions of change means that the meaning of any victory or defeat is always contingent on other struggles. The lines in gender and ethnic access to crucial commercial relations were redrawn in very different places during this century, in large part because of equally striking shifts in gender and ethnic access to other parts of the economy, such as cocoa farming. The power based on achieving a particular gender or ethnic assignment of trading roles or geographical configuration of trade often proves unstable when changes in conventional trading procedures and practices redefine what occupants of those roles or locations can do. Frustration over these complexities accounts for some bitter controversies over seemingly technical details of the trading system, beyond simple access, dating from the early 1700s to today. When power balances outside the marketplace system shift markedly, the trading patterns that reflect and reproduce the old balance provoke energetic attacks and defenses.

The historical dynamics of commercial relations unfold in intimate complicity with transformative shifts in the balance of social power through processes of state formation and class formation in the broadest sense, putting aside the question of whether forms of social control exercised here correspond fully to Western concepts of the state. Both now and before colonial rule, international and local trade were clearly implicated in the progressive concentration of both political and economic power within smaller and smaller circles throughout this part of West Africa. The last chapter presented a detailed account of the mutual construction of political and commercial boundaries in terms of spatial control. Competing trading factions consistently tried to enlist the support of political authorities and institutions to which they had access. Conversely, political authorities (Asante, British, and Ghanaian) used and promoted loyal categories of traders to gain political as well as economic advantage over their rivals. Scott suggests that marketing arrangements are in general a primary site of contestation over the relative power of the state and various sectors of production (Scott 1986).

Political access has consistently been a critical factor in drawing and deepening divisions between men and women, between ethnic groups, and between market trade and other economic sectors. Governments of all periods in what is now Ghana have been openly involved in establishing and protecting ethnic and national boundaries in commercial roles. To the extent that the government controls access to significant resources, in fact and not simply on paper, political access becomes an economic resource. Pellow and Chazan (1986) point out that both the advantages and disadvantages of economic involvement with the state have strongly shaped Ghanaian commercial patterns, both inside and outside the marketplace system. Parpart and Robertson confirm more generally the importance of differential access to state resources and protection for men and women as a factor defining gender-linked economic options (Robertson 1984; Parpart 1986). State mediation of shifts in gender and ethnic assignments of trading roles before and after independence here coordinated those movements with concomitant role shifts in the major productive sectors, agriculture and mining.

Dynamics of Class, Gender, and Race

The interlocking history of these multiple systems of domination makes some discussion of theories of class dynamics essential at the outset. Several distinct approaches to class have each yielded valuable insights into West African commerce. The crosscurrents of these debates have brought out interesting points about the foundations and limits of political and economic power in concrete instances, even when their rival primary conclusions seem beside the point. As Gavin Kitching noted, it is the "relative significance and importance" of a group's strengths and weaknesses, not the nature of these, that leads to the most persistent differences of opinion (Kitching 1985). To varying degrees, analysts of class also discuss its historical interpenetration by ethnic and gender relations.

Rather than settling on the appropriate class assignment for Kumasi market traders at the outset in this section, I will identify significant continuing issues in these debates that identify major indicators of class position for monitoring throughout the historical account that follows. The relative autonomy of traders in commercial practice, their ability to accumulate, and their political alliances appear twice in these debates, as evidence for particular theoretical judgments and as predictions. The chapter then concludes by reconsidering the implications of the historical trajectory of these indicators, as they develop in close coordination, for traders' current class position.

One debate simply argues over classifying African traders as capitalists or workers, matching local specifics with criteria derived from Europe for the orthodox Marxist model of the capitalist mode of production—primarily access to land or other means of production. Whether one agrees or not that the wealthier traders qualify as petite bourgeoisie or the poorest as a disguised proletariat, answering the question requires some precise and useful inquiry into degrees of traders' control over capital and the labor process and the location of accumulation. Latin Americanists arguing for traders as proletarians draw attention to their productive work in transport, sorting, and retailing and their dependence—on larger traders for capital or on wage workers as customers. Their deteriorating standard of living and shrinking chances for capital self-sufficiency or upward mobility convinces these authors that accumulation must be located somewhere else (Babb 1989; Bromley 1979; Moser 1980). Assigning a definitive status to a broad category that includes small-scale manufacturing and service work means denying or ignoring the internal diversity this study keeps at center stage (Moser 1978; Gerry 1979; Scott 1979).

Grappling seriously with the contradictory evidence on control of the means of production has led to perceptive work on stratification within the ranks of small-scale traders or producers that reveals the potential for subordination and surplus extraction through credit, apprenticeship, and subcontracting as well as wage labor. Gerry describes Dakar shoemakers who subcontract for international industrial firms in Senegal, establishing dependence and autonomy on a different basis (Gerry 1979). Vercruissje critiques credit hierarchies in fishing towns near Cape Coast, Ghana, calling fishwives who take seasonal credit from fishermen precapitalist, but wholesalers who give them long-term equipment loans capitalist (Vercruissje 1984). Williams dismissed the whole category as hopelessly diverse and therefore hopelessly unreliable in political organization (Williams 1976).

The driving intensity of these classificatory debates shows underlying motivations also visible in debates over other questions. Judgments about worker/peasant/boss status imply concrete actions and interventions based on moral and political values usually assumed, not discussed (but see Kitching 1985). Orthodox Marxist writers can support traders wholeheartedly only if they are workers, who can be expected to ally with other working-class fractions in time of political need. More conservative writers find equal virtue in the label entrepreneur, a budding capitalist likely to avoid revolutionary activity and ally with local or international business. Actual historical alliances among trader groups made during specific Asante and Ghanaian political crises provide an informative check on theoretical predictions from both camps. Both arguments also depend on the impossibility or possibility of accumulation under those circumstances. Depicting traders as either the disenfranchised poor or as microentrepreneurs could be a strategic choice to increase their access to aid projects, depending on the currently dominant paradigm of foreign assistance.

Other Marxists look with more favor on the indigenous capitalist's ability to accumulate. Independent accumulation lays the foundation for political autonomy, expressed as solidarity with nationalist agendas opposing international capitalism. This debate had roots in the Lenin/Luxemburg debate over the role of Polish industrialists as a national bourgeoisie and continued between Gunter Frank and Cardoso over Latin American industrialists. Within Africa, Kenyan industrialists and commercial magnates provoke the most similar debates over the "indigenous capitalist class," with Leys and Kitching as leading partisans (Leys 1975 and 1978; Kitching 1980 and 1985). While they wonder whether Kenyan capitalists will ally with the state against multinationals, Beckman's background in Nigeria and Ghana leads him to consider the state itself a "comprador," turning over large segments of the economy to international actors through industry and rural development projects (Beckman 1985).

Kumasi market women operate on a decidedly smaller scale, but equally small enterprises have been treated seriously as capitalist accumulation by the Left and the Right. Hill's study of Ghanaian cocoa farmers is classic for its respect for their strategies and growth potential, as well as its early date and neoclassical formulation (Hill 1963). From a Marxist direction, MacGaffey comes to similar conclusions for Zairian women traders (MacGaffey 1987). Hart claimed dynamism and growth potential for his newly conceptualized urban informal sector, although disclaiming them vigorously in later work (Hart 1973 and 1982). The current revival of interest in the informal sector arises from Latin America, making even stronger claims of growth potential as an explicit alternative to revolution (De Soto 1989).

One way to avoid the necessity of finding either accumulation or exploitation along strictly Western lines is by erecting boundaries to the capitalist mode of production and stepping outside of them. Articulation theorists invoke multiple modes of production that articulate with the capitalist mode, now dominant in Africa as elsewhere, but retain some autonomy to organize production and distribution around kinship or other noncapitalist principles. Pioneers of articulationist Marxism considered these enclaves to be relics of precapitalist lineage or tributary modes of production (Rey 1979; Meillasoux 1975; Terray 1979; Coquery-Vidrovitch 1976). Since colonial contact in the nineteenth century or earlier had subordinated and deformed these modes, these authors' "pure" or ideal forms were reconstructions combining historical and logical evidence. They had strong disagreements as to the nature of precolonial economic systems in Africa, particularly over the existence of exploitation, but they shared deeper assumptions that detailed arguments based on the labor process and local property relations, regulated through chiefship, kinship and marriage, would prove their points. The proliferation of modes—domestic, household, lineage, tributary, petty bourgeois, simple or petty commodity—lends itself to parody, but the exercise opened the internal dynamics of African communities to critical scrutiny that did not look for replicas of Western models, leftist or rightist.

The weakness in models of articulation lies in the other direction, in assuming local forms will be necessarily the opposite of capitalist. Meillasoux interprets all differences from the classic bourgeois/proletarian model as archaic survivals from precolonial indigenous modes of production (Meillasoux 1975). Since subordination to capitalism represses the directive capacity of the "other" modes, any recorded change must reflect the expansion of capitalism, and local traditions are doomed to passivity and inevitable withering away. Market traders, along with African farm communities, appear in grand historical narratives as archaic fragments embedded within world capitalism like paralyzed flies in a spider's web, waiting to be dissolved (Meillasoux 1975; Hart 1982). They dismiss the diversity of precolonial or contemporary agrarian systems as insignificant to this transition process, just as Williams dismisses the frantic diversification of urban informal sector activities as "transitional," equally doomed to dissolve into the classic bourgeois/proletarian polarity as soon as dispossession is completed (Williams 1976).

Although these Marxists aim their historical trajectories at a very different goal than modernization theorists, the role and fate they predict for indigenous or informal economic relations looks remarkably similar. Within economic anthropology, the substantivists also argued that Third World economies were organized around principles opposite to capitalism. Not surprisingly, they had links to Marxism, traceable through Polanyi via Sahlins (Polanyi 1957; Sahlins 1972). Bohannon and Dalton extend substantivist arguments to market trading, predicting its demise, along with other backward forms of economic life, after full contact with the international economy (Bohannon and Dalton 1962).

Market trading stubbornly refuses to wither away, however, and with many forms of unwaged labor persists and flourishes in cities and rural areas around the world. Wallerstein incorporates this recalcitrant diversity into his model of capitalism as a world system. Capitalist penetration generates and reproduces diversity because the world system requires central and peripheral nations to fill different roles within it (Wallerstein 1976). A phenomena like market trading, a symptom of underdevelopment, arises precisely from intense contact with the international economy, not from too little contact. Wallerstein avoids the worst victim-blaming rhetoric of the modernization school, but his deterministic portrait is still somewhat patronizing. He sees little scope for agency in the periphery beyond changing places with other poor nations, short of world revolution encompassing the core countries.

Amin, following Rodney, has equally little hope for working within the world system but allows for effective resistance by withdrawal from it (Rodney 1972; Amin 1990a). He expanded Wallerstein's capitalist model by recognizing oppression based on nation, race, and gender to incorporate the contemporary political activism, now more frequently based on these identities, not class. He later responded to the experience of countries like Tanzania by admitting his proposals for delinking were too optimistic (Amin 1990b). Smith argues from historical evidence that past economic resistance in Western Guatemala, sustained partly through marketplace trade, in fact did affect the terms and timing of insertion into the world economy, gaining this area significant (if temporary) protection from colonial appropriation (Smith 1984b).

Another balance is struck between autonomy and exploitation with the concepts of petty or simple commodity production, still used by several authors who grapple with the contradictions posed by concrete relations of work and property. Scott's definition names criteria of local self-sufficiency, autonomy of household heads, and localized exchange retained in later elaborations (Scott 1979; Kahn 1980; Friedmann 1980; Smith 1984b; Roseberry 1986). She locates the fundamental distinction from capitalist production in the level of accumulation. These modes work toward reproduction and propagation of the family unit, not profit accumulation (echoing the substantivists again). Roseberry and Smith extend this distinction to petty and capitalist trading enterprises, establishing a political and conceptual link from artisans and traders to peasants, revalued as a resistant and nonexploitive class, rather than to workers or bosses. Like the peasantry, petty commodity producers are defined as an intrinsically subordinated category, although then the question of the meaningful autonomy of their mode of production arises immediately (Moser 1978).

Bernstein deliberately moves the ideal type of petty commodity production away from stereotypes of the village blacksmith serving local subsistence farmers to the contemporary realities of articulation with more fully capitalist sectors that include wage labor (Bernstein 1986). As Bernstein recognizes, this compromises the independent historical dynamic of reproduction and transformation central to a mode of production in the strong sense, but removes the stigma of being a transitional form, only a way station on the road to capitalism. Vercruissje and Scott drop the term "mode of production" in response to these issues, preferring to talk of forms of production, as defined by Friedmann, operating within the larger social formation (Friedmann 1980; Vercruissje 1984; Scott 1986). Scott and Bernstein find this terminology gives them the flexibility to emphasize the concrete diversity of specific forms. They embrace economic instability, at the enterprise and the sectoral level, as a characteristic feature of petty commodity production rather than a frustration to analysis, because its subordination makes it a vulnerable site of conflict between capitalist sectors over their relative power. Smith argues that its inherent instability extends into its political alliances, since the state largely defines the economic space it occupies (Smith 1986). Several leading authors endorse this emphasis on fluctuating relations with the state in calling for research to focus on microstudies of concrete instances of "class conflict and collusion" and political practice as well as economic diversity (Bernstein 1986; Scott 1986; Peattie 1987).

Feminist Marxists show similar ambivalence toward the mode of production because of its inadequate integration of gender, not to mention race. Even proponents of the lineage mode of production, who give marriage and kinship pride of place within it, manage to take gender for granted and exclude both the prerogatives of gender and actual women from the historical dynamics and contradictions they propose (Rey 1979; Meillasoux 1975). Robertson shows the value of making gender central to this line of analysis in her historical study of Ga women in and around Accra, Ghana (Robertson 1984). She maps out a transition from a communal mode of production, based on fishing husbands and wives smoking and trading fish, to the capitalist system dominated by wage labor by men. This separates Ga men financially and geographically from women, who remain behind in communal residences, trading and producing with their mothers and sisters.

Some feminist critics fired back with their own mode of production, appropriating the terminology of the domestic mode of production to cover women's unpaid domestic work worldwide (Delphy 1977; Bennholdt-Thomsen 1984; Mies 1986). Unfortunately they also appropriated the historical experience of peasant and subsistence farmers and unwaged household workers from the Third World to bolster their ideal type. Dual-system theorists proposed patriarchy as a parallel system to class, articulating with each mode of production (Beechey 1979). Both models drew fierce criticism from Third World feminists for ignoring the specificity of racial and national position (Amadiume 1987). In equating work like market trading with housework, they ironically echo earlier ethnographic accounts that trivialized the economic side of African women's trading by portraying it as socializing, entertainment, "pin money," or sexual rebellion (Nadel 1952; Bohannon and Dalton 1962; Little 1973).

Materialist feminists proposed the opposite strategy, analyzing class and gender as a single system (occasionally adding race or nation). To do this required going back to the drawing board, reworking the existing modes of production through more grounded analysis of concrete instances in all their complexity, presaging the recommendations of petty commodity theorists like Scott and Bernstein. They advocated returning to the level of the labor process to study the gendered division of labor, forms of cooperation, allocation and control of the product, and gendered ideologies (Edholm, Harris, and Young 1977; Beechey 1979). They point out that gender subordination operates in the economy as well as in sexual and family relations, whether these are mutually embedded or not, making gender-blind class analysis inadequate for class as well (McDonough and Harrison 1978). Integrating gender and class in this way involves adopting Marx's method of materialist analysis, but not his or Engels's conclusions about women's place (Young 1980). These debates informed excellently detailed case studies of concrete situations and fed into the broader political economy approach that continued to gain substantial insights from attention to intrahousehold relations (Roseberry 1988; Mackintosh 1989; Guyer 1984; MacCormack 1982; Vaughan 1987).

Black feminists from the United States have an even deeper interest in forms of analysis that give equal weight to class, gender, and race. They argued convincingly in the 1970s against single-issue theoretical frameworks—socialist, feminist, and Black nationalist—that did not recognize the complete involvement of each form of oppression in constructing the others, publishing these debates in the early 1980s (Hooks 1984; Dill 1979; Smith 1983; Lorde 1984). They had practical reasons for the sharpest possible evaluation and prediction of political alliances, since they enacted their own activism by building and rejecting coalitions with feminist White women, nationalist Black men, and socialist groups dominated by White men. Sacks's review article shows how much these writings can contribute to a more precise and sophisticated understanding of class and gender as nonhomogeneous categories, using the domestic labor debate as a specific example (Sacks 1989).

Patricia Hill Collins's recent synthesis takes a form which, while fully grounded in the political and personal experience of Black women in the United States, can easily adapt to the specifics of other historical contexts (Collins 1990). Her matrix model comprises three interlocking axes or dimensions of oppression (race, class, and gender) so that each single point is necessarily located with respect to each one. Where ethnicity and nationality, for example, represent significant systems of oppression, the matrix can accommodate additional axes. While these axes appear metaphorically as separate directions or forces, their connectedness and mutual constitution are her main subject of interest. Whereas orthodox Marxists and radical feminists treat multiple oppressions and cross-cutting loyalties as messy complications to their ideal types, she takes these intersections as her starting point.

In her hands, the intersection of these categories becomes an asset to scholarly analysis and to social action because several or all may be invoked or studied from a single location. They fan out like reins linking Black women to sources of power, anger, and insight in several directions, sometimes hard to keep in harness but creating the potential for rapid forward movement. Based on Black women's history of activism in church and community groups, she argues that members' multiple positioning enabled these groups to address the actual complexities of racial uplift and repression more effectively, even while reenacting some aspects of subordination within their ranks. She emphasizes the centrality of survival issues and everyday lived experience (at home, at work, and in politics) to both Black women's activism and Black feminist thought. African feminists writing on development share these core priorities and epistemologies (Awe 1977; Okeyo 1981). Like the petty commodity analysts just mentioned, Collins endorses a diverse research program that looks carefully at specific historical contexts, but asks for even greater depth and breadth to capture the interaction of multiple systems of domination.

The multistranded analysis proposed here is only feasible as a continuation of a rich historical scholarship on the Asante, spanning generations of Ghanaian and foreign researchers. Delineating the reciprocal influences of gender, ethnic, and commercial transitions, even in one specific case, requires presenting coordinated historical perspectives on all three. Documentation of each set of relations in sufficient detail to compare them is a daunting task for any single researcher, particularly with the disjointed and slanted material typically available for African societies, thus discouraging many such attempts. Fortunately, the renown of Elmina and Asante has drawn historical interest dating from De Marees (1985 [1602]) through Arhin (1975), Wilks (1975), and Kea (1982). The prominence of trade in the local economy encouraged each of these to include thorough accounts of trade and the persons involved in it and to recount in detail the establishment and defense of ethnic trade boundaries. Debates over the class position of traders and cocoa farmers in precolonial and colonial Asante revolve around the autonomy of trading capital from the state and means of access to land and capital (Wilks 1975 and 1979; Arhin 1979 and 1986; McCaskie 1983 and 1986; Austin 1988). Curiously, De Marees pays as consistent attention to gender as any of the more recent authors until Kea. Recent historians of gender in Asante focus on marriage and kin relations, but trade appears alongside farming as a source of income and property (Allman 1989; Mikell 1989; Tashjian 1992).

The following chronological account relies primarily on these secondary sources, although some original archival and oral history research supplements their gaps on gender and market policy. It begins by outlining confrontations from earlier centuries that established the basis for control of major material and social resources and the trends of historical change that continue through the twentieth-century confrontations that constitute the immediate context for contemporary traders' strategic choices.

Early International Trade

Substantial continuities in trading relations, routes, and commodities connect present-day Asantes with an intercontinental trading network flourishing centuries before Europeans visited the Gold Coast and capitalism began. The Asante formed as a political unit during the seventeenth century, within the broader Akan cultural group that already lived and traded in forest and coastal areas in present-day Ghana and Côte d'Ivoire (see map 3.1). Akans first participated in long-distance trade at the southern fringe of an international trading network that crossed the Sahara desert from the West African savannah, or grass belt. These caravan routes brought substantial amounts of goods north through Morocco and Algeria to the Mediterranean, since before Roman times (Hopkins 1973). After the tenth century a.d., Arab merchants and chroniclers traveled throughout the savannah zone north of Akan territory. They report the importance of commodities like gold and ivory, which Akans definitely sent through those channels later, but the mysterious tales they were told obscure the extent of Akan participation then. The volume of trade across the Sahara apparently continued to expand until the mid-nineteenth century (Hopkins 1973).

Europeans exploring the savannah in the eighteenth and nineteenth centuries confirmed the importance of Akan supply areas to the caravan towns just north of the forest. Forest-based traders supplied ivory, gold, salt, kola, and slaves and brought back guns, swords, brassware, cloth, leather goods, and cowrie shell currency. The oldest line of Akan trading *entrepôts* runs along the forest/savannah fringe, including Begho and Bono, (north of Techiman), Bonduku, and Yeiji or Salaga. Ethnic, religious, and ecological factors combined to erect and maintain a commercial boundary at the forest edge. The savannah caravans used donkeys, who lacked fodder in the deep forest and suffered illness and death from insect-borne animal sleeping sickness there. Forest caravans needed head carriers, whose organization and maintenance demanded leaders with strong local connections (Arhin 1975; Wilks 1975).

Widespread ethnic and religious networks among savannah traders made it difficult for Akans to operate there. Ethnic groups like the Hausa, Dioula, and Fulani migrated widely across the savannah belt, partly for trading purposes (Curtin 1984). A shared cultural background eased communication across the relatively open country at that latitude, and these groups gradually came to share religious values also. Most long-distance traders among the Hausa and Fulani had adopted Islam by the nineteenth century, even when other Hausas and Fulani had not. Islamic values and judges laid a useful foundation for mutual trust across the West Africa Sahel and with North Africans. A regular stream of pilgrims to Mecca kept the Arab world aware of the learning and prosperity of West African Moslems (Hopkins 1973). Conversion

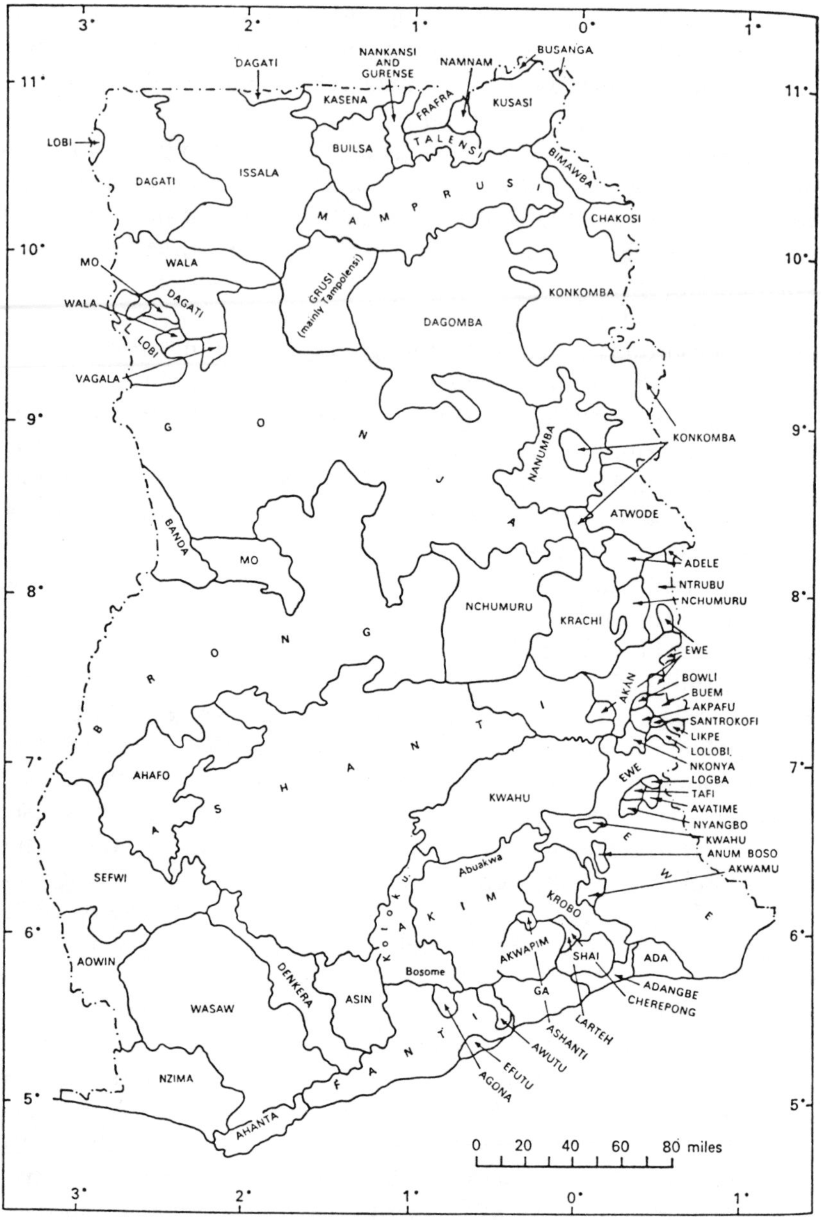

Map 3.1 Ghana: Ethnic Groups (Source: Ghana Census 1960, *Atlas of Population Characteristics*, Government of Ghana, Statistical Office, Accra, 1964)

also increased the local demand for kola, a mild stimulant permitted by Islam, although many non-Islamic peoples also use it widely in ritual and social contexts. As Islam penetrated more deeply into local gender ideals, women were restricted to local markets or home-based trade in these savannah groups (Hill 1969). Documentation of Asante trade with caravan towns includes only a few trips by elite women traders (McCaskie 1980b). Elderly Asantes I interviewed mentioned that the male savannah long-distance networks made it difficult for Asante women to trade effectively to the north, so women went south to the coast more often.

The capital, trading skills, and institutions Akans built up through savannah-oriented trading networks stood them in good stead when Europeans first reached the West African coast. One historian concludes, "Indeed, it was precisely because Ghana had been integrated into the continental trading system that it was so attractive to European traders" (Hymer 1970, 39). Akans supplied both savannah and coastal markets with the same commodities throughout the eighteenth century and utilized the same caravans of head carriers in both directions. An extensive canoe trade east and west along the coast also prepared Akan and other related coastal people to respond energetically to European sea contact in the late fifteenth century (Kea 1982). African traders and coastal chiefs appear in De Marees and other early European traders' accounts as respected adversaries and trading partners, as they had in Arab chronicles. Europeans stayed mainly on their ships before they built forts and landed garrisons in the seventeenth century. Limits on the financial and organizational strength of European traders kept them dependent on indigenous traders for contact with producers and consumers even slightly inland. Because of intermittent warfare and embargoes, inland traders traveled in armed caravans, varied their routes, and relied on coastal African landlords for accommodation, credit, and information (De Marees 1985 [1602]).

While local chiefs held the balance of force on the coast, they or their representatives also controlled access to African buyers and sellers. They stipulated many payments and regulations before agreeing to trade, and Europeans could not dictate prices, commodities, or conditions of trade. Arriving captains opened negotiations with gifts or "customs" that established a host or landlord relationship with local officials, bearing some analogies to the savannah pattern. Ships from many European nations called during the relatively brief sailing season, so towns could and did refuse to deal with captains who refused to meet their demands (De Marees 1985 [1602]). They played traders off against each other to get lower prices, more desirable goods (especially firearms), and more respectful treatment. After notorious episodes of cheating or abduction of bystanders, all the nearby ports might close to ships of that nation. Both sides used intimidation and violence on occasion, and both engaged in various sharp practices, but these did not apparently slow the pace of trade (Hopkins 1973).

The linguistic and material media of commercial transactions confirm the rough equality and relative autonomy in this early period. Traders from other countries had to learn Portuguese because West Africans already knew it; Portugal was the first nation to trade regularly there (Kea 1982). Africans pressed successfully for payment in gold, their currency, and fifteenth-century Portuguese had to bring slaves from Benin to induce Gold Coast traders to pay out gold in exchange (Hopkins 1973). They continued to bring significant amounts of gold during the seventeenth century from Brazil and Amsterdam (Harrop 1964).

The commodities bought and sold also reflected African, not European, preferences. Unless ship captains chose their cargos carefully, goods remained unsold and had to be discounted heavily to unload unpopular items and leave quickly before the winds changed and the fever season began. The Portuguese had catered to Akan customers familiar with Middle Eastern and West African cloths and metal goods by bringing goods from Benin, India, Indonesia, and Morocco for resale at Elmina, their major port. Europeans continued to participate for many years in the established West African coastal trade by carrying craft products and processed foodstuffs like palm oil from at least as far as Benin and Sao Thome (Harrop 1964). The demand for raw materials by thriving local craft industries accounted for a large proportion of the iron bars, brass and copper manilla bracelets, and red Chinese silk imported, destined for melting down or unraveling (Johnson 1966). West African complaints about poor-quality European products induced Dutch and later English manufacturers to modify their designs to appeal to local consumers. They both imitated Indonesian batiks, resulting in the "real Dutch Java print" or the "wax print" from Manchester, now considered essential to African "traditional dress." The English also produced cheap imitations of well-reputed Dutch copper pots, mirrors, and other metalware, called simply "Dutch goods" (Harrop 1964).

The conditions of coastal trade retained for African intermediaries significant control of capital and the organization of trade by defining distinct and interdependent roles for Africans and Europeans in credit, clientship, and licensing. European ship captains trading independently or on behalf of their investors had neither the resources or the expertise to gather exports from inland areas, such as the Asante territory, or to distribute imported goods there in return. Trading magnates mediated between ship captains, inland traders, and coastal polities like Elmina or Fante. They pressed local chiefs to offer better protection, captains to bring better goods, and inland traders to follow accepted commercial procedures. They kept high capital reserves to buy goods from inland traders in preparation for the sailing season and to stock up on European goods to sell during the rest of the year. Relations between individual ship captains and magnates could last for years, with either party extending substantial credit when necessary. Defaults and cheating broke up these relationships, and both sides were willing to deal with others who came along. Coastal magnates still acted as landlords, credit guarantors, and negotiators for inland traders, who preferred not to deal directly with Europeans (De Marees 1985 [1602]).

Coastal political leaders and European trading companies actively negotiated and enforced commercial privileges on behalf of their traders that reinforced ethnic and national role assignments. European captains and inland traders were required to use the services of coastal magnates recognized by the local chief (translated as "nobles" from De Marees's Dutch text). Protective regulations in each chiefdom and the ever-present danger of war embargoes or confiscations gave local citizens a substantial advantage in trade within each chiefdom. For example, local marketplace traders did not pay the taxes levied on foreigners or visiting merchants. Unsettled relations between chiefdoms preserved the value of coastal intermediaries' up-to-date local contacts and information on the best current routes and supplies for Africans and Europeans alike (De Marees 1985 [1602]).

During the sixteenth and seventeenth centuries, the political units that lined the Atlantic Coast were organized around large trading towns and the networks of magnates who dominated them. The ports themselves were not the capitals of these chiefdoms or even their largest towns in most cases. The capitals lay slightly inland, in the protecting forest, where the chiefs and some of the largest traders resided. Production within these city-states was highly commercialized; farm settlements clustered tightly around the towns so that farmers could bring food for sale in the town market to pay their heavy monetary taxes. Craft producers lived and worked mainly in the towns, where their craft products featured prominently in intercity trade, including female crafts such as pottery and cooked or processed foodstuffs (De Marees 1985 [1602]).

Powerful guildlike organizations gave the trading magnates or *abirempon* political influence distinct from the position of chiefly officials (*afahene* or *ahenfo*) whether appointed by merit or hereditary. After an elaborate ceremony involving a feast for current rank-holders, they could trade in slaves, munitions and other luxury goods, display specific symbols, attend town meetings, and enjoy other privileges. The status of an *obirempon* was recognized in other towns, enabling Akani merchants based in Assin to establish regional commercial dominance far beyond its political borders through a network of captains leading Akani expatriate colonies in other cities (Kea 1982).

The nearest parallel to this remarkable regional integration and dominance without central political authority comes from eastern Nigeria. Igbo title-taking ceremonies likewise involved expensive outlays given to current title-holders to acquire an elder status within the local community but recognized outside of it through dress and other symbolic objects. Although these titles were not specifically associated with trading privileges, an Igbo regional network of expatriate communities based in the oracle town of Aro Chukwu did dominate precolonial commerce and finance to a degree very comparable to the Akani captaincies through a region stretching outside Igbo territory (Uchendu 1964). According to Ekejuiba, the Aro had begun land mortgaging and currency exchange activities just before colonial rule (Ekejuiba 1991).

Gender boundaries existed in Akan long-distance trade and were only slightly more permeable than ethnic boundaries. No formal prohibition existed against women in any kind of trade, comparable to the formal regulations about ethnic roles, and women were recorded at all levels of trade, from head carriers to magnates. De Marees mentions that both men and women could have the ceremony performed that formalized their rank as magnates, although he later speaks of the candidate and his wife. Exceptional women also appear in Kea's lists of recognized traders in the Akani companies, but Wilks's typical male coastal magnate and wealthy long-distance trader seem accurate enough (Wilks 1975).

Commoners and women had their main spheres in the trade in foodstuffs and other consumer goods. De Marees describes town marketplaces crowded with women retailing local and imported foodstuffs and inexpensive imported goods, and making and selling cooked food and durable foods like ship's bread. Men brought in palm wine and sugar cane. Some professional women traders visited a round of town markets and had a regular selling location in each. Others traveled to rural markets to collect foodstuffs and sell imports. Village women from surrounding farming areas walked in daily with fresh produce and bought salt and smoked fish to resell in their villages (De Marees 1985 [1602]). Asante oral history describes caravans to the coast that took back salt and smoked fish from coastal producing villages and returning kola caravans that brought down dried fish and shea butter from the savannah (Akoto 1980). Palm oil, vegetables, and grain came in from other West African ports on African as well as European ships.

In the later eighteenth century (also a watershed for European dominance on the coast), the Akan polities of Akwamu, Denkyira, and Asante invented a new dominant role inland that was based on military power. Each one occupied this dominant position in turn, as they pushed the frontier of organized Akan settlement further north along the important trade routes. The rise of these new political units farther inland was accompanied by a change in the relation between trade, production, warfare, and the state. The coastal city-states had relied on slave and mercenary armies, well-trained and rather small in numbers, to defend their borders and attack their rivals. The new inland states relied on mass citizen levies to provide soldiers for their much larger armies, which the coastal states could not have recruited without disrupting food production and tax revenues.

Coastal chiefs taxed farmers heavily so they could buy food for these mercenary guardsmen and pay other officials, which forced farmers to intensify food production for urban sale. Inland governments used slaves not as soldiers, but to produce food and trade goods for official supplies and for sale to compensate for the reduction in revenues collected from free citizens, who now contributed mainly military service, labor, and produce in kind. Wealthy merchants also invested in slaves for production of food for sale in towns and for the production of gold, salt, and other commodities for long-distance trade. The new states controlled trade more tightly, participated in it more directly, and taxed it more heavily because their increasing militarization made them depend on these measures for cash income. Since free citizens now marketed less of their fresh produce, they could live farther from the towns and settle a broader territory under central control (Kea 1982). This enabled Asante villages to spread out into a vast territory only sparsely settled before.

Trade and Production in Asante

The Asante Confederacy gradually united around control of the trade routes which crossed its central forest toward the ancient *entrepôt* cities on its northern border, so long-distance trade played, not surprisingly, a prominent role in economic and political relations. Its autonomy and centrality to accumulation can be judged through its interlocking relations with the major Asante productive sectors—agriculture, mining, hunting, gathering, and crafts. Asante chiefs fought for control of Brong and Gyaman, districts with major supplies of the staple exports—gold, kola, and ivory (Bevin 1956). Asantes committed substantial resources to commercial production or collection of exports and of agricultural foodstuffs in excess of subsistence production. Participation in these activities could bring substantial individual wealth to either men or women, but especially for those with preferential access to finance, land, and labor resources. Women's difficulties in accumulating trading capital were partly based on inheritance rules and labor claims, but partly rooted in their lesser access to public resources made available through the chiefship system.

Asante women found that a wide range of local commercial roles were notionally available for assignment to them through ethnic or gender affiliation. Both men and women participated heavily in marketplace trade and commercial production within Asante, although with distinct commodity specializations. Divisions based on ethnicity or political allegiance were fundamental to the structure of trade; Asante chiefly regulations prohibited foreign traders from penetrating beyond the borders, for security as well as commercial reasons (Wilks 1975). Although the Asante lineage and chiefly systems provided more leading economic roles for men, they did admit some women into the highest ranks in long-distance commercial networks. The lowest rank, that of caravan head-carriers, included men and women, slaves and free persons, employees and entrepreneurs (Arhin 1971; Wilks 1975).

Production for sale was important in its own right and also one means of accumulating capital for trading. Commercial agriculture had begun near Kumasi, the capital, by the time Europeans first reached it as captives (Freeman 1967). Individuals of both sexes used capital or family position to organize a labor force of slaves or dependents for large-scale commercial farming and became wealthy from it (Lewin 1974, 448). Several elderly Asante men and women interviewed mentioned large-scale pig raising; they had been told it was a good way to get quick wealth or trading capital before its prohibition by the British. Poorer rural women gathered kola and oil palm fruits and panned alluvial gold to supply the international trade in these products. Traders purchased kola collected in Asante from wild trees abundant in the forest and also kola grown on slave plantations. Some men hunted elephants for ivory and captured slaves under chiefly sponsorship, but more men could hunt small game, gather snails, tap palm wine, or (toward the end of the nineteenth century) tap wild rubber for sale (Hopkins 1973).

Asante men and women drew power and income from a well-developed internal marketplace system with three distinct types of market, in which chiefly regulations protected their privilege as traders and carriers. Non-Asantes were restricted from trading within Asante during most of the nineteenth century, so goods from outside passed into Asante hands at the officially designated border markets whose location contracted with the limits of effective political control (Wilks 1975). Quantities of imported consumer goods, mainly manufactures and crafts, passed from border markets either to the urban daily markets or directly to the regional periodic markets in leading Asante towns (Akoto 1980). These linked the rural population to the border markets and to other parts of Asante with different food supplies. Urban daily markets in Kumasi and leading provincial capitals served the needs of town dwellers for food and consumption goods of all kinds (Lewin 1974).

The continuity in primary urban food supply patterns is striking: village women walked in every day with fresh produce to sell in Kumasi market and returned home the same day; now Kumasi traders ride out every day to bring it back. Staple vegetables came from each town's immediate hinterland, which produced plantain, cocoyam, and tomatoes especially for sale (Beecham 1968 [1841]). Intensive farming of vegetables, including the starchy root or tuber staples, was visible within walking distance of Kumasi and around regional capitals to a lesser extent (Beecham 1968 [1841]; Lewin 1974).

Fish, game, and snails were traded much longer distances, with constant redrying and resmoking needed. Both sexes brought fish to Kumasi from nearby Lake Bosumtwe and traded in snails. Game was brought to market by the male hunters themselves, who also gathered snails in the forests when game eluded them, or bought by male traders, who also went north for Volta fish. These relatively high-value protein foods passed through the regional periodic markets and also figured in international trade between local states (Lewin 1974). Traders from Kumasi called *adwadifo* bought in these weekly markets, where their namesakes now buy fresh vegetables (Akoto 1980). Wealthier Kumasi men and women, attracted by the larger profits possible from equalizing supplies between different parts of Asante, sent relatives and buying agents around to these markets (Lewin 1974).

Urban populations drew on both marketed and nonmarket specialized supplies for food, so that relations of authority counterbalanced autonomous production for sale. Chiefs received tribute in kind from their subjects and supplied professional hunters with guns and ammunition in return for meat. They distributed these supplies to their subordinates and retainers, in addition to feeding their extended families. Along with other members of the urban elite and subelite, they also settled dependent relatives or slaves on land in the suburbs of Kumasi, either using or selling the crops sent to them (Akoto 1980). Because of the concentration of subchiefs and minor officials in Kumasi around the court of the *Asantehene*, the head of state, these nonmarket channels were especially significant there. The market provided food and consumer goods mainly to the poor, untitled residents, but these were numerous enough (Akoto 1980).

The many wealthy residents of Kumasi also stimulated its market indirectly by attracting craftsmen to the city, who did buy their food in the market. The elite usually bought craft items directly from the craftsman, outside the market, but the same craftsmen and others in specialized craft villages also provided cheaper goods to the marketplace system. Villages for woodcarving, metalworking, cloth weaving and printing, shoemaking, and other male-associated luxury crafts were clustered near Kumasi, with the female crafts of basketweaving and pottery more widely dispersed. A periodic cloth market located between Kumasi and Juaben carried handwoven cloth imported from the savannah and from Benin in addition to the renowned Asante *kente* cloth (McCaskie 1980b). Other Asante crafts, savannah blankets, and leatherwork were also traded in quantity through regional periodic markets.

Chiefship

Asante chiefs intervened to promote, control, or subsidize commerce in three ways. First, the *Asantehene* and other senior chiefs employed people to trade on their behalf. These state traders, called *batafo*, purchased official requirements, such as cloth, slaves, and gunpowder (Lewin 1974; Wilks 1975). They also conducted general commerce for state profit, with state funds. War captives were sold by state traders or distributed to leading figures in the campaign for resale on the coast or local employment. Slaves also traded for their masters or mistresses, including some of the *ahemma*, or female chiefs, and some female slaves (McCaskie 1980b). Second, chiefs loaned out state funds to prominent citizens. The recipient traded with them, either directly or through subordinates, and the resulting wealth added to the glory of the state and potential sources for forced loans (Wilks 1975).

Official caravans, including state loan traders, enjoyed quick passage and exemption from customs duties at the border posts. On the Northern border, guards held up traffic for some time after their passage to raise prices for them (Rattray 1929). State traders used their training and privileges to become wealthy trading on their own accounts. Free men and women enlisted as head carriers to enjoy the royal caravan's prices and military protection as budding entrepreneurs. Women did hire out as carriers, although their domestic responsibilities might interfere. Carriers could put their own goods on top of their official loads, and men could bring their wives or other family members along with additional loads (Brown 1972; Wilks 1975; Akoto 1980).

Asante chiefs also controlled benefits from private commerce by regulating it. Through border controls, the *Asantehene* taxed traders, reserved guns and powder to the state, and restricted the passage of aliens. Subordinate chiefs appointed officials to settle disputes and supervise price bargaining in local and border markets. They also declared boycotts and embargoes in political or commercial disputes with neighboring towns or chiefdoms (Brown 1972; Wilks 1975; Akoto 1980).

Slave trading was kept under strict political control and was conducted mostly by chiefs and their officials. Although private traders selling kola could purchase individual slaves in savannah markets, the majority of slaves sold on the coast by Asantes originated as war captives or tribute. Asante commanders sold captives from northern chiefdoms and occasionally from rebellious Akan tributaries. The Asante also demanded slaves as tribute from the Gonja and Dagomba, their northern neighbors, who purchased them or raided for them farther north. Wars of territorial expansion thus protected Asantes from the worst ravages of the slave trade, while the sale and employment of slaves enabled Asantes to recover more quickly from the financial and demographic costs of war.

The considerable slave population in Asante was especially important for accumulation. Chiefs used their access to slaves to engage in large-scale gold mining, employing them to pan streambeds, work shallow pits, and build deep pit mines. Some slaves were settled in separate slave villages, farming and sending tribute to their wealthy owners. Ordinary citizens brought their fewer slaves into their lineage as second-class members, without the autonomy of free wives and children. Asante women and girls were rarely enslaved but many were pawned when their labor and person served as interest and security for family loans. Their husbands and fathers had first option to make such loans, which gave them rights over the woman's labor, specifically including the right to take them on trading expeditions without the consent of their lineage. Pawns had less rights to their own income and could not leave to reside with their own lineage unless the loan was repaid (Rattray 1929; Wilks 1975; Grier 1989). The cumulative effect of slavery and pawning on stratification patterns will be considered further as part of lineage relations. After Britain abolished the slave trade on the coast, Asantes continued to acquire slaves by buying and selling them locally (Wilks 1975; Hopkins 1973). Pawning continued through the 1930s (Grier 1989).

State participation and intervention in Asante commerce created many male traders in close alliance with the state, but worked to the disadvantage of women because of the preponderance of men in official positions and minor chiefships. Women could not be employed as state traders, and they had reduced chances of receiving official loans, as these often went as rewards to officials and subordinate chiefs, who included very few women. Important nonroyal positions such as the *okyeame,* or spokesmen, and the treasury officials and minor bureaucratic officials, including market supervisors, ranked as nonhereditary chiefships and were always filled by men (Wilks 1975).

The Asante lineage and chiefship system provided for some respected leadership roles for women, but fewer than for men. Each level of community organization had a female leader, a male leader, and a council of male elders. The woman leader or *ohemma* (conventionally translated as queen mother) had important powers and influence not dependent on the male leader, or *ohene* (conventionally translated as chief). Both were chosen from the same royal family, and each nominated the successor when the other died or was removed from office (destooled). Those at the village and town levels were located precisely within a hierarchy that culminated in the *Asantehene* and *Asantehemma* for all of Asante. Each male chief presided over a council of male elders to handle routine public affairs, such as land allocation and civil disputes. The *ohemma* was present at these meetings, but elder women did not attend, although they were respected and consulted on major decisions.

Gender boundaries in these hereditary offices were less absolute than in the appointive bureaucratic offices. The town of Juaben had a renowned succession of women occupying its male *ohene* office, while another woman occupied the *ohemma* office. They kept their female names and identities in office. In contrast, Manuh reports that women occupying male chiefships in Nzima, an Akan area on the Ivory Coast border, take men's names in office and wear men's clothing and behave like men when performing chiefly duties (Manuh 1992).

Besides these rare exceptions, women still gained as Asantes from the military and diplomatic initiatives that extended Asante influence. Raids into the savannah established Asante regulative control over the key caravan markets of Salaga, Atebubu, and Kintampo while collecting intermittent tribute and capturing slaves from savannah chiefdoms as well. Women profited more directly from imperialism to the south, which established an Asante presence in Adanse border markets and regional transfer points like Mankessim, where more Asante women traded. To sustain this expansion at their neighbors' expense, however, the internal structure of the Asante state steadily centralized and formalized, expanding the influence of male courtiers more than territorial chiefs, who included *ahemma* (Wilks 1975).

Lineage and Marriage Norms

Like the commercial and political relations just discussed here, the lineage and marital relations of Asante women show both powerful continuities from earlier centuries and significant transformations in recent decades. Asante cultural norms governing the allocation of property and labor through kinship and marriage, a combination I call "family" for convenience, have their roots in the trading and farming contexts of precolonial Asante. To understand these ideal principles, and how they are compromised in practice, it therefore makes sense to start discussing them within the treatment of that time period. Not only do contemporary Asantes constantly refer to an idealized version of this period to explain and justify contemporary lineal and marital roles, but the actual transformations since that time constitute an important axis of historical change in Asante women's power position.

In present-day Asante, the matrilineage continues to play a major role in the transmission of land and other property and in the allocation of financial and labor assistance. Lineage elders still allocate considerable property and financial assistance through decisions on inheritance, loans or gifts, residence, and schooling, with women participating as elders and as recipients. The patterns of access to capital and labor thus established affect market women through their roles as sisters, mothers, and aunts. Principles of leadership and inheritance give women less access than men to lineage-controlled resources, but ensure women's access at a token or minimal subsistence level. Gender assumptions that limit women's access to lineage funds and land and control over their own labor continue to be obstacles around which contemporary traders build up their enterprises. By restricting Asante women's ability to expand their cocoa and food farms, for example, they encouraged women to divert their energies into market trading and fostered the expansion of that sector in this century. Both their positive entitlements and their negative exclusions from these material resources critical for commercial accumulation shape the conditions under which they enter and work in marketplace trade.

When I began to ask exploratory questions about Kumasi traders' marital and lineal relations, I was surprised at the coherence and consistency of the responses I received. Even women from families that had lived in Kumasi for generations invoked an idyllic, timeless model of life in a farming town, before extensive commercialization of agriculture, to explain how husbands and wives should act and the mutually balanced responsibilities of mothers, children, uncles, siblings, and other important matrilineal kin. The picture of family life they presented contained much less ambiguity and conflict than the daily home experiences I had already shared. Were Asantes indigenous structural-functionalists? A few college-educated acquaintances did refer me to Rattray's work, but the model seemed too widely and firmly held and uniformly understood by unschooled traders to attribute it to external influences. Meanwhile, the same persons departed from it so frequently and cheerfully in practice that they had to find it valuable and instructive as something besides an accurate description of typical Asante family behavior. I call it the "classic" Asante family, because it serves as a meaningful reference point even for arrangements which directly contradict it.

The obvious gap between ideal and practice did not disturb my sources, and they made few efforts to conceal it. They placed a positive value on modifying actual choices in residence, inheritance, and other matters to take individual preferences, capabilities, and circumstances into account. Asante and its precursors took their highly stratified economy into account when formulating expectations in marriage and lineage relations. Behavior appropriate or even demanded of the elite would be deemed ridiculous or condemned as "useless" for ordinary or poor citizens, and vice versa. The twentieth-century Asante maintains this pragmatic attitude in the face of gaps between rich and poor, which continue to widen. Judgmental discussions of specific family actions defend a set of acceptable alternatives and goals rather than a unified law or prescription.

Even the fundamental principle of matriliny, allegiance to the mother's kin, was voided in highly hierarchical situations before conquest. The most ancient and honorable exception applied to the *asomfo,* the courtiers and servants of the *Asantehene* and, by extension, the Asante state. These men were expressly given control of their own children, directly canceling the power of the maternal uncle, so that they could train their own sons without interference as skilled successors to their technical and political offices. Interestingly enough, although these rules applied to substantial numbers of Kumasi residents before conquest, and I knew a few traders with family connections to the palace, none of them mentioned the *asomfo* pattern among marital alternatives. Patrifiliation through slave wives came up more often as a means for wealthy commoner men to gain wives and children with primary loyalty to them, not matrilineal kin. A wealthier man could also acquire pawned wives, who could not work for themselves or go home. Most market women I knew had neither the wealth nor the close royal connections to aspire to elite standards of behavior, so the less hierarchical models had more relevance.

During fieldwork, I focused on aspects of family ideals and practices that affected trading by controlling access to essential resources. A systematic and comprehensive investigation of marriage and lineage would require moving far beyond the market community and was fortunately not necessary to understand the basic framework of these relations. The scholarly literature on Asante kinship and marriage is extensive and of exceptionally high quality and historical depth (Rattray 1923, 1927, 1929; Fortes 1949, 1969, 1970; Beckett 1944). Lineage and marital relations continue to be the focus of richly documented ethnographic, sociological, and historical work on the Asante and closely related Akan people, such as the Brong and Akuapem, in studies that incorporate the effects of urbanization and commercialization, including marketplace trade (Abu 1983; Allman 1989; Bleek 1974 and 1976; Hill 1963; Mikell 1987 and 1989; Okali 1983; Oppong 1983; Woodford-Berger 1981). Rather than duplicating their efforts, the following section draws heavily on them to outline the main points of Asante lineage and marital relations, adding supplementary material obtained from interviews on the interaction with trading. This produced nothing to substantially contradict either the classic ethnographic texts or more recent historically informed analyses. In fact, it was intriguing to confirm that market women differed so little from Asantes in other situations in their primary relations of kinship and marriage.

The Matrilineage

Loyalty to matrilineal kin remains a fundamental moral principle and emotional commitment for these urban women. Asante metaphysics roots the primacy of lineage ties in the common blood (*mogya*) transmitted by the mother during pregnancy and birth. Asantes may try to evade specific lineage obligations, but they cannot deny them in principle without denying the blood in their veins. As one young woman law student explained, "I would have to open my wrists and drain out all my blood first." Repudiating the lineage, or *abusua,* would be like repudiating the gift of life itself. These links reach beyond the grave, forging bonds of duty and power with ancestors still concerned with the future prosperity and purity of the blood they shared. The matrilineage is thought of as the descendants of one woman, including both her sons and daughters, but only the children of her daughters, not her sons. Its primacy is expressed in the proverb "when your mother dies, your lineage is finished" (*wo maame wu aa, na w'abusua asa*). The word *abusua* most often refers to the irreducible unit of maternal siblings and the sisters' children and grandchildren. This minimal lineage is also called the *yafunu,* or womb, for contrast with the larger lineage, which meets more infrequently to consider inheritance or other major decisions (Fortes 1969; Rattray 1929).

Although presented as an irreducible basic unit, even in idealized accounts the composition and orientation of the *yafunu* changes through the life cycle of its senior members. The oldest generation of the *yafunu,* the *nananom,* or grandmothers and granduncles, stay together because they grew up in one house with their mother. They direct the affairs of the group, loan or invest lineage funds, and contribute substantially to decisions made about their maternal grandchildren's marriages, education, and occupational choices. The *yafunu* usually splits after their death, at the fourth generation (Fortes 1969, 195). An Asante woman thus spends her childhood within a *yafunu* dominated by maternal uncles and grandmothers and her elder years leading a *yafunu* group composed not of their descendants but of those of herself and her sisters.

Each lineage should be headed by a pair of male and female elders, analogous to the paired male and female chiefly offices of *ohene* and *ohemma,* selected by consensus of the whole lineage. The eldest sister and brother are preferred, but passed over when necessary due to problems of character or competence. Their titles, the *abusua panin* or lineage elder and the *obaa panin* or woman elder, show that the male elder is considered to lead the lineage as a whole. Male *yafunu* elders also constitute the council of elders supposed to advise the *abusua panin* on matters such as succession and allocation of farmland, although the *obaa panin* of the *abusua* attends and some elderly women serving as *yafunu mbaa mpaninfo* (plural) should be consulted. Very occasionally, women take the office of male elder, due to outstanding personal character or a lack of suitable male candidates. One orange trader told me she was the *abusua panin,* not the *obaa panin,* of her lineage "because none of the men had any sense." I have never found a reverse case, of men occupying one of the female offices. This seems related to women's genealogical primacy, since a lineage with no adult females to take this office would be likely to die out.

Each major lineage is associated with a lineage house, the *abusua fie,* in its town of origin, or hometown. The male and female leaders of the lineage normally live in the *abusua fie,* along with other elderly men and women and some of the younger members living in that town. Lineage members living and working in other urban and rural areas return there regularly for funerals, at which time an heir is chosen and other family quarrels or problems may be settled. Visits during Christmas and other school vacations are also common, and children may be sent for longer stays so they will know their relatives.

The male head of a *yafunu* is called the *fie panin,* or house elder, corresponding to the model of siblings living in their mother's house, although with more frequent migration in this century this minor lineage now rarely lives in a single house. Other houses built and inhabited by lineage kin are sometimes referred to as *abusua fie* to distinguish them from commercial rental properties, especially after they have been inherited by a matrilineal heir. These only become primary lineage houses if that lineage segment separates from the main lineage, which can involve a change of hometown. Lineage fission takes place gradually, as more distant relatives stop attending funerals and meetings. The association of fission with headship of the maternal house partly explains why wealthy men often build their first house for their mothers, since this is the largest *yafunu* they can hope to lead. Establishment of a house makes it possible to hold funerals there and to begin assuming other *abusua* functions. It gives a basis for retaining the allegiance of brothers and the sisters whose children will eventually inherit it.

Although the *yafunu* does not hold or use property communally, it is the basic unit for inheritance and use claims. Land rights, property, and public offices stay within the *yafunu* whenever possible, if a suitable heir is available. The *abusua panin* (for deceased men) or the *obaa panin* (for deceased women) "looks for" a successor first among siblings of the same sex. The *abusua* elders should consider the character of the candidate, past help given the deceased, need, and the ability to make good use of the resource, passing over close relatives of known incompetence or irresponsibility. This ideal legitimizes the particularly broad discretion and flexibility exercised by the *abusua panin* in allocating the virgin or long-fallowed land required on a long-term basis for permanent tree crops such as cocoa or oil palm (Rattray 1929).

Yafunu membership also establishes residual use rights, once houses or land have been inherited matrilineally. The heir enjoys the income from the property but should not do anything to reduce its value or alienate it without the elders' consent. He or she should use part of that income to help these relatives, such as by paying school fees or medical expenses. Kin can also ask to live in such houses at little or no rent, farm small amounts of such land for subsistence, or borrow heirloom cloths and valuables to wear on special occasions. The heir need not agree to every request; in fact part of his stewardship consists of deciding wisely between competing needs. However, sanctions are available if he does not devote a substantial proportion of resources to helping deserving relatives. In cases of conspicuous refusal, his heirship can be revoked in a later family council.

According to Fortes' informants, the larger *abusua* had been a more important inheritance unit for precolonial Asante, and the retention of property within the *yafunu* was a twentieth-century change. Maternal cousins were formerly considered before moving to the younger generation of daughters or sisters' sons, but the order had reversed by 1945. Since then, inherited property should cross to opposite sex kin and even to children of slaves before passing to collateral relatives (Fortes 1969, 175). Land and valuables that leave the *yafunu* then became official or "stool" property of the *abusua panin* or lineage head, used to support his office, rather than passing to an individual heir from another *yafunu* (Fortes 1969, 179)

Depending on how far back connections are traced, the *abusua* can be quite a large group. Its size depends not only on how many daughters are born in each generation, but on how many segments lose contact with each other through migration, quarrels, or other factors. Smaller *yafunu* tend to remain attached longer, because access to backing from a substantial number of people is valuable in economic, political, and legal crises. Substantial amounts of lineage property also tend to retain the interest of collateral branches. Even when they are unlikely to inherit they can hope for access to loans and other forms of sponsorship.

The Asante pattern of lineage leadership reserves offices for women, but integrates them into a joint hierarchy rather than providing full sexual parallelism as proposed by Poewe in a cross-cultural matrilineal ideal type (Poewe 1981). The gender imbalance of power can be counted at the higher political levels; one woman participates at each level with a male chief and a whole council of men. Meetings cannot take place without male elders, while consultation of women elders is informal and optional on issues not specifically concerning women. Land allocation, the central business of rural Asante lineages, was termed "men's business" by some of my informants, although it is critical to the prosperity of women as the majority of food farmers. Women farmers interviewed mentioned difficulty of access to large tracts of good land as one major factor preventing them from expanding their farms. In the few family and lineage meetings I attended, the *obaa panin* sat passively and spoke rarely, and both men and women explained this behavior as normal deference to men. Women elders do not seem to take as dynamic a role in inheritance cases, for example, as matrilineal mothers among the Zambian Toka (Holy 1986).

The gender barriers in Asante monosexual inheritance patterns compound male economic advantages within the lineage: men inherit from men and women from women. When these rules are respected, they keep male property accumulating in male hands. A woman will only inherit her brother or uncle's property when the *yafunu* is totally devoid of male heirs. The advantages and savings men gain from access to wage labor, more school fees, unpaid wifely labor, and better land allocation remain and multiply in the hands of their male successors. Gifts, loans, and farm or business handovers with which wealthy Asantes anticipate or forestall lineage inheritance also rarely pass from men to women. The assumption that men and women will work and associate mainly with members of the same sex prevents male and female relatives from training and sponsoring each other or establishing tight bonds of friendship within the broader lineage. The close emotional bond between brother and sister, both called *nua,* does not bridge this gap when it comes to property, and mutual assistance during life also seems to be weakening.

The security that the matrilineage offers Asante women should not be underestimated, but their access to its resources is premised on a need for subsistence and linked to that level. Unlike women under some patrilineal systems, an Asante need not fear loss of custody or confiscation of working assets if her marriage dissolves, only loss of child support. When she is divorced or widowed, her rights to live in lineage property, farm land, and ask for financial assistance are virtually undeniable because her children are the only future of the lineage. When a woman is married, as most are, lineage brothers and elders will assume that a woman's husband has primary responsibility for her daily support. Because of this presumption of support, a woman's need to accumulate wealth is socially defined as less than men's, so lineage funds and lands above the subsistence minimum are usually distributed to male members. Fortes notes: "Though women can and do own land and houses, it is often said that such types of fixed property should be controlled by men" (Fortes 1969, 175).

Fatherhood

Fathers are also considered to have strong emotional and spiritual links with their children, but these constitute ties between individuals rather than giving a child its group identity. The continuing association of fatherhood with monetary support is conceptualized as an extension of precolonial principles of balance between paternal and maternal responsibilities. The father's contribution to family subsistence was fish and salt, the two staple foodstuffs commonly bought before colonial rule, while the mother supplied starches and soup vegetables from her farm. Rent and clothing hardly figure as expenses for children in this setting, since they lived in their mother's lineage house and wore remnants of adult cloths or borrowed finery when necessary.

Fathers had special responsibility for the moral and occupational training of children, particularly, but not only, boys. A good father took pains to form his child's character through his supervision, companionship, and example. This was easy in the classic village, when sons accompanied fathers to the farm or workshop, and young children ran freely in and out of his family house and often ate there (Rattray 1923; Fortes 1949). Although formal employment now interferes with the fulfillment of these norms, they still have a strong influence on father/child interactions. In my observation, contemporary Asante fathers still seemed to participate more freely in physical childcare than many Western fathers. Fathers regularly played with and cared for infants and young children when they were around, and this was considered central to the paternal role. One older woman described her responsibility to care for her aged father thus: "When I was a baby I wet on his knee, so how can I refuse him now?" When older children were not in school, they might spend considerable time with a father who owned a shop or workshop. Fathers who wished to accept these responsibilities were respected, not ridiculed, by their peers.

Asantes define the spiritual aspect of paternity as the *ntoro* spirit, transmitted at conception to boys and girls. Fathers acknowledge paternity by naming the child with one of the personal names associated with their *ntoro* or paternal line. *Ntoro* affiliation also determined certain greetings, taboos, and ritual observances now largely fallen into disuse. During the nineteenth century, patrifilial ties and *ntoro* identification defined identifiable social groups among the elite, with considerable political importance in royal factions and the ranks of the *Asantehene*'s court bureaucracy (Wilks 1975).

Ideally, the moral and financial duties of fatherhood continue regardless of marriage to the mother. If the father himself dies, or shirks his responsibilities, these are ideally taken over by his matrikin, whom the child can collectively call father. His lineage successor, in particular, should acknowledge the claims of his children as part of stepping into his shoes (and property). Without substantial personal assets, however, a father's support effectively ceases when he can no longer work because of age or infirmity.

Marriage

Asantes see a major dichotomy between the enduring nature of lineage relations, including motherhood, and the inherently unstable, transitory relations of marriage. In a society deeply imbued with respect for ancestral power and loyalty, the phrase "till death do us part" loses much of its weight. One proverb frequently repeated to indicate this contrast is "You can get a new husband (or wife), but not a new brother (or sister)." The frequency of widowhood, divorce, illness, or simple irresponsibility meant that relying heavily on marriage for future security was considered foolish, given the high chance of disruption.

Giving precedence to husbands over kin was actually considered morally wrong and selfish. The ideal model for exchanges between spouses is short-term reciprocity, which is closely monitored by both sets of relatives as well as the spouses themselves (Abu 1983). Marriage serves personal preference, convenience, and pleasure rather than family interest, except in the cases of elite marriages of alliance. For Asantes marriage is structurally optional in a way that motherhood and fatherhood are not, so they talked of it as an individual, idiosyncratic relationship without an absolute moral mandate. Teenagers and young adults under thirty or forty are expected to devote their primary attention to courtship and marriage as part of enjoying a pleasurable stage of life without substantial family responsibility. Mature adults, either men or women, who continue to put a high priority on sexual or marital affairs were described to me by traders as immature, self-indulgent, and frivolous, and they often used sexual insults in such descriptions.

The rituals surrounding marriage are appropriately low key compared to funerals or other lineage-oriented events. Token gifts from the husband's elders to his wife's elders signify their endorsement of the relationship and their commitment to mediating any quarrels that may arise. The essential item, a bottle of liquor, is shared between those elders present so that they cannot later disavow knowledge of the marriage. It is likewise poured in libation to the ancestors to obtain their consent and blessing and to introduce the husband as the future father of their descendants. Customary marriage is legally recognized and entitles the husband to collect adultery compensation, although it is not required for claiming paternity of his children. A married person has ritual obligations in the funeral of a spouse or parent-in-law, although unmarried adults do not have special funeral observances comparable to those of childless adults.

One of the most exotic aspects of Asante marriage to Western observers is duolocality, that is, husband and wife living separately. Both early and contemporary ethnographers devoted considerable energy to investigating duolocal marital residence (Rattray 1923; Fortes 1949; Okali 1983; Woodford-Berger 1986). In the classic Asante marriage, the spouses have met and courted in the village as adolescents and come from families that already know and respect each other. They remain living in their own family houses after marriage as before, but formal customary marriage allows her to visit him openly at night and cook for him. Couples live together when they migrate to a different urban or rural location or temporarily when they move to a nearby farm hamlet to open new farmland. Small-town informants mentioned the farm hamlet as a romantic honeymoon option for newlyweds seeking more privacy. When they return home, on visits or permanently, they return to their respective maternal houses.

Actual residence patterns are rather complex, precisely because of the importance of co-residence in daily power dynamics. Asante women can legitimately live with a wide range of kin, including mothers, fathers, uncles, brothers, sisters, aunts, and children, as well as with husbands. Vercruissje (1972) speaks of "the contradictory requirement that wives should and yet *should not* live with their husbands" among the closely related Fanti. While duolocality is certainly compatible with matriliny, they are not linked exclusively. Patrilineal Ga women in Accra, Ghana, continue living with their mothers after marriage (Robertson 1984). Conversely, matrilineal Bemba or Trobrianders usually move to live with their husbands on marriage (Richards 1940; Weiner 1976). Polygamous Asante marriages are rarely coresidential, except for the wives of chiefs; co-wives usually interact as little as possible.

The permanent social creation linked to marriage is not a new property or residential unit, but the children. Discussions of the role of family elders in approving marriage partners made it clear that they consider candidates' merits primarily as parents of future grandchildren rather than as husbands and wives. They adamantly refuse to introduce "bad blood" into the *abusua* by allowing marriage into families tainted by theft, alcoholism, epilepsy, asthma, and other supposed hereditary problems. These concerns still have wide legitimacy: one highly educated young woman said that romance and fun seemed very important to her now, but she would probably share their preoccupation with such issues when she reached their age. They were soon to be ancestors, she said, and could bequeath little to the family except the purity of the blood itself.

While married, a woman provides domestic services for her husband. She cooks for him, washes his clothes, sweeps his room, brings his bath water, and sleeps with him. Wives who live separately send their husbands food and visit them at night, cleaning the room and preparing breakfast and bath before leaving in the morning. A wife does not look to her husband to share in domestic tasks, except in a sudden emergency. Rather, she negotiates with him the standards of domestic service and the delegation of specific work to her children or maids. As a woman reaches middle age, it becomes less appropriate for her to do these menial tasks. She delegates more of them to her children, now growing up, and accepts that her husband may consider taking a younger wife to supplement her services.

Her husband can also claim unreciprocated farm labor from her, which compromises her ownership of their farm produce. In the sexual division of labor, men clear the land, both men and women plant specific crops, and women do most of the weeding. Clearing the land establishes ownership of the farm and the resulting crop, regardless of who later weeds it. Although husbands and wives each have their own farms, a husband can ask his wife to weed without losing control of the crop. If a wife asks her husband to clear for her, it becomes his farm and she is given only a small part of the crop at his discretion. A woman has to ask a brother or junior relative to clear for her, a man who faces many competing demands, or hire labor to clear it (Akoto 1980). The demands of farm and domestic work for husbands also significantly reduce the time women have to devote to their own farms at optimum times. They consequently make smaller farms closer to the village and use plots with less forest regrowth that are less fertile (Rattray 1929). They also face more pressure to meet the family subsistence needs from their fields. Village women I interviewed mentioned these same problems as reasons they expanded their trading rather than their farming.

Duolocal marriage minimizes the contradiction between the positive value Asantes place on personal autonomy and dignity for both men and women and expectations of female deference to men. Wives are expected to be submissive and deferential in interactions with their husbands and not to dispute their husbands' decisions and requests. This ideal is easier to conform to when such interaction is minimized by separate residence. As women grow older, and their authority in their natal lineage grows, this deference becomes less appropriate. They now are expected to have more serious matters on their minds than sex and marriage with an aging husband and may have borne their target number of children or reached menopause. Middle-aged women often visit their husbands much less often or "retire" from marriage altogether without a formal divorce. When relations with the husband remain amicable, they say he is "like a brother" now, a relationship that involves mutual respect (Owusu 1992). Asante women who have stopped visiting a husband say "I have stopped marrying him," whether this represented a change of partner or an adoption of single elder status.

The processual conception of marriage these phrases imply recalls Comaroff's formulation of Tshidi marriage as "a process of becoming, not a state of being" (Comaroff 1980, 172). In very different institutional contexts, Tshidi also try to perpetuate ambiguities in the status of particular relationships as long as possible for future use to leverage upward mobility. There the practical exchanges of labor and resources between in-laws, rather than spouses, are the critical practices used to constitute and evaluate the marriage, particularly in disputes. In both places, the recognized flexibility and negotiability of marriage can be exaggerated opportunistically. Tshidi argue over whether a sheep given to a woman's father was a marriage payment or a spontaneous gift. Asante argue instead over whether past somewhat irregular gifts of money to the woman were unreliable chop money payments or relatively frequent presents to a girlfriend. Since Tshidi men apparently take their church-endorsed monogamy more seriously than Asante men do, they are highly concerned to delegitimize unwanted relationships. In both cases, completion of marriage formalities often takes place in middle age, as the result of a successful relationship, when the gesture of renouncing further options seems more appropriate.

Some of my interviews suggested that Asante men perceived marriage as more of an event or permanent status than women did. For example, one wealthy landlord claimed to have eight wives, although he freely admitted that only two of them still visited him and several had since married other men. Detaching wives' married status from the debatable quality of men's current financial support had its advantages for men because of the prestige they acquired by polygyny. Women instead tended to disqualify failed marriages retroactively, since it was more respectable for them to have had fewer husbands. The power differential between husband and wife made it a mark of pride to have fewer husbands and more wives.

Individuation

An important aspect of ideal social personhood for men, women, and children is the ability to control autonomous resources. Individuals retain full control of their personal earnings and property and, conversely, only have conditional or negotiable access to the resources of even their closest kin. Personal dignity requires that an adult woman be able to dispose of her own income, however modest, without explanation or permission from others. As a positive ideal, this is shared not only by Asantes and other Akans in other occupations, but found very widely throughout West Africa. Market traders expect to maintain independent incomes and separate budgets after marriage. Both spouses pay for certain expenses related to themselves and their children and maintain allegiance to their natal lineages by supporting relatives with labor and money. Financial individuality is not seen as opposed to lineage or community loyalties, but rather as the basis for forging firm bonds of mutual aid.

Norms for lineage financial contributions assume an independent income for women members, but a smaller one than for men members. It is recognized that the time and money women put into raising children reduces their earning capacity. For this reason, men pay twice the assessment of women toward town and lineage expenses, such as lawsuits or funerals. Informants explained that each gender had one primary responsibility: "Men bring money and women bring children to make the lineage strong." Women are nonetheless encouraged to earn and contribute as much money as possible and respected rather than condemned if they succeed. Brothers feel proud of the wealth and success of their sisters and relieved by their financial independence (Owusu 1992). By contrast, men tend to suspect that the success of their wives was achieved at their expense.

A woman's gender identity depends on her financial independence as well as her fertility, just as a man's does. A woman without an income is not a real woman, but like a child or, more precisely, an idiot. Aidoo puts it succinctly: "In Ghanaian society, women themselves believe that only two types of their species suffer—the sterile—that is those incapable of bearing children—and the foolish. And by the foolish they refer to the type of woman who depends solely on her husband for sustenance" (Aidoo 1970, x). The juxtaposition of dependency with barrenness, the supreme personal tragedy, makes an extremely strong statement, underlined by Aidoo's choice of the word foolish. In Asante this is a much heavier insult than in English, especially for men, for whom it implies sexual impotence. The word thus rhetorically equates female financial impotence with male sexual impotence and with infertility.

Mutual assistance within the lineage should be substantial, but it too stops far short of pooling. Even inherited lineage property clearly belongs to one individual heir, who should use it for the benefit of kin but has virtually unchallenged power to decide what uses will serve their long-term benefit. Relatives can ask for help without offense, and pressures from the *abusua* to agree can be intense, but this help cannot be compelled or assumed. Pleas to wealthier kin are based on needs, not rights, and one certainly cannot use their property as one's own.

British Colonial Rule

British authorities gave much higher priority to manipulating commercial relations than to transforming any other aspect of Akan society. The conquest of Asante had an immediate, sharp impact on trade, but only a gradual influence on lineage and marital relations. On the coast, Europeans had gained clear dominance by about 1750, reducing the autonomy of inland polities like Asante at first indirectly, then directly. Various European trading nations succeeded in imposing more favorable and exclusive trading relations on the coastal port towns commercially during the late eighteenth and early nineteenth centuries. The British then consolidated their administrative and commercial control, taking possession of most of the coastal chiefdoms as the Gold Coast Colony in 1830, and acquiring the remaining Dutch forts, including Elmina, in 1868. Under direct rule, the British legalized and institutionalized these commercial measures, using military actions and territorial annexations to further undermine the position of coastal African intermediaries. Asante intermediaries retained their position until the twentieth century, because Europeans still had little access to Asante itself. After the British occupied Kumasi in 1896 and exiled the *Asantehene* in 1900, they rapidly extended this tighter commercial regime into Asante proper.

During the eighteenth and early nineteenth centuries, informal collegial relations had predominated on the Gold Coast. Many independent European traders operated alongside African and mulatto traders of equivalent scale. Although racist and nationalist status barriers certainly existed, intermarriage and mutual credit were also fairly frequent (Priestley 1969). Independent European traders employed shopkeepers and accepted agencies from larger European firms, but the circumstances of poor communication allowed and required delegation of decision-making powers to the man on the spot. Both European and African subordinates were compensated primarily with a commission on sales and were expected to trade substantially on their own accounts at the same time. Those European "coasters" who had spent long periods of time on the Gold Coast contrasted themselves both to colonial officials and to employees of the larger British firms, who gradually ousted them. European agents of these large firms now returned regularly to Britain and hoped for promotion to the main offices there, and the firms gradually succeeded in forbidding them from trading on their own accounts. The employees' own more subordinate status and lack of personal capital pressured them to have more blatant recourse to an ideology of purely racial separation and superiority. African traders who might well be wealthier and better educated than them contradicted too obviously any more subtle principles of distinction. They established fewer social and economic alliances with elite Africans and were suspicious of those who did.

One episode of this early colonial period, with only coastal enclaves under direct rule, shows the independent and contradictory actions of European merchants and officials, African chiefs and local traders. The Krobos, a small but prosperous ethnic group east of Accra, had rebelled in 1858 when the British tried to implement direct rule by intervening in a dispute between Krobo chiefs. The British levied a fine after their defeat but could not enforce payment. The British merchant firm of Swanzy contracted to collect the debt from the proceeds of a monopoly on buying Krobo palm oil, the major basis of its prosperity. With military backing for their monopoly, Swanzy fixed prices well below market rates so the debt would be paid off more slowly, the monopoly would last longer, and their profits from palm oil resale would mount. After strenuous protests from the Krobo went unanswered, they diverted their entire supply to alternative markets in adjoining French Togo, which the British reports termed "insane competition." After this boycott, the monopoly was revoked and the Krobos promptly paid most of the remaining fine in cash (Wolfson 1953).

Regular steamship and cable service after 1852 enabled the larger British and French firms to consolidate control of import and export trade through more firmly subordinated networks of branch stores with African and European shopkeepers following orders. Wealthy, literate African traders tried to take advantage of improved communication to order direct from overseas manufacturers, cutting out the large British importers, but the latter retaliated by sabotaging their credit, overcharging them, and agitating for direct British rule (Howard 1978, 184). By the mid-1800s, coastal branches of the largest firms dominated local distribution of imports and had reorganized it through a system of passbooks issued to customers, predominantly illiterate women.

British commercial interests drew on gender and class domination, colluding in their intensification to reinforce the increasing racial hierarchy. The new passbook customers accepted less advantageous terms of trade and did not compete as directly with the British firms since, as illiterate women, they had less wealth and a weaker position in local power and communication structures. Passbook holders deposited security with the firm and could then take out goods to the value of their deposit and pay later, after resale. Instead of receiving a wholesale discount, they received a commission on paper, which was added to their credit limit. This system tied customers more directly to particular firms and reduced competition between the firms. The passbook customers could use their accumulated commissions to buy more goods from the same firm, but not from other firms.

Ekejuiba describes a similar historical transition in the palm oil trade in Eastern Nigeria. In the initial stages, chiefs of coastal towns were highly active in trade, forcing European traders of different nationalities to compete for their business. In some cases leading traders founded or took over the leadership of such towns. After the collapse of these coastal city-states, assisted by European military intervention, less politicized large-scale traders expanded their activities for a generation, in a diminished commercial gap between rural producers and the European firms. Ekejuiba describes the career of one such "merchant queen," but her sons did not take over her trading empire. Instead, they took jobs as agents and employees of the large firms who then came to dominate the palm oil trade directly (Ekejuiba 1966, 215).

The large firms organized Gold Coast export buying through subordinate agents as well during the colonial period. Firms advanced capital to local men to travel into the interior and buy up export commodities. This pattern began when colonial officials first promoted the palm oil trade to replace slaves as the major export, lasted through the rubber boom at the end of the nineteenth century and continued for the early decades of the cocoa trade in the twentieth century. Dependent agents never took over completely, but they had to compete with independent cocoa buyers operating with their own capital. After the military defeat of Asante on the coast in 1874, its border controls weakened and Fante men with independent capital or connections to coastal importers and exporters moved quickly into Asante to buy rubber and sell cloth and fish.

When the British imposed direct rule on Asante in 1900, they promptly dismantled the system of commercial controls that favored traders with links to the Asante chiefs. They began to promote the growth of the major British import/export firms in Kumasi and other

Asante towns, giving their branch stores prized locations on the main street near the market and subsidized rail rates (Howard 1978, 63, 76). Their archival comments show more ambivalence toward the Lebanese traders who also set up small import firms in the 1910s and 1920s, competing effectively with the established British firms by importing directly, cutting overheads, and accepting less formal commercial relations with Africans. The government discouraged Lebanese immigration and set up price controls and import quotas during both World Wars to prevent these British firms from losing their market share when European wars hampered their operations.

The British authorities at first confined their regulation of African trading to collecting taxes, preserving and taking over this aspect of chiefly authority. In Kumasi, as in many smaller cities, market taxes laid a firm foundation for the local government treasury. Asantes' stiff resistance to other forms of taxation contrasted to traders' willingness to pay tolls and rent stalls (NAA1). Improved sanitation provided another strong motive, especially after the devastating pneumonia plague of 1924. Popular civic amenities, including piped water and latrines, promised a less threatening outlet for African political energies. The Kumasi Public Health Board (KPHB) became a testing ground for local rivalries and alliances between its appointed African and European members and between Asante factions (NAK4; Tordoff 1965). An energetic building program during the 1920s and 1930s constructed many cement markets throughout Ashanti Region that justified higher rents and fees (NAK5).

Rapid expansion of commerce in Kumasi led traders there to petition repeatedly for market repairs and improvements during the 1910s (NAK6). The British fort built after 1896 had preempted the precolonial Dwaberem marketplace at the top of the hill, opposite the "spirit grove" (see maps 3.2 and 3.3). This main marketplace had not included any permanent buildings, since it doubled as the army assembly ground in time of war, but it was a permanent daily market with royal supervisors and regulations, supplemented by smaller neighborhood markets. The British had designated a market area downtown, near the British firms' branches, with lines of metal-roofed stalls like English markets. Officials first proposed expanding the existing location in 1914, but this plan proved too costly and unpopular, since it required demolition of several adjacent blocks of prime commercial and residential buildings (see map 2.3). The idea of moving the market to an unoccupied area next to the railway line removed these obstacles, and the first sets of stalls were quickly completed.

The new Kumasi Central Market, opened in 1925, expanded stead-

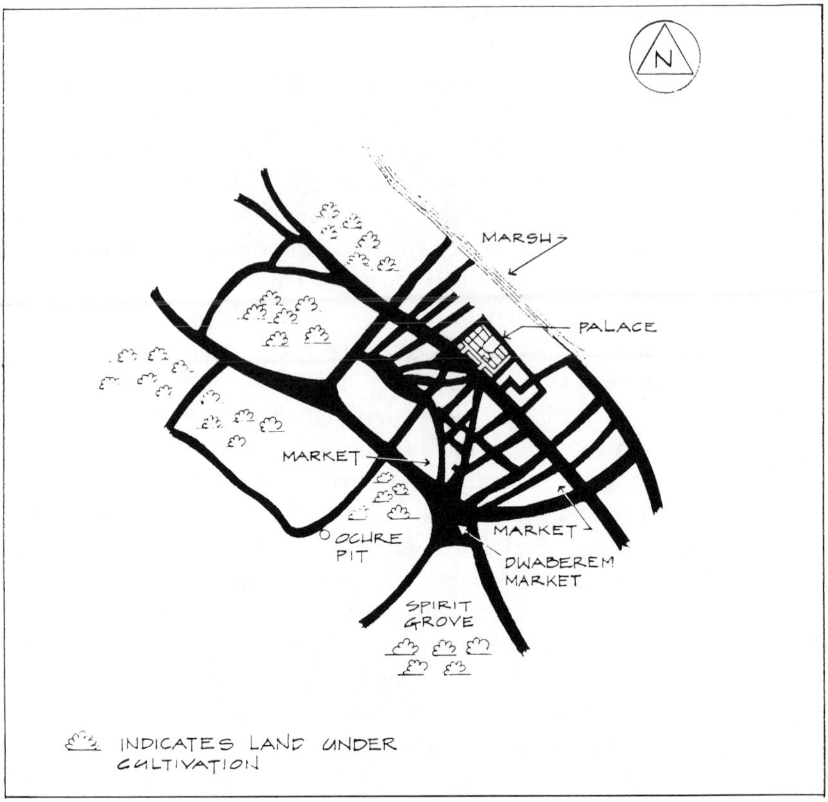

Map 3.2 Bowdich's City Plan of Kumasi, 1817

ily until it held all the traders from the old site, which then closed (NAK11). It lay between the old downtown Adum district and Ashanti New Town, where the new palace and prosperous residential areas were going up, linking the two parts of town across a former swamp drained for the railway. Despite continuing subsidence and drainage problems, traders welcomed the improved facilities and larger spaces and built many extra stalls themselves with government assistance or permission. The current yam queen said her predecessor hired a bulldozer to level ground for the wholesale yards at Bode in the 1930s.

Europeans and Africans still pushed for advantage in trading regulations as members of the KPHB. European members argued for confining African trade entirely to the Central Market, for stricter revenue collection and sanitary control. African members argued for tolerance of neighborhood markets and street hawkers, for convenient shopping and greater revenues for city coffers, over which they had some control.

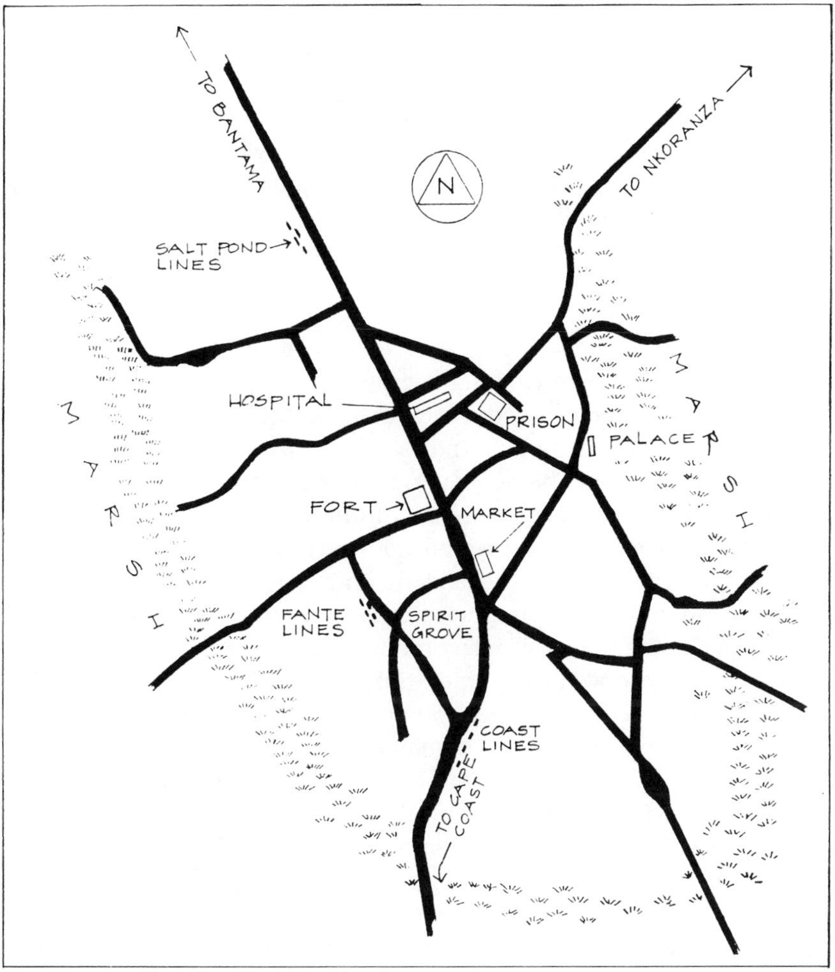

Map 3.3 Kumasi: Market at Conquest, 1900

Licensing and sanitary regulations remained a source of tension; market officials in 1979 still remembered that the army veterans hired after World War II as the first market police, the "sanitary boys," often beat offending hawkers and ate their wares (confirmed by NAK10).

Road building and transport policies of the colonial government had a profound impact on marketplace trade, although these initiatives were aimed at other sectors. Military recruiters during the First World War had complained that Asantes would only enlist in the Motor Corps, to learn truck driving, and road networks and vehicle numbers expanded rapidly afterwards (Tordoff 1965). The introduction of road transport redrew the regional map of market relations, rather than simply reassigning existing roles, since Kumasi could now draw perishable produce from farther than a woman could walk in a morning. A set of more distant markets, including Ejura and Berekum, now became Kumasi's major foodstuff suppliers, outstripping but not closing down the ring of nearby markets, such as Nkawie and Ofinso. Regional trunk roads were constructed over several decades, enabling demand from the mushrooming city to stimulate and tap into substantial surpluses in the virgin farmlands north and west of Asante. Grains, peanuts, chickens, and livestock were brought across the Volta in growing quantities from the Northern Region. New district and regional periodic markets played a key role in organizing this new kind of long-distance trade. They also took over the established trade in kola, smoked fish, salt, and other "traditional" exports.

These changes in the geographical organization of trade brought about complex transformations and innovations in trading relations that increased stratification and concentration among traders and made food farmers more dependent on the market. The new long-distance supply lines supported full-time travelers and farmgate buyers, who tend to be fewer, larger traders than those buying in nearby markets. The economics of truck transport enabled those who could fill one to squeeze out smaller competitors. Farmers committed more resources to cash cropping as demand levels and distribution systems proved stable. They depended on supplementing their family food supplies with market purchases, stimulating rural markets. New avenues of accumulation opened up to men as transport owners.

The Second World War and its attendant transport shortages made only a short pause in this expansion process. After it ended, the marketplace system continued to develop along the new structural lines which had begun to emerge during the 1930s. Commercialization in the South began penetrating the remotest villages as the road network filled in. In the North, commercial production only now began to reach beyond the market centers. As transport to the South became faster, more reliable, and more frequent, fewer intermediaries were needed between Kumasi and the North. The same processes of accumulation and concentration began there as in Ashanti and Brong-Ahafo in the 1930s.

While colonial intervention in the marketplace was limited, policies directly affecting cocoa farming, mining, and government service led indirectly to dramatic changes in market employment and accumulation patterns. Opening the borders of Asante started profound and immediate shifts in the gender and ethnic division of trading roles.

At first Asante men still traded in their old lines, but without their former advantages from chiefly connections they faced stiff competition from Northern and coastal Fante men, who had similar skill and capital levels. Fante men brought with them closer links to the colonial system, longer established there, including lines of credit for rubber buying or imports selling and jobs as storekeepers or government clerks in the new Kumasi branches and agencies. Fante women with Western skills of sewing and baking and coastal passbooks arrived with these middle-class men, joined by Asante exiles returning from coastal towns with similar assets. Resentment of Fante domination of Kumasi employment drew Asante boys into schools despite initial resistance, especially after nonsectarian schools opened in the 1930s. Africanization of the civil service and corporate sectors after World War II greatly expanded promotion prospects for qualified employees. Although aimed at forestalling demands for independence, this policy reforged the alliance between elite or upwardly mobile men and their government, colonial or independent. Western education and adherence to Western principles of government now perpetuated their class and gender dominance, as palace official bureaucracy had entrenched the *asomfo* as a professional elite among nineteenth-century Asante men, with specialized training by their courtier fathers.

The integration of uneducated men into export production opened further space for Asante women in marketplace trade. Asante men planted cocoa with such enthusiasm that they soon exhausted space for food and new cocoa near Kumasi. Women's cocoa farms remained few and small, with their less favorable access to land and labor. High prices brought cocoa farmers rapid accumulation that women shared neither through inheritance or trade. Cocoa replaced palm oil and rubber, earlier major exports collected from wild trees and traded through the marketplace system. With cocoa such an attractive alternative for Akan men, mining companies based in Ashanti Region recruited labor mainly from the distant Northern and Upper Regions, which also sent male migrants south to work as cocoa farm laborers. While the numbers of male traders from these regions in Kumasi Central Market also grew during the 1910s and 1920s, the diversion of many young men into mining and sharecropping very likely reduced local competition while Asante women expanded their trading to the North. In Kumasi, Asante women moved into previously male-dominated commodities like imports and smoked game about this time, in which upward mobility was no longer sufficient to attract Asante men.

During these first decades, with no chiefly officials remaining on duty, the political organization of the market remained informal. New traders simply asked permission to trade alongside established ones and continued to show respect for those who preceded them, as in very small commodity groups today. The limited numbers of traders, intermediary levels, and commodities reduced the need for dispute settlement across group boundaries. By the 1930s, increased volume provided scope for recognized elders and queens in some commodities, and wholesale yards originated at this time for staples like onions, yams, and tomatoes. Capital accumulation was apparent among vegetable traders, even to observers not themselves trading. One such informant compared a well-known family of garden-egg traders in the 1930s to the prominent fish traders of the 1910s, since both coordinated networks of agents in distant collecting markets. However, market leaders still lacked the prestige of public recognition.

Asante women yam traders in Kumasi used their new organization to defend their commercial position inside the new Kumasi Central Market but appealed to the *Asantehene* rather than colonial authorities. Male farmers from near Tamale, in the savannah, where yam surpluses could be produced, had begun to bring their yams in truckloads to sell to the female retailers at the market. Female leaders of the yam sellers brought complaints to the *Asantehene*'s court several times in the 1930s and 1940s about commercial practices they considered unfair. Male traders identified as Gaos, a term referring to men from the French territories north of Ghana, were trying to buy up the arriving yam supplies and insert themselves as middlemen, forcing the market women to buy from them rather than directly from the farmers. Although the *Asantehene*'s court calmed the riotous women without ruling on the commercial issue, Gao men stepped down for the time being, moving into wholesaling grain and other commodities handled outside the marketplace (ARO1).

Colonial Price Controls

If Asante women could invoke ethnic solidarity with the Asante chiefship to protect their commercial position within Kumasi, the large British corporations certainly invoked their close alliance with their national government successfully to protect their interests during times of crisis. The colonial government established food price controls during the First and Second World Wars, when it shared interests with British firms in keeping wages down and reducing costs in workers' canteens. During WWI, prices of locally produced foodstuffs rose sharply because recruitment to the British Army reduced the farm labor supply and raised farm wages. Increased numbers of soldiers and resisters meant that government purchases for the barracks and prisons increased, creating a financial crisis for the administration (NAK13). Workers in government agencies and European-owned mines also agitated for wage increases to meet rising food costs (Howard 1978), and farmers argued that higher prices compensated them for high wage and input costs.

Implementation of these early controls demonstrated limits to government capacity and motivation for enforcement that reflected both the autonomy and the marginality of the national food trading system. Controls were instituted, with limited success, only in the major administrative centers and in the mining towns of Obuasi and Tarkwa, although prices were equally high throughout the country. When government buyers appeared in Kumasi Central Market, all the foodstuffs traders had mysteriously gone to lunch (NAK13). Obuasi traders avoided arrest in markets by selling at roadsides and behind houses. The eventual unofficial compromise abandoned wage workers to inflation, reflecting the higher priority placed on balancing the official budget. Chiefs were made responsible for the delivery of a limited amount of produce to prisons and other government buyers at official prices (Brown 1972). Prices for manufactured and imported goods were never controlled and continued to rise in response to wartime scarcity and transport shortages.

Protests over the worsening terms of trade were loud during the war years and fed into another commercial action during the 1930s. In the cocoa boycott of 1937–38, one of the earliest protonationalist actions, falling terms of trade resurfaced in the grievances of its organizers, who included chiefs and professionals as well as cocoa brokers and farmers. Cocoa prices had fallen while manufactured goods prices continued to rise. An organized boycott of European imports was an integral part of the cocoa boycott and alarmed the government as much. For farmers from the cocoa-producing areas, family financial pressure was significantly reduced by the propagandists restricting purchases to the rural minimum of kerosene, matches, candles, sardines, and tobacco. Laborers and caretakers from the unorganized North eventually broke the boycott by selling their shares of cocoa to buy cloth and other family needs.

The organizers of the boycott attacked changes in commercial channels that restricted African cocoa producers' access to competing buyers and ensured that they would absorb most of the impact of falling world prices. The large export firms preferred to buy cocoa through African agents tied to them by advances of capital renewed at each harvest season. Independent brokers trading with their own capital, often large-scale farmers themselves, might have long-term relationships with one firm but could switch their business to another if prices warranted. Under pressure as the world market collapsed, these large European buying firms colluded to divide the territory and offer a uniform low price, eliminating direct competition between themselves (Hopkins 1965). The passbook system had recently achieved dominance in imports sales and similarly prevented African traders from switching between the few large European importers, who regularly colluded on imports prices. The boycott leaders' economic arguments mentioned both practices and attributed the worsening terms of trade to these restrictive tactics, demanding that they be changed.

The colonial government responded to these demands and to the economic and political threat posed by the boycott organization by changing the organization of cocoa purchases. The reforms implemented so rapidly only made the problems that Africans had complained of even worse. The new Cocoa Marketing Board institutionalized a monopoly on cocoa buying at both the national and local levels, restricting independent African traders directly. It reduced their commercial autonomy even further by prohibiting competition and local alternatives, although cocoa was still bought and sold outside the marketplace system. The full weight of colonial authority now backed the price fixing once informally organized by the export firms, and the Board sold its entire supply to the same few firms.

Although presented to the African public as a strategy for price support during low-price periods, that function never materialized. Excess profits accumulated during subsequent high-price periods were used for higher government priorities, transferring revenues permanently from rural areas to the cities and overseas (Bates 1981). When prices began to fall again in the 1960s, these reserves had been exhausted. The British held the funds back during the 1940s, as a kind of forced loan to finance World War II. During the 1950s, they went into the general budget for industrial development when the funds were released to Ghana at the time of its independence (Howard 1978).

The colonial authorities again tried consumer price controls during World War II, but again manipulated them for the benefit of European firms and the government treasury. Prices for local food crops were again only controlled in the regional capitals and mining towns (NAK3; NAK7). To forestall African protests, price controls applied on paper to manufactured goods as well as to local foodstuffs, allowing a 75 percent profit margin. Unlike official prices for local foods, those of manufactured imports were continually adjusted to compensate for rising costs and shipping losses, doubling and tripling during the course of the war (NAA3; NAA6). Import quotas restricted legal trade to a few British firms based on outdated market-share figures, reversing the expansion of Ghana-based Syrian (Lebanese) and African firms during the 1930s (Kay 1972). These policies affected market traders in imports indirectly, making small-scale imports difficult or impossible and keeping traders more dependent on the large firms.

Commercial policies advocated by nationalist politicians during the 1940s reversed these priorities while still demanding strong government intervention in trade. J. B. Danquah, the leading nationalist spokesman during the 1940s, wanted strict enforcement of price controls on imports. He defended market traders when colonial officials blamed high prices on them and attributed abuses to the monopolistic import quotas. Continued rationing and shortages after the war ended encouraged corruption and black-market activities in the Gold Coast as in Britain. Danquah proposed opening trade in cloth, cocoa, and building materials with the United States, bypassing the established British firms (NAA6).

When Nkrumah's CPP government (1957–66) assumed power after fiercely contested elections, it continued the nationalist policy focus on price controls for imports, especially a list of essential consumer commodities, leaving local foodstuffs alone. As the new nation's financial problems deepened, however, Nkrumah faced some of the same wage and budget pressures the colonial authorities had faced and sought some of the same solutions. Import licensing and foreign exchange controls led to abuses in allocations and resale. Lines, shortages, and black-market activities revived, along with the colonial rhetoric against parasitic market traders.

State Trading Revisited

Policies initiated shortly after independence, in accord with the greater emphasis on central planning and government control of the national economy under Nkrumah's African Socialist government, diverted more commodities from the marketplace system to more manageable channels. The new authorities heavily regulated sales of imported and manufactured consumer goods in ways favoring large, formalized organizations and those with state links through the foreign exchange allocation system and price lists for essential commodities. State distribution agencies included workers' and consumers' cooperatives and department stores confiscated from expatriates. The new Ghana Food Distribution Corporation handled local farm produce, but without monopoly privileges. The State Fishing Corporation sold frozen fish in regional capitals, including Kumasi, although supplies never challenged the smoked fish distribution channels in volume or reliability.

Successive governments have not been able to maintain effective control of distribution, despite a relatively strong economic position with respect to these particular goods. The concentration of international segments of distribution channels for major imports and exports and the demand for modern inputs for fishermen (boats and gasoline) and cocoa farmers (insecticide) creates good conditions for patronage and dependency. The long-term success of efforts to place more of the distribution volume in state hands depended on the reliability of the commercial relations the state could offer rather than on political relations as such. Repeated efforts to concentrate distribution of imported and manufactured goods in the government-run stores, in workers' and consumers' cooperatives, and in registered groups of factory and government employees have not solved this problem. While absorbing disproportionate resources, these agencies also employ or reward large numbers of officials and supporters.

Control of these state corporations and agencies by civil servants placed control of these segments of the distribution system in the hands, predominantly, of the southern ethnic groups and male gender that dominated the civil service. Advisory boards or administrative panels included representatives of managers of state enterprises, union officials, and leaders of formal sector businesses, but rarely market leaders, who were mainly illiterate women. Government policies and development advice not surprisingly favored industries in the formal sector, which the government could more easily control, whether these followed Western capitalist or Eastern socialist models.

Ghanaian traders only found their government trying to promote their enterprises in opposition to foreign traders, who had even less alliance with it. Busia's UP (which otherwise voiced a free market economic philosophy in reaction to Nkrumah) enacted the Aliens Compliance Order of 1969, however misguided, to privilege citizens in small-scale commerce. All foreign citizens had to register and show that their work fell into the allowed categories; many left voluntarily to avoid deportation. The order was reportedly aimed at Yoruba and Hausa market traders and shopkeepers, along with the many Lebanese or Syrians who still ran small shops that competed directly with equivalent Ghanaian enterprises. Small-scale retail trade by non-Ghanaians was specifically prohibited, so all Yoruba and many Hausa market traders returned home and only the wealthiest Lebanese were able to remain. Some Ghanaians acquired small stores or other businesses cheaply from Nigerians or Lebanese at that time, and others took up the customers left by vanished market enterprises. Cocoa farm laborers from across the northern borders also left precipitously, although ostensibly they were exempted (Addo 1969). Capital-intensive operations such as the expatriate-owned sawmills and factories were exempted.

As with the *Asantehene*'s system of state traders and state loan funds, modern forms of government control reduced women traders' access to public capital and limited their control of their conditions of work. Women traders, including market group leaders, were active in all major political parties as individuals and as groups but could not rely on their alliance with the state. Their participation yielded little direct political benefit on critical issues like loans and foreign exchange allocations or commercial regulations, apart from favors for a few individuals. Nigerian Yoruba women traders seem to have had greater success in translating their block votes and demonstrations into better market facilities and lower taxes (Barnes 1986; Baker 1974). As Ghanaian electoral politics lapsed during the 1960s and 1970s, market women lost their last remaining channel of access to political decision-making processes. By 1979, years of military rule had extinguished traders' expectations of participation or consultation, so that they expected only repression from visible political activity. Traders voted individually in the 1979 elections, but most avoided identifiable party allegiance.

Conclusion

The historical record of traders' commercial linkages and political alliances puts the question of their class position in a more concrete perspective. Tracing the continuities and changes through the centuries for which European documentation exists answers some theoretical questions and merely underlines others. The long centuries of contact with European and Mediterranean trade centers argue against articulationist models that propose precapitalist origins for all indigenous or locally distinctive economic institutions. Trade, chiefship, and other local institutions grew up in a context of continual contact with European trading centers, well before these were fully capitalist in the industrial sense. The substantial reliance on West African labor, raw materials, and profits to support successive stages of European capitalism makes these African locations an integral part of its growth process. The differentiation and increasing polarization between continents provides stronger support for world systems arguments that these are central processes of the development of capitalism.

The deep penetration of commercial relations in local trade and production reflects this longstanding linkage, not a recent confrontation between international and purely nonmarket systems. At least in this part of West Africa, commerce and production for the market played a vital organizational role in rural communities as well as chiefly palaces. Asante lineage relations were constructed to be compatible with involvement in cash crop production and trade, as individuals and as unpaid labor, through kinship, marriage, and slavery. Individual accumulation was encouraged and harnessed by kin and chief and institutionalized within the lineage framework through a range of more subordinate kinship statuses. The prominent role of slavery in Asante and of chiefly tribute in labor, military service, or in kind did not survive from an isolated, aboriginal past but developed as an innovation from more market-mediated coastal Akan societies as part of the process of founding and consolidating the Asante nation. Recent changes in lineage and marital relations represent an adaptation to recent changes in the structure of the international economy and Ghana's position within it, not a dissolution of archaic forms and replacement by classic capitalist ones.

Substantial continuities in trading institutions, from the landlord system to marketplaces themselves, could be interpreted as successful resistance—the partial preservation of precapitalist property and labor relations. For Smith, such persistence reflects both the local autonomy ingrained in simple commodity relations and a degree of historic local autonomy capable of reproducing and defending them. In this instance, institutional forms seem to remain far more stable while the degree of economic autonomy visible through other trading practices such as pricing, credit, and alternative channels is much more volatile. Relations typical of petty or simple commodity forms are not directly or rigidly linked to a particular level of local autonomy, even a subordinate one, but articulate with highly autonomous or highly hierarchical social formations.

This makes monitoring the specific locations of control of the labor process, accumulation, terms of trade, and levels of debt doubly important. Through just these issues, access to the state (that is, relations with the various historically constituted governments) was consistently a critical and hotly contested asset for groups of traders constituted along ethnic, racial, gender, or class lines. State sponsorship or recognition could mean access to loan funds, restricted commodities, tax breaks, exclusion of competing traders, and other favorable regulations—before, during, or after colonial rule. Governments also negotiated shifting alliances with specific groups of traders to gain financial benefits (official and personal) and to assert more control over the economy. These led to hostile actions against other commercial interests, including price controls, boycotts and expulsions, in which citizenship or ethnic identity often figured prominently.

The history of traders' political alliances certainly confirms the hypothesis of their volatility and instability and the linkage between state relations and economic diversity. Predictions that market traders will fall into line with urban wage workers, with peasants, and with state patrons all come true at particular moments. Crisis points such as recurrent price control clearly do generate diversity in trading roles to cope with blocked channels and increased needs for either closeness or distance from state agents. In calmer political periods, economic pressures still heavily mediated by the state continue to generate new specializations and associations. In fact, such indirect interventions as creating alternative gendered occupations or expulsion of foreigners affected the marketplace system more deeply over the long run than direct enforcement of commercial regulations.

The importance of racial, ethnic, and gender identities to the strategies and outcomes of these historical struggles makes the need for dealing with all those systems of domination in concert unmistakable. Accumulation processes were highly gendered at all times and places, whether in the context of kinship-based access to land, public office, and labor (including slaves and pawns) or the impersonal gendering of educational and military institutions and the civil service. It was impossible to be a man or woman except by enacting specific ethnic and class expressions of gender, and vice versa—just as Black feminists explained about both Whites and Blacks in the United States. Even if no overt gender struggles had arisen, contests based in other identities would revive them, since they keep invoking gender for better leverage against their other adversaries. Constructing gender as a separate system of oppression or mode of production says as little about the dynamics of these interactions as would subsuming it under race or class oppression. Using distinct principles of analysis for relations of gender, race, and class does not deny their intersection or the interpenetration of these constructed relations in history and contemporary life. It comes closer to taking these multiple interpenetrations for granted by including them among the core descriptive characteristics of each category or group in itself. Even matriliny, conceptualized by urban Asantes as well as ethnographers as an ahistorical ideal type, was heavily inflected by wealth, chiefly lineage, ethnic origin, and slave status, showing its own historical dynamic even before the advent of education and other Western influences.

The mutual inflection of gender, elite status, race, class, and ethnic identity entered into struggles over control of specific Ghanaian trading positions because the interlocking of these systems of oppression was accomplished, in large part, through control of trading position. Social actors or categories stepped in and out of commercial positions, bringing their other identities with them, along with the accompanying resources, obligations, and connections. None of these systems of domination could maintain static or passive hierarchies because the contradictions between them were a constant source of movement as strengths in one system were deployed to compensate for weaknesses in another. Europeans intervened in the gender division of labor precisely to prevent the emergence of a rival commercial class, while nationalists invoked gender norms to justify their own commercial control. The constant changes in the forms and power content of trading relations reflect the changing size and shape of discontinuities between the other major sectors whose relations they mediate and whose relevant categories crosscut their ranks.

One set of relations can even be deployed in contradictory ways, showing the intersection of different systems of domination within a single institution. For example, matrilineage and marital relations supply Asante women with key material and ideological resources despite their increasing subordination to husbands and brothers. Collins speaks at length of the similarly double-edged role of the Christian church for Black women in the United States (Collins 1990). Marketplace trading itself has some of that ambivalent character because its interstitial location enables it to provide an effective basis for resistance at one point and an equally effective instrument of domination at another time or in another way. This confirms Scott's conclusion that economic and political instability are in fact the most consistent aspect of diverse petty commodity forms (Scott 1986).

The mutual constitution of gender, race, class, and ethnicity takes place in the midst of this volatility. While this book addresses broad issues in the social organization of gender, ethnicity, state formation, and the world system, they enter into it as they entered into the lives of traders and, more particularly, into their working lives. It presents a sharply focused account of the intersection of these systems of meaning and domination in one location, a single marketplace in Ghana. As traders undertake to defend and advance their interests, they continually exercise social power from diverse sources, showing the depths and limits of their combined resources. Their potential for success depends on what they can count on from relations in multiple social fields: ethnic relations, urban/rural relations, family relations, national and international political and economic systems. Continuities are paradoxically constructed out of change; the breakdown of gender barriers in an expanding marketplace system enabled Asante women to keep fulfilling their historic responsibilities for feeding their children after cocoa farming undermined their lineage land access. This process does not take place in episodic "traditional" and "modern" moments, but continually through the concrete micropolitics of interaction in every social arena: the home, the palace, the bureaucrat's office, and the marketplace.

4 BUYING AND SELLING

At the structural heart of the market are the commercial operations that ground power relations within it. Just as the labor process of production within a factory is the basis for factory workers' daily and contractual negotiations over working conditions, speedups, wage differentials and subcontracting, the intricate procedures of buying and selling define the points which actors inside and outside the marketplace itself must try to control in order to improve their positions. Buying and selling absorb most of the attention and time of traders themselves, reminding me constantly that these tasks determine pricing, profit levels, and the consequent survival and accumulation of individual traders. Either individually or collectively, traders establish some degree of control within the market by manipulating these practices. Their relative success or failure continually reproduces or undermines the diverse systems of domination and subordination for which the marketplace system is an important arena. Gender, race, ethnicity, and the regional and urban/rural hierarchies penetrate the marketplace system and act through it by appropriating or accommodating segments of its commercial hierarchy to achieve day-to-day capital accumulation. In a highly commercialized region such as southern Ghana, this historical process of interlocking with trade was and remains central to the construction of these other systems of domination.

The very importance of commercial relations to a whole range of systems of domination ensured that they did not remain historically static, inert, or determinate, since they were continually and repeatedly contested as all of the social groups and categories involved tried to improve their overall positions. This constant jockeying for position produces not only historical variation but diversity in trading procedures. Unfortunately, the everyday details of trading techniques are one of the least historically documented aspects of trade, either in archival sources or in living memory. These alternative activities provide the vocabulary, as social relations (discussed next) provide the grammar, out of which traders and their nontrader customers generate the continually fluctuating and contested trading pattern that can be considered as a kind of economic discourse about relative value and power.

The viable range of trading techniques is as historically specific as the range of farming methods or industrial technology. A social formation defines the trading process contingently in terms of the tasks which must be performed in order to accomplish distribution within it, which implies having the resources needed to perform those tasks in one of the usual ways. Traders maintain knowledge of a limited range of alternative trading practices through personal trial, life cycle experiences, reminiscence, and strategic discussions. Although this range exceeds those currently practiced, a trader cannot choose at random from within it. She cannot survive using outmoded techniques that others have abandoned (perhaps for good reason), since she will lack appropriate trading partners. Archaic methods traders are no longer capable of or interested in using fade gradually from the effective repertoire as those with personal experience and skill in them retire. Innovation is equally continuous, but a trader likewise cannot successfully use an advanced technique, however advantageous, without recruiting a sufficient pool of partners who also know their parts. These may include national and international populations, firms, and agencies with contradictory agendas.

Commodity characteristics also constrain the choice of trading techniques, combining physical and social attributes. Limits set by crop seasonality and perishability are not linked directly to biological givens but operate through the infrastructure of transport and storage facilities. The spatial patterns of concentrated or dispersed consumption and production articulate climate and biology with settlement patterns and farming practices. The fiscal structures of importing respond to annual drying-up cycles for foreign exchange tied to the cocoa harvest and to crisis episodes of foreign exchange shortage, devaluation, fluctuating regulations, and political unrest. Illegality, one purely social construct, functions as a commodity characteristic for the time being, from the trader's point of view. Like the others, it determines who can enter trade in a particular commodity and the advantages in doing so as well as the organization of commercial relations in its distribution network.

The detailed look at trading procedures in this chapter makes it possible to estimate the potential for control that exists within current Kumasi Central Market trading institutions, either for purposes of exploitation or autonomy. An overview of the regional configuration of the marketplace network has already identified the key nodal points in the commercial network, such as the wholesale yards or the farmgate, which a trader would find it necessary or advantageous to control in order to dominate the marketplace system as a whole. The specifics of the trading process reveal what kinds of intervention would give her effective domination of these nodal points and suggest the resources she would need to attempt or resist domination. Chapter 5 will discuss the relations through which individual traders gain access to those resources, and chapter 6 considers the social organization of that control.

Traders resist control by others as energetically as they seek to gain it for themselves, and with even more success. The commercial conventions or routines most commonly found in Kumasi Central Market both reflect and place limits on the ability of its traders to establish control. These routines make key nodes structurally and organizationally difficult to control centrally, thereby limiting traders' ability to exert control through the marketplace system over other sectors of the economy, such as farming or urban consumption, but also limiting the ability of external actors, such as the government, to control the marketplace system.

Bargaining

The central moment of buying and selling is the moment of purchase, when the transfer of goods for money defines the level of immediate benefit or profit each party will realize. The process of bargaining crystallizes the differential power of the participants as each invokes or uses directly and indirectly the resources accessible to her through her various social relations, including information and alternative commercial or subsistence channels. Even long-term assets, such as reputation or reliability of supply, must eventually enter the bargaining process at some point in order to affect the "bottom line" of economic advantage. Understanding something of the technicalities of bargaining procedure makes it possible to follow the process of jockeying for procedural and financial advantage and to assess the significance of the small victories that result.

Although specific bargaining conventions may favor one side or the other, having recognized conventions in general assists both buyer and seller. Following accepted procedures streamlines the buying process by removing many aspects of daily transactions from constant renegotiation. The transaction takes less time if only one or two matters need specific agreement, reducing the labor input of both buyer and seller and preventing spoilage of perishable commodities. Reducing the number of changing variables also reduces risk by making it easier for traders to recalculate their expected profits as they contemplate making concessions to each other. Traders familiar with one system of bargaining can estimate their profit quickly and accurately in its terms, but not in terms of another system of bargaining. A woman who usually bought fish by the hundred easily told me her markup and how much profit she expected with her buying price per hundred, as well as her markup with several higher and lower prices. She could not figure these estimates for frozen fish, sold by the pound, so she refused to buy it when it was occasionally available. Holding other factors constant, both parties can more accurately compare one transaction with past or potential others, avoiding unexpected losses. I saw hostile or derisive reactions to buyers or sellers who chose inappropriate styles of bargaining or tried to change non-negotiable aspects of the transaction, as if traders felt they were trying to trick them. They also raised prices sharply to cover the increased risk of miscalculation. One clear sign of domination, then, is that one side can impose a bargaining style unfamiliar or unwelcome to the other.

I learned the general principles of bargaining through trial, error, and general hilarity as I "played" at selling from my friends' stalls. Like a small child, I was gradually trusted to sell small amounts in the trader's absence, when left with strict instructions about prices and the reductions allowed. Neighbors would correct me or laugh at me (usually both) when I contravened the general procedural norms and etiquette of bargaining. On the proprietor's return, she would interrogate me and them. The explanations embedded in these admonitions and teasings made it easier to follow the more complex bargaining over larger quantities that I observed. For example, I discovered that my errors in bargaining strategy might be made by meeting or refusing different buyers' similar demands.

The firmest and most universal convention sets the boundary of the bargaining relation. Once the potential buyer shows an interest in one trader's goods, by as much as stopping in front of her stall, no other trader should address her. When a woman I knew walked up to the next stall, even greeting her before she had completed her purchase drew a sharp look. Traders call overstepping this boundary "stealing" another trader's customer. When I brought up the subject of quarrels between neighboring traders, they frequently used this as their typical example. The customer must take the initiative and turn to another trader, breaking off the first negotiation. Returning later to bid again on the first set of goods is considered impolite; the seller will not usually refuse, but will usually raise her price from her previous final offer. Competitive bargaining between traders would create chaos in a crowded market, since each trader would have to pay attention to many customers at once. It would also obviously weaken the trader's bargaining position.

Bargaining in Kumasi Central Market takes either price or quantity as the primary variable, holding the other aspect constant. The physical divisibility of the commodity into smaller units encourages bargaining over quantity, while a higher transaction price encourages price bargaining by creating a more divisible payment. One cannot see a strict association between retail or wholesale trade and price or quantity bargaining, since examples of each can be found in retailing and wholesaling of specific commodities. Each commodity has its own specific pattern of bargaining conventions, and these often change with the unit of sale. The retail and wholesale conventions for one commodity correspond only loosely, and its bulk, weight, price, perishability, and divisibility at each scale exert a strong influence. Wholesale traders by definition treat the wholesale unit as indivisible, so it is the characteristics of the box or bag that count. Price variations on small retail purchases are useless because the tiny coins required are out of circulation.

The largest number of transactions in Kumasi Central Market are small retail sales of local foodstuffs that use quantity bargaining, the least familiar process for Westerners. The price remains the same, but the amount of goods the customer will walk away with for that price is negotiable. The buyer approaches, stops, selects the pile she prefers, and sets about improving its contents. Retail traders in local foodstuffs like tomatoes or onions set out their goods in small heaps appropriate for a consumer's daily purchase for family meals. In 1979 these were priced at one cedi, four cedis, ten cedis, etc. The uniformity of prices traders call out creates the illusion of price fixing, and is often used as evidence of it. In fact, those authors who have paid closer attention to bargaining procedures note that price uniformity is enforced just as strictly by open competition (Mintz 1961; Trager 1976). Buyers bargain freely over quantity and sometimes quality, which can result in considerable variation in their final cost/benefit ratio.

The exact bargaining procedure varies with the degree of divisibility of the commodity being sold. Where the pile consists of two or three items which vary slightly in size, such as small dried fish or tomatoes, the buyer can ask the seller to substitute a slightly larger or more perfect specimen for one of the original set. Of course, the combination of grades in the original set was carefully calculated, so the seller may refuse, saying "this is how we sell it." Larger foodstuffs, such as yams or papayas, are priced and bought retail as single items with different asking prices for different rough size grades. Here, the seller will offer or the buyer ask to substitute a slightly larger one from the same or from the next higher price range to increase the quantity bought. Quality and size merge in this situation as quantity characteristics, since damaged or rotten portions must be discarded later.

The *to so* or add-on system is popular for quantity bargaining on foodstuffs divisible into very small, inexpensive units, such as beans or chili peppers. After selecting her heap, the buyer may simply stand looking at it doubtfully, and the seller will take the hint and add another small item to it, such as a single dried pepper. More often, the buyer pays for her heap and then asks for the seller to *to so kakra* (drop on a little). This request is so expected for inexpensive vegetables that the seller automatically adds some when wrapping the goods. If the buyer thinks the *to so* amount is inadequate, she asks for more, so the bargaining takes place after the sale, in a sense. The add-on can become a large proportion of the total amount actually taken away by the buyer.

The same add-on principle is used for cooking oil, infinitely divisible physically, which is sold in volume measures the oil traders own and fill before pouring into containers the buyer brings. These range from five-gallon kerosine tins, the wholesale unit, through pint beer and soft drink bottles, on down to an eccentric array of tiny perfume and medicine bottles. Retailers do not allow negotiation on the nominal price for each container below the pint size, but after they pour it into the buyer's container they bargain over the add-on. One retail oil seller I often sold for volunteered an add-on for very small transactions that was nearly as much as the measure itself. She allowed no add-ons for buyers taking one of the more standardized units, a full beer or soft drink bottle, explaining that that price was already lower.

For vegetables like tomatoes and onions, the add-on system was extended and even intensified for purchases of larger amounts, with the effect of a volume discount. Someone buying four or five piles of a given size would expect the seller to throw in an extra pile, or even more. When left minding a tomato stall, I was instructed how many piles someone would have to buy before I should agree to do this. No add-on was permitted for those buying only one of the smallest heaps. Using this bargaining strategy, the seller encourages buyers to buy more by offering to add on generously if they do. This is especially common when she is trying to move perishable goods or as a counter to demands for add-ons she considers excessive.

Quantity bargaining suits the average Ghanaian's low income and fixed daily budget. She lacks the capital to buy food in bulk for more than a few days ahead, as well as the refrigeration or even storage space to keep it. Price variations for such small quantities would require handling obsolete coins not accepted even by beggars, as single and five-pesewa coins were not in 1979. Varying quantity also accommodates the consumer who is already spending most of each day's strictly limited income for food. If the price rises, she has to buy less. If the price drops, she wants to buy more to compensate for previous skimpy meals.

In the public context of an open market stall, quantity bargaining has another advantage for the seller. It offers her more control over information about specific transactions than price bargaining, which can be easily overheard. She can give one buyer a better bargain by adding on, without advertising it to other potential buyers, since only a few near bystanders can observe the actual amount and quality of goods transferred. The extra amount is added at the very end of the transaction, so it is wrapped and removed from public view almost immediately. Giving add-ons rather than direct price reductions makes it more difficult for buyers to compare terms precisely, although I have seen shoppers unwrapping their packages to compare their deals with friends at home or at a resting place elsewhere in the market. Differences in the amount taken home result not only from individual variation in bargaining skill or the stingy personality of the seller—they represent effective discounts given to faithful customers of longer standing or newer but higher volume buyers. Attracting new customers depends on projecting an image of generosity and individual commitment to them, which may require disguising equal or larger add-ons given to others. When legally fixed prices are strictly enforced for local foodstuffs (as in Huaraz, Peru) quantity bargaining helps conceal variations (Babb 1989).

The verbal side of quantity bargaining seems to confirm this association with customer favoritism. Its more personalized flavor includes more remarks with emotional overtones than price bargaining. The buyer rarely breaks off a transaction completely during quantity bargaining. She may embarrass the seller by refusing to leave until given a sufficient add-on, but it is very rare for her to hand the purchase back and demand a refund at that point. Extended emotional arguments appear, with both parties pleading long friendship and near starvation. Both buyer and seller sometimes refer to an add-on as a gift, saying *ma me kakra bedidi* (give me a little to eat) or (in English) "I dash you." The contrast between price and quantity bargaining style was a matter of degree, not absolute. Price bargaining sessions included similar arguments or phrases, for example, *me ma wo one cedi* (I give you one cedi), but this happened less often. Quantity bargaining itself seemed restrained here, in terms of emotional intensity and verbal flourishes, compared at least with bargaining language reported from the Congo (Ngole 1986). Verbal elaboration does not mark emotional intensity in Kumasi, since the price bargaining in larger transactions is terse and tense.

The bargaining itself distinguishes an add-on from a real gift, which traders also make to friends and relatives who come to buy. Unlike ordinary customers, such persons should not ask for a gift, and I heard them criticized for doing so. Although traders complained about relatives who casually dropped by too often, I also saw them insist on giving goods to visitors who tried to buy something, or giving them add-ons so far beyond the ordinary commercial range that the intention was unmistakable. Traders' unwillingness to give friends and relatives substantial price reductions, when they readily offered gifts instead, seems to underline the advantage gifts and add-ons give in avoiding strict comparison and jealousy.

Wholesale transactions almost always involve price bargaining, because the fixed wholesale unit defining them makes it difficult or impossible to vary quantity. For example, sellers in the yam wholesale yard sell only by the hundred, in the tomato yard by the box, and in the cassava yard by the full cocoa sack. Taking some from another wholesale unit to add on would make it impossible to sell the second unit wholesale, but adding on another entire unit would be disproportionate, since most buyers take only one or three. The relatively high price these wholesale units command makes it logical and convenient to ask for price reductions, since relatively small percentages are still useful sums of money.

Traders also price bargain in terms of wholesale units when they purchase entire consignments in bulk. Farmers and villagers bring in produce in all kinds of baskets, basins and bags, which they take back with them. Once the price is agreed, the seller watches as the buyer measures out the goods into her own containers, multiplying to calculate the total purchase price. Garden egg and palm fruit buyers in villages or periodic markets bargain prices "by the bucket," using a mass-produced rubber bucket as a standard measure. Palm oil buyers use the kerosene tin, or *grawa.* Orange wholesalers in the Kumasi Central Market yard receive truckloads of oranges packed loose in the back of the truck. They bargain a price with the travelers in terms of a standard carrying basket, referred to as a hundred but actually containing a variable number of oranges depending on their size. To avoid the delay of counting thousands of oranges, they buy and resell by the same basket used for head transport. During slow periods, the wholesalers keep one or two "hundreds" for retailing in between deliveries. Then they do count out the oranges to sell by the dozen or in threes. Price bargaining also emerges in retail sales of more expensive consumer goods that consumers can rarely buy more than one at a time. Pots and pans, used or new clothing and head scarves, for example, are sold by the piece. Since sellers cannot divide them or add on to a single item, price is the only variable aspect. The indivisibility of twelve-yard lengths of wax printed cloth, called *ntama,* is only sometimes negotiable. The cheaper varieties of printed cloth are sold by the half-piece (six yards) or in two-yard lengths, but traders usually refuse to cut a high-quality piece. Since a full piece makes two women's outfits, one expression of friendship between adolescent girls is to buy a full piece and split it.

Differences in bargaining style between price and quantity bargaining reflect the size of transaction to which they apply. Buying a piece of cloth is a major purchase for the ordinary Ghanaian, who looks carefully for an attractive pattern and bargains at length. It was not uncommon in 1979 for a cloth buyer to return to the same trader over several days of bargaining. When I was doing this, cloth sellers would try to introduce other issues into the bargaining, for example, by substituting an inferior piece of cloth instead of reducing the price. Other buyers also seemed to resist this as confusing. The actual bargaining was the final step of an extended shopping effort for major purchases, which included questioning friends about recent prices, locating the item amid general scarcity, and comparing quality, pattern, and asking price at several locations, before settling down to bargain. From Javanese material, Alexander considers such elaborate bargaining sessions to be typical of trading situations where the buyer does not buy frequently, so that the information gap between buyer and seller is large or unknown, and gives examples from cloth and foodstuffs purchasing (Alexander 1987).

Compared with quantity bargainers, price bargainers stick to economic rather than personal arguments to support their claims. Consumers will not say they need something to eat, but claim others are selling for less, or say they cannot afford to buy at all at that price. Unfortunately, the seller may agree that the buyer cannot afford such a high-quality item and try to substitute an inferior one, so the buyer also has to argue that its quality is not in fact so high. These rhetorical themes confirm Alexander's point that exchange of economic information, or testing of the accuracy of others' information, is a primary function of bargaining (Alexander 1987).

The subdued, tense style of price bargaining reflects the importance of the purchase to the buyer, whether consumer or reseller. In the wholesale yard or the cloth market, buyer and seller both make an offer and wait quietly for a counteroffer. Frequently, they will simply ask the other party to speak again rather than exchanging emotional dialogue. The especially understated style in wholesale yards supports Alexander's contention that high information levels, when shared and acknowledged, lead to abbreviated bargaining sessions with a narrower gap between asking and selling prices (Alexander 1987). Young Kumasi men selling used clothing and other inexpensive imports, such as insecticide sprays and padlocks, did indulge in flamboyant exchanges with potential customers, although their motivation seemed as much to entertain their neighbors as to affect the sales price. When buying smaller, more frequently purchased items, such as toothpaste or shoes, the amount of reduction in price bargaining tended to be small, about ten percent.

A trader who buys regularly for resale in the wholesale yards finds her rhetorical options in bargaining restricted by her need to maintain a good commercial reputation for other purposes. She rarely pleads absolute poverty, for fear of harming her credit rating by suggesting her business is shaky. I heard buyers claim they had insufficient money on hand to pay high prices, to which sellers responded by offering credit rather than reducing the price. Instead, the buyers say they would lose money or be driven out of trading if they were foolish enough to accept the offered price. They invoke professional and gender solidarity, saying that they have the right to make a living and support their children. Each accuses the other person of not wanting to do business or make a deal, of not being serious. Resellers stress the poor quality of the goods less than consumers, since they can resell any quality at the appropriate price, but those preparing most ready-to-eat foods need decent quality to keep their customers. Even half-rotten plantain and moldy tomatoes have their buyers for special dishes or seed, although a reseller may say her regular customers will not like this type. Sellers emphasize the high prices they paid suppliers and their need to buy replacement supplies at that price. They will argue that retailers can easily increase their resale prices and still make a profit. Resellers will argue that their buyers do not have enough money to pay such prices.

Kumasi Central Market traders know of different styles of price bargaining, even though convention prescribes only one for their usual transactions. The most common format, sometimes called Asante style or unnamed, starts with seller and buyer each making offers some distance apart and gradually moving closer until they meet. Another bargaining format, called Hausa style in Kumasi, was reported as typical of wholesaling in kola and other commodities dominated by Northern men. The buyer starts with a high offer the seller accepts and then comes down, making lower and lower offers until the seller refuses one, rather than coming up from an initial low offer. According to Trager, Yoruba women also use this bargaining format in Nigeria (Trager 1991). The fact that each group of traders can use their familiar procedures suggests some basic autonomy in transactions.

The existence of rough quality grades in Kumasi wholesale yards leads to bargaining over the classification of marginal lots, which also indicates the relative power of buyers and sellers. Perishables such as greens and cassava drop sharply in price once unambiguously classified as *abiri,* yellow or fully ripe. They are still good for use, but will not keep long enough for convenient resale. For example, two grades of garden eggs have known prices at a given time: *fitaa,* or white ones, are less ripe and longer-lasting, while *kokoo,* or red ones, are riper and cheaper. The actual fruit ranges from lily-white through bright yellow to orange-red, so quite a few bags have indeterminate status and the classification boundary changes depending on the average quality available. Short supplies in the dry season create a sellers' market, and buyers accept as "white" colors that they could force sellers to discount heavily as "red" in the glut season. Yam buyers also work within a rough framework of small, medium, and large sizes when negotiating prices with farmers. They sort more precisely by size in the Kumasi wholesale yard when stacking their truckloads into hundreds, so that each hundred is of fairly uniform size and bargained on separately.

Conventions on units of measure can have a dramatic effect on real prices and quantities, so variations serve as another index to power balances. The specific container used may be important, since farmers' and traders' sacks can differ markedly in size. The method of filling or measuring can change the volume considerably, for example whether buckets are heaped high or sack ends covered with grass rather than sewn tightly shut. In some instances the distinction between measures used on the farm and in the city represents a major part of the traveler's profit. For example, the "bush hundred" of yams bought by travelers at the farmgate is actually 120 yams, yielding a larger number of hundreds in Kumasi. The extra cassava from a sack heaped "full" in the village is taken off and repacked when the sack is sewn tight for transport to Kumasi. Openly acknowledged village standards that favor town traders indicate substantial urban/rural power hierarchies, although prices do take them into account.

Individualized renegotiation of procedural issues reflects individual vulnerability or power. Both traders and farmers initiate negotiations over the delivery date, which may be important to the immediate solvency of either one. A farmer may have a pressing need for cash for school fees or a funeral. He will reduce his price to attract a trader when buying is slow and to back up his demand for immediate payment. Likewise traders short of goods or cash have to offer a premium price at a time when the farmer can easily hold on to his crop. Traders who advance money to farmers ahead of purchase have moral entitlement to choose the delivery date that suits them, within the limits of the normal farming cycle and the farmer's ability to stall them.

The time of delivery, credit terms, responsibility for transport charges, and other useful services or gifts all affect the ultimate profitability of the sale and so must be shrewdly judged. The fact that conventions about them do vary seasonally in itself indicates that they reflect the relative bargaining power of each side. Gifts and favors are exchanged as use values but, because the embedding relationship is an economic one, their economic value is the most important consideration. Buyers on the farm try to sponge gifts of firewood, fruit, samples, and free meals from farmers, whose tolerance rises when few other buyers are available. On the other hand, I saw traders bring gifts of bread or candy from town to farmers' children and carry firewood back from the farm for a farmer's aged mother when goods were scarce. During times of severe shortage, sellers in stores, farms, or markets can even demand gifts for the privilege of buying. The buyer also becomes more or less picky about the quality of the goods to be delivered. For example, a garden egg trader may want to pay the agreed price only for the best quality white fruit, but the farmer may want to include everything that is ready to be harvested. In the dry season, every old, shriveled, worm-eaten fruit is accepted and easily resold. Some Kumasi Central Market retailers refused to wrap or even make change for small purchases then.

Credit shows particularly strong seasonal fluctuations, reversing its direction as well as becoming more or less obligatory and costly. In this region, extending credit seems to be a sign of weakness more often than domination. When supplies are scarce, buyers lend money to farmers or travelers to secure supplies in advance. When there is a glut, suppliers give credit to buyers to enable them to buy more and keep the goods moving when their capital is stretched to the limit. These credit concessions may be expected at one time of year and out of the question at another. When tomatoes flooded the market, for example, I saw one Kumasi wholesaler extending credit who had told me she never did. She explained that she could not sell without it just then and that others had to offer dangerously low prices for cash they needed desperately. Dominant parties can insist on cash payment.

Either price or quantity bargaining can take delayed payment into account. The seller often holds firmer on prices or reduces the add-on as a disguised fee for credit purchasers, making credit part of the bargain. Conversely, when buyers advance money to farmers or travelers, they expect a good price relative to market conditions when the price is later bargained at the time of delivery. These indirect credit charges must cover a risk of further discount as well as default, since buyers occasionally try to renegotiate the price when they pay. If the buyer has lost money on the transaction, she can claim that she did not recoup the purchase price and present the seller with a choice between a reduced payment or further delay.

Trading conventions for a given situation and commodity usually indicate which options are allowable, but exceptions can be made for individuals. In other words, the negotiability of these aspects is itself subject to negotiation. Since aspects of the farmgate transaction that are negotiable in some contexts are standard in others, there is often room for discussion over which set of rules will apply. When supply or demand conditions give one side a strong advantage, credit expectations do change, but the timing of the change may be contested or gradual. Assessment of transport and harvesting costs changes with location, favoring traders more sharply in the remoter villages, but arguments or outright deception over how remote a given village really is are frequent. Occasional hard bargaining over these peripheral issues suggest that price adjustments do not entirely compensate for their effect on profits or risk.

Price bargaining sessions can become much more elaborate when they include negotiations over non-price issues, as they do between travelers and farmers. Bargaining sessions sometimes invoke several principles of bargaining in turn, resulting in extremely complicated transactions. One session I witnessed between a yam farmer and a traveling trader lasted the better part of a day. We had traveled out the night before from Kumasi to a supply area to collect a truckload of yams and rose early to drive out to the farm on a rutted dirt track. The trader's mother had inspected the yams on a previous trip and already had agreed on a price per hundred for each of two quality groups. On seeing the yams, the daughter accused the farmer of substituting smaller ones for those her mother had seen, which reopened price negotiations. Laborers opened the earth-covered storage piles and counted out the yams into stacks of roughly uniform size, each numbering 120 yams, the "bush hundred." The trader and farmer classified these stacks into three size grades before price bargaining began on a price per hundred for yams of each size.

Intense and dramatic negotiations continued for hours over this transaction involving tens of thousands of cedis (then in the range of

$2,000 at black market exchange rates). Both sides accused the other of fraud and made theatrical gestures, including threatening to drive away or ordering the laborers to unload yams from the truck. The laborer foreman and driver both acted as mediators after particularly heated exchanges, stopping the laborers from unloading after a few token yams. Several times the parties broke off price negotiations to reclassify some stacks. The trader vigorously criticized individual yams and tried unsuccessfully to introduce a fourth category of "very small." The price agreement per hundred that allowed the laborers to load the yams onto the truck and drive off turned out not to be the last word. We also had to unload most of the yams by the roadside, when the truck got stuck in the mud, and reload them again after digging it out.

Further negotiations took place at the farmer's home at the time of payment. First the trader added up the total price for each category of yams and reduced it to a round figure. After adding these up for the total purchase, she asked for a further reduction. After the driver and several neighbors had counted the cash payment, the farmer provided a large yam meal and gifts of substantial yams for all concerned. The trader had arrived with gifts of salt and bread, since she had known this farmer since she accompanied her mother on similar trips as a child. She also had to pay the driver, the laborers, and the broker who arranged for the labor gang; this was not an issue. Calculating exact net profit on such a deal presented a mathematical challenge to which neither the trader nor the anthropologist were equal.

These more leisurely sessions between travelers and farmers, with repeated discussions of a variety of issues, call to mind some of De Marees's descriptions of the courtly bargaining styles of large-scale coastal traders buying from European ships around 1600 (De Marees 1985 [1602]). In these episodes, the exchange of gifts and favors constituted a significant part of the procedure. These amounted to testing the intensity of the relationship, as much as bargaining over the specific transaction, although he complains that they made a sharp dent in the Europeans' profits. Travelers and farmers today also need to test the capacity of their relationships, when the pace of sales permits, since they may need to draw on them rapidly in an emergency.

Barter was hardly used in Kumasi Central Market or the smaller markets its traders patronize. De Marees testifies to the antiquity of currency use in this region, beginning with gold dust and cowries used across local borders (De Marees 1985 [1602]). It was Europeans who tried to insist on barter at that time, to unload unpopular goods, and they only succeeded much later. Only two cases ever came to my attention, one of which was obsolete and both for very low-value commodities. The historical example concerns the green leaves used for wrapping small purchases, before they began to be sold commercially in the 1920s or 1930s. An old lady who had been among the first to sell them said that villagers coming to Kumasi would previously bring along a bunch of leaves to give to a Kumasi butcher in exchange for a morsel of meat, an exotic delicacy in the village. Other items were apparently not wrapped then. In 1990, I saw young girls selling ice water to traders in return for a small sample of whatever the trader sold. They would call out *me gyi adee,* I take goods—instead of money. One trader I sat with contributed a dozen or so peanuts for a drink, after the girl had asked for more. The girl put them in a dish that showed tomatoes, smoked fish, onions and pepper. The trader explained that these girls went home to sell these miscellaneous assortments of goods from tables outside their homes. She said this was a long-established way of starting a tiny trading business and claimed girls earned more this way than the cash price of their water, of course adding a greater labor input with the time spent in resale.

Units of Sale

The dynamics of bargaining show how central conventions of measuring are to the pricing and transfer of goods. Appropriate and familiar units greatly facilitate accurate pricing and convenient handling of goods. The very usefulness of well-chosen units entrenches a multiplicity of measurement systems used to fill specific needs in specific locations inside and outside Kumasi Central Market. Volume units, numerical units, and price units have the widest use within it. Weight units are relatively rare; only the larger sellers of fresh meat use scales. Conventions often specify different principles of measuring for large and small amounts of the same commodity.

The boundary between wholesale and retail sales within each commodity group is defined by its characteristic wholesale unit. This can be a hundred yams, a box of tomatoes, or a sack of rice, but it presents the main internal threshold within a commodity group. Buyers without enough capital to buy a whole one must pay significantly higher prices for smaller quantities. Conventions of display, bargaining, accounting, and transport also divide according to the unit of sale. Traders who sell in both wholesale and retail units use the appropriate conventions for each, frequently in separate market locations, with separate sets of buyers and suppliers for each.

The terminology Kumasi traders use to divide traders into wholesalers and retailers reflects this definition. Yam wholesalers say they sell *oha, oha* (hundred, hundred) rather than *baako, baako* (one, one) and describe wholesale and retail market locations the same way; cassava or maize wholesalers are those who sell by the sack. By contrast, the distinction which Babb finds in Peru and translates as wholesale and retail is defined literally by traders there as big- and small-scale trade (*al por mayor* and *al por menor*). Her respondents named amounts of total capital or turnover that qualified one as a wholesaler, although they disagreed sharply about the actual threshold (Babb 1989). In Kumasi, on the other hand, the defining wholesale units for different commodities were well known and unanimously agreed upon, even by nontraders. They provide clear benchmarks and thresholds for accumulation by individual traders.

Traders in wholesale locations routinely refuse to break this unit, even when the same trader sells retail somewhere else. I often stood beside one yam wholesaler in the yards who also had a retail stall inside the market. When friends or neighbors approached her there for retail purchases, she greeted them warmly but told them to go to her stall to get some yams from her daughter or niece. Wholesale traders' primary concern is to streamline sales, to move the entire truckload before prices fall. She explained, and others confirmed, that small sales wasted her time and left odd piles of goods that could not be sold in the yard lying there to obstruct bulk loading and unloading.

Retailers conversely may well refuse to sell an entire wholesale unit, because this paradoxically interferes with their accumulation strategies. If she cannot offer reliable supplies throughout the day, she has little hope of attracting the regular customers who will build up her business permanently. Since many operate with tight capital margins, one unit may represent most of her remaining stock. Selling it will effectively put a marginal trader out of business for the rest of the day. The marked daily cycle of market sales makes it risky or expensive to acquire new stocks late in the day after prices have risen and quality has fallen. She must obtain her expected retail margin to maintain her daily income, but even an excess profit on one day may cost more in the long run. This distinction by unit of sale contrasts with the "ordinary meaning" of wholesale and retail standard in Western corporate commerce, which distinguishes between purchase for use or consumption and purchase for resale (Bauer 1954, 54). In the United States, plumbing supply houses or upholstery fabric showrooms display notices stating "trade only" to indicate that they welcome only professionals. Many Kumasi hawkers and cooked food sellers buy in amounts well below the wholesale unit level. Hawkers buy in such small amounts for resale that the retailer may not even know if a given child will take the box of cookies home to his family or hawk them in the neighborhood.

Likewise, yam wholesalers sell as readily to a wealthy householder planning a celebration as to a retailer, and at the same price. Small resellers who return regularly do not enjoy wholesale discounts; instead, they gain more access to credit and market information. The Ghanaian usage resembles more the medieval European distinction preserved in the words themselves. Cloth was sold there then in standard lengths, as it is still in Ghana, and a clothier who sold by the whole piece was not willing to re-taille or re-cut the piece.

The most popular units of sale are defined by volume, which of course includes the method of filling, whether heaped or level, as well as the type of container. Jute cocoa sacks serve as the wholesale unit for almost every item safely transportable in them, including grains, vegetables, kola, kapok, and charcoal. Cooking oil and other liquids are sold wholesale in recycled oil drums and kerosene tins. The ubiquitous white enamel basins and black plastic shopping buckets double as measures for intermediate quantities. Cheap and available mass-produced containers are also pressed into service for smaller quantities. The graduated units of grains, powders, flours, gari, onions, peppers, etc. reuse standard sized kerosene, margarine, and evaporated milk tins. The standard liquid measures are slightly imperfect beer and soft drink bottles (perfect ones were too scarce and valuable). For tiny amounts, oil sellers resort to idiosyncratic collections of medicine bottles, miscellaneous tins, and jar lids.

Volume measurement permits easy visual inspection of the unit size by the buyer, who need not then rely on public regulation of weights and measures. Mass-produced plastic and enamel basins and glass bottles are the most reliable, since they are harder to deform with dented bottoms than recycled tin cans. The average Ghanaian buyer, however, considers dents and false bottoms in old evaporated milk or mackerel cans much easier to detect and allow for than dishonest scales. Through practice, they feel reasonably confident of their ability to estimate the capacity of these familiar containers. Local craftsmen produce containers conforming to these industrial sizes—for example, standard baskets holding the same as one cocoa sack or one kerosene tin.

Volume units also save sellers the expense of special equipment, such as a scale, since storage and dispensing require some container in any case. These secondhand containers are not considered disposable, although inexpensive by Western standards. By local standards, the set of container measures can represent a substantial capital investment. No traveler can do business without her set of cocoa bags or kerosene tins, no oil seller without her set of bottles. These belong to the seller, and the buyer must supply her own. Customers bring their own bottle or small pan for liquid purchases such as oil and return sacks or baskets after local deliveries. Retailers wrap purchases in leaves or waste paper bought from hawkers or sell plastic bags to the buyer. Even empty evaporated milk tins are bought and sold by specialists.

The most popular wholesale volume measures are the most popular and practical containers for transport, storage, and handling. Eliminating the need to count or measure at each transaction saves time and reduces damage from repeated handling. For example, tomatoes packed in standard wooden boxes travel from as far as Bolgatanga with only cursory inspection in Kumasi. Some concealment of unripe or damaged tomatoes at the bottom of the box is expected, and each village of provenance has a reputation for the degree of straw padding included. Sellers get very angry if potential buyers start to probe the boxes, not so much because they reveal any secret but because they bruise the good tomatoes without necessarily buying them.

Commodities measured by volume must have an acceptable degree of homogeneity and divisibility relative to the unit size. Sometimes this homogeneity must be taken on trust. The buyer of a full bag of fresh cassava tubers or *gari,* grated dried cassava meal, must be able to assess its quality by opening the end, without pouring out the whole bag to inspect the hidden portions. Cassava tubers are large and unequal enough that smaller quantities must be sold by the heap. Any smaller container, approximating the average daily purchase, would be filled so incompletely that it would be useless as a measure. The consumer can readily compare the size and condition of individual tubers by sight. Gari, on the other hand, can be sold as is by the spoonful, and often is by cooked-food sellers, who purchase by the bag or the "America" margarine tin.

Counted units of sale suit commodities that vary widely in size and quality, so that a hundred or dozen of each lot must have its own price. Traders estimate relative sizes and qualities very carefully, but without standard grades, statistical comparisons have little meaning. It is particularly easy to calculate markups and rates of profit when the wholesale and retail units are both counted. Yams and dried fish are among the goods sold by the hundred in Kumasi wholesale yards. Sellers count them out and buyers recount them as they take delivery, and the seller will correct short counts. Traders then commonly retail them in heaps of three or four for a price. Certain items, including jewelry, children's clothes, handkerchiefs, and shoes, commonly change hands in dozens because retailers want to stock many varieties. Manufactured goods that come in cartons have a standard wholesale count determined by the container.

Numerical units can be deceptive for the inexperienced when the nominal count differs from the actual count. The notional hundred of oranges, already mentioned, is actually a volume measure using the largest size carrying basket, equivalent to a cocoa bag. Sometimes oranges actually arrive packed in cocoa bags, instead of loose in the back of the truck, especially when the total shipment is smaller. The actual count varies considerably with the size of the oranges; retailers allow for this in their own pricing but the skill must be developed over time. Smaller amounts of oranges are counted strictly and retailed at six or three for a price, as well as by the dozen or by twenty.

With quantity bargaining, it makes sense to consider the price unit as the unit of sale. The tomato, pepper, or peanut butter seller displays small heaps or dabs in rows for buyers to inspect. Strictly speaking, the goods are not measured, although both parties closely judge their size, number, and/or quality. The price remains constant while the buyer negotiates the size of the heap and the add-on through quantity bargaining. A tomato buyer cannot choose to buy, for example, four cedis' worth when the seller has heaps for three and five cedis. These displays of heaps appear consistently in early descriptions of Gold Coast markets, suggesting the antiquity of this method of selling small amounts of goods. The indivisible unit is in fact the coin (previously the cowrie shell).

The unit of sale Kumasi traders buy in is variable but not negotiable when a trader purchases the entire stock of the seller. A villager or traveler will refuse to sell unless the buyer takes everything she has, so the buyer may bid without knowing exactly how much she will end up spending. Traders buying crops before harvest may also settle on a price per bag, for example with tomatoes and garden eggs, which are harvested repeatedly. When they bid on the whole field as a single unit, they assume the risk of miscalculating the eventual yield. I only saw this commonly done for cassava, which combines rapid post-harvest spoilage with relatively low unit cost. The trader must pay for harvesting and transport out of her profit, so the degree of overgrowth, hardness of the soil, and distance to a main road enter into her calculation alongside yield.

Like the bargaining system, the measuring system for a single commodity can change many times between producer and consumer. For example, shallots arrive from the Volta Region coast in intricately woven cylinders constructed for ease of storage and transport. Farmers twist the green shallots into fist-sized bunches for drying. The number in one bunch rises if their individual size is smaller. The dried stems enable these bunches to be woven together into flat layers and the layers stacked and joined into tall cylinders, the wholesale unit. In Kumasi, the weaving is undone for bulk-breaking and sale of whole layers or knots of three bunches, mainly to retailers. Dried or green shallots from Ashanti Region arrive loose and therefore are sold wholesale by the cocoa bag or kerosene tin. Consumers buy either kind of shallots in small heaps consisting of three buds to a handful. Wealthier consumers may buy a whole woven bunch or a loose "America" tin full, since they keep well when dried.

Using several different principles of measurement for small, medium, and large transactions is common in marketing systems outside of Ghana as well. In the Dugbe market, in Ibadan, Nigeria, traders in stockfish (dried cod) called wholesalers those who bought the solid bales exported from Scandinavia. Retailers bought by the dozen (Ogunsanwo 1988, 98). In nearby Ilesha, Nigeria, large-scale yam traders used a volume measure called the gage, equal to the freight space created in a passenger truck by removing one row of benches. Sales between traveling traders and market retailers used a counted unit of sixty, comparable to the Kumasi hundred, while retailers sold in twenty or less (Trager 1976).

Although there are understandable reasons for the persistence of diverse units and principles of measurement in different commodities and at different levels of trade, this complexity undeniably presents a serious obstacle to statistical work on Ghanaian marketplace trade. It frustrates the calculation of profit margins in single enterprises and comparison of pricing and profit patterns in different commodities or locations. Yet efforts to use internationally standard measures create even larger problems. Market censuses that seriously attempt to weigh incoming or outgoing goods create such an obstacle to traffic that they seriously distort the flow of goods, defeating their purpose. In Ghana, they would raise intense suspicion of price control enforcement, and rumors of that demonstrably lead traders and farmers to turn around and take their goods back home. Governments have made repeated attempts to encourage sales by weight, but transactors cling tenaciously to the specific units which offer them definite practical advantages, not the least of which is autonomy from official enforcement. They are unlikely to abandon these units until standard units offer equivalent advantages in handling and pricing or until they have other means to solve these problems.

Accounts

Although these commodity-specific units make generalized accounting difficult, they form the basis of indigenous accounting sys-

Two onion traders in the main shed

A yam traveler bargains with farmers

Stuck in the road from the farm

Buyers choosing stacks of yams in the wholesale yard

The orange checker (in striped shirt) records wholesale credit sales

tems designed for traders' own decision-making purposes. Traders in Kumasi Central Market need to assess and compare the profitability of past and potential transactions to monitor their own accumulation rates. Complicated pricing and bargaining systems make it difficult to do this for individual sales transactions, but traders do keep track of their profits and expenses in terms of bulk units. Diverse mental, physical, and written methods of accounting help skillful traders to monitor their current income levels and discover unprofitable situations early enough to take remedial action.

Traders make practical and conceptual distinctions between working capital, capital growth, expenses, and disposable income, although they use local terminology. They struggle hard to keep their working capital separate from their disposable income under incessant pressure from poverty. They will dip into it willingly to meet a legitimate family emergency, such as medical bills, funeral expenses, or school fees for a child, but they are fully aware that this reduces their working capital and future income. A trader who fails to reinvest while enjoying comfortable food and clothing attracts the ridicule of her colleagues, especially when she asks for price concessions or credit.

Western observers have reported market and street traders saying they are not making any money at all and questioned why they keep trading in that case. I believe they misunderstood this concern for capital accumulation, since traders who made that remark to me meant they were not adding to their trading capital. Although they were making a small daily income, it all went out on necessary family expenses. In the same mood, a Western wage worker making a small wage and spending it all might say she was not getting ahead but would still be reported as earning something. In essence, these market women consider their social reproductive costs as part of their overhead rather than as part of their income.

Traders calculate income in two methods, depending whether they want to compare the profits made on two separate purchases or monitor the level of their fixed working capital as distinct from business and living expenses over time. One popular method of accounting keeps the sales receipts for each wholesale unit (sack or tin) which the trader buys in a separate bundle of notes. When it is all sold, she counts up the total and classifies the whole difference between the buying and selling price as income. She has a target figure for this gross income per unit, which allows sufficient margin for her average business costs and living expenses. She takes the replacement cost of the unit out of this bundle, often paying off her supplier at this time, and uses what is left to pay her future expenses. If something accumulates beyond current expenses it is called "savings" and may be taken out to start a new unit fund. This system enables a trader to compare quickly the relative returns of different lots of goods, which is convenient if she frequently considers dropping one line of goods or emphasizing another. The amount of earnings on each unit sold can be compared and income over time estimated fairly quickly by remembering how frequently units turn over—for example, how many tins of oil are bought daily or weekly. This compares closely to the *por producto* (by the product) system described by Babb from Peru (Babb 1989).

The second popular accounting method keeps only the replacement cost separate for each unit. Once this figure has been reached, that money is kept aside to pay off the debt or buy another unit as needed. The additional proceeds are pooled with those of other units currently being sold and counted as daily income. Daily expenses for taxes, rent, transport, and meals come out of this fund before it is counted at the end of the day, so slow turnover and inflation reduce calculated income directly. The "income" remaining in this second system is income after expenses and, as such, would be available for capital growth or major purchases. This would be referred to as "savings" by traders using the first system, but was less easily monitored by them on a daily basis because they would need to add the separate increments from sales of each unit.

Physical accounting methods are convenient for illiterate market traders because they reduce the need to remember individual transactions and to constantly recount cash. Traders use a separate can or box for the retail proceeds from each wholesale unit or the wholesale repayment fund for goods from each supplier. It is often placed near the actual container or pile, convenient for adding the proceeds of each transaction. Depending on which kind of accounts they keep, either the replacement value (or debt) or the entire net proceeds "belongs" to that unit. Physical segregation also helps the trader resist demands for that money from relatives or creditors until she has accumulated enough to pay for the unit or finished selling it. A similar physical accounting system was considered old-fashioned in Huaraz, Peru, where market women bought specially made cloth purses with multiple pockets (Babb 1989).

Physical accounts are not completely foolproof, however. Just as some traders could not remember complicated mental accounts accurately, I knew some who got their cans mixed up and could not be sure that they or their assistants had consistently put the money in the right place. Kumasi Central Market traders seemed to trust written accounts more than either mental or physical accounts, although they made less use of them. The high general level of literacy enables illiterate traders to check the contents of record books and documents with educated relatives or neutral passersby. A few wealthy traders employ "secretaries" (using the English term) to keep their accounts, although they cannot usually become so wealthy without having unusual skill at mental arithmetic and accounts. Poorer traders remarked that written calculations and records would reduce both honest mistakes and cheating, which can cause less skillful traders considerable losses and make them give up credit and other complex practices necessary for business expansion.

Several associations of Kumasi Central Market traders employ young men to keep records for members in connection with other commercial services. The yam traders' association hires a night watchman to guard the parking lot for yam lorries. He registers the owner of each lorry as it arrives, and this list governs the order in which lorries unload at the wholesale yard. Unlike other traders who must stay with their goods to guard them or keep their place in line, yam traders can go home and sleep. Orange wholesalers also employ several young men they call "checkers" (in English). These record the names of buyers and the amount and price of their purchases for each lot of oranges that arrives in the wholesale yard. The wholesalers commonly give credit to buyers who resell in or near Kumasi Central Market, and the checkers make this easy for them by noting it. Later in the day, the checkers take their lists around the market to collect the debts from each buyer. The completely open plan of the orange wholesale yard already makes the identity of buyers and prices paid public knowledge to all involved, regardless of the records kept, but memories can conflict. Orange traders consider that their checkers' written lists prevent many arguments. Babb also reported from Huaraz, Peru, that credit transactions were the aspect of trade most often recorded in notebooks (Babb 1989).

Transport

Traders' profits depend on good bargaining and calculation of marginal returns, but success in these matters assumes that they are selling in a place where demand is higher than where they bought them, when that demand is present. The physical redistribution of goods according to local surplus and need is one of the major functions carried out by the marketplace system as a whole for the national economy. The movement of goods from one location to another is thus an essential part of many traders' commercial operations. Geographical position has already been identified as a key element in Kumasi Central Market traders' power relative to other traders and to farmers and consumers, but taking full advantage of access to key locations requires access to transport. The efficiency and cost of this process obviously dominate the work life of the specialist travelers, who spend a large proportion of it on the road. The price and terms of access to transport facilities is an important technical issue in their commercial success. Reliable transport underpins the profitability of all Kumasi traders, who depend on goods delivered steadily by others at reasonable cost. During periods of desperate transport shortage in 1979 and 1983, access to transport became a critical factor in access to goods. Alleged monopolistic control of transport made accusations of price abuses by either traders or drivers plausible, which a discussion of the actual processes of obtaining transport can help clarify.

Under current Ghanaian conditions, market traders make an essential labor contribution to the transport process by escorting goods from place to place and by arranging and financing transport. Neither large nor small consignments of goods can be expected to arrive at their destination if not constantly accompanied by the owner or someone personally responsible for them. Traders who buy or sell outside the city of Kumasi spend up to half their time escorting their purchases back. These hours have no assigned profit, since the profit comes from buying and selling prices, but theft or excessive transport charges would quickly eat up not only profits but working capital. Extreme transport shortages, common before 1986, meant that timely transport required a high investment of labor in searching for available trucks and negotiating access to them. Efficiency in this process made a large contribution to final profit levels by speeding turnover and reducing spoilage. Transport charges remain high relative to other costs, even though the crisis has eased, so bargaining them down also has a critical impact on income.

Traders traveling to other towns or rural areas use public passenger transport when bringing little or no freight, competing directly with noncommercial transport users but paying standard rates. Each town or city has one or more lorry parks where travelers wait to buy tickets from the driver, union office, or "bookman" (overseer). During acute transport shortages, these bookmen developed an unsavory reputation for fraud, corruption, and extortion from the long lines of anxious passengers. In 1990, lines of half-filled trucks, vans, and buses waiting for passengers were more commonly seen. Most passenger trucks, modified pickups with seats or benches installed in the back under a roof, also stop to discharge and pick up passengers at informal but regular stops at towns and crossroads en route. Villages located on motorable side roads see trucks or vans passing through once or twice daily, stopping on request. Traders also make use of the railways, ferries, and State Transport buses when these serve their destinations. Traders traveling to bring goods from outside of Ghana use every means of transport from air to foot, but usually reside near the border or the airport rather than in Kumasi.

Traders bringing moderate amounts of goods, up to two or three cocoa sacks of gari, for example, use ordinary passenger or mixed transport but get special treatment. These loads are large by passenger standards and require special attention in loading. Traders need to supervise loading and unloading to prevent breakage or theft. The pushing and confusion that were common during gasoline shortages made it easy to lose extra baggage or to lose one's seat while attending to the baggage. Drivers or bookmen will hold seats for traders in anticipation of the high, unstandardized baggage fees they assess on commercial freight. Truck drivers or State Transport employees sometimes step into this position by supervising freight shipments themselves while working, either carrying shipments for friends who are traders or trading on their own accounts.

The traders who frequent village periodic markets often travel in trucks which specialize in this traffic, taking commercial passengers and their freight to a particular village market for each day of the week. In Kumasi these trucks waited for their regular passengers in special loading areas in several gas stations near the market that were used very little during gasoline shortages. They leave at dawn and ply back and forth to the same town all day, taking ordinary passengers to fill up the space not claimed by traders and their goods. Many trucks have removable benches or seats, so the proportion of bulk freight space can be expanded or reduced on demand. The traders who travel out with one truck have a guaranteed seat for themselves and their return freight on the next trip when they need to return. They tend to join the same truck each week or several days in the week (to separate destinations) in order to confirm their relations with the driver. However, I also traveled with other traders going to the same village markets who catch ordinary passenger transport from the main lorry park, which is considerably more frequent on the local market day.

Traders transporting larger amounts of goods hire freight trucks, booking each trip with the driver. Drivers arrange their next trip as they unload at Kumasi wholesale yards, and available lorries also wait at popular supply points in cities or small towns in farming areas. Provisions traders bound for Kumasi from Accra or Tema can join trucks loading at certain Accra street corners, factories, docks, and flour mills. Traders with less than a full load of goods individually benefit from economies of scale by sharing a truck with a handful of other traders bound for the same destination. If one trader has the trust of the others, she will ride in front with the driver and the others can take more comfortable passenger transport back. More frequently, several traders will ride in back on top of the goods, especially when passenger transport is hard to find.

Railway transport used to be heavily used by market traders, especially in and out of Kumasi, where the two lines from Accra and Takoradi converge. Special freight boxcars were set aside for women traders on the slow trains, where they could pile their goods and sleep guarding them. Intense buying and selling took place en route between traders themselves and at most stops. Some villages were on the rail line but had no road, so this was their main commercial outlet. The railway was slower and cheaper than trucks, so it was popular for bulky, less perishable items. In 1979, Kumasi-based traders brought pottery by rail from Eastern Region villages near the line to Accra. Takoradi yam traders also bought yams in large quantities in Kumasi and sent them back by rail, clubbing together to rent a whole railway freight car. It had been common for fish traders based in Takoradi to send up smoked fish, in baskets marked with distinctive cloth, to their partners in Kumasi. Rising rates and increasing railroad delays made this a rare practice by 1979, and it had virtually disappeared in 1983. Smoked fish would spoil before arrival or soon after, traders complained, but with the collapse of direct trunk roads they had to send trucks all the way around through Accra at considerable expense. Railways rehabilitation work started in the late 1980s may eventually revive commercial freight usage, but it was aimed more immediately at facilitating bulk exports.

For the 80 percent of Kumasi Central Market traders who buy their goods within Kumasi, local transport for themselves and their goods is their only direct concern. Those who live in the suburbs have to wait for buses, vans, or trucks in long lines morning and evening with other workers. Even wealthy traders contend with a shortage of taxis. Traders who store their goods at home must pay freight charges each way. Those who buy outside Kumasi Central Market must have their purchases brought to their stalls. Some local factories will deliver large orders, but usually the trader must arrange transport by truck or car from the factory gate. Market head carriers take goods to and from other locations in the central business district, such as stores, the lorry park, and the railway station.

Almost all traders based in Kumasi Central Market make some use of the carriers who use flat wooden carts or carry baskets, basins, or bags on their heads. They connect different sections of the market with the lorry park and nearby street sales areas, charging a standard rate per trip for a standard load, depending on distance. Charges for common destinations are rarely bargained because they are so widely known, although they change from time to time with inflation. The general terms for carriers are *cayafo,* an English loan word, and *Gaofo,* referring to the Gao ethnic origin of the stereotypical adult male carrier, located in the French savannah colony of Mali. Only men and boys handle the wooden carts, mostly owned by Gaos in fact, but men, women, and children all carry head loads. The basket or basin owned by the carrier displays the size of the load he will undertake, since small children carry smaller loads, such as shopping baskets, for less.

Transport within the market causes considerable trouble and expense to its traders. Despite the large number of carriers and their relatively low individual incomes, their charges remain relatively high. One grain trader complained that carriers charged as much to take a sack of grain from the lorry park into the market as the truck had charged to bring the sack from the supply area. Physical conditions within the market make transporting goods inefficient and dangerous. Planners designed the market to be open to truck access between the lines of permanent stalls, but extra stalls have long since blocked these passages. Only one small van still penetrates daily to deliver fresh meat from the slaughterhouse. Handcarts must take long detours even between the wholesale and retail sections of the same commodity to avoid steep, muddy, or narrow sections and cracked or missing pavements. Carts still overturn frequently, injuring bystanders and damaging goods.

Traders resort to head carriers for faster service through crowded passages and treacherous ground conditions which also make the head carriers' work difficult. Heavily burdened head carriers slip and fall on the cracked, slanted, littered pavements or in jostling crowds. In the rainy season, carriers go barefoot for better footing on slippery stairways and eroded slopes, risking illness and injury. Such hazardous conditions put a premium on experienced and reliable carriers who know their way through the market and its environs, but the extra tip paid them is not enough to make this an attractive occupation for those with any reasonable alternative.

Sorting and Processing

Retailers perform several kinds of useful labor that are not usually noticed until they stop doing them. Traders put considerable effort into sorting and processing their goods in ways that save the buyer

Table 4.1 Processing of Goods

Percentage of Traders (Craft Workers Excluded)				
None	Sorting	Trimming	Other	Total
40.0	43.8	11.9	4.3	100.0

SOURCE: 1979 Kumasi Central Market Survey

time in shopping and cooking. Local foodstuffs come out of the ground or the fishing net in a mixed range of sizes, types, and qualities. Used clothing comes in huge bales like compressed rummage sales. Sorting enables a buyer to quickly find the kind she needs or can afford without picking through piles of unsuitable goods. Forty-four percent of traders surveyed at least sorted their goods, while only forty percent simply bought and sold (see table 4.1). Retailing itself makes goods available at a time and location buyers find it convenient to shop, adding value even while traders seem to be sitting idly (or walking aimlessly, in the case of hawkers). One only has to spend hours in line at inaccessible parts of town a few times for goods that turn out to be unsuitable to appreciate the value of these services.

Some lines of trade virtually require sorting or processing goods, but in others traders have the option of expanding or minimizing this work. Goods like smoked fish or grains need periodic sunning, cleaning, and even redrying to prevent spoilage. Bulk kola needs frequent unpacking, inspection, airing, and repacking in fresh green leaves to prevent it from either drying out or moldering. Traders must be willing to devote time and space to these activities when necessary or risk losing their working capital. Displays of cassava and some other vegetables require trimming and cleaning to attract customers at most seasons of the year, but not to the extent of half-peeling onions as has been reported in Peru (Babb 1989).

Traders adopt additional processing voluntarily as a strategy to raise the value of their stock without investing extra capital they do not have. Part-time or seasonal processing gives a trader extra flexibility in her business options. Seasonal drops in supply and demand lead traders to increase processing dramatically to keep their time and capital employed. Slicing okra and yams, for example, not only occupies idle hands but enables traders to salvage edible parts of inferior produce when supplies are short. Brisk trading conditions, with high supply and demand, brought a visible reduction in the effort traders spent processing, sorting, and even displaying goods.

Some traders process their goods to the point of putting them in a higher value category as convenience foods; they are not just more attractive but enter a higher price range. Perhaps some of these traders should be classified as craft workers, since they put as much labor into food processing as some craft workers who also sell their own work in the market. The wide variety of processed foodstuffs found in Kumasi Central Market testifies to the demand for labor-saving in domestic work at home. Powdered and pureed chili pepper and tomato, cornmeal dough, ground melon seeds, peanut butter, and finely sliced okra or greens eliminate the most time-consuming steps in cooking for women short of helping hands at home. Buyers will pay higher prices for these products than whole vegetables; although they are aware of the risks of adulteration, insanitary preparation, and inferior quality, they protect themselves by buying from sellers they have dealt with before. I did not see any traders who cut up or prepared vegetables for cooked-food sellers, as Babb reports in Huaraz, Peru (Babb 1989). Kumasi cooked-food sellers could employ poorly paid helpers at less cost, if they did not do the work themselves. In fact, Kumasi Central Market offers an unusually complete range of these intermediate or semiprocessed products, thus catering to a specialized demand. Hawkers and streetside traders usually carry only ready-to-eat foods or the raw materials, counting on their locations for convenience.

Foodstuffs sellers must sort their goods by quality standards related to different uses in order to reach the best customer for each grade at the best price. For example, plantain sellers buy arriving plantains by the stem, which includes fingers in different states of maturity. When they cut the fingers apart to sell in small bunches or piles of three, they sort more precisely by ripeness, indicated by colors from green through yellow to black. Because many local dishes require plantains of a specific degree of ripeness, retailers often ask the customer what she intends to cook before pointing to an appropriate selection of fingers. Even the squashiest red and moldy fingers have their purchasers, at a reduced price, since cooked-food sellers buy them to prepare a popular fried snack.

Tomato traders likewise have different customers for premium, ordinary, and inferior quality grades. Although large tomatoes cost much more than small ones, quality standards are related as much to keeping qualities as to taste. Consumers buying several days ahead or traders intending to resell will pay extra for slightly underripe tomatoes or the longer-lasting plum variety. Cooked-food sellers snap up slightly bruised or withered tomatoes along with "tired" greens and flabby garden eggs at lower prices, since they will cook them immediately, before the taste is affected. Impoverished consumers also seek these bargains.

Specialist traders buy up the remaining crushed or moldy tomatoes and wash out the seeds to sell to backyard gardeners.

Sorting at the wholesale level takes valuable time but makes goods more attractive by allowing more exact pricing and reducing the risk of miscalculation. When a cassava trader bought and had harvested a field of cassava, she sorted the tubers roughly by size as she and a hired laborer packed them into cocoa bags for transport. Large tubers command the highest price for sale fresh to consumers, but only if sorted for ready identification. A bag of small tubers fetches half the price of a bag of large tubers, but a mixed bag is less salable since each is used for different final uses and a single buyer may not be interested in all sizes. Wholesale buyers did not want to estimate the amount they would have to discard. Small tubers may end up as animal feed, but at the right price they will quickly find a buyer before they deteriorate.

Clothing sellers depend on especially skillful sorting to attract customers. Those selling new clothing or shoes attract buyers by reverse sorting. They collect a large selection of styles by buying a few of each from a number of craftsmen or importers who only offer a few styles each. Used clothing, by contrast, arrived in 1979 in huge mixed bales in which no customer could hope to find his desired hat or shirt. The trader who opened the bale sold hats, shirts, curtains, brassieres, etc. to specialist retailers who kept a range of sizes and styles. By 1989, the increased commercialization of used clothing exports from developed countries had made specialized bales available (for example, only trousers or shirts) which could be resold directly to retailers who only sorted by size and quality.

Display techniques include minor processing used to make goods more attractive, although these efforts may actually either preserve or damage the goods. Periodic redrying of smoked fish, beans, and grains improves their appearance and their storage life. Ironically, fish sellers then brush the carefully dried fish with water to make them plump and shiny for display. Cassava sellers trim and peel their tubers when sales flag, displaying their freshness but hastening spoilage. Filling cracks in yams with earth brings on rapid rotting, but cutting off the rotten part makes the rest more attractive. Arranging displays to conceal a green or crushed tomato under a heap of good ones has little effect on spoilage or on price, since buyers expect it. Washing fresh tomatoes or keeping a clean stall reduces spoilage and contamination.

For other kinds of processed foods, the labor contributed in processing is invisible in the marketplace because they are traded there only as finished products. Some ready-to-eat cooked foods that keep well enter into market commerce as commodities, even crossing regional boundaries. Several Fanti coastal towns export in bulk smoked kenkey and the hard-fried small fish eaten with it, sending them to Kumasi contacts in baskets packed by the hundred, just like Fanti smoked fish traders do. Bread and cakes are baked in clay backyard ovens in Kumasi and sold on credit to hawkers or stall traders, like oranges, dried fish, or vegetables. Long-lasting food products not requiring more cooking, such as oil and gari, are also traded only as finished products. I did not see them prepared in the marketplace or for home consumption in Kumasi, although there was a neighborhood of commercial gari producers in the suburbs. All Kumasi women I knew bought these items ready-made, although many said they knew how to make them and could do so if necessary. The heavy labor investment was not worthwhile amidst other urban opportunities.

Kumasi households make a habit of purchasing some foodstuffs in an intermediate state which they could process themselves, but which urban constraints on space and time make it impractical to produce. They could grind their own corn and cassava flour at local mills, but most families buy it as needed in small amounts. Buying fermented dough for benkum, a popular dish, saves cooks the trouble of advance planning and storage of fermented dough in their crowded urban rooms. Making kenkey also involves a series of steps over several days. Commercial producers, often mechanized, also achieve higher quality or more consistent results than the home producer, in addition to realizing economies of scale. Despite widespread knowledge of the basic processes of making kenkey, gari, or cooking oil, all commercial producers I encountered had trained with an established producer.

Semiprocessed food is rarely sold in wholesale quantities, such as the full enamel basins used to display mounds of peanut butter and carry them into the market. Those who sell processed food buy the raw materials in wholesale quantities and do their own processing. For example, peanut butter sellers buy the raw peanuts by the sack, roast them, and have them ground. Orange hawkers sell them peeled but buy them unpeeled, peeling only enough for a few hours at once to prevent them from drying out. Storing supplies before processing prevents spoilage since processing makes most foodstuffs, even powdered foods and flours, more vulnerable to mold and insects than whole dried vegetables or grains. The small retail quantities usually sold reflect this perishability, but also the fact that small families and single persons more often resort to convenience foods for lack of helping hands. Owners of small restaurants or cooked-food sellers find it more profitable to buy raw items and have them ground at local grinding mills than to buy the processed items wholesale from traders.

Storage

One obvious evidence of power in a marketplace system is large stocks of accumulated goods. Storage is the most straightforward way in which traders or others can control the overall level of supplies in a commodity, an essential factor in manipulating prices. Accusations of hoarding figure prominently in the ideology that holds traders responsible for high inflation in the 1970s and early 1980s. Storage on a smaller scale permits traders to bridge over fluctuations in price and supply which they cannot control directly. Storage techniques and facilities, like processing, also serve to minimize perishability and limit spoilage losses. Since these risks have a strong influence on patterns of commercial relations, storage capability is a critical source of power within the marketplace system that needs close analysis at the individual, commodity-wide, and regional levels.

The physical facilities of Kumasi Central Market put direct limits on traders' ability to store goods in the market. The most favorable storage conditions exist in the permanent locking stalls, which are low sheds six or eight feet square in which only those selling small, valuable items such as jewelry, drugs, or hardware can store more than about a week's supply of goods. Another fourteen percent of traders kept locking boxes like rough wooden trunks in their stalls (see table 4.2). A very few traders with rooms in the market building have facilities comparable to small stores in the business district, with pull-down metal shutters or doors. These supplement their incomes by storing goods overnight for traders from other parts of the market.

Despite these limitations, traders make very little use of storage facilities outside of the market. All of those with locking stalls and 84 percent of those with locking boxes stored their goods in their stalls. Even 39 percent of those trading from tables stored their goods in the sales area, while 52 percent stored them elsewhere in the market.

Table 4.2 Stall Type

Stall Type	Men	Women
Locking stall	62.6	35.2
Locking box	10.8	15.2
Roof, no walls	12.2	7.0
Table	10.1	37.9
Basket or mat	4.3	4.8

SOURCE: 1979 Kumasi Central Market Survey

Traders inside the market walls leave bulky items loose in their stalls, since the gates are locked between 6:00 P.M. and 6:00 A.M. with watchmen inside. Traders selling valuable, light items such as jewelry can take their stocks home at the end of each day without much trouble, but the transport cost is too high for ordinary commodities. Storing commercial quantities of bulky items at home is out of the question for most traders, who live with large families in one or two rooms.

Insecurity definitely inhibits market storage, motivating traders to keep their stocks at a minimum. Despite impressive-looking padlocks on stall doors and boxes, traders fear theft from their stalls by thieves or corrupt market watchmen; watchmen demand high pay to reduce their temptation. The organized wholesale yards hire their own watchmen, who sleep on or near the piles of goods and furniture. Traders outside the walls can patronize self-employed watchmen who erect kiosks as storage facilities. Confiscation by soldiers or police was a constant threat to traders in controlled goods, which included local foodstuffs occasionally.

Inadequate physical facilities also discourage traders from keeping large stocks by increasing their risk of losses from spoilage. Lack of ventilation, leaky roofs, and flooding cause mildew and water damage in the rainy season. Traders in dried fish and beans cannot accumulate more stocks than they can constantly air, sun, and pick over. After heavy rains, sewage water floods the main market several feet deep in places, ruining clothing and destroying paper products, sugar, and salt. Mud in the wet season and dust in the dry season contaminate goods on display, reducing their value. Holding perishable foodstuffs in significant quantities in the market is impossible without expensive cold-storage facilities. Tomatoes and meat, for example, hardly last overnight. Even yams, which farmers can store on the farm for months, last less than one week under mats in the market's rain and sun.

These storage problems constrain the commercial power of Kumasi Central Market traders in several important respects. Lack of space prevents traders from storing enough inside the market to affect major seasonal or erratic shortages either positively or negatively. Risks of theft in the market and costs of transport to storage outside the market that penalize traders for holding stocks discourage them from buying in bulk at lower prices, even when they have the capital. In Zinder, a small border town in Niger, local traders' inability to store means that profits from predictable seasonal price changes in the cowpeas they sell and the millet they buy from Nigeria in return are collected by Nigerian merchants (Arnould 1986).

Spoilage problems prevent Kumasi traders from holding even smaller short-term buffer stocks in the more perishable commodities, which could smooth temporary interruptions or gluts in supply. For example, the orange wholesale yard was occasionally empty during the peak harvest season when heavy rains closed the roads from major supply areas for a few days at a time. The tomato wholesale yard was also notorious for unexpected gluts and shortages when truck arrivals bunched unpredictably. Because erratic supply fluctuations and high spoilage raise both risk and average running costs, traders tie up more capital in covering these expected miscalculations and inefficiencies, leaving less of it active in actual trading and accumulation. The physical and social characteristics of each commodity, including its perishability, its geographical distribution, how long its harvest season lasts, and even its illegality help determine how much these storage problems will translate into sharp supply and price fluctuations.

Perishability

Traders in highly perishable commodities structure their trading practices around reducing spoilage losses. Traders who survive long adopt or avoid certain trading techniques in order to reduce these unusual risks or to compensate for their presence by reducing other sources of risk. One general technique to avoid risk is to delay taking formal possession of the goods (accepting the risk of spoilage) as late as possible. The owner then hands them on to the buyer as quickly as possible, like the proverbial hot potato. Long possession of the goods shows a lack of commercial leverage rather than strength. The relatively time-consuming procedures of bargaining or payment may be displaced out of the more usual order and take place before delivery or after disposal of the goods whenever possible. Traders facing this intense time pressure have developed some ingenious and distinctive marketing arrangements. For example, tomatoes and cassava last only two days after harvest and so must stay in constant motion until they reach the urban consumer. Cassava buyers in one village I visited worked in pairs to ensure speed. One woman made preliminary arrangements with the farmer and located a truck, while the junior partner stayed at the cassava farm to supervise harvesting. The first woman took a nap and arrived at the farm late in the afternoon with the truck to collect the cassava and accompany it on the overnight run to Kumasi. Long-distance tomato companies also take turns to provide a 24-hour escort to their valuable cargos by sending one member to Kumasi with each day's goods. Intermediate changes of ownership would obstruct this continuous flow with repeated bargaining sessions.

Bargaining practices further streamline the selling process for the most perishable commodities. Group bargaining serves this purpose in the Kumasi Central Market wholesale yards for both tomatoes and cassava. Travelers bringing boxes of tomatoes from major supply areas bargain jointly with Kumasi wholesalers for an initial price. Top quality boxes clear quickly at this price, until sales flag and sellers begin to discount those remaining. This is not an actual fixed price, since sellers can discount as early or late as they choose. Cassava wholesale traders bargain on standard cocoa bags individually, but smaller-scale buyers bargain in groups for cassava that arrives in smaller shipments of baskets. The arriving traveler arranges her baskets in a circle around her, numbering from about six to about twenty, filling each identically from those that have fallen off en route. Each buyer chooses the basket she wants and stands behind it, but one of the older traders leads all of them in demanding first more add-ons and then price reductions. Once the price has been agreed on, each carries her own basket off and returns immediately with the money. Again, the common price is not compulsory or strictly fixed; an individual can still refuse to buy her basket. She is replaced by another prospective buyer who either accepts the price or bargains by herself.

Short-term credit of a few hours only is also frequently conventional between Kumasi Central Market retailers and wholesalers in perishable vegetables—for example, for tomatoes and for cassava bought in cocoa sacks. Delayed payment speeds clearance of goods from the open yard by immediate delivery, as well as by enabling retailers to take larger amounts. Buyers pay early in the afternoon, after selling all or part of the purchase, in time for the wholesaler to pay the departing traveler. Although there is still some risk of evasion or delay of payment, sellers sometimes did not even call this credit, but said it was more convenient to collect payments later because of the time required to count their stacks of banknotes. If giving credit is considered a sign of weakness, this would provide another motive for disavowing it. Cassava traders' bargaining procedures only reflect a need for speed in the last stages of a farmgate transaction, providing a particularly sensitive index to this motive. Unlike tomatoes, which will rot on the bush, cassava lasts indefinitely before harvest. A cassava traveler I accompanied bargained slowly for cassava while it remained safely in the ground, making several trips to the farm on successive days to inspect its area and dig up sample plants to estimate the size of tubers. Farmers typically plant cassava on remote, infertile farms, since it requires little attention, so this phase required long, tiring journeys on foot. The trader then arranged for transport and labor for harvesting and packing through another set of complex negotiations before beginning to harvest.

By contrast, yam bargaining takes place at a leisurely pace after harvest, since there is no immediate danger of spoilage. Yams last for months on the farm if stored in earth-covered pits after harvest, and the harvest itself can be easily delayed. Traders can inspect and discuss piles of tubers that have been harvested and stored on the farm over a period of weeks. Traders can dampen long-term price fluctuations by delaying collection of yams already purchased. If they suspect prices are temporarily low in Kumasi from oversupply, they can hold yams a few days in the supply area or even in the Kumasi lorry park, although they must pay for tying up the truck.

Even yam traders must take steps to avoid spoilage from exposure to sun and rain or breakage once they have taken possession of the goods. Traders cover their yams with mats or plastic or store them in rented rooms while assembling a truckload. Yams last only a few days in the truck, wholesale yard, or market stall. Travelers occasionally lose an entire load when the truck breaks down and they cannot find another to send in time. They push hard to arrive in the wholesale yard in the morning, because they will have to reduce prices for any left over the next day to compete with fresh arrivals. They carefully supervise packing of yams into and out of the truck and on and off the carriers' carts to avoid breakage. Yams are rather brittle and rot immediately if the skin is broken. Retailers will refuse to accept cracked or broken yams, and the wholesaler must replace them to make up a full hundred.

The perishability of each commodity and its ratio of value to weight or volume place outer limits on its effective hinterland for Kumasi Central Market. The practical geographical limit for bringing perishable commodities is defined by the time spent in transport rather than absolute distance and so cannot be neatly drawn on a map. Villages off the road or served by poor roads may be within the radius, but simply take too long to reach. Perishability problems are thus partly socially constructed, depending on the commodity-specific intersection of patterns of crop planting, road construction, and vehicle ownership. Unreliable transport increases potential travel time and puts more commodities onto the dangerously perishable list. Plantain traders, for example, regularly unloaded whole truckloads of rotten plantain in Kumasi Central Market after waiting too long for transport from remote districts or suffering mechanical breakdowns. The high risks and rates of loss reduce apparently generous profit margins in perishable goods, in private and official channels alike, as reported by traders for government distribution efforts and as MacGaffey has documented for Zaire (MacGaffey 1987).

In judging the economic limits of adequate transport of specific commodities, the ratio of transport cost to price further modifies absolute or social distance. Heavy and bulky cheap items cost more to transport than their selling price justifies. On the other hand, the high profit margin on expensive smuggled imports easily pays for headloading them across the border through remote villages. Drivers on poor roads charge more for the same distance because of slower travel and vehicle damage, so it matters exactly where the goods are produced. A combination of these factors has left some villages fairly near Kumasi but on very bad roads practically unable to sell fresh produce. I visited one village in 1984 that sold more gari than fresh cassava to Kumasi, and sold both through additional intermediaries, in a pattern typical of much more distant villages. The same ring of villages can sell craft products like handwoven cloth, which is compact and expensive, or lighter, less perishable forms of processed produce that tolerate transport delays.

Seasonality

Seasonality is related to perishability and storage in two ways: goods with a long harvest season create little demand for storage and goods which store well show relatively little seasonal fluctuation. Under tropical conditions, very few commodities store without appreciable loss; even grains and beans deteriorate quickly from insect damage and mold. Wholesale yards of extremely seasonal items like fruits disappear entirely out of season, and their retailers switch to other commodities. Seasonal shifts in the supply of goods consequently transform the marketplace system several times a year, and traders must make radical adjustments to maintain income and accumulation.

Foodstuffs in general become scarce during the months after Christmas and before the first harvests in May. While market stocks as a whole fall in the lean season, more storable foodstuffs like grains, beans, and gari become more prominent as consumers fall back on them. Lack of supplies and higher prices for minimum wholesale units drive some wholesalers into temporary retailing, while others spend more time traveling themselves in search of supplies. Traders adjust to higher capital needs; for example, more travelers start to demand cash advances from wholesalers before bringing them goods. The number of traders sitting in the market shrinks visibly as some turn to secondary occupations or travel in search of supplies. Many traders turn to alternative occupations or commodities when their usual commodity becomes scarce. Some prepare farms in their home villages or take up crafts such as sewing. Others have a habitual second commodity with a complementary season, for example, many orange or mango sellers turn to selling pineapples or avocados.

Not only traders but farmers and consumers take dramatic steps to moderate or compensate for seasonal fluctuations in supply for most local foodstuffs. Farmers extend the harvest season for perishable crops by staggered planting, exaggerating natural variations in the seasonal timing of rainfall. Tomato prices fluctuate enough to justify hand irrigation in the off season, a backbreaking commitment to a daily bucket brigade. Traders stimulate this practice by traveling long distances to collect supplies from areas that succeed in harvesting at times of scarcity. Onion traders, for example, get their main shallot supplies from the Volta Region coast in a three-month irrigation cycle. They supplement these with green shallots from Ashanti Region during the rainy season, while in the dry season they buy large onions from the Bawku area in the far Upper Region.

Consumers try to cushion the effect of annual price cycles on their pocketbooks by changing their eating habits seasonally. Fruits and snack foods have strongly marked seasons because hawkers carry the one currently cheapest. For example, Kumasi residents gleefully fill up on boiled fresh corn and corn fritters after the early maize harvest, switching to yam with even more enthusiasm when the first new yams arrive. During the dry season, they eat more small grains and beans and snack foods made from their flours. Protein foods also shift with the seasons: snails emerge after the first rains in March or April, fish landings peak in August and farmers catch more wild game after Christmas, when they burn their fields for planting.

Yearly demand cycles also call for adjustments from traders, especially around Christmas. Regardless of their religion, Ghanaians buy extra food and gifts at this season, since Christmas follows closely on the main cocoa harvest and the last food harvests. Farmers and farm laborers get their main annual cash income at the same time that they have some leisure time. They pay their debts, make major purchases, and travel to visit relatives. Formal sector workers enjoy their Christmas holidays and bonuses. Visits home mean gifts for relatives and festive meals even for non-Christians. Similar but smaller peaks occur at Easter and the Moslem holidays of Ramadan and the Prophet's birthday. After a holiday, consumption then falls below average levels to compensate for the extra expenses just incurred.

Holidays stimulate demand for both special holiday items and everyday goods. Consumers time needed purchases like new clothing for the holiday period in addition to those they buy as gifts. Lower post-harvest prices for staple foods like yams, rice, and plantain encourage them to cook generous meals at Christmas. Traders stretch their capital to the limit and fill their stalls to capacity. They take on temporary assistants, including vacationing school children and visiting relatives. Open areas fill up with hawkers and squatters as traders send out their assistants and nontraders try their hands at trading. The soaring demand for traditional Christmas gift items, including shoes and children's clothes and treats of cookies and candy, means these goods take over a larger share of the marketplace. The extra supplies of imports and seasonal goods attract many foodstuffs traders away from green vegetables, just then becoming scarce. Traders in other items switch over temporarily or add these lines to their existing stock.

Legality

Traders faced special pressures when they sold commodities that were subject to government regulation consistently or frequently. The imports and manufactures classified as "essential" commodities had been subject to price controls and other restrictions on where and how they could be sold since the First World War, but these multiplied rapidly in the seventies. The effective availability and price of tinned milk and fish, cloth, rice, sugar, toothpaste, and other listed commodities varied over time with the level of legal supplies and the intensity of enforcement of price controls, and with ever more restrictive commercial regulations that eventually banned these goods from the marketplace system for several years. Traders' ability to evade these regulations and keep supplies flowing should not be surprising. Their risk levels were by no means extreme when compared to those of illegal traders in Uganda, Zaire, or even Hong Kong (Green 1981; MacGaffey 1987; J. Smart 1988).

The effects of recurrent confiscations and erratic legal and illegal supplies were analogous to seasonal shortages and spoilage losses for highly perishable produce in some ways. Traders selling these commodities had to be prepared, financially and organizationally, to cope with rapid fluctuations in supply, price, and legal status. Frequent changes in regulations made it difficult to stay legal and in some cases were aimed deliberately to drive traders out of business. Those without strong enough nerves to adjust to such risky conditions switched to other commodities that attracted less government attention. At the same time, surviving traders needed to take quick advantage of lulls in enforcement, so controlled goods were soon displayed openly in the market again after an enforcement episode.

During the 1978–80 research period, traders in these commodities perceived a yearly cycle in price control enforcement within longer historical changes. I could confirm during 1978 and 1979 that legal supplies and the related illegally diverted supplies became more plentiful in November in anticipation of Christmas. Traders referred to a wave of confiscations of cloth and cookies in that same month as "the soldiers doing their Christmas shopping." Enforcement dropped off after several weeks and traders and ordinary Christmas shoppers returned to the market without fear of renewed raids. Legal imports of staples like milk, fish, flour, sugar, and rice tended to dwindle away in midyear as official foreign exchange supplies ran out before the November cocoa harvest replenished the national coffers.

The need for concealment of illegal commodities radically alters normal market practices, which rest on good visual access to price and supply information. The asking price and, in some cases, the physical possession of the item must be kept secret from everyone but the buyer. Only young men and women who could easily pick up their basins or boxes and run still sold openly in the Kumasi Central Market. They often represented older traders who kept the main stock hidden elsewhere. Stallholders selling illegal items displayed one or two empty cans or boxes beside their legal commodity, concealing the item itself in a distant stall. Hawkers carried a few sample cloths or cans in shopping bags or briefcases, supposedly for their own use, and approached people they knew. They could arrange large sales for later delivery, since the quality and size of these manufactured items are generally uniform. Traders in bulky goods like soap and rice closed their stalls or disclaimed ownership when suspicious strangers approached. Those remaining active claimed to know most police informers by sight and had trusted connections in case of arrest.

These conditions promoted unpredictable and disorganized trading practices, since these had the best chance of avoiding detection. Nonmarket locations become more important for illegal sales, and private sales from homes or offices virtually replaced open sales of commodities illegal for long periods, such as *ntama* cloth. In private sales, only buyers known to the seller even hear of supplies. Comparing prices or qualities was virtually impossible for the ordinary consumer, since she was unlikely to hear of more than one source. During 1979, when price control was extended to local foodstuffs, traders temporarily abandoned officially designated markets and set up roadside transfer points for wholesale buying.

Concentration of Supply and Demand

The geographical characteristics of a specific commodity determine the accumulation and stratification patterns of traders trading in it by affecting the technical requirements of trading. In short, a compact configuration of supply or demand makes it easier for a few large traders to dominate it and so provides a crucial basis for their domination of the distributive network in that commodity and their subsequent further accumulation. When supply or demand for a commodity is concentrated, that is, it comes from a restricted geographical area or a few large sources, wholesaling also tends to also be concentrated in the hands of a few relatively large traders (Hodder and Ukwu 1969; Trager 1981a). For example, flour supplies for Kumasi mainly come from several large flour mills in Tema. A few wealthy traders can work to develop preferential relations with these mill managers and effectively control supplies. Supply concentration, evaluated in proportion to the distance from the supply location to Kumasi, represents a relative rather than an absolute value, just as effective distance thresholds integrated time and cost.

Dispersion of supply or demand has the opposite effect. Dispersed supplies give easier access to many small traders who can each contact one or another individual sources. Demand for the commodities handled through the marketplace system tends to be relatively decentralized because it serves the poorer consumers. Demand for cocoa is highly centralized in a single government agency (replacing a few large firms) that monopolizes access to the few major international buyers by the relatively dispersed and small suppliers. Some commodities are drawn from several distinct supply networks with different degrees of concentration, so parallel variations appear within the traders selling it depending on which source they rely on. For example, when legal import licenses were tightly restricted, smuggled supplies of canned foods came across the border at many small points of entry and were often more accessible to smaller rural traders than the diverted supplies obtained through contacts with the very few legal importers.

The degree of concentration of supply at the local level must be assessed in relation to transport access, since poor transport and communication intensify effective dispersal by making assembly of goods more difficult. For example, a distance of ten miles that makes no difference within the Accra-Tema metropolitan area may severely restrict commercial options for off-road farm villagers walking through dense forest. The axis of geographical distance from a city clearly interlocks with infrastructure, also concentrated near the cities, but is not reducible to it.

When supplies are brought to Kumasi from long distances, only the relatively wealthy can remain in business, leaving those who survive in a position to become even wealthier. Economies of scale in transport pay off heavily on long trips, since the transport charges have become a high percentage of the Kumasi sale price. Traders pay considerably lower fees per bag if they can fill a lorry by themselves rather than renting space by the bench unit or the bag. This gives large-scale traders a critical price advantage and makes it difficult for smaller traders to raise their scale of business gradually. In yam trading, travelers must operate on this scale to survive commercially at all. This dynamic helps explain cases like Zaire, where traders who link distant locations seem to be making disproportionate profits, even calculating in their risks (MacGaffey 1987).

Concentrated supply sources compensate for their relatively long distance from major consuming centers by giving more convenient access to supplies. Districts which specialize heavily in one or a few crops reduce the local search time for buyers of those items, since almost every farmer has some available. Traders from more distant towns can spend longer on the road and still return in a reasonable time. When individual farmers specialize heavily in a single crop, they also make larger quantities available more easily. This is most effective when the whole crop is harvested at once, so that yam and cassava travelers, for example, who can buy an entire field with a single visit, can visit more distant locations regularly. Large-scale buyers can buy enough from one or two large farms to fill a lorry. Spatial and temporal concentration to this degree acts as prebulking, which favors large-scale traders and reduces the need for extra intermediaries.

The extremely short traveling distance gives villages very near Kumasi the character of a relatively dispersed source, although they lie within a restricted area. Farmers there take advantage of the transport and spoilage problems that reduce competition from more distant areas to raise highly perishable vegetables as garden crops, for which the price premium on freshness is high. Few economies of scale exist when any villager or Kumasi resident can join a lorry with bags or baskets or produce, so large monocrop farms or wholesale traders are rare. Vendors from such villages swell the villagers' markets near the main Kumasi lorry parks. Villagers who live slightly farther away or slightly off the road network bring their garden produce to the nearest periodic market, where small- or medium-scale traders bring it to Kumasi the same day.

Dispersed supplies at greater structural distance encourage a more complex division of labor and the use of intermediate markets. Small poultry traders operating in the Upper Region, for example, collect a few birds from each producer and take them to local periodic markets. They sell to other traders who follow a circuit of periodic markets up there and shuttle to Kumasi at regular intervals. Supplies of tomatoes or garden eggs are dispersed over time, since growers must harvest them every day or two over several months. Intermediate markets and bulking traders therefore play an important role in their collection, for irrigated tomatoes brought from the Upper Region and for those grown in Ashanti.

The legal supply of imported and manufactured goods becomes more or less concentrated over the years with changes in regulatory requirements that affect social distance. Before trade liberalization in 1984, legal supplies entered the system only through a few Ghanaian factories and licensed importers. This factor encouraged large traders in these items despite the easy physical accessibility of ports and Accra and Kumasi factories to small-scale local traders. A good example of contrasts in concentration comes from the trade in smoked fish, where traders with allocations for frozen fish from the State Fishing Corporation at Tema and its regional outlets then smoke it to compete more directly with the fish landed from canoes and motorboats at many smaller Ghanaian ports and villages. The difficulty of obtaining allocations or other legal supplies favors large traders, who can invest more time and influence in building up their contacts. The same labor-intensive process for obtaining import licenses and legal foreign exchange favored larger over smaller factories and stores.

Illegal trading duplicated these advantages of size, but also exploited countervailing advantages of small scale. Diverted legal supplies remained concentrated, since only a few persons held the critical connections to the few legal distributors. By contrast, smuggled supplies passed through a large number of small traders; larger shipments were split up between many carriers to cross the border, to make them less conspicuous. Dispersed supplies from smuggling acted as an effective brake on black-market prices, especially in regions near borders. A similar movement toward deconcentration appeared temporarily in the trade patterns for local foodstuffs when these became subject to price controls in 1979.

When legal restrictions relax, the level of concentration in imports trading falls. Small retailers reported buying direct from factories or importers in the 1960s. After liberalization in 1984, legal importing still involves considerable red tape, which means economies of scale persist. The numbers of small importers had increased by 1990, but they mainly seemed to import high-value boutique items with enough profit margin to make such small trips worthwhile. The bulk of imports of popular consumer items remained in the hands of the few large firms.

Conclusion

Capital and labor requirements of the trading process erect the most effective barriers within the marketplace system. Access to the Kumasi wholesale yards depends on having the funds to buy at least one of the standard wholesale units, a capital threshold that is relatively high for yams or provisions, but relatively low for *kontommere* leaves or cassava. This usually non-negotiable boundary thus dictates which commodities an aspiring trader can hope to enter and at what scale, with all the implications that choice has for her future profits and other conditions of work. Defining the boundary by unit of sale, rather than intended use of the purchase, lowers the effective barriers between traders and nontraders with equivalent capital. Economies of scale in transport reward higher-capital traders, since fees for renting an entire truck are so much lower than using mixed passenger transport. When a commodity shows a high degree of geographical and commercial concentration, entry to some segments of its distribution network is virtually impossible to smaller-scale traders than those already established.

Effective access to key commercial locations requires constant labor investment. Traders must be present and available at the time the wholesale markets are active in order to buy or sell wholesale. Those buying at the farmgate must be able to leave home for a week or two at a time during the buying season and travel to different regions of Ghana in turn to maintain commercial viability. Even selling retail from within Kumasi Central Market requires daily presence for long hours to buy at the lowest prices, to cultivate steady customers, or simply to justify the rental fee. Capital helps market women support dependent domestic workers to free them for trading, but larger enterprises often involve linking several separate locations and create pressures to obtain the trading services of others.

Skills and knowledge emerge as central requirements for secure profit and accumulation in various commercial processes. Skills in bargaining and accounting are highly significant for the careers of individual traders, causing some to move rapidly ahead of their colleagues who entered at the same scale of trade in the same commodity. Diversity in bargaining conventions and supply areas means that skill and knowledge are highly specific by commodity and location and therefore best acquired on the job. The principles traders use to bargain and judge quality and quantity are the same buyers use, so traders' skill advantage derives from practice rather than access to closely guarded secrets. The frequently different conventions for wholesale and retail bargaining, however, create an additional barrier to upward mobility from the very lowest levels.

Knowledge of supply and demand conditions and the credit reputations of individual trading partners permits traders to use their bargaining skills most effectively. Obtaining the most up-to-date information draws on skills and contacts, but knowledge also accumulates over years of trading experience simply from witnessing the relatively open transactions and disputes in the Kumasi wholesale yards and retail areas. Only illegality manages to force commercial activity into hidden channels that constrain information flow. In times of transport scarcity, all too frequent in recent decades, reliable and prompt access to it also requires significant skill and knowledge. Sorting and handling especially fragile or perishable goods require special techniques as well as constant attention. The losses caused by inadequate skill or knowledge can effectively prevent continued access to a desirable location or trading activity, certainly to wholesaling and accumulation. More skilled and experienced traders have better command of a useful range of alternative trading techniques that compound their advantages by enabling them to respond effectively to hostile or restrictive conditions. Knowledge of dormant techniques and those used by traders in other commodities gives traders an effective repertoire that can be called upon to survive unexpected crises or pioneer unprecedented opportunities. Auxiliary suppliers, specialized buyers, disused locations, and additional processing provide options that can be more quickly activated if they are already somewhat familiar. Seasonal and political changes can make such shifts an expected part of the trading cycle for those selling highly seasonal perishables or usually illegal goods. Just as farmgate buyers move to new supply areas as these come into season, other traders switch to secondary occupations or commodities, which often need supplemental skills. Making these transitions smoothly and efficiently is crucial to long-term accumulation, on which survival often depends.

The boundaries defined by perishability, distance, and legality of supply, and even by commercial conventions, set a strong but elastic framework rather than absolute boundaries. Alternative trading practices can stretch this framework, if sufficient pressure to change and sufficient resources for change are present. The farther individual or group action stretches it, the more pressure it exerts on the techniques and social relations of the traders involved. However, breaking or re-molding its confines remains possible and happens promptly when new economic or social conditions make this necessary or profitable. Traders draw on their social and organizational resources to create these changes, just as they draw on the same resources to maintain the current framework of trade or defend it against hostile pressures from nontraders. Analyzing these social and organizational resources transforms the somewhat static image of common trading procedures and their variations into a more dynamic image of the social processes of personalized and group relations which, after all, constructed them and through which traders continue to use them strategically for survival and accumulation.

5 CONTROL OF RESOURCES

The organization of power within the marketplace not only starts with the daily, weekly, and yearly routines of buying and selling, it is built upon that foundation. Close attention to the way negotiations over prices and procedures are carried out has identified the resources critical to gaining advantage in those negotiations. Some are general social resources, such as capital and labor, which are widely recognized and competed for in other economic activities. Others, like information and transport, are resources shared with users outside the marketplace but disproportionately important in trading. Establishing power along the commercial axis of domination and subordination rooted in the marketplace system depends on establishing control over these resources. Consequently, this chapter focuses on how traders gain access to these resources and the next chapter describes the social relations through which they manage continued access.

The minimum levels of capital and labor needed to start in market trading are low even by local standards. When I asked women why they went into market trading, many, even in this relatively privileged major market, said first it was because they had only low levels of capital. The modest financial capital required for a market enterprise with modest facilities and capital equipment is nonetheless just as central as the larger investment in a factory. Without reliable access to that capital, whether through credit or savings, the business will collapse and must be refinanced on another basis. A woman's continued access to her own labor time must be likewise carefully protected from the claims of husband and children through complex domestic arrangements detailed in a later chapter. This chapter established what kinds of time women must have available for specific kinds of trade. Labor from others as assistants, employees, and more loosely tied clients is particularly essential for a reasonable chance at accumulation. Although market traders value its openness to entrants with low resource levels, they need better access to both capital and labor from inside or outside the marketplace system to maintain healthy enterprises in the face of economic pressures or to expand. Higher levels of investment would increase the efficiency and profitability of most smaller enterprises dramatically, as the examples of successful growth demonstrate.

Market trading procedures also presume consistent access to specifically commercial resources. Physical access to buyers and to goods from suppliers depends on rights of access to markets and other commercial locations. Exercising these rights requires access to transport (passenger or freight) and consequently to information about transport. Effective access to these locations depends on information about supply, demand, and current prices and appropriate trading skills to put this information to good use there. Lack of sophisticated trading skills or information about other individual transactors would prevent an ignorant entrant from participating profitably in trade. The management of information therefore becomes a significant indicator of where power is concentrated within the marketplace system.

Control of these resources is the currency of power within the marketplace system and between traders and specific groups outside the marketplace system. Certain traders within Kumasi Central Market use favorable access to these resources to gain partial control over other traders there or in other markets. In the same way, the extent of their control over these same resources constitutes the limit of their control through commercial relations of nontraders, such as farmers or consumers. Conversely, external economic actors who want to control the marketplace system must do so through control of these resources. The military, government, large firms, farmers, consumers, elders, etc. all have specific relations to relevant capital and labor resources based on their own standing within the wider social formation, but these must ultimately be translated into control of market resources in order to be effective within the marketplace system.

Credit

Credit relations provide an especially sensitive and systematic index to the balance of power. Indebtedness and systematic extension of credit mark relations of inequality and exploitation within trading systems in many other parts of the world. In parts of India, for example, both landlords and grain traders keep chronically indebted families in conditions of dependence and servitude for generations through annual preharvest consumption loans and emergency loans for life-cycle ceremonies or other family crises. Along the Ghanaian coast, fish traders keep fishermen in long-term dependency by extending credit for consumption, nets, motors, and boat purchase and maintenance (Lawson 1960; Vercruissje 1984). These comparative cases awaken suspicions about the widespread extension of credit between traders in Kumasi Central Market and throughout the regional marketplace system that must be addressed through a careful assessment of the terms and circumstances of credit in this part of Ghana and of how much control these relations give to creditors over debtors. Credit for consumption is rarely given by sellers in Kumasi Central Market, but credit for resale was common enough to awaken my concern over its potential for creating credit-based dependency.

Credit between traders based in Kumasi Central Market falls into three categories: advances of goods, advances of capital, and cash loans. Each type has a characteristic form of interest, risk, term of repayment, and moral connotation. Traders understand very clearly the concept of debt and the obligations specific to the kinds of credit they habitually use. This understanding, of course, does not prevent individual debtors from taking various steps to delay or avoid payment when possible, including trying to explain away their obligations. The desire to qualify for future credit generally ensures that most traders pay promptly, despite their virtual immunity from court-based debt enforcement. Informal ostracism or formal expulsion from organized commodity groups turn peer censure into an effective deterrent that can take back the economic cooperation essential to enterprise survival. Strong credit conventions apply to specific locations and categories of traders within Kumasi Central Market, covering the terms of credit and the criteria for granting it. Credit often forms part of the colleague and customer relations discussed fully in the next chapter, but it is also extended outside of them. Traders who refuse to give credit within these contexts, where it is expected, will lose business to those who extend it. When many buyers do qualify for credit, only unprofitable trade with newcomers or with known bad risks remains available to those who insist on immediate cash payment.

The terms of conventional credit accommodate the business cycle of the most important groups of buyers who intend to resell. Credit to them carries less risk because they must return regularly to the wholesale yard to stay in business, so long-term default means losing their business. Retail sellers from Kumasi Central Market or smaller Kumasi markets buy every day or two in the Kumasi Central Market wholesale yards, as do local cooked-food sellers. When I would remark to a wholesaler in the yam or garden egg yard, for example, that she was extending credit, she would explain to me, "I know where her stall is." Such debts must be cleared either by the end of the day or when the buyer returns for more goods. The first system of late afternoon settlement is common in commodities that wholesalers buy from travelers, like yams, cassava, tomatoes, and other local vegetables. The travelers themselves do not demand payment on delivery, but return to collect their money in the afternoons when they are getting ready to return to the supply areas. If a wholesaler has not finished selling or collecting debts from buyers by this time, she must find the money herself, so she makes strenuous efforts to collect from local retailers. Someone who does not pay promptly will not get credit again soon. The second system of payment, when the goods are at least partly sold, adjusts semi-automatically for slow market conditions. It also gives a longer de facto credit term to retailers who buy in larger amounts, since they take longer to sell out. The cassava retailers who had to buy in small baskets not only pay higher prices but must return several times a day for more supplies. Those who can buy a whole bag, enough to last for a day or more, need not clear their debts until later. This kind of short-term credit has been found in a wide range of trading situations inside and outside of marketplaces (Arnould 1986; Alexander 1987; Trager 1976).

The trader extending goods on credit assumes risks of default, delay, and partial repayment. Buyers who agree to too high a price, buy too much, or suffer goods losses from theft or spoilage may actually lack the funds to repay on time or may even go out of business. An unlucky debtor often feels her creditor should share her misfortune, and I often heard traders in this position making such excuses, not only to delay payment, but sometimes trying to renegotiate the amount due. In many commodities, accurate evaluation of quality forms an important part of bargaining. If a buyer has misjudged quality, she cannot sell for the estimated price or as fast as she expects. If she feels the seller has deceived her, she may refuse to pay the total price. Debtors from out of town can simply disappear with the goods; a tobacco and a provisions traders who sold to many rural peddlers were full of stories about such cases. The dependence on market suppliers is significantly reduced by the possibility of going into other kinds of work, as Arnould noted for farmer/traders in Niger (Arnould 1986). Kumasi traders try to learn the buyer's hometown or place of business before extending credit, but chasing such defaulters down is very time-consuming and expensive.

The level and direction of credit changes to compensate for supply and demand variations. When gluts occur, sellers offer longer credit terms to less reputable buyers in order to let them buy more and reduce stocks. This was particularly evident in the tomato yard, when sellers would offer credit to almost anyone on a bad day, to avoid having the goods rotting on their hands. The travelers also had a good chance of getting tomatoes on credit from farmers during the same weeks, so they could afford to return from Kumasi without cash if necessary. This seasonal reversal in credit cannot be taken for granted; in Awe, Nigeria, farmers did not extend credit so travelers also never did (Sudarkasa 1973). Kumasi market sellers demand cash when supplies are scarce, which enables them to replenish their stocks immediately. At times of peak scarcity, sellers even advance money to suppliers to travel in search of goods. Since credit is extended as an alternative to further price concessions, it serves to dampen price fluctuations seasonally or in the shorter term.

Although conventional forms of credit are commonplace in certain Kumasi Central Market locations and at harvest or preharvest seasons, that does not mean that they dominate the market as a whole, or even those locations. More than two-thirds of traders surveyed reported that they did not receive credit from their suppliers, and 89 percent did not give it to buyers. The survey area excluded most wholesale yards, where credit is more common, but wholesale transactions should have shown up as suppliers. Even more men traders, who rarely buy in the yards, reported no credit from suppliers (80 percent). The forms of credit reported were mainly the conventional short-term type for resellers (see table 5.1). Some underreporting may have occurred, since I encountered a number of traders in participant observation who proclaimed a policy of never extending credit but later did so when market conditions required it. The strength of the response, however, indicates that credit burdens do not tie up the market as a whole, although they may overwhelm or subordinate some individual traders.

Handling conventional credit responsibly encourages more individualized forms of credit between those involved. Those with long histories of punctilious payment in conventional credit ask for extra advances of goods or extra delays in payment in emergencies or to take advantage of unusual opportunities. One buyer mentioned this flexibility when discussing the benefits of building a good reputation when one could, since a theft or other crisis could happen at any time. Traders negotiate the terms of unconventional credit transactions when the occasion arises and keep them somewhat secret from competitors.

Advances of capital are another of these accepted, not shameful,

Table 5.1 Traders Giving or Taking Credit

Terms	Given to Buyers	Taken from Suppliers
No Credit	89.0 (%)	69.4 (%)
Same Day	1.1	.8
When Sold	3.6	17.9
Next Purchase	4.4	9.6
Other Terms	1.9	2.3

SOURCE: 1979 Kumasi Central Market Survey

business practices, but less public than conventional credit. Usually wholesalers and large retailers advance money to travelers to purchase goods for them outside Kumasi Central Market. Yam traders, whose high capital requirements made such arrangements relatively frequent, would discuss them quietly in the market or in private, but they avoided mentioning specific names or amounts. Both partners apparently benefit from concealment. Participants in such arrangements report that other traders offer better prices and treatment to someone they suppose to be trading independently. Traders using someone else's capital also enjoy less prestige than if they used their own, but more prestige than if they had no access to any.

The trader advancing capital seemed to consider this a business investment rather than a cash loan, making her something between a partner and an employer. In every such arrangement explained to me, the lender splits the profit resulting from the purchase, sharing in the risk and trusting in the proved skill of the recipient. The money is not considered a debt unless her share is not paid, and these arrangements did not come up in discussions of debts. In times of acute scarcity, traders will advance money and expect only the privilege of buying the goods at a decent price. The supplier is more doing them a favor than the reverse, and they will only talk of fraud if the supplier fails to return within a reasonable time.

Quite a few traders have temporary recourse to outside capital to supplement their own when faced with sudden losses or seasonal high prices. Both retailers and travelers would turn first to the wholesalers with whom they already had longstanding relations of supplier credit. The yam travelers who admitted to this arrangements often mentioned a specific incident, either an illness or the loss of a load through vehicle breakdown. They hoped to regain a viable capital level promptly with their half of the profits, counting on exceptional trading skill. Some did not succeed and became permanently dependent on wealthier traders for working capital, but some did succeed. Others trading with advances, prior to making such arrangements, had been frustrated at their inability to accumulate capital from the typically low profits of very small-scale retailing. They solicited such dependent arrangements as a deliberate strategy to expand their operations, but also hoped to move out on their own eventually.

Dependency of this kind seems to have become more frequent over the last ten years. When I first became familiar with Kumasi Central Market, it was clear that semi-permanent advances of capital were only a minor strategy within the market. Although it seems likely that not all cases would have been reported in the survey or to me personally, very few of the traders I knew well operated in this kind of arrangement. During my visits in 1983 and 1989, trading conditions were so unsettled that it was hard to judge whether advances I noticed should be considered temporary expedients or long-term commitments. Perhaps some of those involved were also not sure yet how they would turn out. In 1989–90, I heard many reports of the increase in credit dependency and particularly emphatic ones about their prevalence in the revived cloth and provisions sections, where many new traders had opened up stalls. Traders I knew from before were concerned to point out to me that the plentiful display of goods presented only an illusion of prosperity, since the real owners would take them back in a few days if they were not sold. Sellers of cloth and manufactured goods I knew or talked with received some goods on short-term supplier credit, paying in about two weeks. Cash payments had been the rule in 1979. Their shortage of capital had not yet made them directly dependent, but they could no longer extend cloth on credit to those buying from them.

Examples of persons trading with cash advances or in employee relationships seemed more conspicuous than before among the larger foodstuffs traders in 1990. One bankrupt oil trader had begun trading long distance to the Upper Region with a friend who arranged a loan for both of them. The supply of potential dependents seems to outstrip the supply of potential employers, since several other bankrupt traders had dropped out of the market. Two wholesalers, one in oranges and one in tomatoes, were still receiving goods from many of the same independent travelers as they had earlier, but they now appeared with small groups of young men who bought for them, whom they referred to as their "boys" or *abrantie* (young men). These hardly qualify as disguised wage workers, since there was no disguise of their subordination, but they were paid by commission or profit-splitting rather than by wages.

Terminology for credit reflects the primary distinction between commercial advances as a form of investment and cash loans, where the money is simply turned over to the borrower. Phrases used for commercial credit specify that the lender has given money or goods for a purpose. Supplier credit is described as *m'ama no nneema ako ton wo nkraase* (I have given her goods to go sell in the village). It usually refers to supplier credit for resale, processing cooked food, or an occupation. Credit for consumption is rare from market traders, although more common among cooked-food sellers near homes or workplaces. Cash advances for purchasing are stated as *m'ama no sika see onko to nneema mbre me* (I have given her money to go buy things to bring me). Again, the noun used refers not to the loan relationship itself but the useful thing, money, given. It is certainly not considered a gift (the verb *ma,* to give, has extremely broad usage), but neither is it considered a debt at this point. Using the verb phrase also leaves the time of reciprocation indefinite, a critical point to leave flexible for later negotiation since this governs the lapse into debt status.

The key distinction in a *bosea* is the loss of control over the money involved, as its extension to contexts of gifts and family obligations reveals. One highly educated informant used the example of begging a relative to pay your school fees. Even when he is producing money from funds he actually has, he will say they are going to *bo bosea,* or borrow the money, to emphasize that the money was already intended for another purpose, from which he has to "borrow" it. It then makes sense that *bosea* not apply to commercial credit or advances, since the lender still has control over the use of the money in loaning it for a specific purpose and, in fact, is using it for business purposes by extending it in credit.

The word for debt, *eka,* is linked closely to the word *bosea,* for loan, in commercial usage. The phrase *m'abo ka* (I have gone into debt) is used alongside with *m'abo bosea* (I have taken a loan) for cash loans, but not for cash advances. These terms are applied to conventional revolving commercial credit only when an unpaid balance remains after the normal payment cycle. For example, when a cocoyam wholesaler had not received payment the first afternoon for the morning's purchases, she returned the next day and started speaking rather loudly of an *eka.* Such default in effect produces an *eka* without a corresponding *bosea,* since the creditor never consented to such a loan. Only an intentional cash loan is called a *bosea,* and traders receive these loans from moneylenders outside of the marketplace more often than from fellow traders. This may come from a desire to conceal one's shaky financial condition or from shame. Shame over cash loans appears in family contexts as well; Asantes avoid approaching relatives for loans if they can get the money from friends instead in order to save face in front of the family (Owusu 1992).

The *eka/bosea* terminology is used much more widely outside of the marketplace. I also heard *bosea* used to refer to funeral contributions, which are entirely honorable but should be strictly reciprocated. In related uses, the verb *ka* refers to amounts, things, or persons left over or left behind, especially when expected to be included. When collecting her friends to go to a funeral, a trader may remark *aka Auntie Yaa* (Aunt Yaa has not come yet). Expecting a payment of six cedis and receiving five, a trader will say *aka baako* (one is left). Buyer and seller calculating the current balance of a revolving credit account will agree *aka cedi oha* (one hundred cedis is left). They would not use the phrase *m'adi ka* as long as the agreed payments continued. Many nonmonetary reciprocal obligations are also called *eka,* especially if they have not been honored when expected. Even in soccer scores, the team falling behind has *di ka.*

The most common usage of *m'adi ka* in the marketplace was not for debts but for business losses on a specific transaction. These might give rise to debt, but only if the trader involved did not have enough reserve capital to pay what she might owe on the transaction. The phrase *m'abo ka* (I have gone into debt) carries a strong negative connotation of mismanagement or misfortune. For example, a trader unloading a truck full of completely rotten plantain after the truck had broken down on the road repeated over and over *m'abo ka awuo* (I have lost money to death). A few days later, when I returned to sympathize with her, she said *m'abo ka awie* (I have finished losing money). She explained that she had cut her losses, cleared what she owed, and was trying not to think about it any more, since she was still able to trade on a considerable scale.

Traders will complain rather openly about losing money on specific transactions, but cash loans are surrounded with secrecy and tension. Small loans imply carelessness; large loans imply dependence and exploitation. Public knowledge of such loans would therefore further damage their commercial credit in the market. Traders usually seek them outside of the market to preserve confidentiality and precisely because they have already exhausted their normal market resources. They would look first to loans from relatives and friends, since the trust derived from that relationship also reduces the interest or other form of charge to viable levels. Only traders disqualified from both commercial and family assistance, presumably for misbehavior, would resort to moneylenders.

The very high interest rates of commercial moneylending reflect the high-risk status of these borrowers. For large amounts, moneylenders would traditionally take family valuables for security. In early colonial days, they still took family members in pawn, which came shamefully close to slavery. In general discussions of such practices, Asantes assumed that individuals or families would go into debt only to pay for court fines or legal or medical bills. Since the shame of such loans falls on the entire family, they are only appropriate for emergencies that threaten family interests, such as land or criminal cases. The high interest makes such loans unprofitable for raising business capital.

Cash loans become more respectable when they are part of another relationship, especially within a junior/senior relationship that already assumes deference and dependence. Relatives and husbands give loans to young traders, either to expand or start their businesses. The recipient uses the income to support other family members instead of paying interest. The donor can reclaim the capital in case of need but often writes it off gradually over the years if the relationship proves satisfactory. These blend almost imperceptibly into the popular forms of premortem inheritance.

Traveling traders also loan money to farmers from whom they intend to buy. Most travelers I knew made some such cash loans each year, but not to a large percentage of the farmers they dealt with. Farmers use the money to pay laborers for weeding and harvesting the crops. In some cases, they do the work themselves but need the money for family subsistence until harvest. The sums involved in loans I learned about were well below the eventual sales value of the farmer's crop. The trader deducts the amount loaned from the total price of the crop when she pays for it after delivery.

Unlike the cases of advance sales described for Zaire, the Kumasi-based traders do not set a low sales price at the time the farmer needs money (MacGaffey 1987). The price is not negotiated at the time of the loan but at the time of delivery and according to the prevailing rate then. The trader should not demand a price which is outside the range of current levels. The farmer retains the right to sell elsewhere and refund the principal only, and the trader cannot bring a case for any interest, either with market or village leaders.

These loans seem to occupy an intermediate status between cash advances and cash loans. Some participants talked of such advances in discussions of normal business investments, such as giving cash advances to travelers when goods are scarce. Traders who made them said that they find them a worthwhile use of money in the preharvest season, when trading itself is relatively risky and difficult. Farmers also use these loans, or the possibility of them, as a risk cushion. They can risk planting larger acreages because they have the option of falling back on traders' capital if necessary for timely labor hire or purchase of fertilizer or insecticide. In other conversations, on the other hand, traders and farmers spoke of loans as a personal favor, helping farmers meet unexpectedly high family or farm expenses without disrupting the production cycle. This places them more in the category of emergency cash loans from friends or relatives.

The level of confidentiality of farm loans was likewise intermediate between that of conventional credit and cash loans. Traders freely discussed individual loans with the recipients in front of other farmers. Although this may have embarrassed the farmers themselves, this was not obvious enough for me to perceive. Farmers were not reluctant to discuss their own loans or loans in general when traders were not present. On the other hand, some traders perceived public hostility to farm advances as a result of government statements presenting loans as part of the traders' stranglehold on farm produce. These traders refrained from discussing their loans in the market and disavowed making them in front of strangers.

Start-up Resources

Financial capital is only one of the resources a trader needs to start up in business. Given the minimal capitalization of many market enterprises, it may not even be the most important. Stall rights or other means of access to market locations and introductions to suppliers are more critical to initial success at the lower levels of trading. Once established in a Kumasi Central Market stall, with an established line of supplier credit, a skillful young trader can build up her business on her own.

Relatives were important, but not the only, sources of these start-up resources. About half of the women traders received their starting capital and half received their location rights through kin (see tables 5.2 and 5.3). Men and women traders had significantly different patterns of access to family resources, suggesting that men and women trading in Kumasi Central Market came from different ranges of family and class backgrounds and were placed differently in those families, which a later chapter will confirm. Few traders reported depending on commercial credit to start their businesses, but current traders did not usually count this credit as part of their working capital. Those who said they relied on their own savings may have also had access to supplier credit.

Table 5.2 Source of Present Trading Capital by Percentage of Traders Reporting Each Source

Source	Men	Women	Both
Self	43.5	26.1	31.2
Same-Sex Parent	24.6	29.1	27.8
Same-Sex Kin	9.4	11.2	13.0
Other-Sex Parent	17.4	4.8	6.2
Other-Sex Kin	1.4	2.7	2.4
Spouse	0	20.0	14.1
Other*	3.6	6.1	5.3

* Includes master, mistress, or credit
SOURCE: 1979 Kumasi Central Market Survey

Table 5.3 Source of Access to Current Trading Location

Source	Men	Women
City Council	41.3 (%)	37.7 (%)
Relative	39.9	50.2
Friend	11.6	9.3
Queen or Chief	0	.9
Other	7.2	3.9

SOURCE: 1979 Kumasi Central Market Survey

One older woman who insisted proudly that she had started trading on her own described receiving a gift of peanuts from a relative who sold them and then selling them instead of keeping the gift. Although such initiatives are not unexpected in an energetic youngster at Christmas, they are different from a request for goods on credit.

Relatives seem to provide commercial contacts more often than they provide assets directly. In life histories, women described relatives as well as neighbors and other contacts introducing them to nonkin suppliers in the market when they began trading. So few reported relatives among their current suppliers and buyers that actual credit from relatives would seem to be rare. Relatives also put new traders in contact with market neighbors or acquaintances who were interested in lending, renting, or selling space. However, traders leaving the market were very likely to transfer their own stalls to a relative if one was available and interested.

The type of facilities a trader has rights to use marks the capital and status position of the enterprise and also defines its location within the Central Market complex. Possession of more elaborate or expensive facilities and locations indicates that those traders have both the social resources to get access to them in the first place and the kind of commercial relations that require or take advantage of them. Permanent, enclosed stalls, for example, provide storage space more secure against theft and the elements, while their congested surroundings and rigid walls limit accessibility and innovative use of space. The Kumasi Metropolitan Authority has sought to limit the potential uses of space within the market by building stalls and buildings according to the original market plan and restricting traders' additions. Traders have worked within and around these limits, however, to modify spatial arrangements in accordance with their own ideas of proper commercial patterns. The present appearance of the market reflects a compromise between neglect and initiative on both sides. The smaller spaces in which individual traders operate are also highly transparent to social relations, since they choose, create, and modify their facilities and use of space to reflect with fair sensitivity shifts in central trading relations. Visual cues serve to advertise these relations as well as to circulate supply and demand information.

The City Council laid a formal pattern for the market with the original market buildings. The three-story cement building, or *abresan*, facing Kejetia Roundabout, remains an impressive contribution. The bottom floors contain spacious storefront rooms with full cement walls and locking doors, with the highest rents of any market location. Shops selling manufactured goods occupy the ground floor, facing either the market or the street. On the next floor, men's tailors' workshops crammed with apprentices take advantage of the clean surroundings, secure small storage rooms, and roomy veranda. Market offices use the small third floor. Another multistory building inside the market burned down in 1976. The meat market, set back inside the market behind the lines of original stalls, shows colonial concern for hygiene in its screened walls, well-drained floor, and then-distant location.

Behind the three-story building the planned part of the market stretches in serried rows of stalls each four to eight feet square. Their tin roofs fill the front section within the cement walls of the market proper. Traders sometimes refer to this central area as the *djum* (lit., market) or *apatem* (lit., stalls) in contrast with the more informally arranged fringe areas or the wholesale yards. The City Council first built the rows of "permanent" cement stalls immediately behind the market building, which were spaced widely enough for trucks to pass between them. More complete drainage of this swampy area reduced malarial mosquitos, partly justifying the expense, although the hasty landfill continued to settle alarmingly and cause structural and drainage problems for the market traders.

Within a few years, traders obtained permission to erect similar wooden stalls at their own expense between and behind these rows, known officially as the "temporary" stalls. These valued stalls, when in good repair, protect goods from rain and sun. Their four walls and locking front shutters offer secure storage. Toward the rear of the market, traders built open- walled stalls with counters and poles to support their tin roofs. Three commodity groups built airy barns, now housing onions, plantains, and stored fish. Traders using open stalls often add a padlocked wooden box to their furnishings. The aisles and corners offer extra space for traders to expand their displays. Those with stalls usually own tables and chairs which they set up in front and stow inside at night. Others without stall space ask permission to set up tables in high-traffic areas, such as near the meat market. In some aisles these extra tables form an intermediary row, with storage boxes left in place overnight.

Outside the market walls, traders erected more stalls in straggling rows that paralleled the walls and gates of the market. Most stalls outside the walls consist of flimsy poles supporting a tin roof over a large table. The wealthier traders invest in kiosks, self-contained rooms which they can move or sell. The overhanging lip of Roman Hill leaves little space for such expansion on the market's southern edge. Traders spread more freely along and across the railway line to the north. This area lacks even the remnants of cement paving found in the market proper, inside the walls. In the rainy season, standing water reduces access to these stalls considerably.

Beyond the lines of informal stalls, open areas provide facilities for thousands more traders. Traders set up their tables, chairs, baskets, and mats in habitual places each morning. In the evening they pack them away in nearby houses or stalls. The very lack of equipment or amenities facilitates part-time use of these open areas by a succession of vendors. On the north side, a mixed retail area jostles truck and van stops where passengers wait for suburban destinations.

The wholesale yards lie in the same outer belt as these mixed retail areas, but use the space very differently. Each yard includes a lane for truck access and an open area protected from through traffic where each wholesale seller demarcates her display and bargaining area with her stacks of bags or boxes of produce. As her goods dwindle, she yields her space to another wholesaler. Sellers use communal facilities like benches and sheds where travelers and wholesalers can rest and discuss business. The commodity group leaders use these sheds to hold meetings and settle disputes.

The Kumasi City Council, now the Kumasi Metropolitan Assembly, mainly allocates unoccupied stalls or open space, not existing commercial facilities. Older traders who moved in when their part of the market was being built applied or registered with the Kumasi City Council. As recently as the 1960s, unoccupied areas remained available next to the market, where aspiring traders could settle and apply for recognition of their holding. Now that traders have filled most of the space contiguous to the market, newcomers must obtain location rights from an established trader. Eviction of traders for nonpayment of city rents was rare. Those unable to pay would sublet, or rent out their stalls, or sell them if necessary, rather than forfeit their rights without compensation. I knew of several cases where commodity groups or market neighbors paid the rent for absent traders until such a transfer could be arranged.

Kumasi Central Market traders subdivide, rent, purchase, and inherit stalls already in use, without reference to city market authorities. In many cases, the stall "owner" or registered occupant negotiates a fixed rent or profit sharing with the new trader, who simply pays the market fees or stall rents in the previous name. Traders will also give or lend space to a relative or friend, who reciprocates less formally with occasional gifts. Outright sales were reported both of kiosks erected by traders and of official stalls in the central part of the market. Market authorities acknowledge sales of stall rights by registering the new occupant, despite regulations prohibiting private transfers. High prices for rent or sale keep poorer traders out of the best locations. Intense demand for centrally located stalls stimulates more subdivision there. Stallholders set up tables in the aisles for themselves or for subcontractors. Some also rent space for limited times of the day. Some traders survive by floating—occupying the space of one or another trader temporarily absent, in return for token gifts.

Traders in fringe squatter areas allocate space by mutual consent. They respect each others' accustomed locations so that regular customers can find them. A new entrant asks permission of adjacent traders before setting up her things. Squatters tend to locate near friends and relatives for mutual assistance in minding each others' goods and children. Rental and sale are less frequent, and whole areas are sometimes rearranged or relocated without formal transfers. These areas are also under the jurisdiction of the Market Manager, however, so formal and informal allocation systems sometimes conflict. Quarrels arose in several cases when one squatter registered her tenancy with the Kumasi City Council and tried to charge rent to later (or earlier) arrivals.

Direct intervention by the city in stall reallocation, although required by law, was considered illegitimate and fiercely resented by traders. One Kumasi City Manager in the late 1980s was attacked by irate traders who poured urine over him, alleging corruption over stall allocations and rents; he was eventually removed from office. In the mid 1960s, Accra traders' resentment over party favoritism in stall allocation apparently was an important factor in turning them against the Nkrumah government (Drake and Lacy 1966).

Although private transfers make the Kumasi City Council's allocation rights seem insignificant, its residual land rights are by no means trivial for Kumasi Central Market traders. Evictions of large groups of traders to improve the appearance of the market, to improve traffic flow, or to discourage illegal sales recurred throughout the research period, especially of traders outside the market walls. Occupation rights were the most important leverage market authorities had over Kumasi Central Market traders. Traders resented what they consider arbitrary evictions, but remarked that reappropriation of trading areas would be valid if actually needed for community facilities such as roads or clinics.

Ownership of market locations by the city government also effectively justifies the collection of substantial rents and daily use fees from traders. Even traders who erected their own stalls pay rent based on their quality, and those squatting in the open areas buy daily tickets. They protested fee increases and complained of neglect of the repairs and sanitary services they were supposed to finance, but did not dispute the legitimacy of city fees as such. Market rents and fees were set by local officials and councils at levels to encourage trade in their locations and did not put an intolerable burden on market traders. Those at Kumasi Central Market were not high enough to put a heavy drain on traders' finances in such a desirable location. Only the poorest hawkers found their survival challenged by the daily ticket, although its per capita nature makes it the most regressive type of taxation.

Market revenues were highly significant to the city, providing about 40 percent of municipal revenue in 1989 (Tackie 1990). This fiscal dependence may have motivated the City Council to allegedly defend Kumasi Central Market from complete demolition in 1979. In fact, the present market was built as much to generate revenue as to relieve overcrowding. The British improved market facilities all over Ashanti in the 1920s and 1930s in order to found local government treasuries to which they could assign most colonial administrative costs (NAK4; NAK5). Official correspondence shows they had realized that Asantes who resisted per capital or head taxes to the point of threatening revolt would pay market fees with little resistance (NAA1). Daily market fees collected by chiefs dated from well before the British conquest, both in Asante and the coast. Although individual traders used tricks to evade purchasing these daily tickets, they more generally paid them than other forms of tax, such as import or income taxes.

Skill

Trading successfully requires not only a location and the appropriate level of capital, but considerable skill. Someone beginning in trading needs to acquire both general trading skills and others specific to the kind of trading she attempts. Particular methods of handling and of judging quality apply to each commodity, as do the complicated bargaining conventions discussed in the last chapter. Skill at acquiring and evaluating up-to-date knowledge of a particular set of supply locations, whether within Kumasi Central Market or elsewhere, is also critical to continued profitability. Building up or taking over an enterprise also requires knowledge of the relevant people at these locations and perhaps the history of interaction with individual suppliers and buyers. Certain trading practices also involve nontrading skills such as languages, literacy, or numeracy. All these skills must be learned, whether in relationships set up primarily for training purposes or in the course of other relationships.

Formal school education imparts skills traders find useful in limited contexts. Written and spoken English and arithmetic are important for traders in imported and manufactured goods, who deal extensively with invoices, chits, receipts, and posted notices in English. Since these commodities in general provide higher incomes than local produce, education gives women an advantage in commodity choice. However, many examples can be found of illiterate women trading successfully in these commodities. Wealthy illiterate traders frequently hired educated people to keep their accounts, or employed their own children, but I never encountered one who took the time to learn herself. Extended Islamic education also enables some Muslim traders to keep their own records (in Arabic script), label their goods, and make calculations. Before colonial rule, the Asante chiefs had hired Muslims from the North to keep records and accounts for them, as well as to provide spiritual support and magic.

Education beyond literacy is less obviously useful in the marketplace. Vocational schools rarely teach girls accounting or other advanced business skills. Continuing through secondary school begins to socialize young people to elite values and habits that have some advantages and some disadvantages for trading. It helps them make elite contacts for legal or illegal supplies and licenses useful to wealthier traders, but can make poorer girls reluctant to follow their mothers into the less prestigious trade in local foodstuffs.

One noncommercial skill many traders found useful was command of several African languages. Almost all Kumasi Central Market traders knew Twi, which is the dominant language of the city. It varies enough from other Akan languages and dialects that travelers who bought regularly in distant regions found it important to use Fante, Brong, or Sehwi for efficient and warm relations with their suppliers there. Asante traders also learned Dagomba, Dagarti, or other major Northern languages, not only if they traded in the North but if they traded in nearer markets frequented by Northerners. Rural-rural migration is extensive enough to bring many farm families of Northern origin into Ashanti and other Akan-dominated regions. Traders with a Northern ethnic background often use Hausa, a Nigerian language, as their trading language. Hausa serves as a lingua franca for traders from different ethnic groups in Northern Ghana and in adjacent former French and English colonies in the savannah zone. Northerners based in Kumasi often speak Hausa more than their mother tongue, and their children grow up speaking it better (Schildkrout 1978). In commodities where one ethnic group dominates supply or demand, traders feel that language is necessary for effective bargaining. For example, although many of the native Ga inhabitants of Accra speak Twi, I heard traders saying they could trade well in Accra because they had learned Ga. Others said they did not try to purchase in Accra markets because their lack of Ga enabled Gas to cheat them. Historical antagonism and wars also lead Asantes to distrust Gas, for the same reason that Northerners distrust Asantes.

Traders both learned languages on purpose and chose trading roles that took advantage of ones they knew. Poultry buyers native to the Upper Region, which contains many small language groups, said that most of them started trading in their own home districts. When they traveled to a new market, they had to go with someone who knew the language until they learned it. Kumasi traders acquired additional languages in childhood from living in multi-ethnic houses or neighborhoods or from living in another region for several years. Adult traders pick up words and phrases from their friends and customers in the market or at their lodgings in the supply area.

Knowledge of basic, as opposed to commodity-specific, trading skills is extremely widespread among the Kumasi population. Urban children need to be able to remember prices, make change, and calculate multiple purchases without supervision in order to buy as well as to sell. They usually have learned this by the age of eight or nine through buying snacks, running errands, and talking with their friends, without special training. More than half of current traders reported learning basic skills by themselves (see table 5.4), since most of them grew up in Kumasi.

With these basic skills, children can hawk goods on a small scale or make small sales at fixed prices beside an older trader who bargains over larger sales and changes large bills for them. These activities put the child in a position to learn more specific and sophisticated skills. Small children, eight or nine years old, often begin to sell things on their own initiative, without consulting any adult. They save small amounts of money from gifts or by running errands for tips. They also

Table 5.4 Learning Trading Skills, by Percentage for Each Sex

Relationship	Men	Women
Teacher of Basic Skills		
Self	51.8	52.3
Same-Sex Parent	14.4	36.3
Same-Sex Kin	20.1	8.1
Other-Sex Parent	5.0	.9
Other-Sex Kin	1.4	.9
Neighbor	3.6	.6
Other	3.6	.9
Teacher of Specialized Skills		
Self	46.0	53.6
Same-Sex Parent	14.4	30.5
Same-Sex Kin	27.3	8.4
Other-Sex Parent	2.9	1.8
Other-Sex Kin	2.9	1.5
Neighbor	1.4	1.5
Other	5.0	2.7

SOURCE: 1979 Kumasi Central Market Survey

beg small amounts of goods to begin selling. Many adult traders and also nontraders told stories of relishing such childhood trading.

Adult traders also explained how they had learned commodity-specific skills without help. One orphaned woman had deliberately sold many commodities one after the other as a girl in order to train herself in all aspects of trading before making a permanent choice. Older traders who had switched commodities recounted first watching successful traders closely to discover which techniques yielded the most profit. Once they started, they expected to make little profit the first few weeks until they became more expert. Such stories give plausibility to Kumasi Central Market traders' survey responses, where about half of them said they learned specific as well as basic skills on their own, by observation and trial and error (see table 5.4). Adults take so much pride in the fact that some overreporting is likely. In conversation, some individuals who spoke of coming to market on their mothers' backs as infants insisted they learned by observation, not instruction.

Observation of children in the market did reveal remarkably little direct instruction. Young children helping their mothers commonly hawk inexpensive items from headtrays away from supervision. Their trial and error in bargaining and mental calculations brings either scoldings on their return or extra profit they may pocket. Direct instruction was readily acknowledged as such when it did occur. On several occasions old women tested young children or hawkers on mental arithmetic, setting complicated hypothetical transactions for them to solve. Another survey of predominantly female traders conducted in Monrovia, Liberia, confirms the importance of self-instruction. There, a comparable 48 percent had learned "by their own efforts," 37 percent from friends, and only 12 percent from relatives, less than in Kumasi Central Market (Handwerker 1973, 291).

Only one case came to my attention of organized training of a small child, but this may have been more commonly done at home. A grandmother who traded in yams said she had brought her young namesake granddaughter from the home village partly in order to teach her trading, although also to keep her company at home. Soon after the child's arrival, I saw the old woman buying some peppers for the six-year-old girl to practice with, since yams were too expensive for practice. For several months, she supervised the girl in buying a small basket full, dividing them into heaps, and selling them in front of her stall without falling asleep over them. Within a year, the girl had graduated to selling pieces of yam, which the grandmother had cut and priced, from the stall in her absence or by hawking them from a headtray.

Adults can also arrange more formally for training with an established trader, usually in order to learn the specific skills needed to sell a new commodity. Several reported asking permission to follow a friend or relative to market for a few weeks or months and helping while observing and asking questions. The current orange queen mother learned to sell oranges after her eight children were born by standing next to a friend of hers, now dead. My own behavior as an anthropologist conformed broadly to this model much of the time, leading some traders to conclude I was learning to sell yams or tomatoes in order to begin selling them back in the United States. In these explicit learning relationships, the learner helps in unskilled tasks without sharing any of the profit, like an apprentice or other young helper, but the experienced trader does not assign her tasks as she would a long-term assistant.

Girls and young women who know basic trading skills can learn more advanced skills by working as assistants to established traders for a longer period of time. Traders were familiar with this possibility, although the survey shows such assistants were in fact rarely employed.

As with craft apprentices, the terms of work are set by agreement but vary widely between cases. Some apprentices receive wages, while others pay fees or work for an agreed period after training as part payment. Successful traders, like well-known craft workers, attract more helpers on better terms. Younger apprentices receive more direct instruction, do more menial work, and expect to stay longer before becoming independent traders.

These long training periods are essential for success in commodities that require accurate and precise quality judgment that cannot be learned quickly. Chicken traders talked about the ability to see when a chicken was about to fall sick and sell it quickly before it became obviously ill. Kola traders stressed the importance of inspecting the nuts skillfully to remove and sell not only the moldy ones, but those which were about to become moldy. Older traders in these commodities run networks of "boys," who stay with them for years in gradually more independent capacities. Fresh-fish buyers had similar perishability pressures demanding reliable judgments to avoid capital loss. One who bought lake fish from her hometown said she knew these things because "it was the work there." A cloth trader from a yam-growing district explained her easy, if reluctant, switch to yam trading with the same phrase; she knew not only appropriate trading procedures and partners but the ins and outs of disguising and recognizing rotten yams. Women growing up in specialized farming or fishing areas acquired expertise others might find hard to match.

Working with a leading trader, an assistant hopes to learn more sophisticated trading techniques than she could afford to try on her own. How much an apprentice learns also depends on the division of labor within the enterprise. The greater the internal division of labor, the less an assistant learns. Those employed primarily as hawkers or as retail sellers, for example, may never have the chance to observe wholesale transactions with suppliers or institutional buyers, which would be essential to establishing an equivalent enterprise of their own. In a smaller business, an assistant may learn all the relevant techniques over time and make the contacts necessary to start on her own or even to take over the business when the older trader retires.

Access to Labor

The apprentice or assistant relationship provides added labor for the enterprise owner as well as training for the subordinate. For craft workers, access to the labor of apprentices is a primary strategy for accumulation. The small number of assistants actually employed suggests that subordinates have relatively limited importance to most traders. Almost half of the traders reported working alone (48 percent) and another 38 percent worked with only one partner or assistant. This is more impressive because the subset classified as traders included some craft masters, such as tailors who had retired from active production to handle sales and supervise their apprentices' work.

Complex centrally managed enterprises including relatives working at different locations seem to have been more common during earlier periods. One provisions trader I got to know fairly well and traveled with said that her mother had headed a family network that was now virtually defunct, although a brother and two sisters still managed stores in other towns. Through the 1960s they had ordered or purchased most of their goods together, taking turns traveling to Europe on buying trips. Now they were still willing to share goods between themselves, but such supplies only came infrequently. For the most part, they bought independently where they could and acted as separate enterprises. When I pressed for descriptions of trading patterns in the 1920s, an elderly courtier mentioned several big families in the garden egg business in the 1920s who sent agents into different parts of the country buying for them. In the 1970s and 1980s, the term agent was not in use for marketplace relations, and even cash advances did not give the creditor the kind of tight control implied by that term.

What work the few assistants found actually did indicates how useful one might be under current conditions. One interesting finding was that the division of labor within an enterprise sometimes did not differ radically from that between independent associates trading on their own accounts. Women who send a daughter to hawk small amounts from a headtray are also selling to other children and adults who hawk small amounts from their own headtrays or sell on commission. The distance and concentration of supply or demand place much stricter limits on the number of tasks a single individual can manage and the consequent patterns of specialization.

As table 5.5 indicates, the most common use for an assistant is to sell alongside the respondent. The two performed parallel tasks most of the time, but the senior trader would handle those which required skilled judgment. These usually included purchasing stock, giving credit, and pricing. Her assistant might be able to mind the stall alone, but important transactions would have to be deferred until her return. Such an assistant is a convenience to the trader; although neighbors would also usually mind her stall, they cannot be assigned to do so. Whether such assistance permits significant accumulation then depends on the terms of remuneration and the trader's ability to finance her own more responsible tasks.

Table 5.5 Division of Labor among Partners, by Percentage of Reported Partners*

Task	Men	Women
Sells Here	85.2	86.7
Sells Elsewhere	2.3	13.9
Craft Work	10.2	1.2
Other	3.3	1.8

* Those working alone not included. One trader could report multiple partners or tasks. Partners included superiors and subordinates.
SOURCE: 1979 Kumasi Central Market Survey

The indistinct dividing line between subordination and independence further blurs comparison. Both kin and non-kin subordinates look after their own interests, including making their own money overtly or covertly. Conversely, independent associates can coordinate their actions closely and share substantial capital through credit. Several groups of relatives I first considered to be extended family enterprises controlled by a senior relative turned out to consist of related traders working on their own accounts. Traders expressed ambivalence about subordination to senior relatives. Their life histories frequently mentioned that a desire for independence led them to stop working for a senior relative.

A young assistant contributes her labor in return for income, training, and access to capital. The other trader provides the location, working capital, and specialized skills the enterprise needs. These assets give the would-be assistant a wider range of enterprises to join than she could hope to finance herself. On the other hand, her choice of employers is limited to those who need extra unskilled or semiskilled labor at that time. If a trader cannot fully employ her own children, as is often the case, she will send them to work with other traders, even in the same commodity, or encourage them to work independently.

Children who assist adult traders expect immediate payment in maintenance and occasional gifts. When the child lives with the trader, she can provide food and clothing in kind but she also gives the child money to buy them. Some mothers paid monthly or daily contributions to savings clubs for their working daughters, using the periodic payouts to buy them clothing and to encourage them to save. The exact level of compensation usually remains at the trader's discretion, but it should bear some relation to the child's ability to work, the child's needs, and the trader's income. A market assistant will leave if she feels her needs have not been met, and several adult traders mentioned in life histories that they had stopped working with mothers or other relatives who were too stingy. Adult assistants get a monthly wage in lieu of support, since they are expected to have their own budgets. Formal apprenticeships are more typical of craft workers such as bakers.

On the other hand, some children assisting an older trader enjoy as much independence, socially and financially, as adults trading on their own. Assistants as young as ten are sent to work without direct supervision as hawkers, once they have learned the basics of making change and bargaining. Like commission sellers, they are responsible for selling out their goods at the set price and can keep anything they make above this. Some turn extra profits in to their mothers to save for them, but others conceal them. One girl who had become a skillful bargainer hawking her father's sugar cane began to sell secondhand children's clothes for an aunt during school vacations. The aunt would set prices for each item, but the girl could usually get more. For example, if a shirt was priced at three cedis, she would ask for five and settle for four. She pocketed the extra cedi, but her aunt was so happy to get the full price that she would give her some money every day and pick out a nice dress her size to give her from time to time. The girl saved her own money for future use and also set money aside daily from her school lunch money and from Christmas gifts from her fathers' friends. She bought cloths and cooking pots as a hedge against inflation, storing them with her best friend's mother so her father would not know.

Gifts of money, though irregular, enable a child to accumulate a small working capital. Traders announced these gifts to the children as lunch money or Christmas presents, but the children themselves expected these to exceed their subsistence needs and thereby permit them to build a nest egg. One could consider these informal gifts as a share of the enterprise profits, especially since they were increased as a reward for good performance or when profits went up. Although they are a small share of profits, they might well exceed what a child could hope to earn by trading independently. They thus increase the scale of business the child will eventually be able to establish, unless the adult uses her own low profits as an excuse to skimp on gifts.

Assistants also gradually establish rights to use the working capital that the senior trader retains. The trader should not dismiss longstanding assistants except for crimes, or if the trader retires or goes bankrupt herself. When an assistant reaches an age and skill level to trade independently, she can ask for capital or credit to start on her own. Since children of eight or nine can make a valued contribution to an enterprise, these use rights begin to accumulate from an early age. Such entitlements are recognized as moral claims, and a child can shame a senior trader into honoring them by complaining to shared relatives or neighbors, but the child has little ultimate recourse against a truly irresponsible employer or one who is simply an incompetent trader except to leave.

Fortunately, the senior trader's self-interest also encourages her to honor these claims. Networks of well established ex-assistants who include kin and non-kin can be a valuable business asset for the trader herself. In one such network, a yam trader, Konadu, apprenticed her daughter Akua to a friend of hers, Frowa, another yam trader with a stall near hers in the market. Frowa already worked with several of her own daughters and a sister's daughter, who traveled to buy for her in the villages. She sent Akua along on buying expeditions with one of her own older daughters to help out and gain experience. After about four years working with Frowa, Akua was making buying trips alone and trading with the older woman's capital. Her terms of profit sharing and degree of independent decision making were very similar to those of Frowa's daughters and niece and to those of others trading with Frowa's capital who had never been her assistants, including some in the older generation. Frowa's daughters remained her close friends, especially the one she used to travel with, and they all coordinated their buying trips according to Frowa's advice. One of Frowa's youngest daughters considered herself apprenticed directly to her older sister, rather than her mother. She accompanies the older sister on her buying trips, handling semiskilled tasks like guarding yams after purchase and making initial contact with farmers wanting to sell.

Alternatively, assistants continue working after maturity with an eye to taking over the business. Usually this is one closely related assistant, such as a daughter or niece. Such an assistant has stronger claims than any other relative to inherit the business under the rather flexible Asante principles of inheritance. She not only deserves reward for helping expand the business, but she is the one most capable of making good use of it, since she has the specific knowledge essential to keeping it profitable. However, these nominated daughters were also dependent on the goodwill of their mothers and families. They could be disinherited by rapacious family elders such as mothers' brothers after the mother's death. In one case, the elderly mother herself distributed the trading capital to a son and other relatives, leaving the long-suffering daughter bitter and virtually bankrupt. The possibility of eventual or gradual inheritance marks the main difference between kin and non-kin assistants in remuneration and degree of identification with the enterprise. Even this distinction is not absolute, however, because a few unrelated assistants took over a trading business when no relative lived near or showed any interest.

School attendance generally prevents a youngster from contributing enough labor to receive the full benefits of assistantship, either in training or capital rights. Public primary and middle schools in Kumasi operated on double shifts that mitigated this conflict. Children could attend one shift and work essentially full time, although at some cost to their schoolwork. Secondary school was the major threshold, usually involving boarding and always substantial homework. This meant that some of the more successful traders, who had educated all of their own daughters, chose apprentices and a commercial heir from among more distant relatives. Poorer traders said they avoided educated girls as assistants, fearing they would prove disrespectful and unreliable. On the other hand, poor employment prospects send many girls back into market trading after secondary school. School attendance may have delayed their trading progress, but it improved their access to more profitable commodity lines than their mothers'.

Distinguishing between the remuneration and conditions of work of kin and non-kin assistants becomes more difficult because of terminology which seems deliberately ambiguous. Local usage of terms referring to trading assistants avoids distinguishing baldly between status categories, even when more specific, accurate terms are available in Twi. The commonest term, *akwadaa* (young person or child), does not even separate trading assistants from other children. Asantes commonly use it around the house to avoid distinguishing between one's own children and neighbor children, foster children, maids, and young visitors. Teachers use it of their pupils, especially in boarding schools. In practice, using such a general term in description or reference draws discreet attention to the fact that no more positive term applies. Traders would introduce daughters and nieces with the more specific word *ba,* for one's own or one's sister's child, adding that "she helps me."

In general use, *akwadaa* has the connotation of inexperience and lack of knowledge, but also the positive qualities of confidence and energy associated with youth (Owusu 1992). This was also the term used for apprentices or trainees in precolonial craft workshops, who were not always relatives, and it places the senior trader in a benevolent, paternalistic light. Traders with numerous associates wanting to refer to all of them will use this term to include close relatives, former assistants, and even adult traders who work with their capital. The last group would be particularly insulted to hear the term applied to them as individuals, even when they are the age of the speakers' actual sons or daughters; they respond with joking and teasing when within earshot.

These Twi terms make no gender distinction; English terms commonly used by Twi speakers are gendered and also encode other more precise status distinctions. In order to distinguish by sex among either employees or young relatives, traders refer to "boys" and "girls." Using the English words not only makes the senior trader sound more sophisticated, it also emphasizes the subordination rather than the paternalism of the relationship by invoking colonial images. When traders refer to young sales assistants, particularly boys, as "apprentices," they still impress listeners with their English, but they include a kind of compliment to the assistant. When present, the youngsters grinned or giggled with pleasure, as the term carries the prestige of upward mobility from its stricter meaning of trainees in craft and skilled industrial work. Not coincidentally, most of these formal sector opportunities were opened to boys and required some Western education. Girls in comparable positions are more often simply called "girls." Ironically, craft masters and mistresses retain the Twi word *nkwadaa* for their actual apprentices, even when these include some older persons.

The English term "maid" applies to girls only and carries a strong negative connotation. It is only used for unrelated girls living in the employer's household and draws clear attention to their lack of kin status or belonging. Polite families refer to even purely domestic maids by the vaguer term *akwadaa,* especially in their hearing. I never heard the more exact term for servant, *akoa* (which implies an unfree relationship of debt pawning or even slavery), used. Maid service is not seen as contributing to the girl's eventual occupational status, although young maids are often promised an apprenticeship after some years of service. Perhaps for that reason, it is also not seen as a fit occupation for an adult woman.

Domestic work has its own association with low status but is somewhat separable from the term maid. I met a few traders who employed several girls, some for domestic work and others for hawking or other sales duties. They referred to all of them as maids, but those selling had higher prestige and pay. Apprentices learning crafts like baking were never called maids, even when they lived at the master's or mistress's house, received food and clothing, and performed domestic tasks. The stigma of domestic work is reduced because of the assumption of up-

Table 5.6 Who Becomes Partner, by Percentage of Reported Partners

Partner	Men	Women
Same-Sex Parent	3.1	26.4
Same-Sex Child	9.3	30.8
Same-Sex Sibling	39.1	22.5
Spouse	13.7	2.7
Other Relative	14.3	13.7
Hometown Non-kin	1.9	0
Neighbor	2.5	0
Friend	13.7	6.0
Other	17.4	4.9

SOURCE: 1979 Kumasi Central Market Survey

ward mobility, although adult apprentices are usually excused from domestic tasks.

Gender influences patterns of partnership and assistance in several ways, operating in the context of specific kin or marital relations (see table 5.6). Women most often worked with mothers or daughters, while men more often joined with brothers, distant kin, or non-kin. This suggests some significant difference between kin and non-kin relations not apparent to observation. In particular, it suggests that men find some quality of parent-child partnerships less congenial than same-generation relations with brothers and friends or purely economic relations with masters and apprentices. Virtually all partners or assistants were of the same sex as the respondent, so this may partly reflect the fact that men would less often find close senior kin, especially fathers, available as partners in a predominantly female marketplace.

The rarity of husband/wife partnerships contradicts not only Western stereotypes of mom-and-pop stores, but market studies from Latin America and Asia that show the most prosperous market enterprises taking this form (Babb 1989; Smart 1988; Szanton 1972). Curiously, more husbands reported working with wives than vice versa. Men like their wives to work with them, saying the wife "helps" them, since the husband usually owns and controls the business in these arrangements. The evident shame wives felt may have prevented some women from admitting that they were not working on their own. The same reason may have led others to work as little as possible in the husband's enterprise, spending less time in Kumasi Central Market and therefore appearing less often in the sample. The one satisfied wife I encountered had recently taken her new husband into the business, which was originally established by her mother in provisions—a set of commodities sold by both men and women. They ran it formally as a "company" and divided the profits equally, although he had made no financial investment.

Individual interviews within and outside of the survey revealed a consistent aversion among women to working with their husbands, much stronger than complaints against working with mothers or other relatives. Wives who worked with their husbands emphasized that they disliked the arrangement and would leave it as soon as they could. Several had entered the husband's business at his insistence when their own failed or after an illness. These were not true partnerships, because the wives had no ownership status and took no direct profits from their work; I saw no examples of wives joining an enterprise started by their husbands as a "company" or considering it a joint enterprise.

Women not only lost autonomy working in a husband's business, they also lost the ability to accumulate for themselves. The long-term or inheritance rights for them and their children were extremely insecure, although "helpful" wives could press more successfully for the profits to be spent on their children. One woman in this position remarked that she would split off as soon as her youngest child finished secondary school. Most women remarked that they would rather go into business with their brothers (also extremely rare) than with their husbands. This is consistent with matrilineal principles, although patrilineal Ga and Yoruba women show an equally marked avoidance of husband/wife commercial enterprises (Robertson 1984; Trager 1976).

Information

Starting a business requires adequate commercial information, defined earlier as knowledge of skills, locations, and persons. Ongoing enterprises also have insatiable demands for updated information about supply and demand conditions, price levels, and persons transacting with them, on which their continued operation depends. In times of acute political or economic crisis, information on recent or planned government policies and actions becomes extremely valuable. No other aspect of trading has as much influence on day-to-day accumulation and survival as the accuracy and timeliness of these kinds of information.

The open layout of Kumasi Central Market and other Ghanaian markets means that physical presence suffices to collect information on supply and demand levels within the marketplace and on the identity of transactors. Traders maximize their information levels by circulating several times daily throughout the market and adjacent commercial areas to check on conditions in competing locations. The terms used to describe supply and demand testify to the central role of visual inspection in the information process. Goods or buyers and sellers simply *wo ho* (are there), implying that they are self-evident. The obsession with truth, deception, and secrecy found in the twisting alleys of the Moroccan bazaar (Geertz and Rosen 1979) would be impossible to maintain here, where goods and the identity of transactors remain continually visible over long distances. The degree of information testing that Alexander reports in Javanese wholesale depots, located outside major marketplaces, is also not as central in Kumasi wholesale yards, since their marketplace location provides a good information base on these frequently traded items (Alexander 1987). One indication of this information flow was knowledge of my own presence. Jellinek reports that a market survey in a Jakarta market toward the end of her stay revealed that many traders were unaware of her identity (Jellinek 1974). By contrast, during my market survey after just under a year in the market, almost all of the market leaders and the traders in the sample had already heard of me and had some opinion of what I was doing there.

Retail prices are especially public within a single marketplace since retailers actually call them out or announce them on request. Bargaining takes place in front of the stall, where subsequent reductions can be easily heard by those standing near, which would include most interested parties. Quantity bargaining makes the exact level of discounts harder to judge, but shoppers do compare their purchases regularly after the fact. Consumers have good price knowledge for foodstuffs purchased daily or weekly, but not necessarily for major and therefore infrequent purchases. With rapid inflation, even research among friends and neighbors who have bought more recently cannot keep pace with recent price increases. Buyers for resale, who normally buy the same items regularly, then have decided advantages.

Good retail price knowledge has the positive side effect of speeding transactions by reducing the length of bargaining. Buyers can easily compare the heaps displayed and prices announced by market neighbors without going through repeated trial bargaining sessions. Retailers notice when their turnover lags behind their neighbors and reduce accordingly. Bargained price reductions observed seldom exceeded ten percent. Wholesalers also ask near the going rate for their goods. In both contexts, buyers and sellers feel offended and may break off bargaining completely if offered prices obviously outside of the current range by someone who should know they know better. Wholesalers use their knowledge of retail prices to counter buying retailers' claims that they will lose money on resale.

The pool of buyers and sellers in a wholesale yard know current prices there and discuss them freely among themselves. Within an hour or so of the yard opening, the standard price for wholesale units becomes common knowledge. Individual lots will then vary from these levels based on quality and size differences. Bringers or retailers talk over prices of individual lots they have sold or bought with colleagues who may have seen them, or at least understand their descriptive remarks. In group bargaining, for example for cassava in baskets, the prices finally agreed upon are completely public. Abstracting the going price from a number of individual transactions is the more common procedure and requires a somewhat longer time commitment. Prices and the status of individual relations could be discussed in quiet voices, to avoid casual overhearing, but traders rarely bothered. Wholesale bargaining for yams, conducted in undertones, was an exception. Offers and counteroffers mention only the tens, not the hundreds column of the price to confuse passing listeners. Those actually bargaining for adjacent hundreds, however, can follow the course of the session. In other wholesale yards, such as cassava or tomatoes, prices and the extension or refusal of credit were settled openly with no attempt at concealment from other potential buyers and sellers standing nearby. Privacy was only sought consistently for very sensitive commodities during price-control episodes and for discussions of problem debts (unless the creditor wished to embarrass the debtor). Highly illegal transactions more often were removed from the marketplace to homes, warehouses, or back streets, another indication of the difficulty of successfully controlling information access within the marketplace.

Since access to price and supply information depends on physical presence at the time of sales, it is more restricted about other locations. Kumasi-bound traders need relations with those who frequent other markets, and vice versa. Even between distant marketplaces the capacity for manipulation is limited, however, since anyone wanting to know badly enough can simply go there if they have the money and the time. The only occasion when traders noticeably attempted to conceal price levels from me took place, not surprisingly, on my longest distance trading trip. The travelers I accompanied to the Upper Region had apparently been reporting substantially different price levels to their Kumasi Central Market wholesale buyers. Most of the Kumasi wholesalers had previously been travelers to the same markets themselves and retired, so it seemed unlikely that they were seriously deceived. In this case, the general price levels were such public knowledge up there that the current travelers could not maintain the fiction even to my inexperienced eyes, as I could confirm my observations with any local participant or passerby.

Travelers can only suggest small deviations from actual market conditions because their Kumasi Central Market contacts have many other sources of information. Anyone in a position to want the information will find out for themselves eventually in one way or another. Both travelers and wholesalers eagerly ask lorry drivers or casual travelers for supply information; they even questioned me when I returned from each trip. Untrained eyes can still see and report the amount of goods piled in the market or at the roadside and the number of traders waiting for lorries. Experienced traders can estimate short-term price fluctuations fairly accurately from the visible quantity of supply or demand described. Travelers normally feigned ignorance rather than try to present misleading information, even about rather distant locations from which few passengers would probably arrive to contradict them. Although my own ignorance was more plausible, I also exaggerated it to protect information I felt travelers were reluctant to share, and they quizzed me when they came to Kumasi about what I had revealed.

Travelers exchange information about general conditions fairly freely because it reduces their absolute cost and risk levels more significantly than it gives relative advantage. They need accurate information from all of the areas from which they buy supplies in order to make travel plans that take into account the location and size of immediate supplies, timing of future harvests, and relative shortages in different consuming areas. Travelers cannot afford fruitless trips, especially in hired trucks, so they follow reports of abundant supplies. They spend their free hours in the wholesale or transport yards discussing the state of crops in the field, the likely time of harvest and the extent of farm storage. All of them reciprocate to some extent because they all need more different kinds of information than any of them could collect individually. They do make preliminary trips purely to collect information, especially when contemplating a seasonal change between supply districts, but these trips would be prohibitively expensive on a routine basis.

Information exchange on market conditions plays an important part in social relations between travelers and their Kumasi wholesalers. Reports or allegations of supply conditions in Kumasi Central Market or in the villages feature largely in bargaining sessions as well as in their socializing and strategy sessions discussing future trips and buying plans. Each side depends on the specialized information about different locations possessed by the other. The wholesaler knows Kumasi Central Market conditions well by virtue of her constant presence there, but this presence itself rules out direct knowledge of the supply district. Each side wants to pass on enough information about her own location for the other to perform well, but less information than she has herself. Information about specific days and people also helps travelers and wholesalers to coordinate their decisions. Those working in close association send messages through traveling colleagues or friends. Wholesalers ask about the movements of their regular suppliers, and suppliers send word of their expected arrival dates. Wholesalers try to coordinate arrivals to even out their supplies, asking individuals to come quickly or delay for better prices. Yoruba traders in Awe, Nigeria, likewise send messages and exchange visits to coordinate their longer trips (Trager 1976).

Travelers may have better information on supply district conditions than their wholesalers, but they are not in the village constantly themselves. They must collect information from rural friends, relatives, neighbors, or landlords living in the supply areas, who keep track of available supplies for them while they are away in Kumasi. These contacts save them valuable time searching for goods on arrival, permitting them a faster turnover of capital. Travelers operating outside their home areas either pay a commission for this kind of brokerage service or use the same broker's paid services for local accommodation, transport, and loading. In less formal arrangements with relatives or friends, they remember to bring frequent gifts from town. Travelers do not share this information on individual potential transactions with each other.

Under conditions of scarcity the search for information intensifies. Provisions traders looking for buying opportunities in Accra in 1979 spent up to a week making the rounds of appropriate Accra streets and personal contacts. On a smaller scale, a garden egg trader in the off-season spent an eighteen-hour day chasing after farmers on their way home to see if they had a few garden eggs in their sacks before she gathered enough in small lots to justify the return to Kumasi. During the harvest season, she explained, she could come from Kumasi to the local market and return with her purchases by noon. Such pressures make buyers quite secretive about their actual sources of goods, buying out of public view in homes and back alleys.

Traders in illegal goods relied very heavily on advance information on raids and policy changes for survival. Even a few hours' or minutes' warning might be essential to enable them to pack up their stalls or at least run away from a police raid. Neighbors and fellow traders cooperated fully in passing on news of the immediate movements of police or soldiers and on the identity of informers. Larger-scale traders also cultivated contacts with officials or soldiers for information farther in advance, which could prevent losses or even allow occasional windfall profits. Advance notice of when and where goods would be sold at controlled prices was as effective and less risky, for example, than receiving diverted supplies and deserved the same reward. During the strict enforcement periods of 1979, this might be only a warning not to come to the market tomorrow, which saved the trader an arrest or a beating. Rumors that some moneychangers had used advance notice of the currency exchange to unload their notes on unsuspecting colleagues provoked great bitterness, since the amount of old notes individual traders had on hand varied so widely with their state of credit and repayment. Sometimes these private tips were confidential, in that traders could not pass them on too widely without endangering their informants. The same contacts might also provide protection after traders were caught, but this was more difficult to conceal.

Market traders will utilize telephones, cables, and other information technologies when these are available. In the colonial period, officials reported that kola buyers from Nigeria were exchanging cables with associates back in Nigeria to keep them informed on price and supply conditions. At that time, they shipped kola through Accra to Lagos as well as over land. In 1979, one provisions trader had a working telephone in the market on which she could call Accra to check on the availability of supplies. This was an impressive display of her personal influence at a time when ordinary citizens had to book calls to Accra days in advance at the Central Post Office, and few home or office telephones worked at all. With supplies so erratic at that time, it saved her considerable search time, although she still had to travel down to Accra to make the actual purchases.

Confidential personal information on individuals can also become a valuable commercial asset in both cash and credit transactions. A trader sharpens her bargaining strategy by knowing the customer's need to buy or sell and which arguments will have the most weight. Making price concessions, she weighs not only general market conditions but the size and good order of the customer's enterprise, which makes her a valuable long-term associate. Extending credit efficiently means saving it for relatively important customers who will appreciate special treatment. Estimation of their creditworthiness requires information on their current capital size, outstanding financial commitments elsewhere, and their past adherence to trading conventions. If they default on debts, it is even more important to know their hometowns or present whereabouts.

Information on individual credit histories becomes public only in case of disputes over unpaid debts. Elderly traders who settle many of these disputes have the advantage of collecting many normally private facts. Long-established traders further consolidate information by attending disputes and gossiping with close associates about past and present scandals. The wide airing of such information during disputes acts as a powerful deterrent to leaving debts unpaid and cases unsettled and constitutes the primary punishment of the debtor.

One case that sprang up while I was sitting in the market showed that the issue of public reputation was considered as central as the facts in dispute. The creditor effectively opened the case simply by bewailing her misfortune in a loud voice in the yam wholesale yard. She complained about her inability to collect a debt, naming the debtor repeatedly. Friends of the debtor quickly sent word to her in her stall and she came immediately. She did not deny the facts, but argued urgently and quietly that the two of them should discuss the matter privately. The debtor was the one who eventually brought the dispute before their commodity group leader, as defamation of character, seeking to avoid worse publicity. Settling the case was a mere formality, since the debtor was not refusing to pay. She asked for a delay on economic grounds, but affirmed her intention of paying and criticized the creditor for making such a public fuss about it. The creditor then took the superior attitude that she had not brought the case in—she could well afford such a minor loss and did not want to create trouble.

When discussing this and other unusually bitter disputes, traders not directly involved are also concerned to minimize the negative publicity. They hesitate to name names and repeat details, using oblique or vague references. My assistant even sometimes hesitated to translate conversations about them. A reputation for quarrelsomeness is one of the most damaging to an aspiring trader, even worse than financial irresponsibility. Wasting time repeatedly in settling quarrels loses a wholesaler far more money than writing off a few bad debts, so they will steer clear of someone who is frequently involved in quarrels, whether she is declared right or wrong. By contrast, land cases and other village or lineage disputes come to chiefly courts as matters of honor, and Asantes have a reputation for tenacity to the point of bankruptcy.

Information about community events and general conditions that affected market trading was also enthusiastically gathered and spread within the marketplace. Government announcements of the annual budget, changes in official prices, wages or regulations, political party speeches, and reports of violence or public disturbances could all affect individual traders' plans as well as the market as a whole. Traders listened to radio and television news and heard of newspaper articles from friends and relatives who read. These were quickly reported and discussed in the marketplace, along with eyewitness or secondhand accounts from travelers. Even weather reports became critical commercial information during the rainy season, when storms periodically made farm roads in one or another district impassable. Traders had to get in and out quickly during brief improvements in driving conditions. Traders' greater need for information and greater access to news from travelers and customers bolsters the reputation of the market as an information center for the community.

Transport

Relations that control access to transport have strong implications for market hierarchies because they dominate the links between locations that reinforce and transmit hierarchy through access to information and goods. Links between urban and rural areas, between different regions of the country, even between formal sector locations and the rest of the country are maintained through the steady physical movement of goods and people. The implications of transport access for commercial power jumped into sharp focus during periods of acute transport shortage created by shortages of gasoline and spare parts. Traders based in Kumasi and other major towns gained leverage over farmers and small town traders because of their greater access to larger transport pools. At the same time, traders' own room for maneuver was severely restricted by their dependence on lorry drivers. Chronic transport shortages were well entrenched when I began fieldwork in 1978 and eased only briefly before trade liberalization in 1984.

Most of the traders with stalls in Kumasi Central Market bought within Kumasi, using porters and riding minivans or lorries. Problems in local carriage could hamper them significantly, such as mud and flooding in the marketplace. Traders bringing goods from one Kumasi location to another prefer to patronize familiar carriers who use head trays or wooden carts. Using an experienced, trusted carrier reduces the traders' work in several ways. When the carrier knows many traders' stalls, they can send the goods to assistants selling in their stalls, who will count and arrange them. They need not walk with him to show him the way, but stay to continue buying more. When the supply of goods is limited, this convenience can be critical to obtaining their desired amount. For example, traders buying vegetables from passengers in Kejetia lorry park compete fiercely for arrivals during a limited period in the early morning. They trust the carrier not to steal their goods because he wants to return to the same place for rehiring the next day. Some commodities such as yams or sacks of sugar also require special handling or stacking on the cart and in unloading at the stall to prevent damage. Experienced carriers with carts can transport several consignments at once, stacking and delivering each to the correct owner without confusion. This reduces congestion and delay in the wholesale yard as well as increasing the carrier's income.

Experience gives the carriers some bargaining power, but not much. One group of young head carriers tried to hold out for higher fees between Kejetia and the wholesale yard. They were well known to the garden egg wholesalers they confronted, and the eldest bargained for all, but they were unsuccessful in raising their fees that day. The pressure from casual head carriers keeps established ones from dramatically improving their level of remuneration. Busy market locations always show many idle head carriers waiting with basket or basin to catch the eye of a customer. Head carrying is a traditional occupation for destitute persons, including homeless children. Certainly many carriers dressed in tattered clothing and could be observed using their earnings immediately to buy food to eat. Several male and female traders reported starting out as head carriers and saving their trading capital from earnings or obtaining goods on credit from traders they came to know through carrying their goods.

Carriers using wooden carts have a stronger organizational base. Only men and older boys handle these carts, which permit much larger loads on a single trip. Some bosses were reported that owned fleets of carts and rented them out or employed crews outright. Traders in locations where the passages are wide enough to permit cart passage seem to prefer using them, although the rainy season forces a return to head carriage in some sections. Carts can easily transport an entire wholesale unit or several at once, while a hundred yams must be divided into smaller loads for head carriage. Freelance carriers have a registered union with leaders based in the main Kejetia lorry park. They settle disputes over payment and occasionally united to raise fees. Yam carters also had a well-organized group, but had only indifferent success in raising their fees.

Due to patterns of task specialization, only a minority of traders personally use intercity transport. Their overall commercial position still depended primarily on the intercity transport facilities focused on Kumasi. Indirect access to these facilities, used directly by travelers, ensured for Kumasi Central Market traders as a whole favored access to goods compared to traders from other towns. The difficulty and importance of obtaining transport was one of the factors that made traveling a full-time specialization.

The most common way of finding a freight truck was to go to the wholesale yard or lorry park and contact drivers unloading their previous shipment. Wholesale travelers in each commodity patronize a pool of specialist drivers attached to their wholesale yard. They prefer to hire drivers familiar with their routes and commodities, ones who can provide special services and handling. Drivers familiar with trading procedures actively mediate in price and labor negotiations and count money for payments. Drivers also travel more willingly to remote farms and villages in areas where they know the current road conditions and can charge accordingly. Information is thus an important resource in effective access to transport.

In a supply area, travelers from Kumasi know each other and can cooperate usefully in transport matters. One pattern is for several traders wanting to return to Kumasi at the same time to join together to fill a freight truck. They obtain the lower freight rate for chartering the whole truck, and each pays a share proportionate to the volume of her own goods. Vegetable traders in Ashanti Region villages commonly do this, traveling outward on regular passenger vehicles. In a few situations, this cooperation frees the traveler from the need to travel back with her goods. When Kumasi Central Market traders buying provisions in Accra share a truck to take their goods back, and the driver or the accompanying trader knows the owner's stall in Kumasi Central Market, a Kumasi associate can take delivery of the goods and the trader in Accra can stay on to buy more. Tomato traders on the exhausting Bolgatanga route have institutionalized this within their company. Each member buys her own boxes of tomatoes to send back to Kumasi in a truck rented by the company every second day. They take turns riding back with the truck to Kumasi overnight. Each share in the company entitles a trader to send a fixed number of boxes, depending on the size of the truck hired that day.

Traders in lower-capital operations tend to organize transport around relations to truck drivers rather than with their fellow traders. Traders buying small amounts frequently become known to the drivers plying their usual routes and receive privileged treatment even without explicit agreements. Drivers or ticket agents who recognize them as regular travelers will let them jump the line in return for inflated ticket or freight payments. In times of acute transport shortage, this can be critical to avoiding crippling spoilage and time losses.

Traders who habitually visit periodic markets often make formal arrangements to travel with the same driver each time. Trucks going to nearby village markets make several trips daily. Traders come out on the first one and leave on the last. Trucks making the longer weekly trip to Techiman, an important regional market, will wait overnight for traders to make their purchases. If a trader goes every week on the same truck, the driver may wait for her to arrive before leaving Kumasi Central Market and send word to her in the Techiman market when he is ready to return. Conversely, she should send word if she is not going that week.

The balance of power in driver/traveler interactions responds quite sensitively to the supply of transport. In 1979, traders told stories of practices twenty or more years earlier that seemed like impossibly nostalgic fantasies but are confirmed by Lawson's comment on an excess of trucks in the 1950s (Lawson 1960). Drivers and their assistants in provincial towns would court customers the night before by offering to carry their goods to the lorry park. The idea of trucks waiting hours to fill while the drivers and "mates" (helpers) tried desperately to generate traffic was hard to reconcile with lorry parks where lines of would-be travelers struggled to board the few trucks who deigned to descend briefly upon them. By 1989, the lorry parks had again filled with trucks waiting for passengers to every destination and drivers insisting theirs would leave first. Visiting some of the same villages I had in 1979, I did indeed see drivers or mates visiting regular customers at home to ask whether they were traveling the next day.

One stable element in these historical changes is the mediation of transport access through the figure of the driver. In Ghana, the skills of driving (which necessarily include vehicle repair on rural routes) are a professional specialty, not a widely possessed life skill. Lengthy apprenticeships with sizable fees restrict entry, and every commercial driver I encountered was male. Since Asante rarely apprentice across gender lines, this effectively bars traders from bypassing drivers to operate their own transport. Only a handful had enough capital to buy a truck, and they reported difficulty in proper supervision of hired drivers. Transport owners often leave it up to the driver to contract for freight loads as well as passengers, but many male owners are ex-drivers familiar with booking practices and cheating techniques who can at least threaten to drive the truck themselves. The only case I heard of booking transport with the fleet owner involved a male exporter who operated outside the marketplace system.

Close noncommercial relations with drivers gave a few individual women traders easier access to transport. Those with drivers as husbands, lovers, brothers, or childhood friends had a great advantage, and women would change their commodities or supply areas readily to exploit such a contact. The woman paid the going rate for transport, in the cases I encountered, but did not expect cheating or overcharging. The driver would also send a message when he expected to be free, greatly reducing the search time which was such a burden on travelers. When their schedules did not coincide, the trader would deal with other drivers and vice versa. In several cases, small-scale traders sent goods unaccompanied with a friendly driver who would hand them over to an associate in Kumasi also known to him.

The same transport scarcity that forced travelers to work longer hours searching and waiting for trucks in 1979 and 1983 and cut into their profits with higher freight charges and spoilage losses paradoxically increased their power relative to their suppliers and buyers. Kumasi Central Market traders can find an available truck more easily because so many pass through the wholesale yards and lorry parks. They even have preferential access to trucks in smaller towns in the supply areas, where they make more attractive customers to the truck driver than the average small-town trader because they operate over longer distances and at higher capital levels.

Truck drivers themselves become very powerful figures in a rural context of severe transport shortage. When few vehicles ply a route compared to the demand for transport, they can set high fares and find customers to accept them. A trader typically looks for transport under time pressure because delays mean loss of income through late arrival and increased risk of spoilage. Farmers confronting the last or only vehicle serving their farm or village road that day are also in a highly vulnerable position for overcharging. Negotiations between traders and drivers in 1979 (described in a later chapter) clearly demonstrated the degree to which drivers capitalized on control over this key resource. Yam traders mobilized an organized national network in 1979 to contest raised freight charges, but the highly organized driver's union successfully held off their challenge with vague promises of future reconsideration.

Farmers' power relative to the traders they supply depends heavily on relative transport access for the two groups. Gore did a systematic study of pricing and marketing patterns in small farm villages near Koforidua just before the first of my fieldwork (Gore 1978). His results show that good road access correlated strongly with higher producer prices. Farmers who have a realistic possibility of taking goods directly to nearby village markets, even if they rarely do so, enjoy a much better bargaining position. Traders buying at the farmgate must pay competitive prices despite their small numbers in any given village. During the 1970s and 1980s, shrinking stocks of functioning vehicles and deteriorating roads constantly raised the numbers of farm villages without regular lorry service. Farmers would then have to make a special trip into town to arrange for a truck to pick up their crops, sometimes without success. They would have to pay for their own trip in, plus the truck's roundtrip journey, further increasing the gap they would tolerate between farmgate and urban price levels.

When transport conditions eased by 1989, direct access became easier between farm and urban center. Persons from either end of the distribution chain could bypass some of the intermediaries previously required. Kumasi traders began to buy at the farmgate in areas near Kumasi where they had previously bought in village periodic markets, since they could more easily get trucks to go out on nonmarket days. Villagers could bring their goods directly into Kumasi themselves more conveniently rather than selling to a Kumasi trader at the nearest market. Farmers themselves only came in from villages very near Kumasi, even after transport became more readily available. I noticed in 1983 and 1984 that farmers farther than one or two hours away from cities expressed little interest in marketing their goods personally. They said they found farmgate sales more convenient, since the all-day return trip would disrupt their work schedule. Reports from Latin America and Asia, in areas where transport was not a critical problem, confirm the rarity of farmers preferring to sell their goods directly in towns (Alexander 1987; Babb 1989).

Instead, farmgate sales were beginning to replace periodic markets as the primary channel for farmers selling foodstuffs in villages near Kumasi. Although Kumasi Central Market traders still came out on market day, the more successful ones used part of the day to meet farmers who were attending the market to shop, or sent messages to them through neighbors that they would return another day with a truck to make their major purchases. Although these women still bought local food crops at the market brought by villagers while they were there, fellow marketers who depended entirely on periodic market purchases complained bitterly that less goods were arriving. Public and semipublic transport to such farming districts was still more freely available on periodic market days than in between, but this also provided easier access to Kumasi for village traders who bought at home or collected from farm hamlets during the week. Traders based in the rural areas increased in visibility at the Kumasi Central Market wholesale yards in 1989, bringing goods purchased or advanced from their neighbors.

Kumasi Central Market traders in more commodities reported bypassing the regional periodic market at Techiman and buying or selling in smaller markets in the Northern and Upper Region towns. On the other hand, Kumasi Central Market traders found themselves increasingly bypassed as through transport became more reliable for outsiders. Traders from Accra and other coastal cities appeared in larger numbers in Techiman rather than buying in Kumasi to avoid arranging rural transport. Those Kumasi traders with the ability to finance longer-distance routes may benefit, but they are likely to squeeze out marginal rural and occasional traders on these longer routes. This concentration of trade may become complete enough that the transition from retailing to wholesaling through occasional traveling will only be practical by working as an agent or dependent of an established trader.

Conclusion

Tracing the control and distribution of resources critical to the functioning of the trading enterprise confirms the pivotal role of the wholesale yard and the traders associated with it. The relations of credit, information, and transport all are structured around these centers. The resident wholesalers in the yards extend credit in both directions to regulate the flow of capital. They manage the seasonal shifts in the direction of credit, from the farmers in the postharvest season and back to them in the preharvest season. They have the best information about local Kumasi Central Market conditions and individuals. Their continual contacts with travelers give the market its portals for information on other commercial locations and supply areas. The travelers themselves are also closely associated with the wholesale yards and base their power on their contacts there. The yards provide the steady volume of business required to support them as full-time specialists. The information they maintain, the credit they can exchange with farmers, and their preferential access to transport are sources of power because they can be turned to advantage in transactions in the wholesale yards.

The conspicuous power visible in the wholesale yard, with its piles of goods and swarms of buyers, is nonetheless vulnerable to competition and destruction from rival locations and systems. The same transport infrastructures and commercial networks that locate and centralize this power center in Kumasi Central Market set definite limits on its traders' control of these vital resources. The volatility of capital relations enables traders to send capital where it is most desperately needed, through credit patterns that ebb and flow seasonally with shifts in supply and demand. Permanent relations of dependency between those in distinct economic or geographic locations are undermined by the flexible response to seasonal needs; those travelers and wholesalers with significant capital reserves cannot preserve their dominant position throughout the year. Open access to skills and information through observation and participation makes it relatively straightforward for Kumasi traders to acquire what they need, but likewise keeps them from easily using secrets to exclude others. Traders suffered from the risks and inefficiencies of poor communication, but they coped through a diversification of sources that left them in no position to restrict access to the most critical points of information when communication improved.

The shifting political and economic environment exposes other kinds of vulnerability, since traders from large urban markets like Kumasi Central Market make such conspicuous symbolic and material targets. Their economic activities, and even their persons, focus tensions generated by relations between rural and urban areas, between waged and unwaged workers, between advantaged and disadvantaged regions of the country, and between Ghana and the international economy. The terms of trade in local foodstuffs and imports provide the most obvious measure of historical shifts in these power balances, and most population groups buy both from market traders. Travelers and wholesalers from the Kumasi wholesale yards are undoubtedly key local participants in price negotiations, so they are alleged to have only too much control over the flow of imports and rural food supplies.

The dominance of Kumasi Central Market traders has also been proven vulnerable to fluctuations in the technology of transport and communications. The regional road network creates a comparatively rigid infrastructure that channels traffic through Kumasi from all corners of the country. Traders based in the wholesale yards take full advantage of their favorable access to transport, as to information and capital, but lose ground just as quickly when conditions change. When transport shortages gave drivers the upper hand, Kumasi traders could not use their geographical position or frequent traveler status to prevent price gouging, nor could they preserve privileged access in the face of increased supply when more vehicles and fuel became available. The intense regional dominance of Kumasi Central Market depends on transport being neither too easy nor too difficult. The flexible transport and information networks that enabled them to survive difficult conditions also kept alternative distributive channels viable, namely, those which could bypass or undermine the dominance of Kumasi Central Market traders in the surrounding territory.

The inherent instability of this dominance results from the unstable meshing of systems of commercial domination with other systems that interpenetrate the marketplace system and interlock with its internal hierarchy at particular moments. As intermediary figures in a number of international and national economic configurations, its market traders remain extremely vulnerable to unfavorable power balances in relations they mediate, for example between farmers and exporters or between national and international finance. The diversity of options within the marketplace system allows traders to change their operations in response to rapid shifts in these wider economic configurations, but these individual strategies are not without cost and risk. Traders establish relations inside and outside of the market to manage these risks, smooth out these fluctuations, and coordinate these seasonal and episodic responses. They work through formal and informal groups of fellow traders to preserve more of the benefits of the long-term continuities in the trading system.

6 WE KNOW OURSELVES

Personalized commercial relations with colleagues and steady customers offer traders definite advantages for capital accumulation and enterprise survival. The impersonal transactions available in the market give traders access to the basic resources needed to start and maintain a small-scale business, and the majority of traders surveyed get by without personalized ties to either buyers or suppliers or membership in an organized group. As fieldwork wore on, however, I noticed that the traders who accumulated more and survived serious crises better had a greater tendency to have stronger vertical linkages with individual customers or stronger horizontal ties with colleagues in formal groups or informal sets than others. Traders without customer networks often mentioned trying to cultivate them in order to expand their volume of business.

A closer look at what customers and colleagues actually do for each other reveals why. Personalized commercial relations give traders a chance to improve their control and utilization of critical market resources such as credit, information, and transport without putting additional capital at risk. Customer relations also reduce traders' actual risk by moderating fluctuations in supply and demand at the individual level through coordinating deliveries and purchases. Even though the majority of traders did not participate personally in such relations, they found their impersonal transactions deeply affected because these relations were strategically located to pass economic fluctuations on to them. Ideological attacks on market traders from the state in 1979 and 1982 singled out these personalized ties as a key to serious abuse and exploitation by traders. Either bilateral (dyadic) customer relations or multilateral relations with colleagues supposedly permitted individual traders and organized commodity groups to fix prices and exclude farmers or outside traders from free access to consumers or inflation and low farm productivity. The controversy surrounding these relations makes it important to assess exactly how much and what kind of power commodity group members and customers actually exercised in Kumasi over each other and over outsiders.

The terms colleague and customer take on a specialized meaning here, referring to two specific models for personalized commercial relations current throughout Kumasi Central Market. For the most widespread model, a vertical dyadic bond between buyer and seller, I retain the word customer, which is used reciprocally for both of them by Ghanaians speaking English and by traders otherwise speaking Twi. It can be applied at any level of the market: for example, between traveler and wholesaler, between wholesaler and retailer, or between retailer and consumer. For formal or informal peer group relations, I use the word colleague—to make an analogy to the relative equality and shared professional identity in these horizontal relations. Traders referring to their own colleagues use the name of the commodity they all sell, for example, *bayerefo* (literally, yam people), or they will call them neighbors and friends. These two models are the most important structurally as well as numerically; other options appear incidentally as isolated cases. I avoid the terms patron and client, although they are often used for similar commercial relationships elsewhere, because they presume an asymmetry which is not a standard feature here.

Voluntary personalized relationships are found in many commercial and noncommercial contexts and are quite a common response to conditions that constantly threaten economic or personal disaster. They reduce risk significantly by making transactions more predictable and controllable, if not always more advantageous. Socially or economically vulnerable groups commonly attach themselves as clients to a powerful patron who offers protection in return for their loyalty and service. One widely discussed complex of examples often involved godparenthood, or *compadrazgo,* when Ladino patrons both protected and exploited indigenous Indio clients in many parts of Latin America (Mintz and Wolf 1950; Beals 1975; Buechler 1973; Swetnam 1988). In the deteriorating economic conditions of Zaire, the asymmetry of commercial client relationships has increased as producers become more dependent on traders for market access (MacGaffey 1987; Russell 1989).

The fact that dependent clientship did not dominate Kumasi Central Market during the difficult period of the late 1970s and early 1980s seems to break this pattern. In fact, Kumasi traders secured many of the benefits linked elsewhere to clientship through egalitarian relations among and between groups of peers. These relations with fellow members of commodity groups and informal sets of market neighbors and competitors were actually more sustainable by traders with relatively modest resources through the intense upheavals of this period than more asymmetrical or hierarchical dyadic relations. Participants in these more diffuse, group-based relations retained more flexibility and made fewer absolute commitments than partners in dyadic relations. The constant influence of egalitarian multilateral relations also acted to keep dyadic relations more equal. When these were repressed and their economic basis undermined later in the 1980s, dependent relations became more prevalent.

Exploring just how influential specific kinds of personalized relations were in Kumasi revealed that they were concentrated in pivotal locations within the marketplace system. At the upper end of the trading spectrum, the minority of traders who accumulate significant capital by local standards rely heavily on customers, and others aspire to having them. At the lower end, personalized relations can be used to cushion marginal enterprises from the full effects of business reversals, which frequently bring the threat of bankruptcy. Horizontal commodity groups perform some of the same functions for middle-size traders. Both customer and colleague relations intensify at points where the marketplace system articulates with other economic sectors and other axes of domination—in farmgate buying, in buying from and selling to formal sector institutions, and in urban/rural contact, as through traveling traders.

It becomes important for traders to construct voluntary, personalized commercial relationships in contexts where access to scarce information, profitable or productive social relations, credit, transport, or other facilities is necessary but cannot be ensured either within kin networks or impersonally. Mutual obligations remain relatively flexible and negotiable within these voluntary relations, as compared with the more absolute obligations between kin or commercial partners or the more absolute authority over employees and formerly over slaves. For example, a trader is liable for debts incurred by employees, agents, or full partners. She need not cover debts or losses by customers or colleagues, although she may lose through credit default or agree to extend extra credit or make other concessions to help them stay in business.

One thing is certain, Kumasi Central Market traders do not emphasize these two types of personalized relations because they are the only commercial patterns they know. The long history of commercialization in the region leads one to expect sophisticated trading relations in Kumasi. Traders and farmers are familiar with a range of commercial relations that stretches from barter through periodic markets to Western-style cooperatives and state marketing boards. Discussions of the relative merits of alternative commercial relationships among traders and nontraders revealed concrete knowledge of many of these, based on previous or occasional participation, observation of visiting or foreign traders, historical accounts, and deliberate investigation. Traders mention costs, benefits, and historical reasons when attributing currently dominant trading patterns to economic or political constraints or when advising for or against particular choices or strategies.

Colleagues

Formal groups or informal sets of colleagues defined by commodity and by location constitute the dominant structure of the marketplace system in Kumasi Central Market and throughout southern Ghana. They help members manage information and credit requirements and allow risk reduction and sharing on a group basis. Fluid group membership, even in formal groups with registered lists of dues-paying members, allows individuals to continually drop out, return, and oscillate between groups in different locations or with different commodity identities. This mobility helps the groups to function effectively in a very fluid economic and political situation while also preventing abuse of their collective power.

The limits and functions of both formal groups and informal sets of colleagues in Kumasi Central Market are more clearly defined by considering the information a trader needs to bargain effectively and to extend credit when necessary. Traders who habitually make the same type of transaction in the same location soon become known to each other and to their opposite numbers in those transactions. Group members say, "we know ourselves," whether or not they have a formal group structure with officially registered members. Each location hosts or defines more than one distinguishable set of colleagues—for example, wholesalers and retailers in the wholesale yards—although these sets may coalesce for some purposes and even constitute one formal group. Peer groups of colleagues emerge not only among traders, but among farmers or other nontraders who frequent identifiable commercial locations.

The wholesale yards provide a central orientation for whole strings of such sets who each "know themselves" but not all of the others. Yams provide a particularly full example of this. The resident wholesalers and local retailers who constantly buy there join the yam commodity group associated with it and expect the trust-based conveniences of delayed payment or delivery extended to all in good standing. The travelers who bring foodstuffs there from producing areas form another, looser group and maintain a subgroup within the same yam traders' association, with their own recognized leader. Each traveler also knows a set of reputable commercial yam farmers in each of the distant surplus producing areas she frequents. Those farmers know a set of traders from different towns who buy in their area and are considered worthy of credit and other mutual favors. Truck drivers and head carriers who specialize in transporting yams also constitute groups that support or confront Kumasi traders on specific issues, such as freight rates. Many travelers keep up known and registered traveler status at more than one regionally important yam market, such as Techiman or Ejura. Leading yam traders from different towns also meet occasionally when they need to negotiate with drivers or install a new local leader.

Being known as a group member carries significant commercial advantages. Colleagues can trust each other to conform to bargaining etiquette, thus streamlining transactions. They know the others will reciprocate favors and pass on helpful information, thus reducing risk. Both retailers and wholesalers take messages and placate customers for each other and watch each others' goods. In serious public crises, such as the 1979 currency exchange, group members met to exchange information and to discuss and coordinate ways of dealing with it.

Immediate market neighbors exchange some of these services on a smaller scale, but not the credit and other services related to buying and selling or the most important information and policy coordination necessarily linked to specific commodities. For example, neighbors from mixed-retail areas cannot help their market neighbors in the wholesale yard or other buying locations since they buy in different yards. They may still develop tight bonds through daily mutual support, but these are based on watching children and goods for each other and sharing food and sympathy (see also Babb 1987; Szanton 1972). Those who buy outside the market cannot exchange information on conditions in their supply areas since they buy from different supply areas. In specialized retail areas, commodity group ties encompass and reinforce those with neighbors.

The important discriminating role of information appears to contradict the apparent ready availability of information about supply and demand within the market boundaries. Given the open layout of Ghanaian markets, the major limitation to mutual information is physical presence. Visual inspection readily reveals the amount of goods and the numbers of buyers and sellers available, even to casual passersby. It would be impossible to maintain the level of deception Geertz reports in Moroccan bazaars, where buyers depend on their contacts to find out when goods have arrived (Geertz, Geertz, and Rosen 1979). Hoarding and concealment of goods and transactions takes place outside the market, in homes and office buildings. High levels of price information result in high levels of price uniformity within a given location.

It is precisely this factor of physical presence which functions as a boundary marker between collegial sets much more effectively than deliberate exclusionary practices, which are rare. A traveler bringing supplies to a wholesale yard where she maintains group ties can freely sell what she brings without offending group prerogatives, but technical considerations make this inadvisable. She could collect fairly accurate supply and demand information within a few hours of arrival, but her goods would deteriorate, and her fatigue after a night on the road would impair her bargaining ability. Selling through a wholesaler puts her back on the road more quickly and in better health. She can check her wholesaler's performance at her leisure by comparison with her own traveler colleagues. She concentrates her main information-gathering activities in her preferred supply areas. This information is not accessible to the resident wholesaler, who must be present in the wholesale yard during all normal working hours to offer information and the other services that attract and keep her customers. Customers buying bulk food for institutions or cooked-food preparation likewise save time for their main work and reduce the risk of acting on incomplete information by using wholesalers as intermediaries. Dyadic customer relations develop only after a lengthy period of impersonal or collegial transactions without mutual commitment.

The boundaries created by information considerations are indeterminate, allowing for intermediate levels of marginality and inclusion. This membership instability paradoxically gives the commodity group structure increased stability in the long run. The permeable group boundaries constantly admit new members, who only gradually filter through to the dense network of relations at the center with maximum information access. Newcomers and less successful traders remain marginal, along with those who deliberately maintain membership in more than one local group. Sponsorship by an established trader helps a new entrant to penetrate more rapidly to the core, but the lack of defined internal barriers permits individuals without sponsors to enter on their own initiative when conditions allow. Only a few wholesaler groups controlling confined yard spaces successfully exclude new entrants and limit their total numbers, and they face constant competition from unaffiliated traders operating out of open locations elsewhere in the market complex.

The tomato yard, for example, was dominated by fewer large wholesalers than the yam yard, but they still did not control total supplies to Kumasi. In the rainy season, substantial amounts of tomatoes reached the mixed-retail areas directly from nearby villages and periodic markets. The Kejetia Lorry Park developed an impressive tomato wholesale yard, as did the large neighborhood market at Bantama. A few irrigated locations dominated dry-season supplies for the whole country, with these being sold through monopolistic companies of traders operating out of each supply area. Although supplies at that season arrived only at the Central Market wholesale yards, the locus of control was in the supply areas rather than among the Kumasi resident wholesalers.

Preserving a discriminatory distinction between core and marginal members in the collegial group permits greater elasticity of response than either could provide alone. The marginal members absorb more than their share of economic fluctuations. As this collegial group sheds or attracts them, they can survive by shifting to and from other comparable groups. The core group of long-established local members can remain unchanged for many years, reaping the benefits of longer experience and longer mutual observation of both successful transactions and disputes, but also preserving these social resources for the market system as a whole. Their continuing presence permits very rapid revival of market institutions when conditions improve, since they then welcome back former participants they remember well.

High levels of information within the collegial set also allow it to govern credit with considerable efficiency. A wholesaler can extend credit to one of the known retailers with confidence, even though there is no exclusive dyadic relationship between them. She knows her buying habits, credit history, and outstanding debts by exchanging information with fellow wholesalers. In case of trouble, she can intercept the debtor on her return to renew supplies from another wholesaler or visit her local retail stall to harass her. Other retailers will encourage payment to protect their general reputations, and other wholesalers will cooperate in penalizing a persistent defaulter by refusing credit and other favors.

Credit was extended when conditions required it to any member in good standing of the appropriate known set, in contrast to its continuous presence in many customer relations. For very perishable foodstuffs, such as tomatoes, rapid clearance of incoming goods during the peak morning hours demanded nearly universal short-term credit. Known buyers had porters carry off their boxes immediately, leaving the sellers to come around to their stalls to collect and count the money during a slack period later the same day. For most local food crops, the direction of longer-term credit reversed seasonally. One yam wholesaler complained of having to sell yams on credit because so many were coming in during the glut season. The traveler had to wait in town for her to collect from retailers after some yams had sold, because a farmer had given her the yams on credit and she could not go back without money to pay for them. During the dry season, the same Kumasi wholesalers were desperate for supplies to keep their capital turning over, so they sent money out with travelers to buy yams for them, and travelers advanced money to farmers for harvest expenses. Rather than establishing domination of the debtor by the lender, traders experienced the need to give credit as a sign of the current weakness of their commercial position.

Credit, dispute settlement, and bargaining procedures all assume a high level of mutual information among a set of colleagues. Buyers and sellers prefer to patronize their wholesale yards and specialized retail areas rather than deal directly with each other because the supply and demand information available there reduces their risk of accepting a bad bargain. Since credit is necessary to move goods at certain times of year, transactors without the information needed to identify creditworthy persons could not survive those periods. The orange group employs credit recorders and collectors, which allows individual sellers to rely more on group knowledge and influence over defaulters. Where recognized commodity group leaders settle disputes on credit and other issues, traders not "known" to the appropriate leader cannot easily bring cases or defend themselves, since she cannot easily judge their actions accurately or bring pressure on them to comply with her decisions.

Farmers and travelers in a supply district also manage mutual credit through collegial sets. The reputable commercial farmers in an area can normally obtain credit from any of the traders who have been coming there long enough to know them. In the same way, traders operating regularly in the area in season become known to local farmers, whether the individual trader is based locally, in Kumasi, or in another town. They also obtain goods on credit from various farmers on occasion, as long as their general credit history has been good. Both farmers and travelers benefit from such credit and retain some control through it. One of the major benefits is influence over the timing of the transaction. Traders with loans outstanding can request delivery of goods from debtors when their supplies run short. Farmers also offer credit to move their goods quickly when they need money urgently or when spoilage threatens. Since the predominant direction of credit reverses seasonally, neither side gains permanent ascendancy.

If either party manipulates the credit terms beyond generally accepted limits she risks social and economic ostracism: in effect, loss of collegial status. These credit transactions may be repeated in subsequent years, but they do not bind either the trader or the farmer to deal only with each other in the future. The farmer who defaults will not easily get advances from other traders later, and vice versa. If the trader demands excessive price or timing concessions, the farmer can sell elsewhere without loss of reputation and refund the loan in cash. The trader would lose reputation instead and later find other farmers unwilling to advance her goods on credit or offer other favors. The trader must forgo immediate advantage to protect her long-term investment in local social relations and information networks, as long as she has competitors in that district. She cannot move to a new supply area and hope to trade as profitably.

Travelers I accompanied on trading trips were well aware that their courtesy, honesty, and good behavior were under observation by the community at large. Yam travelers were careful to speak politely and sympathetically at all times. One young woman visited and cooked with a farm family she had no plans to buy from that year. She explained that they were old friends of her mother and grandmother, and she relied on them to arrange contacts with other farmers. On another trip, a vegetable trader carried back a large tree trunk as firewood for the aged mother of a farmer she bought from on other trips. Yam traders made sure to be conspicuously incensed at a flagrant case of credit fraud brought by a yam farmer before their Kumasi *ohemma.* They openly expressed fears that farmers from that area would begin to refuse them credit, or even bring their goods in themselves, if they could not get satisfactory enforcement of traders' debts.

Horizontal ties between colleagues provide essential support to credit through information and dispute settlement services, but they do not themselves transmit capital. This contrasts with Dewey's description of tightly knit sets of *bakul* wholesalers in Java, who regularly pool their money to make bulk purchases in order to disperse their individual risk (Dewey 1962). Yoruba traders also bought bundles of cloth or large baskets of kola together, taking advantage of the wholesale price but then breaking the unit to sell separately (Trager 1976). All capital transfers observed in the Ghanaian marketplace system were vertical, between buyer and seller, through credit on goods or cash advances.

Colleagues not only gain mutual accreditation, but access to some significant economies of scale through cooperation. For example, it is traveling traders operating out of the same wholesale yard who often get together in a village to fill a whole truck and head straight back to Kumasi rather than waiting for passenger transport. This was critically important to yam travelers when dwindling supplies or cash-flow problems meant they might have to wait weeks to accumulate a full truck load, since their goods were too bulky and fragile to take by passenger truck. Yoruba yam traders in Nigeria even developed stable small groups of travelers who shared trucks back with their yams (Trager 1976). Yam traders maintain a truck parking lot in Kumasi where travelers can leave their full trucks with a watchman until it is their turn to unload. The yam group also supports the services of the full-time market porters who provide expert counting, handling, and delivery services.

Yam carriers using wooden carts had the most tightly organized group of carriers observed. They have a recognized association of their own whose elder negotiated set fees per hundred yams with the yam traders' leader. This group of men contracts to unload every truck that pulls into the yard. They are paid by the seller to deliver the sold hundreds to the buyer's place of business within Kumasi Central Market or place of transport elsewhere. Their unwritten contract excludes only other carters, however. Traders still can and do hire young women head carriers, who carry twenty or so yams at a time (depending on size) in enamel basins. These can walk more directly, down stairways leading from the wholesale yard into the yam retail section, a particular advantage when heavy rains force the carts to take long detours.

The carters' years of experience reduces risk considerably. They count and sort the yams by size, throwing and stacking them speedily but carefully to minimize breakage. Younger men work under the supervision of older men. Each cart-load contains five or six distinct hundreds of different sizes and prices. They know the stalls of the Kumasi Central Market retailers and can reliably deliver the correct hundred to the correct stall. In cases of short count, their evidence is conclusive in disputes between buyer and seller. When they went on strike for higher fees, traders found it difficult to unload and dispatch the normal quantity of yams. The carriers' elder was received with respect for formal negotiations with the yam elders, but they successfully put him off with vague promises of future raises.

Collegial relations did not function effectively to restrict access to key locations such as the wholesale yards in Kumasi, despite the acute pressure on space there. Commodity group leaders have little control over allocation of market locations. Overcrowding prevents them from having empty stalls at their disposal, which they could hope to distribute to favorites. On the other hand, the constant competition from locations outside the specialized area makes it useless to exclude newcomers. Refusing entrance to individual potential traders would only drive them into the more loosely organized lorry parks and mixed-retail areas. Commodity group leaders gain more by welcoming new traders willing to recognize their authority. Trager concluded from several sources that Yoruba market women in Nigeria also have open but compulsory entry into their commodity groups (Trager 1976).

The situation in Kumasi Central Market contrasts with anecdotal reports from Accra and some other Ghanaian locations that commodity groups operate as cartels to exclude or ration access by outsiders. Tomato traders in Accra's Makola #2 market, the major location for vegetable wholesaling, scheduled deliveries by women traders from specific supply towns on different days of the week and limited how many boxes they could deliver each day to even out supplies and maintain price levels during the glut period. These practices were recorded when traders from one of the supply towns complained to a government agency. The overwhelming regional dominance of the capital city as a center of demand meant that travelers did not have a realistic option of bypassing it or its single primary wholesale location.

Reports from other markets in and around Accra show that at least one group of colleagues became so cohesive that they could switch commodities as a group. When Accra's Makola #1 market was demolished in 1979, its wealthy and powerful traders in cloth and provisions were advised to begin trading local foodstuffs to make an honest living. Fish smokers from nearby coastal fishing villages reported in 1983 that these traders had moved en masse into fresh and smoked fish trading, whose large volume and price variations offered substantial profits for their substantial capital. The fish smokers liked the change, citing the convenience of selling to them in the village rather than having to transport smoked fish to market towns near and far, as the "Makola women" pushed aside smaller-scale fish wholesalers in villages and towns surrounding Accra. Their economic weight was also sufficient to push their way into Makola #2, Accra's leading fish wholesale location, creating a domino effect. The smoked-fish sellers already established at Makola #2 in turn moved in on those in the smaller suburban Malata market. This market also specializes in local foodstuffs and has a strong biweekly periodic cycle. The Makola #2 fish traders intimidated those at Malata into allowing them to trade there on the main market days by threatening to drive them out of business. No Kumasi Central Market groups observed could exert this kind of influence over other locations.

Monopolistic practices based on descent also were not confirmed by interviews in Kumasi or the survey. Although almost half of traders did obtain their stalls through relatives, this practice did not result in exclusive kin-based trading groups. The absence of large family enterprises or networks in general ruled out control of substantial sections of the market by a few extended families. Kinship recruitment therefore spread access widely rather than concentrating it in a few specialized trading families.

One comparatively rare form of horizontal grouping did have a rigid membership with the potential for exclusivity. Kumasi traders used the English word "company" to refer to formal partnership organizations with strict equality between members. Several of these encountered were simply two-partner enterprises. Profits were divided in half or each partner retained responsibility for his or her own purchases and profits. They gained some economies of scale by sharing transport or facilities and coordinating deliveries. Small companies like this had no monopoly potential in most commodities.

Where the conditions of trade favored a high degree of concentration, companies did become cartels. Tomato traders on the long routes between the irrigation projects of the Upper Region and southern cities have successfully established limited monopolies on this basis. In the markets around Bolgatanga, companies from Accra, Kumasi, Tamale, etc. buy in competition with each other, but each monopolizes access to its own city. Traders from Ada, where the Volta River makes irrigation possible, also formed a company to handle sales to Accra, their nearest large city. The tomato companies charge high entry fees, limit numbers, and enforce quotas for individual purchases. Unlike tomato traders based in Accra markets, they do not directly control access to any Kumasi locations by traders from other sources of supply. However, in the late dry season the Bolga companies have little competition in Kumasi because other sources of tomatoes literally dry up. The current leader of the Bolga women's company is a daughter of the former Kumasi tomato leader, further reinforcing their connection, although she was not the original leader of the Bolga group.

Such monopolies have been vulnerable to challenge, however. On the Kumasi-Bolga route, a men's company started by local men predated the women's company started by Kumasi women. One of the founders described to me how they approached the men's company leaders in the 1950s, threatening to drive them out of business unless they shared access to Upper Region markets with the women. The compromise agreement has the two companies each sending a truck to Kumasi on alternate days. Kumasi traders further bought shares in both these companies from retiring members. Each share entitled the holder to equal space in the truck their company sent on the twelve-hour trip to Kumasi, under the escort of one member.

Restricted sources of supply in the dry-season have generated similar tomato companies for delivery to Accra, the capital city, as well. On the Ada-Accra route, the overwhelming dominance of one single destination city meant that the Ada women were dependent on access to the Accra tomato wholesaling facilities, located at Makola #2. It was the wholesalers there who enjoyed monopoly status, assigning volume quotas and delivery days to the companies from Ada, Bolga, and other supply areas. The Kumasi tomato *ohemma* was familiar with these Accra policies and remarked rather wistfully that she wished they were able to enforce such regulations in Kumasi.

Kumasi Central Market wholesale and retail traders' practices conformed to an ideology of open access, which they expressed forcefully, based on the imperative of survival. Already in 1978 traders recognized that the unprecedented number of new entrants was cutting into the profit levels of established traders. Still, both leaders and followers said that any woman had a moral right to try to earn a living for herself and her children, as long as she respects market conventions. These conventions do include some costly ones, such as funeral donations, that bar the poorest traders from full participation in the highly organized groups. However, many yam traders in financial straits hang on without fulfilling all of these obligations on the strength of apology, just as some traders from Moslem backgrounds remain members though unable to fulfill Akan funeral attendance obligations. Expulsion from the yam group was only mentioned when repeated defiance of market norms of dispute settlement made one trader an economic and moral liability, and then it never even reached the point of verbal threat.

By 1989, traders had extended the survival argument to cover the increasing numbers of male traders. Market leaders explaining the presence of men in the yam and tomato wholesale yards, previously all-female locations, said these men now also had no jobs available to them, for lack of education. Even when a few of these men did not conform acceptably to group norms of market etiquette, the yam traders felt unable to exclude them from access to wholesale yards or other desirable locations.

Customer Relations

Kumasi traders also recognize and value stable bilateral or dyadic relations, which have a long history in Ghana and West Africa generally. Traders refer to both regular buyers and regular suppliers with the English word *customer,* describing their specific tasks with Twi verb phrases, such as, "she brings me goods" or "she always buys from me." The word customer was apparently adopted from its use by British traders on the coast in precolonial times, when they regularly bought slaves and local goods from the same African magnates who regularly bought imports from them. Living Kumasi traders associated it especially with the passbook system linking import firms with their regular customers, which flourished in Kumasi from the 1910s through the 1960s.

Customers' obligations are mutual but not identical. On one side, the relationship is exclusive, with the buyer or supplier dealing only with her customer whenever she comes to the market. This exclusivity is not universal; in Java, a wholesaler's regular suppliers will be casual suppliers on less frequent visits to other wholesalers when supplies were plentiful (Alexander 1987). On the other side, the relationship is necessarily nonexclusive; if the Kumasi trader restricted herself to that one customer she would be useless even to that one, since she could not maintain a sufficient volume of business to meet her needs reliably. Instead, the Kumasi resident wholesaler or retailer must be prepared to buy or sell whenever her customer appears in the market. Other aspects of these relationships include providing reliable price and quality standards, credit, and the exchange of small services and information. These reduce important incidental risks, but the main risk addressed is not being able to do business due to lack of supplies or buyers. This principle makes sense of seasonal shifts in customer relations in Java, where they become more dominant and more hierarchical at the beginning and end of the harvest season when supplies are more scarce (Alexander 1987). Except for actual debts, these mutual obligations cannot be enforced in Kumasi, but either party can break off the relationship if she is not satisfied.

Attracting and holding customers helped wholesalers accumulate capital by smoothing out short-term fluctuations in supply and demand through coordinating the buying and selling decisions of their customers. Wholesalers sent messages to customers among the traveling traders advising them to rush or hold off on their arrival with new supplies, depending on Kumasi supply conditions. They could not compel compliance, but travelers usually tried to cooperate because they shared the profits from favorable prices. Under the current difficulties of communication and supervision, coordination was often accomplished more easily through customer networks rather than through true subordinates. With less risk from unexpected price fluctuations, the wholesaler with customers could reduce the amount of capital she held back to cover possible losses, invest more fully, and accumulate more quickly.

When a customer did arrive with goods at a bad time, she relied on her own wholesaler to make special efforts to dispose of her goods and minimize her losses, if necessary by extending credit or making other concessions to her own buyer customers. The wholesaler's customers among institutional suppliers and retailers helped ensure a steady basic level of purchases that made this protection possible for her traveler customers. Conversely, the retailers and institutional customers counted on her traveler customers to bring in at least some supplies when they were scarce. If necessary, wholesalers will hold scarce supplies for regular buyers' arrival or even buy them from colleagues for resale at cost. The guaranteed turnover reduced risk for the wholesaler's customers as well as herself, ideally promoting everyone's prosperity.

Through customer relations, independent traders share some control over each others' capital and labor through voluntary cooperation and coordination. This gives them access to some of the benefits of vertical integration, without its disadvantages and rigidities. In fact, the points of division of labor or specialization remain consistent whether the personnel involved are subordinates, customers, or completely unassociated. The number of tasks an individual can manage depends on the configuration of information and transport and the concentration of supply and demand for that specific commodity. Contractual commitment to a more permanent relationship seems to be a handicap under the current unpredictable trading conditions, which demand considerable flexibility. More rigid, hierarchical relations collapse when participants are simply unable to fulfill their promises. Autonomous customers have the authority as goods owners to respond flexibly and rapidly at various points along the distribution chain. Those with initiative and shrewd insight are valued assets for the long run of accumulation and can renegotiate their obligations retroactively if necessary.

Substantial traders typically combine a high volume of both impersonal transactions and transactions with customers. A leading onion trader, for example, maintained diverse supply relationships for different sources of supply. She still uses links with her hometown, Dunkwa, but not for the greater part of her business. She grew up there, where her mother and all of her sisters farmed, and still has a cocoa farm there. She married a hometown boy but they moved to Kumasi, and she began by traveling to the nearby villages herself to buy onions to sell in Kumasi. When she traveled, she shopped for extra food and left all but the youngest child at home in Kumasi with her eldest daughter, aged eight or ten. Even at that time, she also bought onions from the extreme southeast, around Keta. Their trucks came to the market in Kumasi, and "you could buy if you wanted some," that is, without knowing anyone, just like now.

After she got too old to travel, she relied more on dyadic relations.

She gives her money to "young girls" to go and buy with, who include some of her children and some nonrelatives. One daughter had gone to nearby Mampong to buy some shallots, but those she was currently selling were from Bosumtwe, in the opposite direction. She remarked that she has a separate set of customers from each supply area. For example, she has good customers in Kwahu, between Kumasi and Accra, where the crop would come in soon. "Even if you give them money in advance, they will still show up with the onions." Another customer had brought her small red onions from the northern border town of Bawku. She regularly bought larger red onions from farther north, in Mossi territory, but they were not in yet.

With customers, traders intensify the trust and exchange of services seen with reputable members of their complementary sets. Cheating or deception on quality should not occur. Prices offered should follow current levels with minimal bargaining. This trust substantially reduces time spent on inspection of goods, price comparison, search and bargaining. For example, orange hawkers buying regularly from a customer can return oranges found too soft for peeling for replacement the following day. Given their minuscule profit margins, this is an important privilege for hawkers.

Seemingly trivial services can be important in reducing or preventing losses and costs, for example, storing customers' purchases while they shop or having them carried to the truck stop. One cooked-food seller was too ill to come to market for more than a week, but well enough to cook and sell food from her house as usual. Because she bought from regular customers, she could send her young child to purchase her usual supplies from them and adjust any outstanding balance when she recovered. This maintained her income and her relations with her own steady customers. Customers can also ask for extra credit temporarily to recover from a business or personal disaster, such as a theft. The majority of traders operate at such low capital levels that relatively minor incidents can put them out of business.

Several analogous systems of relations using reciprocal local terminology implying a more egalitarian relationship have been fruitfully analyzed elsewhere within the literature on clientship. The most detailed presentations include the Yoruba *onibara* relation described by Trager, the Javanese *bakul* relations described by Dewey, Geertz and Alexander, and the Filipino *suki* relation described by Szanton and Davis (Trager 1981b; Dewey 1962; Geertz 1963; Alexander 1987; Szanton 1972; Davis 1973). It bears such a close resemblance to relations described for Haiti and Jamaica that a direct legacy from West African models seems plausible (Mintz 1957; Katzin 1959). The use of a terminology of equality is consistent with the content of these relations, since information, credit, and unpaid services pass in both directions.

The reciprocal terminology used in Kumasi Central Market masks the one-sided exclusivity of many customer relationships which carries a potential for exploitation. Resident wholesalers in particular try to coordinate the behavior of supplier and buyer clients to achieve a steadier flow of goods. This is essential for their own capital accumulation, but this personal benefit is tolerated by their customers because they also benefit from more reliable supply or demand. Mutual benefit need not imply equality. For example, Barnes describes Lagos, Nigeria, neighborhood patrons coordinating clients' actions for mutual benefit in electoral politics and land litigation (Barnes 1986).

Patterns of access to particularly scarce resources dominate the structure of clientship, making such ties essential for some locations and irrelevant to others. For example, in Moroccan bazaars traders buy and sell through clientship to bridge gaps in information on supplies and prices (Geertz, Geertz, and Rosen 1979). Hausa traders move through Nigeria and West Africa along a network of landlords providing local accommodation, credit, information, and bargaining services (Cohen 1969; Hill 1966; Schildkrout 1978a). Filipino vegetable traders depend on Chinese storekeepers' links to urban demand centers through their kin associates (Davis 1973). Dewey stresses the importance in Java of peer relations between wholesalers who depend on vertical client relations for other purposes (Dewey 1962). Dependence on individual patrons is muted if alternative patrons are present and accessible.

Culturally based asymmetries can generate or exaggerate commercial clientship by defining barriers to personal access and information flow. Throughout Latin America, Ladino patrons base their dominance on language and social skills that exclude or victimize Indios (Smith 1972; Chinas 1973; Buechler 1973; Seligmann 1989). The Ladino patrons offer protection from dangers largely created by people like themselves. In the same way, political officials or soldiers in Zaire protect individual illegal traders from arrest and arrange licenses (MacGaffey 1987 and 1991; Russell 1989). In colonial Rwanda clientship between Hutu and Tutsi became both more unequal and more necessary as land rights deteriorated under colonial rule (Newbury 1988).

The brittle relations between Asante market women and their regular customers substantially reduce the potential for abuse of the relationship. The length of customer relationships they reported, two to four years, is less than half the median length of time they had been in their present trade, 7.3 years. Customers readily compare notes on each other's performance with their own colleagues, so that neither partner can consistently maintain terms out of line with those offered by potential rivals. Customers can be rather easily replaced because they can be recruited from the familiar colleague set and need not share other ties. Traders select their customers in the market from among those sets of buyers and suppliers with whom they have dealt regularly. Like Yoruba traders, they rarely socialize with customers outside the marketplace or the trading trip (Trager 1981b).

This pattern contrasts sharply with Robertson's findings for Accra, where most of the fish, produce, bead, cloth, and kenkey traders depended on relatives and husbands for access to customer relations, although in different ways for each commodity (Robertson 1984). Kumasi traders reported noncommercial ties with only 3 percent of buyer and 16 percent of supplier customers, whether as relatives, neighbors, friends, or hometown folks (see table 6.1). Almost two-thirds had no relatives trading in their commodity as potential customers (61.9 per-

Table 6.1 Traders with Regular Clients

Number of Clients among Suppliers or Buyers		
Number	Suppliers	Buyers
None	50.0	48.5
One	14.6	.4
2–9	31.8	29.7
10–19	1.9	10.6
20 or more	1.7	10.8
Duration of Clientship with Present Clients in General*		
Years	Suppliers	Buyers
One or less	26.6	33.3
2–4	32.7	31.5
5–9	19.4	19.4
10 or more	21.3	15.8
Client Recruitment of Present Clients in General		
Method	Suppliers	Buyers
Came with business	66.7	60.5
Met in market	17.4	36.4
Relatives	7.2	2.7
Others	4.1	.5

* Traders reporting no clients are not included in percentages
SOURCE: 1979 Kumasi Central Market Survey

cent) and 20.9 percent had only one (see table 8.7). Large family networks were extremely rare, and even rarer among women than among men.

When Kumasi traders accumulate large numbers of dyadic relations, some will be with relatives and some not. Likewise, some relatives generally remain outside a trader's own commercial network. One tomato trader, whose mother also had sold tomatoes, had ten children, but only two daughters sold tomatoes. One of these was an independent retailer, while the other traveled up to Bolga seasonally and sold through her as a wholesaler. One son also sold her tomatoes wholesale on a commission basis, and three others were carriers for her. She employed two other male carriers and had ten other people who brought her tomatoes, besides four who brought her garden eggs and three who brought her chili peppers.

Traders' attitudes about customer relations parallel in some respects Asante attitudes to marriage. A long, satisfactory relationship is ideal in both cases, but a short, bad relationship is considered better than a long, bad relationship. Both parties should seek mediation and make sincere efforts to improve the relationship before reluctantly breaking it off and particularly before approaching possible replacement partners. In fact, surreptitious testing of alternative partners often preceded a formal break between customers, as between spouses. Discovery in either case leads to recrimination, public scandal, and sometimes to formal dispute settlement procedures. Compelling the return of an unwilling customer is neither possible nor of much benefit, and both parties are mainly concerned to preserve their reputation with third parties, including potential replacements.

The fluid character of customer relations in Kumasi contrasts dramatically with conditions in other Ghanaian markets, bigger and smaller, revealing that it arises directly from the relatively equal power of participants in Kumasi. Tomato traders bringing supplies from Ada to Accra's Makola #2 market complained in 1978 of their inability to change wholesale customers when they wished. If they brought a shipment to their new choice, the original wholesaler would forcibly seize the goods and sell them (Manuh 1991). Gore reports small rural towns around Koforidua where only one buyer was effectively available, since she was the only trader visiting that area with any regularity (Gore 1979). Under these conditions, abuses of price and risk factors are very likely, but not under the more flexible supply systems centered on Kumasi.

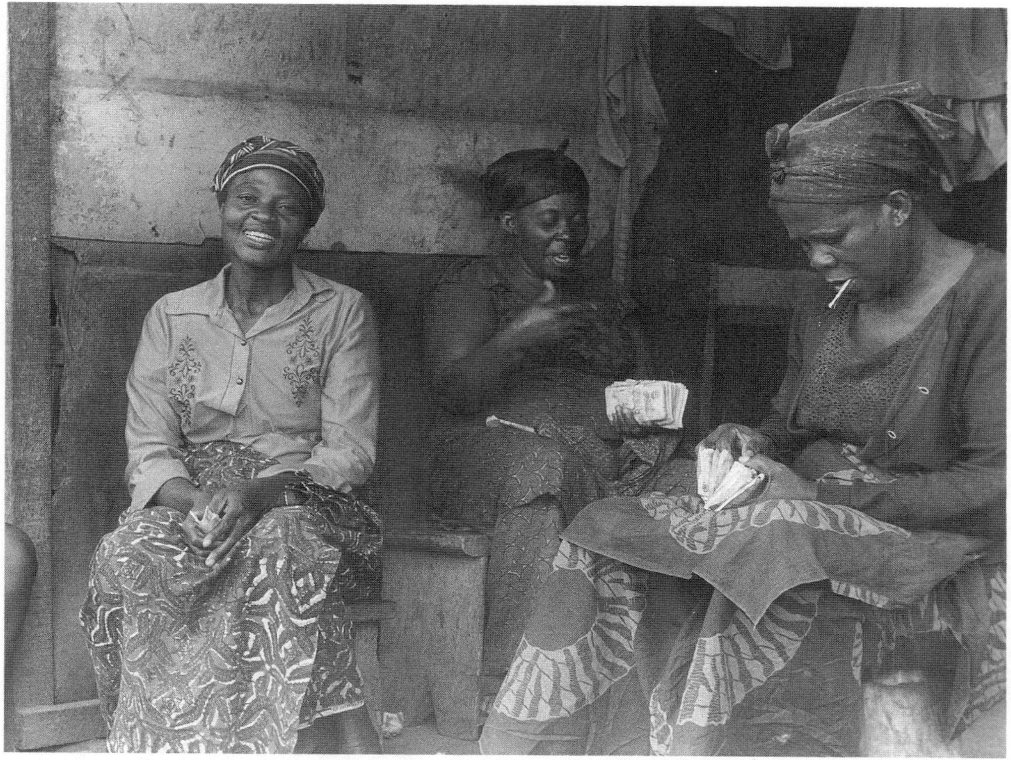

Yam travelers rest and count money in a shed beside the wholesale yard

Yam travelers discuss business in the wholesale yard

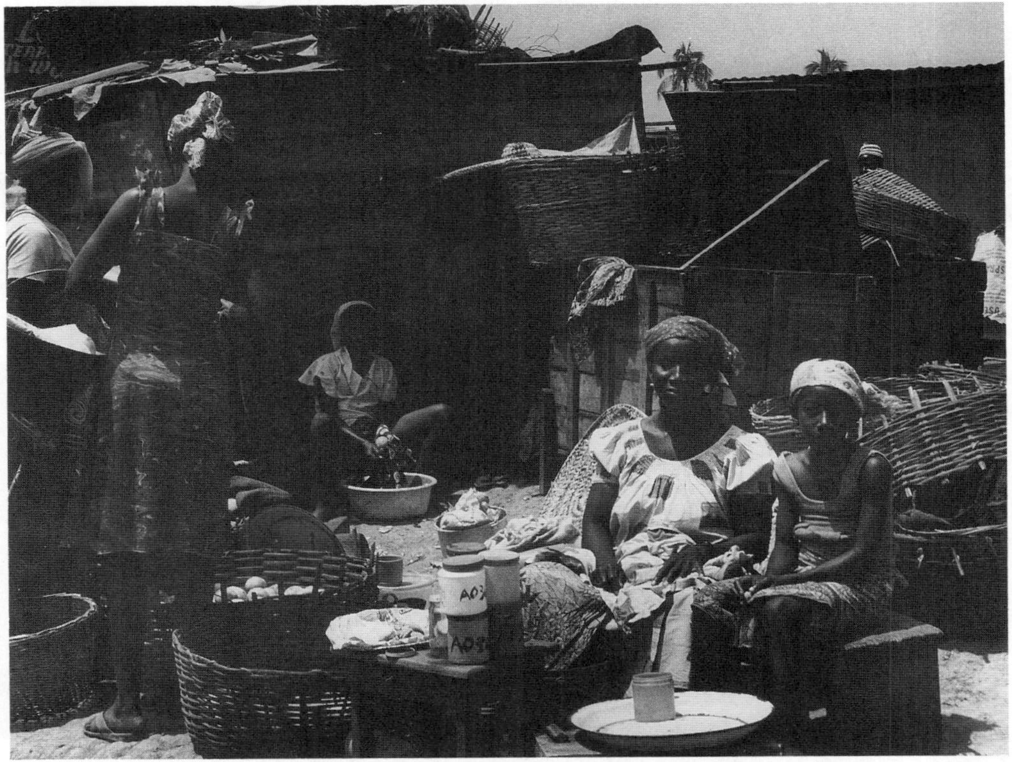

A small-scale orange trader whose daughter sells ice water

A wealthy provisions trader phones her Accra contacts

Historical Trends

Historical changes in personalized commercial patterns in southern Ghana demonstrate how important traders were in mediating the structural relationship between the sectors they linked. Shifts in this articulation, and especially shifts in relative power, brought dramatic shifts in commercial forms. During the early precolonial period, relations of rough equality characterized contacts between European traders, coastal Africans, and caravan traders from longer distances, such as Asantes. The landlord system of clientage organized both the Northern and Southern connections. Sedentary traders in the Northern caravan towns hosted visiting traders from Asante and distant parts of the savannah. They offered credit references, information, and bargaining skills in addition to accommodation. Leading African traders in the coastal ports offered the same services to inland traders from polities like Asante who arrived by caravan through the nineteenth century. De Marees's description of bargaining sessions around 1600 suggests that inland traders were highly dependent on coastal traders' familiarity with European procedures, making the concept of clientage very appropriate (De Marees 1985 [1602]).

The landlord model persists or appears today in long-distance trading situations where such services are required. Male traders from savannah-based Mossi and Hausa ethnic groups still maintain such landlord relations in Kumasi today, passing down the link to their heirs or apprentice successors (Schildkrout 1978a). Fanti women traders in smoked fish reported staying with landladies when delivering fish to customers in widely scattered cities and market towns. Asante women traveling to buy tomatoes in the Upper Region also depended on arranging congenial housing with people there, although the commercial services landladies offered seldom extended beyond storage and message transmission. In the Brong-Ahafo region, Kumasi-based yam travelers used the landlords of the houses where they stayed overnight as formal or informal brokers. They would enquire who had goods for sale on arrival, and potential sellers could leave messages for them.

Collegial relations also find their precursors in the early coastal period. Ship captains and coastal magnates depended on their personal reputations, built up over many years, to move a large volume of accumulated goods during the limited shipping season, through credit and other privileges extended on a reciprocal basis without binding dyadic ties. Fanti chiefs ritually accredited large-scale traders as compulsory intermediaries for slaves, munitions, and luxury goods (De Marees 1985 [1602]). The captaincy network maintained by Akani traders during virtually the whole of the seventeenth century coordinated a fluid diaspora of recognized groups of traders from Assim in major towns throughout the Gold Coast, within which individuals could move from town to town (Kea 1982).

A considerable degree of collegiality was maintained between European and African traders along the coast well into the early nineteenth century. Without reliable communication with the head office, both European and African employees or agents of British firms had to make major commercial decisions on the spot. A large addition to their salaries came from trading on their own accounts, and they aspired to eventual independence. Both factors encouraged European traders to develop long-term local contacts, including marriage into local trading families. In the later nineteenth century, after direct colonial rule began in 1830, British firms deliberately discouraged such collegiality by directing policy more centrally, rotating their European employees regularly back to Europe and gradually forbidding them to trade on the side. They now aspired to promotion within the company, and further intermarriage became very rare (Priestley 1969). This social transition accompanied a transition in commercial relations away from dealing with large independent African traders, both men and women, who were then starting to order directly from European manufacturers.

These colleagues were replaced by dependent buyer customers through the passbook system, which channeled cloth and other consumer imports through primarily female, firmly subordinated passbook holders, who challenged European firms and employees less directly. Passbooks were clearly designed to turn African buyers into dependent clients, although passbook holders used various tactics to avoid complete control. The larger women traders established several passbook accounts at competing firms or branches. Accra passbook holders established an association with considerable leverage due to their limited numbers. Longstanding passbook holders enjoyed preferential access to goods which gave them a virtual monopoly over scarce items or the most popular cloth patterns. These privileges virtually ensured eventual capital accumulation and also public resentment.

During the same early colonial period, sales of exports were also reorganized through tied buying agents. Export firms advanced capital to African men to travel into the interior and buy up export commodities —palm oil, then rubber, and finally cocoa. Fanti men with connections or capital from the coast moved quickly into Asante as its border controls weakened. Dependent agents operated alongside independent cocoa buyers, using their own capital, until state marketing boards were established.

Chiefly connections dominated trading patterns inside Asante during the nineteenth century, establishing a hierarchical framework that included employees, agents, and clients. State traders were chiefly employees and enjoyed as such a monopoly of munitions and other strategic commodities. Like European company agents, they retained enough autonomy to gradually accumulate their own capital (Wilks 1975, 703). Independent traders who traded with public loan capital escaped direct supervision but remained vulnerable to forced loans in time of public need. Loan recipients and even head carriers invested their own capital when joining royal caravans, accepting discipline in return for protection, a typical clientship pattern.

After the conquest of Asante in 1900, the chiefly trading system and border controls were suspended and collegial and clientship relations expanded and diversified. Northerners moved in to trade directly with kola producers, extending their landlord system to Kumasi and other Asante and southern towns. Fante women had traveled to Kumasi before conquest to sell smoked fish, but their numbers increased dramatically and more settled permanently in Kumasi. Fante men also now entered freely to sell imports and to buy rubber and cocoa, often with cash or goods advanced by expatriate firms. Fante women and Asante former exiles who had passbooks on the coast now introduced the practice in Kumasi at the new store branches there. As the Kumasi vegetable supply network expanded spatially with rapid urban growth, the more dispersed sources of supply intensified colleague and customer relations among the women collecting foodstuffs from farmers, as geographical models would predict.

Sources of supply for imported and manufactured goods continued to become fewer and fewer through the colonial and independent periods in Asante, with the merger or bankruptcy of smaller European firms and the nationalization of some Lebanese firms. This concentration in fewer hands provided a firmer economic basis for subordination up and down the customer hierarchy. In the 1950s and 1960s, the terms of passbook sales deteriorated, including lower credit ceilings and conditional sales (Robertson 1984). Conditional sales, first seen during wartime shortages, compelled traders to buy some unattractive, slow-moving items in order to buy popular goods that were in short supply. Passbook holders with solid connections could expect nearly automatic profits by reselling the scarce items at high margins.

By the 1970s, passbooks themselves were suspended and then revoked, to be replaced by even more personalized and hierarchical forms of clientship. Import and foreign exchange licensing procedures limited legal supplies to a few large firms, government agencies, and local factories. Traders needed to obtain allocations from these sources, or establish patronage relations with government or corporate officials who controlled these supplies, or with intermediaries with contacts. Sexual relations might be extorted or offered alongside substantial kickbacks. These supply relations were reported in 1979 to be very asymmetrical since many potential clients vied for the few powerful patrons.

This extreme dependence effectively destroyed the marketplace leadership structure previously rather strong in these commodities. As one Kumasi Central Market canned goods dealer put it, "If we had a chief, he would be someone in a store." In Kisangani, Zaire women business owners found it equally difficult to use an association to negotiate for better legal supplies for all rather than good connections for a few (MacGaffey 1987). The concentration of supply through a few big wholesalers creates similar dependency when it occurs within a marketplace system, although these conditions could not be detected within Kumasi Central Market (Babb 1989).

During the late 1970s and early 1980s, supplies of imports became so erratic, with periodic crackdowns affecting both diverted and smuggled supplies, that no single patron could provide a reliable supply. This actually undermined the stability of the illegal patronage hierarchy. A kind of parody of collegial relations emerged as the surviving traders circulated frantically to maintain contact with a number of potential sources of supply, buying what they could. Their status as "known" buyers did not secure credit in this sellers' market but was necessary before suppliers were willing to trust them in such highly illegal transactions. Kumasi traders also checked with colleagues on the reputation of new sources of illegal supply before venturing to buy from them. Smuggled supplies also played an important role in mitigating absolute dependence on official patrons for diverted or legal supplies. Although total quantities seemed small compared to diverted legal supplies, this steady trickle provided a price ceiling. Kumasi traders could establish their own customer relations with smugglers or intermediaries through commercial channels without special connections, although actual smugglers needed border contacts.

If the revocation of passbooks in the 1970s marked the end of one era, the lifting of import and foreign exchange restrictions under World Bank pressure in the 1980s marks the beginning of another. The steadier, although more expensive, legal supplies now available may have far-reaching repercussions on relations between traders by reestablishing hierarchies based on international connections. As of 1989, these changes seem to have led to greater concentration of trade in fewer hands and more frequent and more extreme subordinate dyadic ties involving market traders in these commodities. A similar intensification of dependent trading relations during periods of economic austerity is reported for Zaire and Peru (MacGaffey 1989; Babb 1989).

Asymmetry and Accumulation

Notwithstanding the dominance of collegial relations in the market, statistically and structurally, the potential for subordination and dependency lies primarily with customer relations because these are strategically located at the top and bottom of the market hierarchy. Half of the Kumasi Central Market traders surveyed reported no regular suppliers (50 percent) and 48 percent reported no regular buyers. By comparison, Handwerker reported that of the traders he interviewed in Monrovia, Liberia, 76 percent had regular suppliers and 53 percent had regular buyers (Handwerker 1973). Developing strong customer relations is considered by traders to be an essential factor in capital accumulation and upward mobility for the fortunate few. Customer relations can also make the difference between survival and bankruptcy for small, precarious operations. For dependency to become exploitation, asymmetries in the relation would have to give the dominant customer the ability to control the terms of transactions, establishing a patron/client relationship. To conclude why this potential for subordination remains unrealized, it is necessary to examine the asymmetries in customer relations in the specific locations within the marketplace system where they are most prevalent.

In the distribution of locally grown foodstuffs, the wholesalers operating full time from the Kumasi Central Market wholesale yards are the focus of trading relations for that market and the surrounding region as well. Those interviewed maintained a considerable number of customers among both the travelers who supplied them and the Kumasi retailers and institutional suppliers who bought from them. These resident wholesalers unquestionably wielded considerable economic power and earned some of the largest incomes in the market. The commodity group leaders were invariably drawn from their ranks, although for reasons discussed in a later chapter leaders were not the wealthiest of them. In commodities without wholesale yards, some of the larger traders in the specialized retail areas had similar wholesale customers.

Descriptions of entrenched commercial dependency elsewhere often feature long-term credit or indebtedness, so the extension of credit within Kumasi customer relations merits attention. The most common types of credit in Kumasi did not establish dependency between debtor and creditor. Retailers often collected goods for payment later the same day. In several commodities this was not considered credit, but it helped very capital-short traders buy in larger quantities, since they could sell at least part of the goods before payment. These kinds of credit were governed by the balance between supply and demand and collegial relations rather than the relation between customers. Wholesalers could not force unfavorable terms on their customers since other colleagues would offer them credit under the same conditions. This conventional credit instead made travelers dependent on wholesalers to provide it to retailers for them. Travelers often delivered their goods and returned later to collect the proceeds before they caught a truck back to the village. The wholesaler undertook to pay the traveler in full at that time even if she had not succeeded in collecting all the money by then. When longer-term credit to retailers was required by market conditions, usually on a when-sold basis, the traveler could have wasted several days waiting to collect her money. Each side in a sense depended on the wholesaler to manage credit between them, paying and collecting at the appropriate times and absorbing any default.

Wholesalers and larger retailers in Kumasi Central Market extended revolving credit to those buying for resale in locations outside Kumasi Central Market. Food processors and peddlers normally received credit through customer relations, since they are too dispersed to form collegial sets. They paid for their purchases on their next visit to the market, ranging from the next day for cooked-food vendors in Kumasi to two or three weeks for fish peddlers in the more remote villages. Institutional buyers also often paid on their next buying visit, clearing the old account and taking the new goods on credit.

A customer relation in this context normally began with cash purchases on a regular schedule. The buyer then asked for partial credit to increase the scale of purchases or when prices went up seasonally. For the smaller traders, this credit limit could gradually rise to form the bulk of their working capital. Village peddlers especially depended on this form of credit to build up their businesses. They would cease buying from a supplier who refused it after an appropriate length of time in order to start over with someone else. A growing customer of this kind was an asset for the supplier, who figured her increased turnover gave adequate return for the capital invested.

Although the wholesaler or large retailer clearly had more economic strength than the reseller (with the exception of institutional suppliers) her ability to control the reseller directly was extremely limited. While the level of eventual credit might be beyond the debtor's ability to pay off in order to switch suppliers openly, it was quite easy for one to simply disappear with the goods. Suppliers hoped the person would eventually reappear in Kumasi to reestablish themselves in business, which was likely unless she could find a new source of goods in another market. Collegial loyalty would then prompt a neighboring supplier to turn her in. Alexander reports the same problems with runaway debtors in Java, another diverse economy with many alternative earning activities (Alexander 1987).

Wholesalers and large retailers sometimes advanced capital to travelers who brought them goods. As a temporary response to seasonal shortage, such advances only bound the traveler to sell the goods bought with this money to the one who had given it, at the price current when they arrived. They did not presuppose or create a customer relationship, although the wholesaler would want to know the individual traveler very well. Travelers and other customers can ask for advances of capital or goods to take advantage of unusual opportunities or to recover from a theft or other occasional loss. If repaid promptly, these longer-term advances do not necessarily lead to customership, let alone chronic dependence.

A few wholesalers keep substantial amounts of capital on semipermanent advance to traveler customers for greater returns. They then get half of the traveler's profit on top of their profit from wholesaling them. The investor shares part of the risk of bad judgment or other losses, but these amount to less than if she had sent a subordinate. Although conditions allow some deception, pricing should conform to current levels. Wholesalers solicit such arrangements with trusted clients if they accumulate more capital than they can easily employ in wholesaling alone. Travelers receiving advances usually also trade with their own capital on the same trips, but they may become dependent on the extra capital to maintain their operations at a competitive level. This situation can arise after a catastrophic loss, when an individual requests an emergency advance but cannot repay it later out of her halved profits. Permanent capital dependency relations seem to affect relatively few traders in Kumasi, perhaps because of the easy availability of less restrictive supplier credit. This contrasts to widespread capital dependency reported for Latin America (Babb 1987; Bromley and Gerry 1979). Farmers did depend on credit in the sense that they planted higher acreages in anticipation of the availability of credit to get them through the cycle if their own finances ran short. Traders made these loans as a kind of alternative investment during a season when trading was less profitable. They could only tie up their capital if they had enough other income to maintain their subsistence until harvest.

Farm loans facilitated accumulation by traders indirectly, since they did not make the debtors dependent on individual traders or give traders much control of the terms of sale. The amounts involved did not represent a large percentage of the expected proceeds of the harvest, and the farmer might later extend goods on credit to the same or other traders. The creditor could exert some influence on the timing of the repayment sale but could not expect major price concessions. If the creditor demanded unreasonable prices, she might suffer later when seeking goods on credit or other favors from local farmers.

Far from demanding that the farmer sell at low prices when supplies are abundant, traders were observed trying to schedule these promised goods at a time of scarcity, when the farmer reaps the major price benefit. Farmers who sold at low prices immediately after harvest did not mention debt or pressure from traders as their motive, but their poverty, which left them without cash savings to pay urgent school fees or medical expenses. Farmers desperate for money press the trader to take delivery soon and may have to extend goods on credit or commission, even to a creditor. Traders needing to fill a truck in a hurry may agree to taking only part of the farmer's crop to cover the debt, if he wants to wait longer for his major sale.

In Ghana, the climate puts Northern and Upper Region farmers most at risk for drought, famine, and chronic food deficits, leaving them particularly vulnerable to debt dependency. They primarily grow grain, which they sell to Muslim middlemen based in Northern towns and the regional periodic markets of Techiman and Ejura, not directly to Kumasi-based traders. These grain trading networks supply Kumasi through storefront warehouses and extend across Ghana's northern border. Studies from Mossi territory across that border in Burkina Faso therefore carry considerable weight in denying or not finding the presence of significant indebtedness, despite very significant rural suffering (Sherman 1984; Saul 1988; McCorkle 1988).

Another indication that rural areas retain control of their food crops comes from the 1982–83 drought period, when crops failed throughout Ghana. Food did not apparently drain away from poor farming districts already short of food toward wealthier urban consumers, despite their stronger buying power and the desperate shortages of urban food. One would expect such movement if debt constrained farmers to sell food they needed, since the wealthy would have less money left over to renew consumption loans to the poor. In 1983, food supplies in the

Ghanaian countryside remained consistently higher than in the cities, as they had during the political food crisis in 1979. Urban families sent their children to stay with rural relatives both years in order to eat proper food, since city residents were going hungry.

When I visited the Northern Region in 1984, I asked about the availability and the price of food during the previous year's crisis. Cassava producers from Damongo recounted eating less preferred foods like *gari*, which they had intended to sell in 1983. The region imported most of this *gari* from the South, although the experience convinced many Damongo farmers to begin planting drought-resistant cassava. The substitution of cassava for cereals, although a nutritional loss, seems mild in comparison to the consumption of coconut husks and other dangerous non-food items by desperate urban residents that year. Prices were higher in the cities, which did draw grain there from drought-affected areas. Those farmers harvesting some millet or sorghum did sell it for consumption by urban elite consumers, at very high prices, but because they could buy proportionately more of the cheaper cassava with their money. Very low farm prices mark the extremely unfavorable urban/rural terms of trade that can threaten rural survival capacity and yield extractive profits, even within a single country (MacGaffey 1987). Earning power was more of an issue here; the farmers hardest hit suffered because they had nothing to sell, not because they had sold what food they had. These farmers continued to suffer for the same reasons in subsequent years, as structural adjustment policies of credit and wage restraint prevented them from expanding either their farming or their off-farm employment, including trading or wage work.

In Ghana, the pattern of food shortage during drought and during political upheavals shows that farmers, rather than traders, can hold food supplies back. In 1979 and 1983, strict price control enforcement on local foodstuffs quickly degenerated into indiscriminate confiscations and physical attacks on anyone transporting commercial quantities of goods, very broadly defined. Farmers were afraid of both the violence and the loss of revenue, and urban food supplies dried up abruptly. Highly perishable vegetables, which had to be sold when ripe, recovered most rapidly after June 1979 because farmers could not store them. Yams could be stored on the farm for months, so farmers delayed the harvest in 1979 until they needed to prepare their fields for the next year, and some stored them in pits even longer. Urban yam supplies stayed very low during the whole normal harvest season but remained steady long after they were normally exhausted as farmers gradually released their stocks. Corn farmers also delayed their harvest that year, passing up the high early prices for green corn in favor of the more storable mature crop.

When farmers are overly dependent on a few buyers, through debt or lack of alternatives, serious distortions in supply and demand can and do result. Examples from elsewhere in West Africa suggest that this would have happened in Ghana if these power imbalances had existed. In Northern Nigeria, oligopolist grain traders from the largest cities did succeed in draining grain from districts with acute shortages (Watts 1987). Arnould's work across Nigeria's northern border in Niger suggests that the same dominant trading network still drains foodstuffs out of Niger at harvest and returns inadequate quantities during the hungry season (Arnould 1986). Village traders have relatively small profit margins. In similar circumstances, retailers in Peru say "we just work for the wholesalers" (Babb 1989).

As close by as Burkina Faso, the presence of urban traders actually improves the urban/rural terms of trade. Trade in staple grains dominates the food system, and wealthy grain traders, usually Muslim men, dominate the grain trade. Saul and McCorkle report villages where grain prices are actually higher just after harvest because traders from more distant cities who buy in bulk only find it worthwhile to visit the district when supplies are plentiful (Saul 1988; McCorkle 1988). In Java, Alexander likewise reports higher prices during the glut season for chilies, due to the presence only then of buyers from distant cities (Alexander 1987).

The main brake on Kumasi wholesale traders' ability to manipulate these relations to their own disproportionate advantage comes from the existence of multiple alternative channels within the marketplace system. Each wholesale yard in Kumasi contained at least a dozen large wholesalers capable of providing for the needs of each others' customers. While customers would have found it difficult to perform some of their wholesalers' functions themselves, especially extending and collecting credit, they could have found a replacement easily enough or operated successfully without a continuing dyadic relationship, as many did. Only a long series of rapid substitutions would have seriously impaired their reputations as customers. Institutional suppliers, whether employees or independent contractors, were especially independent because their large, year-round purchases made them extremely desirable customers.

Buyers and sellers did not depend on establishing customer relations with Kumasi wholesalers for physical access to supplies because the wholesalers could not effectively control the supply situation. Effective competition extended between locations, preventing Kumasi

Central Market wholesalers from combining to force price or other concessions. Buyers and travelers constantly monitored prices and supplies at the adjacent Kejetia truck arrival area and major markets in other towns easily accessible by road. They occasionally bought and sold at them when prices warranted. The fact that trade shifted within days to other locations when price control artificially lowered prices in the Central Market suggests that it would shift as swiftly if traders artificially raised prices.

Only a few cases were found where collegial sets of trading peers could accumulate significantly by monopolizing specific commercial positions as a group. The "companies" of traders bringing in irrigated tomatoes from the Upper Region are effective because they tap relatively distant, concentrated sources of supply. The combination of high seasonal prices and high perishability made this a very high-risk, high-capital operation. It seems unlikely that individual traders would be economically viable on these routes without the support of the group monopoly. However, it was undoubtedly very lucrative for the individuals involved. Passbook holders in their heyday also profited from the social distance and limited number of sources of imports through large European firms.

MacGaffey's work in Zaire explores an extreme case of alternative channels, analyzing both the extreme power inequalities and the safety net potential revealed in illegal trading when legal channels break down almost completely (MacGaffey 1987; 1991). In that situation the bureaucratic elite around the capital takes ruthless advantage of clientage opportunities based on state power, but clientage based in more remote rural areas has built up new elites. They interact only marginally with state functionaries, such as border guards, but they can be equally exploitative in areas where they are the only functioning commercial channel (Russell 1989). Both emerge as key aspects of the "real" national economy, providing unorthodox alternative channels that provide food when more orthodox ones cease to function.

A more sudden shift from concentrated, state-authorized channels to decentralized, unauthorized channels occurred in the Somali cattle trade during the last decade (Little 1989). Legal exports to Saudi Arabia, dominated by relatively few licensed exporters based in major ports, were prohibited by the Saudi authorities after 1983. Rural middlemen reoriented their transactions to feed more diffuse export networks sending cattle "informally" to neighboring African countries. These gave more advantageous terms to the herder, who lived near the land borders. Because this shift had occurred already several times in this century, these alternative channels existed and could be expanded with relatively little disruption to producers, although with considerable disruption to port-based exporters.

Historical studies comparing urban food supplies in different parts of the African continent confirm that the existence of viable alternative channels makes a consistent contribution to long-term food security. Guyer identifies flexibility as a characteristic of food marketing systems that respond adequately to droughts or simply to rapid urbanization (Guyer 1987). Rigid trading hierarchies in Hausa cities provided stability to traders, by holding trade tightly in the hands of small numbers of traders defined by ethnic, class, gender, and geographic identities but contributed to more severe and frequent famines (Watts 1983; 1987). By contrast, trading networks centered on Yaounde kept food supplies steady by dramatic changes in personnel and sources of foodstuffs that stimulated commercial production in both near and distant regions (Guyer 1987).

Conclusion

The pattern of collegial and customer relations in Kumasi Central Market does not permit traders to dominate others, nor does it permit others to dominate them. They do not depend on outside capital; on the other hand, they have very little access to public or private capital except from other traders. With few exceptions, they have enough capital to employ themselves, but rarely enough to employ others. The structure of relations between other national economic sectors, especially farmers and industrial producers, sets limits to the influence of the marketplace system as a whole, but reproduces a steady demand for its services. The commodity groups and informal collegial sets of traders forming official or ad hoc commodity groups play an important role in preserving this relatively autonomous position for traders. Credit and other services exchanged within the group structure enable small individual enterprises to survive economic shocks at the personal or societal level that might easily topple them over the edge into direct dependency. They gain access to economies of scale more often through group activity than from joining or founding enlarged single enterprises.

Current patterns of clientship within the marketplace system reveal both strengths and weaknesses in traders' current status. Traders have largely succeeded in maintaining their fiscal independence from outsiders and each other. They prefer trading on their own accounts at however small a level to more dependent relations. They can generally manage to do so, partly through relatively free access to supplier credit. The existence of multiple alternative channels for obtaining and disposing of goods means that participants need not remain in highly exploitative relationships.

The same dynamics that prevent traders from putting each other out of business preserve some measure of autonomy at the boundaries of the marketplace system. Multiple channels within the system protect nontraders from potential exploitation by traders, while customer and colleague relations give them a basis for some access to traders' capital, information, and other resources. Despite considerable seasonal transfer of resources toward the farm sector, for example, traders have not established enough control over it to accumulate significantly at the expense of farmers or consumers. The same flexibility and potential decentralization protects the resources traders control from total expropriation at the hands of national and international institutions. This incidentally improves the capacity of the marketplace system to buffer or insulate farmers and other local producers and consumers from absolute control by those same institutions.

This remarkably resilient distributive system recovered with startling swiftness from apparent total collapse during 1979 and again in 1983. Although capital shrank and individuals suffered or went bankrupt, market institutions themselves resumed very nearly their previous form. In particular, the commodity groups and informal collegial sets showed themselves to be the backbone of the marketplace system by reconstituting themselves as soon as trade was possible. This rapid, elastic response suggests their present form is well suited to the task of adapting to dramatic, recurrent shocks to the commercial system. More flexible, less hierarchical commercial formations like these provided for more alternative supply and disposal channels than the official formal sector and thus weathered both social and ecological challenges more smoothly.

7 QUEENS OF NEGOTIATION

The leaders of the organized women's commodity groups in Kumasi Central Market have the most structural potential for coordinating and exercising the diverse strengths that market women draw on from ethnic, gender, and community connections as well as their commercial positions. These groups are the most cohesive collegial sets within Kumasi Central Market and thus provide something of a test case for the efficacy of collegial relations. As leaders of those groups, they can call on the collective support of their members but are sometimes accused of manipulating members' loyalty for personal financial gain at their expense. Since their authority turns out to be based on rendering services in dispute settlement and negotiations, services that can only be effective in full support of the members' interests and with substantial consensus, a strong argument can be made that this exploitative potential either does not exist or has not been realized.

Limits on market leaders' ability to abuse their authority come from outside as well as inside of the market, through the same channels of subordination which also affect their followers. Their leadership draws on Asante chiefly precedents for legitimacy but is illegitimate on other ideological grounds. As prominent urban public figures, they are lightning rods for tensions and conflicts based on urban/rural and international/local systems of domination. They also exemplify the independent urban woman who symbolizes the problematic changes in relations between waged and unwaged work. They played a critical role in facilitating the swift rebound of the market from the wide-ranging series of political and economic crises that brought trading to a virtual standstill repeatedly in the 1970s and 1980s by coordinating traders' responses. Nonetheless, their economic autonomy had strict limits, internal ones from checks and balances rooted in the diversity of the marketplace system and external ones from interlocking systems of domination that affected traders' access to social and material resources.

The loyalty and discipline that give leaders their effective power derive from their presiding role in internal dispute settlement. Group members value this service highly as being essential to long-term efficiency in market transactions. Dispute settlement often appears in the historical and ethnographic record as a key aspect of organization for traders or urban residents. Medieval European cloth merchants began to develop bourgeois institutions of town government at fairs, where they needed speedy dispute settlement outside of the feudal courts. Zairian smugglers set up informal tribunals in remote border regions to regulate their illegal activities (MacGaffey 1991). Yoruba women traders in small towns and villages have leaders who settle disputes, even where more elaborate functions have not developed (Sudarkasa 1973; Trager 1976). In Ghana, Cape Coast market association members and leaders both agree that commodity queens have been needed as long as there were disputes between market traders (Amonoo 1974). Routine disputes also hone Kumasi market leaders' skills of argument and negotiation on a daily basis. These were taxed to the full in external negotiations with government and military officials and with other economic actors, such as drivers and porters.

Other aspects of market leadership are subordinated to negotiations and dispute settlement. Skills and values important in negotiation were listed by traders as primary criteria in selecting new leaders, and the need for negotiation had often sparked the formalization of the commodity group. A candidate's wealth, for example, which enhances ceremonial display, takes second place to personal qualities required for dispute settlement, which inhibit accumulation. Group members did highly value leaders' ceremonial functions, however, in attending funerals and community celebrations. This public visibility cements group loyalty and also maintains the leaders' prestige and connections, which were drawn upon during crises. Market leaders gain legitimacy and enhance group discipline by adapting titles, ceremonial and court procedures from both traditional and modern models.

Commercial regulation by leaders of prices or access to goods turned out to be relatively minor and rare, despite widespread controversy and allegations in popular and academic publications over the years. Other authors have looked for price manipulation by market leaders or groups in Cape Coast, Koforidua, and Western Nigeria and found equally negative evidence (Amonoo 1974; Gore 1978; Trager 1976). Routine enforcement of conventional rules of bargaining and credit formed part of the leadership duties through dispute settlement, but legislation was minimal. Extremely rapid economic changes or crises did bring leaders to expand their regulatory roles temporarily. They still innovated within the framework of negotiation, rather than fiat, by coordinating negotiations between different categories of members and nonmembers on new rules or procedures to deal with the new conditions.

Structural Models

Kumasi market traders have drawn on aspects of culturally legitimized patterns of leadership from both contemporary and traditional Ghana, reassembling and modifying them to meet their commercial and political needs. From Akan culture, Kumasi traders have incorporated the offices of *ohemma* (female chief), *ohene* (male chief), and *opanyin* (elder). From Northern Ghana, traders draw on the *sarkin* model of chiefship. Western models of cooperatives, with committees and secretaries, supplement but do not supplant those of chiefship. The current structure of market leadership does not conform to the precolonial chiefly offices that supervised Kumasi and other markets, nor do particular commodity groups conform substantially to either precolonial or Western models. These leadership institutions constitute innovations that integrated conflicting principles, procedures, and titles. Each group has adopted or refrained from asserting organizational forms and statuses according to the ethnic and gender identities of traders and the economic relations specific to their chosen commodity and location.

Since Asante women predominate numerically in Kumasi Central Market, it is no surprise that the political offices Asante culture reserves for women provide a powerful model for market leadership. The formal commodity groups for traders in locally grown vegetable foodstuffs, which are sold overwhelmingly by Asante women traders, have adopted the *ohemma* title of female community leadership and many of its procedural elements as a precedent for their elected female leaders. These leaders are *ahemma* in the plural but *ahemmafo* when acting as a group. Each market *ohemma* adds the name of her commodity to her own title, in the same place that a town or village *ohemma* uses the name of her town. For example, the leader of the traders in *bayere* (yams) is called the *bayere-hemma,* and the leader of the tomato (*ntos*) traders the *ntos-hemma.* These offices are linguistically parallel to the *ohemma* of the town of Mampong, the *Mamponghemma,* and the *ohemma* of the people of Asante, the *Asantehemma.* The male chiefly title of *ohene* is modified in the same way—for example, in the titles of *Mamponghene* and *Asantehene* (male chiefs of the town of Mampong and the Asante nation).

Market *ahemma* follow the chiefly pattern in some respects, but deviate significantly in others. Like community *ahemma* and *ahene,* they are elected by their elders for life and can be destooled by them in case of bad conduct. They must consult these elders, called *mpanyin-*

fo, regarding important decisions and disputes. The larger commodity groups choose a council of elders, while in the smaller groups every trader of generally accepted mature age and stature attends all such meetings. Most significantly, market *ahemma* define their followers by occupation rather than by residence or citizenship, as in community leadership, or kinship, as in lineage leadership. When an *ohemma* dies or is destooled, her successor is elected from among the council of elders rather than the royal lineage. Her constituency consists of women rather than a community of men and women. She also rules alone rather than in tandem with a male chief or lineage head. Unlike town and village chiefs, she has no official place in the chiefly hierarchy and needs no approval or installation by a superior.

The market *ahemmafo* stepped into a vacuum created when the colonial authorities put aside a set of chiefly offices that governed Asante markets before direct colonial rule around 1900. Specific court officials under the Asante treasury kept order, settled disputes, and collected taxes in the main Kumasi market, in addition to those that regulated border markets and supervised the state traders. These titles still exist, but their functions have been taken over by government employees, such as the Market Manager, or by the *ahemmafo*. The only remnant of chiefly authority was with the *Asantehene*'s police, who participated in keeping order in the market alongside the Ghanaian police.

The current commodity group structure was gradually formalized between the 1930s and the 1950s. Some leadership structure was apparent in the records of negotiations for the transfer of traders commodity by commodity from the old downtown site in the 1920s. Another indication was the establishment of commodity wholesale yards, now closely associated with formal commodity groups. The first wholesale yard originated at the old downtown site, when the Kumasi Public Health Board set aside an area for fish unloading. As strangers, Fante women trading in smoked fish may have developed a tighter organization earlier. Yam traders built the first vegetable wholesale yard in the 1930s, at the new site, hiring equipment to level a hillside to accommodate trucks arriving from the northern farms. Older traders also reported that commodity groups had erected many of the new lines of wooden stalls built to supplement the original city construction. In Nigeria, commodity traders' associations in Ibadan's Dugbe market also originated in the 1930s and 1940s, in response to the need for negotiation with the colonial government over wartime quotas and new taxes (Ogunsanwo 1988). Market union members in Huaraz, Peru, also recalled activism in their early years over taxes and community political issues, suggesting that external challenges often trigger the formalization of collegial ties (Babb 1989).

Without formal recognition by chiefs, market *ahemma* cannot invoke their political or ritual authority directly. In attending funerals and settling disputes, they follow general Asante procedural models rather than the specific chiefly ones. For example, they have no authorization to use ritual oaths like those attached to specific chiefly courts in hearing disputes. When they appear at the palace on public holidays or ritual occasions they do so as private citizens, although important ones. *Ahemma* do sometimes follow less tightly regulated aspects of Asante court procedure to create an image of grandeur and prestige, for example, by speaking through an *okyeame* (literally, a speaker or linguist) in formal negotiations with outsiders.

The term *ohemma* has been commonly translated into English as queen mother, following the practice of Rattray, the original British ethnographer (Rattray 1923). He invoked the prestige and respect given the dowager Queen Mother of Great Britain by her imperialist subjects for these Asante women, whom he frequently refers to as "the dear old Queen Mothers," while arguing for their salaries and other recognition by colonial authorities. Ghanaians speaking and writing in English generally follow his form, using the title of queen mother not only for the female community leaders, but also for the female market leaders who use the same Asante title of *ohemma*. They are often distinguished from the chiefly *ohemma* by English modifiers, in the phrases market queen mother, market queen, or mammy queen, the latter often derogatory. Sometimes these English terms are applied rather loosely to any wealthy or powerful trader, not just the actual *ohemma*.

Women traders selling each of the important Asante staple foodstuffs in Kumasi Central Market have an organized commodity group with an *ohemma*. Each has complete authority within her own commodity group. She normally does not consult the others about internal affairs and resents any such interference. It is these *ahemma* who act in concert when conditions warrant. The head of the yam traders, the *bayerehemma*, has seniority over the others, and in joint actions she takes the lead. On ceremonial occasions or in negotiations with high officials, she leads the delegation of *ahemma* and speaks for them. This seems to reflect the economic importance of yams in this market, which is centrally located for the interregional trade in foodstuffs. In coastal markets, such as those in Accra, the head of the cloth traders takes the leading role.

Although the other *ahemma* do not acknowledge her everyday authority, they act as her council of elders in some respects. The *ahemma* of yams, cassava, tomatoes, kontommere, cocoyam, oranges, and snails constitute a senior set who remain in informal contact about market affairs. The *bayerehemma* could not make a major decision without consulting with them; they must be summoned and have a duty to appear at formal meetings of the *ahemmafo.* She calls them to meetings and presides over their deliberations. Following Asante decision-making norms, she hears each of them speak before summing up the discussion in her decision. The membership in this senior council appears to represent the historical importance of the foodstuff in the market, although it lags behind some recent expansions and contractions in specific commodities—for example, the decline in snails. Those omitted from this senior council were as interesting as the attendees. The leading fish *ohemma* is invited to these formal meetings but not expected to appear. Her office has the requisite seniority, but, since she is old and bedridden, she no longer comes to market. Unlike the tomato *ohemma,* she did not name an official representative before lapsing into senility. The organizational complexity of fish traders, who divide by fish species and origin, may have prevented this. The plantain *ohemma* was not even invited, apparently because of her anomalous political status, which will be discussed later. She was not a market trader but had been installed from outside due to her connections to the Convention People's Party when it was in power at independence.

Also absent from these meetings were the leaders of organized commodity groups for commodities sold primarily by men. The leading *ahemma* consulted them informally, but they did not take part in group meetings or ceremonies. In Kumasi Central Market, Northern men sold kola, cattle, and meat in sufficient numbers to justify formal group organization. Craftsmen working inside of the market also had organized groups. Men's groups followed different organizational patterns, which are discussed below. Mixed commodities, sold by both men and women, were also not represented. Traders in most of these commodities remained without formal organization or acknowledged single leaders.

Perhaps in recognition of their experience and the size and strength of their groups, the leading *ahemmafo* have a disproportionate influence in external negotiations. They represented Kumasi Central Market traders as a whole in negotiations with the Market Manager and other nontraders during periods of crisis, such as the price control enforcements of 1979, and during periods of peace, as in 1989. Leaders of male or non-Akan market groups maintained their own external relations with co-ethnic or male hierarchies, but speak only for their own members. On market-wide issues they follow the lead of the *ahemmafo.*

Concentration here on the *ahemmafo* is justified by both their structural and demographic importance within Kumasi Central Market. A large majority of the traders are female, a large majority are Asantes, and a large majority sell various local foodstuffs. These overlapping majorities define Asante women foodstuffs sellers as the core group of traders. Since more than 60 percent of Kumasi Central Market traders do not recognize commodity leaders, actual constituency group relations only link them to a minority of traders (see table 7.1). These groups are among the strongest in the market, however, for both economic and cultural reasons.

The commercial relations specific to traders in agricultural commodities foster relatively strong groups with stronger leaders among them. Traders in farm produce have more autonomy in relating to farmers than those buying imports or manufactures presently have from the large import firms or factories. Both leaders and followers have more scope for developing loyalty through effective negotiations and dispute settlement. Among traders in imports like cloth and provisions, dependence on powerful sources does not permit the emergence of independent negotiating figures. Even traders in the local foodstuffs whose supply or sales relations or stall locations place them outside of the reach of effective dispute settlement do not join the appropriate commodity groups.

Some commodity groups combine in formal or informal alliances with traders selling the same commodity in other markets. Yam traders have a formal nationwide network, founded and headed by the Kumasi *Bayerehemma,* which holds meetings of representatives at least once a year. Orange leaders from markets throughout the Kumasi area hold occasional meetings to discuss common issues. Cloth traders from Kumasi Central Market, Asafo Market, and the downtown Kumasi streets formerly had separate groups that consulted regularly. Market *ahemma* from towns trading heavily with Kumasi make occasional formal visits to greet the Kumasi Central Market *ahemma,* in addition to consulting with them over disputes or shared crises that arise. Travelers bringing commodities from long distances also link these groups, since they often hold de facto membership in the local market groups in several supply towns they frequent as well as in Kumasi.

The strongest and most elaborate groups arise in commodities where a large proportion of the traders are of one sex and one ethnic

Table 7.1 Commodity Leadership

A. Queen or Chief

Percentage of Traders Reporting One in Their Commodity

Commodity Type	Men	Women
Perishable Food	33.3	74.3
Nonperishable Food	0	37.0
Canned Food	0	9.1
Craft Products	10.8	17.6
Industrial Products	3.8	16.5
Clothing	11.1	7.1
All Commodities	10.8	40.6

B. Elder

Percentage of Traders Trading Under One

Commodity Type	Men	Women
Perishable Food	100	77.9
Nonperishable Food	100	43.2
Canned Food	0	0
Craft Products	51.4	32.7
Industrial Products	37.5	38.3
Clothing	59.3	30.4
All Commodities	56.8	53.2

C. Copresence of Queens and Elders

Number of Responses

	Queen or Chief Present			
	Men		Women	
	Yes	No	Yes	No
Elder Present				
Yes	14	65	113	63
No	1	59	21	134

SOURCE: 1979 Kumasi Central Market Survey

background. This ethnic and gender homogeneity brings general agreement on correct leadership styles and procedures and facilitates shared ceremonial observances. The few non-Akan women in the yam traders' association, for example, could not attend Asante funerals or expect Asante market elders to attend theirs, which led to remarks from yam elders about their marginal status. Most ethnic cultures make close interaction between traders of opposite sexes uncomfortable, hindering leadership in commodities sold by both sexes. An *ohene* of secondhand clothes dealers, self-proclaimed in 1978, did not last until 1989, and the male leader of provisions sellers had retired by 1979.

The unwillingness of Ghanaian women traders to follow male leaders is a marked contrast to widespread examples from other continents of male leadership in mixed-sex trader associations or even in predominantly female ones. Lessinger discusses dynamic male leadership of urban traders, including of some women in an Indian city (Lessinger 1988). In Peru, predominantly female trader groups selected male spokesmen (Babb 1989; Seligmann 1989). Although these male leaders did neglect some issues specific to women, replacing them with women did not seem to be a viable option.

The Asante system of community *ahemma* is less thoroughly separatist than Nigerian Igbo and Yoruba systems, where women leaders represent the female population as a group (Van Allen 1972; Sudarkasa 1973; Eames 1988; Amadiume 1987). Still, single-sex voluntary associations are the rule. A woman organizer for the Ghana Trades Union Congress in the 1960s told me that she had tried to recruit market women's groups. They were offered membership in the commercial worker's union, which was dominated by shop assistants and led by men. They told her that rather than follow a male leader they preferred to join the Ghana Assembly of Women, dominated by church women's groups (Addo 1980).

Much of the observed variation between commodity groups in leadership titles, norms, and relations can be traced directly to the ethnic and gender identity of the member traders. Northern Moslem men dominate trade in cattle and kola, widely traded across the Northern savannah. Male chiefs of these commodity groups take the Hausa title of *sarkin*. They report to the chiefs of Northern ethnic groups in the Kumasi Zongo for ceremonial purposes and to settle difficult disputes alongside other *sarkin* from the cattle and kola markets located outside of Kumasi Central Market. Subordinate kola elders represent the different home areas in the North and report directly to their ethnic *sarkin* for some purposes. Islamic traditions govern their dispute settlement norms and procedures. When the *sarkin kola* discussed his criteria for choosing a leader, he described a hypothetical dispute and placed the same emphasis on truthfulness that Geertz found among Moroccan traders (Geertz, Geertz, and Rosen 1979). While Asante women did not expect their leaders to lie, they never mentioned truthfulness as a positive criteria. Leadership patterns among male poultry traders reflect their ethnic origin in Ghana's Upper Region. Only a few poultry traders spoke Hausa, not including the recently elected chief. Their localized supply networks admit of less influence from international savannah connections that promote Islam and the Hausa language. Their Kumasi chief reports to the Hausa *sarkin* of the Kumasi Zongo, since a Northern/Southern division overwhelms other ethnic differences in Kumasi, but he also maintains direct relations with local chiefs in the Upper Region hometown supply areas.

The organized groups of Asante men in Kumasi Central Market are groups of craftsmen operating there. Butchers drawn from the tiny Asante Muslim community bridge the gap between Northern Moslem cattle dealers and Asante consumers. The numerous shoemakers still retain a craft *ohene* placed in the Asante chiefly hierarchy. For ceremonial purposes, they recognize the seniority of the *mpaboahene,* who makes the Asantehene's sandals and leads shoemakers throughout Asante. Those who make many other kinds of shoes (predominantly men) and shoe sellers of both sexes in Kumasi Central Market acknowledge a citywide organization with both *ohene* and *ohemma,* for male and female members. Its dual leadership conforms to the Asante community pattern, but it also functions as a modern pressure group to lobby for increased importation of raw materials and favorable pricing.

The institution of eldership (in Asante, *mpanyinfuo*) is flexible enough to cover a wide variety of commercial situations and organizational needs. Market *ahemma* or male chiefs usually have supporting elders that represent small geographical or network sections of their commodity groups and settle minor disputes within that section. Market elders also provide more informal leadership to traders whose commodity has no queen or chief or who sell in fringe locations among neighbors selling many different commodities. These independent elders settle disputes and lead delegations to funerals, but they have no authority to enforce decisions or contributions. They do not attend marketwide meetings.

Men traders stopped at the elder rather than the chief level of organization more often than women traders for several reasons. A larger proportion of the men traders sell commodities sold by both sexes, which are difficult to organize centrally. Predominantly female commodities outnumber predominantly male ones. Men reported having market elders as often as women did, but they seem more hesitant to call single leaders by the chiefly titles of *ohene* or *sarkin.* In interviews, several male traders emphasized that their commodity leaders were only elders, not real chiefs, and did not claim jurisdiction over all of the eligible traders. Male chiefly titles carry greater political weight, so adopting them without clear authorization from superior chiefs in the appropriate hierarchy or without government permission may seem defiant or invite retaliation. Among the extremely small commodity groups, the five or so male kapok traders were content to call one of their number an elder. The same number of female traders selling snails or green leaves had an *ohemma* or a *magasia* (the Hausa title), but no formal council of elders.

Official cooperative status was worth seeking because it improved relations with the national government. Yam traders expressed the hope that this public endorsement of the legitimate status of their group would deflect government hostility to its existence, although any such effect was imperceptible in 1979. They also hoped it would improve their chances, admittedly slim, of receiving a cheap loan for a truck or other major improvement, since these seemed to be extended to cooperative groups only. Cooperative status had brought tangible benefits to others in the past. For example, a defunct tobacco traders' cooperative had once received a regular bulk allocation of government supplied tobacco, plus other commodities.

Traders show considerable creativity in incorporating Western terms and institutions into indigenous patterns of chiefship and elderhood without disrupting them substantially. In the all-male butchers' cooperative, the two hierarchies coexisted. The younger, Western-educated cooperative officers negotiated with the government concerning prices but showed careful respect for the prerogatives and dues of the ancient chief and his elders. More frequently, an indigenous hierarchy simply layers on extra Western titles. When yam traders registered their commodity group as a cooperative, their *ohemma* became the president, various elders became vice president, treasurer, etc., and the council of elders became the executive committee. The male secretary (employed since 1958) now keeps minutes of meetings, accounts of monthly dues and funeral contributions, and issues membership cards with photographs. Market women also become familiar with committee ritual through church women's groups. They continue to welcome new titles that give access to new forms of legitimacy—for example, when the yam *ohemma* became a member of the Kumasi District Assembly, which assigned her an air-conditioned office.

Superficial addition of Western models had little effect on the day-to-day activities of the commodity groups, either in functions or procedures. Their attraction to Western titles and trappings of office suggests some parallels to the classic examples of imitation of European organizational styles, such as the Kalela dance groups on the Copperbelt (Mitchell 1956). In this case, the balance of power remained with the indigenous aspects of function and legitimacy. The Westernized elements were adopted instrumentally and were not a major purpose of group formation. The process bears a deeper resemblance to the "reinvention of tradition" that took place during the codification of customary law (Wright 1982; Moore 1986). Africans presented institutions that were sometimes highly innovative as longstanding traditions and inserted them into respectable European classifications, both for more prestige and for self-defense when operating within the Eurocentric framework of the colonial and national political arena.

Dispute Settlement

Traders themselves rank internal dispute settlement first among the duties of market leaders and mention it first when they list those duties. They consider the need for speedy, impartial dispute settlement to be the main reason they join groups and accept group discipline. The most common types of dispute settled between colleagues show how this service maintains key social relations and the steady flow of business. The skills and personal qualities required for dispute settlement vary according to ethnic-specific norms, but provide the primary criteria for choosing new leaders.

The smooth conduct of transactions in retail and wholesale areas alike depends on mutual respect for a complex network of trading etiquette and conventional procedures. The ability to take disputes immediately to a nearby elder or to the *ohemma* if necessary for final settlement reduces the uncertainty over general compliance. Rapid local settlement avoids the loss of time involved in a protracted quarrel and the high cost and risk of complaints to police or courts unfamiliar with trading procedures. Traders find formal legal channels virtually useless. Market *ahemma* have no enforceable legal jurisdiction and many commercial conventions have no legal standing. Creditors could take their debtors to court, but the expense and time of a lawsuit would cost more and disrupt more social relations than losing the case in the market. Traders distrust the impartiality of the courts and suspect someone bringing a court case of wanting to ruin her opponent at any cost. One would not want to do business with such a person.

Group leaders both enforce well-known trading conventions and publicize correct procedure in doubtful cases. For example, when a neighboring seller "steals" a customer before she stops bargaining, she will have to refund the expected profit to the first seller. In one more ambiguous case, a yam buyer in the wholesale yard had promised to buy a hundred and then wandered away. She complained when the seller sold them to someone else, while the seller blamed her for not returning until the next day. The *ohemma* plays an important backup role in credit extended between colleagues, which is often necessary to keep goods moving. Creditors count on her ability to locate a defaulter, summon her, and enforce payment. Once the debt is proved, the *ohemma* tries to collect it immediately to finish the matter. The publicity itself constitutes the only punishment for default. The *ohemma* only imposes an extra fine if the debtor refuses to pay after her decision, as a kind of "contempt of court." The pleas of insolvency the debtor normally makes, while perhaps effective in delaying payment, weaken her credit rating with other traders.

Disputes between customers are another common source of cases before *ahemma*. Relations of customership are essential to capital accumulation, as shown in the previous chapter. Although completely voluntary, they carry enforceable obligations while the customership remains. A customer thinking of breaking the relation often furtively deals with other traders. I witnessed several disputes with unfaithful customers, who responded with counterclaims that they had never promised to be a steady customer or had already dropped the relationship. At that point, neither side wants to enforce or renew the relationship, but the public hearing enables them both to protest that they did nothing to justify ending the relation, defending their reputations in front of other potential customers. One orange wholesaler spied her customer delivering a truckload to a rival and protested that the woman always brought her goods to her. The traveler replied that she had not specifically promised this shipment to her, implying that she was not a long-term customer but disposed of each shipment by arrangement. Since oranges were scarce, the wholesaler was willing to fight for one last shipment, or at least hoped to be awarded the profit from it.

Like other Ghanaians, traders prefer to settle disputes within as small a group as possible, considering the social distance between disputants. Disputes between neighbors or within the family should ideally not be taken to outsiders, since the bad behavior of at least one party and their inability to discipline him and reconcile the injured one lowers the prestige of the family or neighborhood involved. Correct market dispute procedure begins with taking the case to a neighbor or elder. In the dispute between orange traders just mentioned, the defendant took the case to the *ohemma* after neighbors had failed to settle it.

This particular dispute happened while I was sitting with the orange *ohemma*, so I was able to observe the settlement procedure in more detail than participants included in descriptions of other disputes after the fact. The accused trader came up to the *ohemma* as she sat in her shelter to one side of the wholesale yard with a complaint that the other trader was telling lies about her. She asked the *ohemma* to clear her name, presenting her accuser as the instigator of the quarrel. By the time she finished telling her story, the other trader arrived and began to present her own side.

Both parties received a full hearing, repeating their stories several times at length at different points during the case. The *ohemma* asked questions and called for witnesses, but said relatively little. I was at first confused by these repetitive accounts of the facts of the case, seemingly pointless and much too frequent simply to inform newcomers. Then I became fascinated as I heard the settlement emerge gradually from them. Each disputant gathered a small set of supporters, to whom she repeated her story and complaints during breaks in the proceedings and during her opponent's speeches. Most commodity group members came to hear at least part of the speeches, although only a few contributed directly to the decision as advocates or discussants. Friends of each disputant comforted and calmed her, while encouraging her to drop some of her wilder statements in subsequent recitations. A less partisan, older trader from each supporter group took the lead in admonishing that trader and proposing compromises. Each disputant could express her feelings fully about these potential settlements while they were still private suggestions and not decisions coming from the *ohemma*.

At this stage, the *ohemma* took a more active role and began to repeat the facts of the case herself to elders arriving late from distant sections of the market. Surprisingly, her first resumes were the shortest and also seemed strangely incomplete, until I realized they included only those facts not in dispute. Further repetitions soon followed, and each became longer and smoother, as she removed more and more facts from contention. The disputants began conversely to shorten their own accounts and to respond directly to several proposals for settlement presented by different elders. When the serious proposals had narrowed to two, the *ohemma* announced her decision. She would divide the disputed shipment between them.

Then the two traders shocked their colleagues by refusing to accept this settlement. Their refusal represented a direct insult to the authority of the *ohemma* and the solidarity of the group. The *ohemma* went silent as their supporters went through several rounds of exhorting them to agree. Finally, the *ohemma* announced that she would take the shipment and sell it herself. This was a novel solution I never encountered before or since. The confiscation seemed a creative gesture to them because it not only compensated the *ohemma* for the insult but saved the oranges (then very scarce) from further deterioration. The surrounding traders immediately began clapping and cheering, drowning out the disputants, now shocked in their turn. The traders took time for a small celebration, clapping, dancing, and singing impromptu songs praising their *ohemma,* before returning to their stalls. They needed time to restore their equilibrium and hers after this disturbing incident. Other disputes over shipments were taken in stride, but the bitterness of these disputants and especially their refusal to accept settlement were unusual. The celebration in effect asserted that the dispute had been definitively settled. Orange traders remained upset for several days and refused to talk about the dispute afterwards, repeating that it was settled, it was finished.

Market *ahemma* depend on peer pressure and the disputants' mutual interest in consensus to maintain an orderly market. The *ahemma* have none of the authorized court oaths central to Asante chiefly dispute settlement procedure, which invoke ancestral disasters in order to threaten ancestral anger. Other spiritual enforcement measures available to traders are considered inappropriate for market use. Any person can swear an oath by ingesting earth or pouring water on it, which will cause the death of the guilty party, whether a thief or liar. Traders consider these oaths too serious for the market, where disagreements and even thefts are to some extent an inevitable product of commerce.

Twice I saw traders threaten to use these oaths in market disputes, and their colleagues forcibly restrained them. In one case a woman trading vegetables from a stool and basket missed some money she had left tucked under her ground cloth. She was among the squatters who moved into regular locations in the wholesale yard after wholesale operations finished and apparently had some reason to suspect her usual neighbor. Since she lacked proof, her willingness to swear served to dramatize the incident and give an indirect warning. Other neighbors laughed at her flamboyant gestures but also made sure to grab her arms and release the dangerous pinch of earth each time before it came near her mouth. Their comments made it clear that they thought the oath would work, even if inappropriate. As one said, "If we swore an oath every time something was stolen, there would be dead bodies lying all over the market."

Another incident had even more direct comic intent, but the oath gesture itself was likewise carefully avoided. On a hot, dull day with few yams in the wholesale yard, one of the middle-aged wholesalers came into the association shed with a complaint against an elderly yam porter, also something of a clown. He had ruined her reputation, she claimed, by bragging to people in the yard that he had married her at some unspecified time in the past (a common euphemism for sleeping together). She entertained us all with a forceful counterclaim that not only had he never touched her but was clearly incapable of doing so. Threatening to swear an oath on it seemed only the ultimate theatrical pose. But I noticed that when she dramatically called for a water-seller and bought a jar of water for the oath, the water itself was treated very carefully to make sure none of it did spill on the ground. While continuing to laugh heartily, the *ohemma* herself took the jar away from her and drank it off to the last drop.

Traders abide voluntarily, if not always cheerfully, by their *ohemma*'s decisions because they need a speedy decision by a panel familiar with market conditions, both in their present dispute and for the future. The paramount aim of dispute settlement is to preserve the smooth flow of business for the disputants and other traders. The loss of time and income involved discourages traders from appealing often to the *ohemma,* for fear others will avoid dealing with them. Even traders in the middle of a dispute exclaim at frequent intervals their great reluctance to press the issue with the refrain, "I don't like to argue," even if they are screaming it. Disputes multiply when the flow of business is already threatened by other factors during the dry season. Short supplies and high prices put traders under severe capital and income pressure. Loss of one shipment at such times can leave the loser with nothing to sell for several days. The slow pace of the market then also allows plenty of time for noticing offenses and prosecuting disputes.

Farmers and other nontraders can also bring disputes with Kumasi traders before the commodity *ahemma.* One elaborate case involved debt collection from a yam traveler for a farmer. The farmer had advanced goods on credit and expected the traveler to pay when she returned. When she made repeated excuses, his elder brother brought him to Kumasi to find her. The *ohemma* located her and forced her to appear, although she was not a formal member of the Kumasi association. The hearing, although not involving other *ohemma,* was conducted very formally compared to disputes between traders. A trader collecting from a farmer would have to approach his or her village or town chief. The proceedings illustrated the value traders place on an atmosphere of mutual confidence based on reliable dispute settlement. The market elders made special efforts to treat the visiting farmers respectfully and exhorted them to return with any future problems.

When the defaulter appealed for support to other travelers, saying they all did the same, their elders rose with scathing diatribes. They criticized the trader for taking advantage of an exceptionally gullible farmer, whom some speculated later might have been mentally retarded. Travelers also explained later that they wanted their own farmer contacts to continue extending credit and bringing disputes to the *ohemma* instead of to less sympathetic rural chiefs. This trader's worst crime had been trying to scare him away from Kumasi by warning him the *ohemma* would beat him. When they heard this from him, the elders exploded that she had insulted the *ohemma*. There was serious talk of a fine for this offense, although in the end they settled for having her pay the entire debt on the spot, by borrowing from a friend in the market if necessary. Traders considered later that the insult would have justified her expulsion had she been a member of the group, and they expected her to avoid Kumasi voluntarily.

External Negotiations

Representing traders in negotiations with outside institutions or groups is another primary function of the market *ahemmafuo*. Market leaders spent considerable time in negotiations with government officials, military representatives, chiefs, farmers, drivers, porters, and other nontraders during the 1978–80 period of close observation. Traders also mentioned external negotiations as one of the major services provided by leaders, since as individuals they could not afford to leave the market for these frequent summons.

While dispute settlement between group members was the day-to-day priority generating and maintaining group solidarity, external negotiations seem to have provided the historical impetus toward starting the current commodity groups. The earliest groups reported in Kumasi after British conquest were formed by immigrants who needed to negotiate their guest status and loyalties. These were the dried-fish traders, mainly Fante women from the coast, and the Northern men trading cattle and kola. Group formation by Asante women traders saw two surges: in the late 1930s, when the women yam traders were seeking protection from immigrant Gao wholesalers and negotiating to level space for their wholesale yard, and in the 1950s, when rival nationalist parties struggled for control of the market and the country and yam traders fought Gaos again in 1958 (Drake and Lacy 1966). A richly detailed historical study of Dugbe market in Ibadan, Nigeria, also concludes that groups formed in response to the need for external negotiations, at independence or when specific hostile policies were proposed (Ogunsanwo 1988).

Almost all of the negotiations observed could be considered a form of dispute settlement. They took place in response to a dispute or problem between the traders and outside groups or institutions, which they aimed to resolve. The *ahemmafuo* tried to implement the norms and procedures of dispute settlement between individuals in these intergroup negotiations, but could only do so to the extent that nontraders respected them. This was occasionally problematic in negotiations with male groups because of the deference men expect in impersonal male-female relations, making an analogy to marriage rather than to lineage relations. Intergroup negotiations do not always have a single presiding figure whom both sides recognize as senior and impartial, although sometimes such a figure was sought out by approaching the Market Manager, the Regional Commissioner, or even the National Council on Women and Development in cases over which they had no official jurisdiction. In addition, the group negotiations observed rarely reached a definite end or settlement. Since they fundamentally concern the relative power of the two groups, the settlement would be continually reopened and adjusted, or such adjustment promised but deferred.

This consistent pattern of group negotiations shows clearly even in informal negotiations not involving the *ahemma*. One dispute between small numbers of traders and carriers involved only ad hoc leaders on both sides. Garden egg traders who regularly buy at the adjacent Kejetia Lorry Park prefer to hire head carriers they know among the young men and boys swarming there so that they can send goods back to the market unaccompanied and remain to buy more. One morning, four or five of these carriers arrived simultaneously in the wholesale yard with goods from several traders. They demanded a higher payment than the rate previously accepted. The carriers chose to demand higher pay in a group situation outside of the lorry park, which gave them the benefit of numbers, removed immediate competition, and would set a public rate for future reference.

The oldest of these young men and the most aggressive among the traders conducted the whole negotiation. Other members fell quiet without overtly choosing their leaders. They argued fiercely, each threatening that their whole group would break off relations. This particular episode ended inconclusively, when the fragile coalition of carriers cracked. The youngest, a boy of twelve or fourteen, began to cry because he had not eaten and needed the money to buy his lunch. The leading trader ostentatiously paid him a generous amount, although he had not actually carried her goods. Both sides closed by threatening to insist on their rights the next time.

Formal negotiations ensued when organized groups of traders and carriers took up the same issue of transport fees. The yam traders employ a standing group of carriers, called porters, who unload the yams from trucks in the wholesale yard and then cart the resold yams into the market to the buyer's stall. A porters' elder allocates work and stands responsible for thefts or breakages. One morning the porters demanded a rate increase and struck, forcing the traders to unload their own yams. The yard had to close down for a formal meeting of the yam elders, so negotiations waited until the next day. The porters' elder appeared in immaculate robes, accompanied by the head of the drivers' union. The driver, although much younger in age, was supporting him as his elder, because of drivers' stronger economic position and negotiating experience. The yam *ohemma* and her elders showed extreme courtesy in receiving their visitors. In a series of speeches, they commiserated with the porters' pleas of poverty and inflation while themselves complaining of the unsettled conditions of price control and its confiscations. They could afford to sympathize, given their power advantage over the relatively impoverished porters. After lengthy polite discussion, the porters agreed to wait for their increase until the new yams came in. In fact, they did not strike again after the harvest.

The yam traders' negotiations with their truck drivers over transport charges were much less polite. This dispute pitted two powerful groups against each other, and they manipulated the full range of procedural and economic points at issue. The Kumasi talks followed intense negotiations in Accra between yam traders and drivers there. Accra traders who brought yams from the supply areas had gone to their *ohemma* threatening to stop traveling because of ever higher freight charges during a period of gasoline and transport shortage. At this point, the Accra *bayerehemma* notified her superior, the Kumasi *bayerehemma* (according to the latter). The Kumasi *bayerehemma*, as head of the national association, called a full convention in Accra with great speed and secrecy. The *bayerehemma* and two elders came from each major town in Ghana, and the drivers reportedly made some concessions.

If the yam traders had hoped to settle the issue by assembling their full association, they were soon disappointed. Within two weeks after the Accra meeting, Kumasi drivers announced an increase in the mileage charge for bringing yams from the farms. Although traders negotiate each trip separately, taking the quality of the roads into account, they consider the mileage rate an influential starting point. Drivers' leaders first tried to manipulate the meeting day as a show of strength and to avoid the presence of an Accra delegation. Since yams were selling slowly, the traders wanted to close the market for a meeting on Thursday, their usual meeting day, while the drivers insisted on a Sunday meeting. The drivers' elders appeared at the meeting called by traders, but walked out. They said they had work to do, but before leaving they asserted their right to set prices unilaterally according to their costs. They taunted the traders openly by saying, "Can you drive a truck?"

Instead of confronting the drivers directly, the *bayerehemma* appealed to the Market Manager. The Market Manager did arrange an impressive meeting attended by the yam delegation, the yam drivers, the Motor Union, and the Regional Commissioner. At this meeting he did not propose any compromise, however, but simply told the drivers to attend the traders' meeting. He left the issue of transport charge levels untouched, and no further meetings took place. The extreme transport shortage seemed to give drivers the upper hand. In appealing to the Market Manager, the *bayerehemma* invoked a standard dispute settlement norm, taking the case to a mutual superior. The weaker party usually appeals to an authority presumed high enough to be impartial, just as the accused orange trader appealed to her *ohemma*. In such circumstances, the *bayerehemma* becomes one of the disputants and the superior takes the presiding role. To settle the case effectively, the senior figure must have ties to both parties. These enable him to ensure that both sides abide by the settlement when they have agreed to it. Market leaders had been known to take disputes before the Regional Commissioner and the *Asantehemma,* depending on the kind of settlement they wanted. In disputes involving farmers or markets outside of Kumasi, they could also approach chiefs with local jurisdiction. The government also used the *Asantehene, Asantehemma,* and local chiefs to mediate with traders in Kumasi and elsewhere.

Market traders expected external negotiations to conform to general procedural norms of Asante dispute settlement, whether or not there was a presiding senior figure. Both sides should be given a full hearing. They should negotiate in good faith, with some willingness to compromise. The settlement should be accepted by both sides, not imposed by one, and both should abide by what they agreed upon. Traders became furious when the Armed Forces Revolutionary Council (AFRC) government broke these norms of negotiation blatantly and repeatedly in meetings held on price control during their brief rule in 1979. Market *ahemma* claimed that "they don't want to talk" despite incessant summons to meetings because these meetings did not follow norms of legitimate talking as they knew them. They often referred to one most basic deviation, that the AFRC commonly scheduled these meetings after the decisions had been made. Rather than negotiations, these seemed to them to be announcements or occasions for intimidation. "How can you talk to a gun?" one *ohemma* explained, implying that soldiers were not behaving like people, who talk.

In one early example, the *ahemmafuo* dutifully brought samples of size and quality grades of various staple foodstuffs to a meeting arranged by the Regional Commissioner and agreed to prices for each grade. The next day, soldiers in the market ignored this price structure when seizing and selling off yams. By contrast, soldiers respected the prices set at similar meetings between AFRC representatives, male producers of adinkra cloth, furniture, and poultry, and their raw material and feed suppliers.

The most elaborate meeting during this period led to the most intense resentment. Traders saw both its procedures and its rhetoric as insults to their leaders. *Ahemma* were summoned to the meeting in their own shed, not given a choice of time or place. Robertson confirms in a rural setting the importance of conforming to accepted, familiar meeting styles and procedures in order to ensure effective and recognized participation (Robertson 1976). The president and secretary of the National Farmers' Association and a leader of the official farm laborers' association made no pretense of consultation or of seeking mutual agreement. They harangued the traders about their stubborn refusal to lower prices and threatened that traders would suffer for their evil ways. The opposite side did not even acknowledge points brought up by traders by agreeing or disagreeing. One trader complained, "They treat us like children, when we are old enough to be their mothers." A particularly offensive speaker repeatedly asked, "*Wati*?" (literally, have you heard?), a phrase commonly used to instruct or scold children or subordinates. The most militant *ohemma* repeated this sarcastically in an answering speech, saying *mati* and *yati* (I and we have heard).

Ceremonial Duties

Such points of ceremony in important economic negotiations are not the main ceremonial functions of market *ahemma*. Relatively few market events or social relations have a ceremonial aspect. Market traders instead put a high value on ceremonial representation by leaders at events outside of the market, especially funerals. By contrast, Moslem craft groups reinforced group solidarity by praying together daily in the market and holding elaborate graduation ceremonies for apprentices. A Bolivian example demonstrates a fully opposite possibility, where elected market leaders used market ceremonies and market-sponsored fiestas as a central activity for building and demonstrating political support (Buechler and Buechler 1977).

The scale of funeral attendance marks structural divisions within the market. When a commodity group member dies, her *ohemma* leads all the group members to attend her funeral en masse. The individual *ahemma* also attend funerals of group members' close relatives, accompanied by several elders and near neighbors of the bereaved, presenting a group contribution. The funeral of an *ohemma* would be a marketwide event, I was told, with the entire market closed and all traders attending, as they did when the aged tomato *ohemma* died. When an *ohemma* held a funeral for a close relative, such as the *bayerehemma* did for her mother, her entire commodity group and the other *ahemma* attended. For the 1979 funeral of a yam trader held in Kumasi, the yam wholesale yard and stalls closed for the day. Traders marched together to the house, brandishing yams and singing funeral songs referring to the group. The *bayerehemma* led chanting there, presented a cloth and other gifts for the burial, and made a substantial contribution. The traders stayed in a group for the rest of the afternoon in the street outside of the house, which was crowded with mourners. They made a show of selling the yams they had brought to other mourners and kept on singing and dancing together when other mourners were standing quietly.

Traders expect leaders of commodity groups to offer them ceremonial services similar to those from leaders of other Kumasi voluntary groups. Funeral attendance is a primary benefit of membership in any group and demonstrates its strength and cohesion. The drivers' union sends representatives to drivers' funerals in their hometowns and attended en masse the funeral of one driver killed in a Kumasi robbery, with everyone honking their horns. Associations based on region or clan of origin provide financial assistance for illness or family funerals and also hold annual parties. Many traders also belong to church women's groups and choirs that attend members' funerals in uniform, singing. They gain further prestige by fundraising and attending church services together in uniform. Asantes value group membership as such, since for many ceremonial purposes groups are virtually interchangeable. At one funeral I attended, a middle-aged woman remarked appreciatively that the dead woman had belonged to four *ekuo,* or groups: two church choirs, a commodity group, and a benevolent society. All four groups attended en masse to make a grand funeral such as anyone might aspire to.

Market *ahemma* also should keep up the public image of market traders by taking part in community events. The senior *ahemmafuo* went to greet the *Asantehene* and *Asantehemma* at Christmas and other public holidays. They attended the durbars or public festivals held for heads of state or distinguished foreign visitors. They attended the annual New Yam festival and the historic Outdooring of the Golden Stool (the Asante symbol of nationhood), which had not been held for twenty years prior to 1979. The entire market closed to attend the second funeral of the *Asantehemma* in 1979. At all of these events, the *ahemmafo* were introduced as such and given respect as prominent citizens, such as special seating, but had no ceremonial role other than making an appropriate financial contribution. Group members might also attend such events in large groups, if not en masse. Formerly, yam traders attending events such as funerals in a group wore a uniform cloth, chosen with a pattern resembling yams. Shortages of cloth and money in recent decades had prevented younger members from obtaining it and only a few faded outfits remained.

Small ceremonies are held to mark events inside of the market. The Sunday after the yam trader's funeral just described, the committee of elders met privately in the wholesale yard shed to pour libation and pray for or to her. When a new yam trader joins the group, her sponsor formally presents her to the *bayerehemma* and elders. She asks for their protection and presents a gift, and the *bayerehemma* invites her to complain if anyone cheats or mistreats her. Yam traders celebrate the arrival of the first new yams after harvest each year by pouring libation in their shed, which I attended in 1992. The date was fixed a few days in advance, with reports of the new harvest. All the mature traders gathered inside of the shed in the morning in their fine cloths, while the younger ones and carriers crowded outside, waiting to begin sales until the ceremony was over. When the *bayerehemma* arrived, she wore a blue and white cloth outfit over which she put on a new pure white brocade overdress made for the occasion. She also showed around an uncut blue and white cloth and several bottles of schnapps. The travelers' leader, some elders, and the leaders of the drivers and carriers groups brought up bottles of schnapps and presented them with short speeches. After a Christian prayer by one of the more devout elders, the *bayerehemma* poured a lengthy libation to the earth goddess on the cement floor of the shed, with thanks and requests for a good harvest, low prices, and no harassment. The remaining schnapps was passed around, first to the elders inside and then to those cheering outside.

Commodity groups also gather to celebrate public holidays. At Christmas and Easter, the yam elders gather at the *bayerehemma*'s house to pour a libation for peace and prosperity. When circumstances permit, they hold a party. The yam travelers hold a separate and rowdier Christmas party, suitable to their youth and strength. Market *ahemmafo* send foodstuffs to the Asantehene for the *Akwasidae* festival held every forty days. Moslem trader groups celebrate their own major festivals, such as the Prophet's Birthday, with prayers and feasts.

A good leader should also act with as much formality and dignity as possible on any public occasion so as to enhance the status of her group. She should dress well and exchange visits and gifts with other *ahemma* and local leaders. One trader remembered with satisfaction a previous *ahemma*, her relative, who "always went places, so that everyone was mentioning her name." These standards are goals, by no means ritual obligations. No one condemns leaders of smaller, poorer commodity groups for having to economize or even carry heavy loads on occasion. On the other hand, the ideal encourages traders to choose leaders with enough wealth that they can afford leisure for ceremonies and visiting and can support dependents to handle their less prestigious tasks.

Commercial Regulation

Market leaders only play a limited role in regulating daily commerce. They exercise their authority mainly through settling disputes over the interpretation of commonly acknowledged rules and rarely take positive legislative action. *Ahemma* also clarify or emphasize established norms by proclamation when repeated disputes show confusion on a particular subject, perhaps under changing conditions. In the wholesale yards, the *ahemma* make sure each arriving truck pulls up in line so the wholesaler has a distinct place to unload her goods. This prevents physical confusion and consequent disputes and can require constant supervision during the crowded harvest or Christmas seasons. *Ahemma* in neighboring yards coordinate shifts in the yard boundaries to accommodate seasonal changes in daily volume and episodes such as floods, demolitions, and expanding garbage heaps.

The potential for selective or distorted enforcement of rules by the *ohemma* is sharply contained by the procedures for dispute settlement and the role of the elders. Constant consultation with elders is required in disputes and policy decisions. For example, when one *ohemma* wanted to monetarize her customary dues she had to negotiate the rate with her elders and put up with delays in collection when traders pleaded slow sales. Ordinary members can passively refuse to comply or to enforce unpopular decisions and elect different elders if necessary. In the last instance, they can destool the leader or withdraw from the group. As already shown, the *ahemma* do not control access to market stalls, the basis of group membership. Consequently, they cannot pack the group with their own dependents or supporters in order to force through unpopular changes or avoid destoolment.

Group discipline becomes semicompulsory because of the threat of withdrawal of services and mutual support. An uncooperative trader may find only lukewarm support from elders or the *ohemma* when she brings her next dispute before them. Traders consequently hesitate to oppose leaders in minor matters. A trader who refused to accept a judgment against her could not later complain to the *ohemma* about mistreatment by others. A reputation for solidarity and trustworthiness constitutes good character and helps one to be believed in future disputes, especially internal ones. Loyal behavior also reinforces informal mutual aid between neighbors. Reluctant neighbors can find many excuses to avoid doing commonplace favors, like watching one's goods during a brief absence. Routine commercial transactions presume some degree of trust, and several groups provide valued trading services in storage or credit collection. Traders can operate successfully completely outside of the organized commodity groups, but this may require relocating to a different part of the market complex. The fear of complete ostracism encourages member traders to accept lighter punishments or fines.

The routine functions of the *ahemma* nonetheless positioned them well to rapidly expand their regulatory role temporarily in time of crisis. Trager makes a similar distinction between the relatively restricted routine functions of market leaders in a Yoruba town in Nigeria and their ability to mobilize quickly and expand their jurisdiction dramatically in time of crisis (Trager 1976). Many commodity groups there hardly ever held formal meetings, although leaders frequently settled disputes. They could still respond within hours, however, to either economic threats of commercial restrictions or to the public safety threat implied by a kidnapped child.

The Ghana currency exchange exercise in March 1979 demonstrated clearly the importance and limits of leaders' responses by posing direct challenge to commercial transactions. After closing all of the borders, the Ghana government announced on Friday evening, March 9, that all existing banknotes would become valueless on March 26. The entire population had to exchange its old notes for new ones through the banks, at a rate of ten old to seven new cedis. Although the deadline was extended and extra facilities for exchange set up, the basic procedure remained the same. Commodity group leaders, both *ahemma* and others, coordinated discussions within each group of the

The orange *ohemma* (bottom left) hears a dispute

The yam *ohemma* receives visitors at home at Christmas

Children help pound fufu in a shared courtyard

Days after the 1979 demolition, men return to sell Hausa caps and local medicines

practical implications of the change. Each group formed a consensus on joint strategies for weathering the transition period. Leaders then publicized these decisions so that individual traders would not suffer disproportionately. The *ahemmafuo* visited each other to compare notes and commiserate but did not call a general meeting or formulate any marketwide guidelines or response.

In the onion shed, the onion traders met informally in the aisles Saturday morning to discuss the announcements. Some continued to do business at normal prices, as the radio statements had instructed. The onion *ohemma* collected information on the exchange procedures, which varied for different amounts of cash. The rate of exchange also ranged between five and seven new cedis for ten old cedis. One woman brought a poster of the new money which the *ohemma* showed around. The onion shed nightwatchmen, all Northern men, held their own conclave, which the *ohemma* visited. As traders began to realize the old money had been effectively discounted, they stopped selling unless customers could pay with coins. They decided individually either to stay at home or to adjust their prices to charge ten old cedis for seven in the original price.

The relatively calm response in the onion shed made quite a contrast with the havoc created in the wholesale yards. Commercial credit was a prominent feature in transactions here, and many traders owed or were owed a substantial proportion of their working capital. Hysterical wholesalers sought advice from the *ohemma* when their debtors tried to force them to accept payment in old notes. Travelers would not accept the old notes from wholesalers, since they expected farmers and drivers to reject them, but were stranded until they could be paid off. In hardship cases, leaders negotiated reasonable discounts for the old notes. The cassava yard closed down first because drivers doubled charges in old note terms, and reopened only when traders obtained new notes. Although most of the yards closed, the *ahemma* came to market daily to monitor conditions. The onion yard only closed in the second week, when traders decided to take a break to finish changing.

After the initial shock phase of the exchange exercise, commodity *ahemma* resumed a passive role. Traders simply decided whether to accept old cedis or not, or to stay home, depending on whether they had savings to eat from and bank connections to ease further changing. Some sellers extended credit rather than accept old notes. Sellers stated prices either in new or old cedis, the latter prices climbing as the deadline approached. The ohemma could enforce these terms just as she did normal agreements. A few traders with close bank connections continued accepting old cedis to the end. Customers struggled over who would receive new notes first in payment when they arrived. Some brought these arguments to the *ahemma*, but priority depended on the strength of personal ties, not a rule they could enforce. Wide fluctuations in food supply from day to day raised tensions. The level of commercial activity dropped to about half, since traders, drivers, suppliers, and consumers all were spending most of their time trying to exchange their money. Perishable vegetables had a glut, since farmers could not easily delay harvest, while cassava, fish, and plantains stopped coming. Stress and hunger shortened tempers, and disputes multiplied. During this crisis, the ordinary duties of the *ahemma* were as much in demand as these extraordinary functions.

Succession to Market Offices

All mature traders participate in electing a new *ohemma* when death or destooling makes it necessary. In the larger, more elaborately organized groups there is a formal roster of these, but in most groups consensus recognition of maturity follows achieving some combination of age, emotional reliability, familiarity with market affairs, and financial independence and stability. The new *ohemma* must be chosen within a day or two of the death of an incumbent. In fact, traders have begun to evaluate potential candidates if their *ohemma* shows signs of old age or weakness. When a younger *ohemma* dies suddenly from accident or acute illness, the lack of preliminary politicking and alliance formation means an unusually stormy election.

The appropriate criteria for selecting the best candidate are very widely known. Interviews with leaders and followers, men and women and participants and nonparticipants, elicited very consistent lists. Controversy and competition focuses on which among the elders eligible actually has most of these desirable characteristics and on which criteria are the most essential, since it is likely that no candidate has all of them. Specific criteria were explained and justified with reference to the internal and external duties of market leaders. Traders initially volunteer the character traits and skills they consider essential qualifications for performing internal duties, especially dispute settlement. Qualifications useful for external duties, including influential connections and wealth, emerged from discussions of specific past candidates. Traders sometimes condemned or minimized the importance of external criteria, but acknowledged their influence on specific past elections. Those who justified considering these criteria cited the advantages they brought a leader in external negotiations.

Traders emphasize impartiality, patience, and honesty as the personal qualities of a good market leader. Electors judge these qualities from a candidate's previous behavior in disputes. A trader who rarely starts disputes, refrains from exaggerated statements, shows little anger, and seeks no revenge shows the correct personality. Experienced traders demonstrate their character and skill by settling small disputes informally among their neighbors and associates. They should listen carefully to all parties, refrain from taking sides, and propose compromises which satisfy both parties. Quick and permanent dispute settlement requires a reputation for fairness as well as the mental ability to find a fair solution. Traders also mention speaking ability as an advantage in a leader. Effective speakers more easily convince disputants of their own interest in abiding by a decision. In negotiations, polished and articulate speeches raise the prestige of traders and gain concessions for them. Finally, graceful language embellishes the many occasions which call for short addresses, including libations, funeral contributions, social visits, and reports of journeys.

Potential *ahemma* must have passed a threshold age, approximately forty years. Younger leaders would not get sufficient respect from inside or outside of the group. In the eyes of traders, they would lack the wisdom and mental stability to perform well. In addition, menstrual restrictions and the demands of husbands and young children would conflict with some of their official duties. Women over forty usually have a child old enough to cook and look after the others. They may well have reached their target number of children and be withdrawing gradually from marriage. Age is not an absolutely positive criterion, however. Traders rarely elect a very old *ohemma,* because they prefer infrequent elections and long terms of office to reap the benefits of experience. They also recognize that physical weakness interferes with daily market attendance, negotiations, and funerals. Infirm *ahemma* were represented by a surrogate, usually one of the elders, in some or all of these activities, although a new election will not be held until she actually dies.

Length of tenure in the market also serves as a threshold rather than an absolute ranking criteria. Candidates must have sufficient experience as independent traders to understand fully all of the common commercial relations and to know the personalities and weaknesses of the other traders. Among the snail sellers and other small groups, the incumbent *ahemma* had qualified by pure seniority, since she had begun trading before all of the others. In very large groups, candidates must have demonstrated their leadership qualities by previously serving in the executive committee or some other office.

Income is also not an unambiguous criteria. Market leaders must have a respectable level of wealth, relative to standards within their commodity group. Traders presume an unsuccessful trader too lazy or naive to make a good leader. Her competence ensures her long-term survival as a trader and her financial independence from other traders, which could compromise her impartiality. This concern leads traders to select *ahemma* with higher than average, but not the highest incomes. This practice may be possible because of the rarity of true commercial dependence on wealthy traders and, as such, may change in the near future if that dependence spreads. In Lome, Togo, the wealthiest cloth wholesalers are continually re-elected as heads of the cloth traders' associations, which they took the initiative to organize in the 1950s. They monopolize the most popular cloth patterns, and each employs many agents and "filles" (Cordonnier 1982).

Poorer than average Kumasi traders say they cannot afford to accept offices that involve extra expense and time off, and the office itself does not improve their economic position enough to provide the resources to carry out its duties. *Ahemma* collect only token dues of a yam or two from each truck or a handful of tomatoes from each box. These are sold from their stalls, but hardly compensate for the amount of work time they spend in dispute settlement or meetings. Candidates with larger capital levels can turn retailing over to a daughter or other assistant when necessary and put some of their capital out in advances. Leadership of the smaller commodity groups involves proportionately less time, allowing poorer traders to function as their leaders.

The wealthiest traders also rarely obtained or sought high office. Their degree of economic success implies a more aggressive pursuit of self-interest than traders consider appropriate to leaders, since it is usually incompatible with the desired judicial temperament. In the process of active accumulation, they have inevitably alienated some envious competitors, thereby losing potential votes. These high-volume traders typically expressed little interest in market leadership. They work long hours and have many steady customers who are arriving at all times. They say they have no time to gain the necessary experience and reputation by offering advice and settling small quarrels among their neighbors. Time lost attending funerals and meetings outside of the market would significantly reduce their incomes. Their wealth alone brings sufficient prestige, and the office brings comparatively little financial reward.

Most Kumasi market traders interviewed count connections to powerful political, military, or palace figures as illegitimate criteria for choosing new leaders, just as they do exceptional wealth. Nonetheless, they freely discuss how these factors operated in specific recent elections. Electors in the larger, more senior commodity groups feel considerable political pressure from wealthy, influential quarters in Kumasi. Less prestigious groups attract little outside attention. To justify supporting candidates with powerful backers, traders remark that a well-connected leader does bring more prestige and life experience to the office. Constituents hope the new *ohemma* can use these connections to protect group members individually and to influence public policy on their behalf.

During the mid-fifties, market offices were incorporated into the rivalry between two nationalist political parties. The National Liberation Movement (NLM) was strongly associated with Asante nationalism and cocoa, but the Convention People's Party (CPP) also had considerable support in Kumasi among immigrants and the working poor. Market women were active in both parties, collecting substantial financial contributions, and addressing and attending rallies. Market *ahemma* known to back one or the other party could be expected to deliver a sizable block vote for their candidate. When a market office fell vacant, supporters of each side fielded their own candidate or tried to enlist one of those likely to succeed.

Instead of building political sophistication and commitment among the market leaders, this period had the opposite effect on those who had come through it. It convinced many of them to avoid national political involvement on principle. There was considerable political violence in Kumasi before and after the 1956 elections. Armed thugs from both parties roamed Kumasi, beating up partisans of the other and defending their own (Allman 1993). Several current *ahemma* mentioned having to leave town for as long as a year to escape retaliation. Even those supporting the then victorious CPP, led by Kwame Nkrumah, felt they had received little in return for the danger and effort. When parties and elections briefly returned between 1979 and 1981, they voted, but refused even to discuss their party preference publicly. They seemed more willing to run for the large numbers of nonpartisan positions in the 1989 local government elections, after which the *Bayerehemma* joined the Kumasi City Council.

Descent is not an acknowledged selection criterion and so plays an irregular and indirect role in market succession. Leaders can give their relatives valuable experience as their formal or informal assistants, but the elders have no obligation to choose these qualified relatives to succeed them. Daughters rarely succeed their mothers because of close generational timing. If ambitious and successful enough to be viable candidates, they become independent traders while the mother is still middle-aged and would not want to remain in her shadow for so many decades.

Passing on the title to a descendent proved elusive even in a case where many factors seemed to favor it. The aged, bedridden tomato *ohemma* had named a granddaughter as her representative when she became bedridden. Her daughter was not available because she had left decades ago to found the Bolgatanga company and was now its *ohemma*. The granddaughter had taken over effective leadership as the old *ohemma* declined into senility after several strokes. Her authority went unchallenged, although she was still rather young compared to other *ahemma* in 1979. Perhaps this explained her relatively aggressive and pushy leadership style, but it seemed well within the range of acceptability and attracted no comment I noticed. I thought of her as the heir apparent, but elders in other groups insisted that "you never can tell." She had no assurance that the elders would confirm her position after the aged *ohemma*'s death. Interestingly enough, in a 1981 film interview she asserted quite positively that market *ohemma* positions were inherited from mother to daughter (Granada Television International 1983). When I last returned, in 1990, the grandmother had died and the tomato elders had in fact elected someone else, a bit older, as their current *ohemma*.

Another anomalous case underlines the difficulty of imposing effective candidates from outside the ranks of the experienced elders. During the Nkrumah period, a woman had been installed as *ohemma* of the plantain sellers because of her connections to the ruling party. She had never even sold plantains and only had a few distant relatives in the group. After Nkrumah had been put out of office and his CPP outlawed, she had no more basis for remaining in the market. Her influential connections remained strong enough to prevent the plantain sellers from installing anyone else in her place, although the fact that they were dispersed in several unloading locations also made unity difficult.

When I asked plantain sellers to introduce me to their *ohemma* in 1978, they responded with confusion or suspicion. At first they said they did not have one, then they sent me to one of the larger wholesalers after arguing among themselves whether she was an elder or *panyini*. I talked to her several times before she explained about the CPP *ohemma* and arranged for someone to take me to visit her at home. From 1978 to 1980, the plantain *ohemma* never appeared in the market to participate in daily dispute settlement or negotiations, nor did she attend traders' funerals. She attended the *Asantehemma*'s funeral and other court occasions, but not with the group of market *ahemmafuo*.

Her fortunes rose again briefly under civilian rule from 1979 to 1981. The People's National Party, widely considered a successor to the

CPP, won the 1979 elections with their candidate President Hilla Limann. When interviewed for British television in 1981, she was back in the market and clearly enjoying her reclaimed status (Granada Television International 1983). However, her inexperience in market procedures contributed to her problems in controlling the group. In a staged dispute sequence filmed, her elders can be heard protesting, "We don't do it this way!" as she was clearly unable to follow normal procedures. She not only fined a trader for selling rotten plantain, which specialized processors commonly buy at a lower price, but kept the fine herself instead of giving it to the offended party. When I returned in 1990, the PNP had been overthrown and she was at home again, although also in frail health by then.

Conclusion

Examination of the concrete relations between leaders and followers in Kumasi Central Market commodity groups confirms the central role of dispute settlement in the continuation of the groups. The way age, experience, and wealth appear as threshold rather than absolute ranking criteria for candidates for leadership is directly linked to the norms and tasks involved in dispute settlement. The dominant Asante style of dispute settlement demanded *ahemma* who were not among the oldest, wealthiest, or most aggressive traders. Ceremonial considerations favor the selection of wealthy traders as leaders, but elders considered this criteria illegitimate and detrimental to group unity. In fact, very wealthy traders tended not to seek group leadership for economic reasons. Drawn from traders of middling status, *ahemma* do not acquire a distinctive economic position as queens, based on regulatory advantage, fees, or even court fines. Dispute settlement gives *ahemma* a reactive role in commercial regulation, conservative but not passive in the face of crisis.

Ceremonial functions, especially funerals, are important to strengthen members' emotional commitment to the groups; however, they did not provide the primary basis for group formation or for the exclusion of nonparticipants. For example, Asante yam traders expressed resentment of non-Akan traders because they did not participate fully in the funeral ceremonies of Asantes, the dominant group. Although the Asante leaders suspected them of disloyalty, they retained functional membership in the group as long as they abided by dispute settlements.

A comparison of strongly and weakly organized commodities and locations confirms the primacy of dispute settlement in group dynamics. Wholesale yards put the highest premium on fast dispute settlement. In commodities with wholesale yards, the *ohemma* spends the peak trading hours there, in a small kiosk or "office." Commodity group leaders have the tightest control of the wholesale yards. Even in the specialized retail locations, stall-based traders emphasize neighborly relations, independent of the complexity of their groups's leadership roles. Commodity groups without wholesale yards have less authoritative *ahemma* whose style and actions are often hard to distinguish from those of the independent elders recognized only by their neighbors.

Concentrated retail areas also show firm allegiance to commodity groups. In commodities without wholesale yards, traders select a leader from among the stallholders. Regular buyers do not join such groups, as retailers in other commodities would join the yard-centered groups, but they can take grievances to the *ohemma.* The concentrated retail area offers enough advantages in information access and potential clients that both stallholders and their patrons take care to maintain their social relations there. This provides the necessary motivation to achieve consensus and abide by dispute settlements. Significantly, when there is monopoly control of supplies, for example in an imported commodity, or when there are sellers of both sexes, effective settlement of the most common disputes or problems through negotiation is more difficult. Commodities like enamelware or secondhand clothing, with both of these problems, have concentrated retail sections but no groups.

Only locations with stable trading populations specialized by commodity can support an organized group at all. In locations that mix traders selling many different commodities, ties of neighborhood alone support leadership functions. Disputes between neighbors cross commodity lines there, so localized elders rather than commodity group leaders are appropriate senior mediators. Disputes between neighbors more often concern personality clashes, which a leader can rarely resolve definitively.

Transience and intermixture by commodity in marginal sections without permanent stalls both prevent the development of group loyalty based on locality. Trading neighbors in the mixed commodity areas attend each others' funerals and take care of each others' stalls, but this is not sufficient for group formation. They may respect local elders, but they take little interest in commodity groups even in commodities they sell. Individual traders have low commodity commitment, since their commercial relations depend on casual, walk-through traffic rather than repeat transactions. Among squatters, lorry-chasers, and hawkers the high seasonal turnover and low capital investment creates an opportunistic pattern of commodity and schedule choices that makes mutual accountability and support extremely difficult.

Active participation in a commodity group is impossible for traders located primarily outside of the locations forming its geographical base. Attendance at funerals and group meetings at short notice becomes difficult and expensive. Dispute settlement and other decision-making procedures presume face-to-face negotiations. Acceptable levels of speed and accuracy depend on the availability of all interested parties and witnesses. Enforcement of these decisions also requires group proximity, so that interested and impartial observers alike can monitor traders' behavior. De facto geographical boundaries arise for commodity groups without defined ones because inaccessible traders cannot participate effectively, even when they are supposedly included.

Neighborly relations between those with adjacent stalls create the basic units of trust and respect a tight organization needs. They intensify group loyalty when one exists, although they do not require one. Traders maintain the smooth flow of business through the help of neighbors who mind their stalls, relay messages, and share advice and information. In times of disaster, such as illness or theft, they stay in business by turning to their neighbors for credit and donations. Mutual aid gives added weight to the threat of ostracism by fellow members. While the group cannot evict a trader from her stall, she cannot survive long without reciprocal favors from her neighbors.

The economic pressures accumulating under Ghana's structural adjustment program reinforce the need for neighborly solidarity, but at the same time undermine traders' capacity to show it. As more of the poorer traders are pushed closer to the line of business failure, they depend even more on informal mutual assistance to bridge the small crises that now loom larger. As more of the medium-scale autonomous traders who are the backbone of the organized commodity groups go over the edge into capital crisis, however, these groups may gradually change their character. A larger proportion of traders will be partly or wholly dependent on credit or other connections to the few wealthy traders remaining, reducing the economic space for independent maneuvering. This is likely to either weaken the current commodity group structure or turn it in the direction of more hierarchical networks dominated by wealthy traders, as in Lome.

If leaders and their groups have shown considerable creativity in combining and transforming varied cultural models of leadership to suit their changing economic and political environment, they still face very real constraints. Factors affecting the character and potency of external negotiations have been especially influential on the strength of market groups. When they formally emerged during the turbulent preindependence period, they were allowed or even compelled to join in contestations over Africans' and traders' roles in the new national power structure and in competition between political parties. As political parties were repressed in the 1960s, 1970s, and 1980s, government hostility intensified against traders and their leaders in particular. They seemed the chosen symbol for frustratingly incomplete government control of economic and organizational life. A later chapter shows that formal market leaders provided easy targets for physical and ideological attack.

These incidents and campaigns not only reduced their prestige but their ability to function effectively. Their negotiating role as traders' representatives presumed tacit recognition of their standing by other social groups, which never ceased entirely but which was seriously attacked and muted during the periods of military rule. Even internal dispute settlement required traders to assemble openly and conduct business within calling distance, which was impossible under constant threat of confiscations, beatings, and arrests. The office became much less attractive to potential candidates and lapsed completely in groups selling the imported and manufactured commodities subject to particularly extended attack, such as cloth. While expecting and usually enjoying a considerable degree of autonomy in their normal operations, therefore, the market leaders also depended on the acceptance of orderliness and tolerance as underlying norms in their society at large to maintain those operations.

8 MULTIPLE IDENTITIES

Far from stepping outside of their identities as Asantes, as women, and as Africans while at work, Kumasi Central Market traders invoke these identities in their work and constantly find others invoking these identities against them as well. Gender, ethnic, and international systems of domination enable traders to gain access to significant resources in some respects, while contesting or blocking their access in other respects. These crosscutting identities interact with trading relations to create lines of cleavage and solidarity both within the market and between traders and outsiders. The importance of multiple directions of contestation makes it essential to locate Kumasi Central Market traders as precisely as possible within each of these systems of domination. This chapter compares information on traders' social location obtained through the market survey with relevant Ghana Census results to identify their distinguishing characteristics. The implications of these differences for known trading relations is discussed, along with historical trends for the most significant ones.

Each of these overlapping social identities contributes to the definition and redefinition of the others over time through the historical process of mutual construction. What it means to be an Asante, a woman, or an African depends partly on the aspects of trading then associated with those social categories, just as the significance of a trading role changes historically along with its social reassignment. Gender, ethnic/racial, and urban/rural divisions are those most influential within Ghanaian marketplace trading relations and therefore define the most hotly contested boundaries.

Asante women and men gain access to specific trading positions through political institutions (for example, local chiefships and public or military office) to which gender, ethnicity, and Western education mediate access. Inheritance, kinship status, and marital duties control access to capital and labor directly, in ways specific to gender, ethnicity, and family wealth. Gender and ethnic cleavages tend to reinforce each other, as when commodity specialization follows the sex and ethnicity of the consumers. All of those commodities strongly identified with a single ethnic group are also sold by one gender only. Subtler positional factors such as family occupational or urban experience provide access to human resources of skill, information, and labor that give advantages in trading. The degree to which these qualifications, related to birth and wealth, govern resource control is itself continually renegotiated, not least within the state itself.

The prevalence of single-person enterprises already noted means that these background factors rarely operate directly within trading relations. Few Kumasi Central Market traders enjoy these privileges through joining kin or neighbors in trading networks that share capital and labor, since they report relying mainly on their own efforts. Kinship, gender, and ethnic identity instead condition those individual efforts by affecting their ability to gain the training, save the income, and win the respect needed to succeed. Direct contributions to their startup capital, including providing credit references and stall space, were mainly reported at a young age, when the indirect factors were also most influential. This chapter therefore focuses on the childhood environment of current traders and how these demographic indicators operated at that time in order to present this formative process most accurately.

Assessing factors that distinguish traders from the general population will be important in analyzing their recent political problems. When highly charged social attributes like gender, ethnicity, race, or education make a group of traders easily identifiable, tensions generated by their commercial relations are compounded by tensions over the distribution of social resources along those other axes. These effects can be seen in Ghana for market women, for foreign traders, and for privileged groups such as passbook holders. Sharp distinctions based on nonmarket relations that divide off particular commodities or types of enterprise from traders as a whole set them up for victimization, giving leverage to farmers, the military, and government officials in actions against them. Social isolation invites political isolation, whether the distinction is made using positive criteria, such as group membership or high investment requirements, or such negative "qualifications" as low prestige, meager resources, and exclusion from viable alternatives. Conversely, ties that traders share with each other and nontrading compatriots provide potential channels of unity and solidarity in times of personal or social crisis.

Gender

The social division between men and women is one of the most active throughout the marketplace system, creating specific kinds of divisions and solidarities within and outside of it. It serves at the broadest level to separate traders from nontraders while also marking boundaries between commodities and enterprises within the market.

The high proportion of women traders (70 percent) supports a strong public identification of market trading with women, but the intensity of the ideological association of women with trading far outweighs the actual sex ratio. The female leaders representing the market as a whole, incorporating both male and female traders, reinforced its female image. In Indian, Peruvian, and United States examples where male leaders represented groups made up of mostly or partly female traders, gender issues were obscured or avoided (Lessinger 1988; Babb 1988; Spalter-Roth 1988). In times of high tension, such as price control enforcement, Kumasi traders were consistently referred to as "the women," even when the commodity at issue was one sold by both men and women, such as provisions (Clark 1988).

Ideas about gender articulate powerfully with ideas about trading here because the relations affected by the articulation are central ones for each system of domination. Income and autonomy, such as those generated in trading, are essential to maintenance of expected marital and lineage relations for men and women, but in gender-specific and somewhat conflicting ways. Likewise, gendered lineage relations directly affect access to capital and labor critical to trading. The female identification of trading implicitly invokes ideals of motherly and wifely behavior so that the direct linkages between trading and non-trading gender issues such as income implicate trading in tensions over shifting gender roles outside of the marketplace system.

Gender stereotyping justifies gender segregation by reference to the prestige and the physical demands of specific trading tasks, a correspondence maintained despite visible contradictions. For example, the one male tomato wholesaler remarked that only men unloaded trucks because women could not lift the heavy wooden boxes out of the trucks. As he spoke, he could see women buyers lifting those same boxes to carry them an even longer distance to their market stalls. Biologically based arguments like this one are also weakened and partly contradicted by prestige considerations.

Another common line of argument refers to the low prestige and income of most market trading—enough for women but not for self-respecting men. Men who do trading or take even lower-status jobs, such as carrying loads or cleaning latrines, must be illiterates who cannot get a proper job. This logic helps explain the strong female appropriateness of trading now, despite much trading by men in historical and contemporary Asante. Certainly the Asante men currently selling from stores would consider market trading beneath them. Their status, derived partly from gender and partly from class and ethnic identity, demands an elite clientele and little physical labor. These values also help explain the special outrage expressed over wealthy female traders, even in female-identified commodities. Further segregation by gender in relations of capital, partnership, and group formation within Kumasi Central Market makes it a doubly important organizing principle. It affects most traders at the level of commodity or occupation, since they work alone. Commodities permitted or reserved for men, like male-dominated nontrading occupations, present higher levels of average income and capital accumulation than predominantly female commodities. Isolation and ridicule prevent traders from establishing normal commercial relations in a commodity rigidly assigned to the opposite sex. Even then, no formal prohibition or expulsion takes place. In commodities with softer sex-typing or looser organization, more subtle disadvantages arise.

Gender segregation of the social relations of trade is far stronger than segregation of the occupation as a whole. At the commodity level, men are concentrated in a restricted number of commodities or commodity types, which include housewares, drugs, hardware, used clothing, kola, meat, and chickens. Local products tend to be exclusively male or female, while imports and manufactures are open to either gender because the racial distinction is more dominant. Women outnumber men even in the mixed commodities, but by more than thirteen to one in the local foodstuffs consumers buy most often (see table 8.1). Customer relations also tend to be segregated; women sell foodstuffs, cosmetics, dishes, jewelry, and other products bought by women; while men sell hardware, stationery, drugs, and records bought by men. Within the clothing section, men sell men's clothing and women sell women's clothing. Concentrated retail areas in these

Table 8.1 Sex Ratios: Women to Men by Type of Commodity

Commodity	Ratio
Perishable foodstuffs	9.13
Nonperishable foodstuffs	81.00
Canned food	1.38
Craft items	1.40
Industrial items	1.44
Clothing	1.05
Total	2.32

SOURCE: 1979 Kumasi Central Market Survey

commodities encourage physical segregation of both buyers and sellers.

The more elaborate social relations of commodity group organization even more rarely cross gender lines. The best organized groups have strong gender and regional identification. Northern male craft groups, including tailors and butchers within Kumasi Central Market, correspond to the female vegetable groups in this respect. Economic characteristics of a commodity that encourage tight organization, such as concentration of supply or long-distance linkages, put a premium on gender and ethnic/regional specialization. Traders selling commodities sold by both men and women are notably less organized, including provisions, used clothing and enamelware traders, corresponding to their dependence on relations with large import firms rather than internal coherence for power. Commodity group functions like dispute settlement, funeral attendance, and external negotiations are weakly established or have lapsed.

The avoidance of mixed-sex work has the most drastic effect on the recruitment of assistants and partners. Even in mixed-sex commodities, men and women rarely work in the same enterprise. Traders reported 77 percent of partners unambiguously as being of the same sex (see table 5.6). This effectively segregates access to the training and capital which come from working with experienced traders. Commodity segregation undermines the effect of occasional exceptions. In the few cases where fathers trained their daughters in predominantly male crafts, such as a shoemaker, the daughter proceeded to train her sons rather than her daughters to follow her.

Segregated distribution of stalls and capital seriously affects the range of enterprises a new trader can establish. Loans, gifts, and inheritance all follow same-sex lines, with more female-to-male transfers than the opposite. This multiplies any accumulated advantage of men, as well as restricting both sexes to gender-appropriate commodities. Better access for men to education and higher-paying jobs in government, factories, or expatriate firms thus primarily finances the education and establishment of younger men. The median male trader has more than 1,000 cedis invested, while the median female trader has between 100 and 500 cedis invested and is less likely to enjoy a locking stall (see table 8.2).

Gender also influences recruitment patterns through its articulation with hometown and childhood residence. Migration has different effects on men and women. For example, relatively few of the women traders from Northern and Upper Regions had grown up in their region

Table 8.2 Capital Reported Required to Trade at Current Level

Goods	0–99	100–499	500–999	1000–4999	5000–9999	10,000–more
A. Women — Amount of Entry Capital (in Cedis)						
Local food	21.0	27.6	9.6	6.3	0.9	0.3
Canned food	0.6	1.8	0.3	0.6	0	0
Craft items	4.5	1.5	3.6	3.9	1.5	0.6
Industrial items	6.1	9.4	6.1	7.6	2.7	2.7
Clothing	0.3	6.7	4.2	4.8	0.9	0
B. Men — Amount of Entry Capital (in Cedis)						
Local food	0.7	4.3	0.7	2.9	2.2	0.7
Canned food	0.7	0	0	2.2	0.7	2.2
Craft items	2.9	6.5	5.1	6.5	2.9	2.9
Industrial items	5.1	7.2	10.1	22.5	6.5	6.5
Clothing	2.9	10.1	10.1	12.3	2.2	0.7

SOURCE: 1979 Kumasi Central Market Survey

Table 8.3 Regional Background of Traders

Town or Region	Family Hometown: Men	Women	Both
Kumasi	8.7	7.3	7.7
Ashanti	54.3	58.3	57.1
Northern	8.7	7.3	7.7
Upper	11.6	3.0	5.5
Other Ghana	12.3	22.9	19.9
West Africa	4.3	0	2.1

Town or Region	Childhood Residence: Men	Women	Both
Kumasi	36.2	59.5	52.7
Ashanti	34.8	25.4	28.1
Northern	6.5	2.1	3.4
Upper	8.0	1.2	3.2
Other Ghana	10.9	10.6	10.7
West Africa	3.6	1.2	1.9

Birthplace
Of Kumasi Residents, All Ages, in 1970 Ghana Census
Compared with Childhood Residence of Traders

Category	Kumasi	Ashanti	Ghana	Other
1970 Women	44.6	24.9	27.2	3.3
Female traders	59.5	25.4	15.3	1.2
1970 Men	41.3	23.2	29.5	6.0
Male traders	36.2	34.8	25.2	3.6

SOURCE: 1979 Kumasi Central Market Survey

of family origin (see table 8.3). Women traders reported far more Kumasi childhoods than the Kumasi average, while male traders reported slightly less. Gender differences in child migration explain part of this difference. Censuses show girls outnumbering boys in Kumasi in 1960 and 1970, peaking at 1.32 girls per boy for ages ten to fourteen in 1970 (Ghana Census 1970). It seems more likely that adolescent girls came to work as traders and domestic workers than that boys left, judging from life histories and contemporary residence practices. Once established, both men and women are generally acknowledged to favor their own sex in trading relations. They often extend credit and other concessions more quickly to members of their own sex, considering them more reliable or needy. Friendships between buyer and seller, very rarely established with the opposite sex, allow traders to ask for favors because of gender-specific personal problems otherwise embarrassing to explain. Women traders admit they routinely charge men higher prices, because they assume men make more money, and reduce the prices for women, explaining that they buy to feed their children (whether by immediate consumption or resale).

Traders establish commercial relations across gender lines more readily with transactors located outside of the marketplace than within it. Women traders take for granted buying from male fishermen and farmers and store and government employees, exchanging credit when needed, and dealing with men as drivers and carriers. Men traders have fewer relations with women, keeping more closely to goods produced and sold by men, including male crafts, male farm crops and factory and imported goods. Those men based in Kumasi Central Market rarely used female head carriers, since men were available. Men do buy from women when necessary—for example, buying kola from rural women in forest hamlets and markets.

The female identification of trading itself has the effect of sexualizing commercial relations between female traders and male nontraders, with several negative effects. Traders' most important external relations, with drivers, farmers, and store and market employees, were conceptualized as male/female relations. For interactions between these unrelated persons, norms of female respect and deference were invoked to the traders' disadvantage through reference to husband/wife relations, perhaps the least autonomous for women within their domestic repertoire. Jokes and serious allegations about sexual misconduct were commonplace among traders themselves as well as among observers. Female traders dealing with predominantly male supplier groups complained that sellers often demanded sexual relations; I heard this from women buying canned goods from elite government officials and from women buying plantains from cocoa farmers in remote frontier areas.

The principle of gender segregation in Akan social relations is farther reaching and more consistently implemented than the gender division of labor. In Akan rural areas, for example, where both men and women farm, they rarely establish farms with members of the opposite sex, even siblings or spouses. Only nonreciprocal labor exchange crosses sex lines, when wives help on their husbands' farms or hire male laborers for their own farms. Men and women separate spontaneously in many contexts where no division of labor is involved. For example, residents of a multifamily house in Kumasi faced a crisis when the landlord cut off their water and light unexpectedly in an attempted eviction. Men and women from the families affected met separately to discuss their joint response.

Men doing domestic work maintain gender segregation even when they openly break the ideal division of labor. When a young man lives with an older brother or craft master, he can cook and clean without any stigma. When the older man marries, or a female relative comes to live with them, these tasks turn into helping a woman and become shameful. The younger man no longer cooks, although he may continue to perform more acceptably masculine tasks such as ironing or laundry. When single men cook for each other, they do so on the veranda or in the courtyard to avoid associating with women in the house kitchen.

Gender segregation in public services can also create and maintain de facto inequalities for traders in access to very scarce goods. For example, separate men's and women's lines formed in front of stores selling controlled commodities, transport stations during petrol shortages, and banks during the currency exchange in 1979. Women and men standees both endorsed this segregation because they considered the full-body pressing together and physical struggles that took place in both lines separately inappropriate for a mixed line. Employees served each line alternately, but since more women usually waited for goods and transport their line was longer and they waited longer for the same "separate but equal" service.

Life Cycle

Several other hierarchies besides gender intersect within Asante lineage and marital relations. Age, seniority, and number of children affect not only prestige within them but control over material resources vital to trading. Several studies suggest that market women in Nigeria, for example, typically have seniority within the fairly representative families they come from. Yoruba and Igbo ethnographies mention that senior wives and middle-aged mothers are the most prominent traders (Uchendu 1967; Sudarkasa 1973). Sudarkasa suggests that older Yoruba wives enter long-distance trade when they stop childbearing and delegate domestic work to junior co-wives. Her later work in Kumasi confirms that many Yoruba traders were first wives (1975). Nadel asserted decades ago that barren and divorced women made up a large percentage of the Nupe trading population (Nadel 1952).

By contrast, Kumasi Central Market traders' individual and household characteristics fall within general Asante and Kumasi norms. Most women traders are married and live with a spouse, several young children, and/or other relatives. Their marital status (men 73 percent;

women 65 percent) and average of three children are reasonable for their modal age (15 to 35). Demographic restudies based on subsamples of the Ghana Censuses investigated household composition and yielded very similar percentages (Gaisie and de Graft-Johnson 1976). The reported ages of current traders are also broadly distributed across the adult life span, with no sign of the double peak produced when women trade before marriage or pregnancy and then leave, returning after their children have grown older.

Traders' ages in Kumasi Central Market instead show a single peak pattern, concentrated in the middle years both absolutely and when compared to other Kumasi residents (see figures 8.1 and 8.2). The age pyramid for men peaks sharply from ages 25 to 35, while that for women shows a high plateau from ages 15 to 35 and dips slightly below men from ages 35 to 45. Asante women begin trading earlier than men, in keeping with their earlier social maturity. They trade most often during their peak childbearing years and slack off later, if at all. Analysis based on number of children born had similar results, but these were less clearly defined. This suggests life-cycle considerations that affect men more sharply than women and tend to keep younger adult men out of market trading.

The relationship between trading and manual or nonmanual work through the lifespan is especially strongly affected by gender. Young men in 1979 often operated market stalls after a craft apprenticeship, while ostensibly saving capital to buy the equipment for a more acceptable male occupation, such as a welding machine for auto repair or even a sewing machine for tailoring. These boundaries, although blurred by individual cases, reconfirm the difference in capital status between acceptably male and female occupations. Although some women traders achieve ownership of stores or power machinery, or the equivalent capital levels, the majority do not approach the levels considered minimally respectable for a man.

Women traders more often enter manual or nonmanual employment before they begin trading. Despite constitutional protections, employment practices force them to retire at marriage or after the birth of children. One woman had been employed at the Bank of Ghana for many years when she unexpectedly became pregnant again and was fired. She quoted her supervisor as saying, "Yes, we have maternity leave, but you are not supposed to get pregnant." These women's relatively young age and low wage levels as teachers, nurses, and clerks meant that they could not bring substantial savings or pension funds into trading compared to male retirees, who could hope to start larger businesses outside of the marketplace.

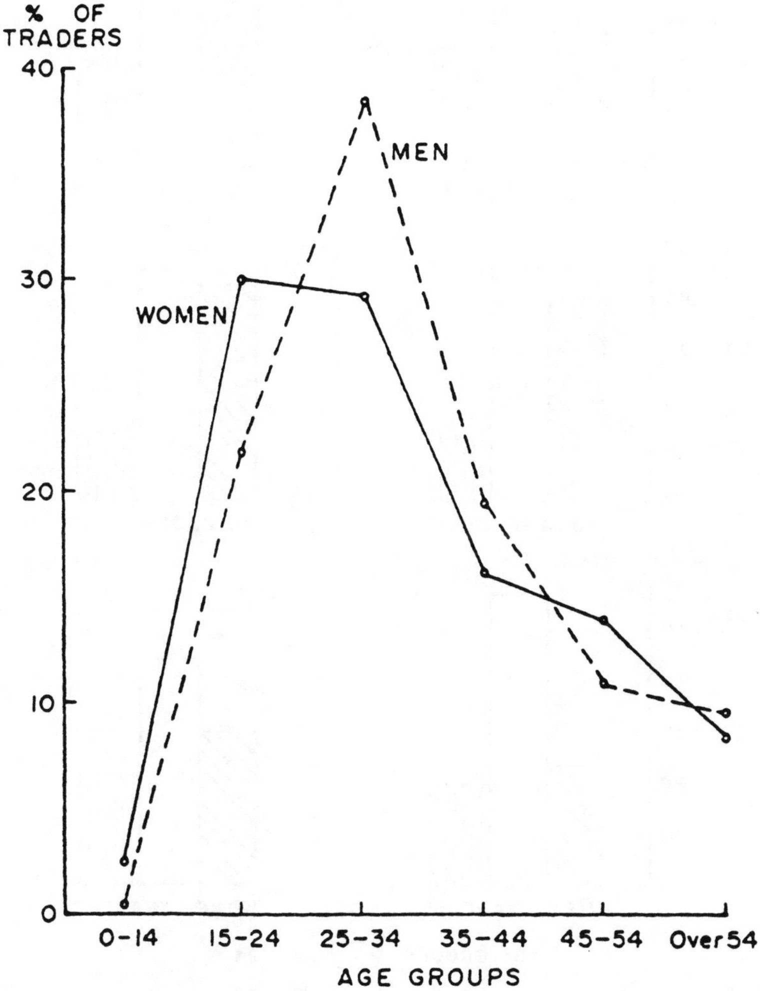

Figure 8.1 Age Distribution (Source: 1979 Kumasi Central Market Survey)

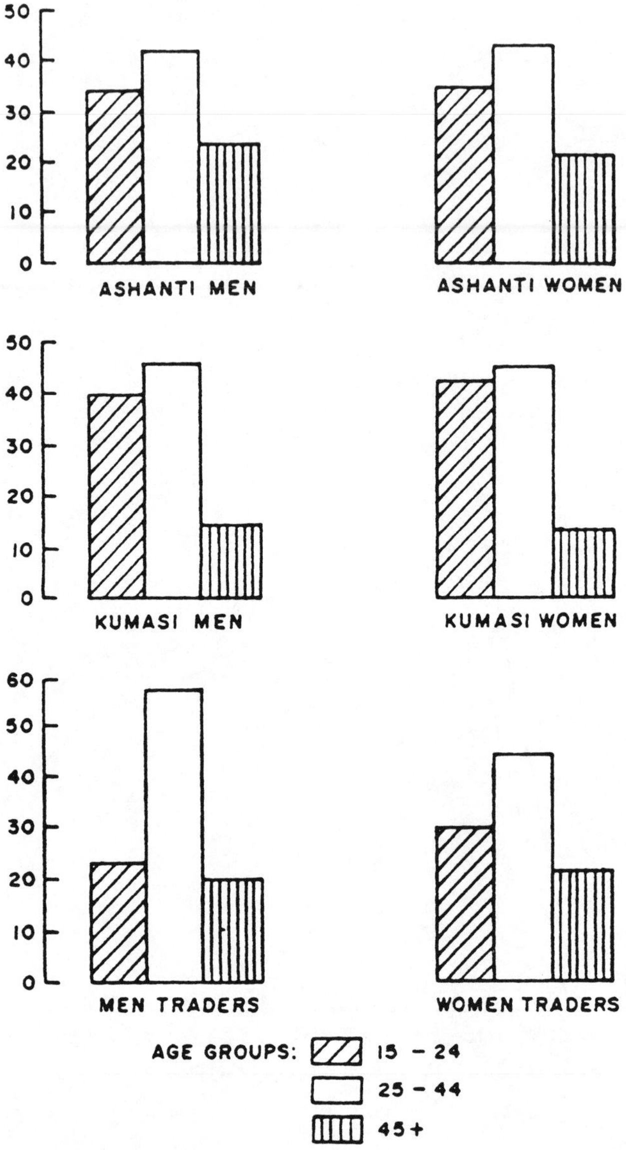

Figure 8.2 Comparative Age Distribution (Source: 1979 Kumasi Central Market Survey; Ghana Census, 1970)

In order to trace how both men and women adjust their work to family responsibilities in different ways, one section of the survey asked traders for the reasons why they had begun trading or changed between types of trade. Women frequently reported dropping school or salaried jobs upon marriage, either because of official policy or in order to cook for their husbands. When family expenses, usually pregnancy, force them to work, they turn to trading. Some men also reported starting trade in response to unexpected pregnancy, but this was rare. "I impregnated a girl, therefore my father decided not to pay my school fees again and gave me some capital to start a trade." Men more often began work in preparation for marriage and fatherhood rather than in response to it.

Either marriage or divorce could disrupt a women's work by precipitating a change of residence. "I was farming with my husband, so after the divorce I left to come and trade." "When I came to Kumasi I had to change because I couldn't get a regular supply of fish." Women did not passively accept male-defined residence; several traders I knew well lived away from their husbands in order to continue their trading. Women could also manipulate marriage ties in order to reside where they wanted, if they were willing to marry or divorce on that basis. Young women could marry a city husband or a farmer or leave a partner who was unwilling to relocate. Traders in general show only moderate differences in age from the overall Kumasi population, comparing traders' age distribution to that of Kumasi residents over the age of fourteen in 1970. Few traders were under the age of fifteen, most of them girls, confirming that the unbalanced sex ratios for children come from causes other than trading apprenticeships. Both male and female age peaks are sharper than those for the general Kumasi population, but located in the same active adult years. Market traders include more elderly persons than the Kumasi average, suggesting that traders retire to rural areas less often than nontraders. This seems logical considering that more traders spent their childhoods in Kumasi. Historical expansion and contraction of the market—for example, its rapid expansion during the 1950s—may also have brought this particular cohort into trading in unusual numbers.

Ethnicity

An especially strongly marked boundary is set up inside or around the trading community when a commodity, or trading itself, is identified with a recognized ethnic group. It has been argued from the many examples of trading diasporas, including European Jews, that minorities sharing cultural and family ties find it easier to establish and enforce mutual trust and cooperation than is the case in a majority culture (Curtin 1984). Minorities also can organize tightly to maintain their commercial dominance; Cohen's classic study of Hausa traders in Yoruba Ibadan shows how exclusive such communities can be (Cohen 1969). Both exclusionary tactics and sheer commercial effectiveness can provoke a backlash, as seen in Ghana in 1969 against Yoruba, Hausa, and Lebanese traders. In more extreme examples, Chinese traders in Southeast Asia and Indian traders in East Africa have attracted hostility in several countries because of their use of minority cohesion to build commercial monopolies. In Kumasi, marketplace trading as a whole is not now associated with any such ethnic minority, and the locally dominant Asantes constituted a clear majority of traders of both sexes. They predominated in Kumasi Central Market even more than in the city itself, although traders from all regions were present. The Central Market is clearly a locally rooted institution, although the same cannot be said of all of its parts (see table 8.4).

Ghanaians typically acknowledge ties with several locations established by former residence and ethnic origin and maintained through periodic visits and relations with other migrants. Identification with the town of family origin, called the hometown in Ghanaian English, remains strong even after several generations of migration, and elderly people in particular consider moving back there. Other towns and vil-

Table 8.4 Trading versus Craft Production by Hometown and Gender

	Percentage		Proportion	
	Trade	Craft	Trade	Craft
Asante				
Men	52.9	47.1	19.7	57.1
Women	92.4	7.6	50.7	13.6
Both	76.4	23.6	70.4	70.7
Northern				
Men	53.8	47.2	6.1	17.9
Women	100.0	0	7.5	0
Both	71.3	28.7	13.6	17.9
Coastal				
Men	57.1	42.9	2.8	7.1
Women	87.5	12.5	13.2	4.3
Both	78.3	21.7	16.0	11.4

SOURCE: 1979 Kumasi Central Market Survey

lages are familiar from frequent visits or stays with close relatives or from temporary migration there. High rates of migration and visiting meant that few Kumasi Central Market traders had intimate knowledge of Kumasi only. Each location can provide skills significant to trading and contacts through kin and former neighbors.

Heavy rates of migration in both urban and rural Ghana called my attention to childhood residence, a major potential source of group solidarity and trading contacts. Local contacts provide a valuable introduction to suppliers and buyers living there for credit and other forms of trust, and perhaps for information on a market stall left vacant by neighbors or family friends. The shared social relations, cultural values, and even the shared language that ethnicity implies are acquired during childhood. Substantial residence outside of the hometown brings secondary or even primary familiarity with aspects of those local cultures. For example, Schildkrout (1978a) shows how ethnic origin, residence, and occupation articulate to produce intricate patterns of cultural identity in the Northern community in Kumasi. Both hometown and childhood residence variables in the market survey showed high representation from Kumasi and the surrounding Ashanti and Brong-Ahafo Regions (see table 8.3).[1] Childhood residence in Kumasi was exceptionally common among female, rather than male, traders compared with the general Kumasi population. A survey of the same market in 1989 showed the same 58 percent of all traders born in Kumasi (Tackie 1991).

Hometown and childhood ties both operate powerfully in the traders' choice of commodities, which reflect both local and ethnic variations in supply and demand. For example, Northern Muslims sell veils and other Muslim clothing, while Asantes sell the adinkra funeral cloths they wear. This practice gives sellers the advantage of a common language with consumers and familiarity with the goods sold. The same principle puts long-distance cattle and kola trading in the hands of Muslim men culturally similar to their counterparts in the savannah north of Ghana (Hill 1966). Shared culture is a more powerful bond in commercial relations inside of the market than outside of it. Asante women predominate in the foodstuffs trades, which make up most of the market, even when these commodities come from non-

1. The census category of birthplace approximates the survey variable on childhood residence more closely than it does hometown. Census instructions told interviewers to record the mother's habitual residence at the time of birth, precisely because pregnant women often went back to give birth in their hometowns. Another source of discrepancy remains when traders moved after infancy to spend their formative years in another place, which they then reported in the survey as their childhood residence. Ethnic origin was not recorded in 1970.

Asante supply areas, such as Northern yams and irrigated tomatoes, because of their solidarity with other Asante traders in the distribution chain. Asante women wrested control of yam and tomato routes after these were pioneered by non-Asante men from the producing areas. The only exceptions are a few items consumed by Northerners and sold by Northern women, including certain greens, different from those preferred by Asantes, shea butter, and veils worn by Moslem women. Since Northerners also gather, process, or import these items, ethnic ties with consumers reinforce those with suppliers.

Northern men only dominate in locally produced foodstuff trades for which the savannah trading networks remain important. Cattle and kola are still brought in and out across the northern boundary of Ghana, although kola is actually gathered or planted in the forest zone and mainly by Asante women. Kola traders mentioned that some rural women bulked and stored kola in the villages, in anticipation of the trading season, but none had interurban roles. Northern men also take advantage of their ethnic-based commercial ties to retailers and consumers when they take imports and manufactured goods north from Kumasi. Some of these items also find their way into international trade, although not legally.

The trade in poultry, dominated by men from the Upper Region, referred to in Kumasi as "Frafras," makes only an apparent exception. Poultry traders are not tied into the international savannah networks, yet they maintain a tight monopoly of their commodity. Although these men grow up familiar with chicken judging and transport in their home areas, which export chickens to Kumasi, they range outside these home areas once they become professional traders. Like the Asante women, they maintain extremely solid commercial relations with colleagues based on their shared heritage and funeral attendance.

Supply areas with strong commodity specialization in commercial production teach children growing up in them trading techniques and quality variations of the local specialty almost automatically through observation and practice. Poultry traders from the Upper Region and fish traders from the Fanti coast or Lake Bosumtwe, for example, said they needed no commodity-specific training since this was the main occupation in their home villages. Former neighbors and relatives provide steady supplies to the new trader, and it becomes very difficult for an outsider to overcome such advantages. For the same reason, a local boy or girl who enters trade in another region, such as Kumasi, has little incentive to start by selling a different commodity where she has no such advantage.

Growing up in Kumasi offers similar advantages specific to trading in Kumasi. Local children continually visit Kumasi Central Market to shop or talk to friends and relatives. Familiarity with important commercial locations and personalities speeds their assimilation of knowledge specific to their later trading. City children have more opportunities to begin hawking or petty trading at an early age, thus building skills, capital, and social relations. Kumasi children also are more likely to have neighbors and relatives who trade there, who may train or sponsor them or help them obtain rights to a trading location. The regional dominance of Kumasi Central Market makes local knowledge of that market more valuable than knowledge of most others. Children growing up outside of Kumasi will have similar advantages in their local markets, but these give fewer opportunities. The size and central position of Kumasi exposes Kumasi children to more sophisticated and therefore attractive trading methods than village children, who may only visit the small periodic market in a nearby village.

These factors may encourage Kumasi children to enter trading as such. Without more strictly comparable statistics for the general population, one can only speculate that Kumasi-based children enter market trading in disproportionate numbers. The relatively large proportion of traders in the Kumasi working population would steer a large proportion of Kumasi children into trading in any case, if they wished to stay in the city.

Family Connections

Kin-based trading networks are rare and localized within Kumasi Central Market, and connections through immediate kin have relatively little influence within the marketplace system as a whole. This finding has important implications for commercial policy and political coalitions. Even where trading families do not belong to a distinctive ethnic or geographic group, they can constitute an identifiable group in themselves if they monopolize advantageous or leading positions within the marketplace system. Kin solidarity becomes an important source of trader/nontrader tension if such monopoly or dominance is conspicuous and resented as undeserved or enviable. Families with such historical connections to trade can offer special skills and key social relations which overtly exclude outsiders or make it impossible for them to compete with family members, quite apart from any capital transfers. Commercial reforms should then focus on eliminating restrictive arrangements and establishing alternative channels of open access to suppliers and buyers. Many commercial policy measures of the seventies and eighties followed this pattern, implying that such restrictions existed.

The survey conclusively eliminated this hypothesis because it found so few specialized trading families. In order to benefit from such a family tradition, traders would have to trade in the family commodity, at least, and perhaps join the family enterprise, as happens in Asante specialist craft villages. Many parents of traders had traded, but so had a large proportion of the 1960 Kumasi population. Only mothers of female traders did so much more frequently than the Kumasi average (see tables 8.5 and 8.6). Men's mothers usually farmed, while women's fathers followed the normal spread of Kumasi occupations. It would take a large family where all or most of the members traded together to create and hold a dominant position in Kumasi Central Market. Partnership patterns alone ruled this out, since almost half of the traders work alone and another 35.1 percent have only one partner. Traders of both sexes reported few relatives even traded in the same commodity (see table 8.7). Although female traders had more mothers trading, the smaller percentage of sisters reported shows that many daughters of traders chose other occupations or commodities.

The relatively minor family support traceable in Kumasi Central Market commercial relations suggests that trading tends to attract persons who lack substantial family backing, since few market enterprises demand it. This lack only eliminates those few choices which

Table 8.5 Father's Occupation During Male and Female Traders' Childhoods Compared with All Men Over 15 in Kumasi and Ashanti Region 1960

Category	Traders	Farmers	Manual	Nonmanual
Fathers of men	18.2	57.7	12.4	11.7
Fathers of women	16.8	39.4	28.7	12.3
1960 Ashanti men	5.1	46.5	26.0	5.8
1960 Kumasi men	12.6	5.9	48.9	11.4

SOURCES: 1960 Ghana Census; 1979 Kumasi Central Market Survey

Table 8.6 Mother's Occupation During Male and Female Traders' Childhoods Compared with All Women Over 15 in Kumasi and Ashanti Region 1960

Category	Traders	Farmers	Manual	Nonmanual
Mothers of men	38.1	54.0	3.6	.7
Mothers of women	61.5	32.4	3.4	.9
1960 Ashanti women	13.2	44.7	6.6	.9
1960 Kumasi women	34.4	6.7	12.4	2.7

SOURCES: 1960 Ghana Census; 1979 Kumasi Central Market Survey

Table 8.7 Trading and Kin Relationships

Kin Trading Same Goods	
Number of Kin	Percentage of Traders
None	61.9
One	20.9
2–5	12.3
More than 5	4.9

Specific Relationship among Those Reporting Kin as Colleagues			
Relation	Men	Women	Both
Same-sex Parent	10.2	26.9	22.4
Same-sex Child	6.1	14.9	12.6
Same-sex Sibling	59.2	29.1	37.2
Other Relative	28.6	38.8	36.1
Spouse	16.3	.7	4.9

SOURCE: 1979 Kumasi Central Market Survey

require high capital levels or specific kinds of connections. For traders not counting on these resources, less personal relations of gender and region of origin determine their choices of commodity and type of enterprise directly, with minimal mediation through family or household relations.

In a relatively open trading system, lineage and marital relations still give some traders much better access than others to income, capital, education, and other valuable resources that influence their commercial relations. They are more often found in the commodities and roles that require and reward these resources and enter higher levels of trade and accumulate faster than less well-endowed traders. Traders with exceptionally low access to such resources likewise are noted in the less profitable corners of the market or in roles like hawking. Such capital and prestige factors do mark identifiable areas within Kumasi Central Market, such as the high-status provisions and cloth lines and the low-status charcoal and villagers' markets. Given the diversity within the market itself, they do not cut market traders as such off from the bulk of the city population.

Capital

Capital level has a determining influence on traders' commodity choice. Traders with capital concentrate in the commodities where capital gives them the most advantage, pushing low-capital traders into less desirable commodities. Those commodities which fail to reward additional capital usually yield lower incomes on small amounts of capital as well. Work histories collected as part of the survey provide many examples of traders switching commodities because their capital had increased through family gifts or inheritance. "When I got married, my husband gave me 1,000 cedis, so I decided to sell bowls instead of pepper." Family relations can also cause loss of capital, through crisis expenses such as illness or when other family members stop contributing to the family expenses, as after the retirement or divorce of a husband. These losses can force a shift down to a less capital-intensive commodity.

Market assets in the form of stalls or other location rights are often commodity-specific. Traders who inherit or take over a desirable location in a concentrated retail section must sell the dominant commodity of the section to realize its full value. Sometimes the commodity mix of a section changes over the years, affecting traders dependent on walk-through traffic. One former scarf seller found that people looking for scarves now went elsewhere. "The traders on that line had changed over to selling children's clothes, so I had to change because selling shoes was not popular on that line." Family assistance with working capital usually is given during the lifetime of the donor. The donor thus controls who will receive the gift of cash or a stall, and when. A senior trader can set up a younger relative when she is ready or needs it or choose to delay until she is ready to retire. Although such premortem gifts intentionally bypass matrilineal inheritance rules, they are widely accepted in Asante lineage practice. Men use them to transfer personally acquired property to their children, especially sons, and wives. Female traders do not face the same conflict, since their children are also their closest matrilineal heirs, but they may feel themselves better able than their lineage elders to choose the one most deserving or most capable of profiting from the gift among several potential heirs, especially now that lineages sometimes pass women's assets unexpectedly to brothers.

Money transfers take the form of either gifts or loans, but often represent a compromise between the two, as when one trader reported: "Given by my sister. I can pay if I get enough money." Commercial sponsors without money capital also give indirect access to working capital by guaranteeing credit with a third party (see table 5.2). Young traders also take over all or part of the enterprises where they work as assistants in stages. The older trader sets up earlier assistants in business independently and hands the remaining capital or credit line over to the final assistant on retirement. Living donors or lenders retain some influence over the use of the resulting income—for example, they can require that it be used to support other family members. The elderly donor has a particularly strong claim for support from the profits of an enterprise she might otherwise have to abandon and can still try to claim or borrow back the capital in case of an emergency.

Extended family relations seem strong in Asante, but collateral relatives contributed surprisingly little to traders' starting capital. The majority began trading with their own resources or those of the same-sex parent. Men relied more on their own savings, but also received help more often from mothers than women did from fathers. Women received more capital from spouses (in lieu of other support) and less from other kin. The very similar capital sources presented by Osirim for patrilineal Lagos and Benin female traders suggests that most Asante women derive little distinctive financial benefit from their central position in their extended matrilineages (Osirim 1989).

The retrospective picture of traders' family resource distributions given by current traders' surveyed confirms the anti-female direction of changing patterns of Akan inheritance and financial responsibility indicated by historical research on the family (Mikell 1989). Men feel less obligation to sisters and the sisters' children but retain tighter solidarity with their brothers. Brothers inherit more often than sisters' sons and often claim inheritances from their mothers and sisters that would earlier have gone to their sisters. They take only somewhat greater responsibility now for their own children and wives, leaving women with markedly lower access to all resources held by men or women. I heard anecdotes about women receiving substantial capital inflows from inheritances or from the proceeds of lineage funerals after they were already trading on a large scale, but these transfers were evidently not frequent enough to appear among the survey responses.

Parental Status

The relatively weak contribution of the extended family to traders' enterprises through providing connections or capital redirects attention to their own parents. The Asante extended family seems to soften the impact of exceptionally low or high parental status on children's subsistence levels, but parental income and education remain the strongest influences on the child's environment and access to food, clothing, education, and capital resources. It seemed unlikely that accurate information on parental income some twenty years earlier could be reconstructed in a survey context. Parental occupation and education, on the other hand, were readily remembered and reported. Measures of class background drawn from European models are not very applicable here because of the persistence of communal and lineal control over major means of production, such as farmland.

Using occupational and educational variables as indicators of childhood environment and resources has its strengths and weaknesses. The broad census categories of farming, trading, blue- and white-collar work each contained wide variations in parental income. Among farmers in Ashanti Region, for example, cocoa farmers could earn large incomes before 1960, while subsistence farmers earned little. These indicators are more significant for nonmonetary resources, however. The connections and training important for trade were linked to type of work and education as much as to income.

The goal of these rough comparisons is to see whether young traders' family backgrounds had put them in a distinctive position or placed them at a marked advantage or disadvantage to their peers. Consequently, survey information about their parents was compared with census figures for the decades in which traders were growing up, since the most significant transfers and influences took place before adulthood. The largest numbers of traders surveyed in 1979 were aged 15 to 35, followed by the 35 to 45 age group, so the 1960 rather than the 1970 census found more of them in childhood. Sixty percent of female and 36 percent of male traders reported spending those years in Kumasi, with the next highest number from Ashanti Region (still including Brong-Ahafo Region then), so these locations were selected for comparison.

Family backgrounds reported by Kumasi Central Market traders place them firmly in the mainstream of urban Ghanaian life. Modest parental resources limited traders' access to education and capital, although their level of school attendance indicates their families were not exceptionally poor. In fact, few traders' parents enjoyed the occupational or educational advantages shown by the average Kumasi resident over rural compatriots in census tables. This kind of parental background gives little basis for separation or hostility between traders and the general public.

Traders' parents ranked neither grossly high nor low compared with their peers, by the rough measure of occupational category, but showed some interesting divergences. Traders' parents' work during the traders' childhoods approximated those of largely rural Ashanti Region more closely than those of Kumasi, where many future traders were then living (see tables 8.5 and 8.6). Female traders had nearly as many farmer parents as the regional average and male traders exceeded the regional average. Manual, or blue-collar, workers were strongly underrepresented; only fathers of female traders approached even the regional percentage, much lower than the Kumasi percentage. This suggests that blue-collar fathers were likely to bring their sons into blue-collar work or better. In general, fathers showed urban levels of trading and white-collar work and rural levels of farming and blue-collar work. Mothers of both men and women traders showed low rural levels of blue- and white-collar work and farming, with urban high levels of trading. This suggests an informal/formal sector divide that persists across generations.

Spouses in other occupations provide traders with stronger ties of cooperation and financial support across occupational boundaries. Spouses covered the full range of adult occupations for both sexes. Wives of blue- and white-collar workers evidently find trading neither unnecessary or unthinkable. Few male traders marry white- or blue-collar workers, in accordance with the small numbers of such women available and the low status of men market traders.

Education

Since Ghanaian families have placed such a high priority on investment in education for many years, education provides a valuable rough approximation of family wealth. It contains a de facto control for family position, since the child's ability to actually draw on resources from any wealthy relatives enters into the result. It is particularly appropriate for traders because school fees require ready cash, also a critical resource for beginning in trade. Free primary education and numerous scholarships for further education awarded after independence provided significant access for poorer children, but did not remove the pressures poverty creates to keep children at home to contribute labor or earn income. Parental occupation and education also reflect the parents' own effective extended family resources, which form the basis of those available to their children.

The low levels of traders' parents' education suggest extended family backgrounds with relatively little wealth. Fathers' education indicates family resources somewhat more sensitively than mothers' education because of the gender gap in keeping children in school. Wealthy farmers of the grandparental generations invested heavily in educating their sons and young male relatives, but only elite families educated their daughters at that time. Traders' mothers and fathers both attended school less often than regional, let alone Kumasi, averages (see table 8.8). Women traders reported more educated fathers than men traders; together with women's fewer farming parents this suggests that men traders were drawn from more exclusively low social strata than their women colleagues.

Table 8.8 Parental Education: Percentage Never Having Attended School—Traders' Parents Compared with All Men and Women 25 and Older in 1960

Category	Percentage
Fathers of men	74.5
Fathers of women	68.5
1960 Ashanti men	64.8
1960 Kumasi men	48.6
Mothers of men	90.6
Mothers of women	92.4
1960 Ashanti women	92.4
1960 Kumasi women	76.1

SOURCES: 1960 Ghana Census; 1979 Kumasi Central Market Survey

Table 8.9 Traders' Education: Percentage Never Having Attended School Compared with All Males and Females 6 and Older in 1970

Category	Men	Women
Traders	28.8	51.7
1970 Kumasi	31.6	49.1
1970 Ashanti	39.7	57.2

SOURCES: 1970 Ghana Census; 1979 Kumasi Central Market Survey

Table 8.10 Level of Education Attained by Traders

	Men	Women
None	28.8	51.7
Primary	4.3	6.9
Middle	45.3	36.0
Secondary	15.8	3.0
Other Higher	5.8	2.4

SOURCE: 1979 Kumasi Central Market Survey

Traders' own levels of education reflect the disposable income of their families at a more recent period and show their degree of personal privilege compared to their agemates more accurately by allowing for differences between siblings. Traders working in the market in 1979 would have appeared in the 1970 census as aged six and above, since almost all were over fifteen. Both sexes report attending school at rates similar by gender to their 1970 Kumasi peers. Women fall below and men exceed these average levels slightly, but not significantly (see table 8.9).[2]

The implications of these relations are less clear, since education articulates with trading in complex ways. The high prestige of education and low prestige of trading in general suggest a negative correlation between the two, and many uneducated traders from Kumasi Central Market commented that they chose to trade because their lack of schooling disqualified them for other jobs. Educated parents wanted to keep their children out of trading, but educated people also did trade in substantial numbers. The range of reported educational levels shows that no degree of education rules out trading entirely (see table 8.10).

Education affects commodity choice more straightforwardly, with more educated traders trading in imported and manufactured goods. Literacy gives a practical advantage in dealing with factory regulations, wholesalers' invoices, customs papers, chits and package labels, although prominent illiterate traders do manage well without it. Imports and manufactures are also the most lucrative commodities to sell, so that education steers traders into the more promising parts of the market. Wholesaling provisions or other manufactured goods requires substantially more capital than wholesaling farm produce and gives a higher return on that investment. Traders in these goods approximate the work expectations for and by literates, with formal-sector associates, clean working conditions, and a potential for higher income—thus mitigating the status contradiction. Wholesale foodstuffs traders make the same or higher incomes than provisions retailers, but have less prestige through association with the farm. Packaged goods normally require less handling, carry less dirt, and generate more prestige

2. This comparison underestimates the school attendance of traders' actual cohort in two ways, both of which would have fairly small effects. Very elderly persons alive in 1970 but deceased or retired in 1979 would have had few educational opportunities compared with the slightly younger 1979 traders, bringing census averages down. In addition, some children over the age of six in 1970 would have started school after the census.

as symbols of Westernization. These traders spend more time in contact with wealthy, educated persons, including store and factory managers and government officials. Socialization in school prepares them for the elite social relations that promote and protect their business dealings.

Looking more closely at the range of variation, however, reveals that educated traders' high incomes depend more directly on capital than education. The two effects can be separated most easily when they contradict each other, since the same families that could invest in their children's education usually also give them capital advantages. Educated girls from borderline families can face problems when the elite-centered socialization of the educational system raises expectations of employment higher than the current economy or family finances can meet. Graduates with qualifications that would have brought secure and respected positions a generation ago now compete for a restricted number of job openings, making family connections and business capital more essential. Some girls and boys drop out of school before they need to because they do not foresee the kind of family support required to benefit fully from it. Young women may show less reluctance to trade after advanced schooling in Ghana than elsewhere, since older elite women often left white-collar work for trading after marriage, but poorer schoolgirls may disdain the kind of trading they can realistically afford to start.

Children who trade instead of attending school generally acquire skills and knowledge that will benefit them in later enterprises, but not enough to give them an overall advantage. Schoolchildren also often learn adequate basic trading skills by trading part-time, for adults or themselves. Without full-time involvement, however, they are retarded several years in acquiring the savings, credit reputation, and network of work-related obligations essential to an established business. The small number of child assistants in Kumasi Central Market enterprises suggests that more children, especially girls, are kept out of school to help with domestic work, which does not build up profitable personal skills and connections.

Children not attending school are not entirely dependent on their parents and accumulate their own capital resources in several ways. Some save enough as independent traders to finance small but respectable enterprises by the time their peers are leaving school. Such accumulation still depends indirectly on their families' ability to feed and clothe them, however, since truly destitute children spend all of their earnings on food and save little. Only children who work unpaid for adults accumulate moral rights to working capital, which depend on the adult's good faith but not on charity. Survey results show that the advantages of working fail to compensate most working children for the greater poverty of their families. Educated traders in fact received more capital assistance than uneducated traders. Ghanaians value education highly and send their children to school if at all possible. While the burden of school fees may prevent particular families from providing adequate working capital, families that could not afford to educate their children usually could not give them much capital either.

Further education carries some risk by keeping a child dependent longer on parental assistance, which may dry up. It drains the finances of a parent or other sponsor but does not substitute for working capital. Families try to calculate closely the most effective and realistic strategy for setting up their children in life. Craft apprenticeships present a compromise for poor but not destitute families aiming to strike a lower but still useful balance between training expenses and working capital. A young person graduating from school or from a craft apprenticeship still needs further help to find a job, to buy tools, or to buy stock. Parents or other sponsors caught short at this time waste the money already spent on the training. Discrepancies between training and capital most often occur when the family fortunes fall or rise sharply between early and late childhood. This can happen when the father dies or retires or, conversely, when long-awaited prosperity arrives for a parent or older sibling. The rapid economic decline of the 1960s and 1970s put many families unexpectedly in an unfair position as inflation devoured the savings and income they planned to use to educate and establish their younger children. The more fortunate elder children could not find jobs earning enough to compensate by financing younger siblings. Structural adjustment policies on revenue and devaluation after 1985 brought further sharp jumps in school fees and expenses and the capital sums needed for equipment and stock in specific occupations. These trends disenfranchise the younger generation economically to the point of threatening reproduction of the fragile middle classes.

Professional Identity

The purely occupational identity of traders also serves as a primary basis for sociopolitical isolation or solidarity. This requires above all a relatively stable set of persons in that category; if individuals constantly move in and out of trading they can hardly be ostracized on the basis of group membership. Occupational stereotyping by linking traders with characteristic nontrading relations also becomes more difficult with a highly fluid population. Real or even imagined characteristics of traders must be assigned to a concrete reference group for plausibility. Large-scale circulation in and out of the marketplace system would mix up current traders with past ones and potential traders presently doing other work. Once nearly every woman had traded at one time or another, one might expect public hostility to be muted, although the high total rates of trading in Ghana's urban populations did not seem to have this effect.

High expectations of leaving trading should also reduce political or other forms of solidarity and social action among current traders by leading them to devalue interests and relations specific to their present position. Traders must be an identifiable group to themselves to act as such. Several authors interested in the political potential or likely class allegiance of traders have drawn negative conclusions from occupational instability. In influential case studies, frequent changes of work and social relations were found and generalized as the defining characteristic of informal sector employment (Hart 1973) and of casual work (Bromley and Gerry 1979). These authors specifically include market trading in their categories, which embrace small-scale production, sales, and services.

In order to assess traders' professional commitment, the survey included questions about their work as children, before marriage (if ever married), and just before their present work. It also asked for the reasons for changes reported at any of these points. These work histories indicate considerable retrospective stability. The average length of time of 7.3 years in their present commodity and location seems fairly long considering the age peak around twenty-five and the disruption of the economy in recent years. The modal length of tenure is four years for women and five for men. Current traders had more experience as children and young adults in trading than any other work. Older traders had often made their last change from another kind of trading, not necessarily in Kumasi Central Market. These traders have thus stayed with trading to a considerable degree, although they switched commodities and locations with more frequency. This pattern raises serious questions about the instability hypothesis, since commodity and locational groups are more cohesive than broader-based groups.

Women show a stronger commitment to trading than men, reporting less school and farming and much less blue-collar work. They also report more unemployment at all ages, probably representing domestic work. Differing economic conditions in male-dominated compared with female-dominated commodities could have generated some of this difference, since in gender-mixed commodities men and women had similar median lengths of tenure. The few men recorded in female commodities had exceptionally long tenures, perhaps remaining from earlier times when those commodities had also been mixed.

The reasons traders give for past job changes give a subjective picture of the forces acting on the boundary between trading and other career choices. The choices individuals make represent a compromise between their aspirations and general economic conditions that expand and contract the market. These reasons indicate potential stability when they refer to conditions or motives not likely to change—for example, some of the negative factors keeping potential traders out of alternative occupations.

Occupational decisions take place in a context of family negotiations and advice, like or as part of decisions about fostering, marriage, and inheritance. Comments from traders about their own life changes reveal this family input. "She was doing no work, so her parents decided she could go and stay with her aunt and trade with her." On the other hand, individuals reported they had the deciding vote on such decisions from a surprisingly early age. "None of the friends I had at that time were going to school, so they laughed at me until I couldn't stand it." "I preferred trading to school." "I was interested in sewing." "I wanted to trade with my brother." The absence of family support in household duties could prevent a woman from working or force a change in her occupation. In these cases, she usually perceived the problem as a domestic labor shortage rather than a work problem. "At first I was a housewife, but now there is a cook in the house."

Certain reasons traders gave for work changes (see table 8.11) beg the question of choice between trading and other options. The four most common reasons traders gave justify working as such and account for 43 percent of responses. For example, the comment "I acquired a little capital through my daily jobs to start my own trade" leaves unsaid the desirability of trading or the impossibility of other work. Cash that enabled her to begin trading could have been used to finance other occupations. In such instances, ease of entry and previous childhood experience (see tables 8.12, 8.13, and 8.14) make trading a virtually automatic choice. Inheriting family-owned stalls or taking over going enterprises indicated a response to capital assets only useful for that kind of trading. "My aunt gave me a stall." "My sister was traveling, so I took over." Trading was such a dominant occupation in Kumasi, especially for women, that these trading-specific forms of capital would have been the only major assets many girls' older female kin had to pass on to them.

Scarcity of resources led traders into the market as surely as sudden acquisition of resources. Lack of capital, space, or labor needed for

Table 8.11 Work Changes: Percentage Giving Each Reason* for Any Change of Work

Reason	Men	Women
Finished school	17.8	10.0
Needed money	21.7	15.4
Got older	7.0	5.6
Got capital	7.8	7.2
Liked new job	10.1	7.8
New job paid better	3.1	1.6
Disliked old job	7.8	8.8
Did not do it well	11.6	9.7
Lacked supplies	3.9	5.6
Government trouble	3.1	2.5
Moved	3.1	6.3
Married	0.8	4.7
Did not change	4.7	13.5
Other	17.8	19.7

* Coded after recording as told.
SOURCE: 1979 Kumasi Central Market Survey

other occupations forced some into trade. This answer seemed especially common among trained craft workers. "When I qualified as a welder, I could not get money to buy a machine." "I stopped because I could not find a room or any other place to continue sewing." "I changed because there was no one to look after the children in the house." Ex-farmers reported problems obtaining land as well as labor. "The land owner collected the land." "I wasn't getting help farming." Traders often reported leaving school for lack of money as their reason for first starting work. The current economic crisis compounds all these factors because it makes individual poverty more widespread and harder to overcome. Tools, rooms, land, and helpers can be obtained with sufficient money, and prosperous relatives are approachable for loans to finance such productive enterprises.

Traders entering by default constitute a more unstable trading population, at least theoretically, since they might move into other work they prefer if economic conditions improve. However, structural adjustment policies of credit and wage restraint and devaluation since 1985 have intensified the problems of establishment in craft enterprises and waged work. Shortages of raw materials, equipment, or spare parts due to legal foreign exchange shortages before 1985 have been re-

Table 8.12 Work Prior to Marriage, by Percentage of Each Sex*

Work	Men	Women
Trading	41.2	43.1
Farming	16.7	11.3
Blue-Collar	28.4	9.1
White-Collar	9.8	4.4
School	2.9	9.1
None	0	22.6
Other	1.0	0.4

* Unmarried persons gave present work.
SOURCE: 1979 Kumasi Central Market Survey

Table 8.13 Previous Work, by Percentage of Each Sex

Work	Men	Women
Trading	14.5	40.1
Farming	14.5	7.5
Blue-Collar	29.0	9.0
White-Collar	9.4	3.0
School	25.4	20.4
None	5.8	19.8
Other	1.4	0.3

SOURCE: 1979 Kumasi Central Market Survey

Table 8.14 Childhood Work, by Percentage of Each Sex

Work	Men	Women
Trading	2.2	22.8
Farming	17.3	11.4
School	69.8	43.1
None	5.0	43.1
Other*	5.8	3.9

* Includes blue-collar and white-collar employment.
SOURCE: 1979 Kumasi Central Market Survey

placed by high prices and lack of credit as barriers to entry. Personal savings and loans from relatives are reduced by low wages and layoffs, while the prices of imported manufactured equipment and raw materials have continued to increase, all trends that seem unlikely to reverse in the immediate future.

Other traders had to leave their previous occupations because of poor performance due to lack of skill or physical weakness. Comments like "The crops were not growing well" or "I was finding it difficult to produce nice sewn dresses" made this explicit, but complaints of lack of income or dislike of the old job or of schooling sometimes masked ineptitude. Illness forced changes because of either permanent and temporary physical disabilities. Farming and constant traveling were referred to as particularly strenuous and actually causing health problems. Several yam travelers had serious bouts of malaria from exhaustion, although other individuals even older could continue traveling. Survey comments included "I was getting weak walking around (hawking)" and "I got tired and couldn't work any more." Other illnesses or old age ruled out specific jobs. "I was operated on, so I had to do work where I could sit down." "I have eye trouble." "Carpentry, no strength for that." Those who leave salaried jobs or drop out of school during a serious illness cannot always resume them after they recover. "I took sick leave and was then sacked." Medical expenses and lost income from an illness can also reduce capital below the critical level, curtailing operations after the trader recovers.

Working conditions in some previous jobs were experienced as painful, antisocial, or humiliating. "Sitting by the fire all day made my face burn." "I didn't come home early, and I wanted to see my wife more often." "I was against being a maid, as I felt as a married woman I had to stop it." Occupations suitable for children were undignified for an adult. "I was hawking groundnuts, then I became too grown up for that." Changing to trading from such an unattractive occupation is a positive act likely to raise self-esteem. These changes might be more stable across the life span, because traders would resist moving back unless trading became impossible or the cultural values or social relations stigmatizing those occupations changed substantially.

I was also interested in the traders' prospective commitment to trading—whether they wanted and expected to remain in it. Since acquiring more capital was a common reason given for past occupational changes, I presented survey respondents with a hypothetical capital windfall to see if they would use it to leave trading or change their type of trading (see table 8.15). Its impersonal origin as lotto winnings avoided the obligation pilot respondents expressed to spend a cash gift

Table 8.15 Proposed Use of Windfall Capital

Purpose	200 Cedis	2,000 Cedis
This Work	71.7	67.0
New Work*	5.4	12.0
Save	3.6	10.1
Consumer Goods	9.0	3.4
Food	6.4	0.4
Other	3.9	7.1

* Includes another kind of trade.
SOURCE: 1979 Kumasi Central Market Survey

on a physical object that would remind them of the donor. This question aimed to assess their subjective commitment to both their current line of trade and trading as such, incorporating both positive and negative attitudes and opinions, such as pessimism about the prospects in other work. Their replies indicate ideals and expectations rather than predicting their actual behavior.

Traders stated how they would use two hypothetical windfalls. The lower amount was chosen to represent twice the weekly food budget of an ordinary household—a significant but not earth-shattering lump sum. The higher amount was twice the estimated working capital of 68 percent of the enterprises surveyed, so that it offered a majority of traders a practical possibility of changing lines of work within the market if they wished. A large majority of traders of both sexes chose to invest both amounts in their present work, showing that they feel a high personal commitment to trading and a willingness to reinvest.

Both positive and negative factors contribute to the high expectation or preference traders show for remaining in their current work. In interviews, traders spontaneously expressed pride in the independence and skill trading displays and in their ability to provide for their families. These values will continue to hold them in trading, not least because the lack of attractive alternatives is also likely to continue for some time. Traders know the drudgery, capital barriers, and uncertain supply and demand in other occupations from their own experience and that of family members. They make the same complaints about trading, but realize that a change of occupation would make little improvement. The living example of their own and their colleagues' persistence in trading also makes continuation seem likely. Switching commodities appears a much more realistic alternative than entry into another occupation because they have seen and done it more frequently already.

Historical Dynamics

The radical shifts and intense struggles over ethnic and gender boundaries in the marketplace system demonstrate both the strength and situationality of Kumasi market traders' identification as Asantes and women. Asante men exited from marketplace trade within a few decades after British destruction of chiefly trading institutions and the rapid expansion of cocoa farming. Asante women replaced them in important commodities and accomplished a rapid expansion of urban foodstuffs trade in the 1930s, gaining ground against other ethnic groups. Particularly rapid response to changing ethnic and gendered opportunities for education and employment suggest that adjustment along ethnic and gender lines strikes the most critical balance between commercial power and other systems of domination.

The initial shock of conquest and the dismantling of Asante border controls brought in several decades of rapid fluctuations in the ethnic and gender organization of trade as traders tested and negotiated changes in the regional balance of power along other lines. Many new income opportunities opened up for men with the expansion of jobs in European enterprises and the widespread adoption of cocoa as a cash crop. The stricter subordination of traders through the extension of the credit customer system meant that these new sectors now offered better returns and advancement than trading. Starting in the 1910s and 1920s, fundamental reorientations in the gender assignment and geographical structure of trading roles began to stabilize, laying a new foundation for the massive expansion of the 1930s. Fante men filtered into Asante in large numbers to sell imports and buy exports, beginning in the 1880s, when political upheavals weakened the *Asantehene*'s effective border controls. Their previous commercial experience on the coast gave them advantages over Asantes in several expanding commercial roles. Some had established lines of credit with coastal stores, which they used as itinerant rubber buyers or selling cloth and other imports in rural Asante. Their literacy rates and familiarity with store and office procedures were higher from living under British rule on the coast since the early 1800s. After 1900, some worked as clerks in the new government offices and as storekeepers in the new Kumasi branches of expatriate stores.

Throughout these first decades, immigrant Fante men virtually monopolized white-collar job openings in Kumasi, as they had in Accra three decades earlier. The basic reason was also the same: they were the only ones to qualify because of the long tradition of education in their home region. Educated Fante men had actively traded in the early nineteenth century, the first years of colonial rule on the coast, but now the tighter control by European firms led ambitious young men to seek salaried or professional jobs. Few Asantes had educated their sons and nephews, resisting mission education out of distaste for Christianity. Chiefs petitioned for a nonsectarian schools in Kumasi, and enrollments surged after this opened in 1909 (Brown 1972). When these students began graduating and completing technical training, by the 1920s, Asante men began to move into local white-collar positions in substantial numbers.

Asante men's desire for jobs was also tempered by their strong preference for cocoa farming, then offering high incomes. Their gender and ethnicity gave them favored access to the type of land required, and their farms rapidly extended through the Asante heartland and most of the present Brong-Ahafo Region. Women's farms were markedly smaller and fewer than men's farms, in both the old and new cocoa-growing areas (Okali 1983). Women lacked the substantial capital needed to acquire land, pay laborers, and supply food until trees matured, while men had better access to lineage loans and lands, unpaid labor from subordinate male kin, and food supplies from wives. Increased cocoa production brought additional employment for Asante men as cocoa traders and brokers. From the first, cocoa was bought and sold outside of the marketplace system through links to expatriate trading firms. When later transferred to the government Cocoa Marketing Board, cocoa buying and resale remained in male hands, now government employees.

Government and private clerical employment for men in Asante expanded rapidly during the first decades of this century, but the small size of the local official and commercial establishment, based mainly in Kumasi, meant that such employees remained a small proportion of the labor force, even in the city itself. While women were certainly excluded from Asante white-collar jobs, at least as strictly as Robertson documents for Accra (Robertson 1984), their labor-force position was determined more significantly in Asante by their exclusion from other lucrative sectors: notably from cocoa farming, but also from craft and industrial jobs. In Accra, the national capital, a relatively high proportion of men had the European-recognized skills needed for white-collar or blue-collar work, and the land base for cocoa was absent (Robertson 1984, 31).

Fante immigration also included women skilled in trading and craft work, who came alone or with male white-collar relatives. These Fante women baked bread, sewed clothes, and sold fish, foodstuffs, and imported goods in Kumasi, as they had on the coast. Asante families who had left for political or economic reasons to become landlords or brokers in coastal towns had also raised children in that more Westernized environment, who now returned to Kumasi with their skills and contacts. Both sets of coastal women included credit customers of coastal branches of expatriate stores, who still bought there for resale in Kumasi or established accounts in Kumasi branches with their sound credit histories.

Asante women began to move into previously male-dominated roles in market trading in the 1910s, replacing the men moving out and into cocoa farming and wage work. Accounts of eyewitnesses agree that the first new commodities women took up were the staple imported goods: liquor, tobacco, and cloth. The first Kumasi women began to sell these items in the 1910s, and they had expanded into the full range of imported goods by the 1930s. Women sold imports in the markets, and to a lesser extent in stores, while men bought exports and sold imports outside of the markets. This put them in a commercial position comparable to coastal women, who had completely replaced local men in the import trade in coastal areas by the mid-1800s.

The rapid multiplication of branch stores and transport facilities in Kumasi improved Kumasi traders' direct access to supplies of cloth, coastal fish, and forest vegetables. Kumasi-based Asante women obtained imports from expatriate import firms in Accra, Cape Coast, or Kumasi itself. The passbook system used by British firms favored women with educated male connections, since salaried husbands or relatives guaranteed credit for new passbook holders, but other women deposited their own passbook security in cash, gold jewelry, and other valuables.

Asante women also replaced men by trading in some locally produced commodities, gradually taking over all of the larger market sections selling foodstuffs. Fante men and women both had actively traded fish to Asante since precolonial times. During the 1920s and 1930s, both fish and game sales gradually became female-identified, to the extent that present informants refer to fish-selling as a stereotypically female occupation. Those who traded or shopped during this entire period observed that Asante women achieved their present numerical dominance of the markets only in the 1940s, trading in more items and with more regions than ever before.

The ideology generating feminization of marketplace trade did not devalue trading for men as such, but consistently steered men into the most profitable, upwardly-mobile occupations, closely linked to the major power centers of their society. In precolonial Asante these had included market trading, but that was no longer the case after 1900.

Shopkeepers and local agents for European firms, government and industrial employees enjoyed stable and relatively high incomes at first, but their jobs now depended directly on the favor of employers and international financial conditions. Even elite men in the learned professions—ministers, lawyers and doctors—usually depended on formal qualifications and external linkages for jobs appropriate to their training.

Contemporary statements about male and female trading roles highlight the importance of new, higher-prestige occupations for men in naturalizing this gender transition. One prominent onion trader explained that trading was too dirty and physical for men, an important prestige indicator for both male and female occupations. "Men should instead sell in a clean store, sitting down, for high prices." Two pervasive values converge in these twists of ideology: that dirty jobs have less prestige and pay less and that men have more prestige and earn more. When I mentioned that men in fact had the dirtiest occupations in the market, as carriers, she explained that such work was all right for low-status Northerners and impoverished young boys, but a man should aspire to more. Clearly only Asantes from decent families qualified as "real men." Those Asante men remaining in the market after the 1930s sold imports and manufactures, the type of goods they also sold in stores. Male craft workers also kept their workshops in the market stalls.

Women traders also gained in numbers and wealth through the growing volume and concentration of the local foodstuffs trade, which they continued to monopolize. During the 1910s and 1920s, volume increased within the old geographical and organizational framework. Vegetable foods still came into the growing towns from their immediate hinterlands, without the need for multiple or specialized intermediaries. Village women still control supplies from these sources today. A smaller range of vegetables reached the market than at present because many forest products and minor foods were not yet fully commercialized. Formal market organizations, with recognized queens and elders, belonged to the later stages of marketplace development. The elderly queens of several minor commodity groups asserted in 1979 that they had been the first to trade professionally in their commodities, during the 1930s or 1940s. The very rapid expansion of marketplace trade meant plenty of customers for all and put some premium on the skills of the few experienced traders.

The expansion of Asante women's dominance in the local foodstuffs trading range brought them into direct conflict with Northern men traders who were expanding southward. Northern traders at first simply brought their kola caravans into producing areas near Asante's northern borders instead of stopping at the official border markets. After 1900, Northern men ventured down to Kumasi to buy imported and manufactured goods and coastal fish and also brought dried Volta fish, blankets, shea butter, chickens, cattle, and sheep from the Northern and Upper Regions into Kumasi. Northerners settled in Kumasi with their wives and families in greater numbers by 1910, when peaceful conditions seemed likely to continue. This influx greatly expanded the demand for foodstuffs in the city, since these newcomers had no access to farmland or food from farming relatives.

Men from the Northern and Upper Regions traded in Kumasi Central Market, and even expanded their operations during the 1920s and 1930s, but were separated spatially as well as culturally within it. The foodstuffs that they dominated were wholesaled at the outside edges of the marketplace. Cattle and kola traders had their separate areas beside the main market, with the chicken market just inside. Northern men also sold beans and grains wholesale in sacks from storefronts in nearby streets.

Expatriate Muslim merchants moved into Ashanti Region in large numbers during these decades and were incorporated into the "Northern" ethnopolitical grouping evolving in Kumasi (Schildkrout 1978a). Gao traders from Mali and Mossi from Burkina Faso filtered in across the Northern border as far as Kumasi, trading in grain and yams and carrying loads. They dominated the trade in imported and exported agricultural produce, especially kola, cattle, and grains. Much of this trade was technically illegal because it bypassed formal import regulations, so cultural and religious solidarity was important in establishing trading links across national frontiers. Hausas from Nigeria and "Ghana Hausas" from settled communities within the country came to dominate these urban communities linguistically and politically, partly because of their commercial strength as a diaspora through many Sahelian countries.

Cocoa and industrial employment also brought large numbers of Northern men into Ashanti Region. Young men migrated to Asante to work as laborers on cocoa and food farms, either seasonally or semipermanently. Others came south to work for wages in mines and sawmills, swelling the commercial demand for foodstuffs. These new employment opportunities may have diverted significant numbers of young Northern men from entering trading careers and therefore reduced the competition faced by Asante women in their newly expanding trading roles there.

Asante women not only stretched gender boundaries in the trading system, but ethnic boundaries as well, by expanding their commercial position relative to coastal Ga and Fante women. They moved into larger-scale intermediary trading positions, either formerly occupied by coastal women or newly created by the intensification of trade in some commodities. Asante women supplied cloth and other imports to traders and consumers in Asante and the North, who previously had to travel to the coast. They also collected foodstuffs such as yams and beans from those regions to supply Accra traders, who bought increasing amounts for their growing populations in the markets of Accra or Kumasi (Robertson 1984). Coastal women seemed to concentrate their efforts on retailing and wholesaling within their own growing cities. Robertson reports that fewer Ga women did long-distance trade in cloth, fish, and vegetables after the 1960s, and more engaged in local retailing and processing. While this fall in numbers might be explained by increased specialization and concentration among Ga traders, a number of the life histories I collected from Asante traders reported starting to buy and sell in Accra during that period. Fante women had continued and expanded the trade in smoked fish and bread they had established before British conquest, but higher volumes also made room for more Asante women as retailers and producers. On the other hand, Ewe women traders from Volta Region admitted no outsiders on their route, bringing truckloads of shallots to Kumasi from irrigated farms near Keta and Anloga to supplement seasonal supplies from Asante villages, which began in the 1930s.

By that decade, Asante women also began to expand their trading networks into the North by venturing out to sell imports, manufactures, and southern produce in the markets there. One of the first pioneers described rather nostalgically the excitement of traveling from town to town with her truck driver husband as a young married woman in the 1920s, buying and selling opportunistically. She returned to Kumasi from time to time to sell her purchases, usually yams and game meat, and to renew her supplies of cloth and enamelware. She explained that she could not then find an Asante-speaking maid in the North, so her several children made traveling difficult and she settled in Kumasi to sell yams in Kumasi Central Market. After a few years, she went back to Northern villages regularly as a yam traveler, leaving her children in Kumasi in the care of relatives. Increased knowledge of commercial conditions in the north led to more organized routes and practices by the 1940s.

Toward the end of the 1940s, Asante women began to trade actively in major markets in the Northern and Upper Regions in direct competition with local men. They displaced the Northern men who had brought yams from their farms by buying not only in markets but directly from farmers in the main supply areas. Aspiring Gao intermediaries, ousted in the 1930s, renewed their attempts to dominate Kumasi wholesaling, leading to another riot in 1958 (Drake and Lacy 1966). Northern men had pioneered the trade in dry season tomatoes from irrigation projects in their hometowns in the Upper Region. Their cartel-like companies, based in Bolgatanga, supplied tomatoes to all of the southern cities, including Kumasi. During the late 1940s, Kumasi women challenged the dominance of this all-male company. They succeeded in forcing the men to share the trade with the "women's company," founded by a daughter of the tomato *ohemma* in Kumasi. Now southern women have purchased a majority of the memberships in the "men's company" as well. Similar companies of women now supply all the major southern cities.

Yorubas and Lebanese took a conspicuous part in the trade in imports from Europe in the Kumasi hinterland during the whole colonial period, although they were conspicuously absent during my fieldwork because of their expulsion in 1969. Poorer Lebanese immigrants had started out by selling in Adum market stalls in the 1900s and 1910s but did not get allocated stalls in the new Kumasi Central Market. Those who were successful or arrived with more capital set up small import firms in the 1910s and 1920s in most major towns in Ashanti Region.

A sizable Yoruba community was evident by the 1930s, comprising men as craftsmen and traders and women as traders. Yoruba men often set up small stores selling consumer imports, such as bicycles or provisions. Their wholesale shops supplied imports to smaller Yoruba traders who circulated through every recognized town and village market in Ashanti Region. Yorubas also traded actively in Tamale and other Northern towns, forestalling Asante or Fante expansion in that direction (Eades 1983). They advanced goods on credit to Yoruba women, who became a common, even stereotypical sight in rural and urban marketplaces in Ashanti Region. Although they remained a small minority in the region, Yoruba women were the largest ethnic group after Asante women represented among Kumasi Central Market stallholders in 1968 (Sudarkasa 1975; 1979). Men with little capital preferred to peddle goods from village to village, perhaps because marketplaces were so identified with women in Ashanti Region and Yorubaland. Returning male migrants helped to establish cocoa production in Nigeria.

Another period of dramatic change in the ethnic and gender divisions of labor started in the late 1940s and early 1950s, with the expansion of the rural road network and official policies promoting

Africanization in the civil service and business sectors. Many more jobs opened to educated Africans, and Asante men were graduating from schools and colleges in larger numbers, intensifying the withdrawal of men from market trading. A few women also benefitted, most moving into the lower levels of white-collar work at this time. These women came predominantly from coastal Fante families with long traditions of education, as had the previous generation of educated men, but some Asante women also became teachers, nurses, and clerks. Educated women also traded later in their careers, however, when employment practices forced them to retire at marriage or after the birth of children. Women workers' lower wages, marginal status, and shorter careers reduced their expectation of accumulating significant resources on the job, so their alliance with state interests was even more conditional than male workers.

As Asante had followed the coastal pattern with some delay, now the North followed Asante. Asantes moved into some of the same administrative and professional positions in the Northern Region that Fantes had monopolized earlier in Kumasi. The establishment of more elaborate administration and better schools in the North at first created more openings for Asantes, but eventually trained Northern men with the qualifications to take up the new jobs. Northern women also began to push against their gender boundaries in trade. Very few Northern women had been educated by then, but local women began to take over small-town trade in items such as shea butter and chickens from local men. As more Northern women continued to move south with their families to live in Kumasi and grow up there, they began to trade in Kumasi Central Market in larger numbers and to work as travelers bringing goods from their home areas.

Hiring practices in the civil service had a greater direct impact on trade after independence in 1957, as governments participated in commerce more directly. Although the British government had removed cocoa trading from private African hands, it concentrated on promoting and protecting the market share of British firms, for example, during both World Wars. Soon after independence, the national government diverted more commodities from the marketplace system. In accordance with its greater emphasis on central planning and control, it established state distribution agencies, but without monopoly status. The Ghana Food Distribution Corporation sold local farm produce and the State Fishing Corporation sold frozen fish in regional capitals, including Kumasi. Workers' and consumers' cooperatives were promoted and department stores confiscated from expatriates were changed into the Ghana National Trading Corporation. Although state-distributed supplies never challenged marketplace channels in volume or reliability, these institutions did provide substantial incomes for employees and officials.

With accelerating inflation and economic decline in the 1970s and 1980s, economic returns from other occupations fell sharply, making trading relatively attractive again. Cocoa farmers and formal sector employees suffered from their dependence on government-set prices and wages, and these occupations lost much of their survival value. Market traders, although also losing a high proportion of their real incomes, could compensate more directly for the rising cost of living. The high cost of food made food farming, for example, more profitable than cocoa farming. Wealthy men turned to trading and also to commercial food farming in an attempt to protect their capital from rapid erosion by inflation. Stagnant or bankrupt industries could not employ capital, absorb more workers, or pay living wages. Housing and transport also become more difficult investments because of extreme shortages of imported materials and supplies.

Large numbers of school-leavers and unemployed or underpaid wage workers, both males and females, entered the market as a refuge employment in the late 1970s and 1980s. Women continued to dominate the trade in local foodstuffs, although a few men could be seen even there. In imports and manufactures, where once only a few older men remained, young men abounded at the lower retail levels. They sold used clothing, provisions, and manufactured goods, where their education would be an advantage in dealing with suppliers. Educated women also gravitated to imports and manufactures, since these "clean" trades had higher prestige and substantially higher incomes than the jobs most available to women.

Structural adjustment policies in the later 1980s intensified movement in this direction. Massive layoffs from the civil service threw men and educated women back onto the informal economy. Rehabilitation of the mining industry along more capital-intensive lines meant less employment there as well. Those "redeployees" with some capital could aspire to start small businesses, but the stresses of previous decades of inflation and food shortages had left very few in this category. Credit and demand restraints central to fiscal stabilization prevented the private sector from expanding production in response to the incentives supposedly created by structural adjustment. Extraordinary numbers of new entrants to Kumasi Central Market, in a context of declining total buying power, depressed income levels appreciably. Younger men stopped paying even lip service to the eventual welding or sewing machine. They flooded into secondhand clothes, one of the few expanding commodities, but their presence was especially conspicuous in the local foodstuffs, hitherto virtually reserved for women (Clark and Manuh 1991).

During the twentieth century as a whole, the trading system itself has grown, with increased volume and capital that should translate into more economic influence. This expansion generated some powerful new trading roles, which Asante women promptly occupied. As farmers committed more resources to commercial farming, they depended more heavily on the market system, although not here on specific sets of traders. Asante women also took over trading functions or positions from men traders, Northerners, self-marketing producers, and even immigrant Yoruba market women.

Paradoxically, the power of the trading system and of Asante women was shrinking with respect to the overall social formation during this same period. The increasing female predominance in marketplaces corresponded to an accelerating marginalization of market traders and of women, in a mutually reinforcing pattern. European firms had replaced African men with African women as their main client group because their disadvantages in education, capital accumulation, and political connections made them a more reliably subordinate group. By removing the leading social elements and the principal items of export trade, such as cocoa, from market trading, the British put more distance between market traders as a occupational group and the main sources of capital and influence within African society. The separation of trading from chiefship was compounded by the separation of women from the civil service, and thus from state distribution work.

Educational, industrial, and political policies cut off women traders from the major centers of economic power in the Ghanaian economy by deepening and rigidifying a gender division of labor in market and extra-market trade that was largely new to Asante. Through the worsening terms of trade and more subordinate commercial relations, market traders lost ground to the expanding European and Lebanese import firms. They also lost ground consistently to state institutions, controlled largely by Asante and coastal men. Women had less access than before to these official channels, as even their restricted participation in education, electoral politics, and chiefly office was overshadowed by military rule.

Contemporary female dominance in market trading in Asante thus is not rooted in a conservative tradition of female trading reproduced unthinkingly or inescapably. The current disapproval of Asante men engaging in marketplace trade is historically contingent, based on the low returns and limited upward mobility in trading after British conquest. This ideological situation created an unstable gender division of labor that responded quickly to changing economic pressures. The coordination of shifts in gender and ethnic participation in trade with overall economic conditions confirms that men and educated women consistently moved out of market trading during the first half of this century whenever more attractive options opened for them. Ethnic groups began to exit in the order that they could take up these options, although not even southern men managed to leave completely. As these outside opportunities shrunk, these groups reentered market trading without much delay.

Conclusion

Gender takes on additional importance in forging market traders' distinctive identity because other distinguishing attributes are so little generalized in the Ghanaian marketplace system. The use of gender as an organizing principle in commercial and leadership relations inside of the market reinforces its significance in trader/nontrader relations, especially in urban settings where large proportions of the women trade. Class or ethnic relations provide little basis for dividing Kumasi Central Market traders from the general population, although they do mark commodity groups strongly. The majority of Kumasi Central Market traders belong to the locally dominant Asante ethnic group, which leaves ethnic minorities monopolizing certain commodities vulnerable to victimization and adds an interethnic edge to many interregional commercial interactions. Traders' family backgrounds reveal no unusual connection with low or high income, education, or access to other important resources.

The intensification of traders' marginality, to the verge of stigma in recent decades, both depends on and reinforces stable occupational group membership. Individual traders showed a high degree of objective and subjective commitment to their occupation that confirms their professional identity. This long-term commitment made it critical that few distinctive family or other nontrading relations were present to contribute to isolating traders. Trading relations rarely use kinship relations as such to organize trade within the market, and age or other aspects of traders' position within the family also have relatively little impact.

The pattern of ethnic boundaries in trading role assignment also shows far greater persistence of divisions based on current commercial and economic circumstances than on extra-commercial or affectional links. Ethnic solidarity with other traders proved much more effective than ethnic solidarity with the producer group in creating and defending ethnic niches in the distribution system. This reflects a situation where producers have relatively free access to markets, so that no one group has a monopoly on access to them. Asante women predominate in the foodstuffs trades, which make up most of the market, even when these come from non-Asante supply areas, such as Northern yams and irrigated tomatoes or plantains from Sehwi. Asante women wrested control of yam and tomato routes after these were pioneered by non-Asante men from the producing areas. The only exceptions are a few items consumed by Northerners and sold by Northern women, including certain greens, different from those preferred by Asantes, shea butter, and veils worn by Moslem women. Commercial ties with consumers (not producers) apparently compete successfully with non-specific commercial dominance.

Northern men dominate only in foodstuff trades where connections to the old savannah trading networks remain important. Kola and cattle are still traded across national boundaries, in opposite directions. Kola is actually produced or gathered in the forest, mainly by Asante women. Kola traders mentioned that some rural women bulked and stored kola in the villages, in anticipation of the trading season, but none had interurban roles. Northern men also exercised their ties to consumers when they took imports and manufactured goods north. Some of these also find their way into international trade, although not legally. The trade in chickens, dominated by Upper Region men referred to in Kumasi as "Frafras," is only an apparent exception. They are not tied into the international savannah network, often not even speaking Hausa, but maintain a tight monopoly of their commodity. Although these men grow up familiar with chicken judging and transport in their home areas, which do export chickens to Kumasi, they range outside these home areas once they become professional traders. These men will learn local languages in order to develop trading contacts in a new area, just as Asante women do. They maintain extremely solid commercial relations with colleagues based on their shared heritage, funeral attendance, etc.

Traders' strongly urban background suggests a possible alternative cleavage, placing urban market traders in opposition to rural farmers and tapping into the social tensions associated with rural/urban inequality. Local identification does figure in their organizational framework and their situational alliances in some incidents of disputes and competitive rivalries. Within the urban Asante context, locality-based social relations implying isolation coexist with a multiplicity of cross-cutting ties which tend to compromise the boundary around traders as a social group. High occupational commitment of current traders is also balanced by the ease of entry into trading, so that nontraders can easily see themselves as potential traders. The identification of powerful traders with dominant ethnic groups and urban centers is balanced by shared interests with traders drawn from their own communities and income levels. Close ties between traders and family members of both sexes in the most common other occupations should likewise undermine gender stereotyping.

This complex result suggests that the ideological and practical isolation of traders depends on strong antagonisms that undercut these bases of solidarity. Family solidarity with traders was less effective because of deepening and increasingly conflictual cleavages on the basis of gender within lineage and marital families. Communal support of local traders implies a deemphasis on class or ethnic antagonisms within the local community. This line of argument predicts that hostility and actions will focus on commodities or other subgroups of traders where stricter ethnic or gender assignment or economic barriers limit entry or where economic factors highly reward the high capital levels and long tenure of established traders. This is confirmed historically by the special targeting of cloth and provisions traders and foreigners (Gaos, Yorubas, Hausas and, in 1979 and 1983, Lebanese and "French Line" Gaos and Mossis).

Political access has been a critical factor in drawing and deepening divisions between men and women, between racial and ethnic constituencies, and between market trade and other economic sectors. Government attempts to monopolize distribution of imports or farm produce confirm the primacy of commercial over noncommercial factors. They have failed for lack of technical coordination despite the popularity of the idea with farmers when first promoted, and even with urban consumers. Unfortunately, state distribution personnel lacked the skills and resources to judge quality, estimate supplies, and price fresh produce, or to store and transport it without massive losses through spoilage and theft. Neither farmers or consumers could afford to rely on them, so both continued to patronize the market system. By contrast, successive governments have been much more effective in reserving commercial roles for their constituents: first for precolonial Asantes, then for expatriate British, and recently for Ghanaian citizens.

A clear contrast emerges between the pattern of contest of ethnic and of gender boundaries within the marketplace system. Gender boundaries have mainly shifted in response to changing access to opportunities and resources outside the marketplace system. Ethnic boundaries (which are also gendered in many cases) have been more overtly contested on that basis, and invoking ethnic solidarity with fellow traders or local authorities has proved effective. Ethnic-based hostilities have been intermittent, but gender-based hostility has consistently generated widespread public support for government attempts at price control and direct distribution from the 1960s through the 1980s.

Gender attacks hit hard at the ideological level but had much less effect on the actual division of labor in commerce than, for example, deportations or restrictions of foreigners. The high incomes and prestige available to illiterate women through market trading functioned as a powerful symbol of national degeneracy in 1979. Direct government distribution would return these incomes and positions of power to the educated male civil service or the public-spirited military, where they belonged. Harsh polemics and policies could not expel women from the trading roles in question because the government could not provide either a viable alternative in distribution or in occupations for women. Instead, these campaigns simply intensified the gender isolation of women as traders. It was left to structural adjustment to undermine female control of market trading indirectly by sending more men back into trading and by subordinating the locally based economy more deeply.

9 HOME AND HUSBAND

Gender negotiations within the relations of marriage and lineage are essential to the survival of Asante women as market traders. Tensions these unresolved domestic struggles create may intensify societal tensions about commercial issues, but without the personal autonomy Asante women expect, construct, and defend the trading system would collapse. Only a minority of traders brought much labor or capital directly into trading from husband, children, or other family members, but their enterprises depend on their ability to juggle successfully the competing demands their responsibilities to husband and children make on the same labor time and capital they need for trading. They manipulate the complex interaction of these diverse and sometimes conflicting relationships, each of which gives them control over some people and resources and subordinates them in other respects. Life-cycle dynamics interlock with differential class resources to construct distinct sets of strategies for wealthier and poorer traders, elders and adolescents, and for those who depend more on husbands than kin.

Gendered capital accumulation processes take place as much at home as at work within the context of gendered lineage and marital relations that establish claims for unpaid domestic labor and subsistence support but also generate resources that affect trading patterns profoundly. Access to inherited capital assets and to loans, gifts, and other transfers of resources from kin, parents, and spouses is tightly linked to these gendered exchanges of labor. Even when these resources are not used directly for trading, they reduce competing demands on traders' capital and income. Juggling long- and short-term entitlements and reciprocities involves balancing contradictory norms and ideological principles applicable to kinship, parenthood, and marriage, as well as balancing a restricted budget.

Matrilineal traditions remain strong, even for those traders not actively using lineage land, houses, or other property. Most Kumasi market traders have their hometowns in the smaller towns and villages in Ashanti Region or adjacent Brong-Ahafo Region. They can keep in touch with relative ease through visits and by sending messages via other visitors. More frequent contacts with kin who live in Kumasi also reinforce lineage loyalty. When no close genealogical kin live there, relations with more distant aunts and cousins may intensify.

Some large lineages have organized mutual-aid groups of lineage members living in Kumasi, with monthly dues, monthly meetings, and standard benefits in time of illness or bereavement. Traders call on individual kin for support in financial need, political initiatives, and legal trouble and take refuge with them in old age, illness, and bankruptcy.

The matrilineage provides a real safety net for most urban Asante women against the risks of divorce, illness, or bankruptcy. This safety net can also help a trading enterprise survive, but helping to maintain it for other kin requires commitments of time and income that inhibit capital formation. Raising children is an Asante woman's most important contribution to her lineage, since they are its future members. She trades in order to keep them alive, but they also take her income and time away from the market. Conversely, both men's and women's trading profits also contribute to the accumulation of human and financial capital ultimately located in the kin group, especially when spent on the education of young people expected to help the wider kin group later or on building assets to be inherited within the lineage, such as houses and cocoa land. The timing and direction of exchanges of labor and financial assistance with kin are analyzed in detail here because this aspect of kinship ideology and practice is one of the most influential on trading itself. Trading gives the market woman valuable leverage in her lineage affairs, and her position in her matrilineage gives her a more solid point of leverage in the market.

Household analysis usually presumes substantial pooling of income and labor within a co-residential unit that centers on a married couple, their children, and collateral relatives. Asante presumptions of co-residence and resource sharing lead to very different configurations of domestic demands on labor and income. The clear acceptance of duolocal marriage and individuation in both kinship and marriage, recognizing claims for assistance but not strict pooling of resources, leaves interesting and crucial choices for individual women in each arena. Children and husbands compete for some of the same labor and emotional resources. Kumasi women traders consciously weigh direct and indirect financial returns from an active marriage against its costs in personal domestic labor commitment. This chapter focuses on the interactions and contradictions between the demands of marriage, kinship, and trading.

Kumasi Central Market traders do not resolve the conflicts between domestic and commercial work by integrating the two spheres of activity by, for example, seeking to reorganize their trading so that they can cook or care for children at the same time. Those who take this route must leave the market altogether and limit their trading to roadside stands or home-based cooked-food preparation. Those who remain Kumasi Central Market traders instead act to separate the two arenas more completely by reorganizing their domestic arrangements so that they can withdraw further, although never entirely, from personal performance of domestic tasks. They delegate as much domestic work as possible to children, maids, and adult kin who do not trade. Only women who have achieved substantial success in this direction can keep the full, stable trading schedules essential to building and maintaining substantial levels of business volume and capital.

One middle-aged trader, not exceptionally wealthy, exemplified the ideal that children take over housework entirely. Her nine children, aged three to twenty-six, lived in a house built by her deceased maternal uncle which was shared by other lineage relatives. The oldest, a daughter, had left home to live with her husband, but the trader convinced her to quit her white-collar job and move back in to run the home when she became pregnant. Younger daughters and a maid did most of the physical work and cared for the youngest girl, who never appeared in the market. The mother declared proudly that she did nothing at all when she went home, and she spent most of her nontrading hours at her husband's apartment, even while her husband himself was working in Nigeria.

Disengagement from housework turns out to be vital for business expansion because of direct conflicts between trading and the timing and quantity of labor required by culturally specific standards of cooking and childcare. Strategies for accomplishing this disengagement rely on intensive management of nonmarket entitlements and responsibilities governed by kin and marital relations. These relations thus exert a powerful, but primarily indirect, influence on eventual commercial success and failure. Unpaid domestic labor from children and kin paradoxically gives most women their best opening to withdraw from unpaid domestic labor for kin and husbands themselves. The desire for substantial financial assistance from husbands pulls in another direction by encouraging co-residence with husbands, which inhibits recruiting assistance from live-in kin and thus favors commercialization of domestic labor through hired maids and processed food purchases.

My investigation of domestic relations during fieldwork focused on three issues: defining which aspects of domestic relations were most crucial for these Kumasi traders, verifying to what extent they conformed to the dominant Asante patterns documented by other researchers, and examining their interaction with market trading. It does not address directly Asante domestic relations in general, since the traders I visited and surveyed were drawn from a range of trading roles and commodity groups rather than the full range of the larger Kumasi community. I investigated cooking and childcare in particular detail, once I found they posed the most direct challenge to trading. Contrasting strategies for dealing with these two challenges underline sharp contrasts in the gender power balance within marriage, which embeds cooking, and lineage relations, which embed childcare. It proved intriguing that traders in fact differed so little from Asantes in general in the primary features of their kinship and marriage relations. It seems that even unusually intense trading activity, associated with participation in a major urban market like Kumasi Central Market, is not incompatible with mainstream Asante female roles and did not distort them unduly. On the contrary, market women found the flexibility Asante marital and kinship norms provided them to be a critical asset for surviving economic stresses.

The Individual in Relation

The economic position of Asante market women cannot be derived unproblematically from their status within the household and that household's status relative to others, because they do not have unobstructed access to household resources or allow such access to their own. Instead, they participate in a complex articulation of systems of access to resources based on lineage, marriage, co-residence and gender, which are subject to constant manipulation and negotiation by everyone involved. An advantageous marriage or lineage connection can certainly be turned to advantage within the trading system, and vice versa, but other configurations of interaction are also common. Traders frequently talk of compensating for poor position within one system, especially marriage, by relying primarily on another, in that case kinship or trading, although a collapse in any one also tends to trigger deterioration within the other systems.

The scope for individual negotiation within the locally specific normal framework of kinship and marriage does not make these relations trivial or weak. They seem to retain their importance because of, not in spite of, their ability to adapt to individual capacities and inclinations. The matrilineage continues to play a major role in the transmission of property and financial or labor assistance, so it is important to assess how fully women, including urban market women, participate in that transmission. Marriage still represents a key channel giving women and children access to male incomes and social sponsorship, although not an effective channel for all women and children. Individual autonomy is seen to reinforce, not contradict, the capacity and desire to strong bonds of mutual benefit with kin, spouse, friends, and community members.

It is not entirely clear that Asantes *have* households in the usual sense of the term; at least one prominent analyst specifically exempts them from his general model (Laslett 1972). The domestic unit portrayed in the work of Chayanov, Sahlins, and Hyden, with resources pooled and allocated for joint benefit, is contradicted in Asante by strong themes of multilocality and individualism already evident before the colonial period (Chayanov 1966; Sahlins 1972; Hyden 1980). The Asante emphasis on matrilineal kin as a residential and property group decenters the married couple and unsettles Eurocentric images of the household, but shifting the nucleus to a brother-sister or mother-child bond does not solve all of these analytic problems. More sophisticated and abstract definitions of households are still based on resource sharing and joint decision-making, which Asante ideals and practices throw into question for kin as well as spouses (Friedmann 1986; Yanagisako 1979; Wilk and Netting 1984). The labor and capital resources generated by co-resident family members in Kumasi Central Market enterprises described in the preceding chapter are not freely available for communal use, and they often work in distinct enterprises that do not share resources. This key characteristic of the household enterprise or household mode of production is openly disavowed.

The negotiability and contingency so prominent in Asante lineage and marital obligations means that Asante women are not flatly excluded from access to capital resources, but this does not result in their gaining access on equal terms to their brothers or husbands. Patterns of trading and capital formation in Kumasi Central Market confirm a systematic disadvantage of women in inheritance and premortem transfers that studies of rural areas reveal in patterns of cocoa farm devolution (Okali 1983; Mikell 1989). Men traders reported financial backing from their mothers much more often than women traders reported help from fathers or male relatives such as matrilineal uncles. Transfers from husbands came with strings attached; women traders actually said they would avoid accepting capital from their husbands because this would end their claims to child support and allow him or his heirs to claim ownership of the business later.

For the typical Asante market woman, the amount of lineage property is not substantial enough for succession to be a primary concern. Use rights they retain in lineage resources are more important to their long-term work and survival strategies. They are more likely to live in houses owned by lineage kin than to inherit them. Returning to the hometown remains an important fall-back strategy, whether as a short-term refuge, a long-term career change, or a retirement option. Hometown land claims preserve the possibility of food farming, at least at a subsistence level. In larger hometowns where nearby land is fully occupied, local small-scale trading opportunities tend to be greater. Many traders expressed thoughts of retiring to the lineage house or hometown in frail old age. Family accommodation and domestic help, combined with the lower cost of living, would help their children's financial contributions stretch farther there. On visits to hometowns I met elderly women who had retired there successfully after a lifetime of city trading, although I also met many other elderly traders who had remained in Kumasi.

As traders, they may borrow or share market stalls that kin control or inherit lease rights. Trading partnerships are rare, but when assistants are needed they will usually be recruited from among kin. In case of bankruptcy, by no means infrequent, the ability to call on kin for loans, business connections, selling space, and other forms of sponsorship may be the only practical way to reestablish independence. Domestic labor from kin is also a critical resource. Adult and child kin can move in briefly to deal with sudden health crises or supply long-term household assistance through fostering or co-residence. Relatives feel an obligation to help, but this gives them the authority to offer other less desirable solutions to the problem.

Siblings, especially of the same sex, tended to be the first asked for help or advice in the commercial and public crises that abounded, and many did provide valuable help. They found it hard, although by no means impossible, to turn down requests for money, a place to stay, or a word in the right ear. But even their support is not completely unconditional. Assistance rarely continues beyond the short term without definite reciprocation, although not necessarily of the same kind given. Unreliable or incompetent siblings cannot be totally disavowed, but they can be gradually excluded from all but the lowest level of subsistence support. Persons with small, absent, or unhelpful sibling sets reported cultivating closer ties with cousins or more distant relatives who lived nearby and showed interest.

Exchanges and cooperation between kin beyond the subsistence level are negotiated between the individuals involved on the basis of mutual trust and proven reliability rather than extended automatically because of a given blood relationship. Cooperation is established for specific, limited purposes, even between kin who live in the same house. Demonstrated reliability in short-term exchanges lays the basis for longer-term relations with long-delayed reciprocity. Differential results of such negotiations could be seen even between those with the closest ties imaginable to market women: between mother and daughter or between sisters living in the same house.

Individuals select several from among their siblings for close cooperation and mutual confidence, whether in trading or other concerns. The market survey found pairs of same-sex siblings trading together, but not full or nearly full sibling sets. High rates of migration break up most sibling sets geographically, making continual consultation impractical, but there are other obstacles. Even when sisters lived in the same house, they did not consistently pool resources. Each had her own budget and timetable, from which she could offer help to the other. Two sisters in this situation usually cooked separate meals and then shared the cooked food freely with each other and with other neighbors, unless they had quarreled. They would exchange help on an ad hoc basis with domestic tasks, watching each others' children and boiling pots as needed for short periods. There was no careful accounting of who did what, but each returned the same kind of aid when requested. When one sister takes an unbalanced share of financial or domestic responsibility, the reciprocity is formally negotiated.

Resources are shared more freely between mother and child than in any other Asante relationship. Adult children refer to the unconditional pooling of food in asserting the priority of their tie to their mothers. The statement, "She would not eat if I was hungry," both defines and distinguishes the maternal bond so clearly for Asantes that one suspects it need not hold true for other close relatives. Men as well as women work hard to provide for their children's subsistence and advancement, but fathers acknowledge other goals more openly as well.

Fatherhood also is very important to contemporary urban Asantes. While none of those I knew carried out *ntoro* rituals and many did not know their affiliation, the influence of Christian values and Western paternalistic institutions has replenished the moral charge of fatherhood. Asante men and women in Kumasi had a clear image of the ideal responsibilities of an urban father. In the modern monetary economy, his traditional responsibility for their moral education and occupational training means paying for formal schooling and apprenticeships. He should provide his children with food and shelter and contribute generously to their clothing and other expenses.

Parental relations, like lineage ones, become more conditional when it comes to allocating support and property transfers above the survival level. Although parents might like to offer maximal support to all of their children, their actual resources are always limited. Demonstrations of individual character and intelligence such as good grades, conspicuous obedience, and helpfulness can tip the balance when hard choices must be made.

Children also develop individual resources not pooled with their parents or with their brothers and sisters. A child automatically has some degree of separation from each parent because of its relation to the other, who often gives money, clothes, and other goods directly to the child. Half-siblings may get quite different levels of support from their different fathers or mothers. Closer relations with the same parents may also give one full sibling more effective resources than another. In addition, even quite young children develop relationships with more distant kin, neighbors, teachers, and other adults that distinguish them from their brothers and sisters. These can complement parental support or provide a virtual alternative to impoverished or irresponsible parents. In some cases, relationships initiated by the child led to fostering and other acceptable quasi-parental arrangements. Parents themselves sometimes arrange or encourage such special relationships for one or more of their children.

Parents also frequently encourage even young children to develop independent sources of income. Small children who begin to trade take pride in their first earnings and receive lavish praise for them, but they also discover the other side to independence. One eight-year-old on her first day of hawking showed her proceeds to her mother, who congratulated her and told her to buy her own lunch. Many children in Kumasi trade independently to earn pocket money, and some poor children are virtually self-supporting as low-capital traders and carriers. Accomplished child traders can make sizable incomes relative to their consumption levels. I stayed with a middle-aged fish trader whose twelve-year-old daughter hawked daily and took over the market stall when her mother went on buying trips. She and her mother both bragged about how much she sold, compared with older children with less skill. If family finances allow, children are encouraged to save their earnings and casual gifts. Many traders reported such savings as their major source of initial trading capital.

Although mother/daughter ties remain tight, Asante girls and women unfortunately seem to be increasingly marginalized within their lineages, in leadership, residence, and inheritance. As migration disperses the lineage geographically, informal consultations with female elders are more often neglected. Women find it harder to take advantage of rights to lineage-controlled farmland and housing, since they must follow migrating husbands to maintain a regular flow of financial support. Brothers scattered around the country in rented accommodations find it more difficult to take in unmarried sisters and easier to evade their financial demands.

Inheritance from women to men has become much more frequent, to the point that the ideal of monosexual inheritance seems to be seriously compromised for women's property. Okali and Mikell demonstrate that the cocoa farms Brong-Ahafo women establish are often inherited by sons or brothers rather than daughters (Okali 1983; Mikell 1989). Mikell had interviewed many elderly women farmers before their deaths. They had expected these farms to pass automatically to their daughters, so they had not made wills or gifts before death, with which men often forestall lineage control of property division. Elders could justify their choices of male heirs by arguing that men were better able to manage cocoa farms for the benefit of the whole lineage. Land and housing transfers to women as wives, from their husbands, were too minor to compensate for this drain.

Market traders presented their need for independent incomes in relation to marriage rather than lineage kinship. They constantly referred to the unreliability of financial contributions from husbands in any discussion of their economic prospects or marital relations, mentioning the possibility of death, illness, divorce, or unexpected polygyny in a kind of litany of risk. These considerations clearly inhibited their own emotional and economic commitment, even to marriages that currently seemed stable and satisfying.

Although it is not financially or socially central in Asante, marriage is still personally important in a woman's life, especially for the allocation of domestic work. Asante women expect to be married for a major part of their adult lives and to adjust their trading and other relations accordingly. In Kumasi Central Market, 65 percent of women traders were currently married. They look to marriage to provide them with children, economic support, and sexual satisfaction. Although all of these can be secured outside of marriage, marriage makes them more respectable (McCall 1956, 76). One trader pointed out that having children with many different fathers was slightly shameful as well as logistically too complicated. I later discovered she had edited her own marital history to omit the father of her eldest daughter. Asserting that all of her children had one father seemed to compensate her for her current marital dissatisfaction.

Asante women value sexual satisfaction and companionship within marriage, although they seem to consider reliable financial support more essential and more likely. Outright sexual neglect leads rapidly to divorce or adultery for young women, not least to conceive additional children. Women asked to describe a good husband switched out of the financial key in which they usually discuss bad husbands and said that "he sits and talks with you on the veranda in the evening." One elderly woman described nostalgically a short, early marriage where the two of them went everywhere together, "like twins," even attending the same church. She repudiated him when he took another wife and still remarked sarcastically on his status as an elder in the church. A good husband also takes your advice seriously on major decisions, especially concerning the children. These more companionate marriages lasted longer and into old age. Other women had little to do with their husbands after they stopped wanting children and expressed more cynical opinions about marriage.

Independence within marriage is rated a virtue and not just by those who have a poor opinion of the institution. Kumasi traders disapproved of women who did not work, even when their husbands could and did support them completely. They were "mmere" (soft) and lacked ambition for themselves and their children. They were also bad mothers and stupid, because they did not consider what would happen to themselves and their children if their husbands died, lost their money, or divorced them. The traders' ideal was for even elite women to take advantage of their elite husbands' connections or generous support to build up a substantial business of their own (Oppong 1974). Mothers also said they would feel justified in challenging their husbands' demands for domestic service if these seriously interfered with their earning capacity. For example, some traders had refused to follow husbands transferred to another town where they felt they could not trade effectively.

As husbands and sons, men are somewhat ambivalent toward women's incomes. It is often said that a man wants his mother to be wealthy, but not his wife. Brothers will also brag about their wealthy sisters, who are "carrying" the lineage (Owusu 1992). In practice, many men openly appreciate their wives' contributions. One male trader said he would feel ashamed as a father to satisfy his vanity and convenience by keeping a wife at home to wait on him at the expense of his childrens' higher education or food supply. Both sexes admit the autonomous decision-making ability which independent earning capacity gives to wives. Women consider this a positive side effect, while men consider it negative but unavoidable. They have neither the inclination nor the capacity, in most cases, to support their wives and children totally.

Duolocal residence is a dramatic expression of the financial and emotional independence expected between husband and wife. Market women frequently discussed the relative merits of joint and separate residence among themselves, suggesting that the choice was often a conscious strategy. Kumasi market women could and did exercise both options: to live or not live with their husbands. Of those currently married, 59 percent lived with their husbands. This is comparable to the co-residence rates in farming towns studied by Fortes (1949) and Beckett (1944). Market traders are apparently not anomalous among Asantes in their practice of duolocality, so perhaps not in their attitudes toward it as well.

Both men and women informants who preferred duolocal marriage claimed that the social distance it preserved created a more peaceful, longer-lasting marriage with greater mutual respect. Specifically, living separately "prevents quarrels" over use of money, time, and personal movements by reducing knowledge of each others' decisions. Virtual ignorance of the husband's amount and sources of income is not uncommon, and some of the women openly recommended it. As long as he contributed adequately to the children's expenses, it was better not to know about the rest. Besides, he was more likely to pay his share if he did not know the full extent of your own income. Living together would lead to jealousy "when you see each other going out and coming in," implying suspicions of adultery. Some couples even went to the trouble of finding and renting separate rooms despite the local housing shortage. Living separately also gave a woman more freedom to live with lineage kin or invite them to live with her, although this would be subject to her elders' authority in a family house.

Those supporting joint residence reminded listeners that it avoided extra expense in nightly transport and in rent, especially for those without childhood homes in Kumasi. Women also mentioned that it gave them easier access to their husbands' income. As budgets contract, bills cannot always be assigned as planned. Husbands living with the children are more often available when urgent financial needs must be met, such as overdue school fees, replacement of torn uniforms, or medical bills. But co-residence also gives the husband more access to the wife's time and resources. Many women said they would rather forego some support than allow these reciprocal claims.

If a shared residence is debatable, a shared budget is almost unspeakable. Kumasi market women react with amusement to the idea of pooling resources with their husbands, which is often promoted by local Christian churches. One woman about sixty asked me for an explanation of the joint bank accounts she had heard about. After listening carefully, she was still dubious. "Maybe you have a different kind of husband in Europe," she said. Another elderly cloth trader sitting with us, still living with her husband, added that it would present too much temptation even for the most honorable husband to spend the money on his relatives or other women. In a more serious mood at home, some older women explained how keeping a joint budget would always lead to quarrels, since each partner would want to spend the money on different things. Divergent interests are taken for granted; the common interest in their children cannot outweigh lineage identity. In the words of one middle-aged trader, marriage is "like two trains colliding" because the partners come from different lineages (Granada Television International 1983).

The two cases that came to my attention of spouses sharing resources beyond the limits of short-term reciprocity were told to me with embarrassment bordering on shame. The supportive spouses spoke rarely, softly, and privately of their actions, only mentioning them after nearly a year of close acquaintance. They immediately stressed that they were only reciprocating past unusually favorable treatment. One elderly woman explained that she now fed her aged husband, long past earning, because he had been very generous in support of the family before his retirement. A legal clerk excused using his precious savings to buy food when his wife's cloth trade collapsed during price control by saying that she had enabled him to save the money by contributing heavily when she was earning well. By contrast, many traders complained freely and openly of neglect by their husbands and of the inordinate demands of poorer kin, situations that transgress other short-term and long-term norms of reciprocity. Asantes can justify supporting poor lineage members to enable the recipient to help other kin in future, or even to avoid future trouble from an undeserving deadbeat. Apparently, seeking selfish short-term advantage in the inherently short-term marriage relation may be understandable, although not praiseworthy, but creating or honoring long-term obligations there is simple foolishness and makes observers wonder about witchcraft.

Tensions over short-term advantage and obligations are rising because the division of contributions to subsistence, conceived of as complementary in the classic model, has become unbalanced under contemporary economic pressure. The wife contributed staple vegetable foodstuffs from her farm, while the husband contributed the sauce ingredients: meat, fish, and salt. As vegetable food prices have risen precipitously, consumption of fish and meat has dropped sharply. The emblematic fish and salt have been translated into giving a food allowance called "chop money" to the wife. Her subsistence farming has been translated into financial responsibility for a high proportion of family living expenses.

The current economic crisis also keeps husbands from fulfilling their defined responsibility for major cash expenditures, such as rent, school fees, and new clothing, since these purchases are the most likely to be cut back when money is tight. As food prices soared in the late 1970s and early 1980s, household budget surveys showed up to 90 percent of income going for food, to which women were expected to contribute heavily (Ewusi 1984). New clothing, school fees, and even private medical care had become things of the past for all too many families. Charges for utilities and for public clinics and hospitals remained low until 1985, although services and supplies were unreliable. Rents also remained relatively low, despite a shortage of housing, because many residents still rented from relatives or other personal connections and because rents were a prominent target of price control. After structural adjustment began in 1985, user fees and rents rose to the point of reducing demand, but the pressure of high food prices still kept non-food expenditure levels low.

Although Asante cultural standards allow polygyny and even elevate it as a goal for men, women I interviewed saw it as a serious threat to their economic and personal interests. They mentioned it as one of the disasters, like widowhood or crippling disease, that all too often afflicted a seemingly good marriage without warning. The new wife and her children, at best, divided the financial support a husband could give and, at worst, became his favorites, displacing the first wife entirely. For Asante women, polygamy held none of the compensations of senior wife status or domestic help. Asante co-wives interact as little as possible and only important chiefs' wives will live in the same residential area. One middle-aged trader, shocked at the very idea of coresidence, described the glacial correctness she considered the best possible relation between co-wives: they meet and nod at funerals, asking after each other's children. Several older traders told of divorcing husbands because they had taken other wives, formally or informally. This seemed more common in romantic partnerships contracted in youth, and one of the same women later stayed in another polygamous marriage. Wealthier older husbands, like chiefs, could satisfy several wives financially, so they had more prospects of keeping several wives at once.

Divorce threatens the paternal relationship by making contact between spouses uncomfortable and infrequent. Since chop money is linked conceptually to the personal relation between spouses, it stops completely. In many cases, estranged fathers paid the childrens' school fees and sent gifts of clothing but contributed little or nothing to their daily subsistence. Women mentioned the difficulty of collecting support from ex-spouses as one of the primary disadvantages of having children by several different fathers. Suing for child support has been prohibitively expensive until very recently, and the special family tribunals still award very small amounts and give little chance of collecting them (Mikell 1987). Several divorced couples I encountered tacitly acknowledged that money transfers would be unlikely by instead dividing the large number of children equally between the two parents, quite contrary to matrilineal principles. In practical terms, this meant that those in the father's custody were sent to be cared for by his mother or sisters.

Ideally a man's matrilineal relatives should step in to fulfill his paternal responsibilities if he is unable to do so, although women I talked to rarely mentioned this as a realistic outcome of widowhood. Public media more often publicize the opposite, with lurid complaints about the dead husband's relatives descending on the grieving widow and orphans to take all of his property and leave them homeless and penniless. One assumes most heirs fall somewhere in between, and the stories I heard from men classified a wide range of responses as conscientious. One wealthy man received several visits I saw from the wife of his dead brother, who called him husband and asked for money for the children. He claimed to have given her money repeatedly in the past, but did not feel obliged to take over their primary support. One man with a young family of his own said he had declined the inheritance of several lineage houses and farms in his hometown because accepting them meant raising the maternal uncle's ten surviving children. Another man who had received the level of support one might have expected from a birth father, including school fees, from an uncle with children of his own, singled the man out for overwhelming gratitude and praise. Heirs are apparently expected to keep the "inherited" children from starving, but save the school fees for their own.

With men less able to meet the financial responsibilities ideally linked to marriage, urban Asantes often delayed or neglected the formalities of marriage and divorce. The term for marriage was very broadly interpreted in everyday usage. Asking the question, "Have you ever been married?" drew the kind of reaction one would expect from the question, "Have you ever had sex?" Relationships that were later formalized would be back-dated as marriages to their beginning. Similar relationships that ended up failing were often classed as non-marriages and left out of marital histories. Spouses and their respective families had grounds for expecting and enforcing conformity to marital roles once public domesticity had been established by open cooking and sleeping. Formal divorce through the families was only needed by younger women intending to remarry (to prevent adultery charges) and then only if customary gifts had been presented. Civil or church ceremonies, which made subsequent divorce very difficult, were more frequently held at the end or culmination of a marital career, with the numerous children in proud attendance. Although this ambivalence toward marriage has become more pronounced in Asante under recent economic pressures, the ambiguities surrounding marriage were already there when more effective lineage structures provided more of a safety net for women.

Cooking as Marriage

The defining element that distinguishes marriage from a more casual heterosexual relationship is the exchange of a regular cash allowance for food (called *akroma* or chop money), on the male side, and cooking the evening meal (implying sex), on the female side. The urban Asante women who were my main informants considered marriage a process rather than an event. The appearance of chop money paid daily, weekly, or monthly (at least in intent) frequently marked the beginning of marriage as a socially recognized pairing, and its cessation marked the end of marriage, especially when customary or civil formalities are so often delayed or omitted. In the classic duolocal marriage, a wife cooks the evening meal in her own house as a preliminary to visiting her husband for the night at his house. In Kumasi, dusk brings a noticeable traffic in children and young to middle-aged women carrying large covered dishes. In polygynous marriages, evenhanded rotation in cooking schedules removes the necessity to discuss sex directly.

"Cooking for" a man seems to take the place that "living with" a man occupies in contemporary United States society, as a trial or quasi-marital relationship. For some relationships it will turn out to be a stage of courtship, formalized eventually through lineage, church, or legal rituals. Other similar relationships will be broken off due to incompatibility or remain informal, with less than full family and public support. Couples in a relationship including daily cooking accept some degree of public recognition of the relationship and also recognize mutual responsibilities similar to marital roles, although less binding. For example, it would be extremely difficult for a man in such a relationship to disavow paternity of any children conceived during it, unless they resembled someone else very closely indeed.

The sexual connotation of cooking is so strong that Asantes use it as a euphemism as well as a symbol for sex. As in many languages, Asante Twi uses the same verb (*di*) for eating and sex, a verb which has many other meanings of possession, taking, inheriting, etc. It must be reduplicated (*didi*) to unambiguously mean eating, although this is also conveyed by the context. One woman trader with a new boyfriend she hoped to marry made a great show of departing early to cook for him, complete with bawdy gestures. Another trader tried to deny accepting goods on credit from a male farmer (a type of transaction associated in jokes with sex), by loudly maintaining, "I am not cooking for anyone!" The ubiquitous street comments from young men of "my wife, my wife" change to "ah, you are bringing me food" for a girl carrying even the smallest dish.

Asante women in the market also identified cooking as a disproportionately problematic domestic task through discussions, surveys, and specific incidents that made it clear these problems arose from its connection to marriage. Although childcare requires more labor hours, traders can adjust its standards and timing more easily to accommodate their work and delegate it with fewer repercussions. The symbolic and practical connection between cooking the evening meal and marital sexual and financial exchanges makes it risky for married women to delegate cooking or utilize widely available shortcuts. Compromising standards of quality and timing for the evening meal threatens the continuance of a marriage and of the financial support a husband provides, because women have less latitude within marriage than as parents. These considerations create pressures to conform closely to ideal meal patterns that interfere quite directly with market trading.

Cooking the evening meal is linked as tightly to chop money, the main financial contribution from husbands to wives, as it is to sex. Chop money is often the only money a husband gives directly to his wife to cover his obligation to feed his children and help her. The wife must pay for foodstuffs and any other expense related to cooking from this money or supplement it with her own earnings. She is expected to save something out of what she is given to cover days when it may not be paid. When discussing the dangers of potential polygyny, women assumed that if a husband took a second wife he would split the previous chop money between them, paying it to the wife cooking for him that week. Temporary interruption in cooking also usually suspends it as, for example, during the husband's travel or illness.

Wives apparently took for granted that any interruption in the marriage relation would substantially reduce the paternal contribution to the children's expenses, as well as the wife's. For example, women whose husbands had migrated temporarily to Nigeria or Europe accepted the complete cessation of support as normal, and it did not necessarily break up the marriage. Fathers brought back gifts or lump sums on their return rather than sending money regularly. Even a transfer to a distant town within Ghana, where the wife did not wish to follow, suspended chop money for the duration. Retirement also typically ends child support from waged workers, regardless of the age of the children or the size of the pension. Women with retired husbands did not express resentment or surprise, but the marital relationship also stops at this point, which can leave the father with only a minimal personal relationship to children born late.

Asante traders remarked that either sexual competition or pride could lead women to provide higher-quality, more ample meals to their husbands at their own expense. Low or irregular chop money signifies sexual disinterest, which a wife may prefer to conceal (see also Robertson 1984, 190–92). According to Abu (1983), some Asante women were reluctant to admit that their chop money is inadequate, although the traders I interviewed seemed to show no such inhibition. Several traders mentioned that their chop money was not enough to pay for their husbands' own food, let alone buy food for the family meal, as it should.

The act of cooking can express either positive or negative sexual feelings. Preparing prompt, attractive, large meals for a husband symbolizes respect for conservative standards in other aspects of the relationship. Wives express their satisfaction with a warm relationship by taking extra care in cooking, just as husbands enjoy giving beloved wives extra gifts. One trader in early middle age described with rather intense emotion how a wife chooses her finest bowl, puts a beautiful fufu in it and arranges the fish to look big and plump. Then she bathes carefully, rubs herself with cream and puts on her good cloth to take the dinner to her husband. I later saw her going through this ritual herself to visit her husband in another neighborhood. They were apparently monogamous and got along well. When I returned several years later, he had asked her to move in with him "to avoid the young children having to carry food every night."

The sexual charge given cooking means that women compete sexually in the evening meal, with hypothetical rivals even when no co-wives exist. A wife becomes extremely suspicious if her husband loses his appetite for her food, especially in the evening. She will accuse him of eating somewhere else (with someone else) or of not liking her food. This personalized competition makes women more reluctant to delegate cooking to potential sexual rivals, such as housemaids, in case the sexual implications prove too strong to resist.

Women also express anger and defiance by persistent carelessness in cooking or by refusing to cook altogether. This expresses the threat or intention of breaking off the relationship, either temporarily or permanently. It is particularly embarrassing to the man, because it signals lack of sexual access in a form highly visible to his neighbors and friends, who might normally eat with him. Women wishing to send more subtle warnings will "accidentally" double-salt the soup or forget some key ingredient, because the quarrel is worrying them (Owusu 1992). Robertson reports that Ga women similarly stop cooking to signal imminent separation (Robertson 1984, 183). Refusing to cook seems to be considered a relatively respectable response to outrageous conduct or neglect. One evening, I sat with a group of Kumasi traders who were sympathizing (behind her back) with a middle-aged friend who had stopped cooking for her husband because of his continual adultery. Although not endorsing it as ideal wifely behavior, they found his complaints ridiculous. Since he no longer came home to eat dinner, they argued, cooking for him was a waste of food. At any rate, they thought this more appropriate than her other reaction, which was to take several lovers herself.

The tight connection between cooking, sex, and financial support entangles sexual and economic jealousy. A wife fears rivals will be spending money she would otherwise receive for her children. In itself no trivial issue, the expression of economic outrage on behalf of her children shows more self-respect and propriety than voicing sexual jealousy (see also Robertson 1984, 189). A man likewise complains more publicly about his wife's laziness in cooking than of the dissatisfaction or infidelity that may have motivated it. Jealous scenes between women and their rivals are also considered less than dignified, since mature women (and men) should focus on more serious issues than sex. A really angry woman would also want to avoid the backhand compliment implied by fighting over him. As a trader filmed in late middle age said of her husband's affairs, "If you are eating a piece of rotten pawpaw, you don't mind sharing it" (Granada Television International 1983). Ideally, she acts almost relieved that such a worthless man is no longer interested in her. The preferred image aimed at by either husbands or wives seems to be that of course they could find many better sexual partners (and perhaps already have), but they must correct the spouse's behavior for the sake of the children.

The sexual connotation of cooking also extends to commercial sources of the same types of food served at evening meals. Informal restaurants serving these heavy meals to patrons with ordinary incomes are called chop bars. Single men and travelers such as truck drivers depend on them. Although many are perfectly respectable, the suspicion persists that the proprietor or her assistant provides sexual services along with the evening meal, as a wife does. Some chop bars serve alcoholic drinks and are neighborhood centers of partying and/or prostitution. The proverbially named "Don't Mind Your Wife" chop bar found in many neighborhoods acknowledges the economic and sexual rivalry between wife and street. If a man buys his dinner at the chop bar, he may "eat" more than food before he comes home. He may be tempted to go out if his dinner is late or if its quality is not clearly superior to chop bar food.

Cooking as Work

Important as cooking is as a symbolic act, it is also work. It interacts with market trading primarily as work, through the time and other demands it makes on women traders that compete directly with the demands of trading. Culturally specific ideal standards specify the timing of meals and the persons who can make them, as well as a limited number of fully acceptable dishes. Looking at the labor process of cooking different dishes in some detail makes it possible to define the difference between cooking for a husband and cooking for children or other relatives. Cooking personally to the high standards likely to ensure marital stability interferes appreciably with trading, but not every married woman conforms to ideal standards, and not every woman is married. A glance at the wide availability of commercial and noncommercial means of reducing or delegating work indicates that many women are taking up meal options others consider too risky. Discussions of the compromises in actual meals made by wives and accepted by husbands define the area of conflict between cooking and trading in practical terms, as imbedded in marital and other relations.

The ideal Asante evening meal consists of fufu and soup. Yams, plantain, or cassava are peeled, boiled, and then pounded in an immense wooden mortar with a pestle up to six feet long. A light soup can be prepared while the tubers boil, since the most labor-intensive step, finely grinding the vegetables, takes less than half an hour. The entire process takes two or three hours, depending on skill and quantity. Only palm-nut soup requires a multi-step process of boiling, pounding, and squeezing comparable to making the fufu. Other dishes eaten with soup or stew in the evening make significantly less labor demands. For example, beaten porridge dishes like benkum take less than an hour.

The devotion to fufu of men and women alike is such that eating anything else is a significant compromise. Asantes consider fufu not only their favorite and most characteristic food, but the only completely satisfying food. A middle-aged woman accustomed to this extremely heavy, slow-digesting dish once asked if I could really sleep properly after eating only a huge plate of rice and stew. "Don't you wake up in the middle of the night hungry?" Funeral participants consider themselves to be fasting as long as they refrain from fufu, taking only rice or lighter foods. Although young married women may make fufu nightly to please their husbands, divorced and widowed women with sufficient income and household help also eat fufu as often as possible.

The traditional home-cooked dishes for breakfast and lunch are much simpler than fufu. Mashed or boiled yam or plantain take less than half and hour to prepare with stew for breakfast. Interestingly enough, it is these dishes that appear in ritually significant uses, especially mashed yam with boiled egg. The noon meal hardly features in the ideal pattern. The classic farm family referred to by urban Asantes in describing the ideal have all gone to the farm at this time of day. Those farm families I observed would snack on roasted plantain and fruit, take leftovers along to reheat at a campfire, or purchase snacks in farm hamlets near their fields.

Timing is as significant as content to the ideal meal pattern. Women should rise well before dawn to clean the house, bathe, and prepare *ampesie* before family members leave for the farm at dawn. Fufu should be ready before dark, when they return. Correct meal timing carries a strong moral connotation of industriousness and a well-ordered life. Women said they would be embarrassed if neighbors saw them rising late or cooking late. Technical considerations reinforce the cultural value on prompt evening meals. Preparing an elaborate fufu-type meal after dark in the typical compound kitchen with no electric light or a single bare bulb is no easy feat.

These meal times conflict directly with the daily commercial rhythm of the market. At the time family members should eat breakfast, before work or school, traders should be at the market already or standing in line for a car. They need to buy their supplies when prices are lowest, around 8 A.M., when the villagers and travelers arrive from the supply areas. Lunch would come at the peak of rush hour, from 10 A.M. to 2 P.M., when traders count on their highest volume of sales and rarely leave for any reason. Serving fufu by 6 P.M. means arriving home by 3 or 4 P.M. and leaving the market at 2 P.M., after shopping, to stand in line for transport. Cooking popular fufu substitutes delays this schedule by one or two hours only, so the trader still must leave by 3 P.M., although the trading day continues until 5 or 6 P.M. Cooking close to ideal standards thus interferes with trading by limiting the amount of trading women can do and by ruling out the most lucrative trading roles. Personal performance of cooking is only compatible with retailing and appreciably hampers even this. Retailers generally have lower capital and income levels than wholesalers and travelers in the same commodity. Travelers obviously must delegate daily cooking while they are out of town. Specialist travelers are only supported on routes to the more distant supply areas, where they spend between one and two weeks before returning.

The local wholesalers, who earn the highest incomes in Kumasi Central Market, must also make arrangements to delegate cooking. The success of wholesalers in building up a steady clientele depends upon their constant availability in the wholesale yard during all normal working hours. They must be ready to receive travelers' goods when they arrive and must have supplies ready for buyers at convenient times. The full complement of wholesalers in any Kumasi Central Market yard arrived early and remained until business had stopped for the day. They showed great haste to return to the yard if they left for any reason.

Among food retailers, those who cook personally buy less goods, even if they have the capital to buy more, to be sure of clearing perishable stocks before they leave. Observed cases of temporary or long-term restrictions for that reason were reinforced by traders' own generalizations or presumptions. An inquiry about normal working hours elicited these two categories: "Some women have to leave early, because they have to go home and cook dinner. Others have children at home, so they can stay until the market closes." Traders openly and frequently attributed their own or others' restricted trading to conflicts with cooking, specifically to the need to leave early, and only rarely mentioned any other domestic task as a reason. For example, one woman left the cassava buying area with noticeably less total stock than her colleagues. They explained, "She can't buy as much because she has to sell quickly to go home and cook, because no one is at home." Another young yam trader frequently reduced her prices below the prevailing rate in early afternoon. Market neighbors who did not know her personally commented that, "She probably has to go home and cook, so she has to sell quickly." Rather than resent her for undercutting them, they pitied her lower profits.

The conflict should not be exaggerated; Asante meal times do not make trading impossible or force market women to rearrange the trading day. Yoruba women in Nigeria, also very active traders, must work around a cooking schedule that focuses on a hot meal in early afternoon, with the morning and evening meals purchased from vendors.

Yoruba markets begin at dawn and finish in time for women to go home and cook, after which they return to separate night markets. This schedule makes it difficult for young wives to do more than prepare cooked food or sell in local markets. Long-distance or large-scale trade is reserved for senior wives or middle-aged women in general (Sudarkasa 1973).

Kumasi Central Market traders cannot resolve cooking conflicts by doing much of their food preparation at their stalls, as some vendors in roadside stands or tiny markets do. Such a highly desirable business location is very crowded, and the fast pace of trading does not leave enough attention free to cook a proper meal. If a trader had the space needed to cook safely in her stall, she would have already sublet it to another trader. Besides, cooking fires in the market were prohibited after a disastrous fire in the early 1970s that destroyed money, goods, and a complete market building. Feeding the whole family in the market would be impractical, since other members would need to spend scarce time and money traveling to the market for meals and would have to eat in noisy public surroundings. Husbands in particular might as well spend their time and money in a noisy chop bar as eat in the market. Children stopped by to help at the stall, or for afternoon snacks on their way home from school, but were usually sent home to begin preparing the evening meal.

Delegation of cooking is made easier, however, by other technical aspects of Asante standards. The restricted set of acceptable menus leaves as little scope for elaboration as for corner-cutting. A young girl can master all the acceptable dishes within a year or two of acquiring the needed dexterity and strength. The lack of variation or discretion also facilitates turning specific tasks over to children. Girls begin grinding vegetables for the family soup at age six or eight. The ability to judge cooking times and ingredient quantities develops by age ten or twelve. Pounding fufu requires more strength and coordination, turning the lump in rhythm between each stroke of the pestle and reaching each family member's preferred soft or hard consistency. A girl is ready to take charge of the entire process by age twelve or fifteen, depending on her aptitude and interest. Further experience adds little to quality, which depends more on conscientiousness than additional skill.

Traders calculated the skill levels of each task closely to construct ingenious divisions of labor that enabled even younger children to do most of the cooking. One woman made her soup every morning before leaving for the market by rising very early. Her children were old enough to peel and boil the cassava and plantain, and she pounded the *fufu* when she came back in the evening. Most women returned from the market in time to complete the final pounding, which involves judgment about portion sizes for each family member as well as their preferred texture.

Adult skill levels make a more significant contribution to meal quality through shopping. Without home or market refrigeration, shopping is part of the daily routine. Including travel between home and market, it can take time equivalent to the time for cooking. Considering the limited daily food budget of most traders, the taste of the meal improves more sharply with greater amounts or quality of key ingredients like fish and tomatoes than with better preparation. Experience, motivation, and personal contacts all continue to improve shopping results over the years. Traders in the market could shop themselves or supervise shopping minutely without disrupting their work.

Compromises in shopping skill and time usually cost money. Some cloth and imports traders bought lower-quality, higher-priced foodstuffs from passing hawkers in the market and sent them home with younger children. They had higher incomes than average and saw heavy business in the afternoons, when customers had time to shop for major purchases. They also had valuable inventories they did not like to leave unattended. In another case, the children were old enough to buy from neighborhood markets and streetside tables near home, but not to travel to the Central Market for better prices. This mother left her children home with money and strict instructions on where and what to buy for dinner but purchased the more expensive items in bulk to bring home with her.

From a woman's point of view, the ideal solution is to delegate home cooking to her own child or a close lineal relative. After a year of practice they may even cook better than she does. They can be expected to take a personal interest in careful preparation and economical use of ingredients, while incest prohibitions on intercourse with the husband minimize their sexual threat. The adult woman loses some intimacy in the marital relationship, but not much if she lives apart from her husband and still brings him the meal herself. Keeping one's own child home to cook entails some opportunity cost for the child. Very poor families cannot afford to carry the subsistence expenses of a full-time domestic worker, so every member must try to make some income, however small. A child who cooks can still go to primary school, although domestic work does make a difference in the amount of time girls can spend on homework. Secondary school usually requires full-time attention to homework, and most are boarding schools in Ghana.

A young daughter's aptitude and interest in cooking or, conversely, in school or trading is a factor in the length of her cooking career. In one family, each daughter took over the family cooking in turn as the older one went off to secondary school. The father was a principal of a public middle school, but they did not have a maid. In another family of traders, one sister had stayed home to cook and take care of her younger sisters and brothers. Several sisters eventually became traders, but she remained on at home to care for their children. They in turn contributed financially to support her children and a young maid to help her.

Children who cook (usually daughters) do receive benefits not shared with siblings, especially those who refuse to help in cooking. They usually increase their personal share of food through generous sampling and enjoy exchanging samples with neighbors who help each other in watching pots, pounding fufu, etc. One teenage daughter, a very enthusiastic cook, was severely scolded when discovered to be holding private feasts for her friends with a major part of the family's daily ingredients. Since daily cooking places a child in more intimate contact with adults and demonstrates the positive character traits of reliability and helpfulness, it can also secure long-term benefits from better sponsorship in school or work.

The most difficult domestic years for a woman come when she is between twenty-five and thirty-four years old. Her children have become numerous, but the oldest is not old enough at eight or ten to take over cooking. Her financial burdens are also growing as the older of perhaps four or five children start school. She is likely to co-reside with her husband at this time, in order to maximize his financial contribution and to have more children, so help from lineage kin drops very low. At the same time, she wants to expand her trading to provide income for future demands for secondary school fees or other sponsorship. This age group also furnishes the greatest numbers of women traders in Kumasi Central Market.

The most fully accepted strategy in this situation is to bring in older children or adolescents from closely related families as foster children. School leavers or uneducated young girls from rural hometowns are often quite willing to move to Kumasi, which offers more excitement and job prospects. As they grow older, they become familiar with the city environment and move into their own work. Close relatives are folded into the family and were referred to as children in conversation and in the survey. Although they may not receive the same financial sponsorship as her own children, the foster parent will provide food, clothing, and pocket money and arrange for eventual training or employment. Some traders mentioned avoiding such kin help because of the unspecified future obligations it created; others simply could not afford to support additional dependents at home.

Another possibility for bridging this domestic labor gap is hiring a maidservant, by definition a nonrelative. Employment of maids in cooking reaches its peak of 10 percent in the 35–44 age group. Female-biased sex ratios in the Kumasi census for the 10–15 age group suggests a considerable movement of young girls into the city, although they do not distinguish maids from foster children. Maids receive less in short-term subsistence and long-term sponsorship, but they are the focus of considerable sexual anxiety and tension. Married women expressed the fear that a maid will become an obvious sexual target for her husband, especially if the wife is absent on long trading trips or usually returns late from work. The theme of the maidservant and the husband appears often in serious newspaper editorials and in popular comics. One common strategy to minimize sexual competition is to hire girls as young as seven years old, so they have the loyalty and familiarity of relatives long before sexual maturity. This involves a long training period before the child can work without supervision, so more prosperous women keep two maids on at once.

The relationship with maids can be extremely exploitative, because conditions of work and recompense are too often left to the discretion of the employer. Long hours, inadequate food, minimal or irregular pay, and broken promises of vocational training feature in stories and observations. Obligations that seemed easy to meet when the maid was hired may become truly impossible due to economic pressures when they come due. If the maid has left her own family at a very early age, she may lose contact with them altogether (Dzidzienyo 1978). More often, they are so impoverished that they cannot keep her at home if she runs away to them. The historical continuity between maids and children "pawned" for family debt cannot be ignored. Employers who treat their maids well sometimes make a point to recruit them through distant relatives or hometown connections and refer to the girls politely as their foster children.

Given the range of alternatives possible, it was notable that a majority of Asante market women reported usually cooking the evening meal themselves. Delegation increased with age, but much more slowly than with other domestic tasks, dropping sharply only after age thirty-five, near menopause (see table 9.1). Age of the mother proved a more reliable indicator of personal cooking than number of children, although the two were closely correlated, as might be expected (Clark 1984). This confirms evidence from observations and interviews that

Table 9.1 Cooking

A. Usual Cook
Reported by Ashanti Women (Percentages)

Self	Child	Adult Kin	Maid	Purchased
58	28	9	4	.4

B. Marriage and Cooking
Usual Cook Reported by Married and Unmarried Women (Percentages)

Status	Self	Child	Adult Kin	Maid	Purchased
Married	58	32	4	6	0.7
Unmarried	57	23	18	2	0

C. Age and Cooking
Usual Cook Reported by Each Age Group (Percentages)

Cook	0–14	15–24	25–34	35–44	45–54	over 54
Self	57	70	69	45	33	25
Kin	29	14	4	0	6	19
Child	14	11	21	45	58	50
Maid	0	1	5	10	3	6
Purchased	0	0	1	0	0	0

SOURCE: 1979 Kumasi Central Market Survey, Asante subset

the age of the oldest child is the critical factor. Firstborn boys sometimes step in temporarily until a younger sister is old enough, but not consistently. One woman explained why her main problem at home was exhaustion by saying simply, "I gave birth to four boys."

Marriage and co-residence with the spouse had the most effect on which other substitute cooks were recruited. Unmarried women were twice as likely to have adult kin cooking for them (18 percent), mainly at older and younger ages. Married women relied slightly more on their own children and accounted for most of the small percentage (7 percent) using maids. Married women living with their husbands had no help from adult kin. They explained that it was difficult to invite kin to live with them in the husbands' home. They relied much more on maids, even though maids were actually more problematic sexually when husbands lived in the same house.

An ongoing marriage also increases labor demands by keeping up higher quality standards for cooking. The difference created by cooking for a husband emerges most clearly when he is not present for the evening meal. Women cooking only for themselves or their children can treat it like a noon meal. One exhausted young mother of four preschoolers said that she never cooked when her husband, a minister, traveled out of town. "We eat anything," so she often purchased rice or other cooked food from nearby vendors. Small children actually prefer and need small, light meals rather than fufu. Another middle-aged trader long past marriage took her fufu at noon at the market, cooking fried eggs or other snacks for herself at home in the evening. Her children were old enough to feed themselves and ate fufu at a normal hour before she got home. Other middle-aged traders had full meals prepared for themselves and their children, but could worry less about their precise timing and could substitute other starchy dishes for fufu.

Because the sexual and financial pressures associated with cooking focus so heavily on the evening meal, they leave married women relatively free to compromise ideal standards for the morning and noon meals. Kumasi residents almost invariably purchase both morning and noon meals from cooked-food vendors; this is taken for granted and has no moral or relational repercussions I could perceive. Even women staying at home for the day will buy food from nearby vendors rather than light the stove to cook. I was intrigued to hear a Muslim trader whose wife observed propriety by working as a seamstress in their home near the market remark that he would not think of going home for lunch, since his wife was too busy with her work to stop and cook for him. An added advantage to women of bought breakfasts and lunches is that husbands and other employed family members pay for their own, whereas home cooked foods would be paid for from the chop money.

When people leave for work or school very early, they begin the day with a thin maize gruel sold from immense kettles near homes and transport lines. Tea and bread had been standard before they became very scarce and expensive. The traditional boiled yam and stew breakfast was exceptional enough that one young woman made it as a Christmas treat for her neighbors. More substantial foods including kenkey and fish, rice, gari and beans, or boiled yam or plantain and stew serve equally well for a later or second breakfast or an early lunch. A very wide variety of steamed, fried, baked, or boiled items of diverse ethnic origins are relished for lunch and snacks by Asantes very conservative about their evening meal.

In addition to ready-to-eat foods, foods that have already been partly prepared for cooking are available in the market, reducing meal preparation time considerably. These include sliced, machine-ground, and powdered vegetables used to make soups and stews, and premixed doughs for cooked porridges. Their visible presence along market exit routes constantly tempts the harried trader to lower her standards of meal quality in this less obvious way. These convenience products are priced higher and may conceal adulterated or lower-quality ingredients, but create the same dishes prepared by hand. The number of vendors testifies to a ready market for such items, at least among unmarried women, and they provide a valuable backstop in case a trading or domestic emergency throws off the cooking schedule. Chop bars rely heavily on machine-ground vegetables and other prepared foods, so by using them a wife threatens to blur the distinction between her own cooking and commercial food. I heard jokes about the wife who even bought fufu from a chop bar to send to her husband when kept late at the market or a lover's house. Women do consider the health risks involved, especially for their young children, in buying prepared foods which may be spoiled, contaminated, or adulterated. On this scale, market hawkers and chop bar operators rank lowest in reputation. Traders mentioned fear of illness as a reason they avoided buying market snacks for preschool children and therefore avoided bringing them to the market. Vendors near home seem safer, since their cleanliness of preparation and any frequent health problems among their regular patrons are open to observation and gossip. Small children are quite frequently left home alone with lunch money and careful instructions to buy from familiar vendors.

Childcare

It is the lack of problems with childcare that underlines the importance of relational rather than absolute time demands in constructing conflicts with market trading. Childcare undeniably requires many more hours of time and attention than cooking. As a technical labor process, childcare is also much less tractable; children cannot be subdivided or rushed or done before or after work or school. Working shorter hours or choosing less demanding trading roles does not resolve the conflict either, since children need continuous care. Childcare, not cooking, is often selected as the plausible primary constraint on women's occupational choices, for example by Brown (1970). Several cross-cultural analyses of market women imply that women trade because it is unusually compatible with childcare (Mintz 1971; Bohannon and Dalton 1962). Market ethnographies from several parts of the world show women caring for the whole family in the market (Babb 1989; Szanton 1972). Contrary to this suggested pattern, less than half of the Kumasi traders who have young children bring them to market (see table 9.2). Instead, they resolve the conflict by delegating childcare to others at home; in every age category, women delegate child minding at least twice as often as cooking. They can do so with relatively

Table 9.2 Care of Young Children

A. Age and Market Childcare
Percentage Bringing Young Children to Market*

Age Groups					
0–14	15–24	25–34	35–44	45–54	over 54
20	46	54	28	44	60

B. Child Minder
Primary Child Minder at Home*

Self	Child	None	Own Kin	Spouse's Kin	Maid	Other
22	22	19	13	5	7	9

C. Marriage and Child Minder
Primary Child Minder for Married and Unmarried Women

Status	Self	None	Child	Own Kin	Maid	Other
Married	28	18	21	6	9	18
Unmarried	10	16	22	28	2	16

D. Age and Child Minder
Primary Child Minder Reported by Age of Trader

	0–14	15–24	25–34	35–44	45–54	over 54
Self	0	30	24	26	9	0
None	25	17	13	30	30	0
Child	0	13	21	13	44	50
Own Kin	25	28	6	0	9	25
Maid	0	2	11	17	0	0
Other	50	9	25	13	9	25

* Women without young children at home not included.
SOURCE: 1979 Kumasi Central Market Survey

few negative repercussions because Asante culture embeds childcare in lineage relations, within which women have more autonomy and authority than in marriage.

Traders themselves emphatically denied the compatibility of childcare with trading in Kumasi Central Market. Above all, they did not consider the market a safe place for young children. Nursing infants could suffer fevers and dehydration from exposure to sun and rain. Toddlers could wander off into the crowds and be trampled or fall into the deep open drains. They could eat something sharp, poisonous, or filthy. The wholesale yards are hazardous even to older children, with huge lorries, carts, and loaded head carriers passing constantly.

Traders also complained that childcare interfered quite directly with trading by distracting the mother from her work. This is particularly problematic during the busy periods of the day, when she needs full attention to maximize sales. The mother must watch her child constantly to avoid accidents and must stop to wash or feed it. Children also made trouble by disarranging the goods of neighboring traders or fighting with other children. No trader brought more than one child to market, so she had to make childcare arrangements at home for the other children and might as well leave the youngest there as soon as she could eat food. Even one child with a demanding personality could be too many. One young fish trader sent her older child back to her mother in a lakeside village when the second was born, to stay until school age. She intended to keep the younger girl with her longer, since she was now divorced and did not expect a third soon, but this toddler constantly cried and demanded to be held and entertained. She was impossible to handle in the market, so she was sent off with some regret to join her sister and grandmother.

A few women reported not bringing children to market because they came to market to get away from them. One middle-aged trader with a terrible cold said she had come to market to get some rest. At home "the children are always quarreling and asking me for things." Another middle-aged trader admitted she spent as little time as possible in the house where her children lived, "because of the noise." This image of the market as a haven of peace and quiet contrasts oddly with the stereotype of a bored wife taking up petty trading for excitement or entertainment (Bohannon and Dalton 1962).

Many traders nevertheless bring their young children to market under these adverse conditions, but they regret that economic pressures force them to compromise their children's health. The critical factor seems to be the availability of domestic help at home. Those who cared for their children themselves when they were home brought them to market more than twice as often (83 percent) as the average (40 percent). Impoverished squatters or head carriers explain that they cannot afford to support an older child at home to care for their infants or toddlers. Not surprisingly, the heaviest burden fell on those aged twenty-five to thirty-four, who also cooked most often. Women with secondary education, presumably from wealthier families on average, brought their children less than half as often. Married women brought their children more often than unmarried women, perhaps an age effect since the residence of the husband had no effect. Traders go to considerable lengths to arrange for caretakers at home. They invite relatives to stay with them, change their own residence, or hire maids. Even nursing babies were left at home and brought to the market to nurse several times daily. When substitute caretakers cannot be found, mothers will move to be near relatives or leave market trading altogether. One woman who had traded successfully in the Upper Region moved back to Kumasi after she had several children because "you could not get maids there," meaning girls who spoke Twi.

Neighbors provide essential informal assistance in childcare that often remains an unspoken assumption in the arrangements reported. Women do not expect neighbors to show the concern of a relative for their children, but they trust older children and adults present in the house to keep toddlers from wandering into the street, play with them safely, and call the mother or intervene in case of trouble. This enables the mother to cook, work, or converse without paying them constant attention. One mother who hesitated to allow her four preschoolers to play with house neighbors who did not share her strict Christian values became so exhausted and irritable with the effort to watch and amuse them that she finally had to move back in with her mother in another town. Children of school age have enough sense to run to neighbors for help in case of emergency but not to bother them constantly. This enables children to be left at home alone from age five or six, and left in charge of preschool siblings from age seven or eight, depending on how much sense they demonstrate.

Less exacting standards of childcare combine with less emotional significance assigned to physical care of children to encourage its delegation. An Asante child needs reliable care from a competent person, not a mother's care as such. Although a mother accepts the responsibility to provide for physical care of her child, her financial responsibility takes emotional precedence. As one mother explained, "Everyone likes children, so they would not let them stay hungry or hurt themselves, but no one would work for them the way I do." In contrast to middle-class families in the United States, Asantes do not seem to consider full-time interaction with the mother or another intelligent, devoted adult essential to normal intellectual and psychological growth. When I brought up the idea of staying home to give children continuous attention, they seemed to find it ridiculous for an adult who was not herself retarded. Mothers feel they can ensure the children's proper moral development by making rules and by talking with them at night and on weekends.

Cultural norms accept more potential surrogates for childcare than for cooking. The technical standards for childcare resemble those for cooking in that conscientious attention is essential, not mature judgment. Mothers can leave their children in the hands of substitutes with little anxiety, because they are concerned mainly with physical safety, including prevention of accidents, adequate food and water, and cleanliness. Once a toddler can walk and eat, another child of eight or nine can look after it. In an emergency, adult relatives or neighbors in the compound can give advice or take necessary action.

Asantes consider older siblings the natural caretakers because of their concern for the child's welfare. They fear a maid may be careless rather than unskilled, letting the child remain thirsty or hungry or fall into the fire while she falls asleep or gossips with friends. As long as one of their children is old enough to look after the others, the arrangement requires no comment other than "there are children at home." It also probably accounts for the 19 percent of small children reported home with no child minder. Other children emerge as the leading child minders for women over the age of forty-five, or those with more than four children (compared to five children for cooking). By extension, collateral kin such as cousins and mothers' younger siblings are logical substitutes when the older siblings are still too young.

Market women expressed no apprehension about weakening parental bonds by delegating childcare. For Asantes, parenthood is a very different kind of relation than marriage. It is naturalized in terms of the biological facts of conception and birth, which cannot be revoked or denied. The more diffused affective and moral bonds shared caretaking creates are considered a positive consequence, serving to draw the family together. Some women did complain of adult kin who had their own ideas about how to raise the child, but this seemed to be a relatively rare source of conflict.

Older children who take responsibility for physical childcare build up more intimate ties to their charges than other siblings do. Asantes acknowledge a special relationship with the sister who "carried me on her back." One woman described visiting this sister every week or two, while she had not seen another sister in Kumasi for a year. "I hardly know her, since I left home while she was so small." A young relative who is fostered in to care daily for her young maternal cousins or sisters' children establishes the same kind of bond with them as if they were her own younger siblings. Boys also play enthusiastically with younger siblings and can be named as their primary caretakers in the absence of girls.

Patterns of assistance from adult kin reinforce the subtle conflicts between marriage and lineal relations reported for cooking. Adult kin most commonly help unmarried women (28 percent) with childcare, whether these unmarried women are older or younger. Young unmarried women often still live with or near their mothers and younger siblings. They can add their first child into their mother's childcare arrangement for these young siblings, since it means only a little extra work for this older daughter, maid or foster child. Older women traders were likely to have adult children or nieces living with them who could care for younger children along with their own. Maids, while minor overall, give significant help to women aged twenty-five to forty-four (11 percent and 17 percent). Marriage has a similar effect on child minding as it does on cooking patterns. Currently married women rely more on maids and less on their own kin and do more childcare themselves, although still only 28 percent. Wives living with their husbands also rely more on themselves than do those living separately, even when they are the same age.

Kumasi traders rarely solved their childcare problems by sending their own children elsewhere to be fostered by relatives, although this was culturally quite acceptable; only 10 percent of traders' own children were living with relatives. They prefer to bring them up in Kumasi to take advantage of the concentration of better schools and health facilities there. Two women complained that children living in the villages refused to attend school, since many of their playmates did not. In several cases where traders had sent preschool children to their village-based mothers, they planned to retrieve them at school age. They were more willing to foster children out with relatives who also lived in Kumasi. During severe urban food shortages, however, urban children were sent temporarily to stay with relatives in farming districts. Also, some specific rural hometowns that had exceptionally good schools or mission hospitals located in them attracted the studious or sickly children of migrant citizens.

Asante women make relatively little use of their own mothers for childcare, still less for other domestic help. Older women have relatively high prestige here, and physical childcare holds rather little. Elderly women are still capable of coming to market daily and taking leadership in lineage and community affairs at quite advanced ages, though they may have curtailed their traveling. Young women cannot depend on the availability of their own mothers during the specific years when they need help most desperately. The short period of years when the mother is still strong enough to look after children but too feeble to go to market is unlikely to match the crisis period of more than one of her daughters. Grandmothers are much more likely to foster grandchildren in order to receive domestic help than to give it.

Cleaning and Errands

The way Asante families handled other household tasks reveals the same interpenetration of technical and social factors in determining the degree and form of conflict with trading. Taken together, the major cleaning tasks of laundry, sweeping, and dishwashing occupied a comparable amount of time as cooking (about three hours per day in weeks traders described as typical). Cleaning created far fewer problems in terms of labor time and social control than either cooking or childcare and caused much less disruption of trading because Asante women can manipulate the timing and delegation of cleaning tasks with even more freedom. These tasks either break up into small units of time or can be easily postponed to a more convenient time. Delegation is made easier because a wide range of surrogates are considered appropriate, including both boys and girls from toddlers to teenagers.

Laundry stood out as the cleaning task easiest to isolate for analysis and most likely to conflict with other commitments, including trading, because once begun it had to be finished. It appeared in narratives and remarks as the primary occupation of a block of two or three hours, preferably in the early morning to allow time for clothes to dry. Traders would explain, "I came late because I did my laundry today." "I spent the morning doing my laundry." "Some of us stay home on Sundays and do our laundry." Traders did adapt their trading and churchgoing schedules to fit in laundry, but at least they could delay it and choose to forgo a nonpeak trading period, usually Sunday morning. Perhaps for that reason, they rarely reported relying on maids for this task.

Hand laundry is notably heavy work, involving carrying water, hand scrubbing and wringing between a series of three buckets. Laundry requires enough physical strength that elders or youngsters may need someone to do it for them, even though they can handle cooking and lighter routine tasks. Women complained of exhaustion, and one even refused to cook dinner after washing the clothes. Kumasi residents living far from a water source had to carry water home instead of taking the clothes there for washing and drying, as villagers do, because of the danger of theft. Two or three women and children often do their laundry together, from different households if necessary, in order to share labor, water, and buckets. Less than half of the women with five children or over forty-five years of age did laundry, but almost 80 percent of those aged fifteen to thirty-four did (see table 9.3).

Fortunately, help was available from many sources. Other domestic tasks need not wait for the laundry to be finished, so it makes an appropriate labor contribution by persons outside the normal domestic rou-

Table 9.3 Traders' Performance and Delegation of Domestic Tasks

A. Laundry

Percentage Doing Own Laundry in Age Group

0–14	15–24	25–34	35–44	45–54	over 54
57	78	79	52	30	38

B. Domestic Tasks Observed

As Performed from 1:00 to 6:30 p.m. in Four Compounds

			Females		
Task Type	Incidents	Males	under 20	20–30	over 30
Cooking	43	0	5	37	1
Carrying	37	5	13	14	5
Childcare	32	5	6	20	1
Dishwashing	13	1	6	6	1
Sweeping	12	1	3	7	1
Laundry	9	0	4	5	0
Pounding fufu	8	2	1	5	1
Other	3	1	0	1	1
Totals	157	15	38	95	11

SOURCE: 1979 Kumasi Central Market Survey

tine. The minimal clothing worn by very young children eliminates the pressure they create for frequent laundry in United States households. Laundry can be saved up (to the limit of the clothing supply) and done on weekends by children who work or attend school or by nonresident kin who visit for the purpose. One young adult daughter, for example, cited this heavy work as the reason she returned to her father's house on Sundays. She said she went to do his laundry and refill his water drum, although she also cooked a meal while she was there.

A woman trader also gets more help from her male relatives for laundry than for other housework. Laundry appears less gender-linked than cooking or childcare, perhaps because the few commercial laundries have male proprietors and employ young men. Boys and young men could be called on to help with the laundry and ironing even when women lived in the house, although they would only cook or take care of children when there were no women or girls available. In several mixed-sex households I knew well, young unmarried men who were working as apprentices or in other jobs during the week did the laundry and ironing at weekends as their major labor contribution, without loss of masculine dignity. Men also frequently did their own laundry when they were not living with any women. In fact, men traders reported doing their own laundry almost half as often as women did.

Housecleaning is unproblematic for both technical and social reasons. Sweeping the house also takes up considerable labor time, but in small amounts throughout the day. Asante standards of cleanliness require that rooms, verandas, and courtyards be swept every morning and after any activity creating rubbish, such as cooking or eating. Although adult women will sweep, they usually ask the nearest child to do it for them. Children as young as five can handle the short brooms used here and should get used to being helpful and responsible. One mother remarked on the good manners her son showed by sweeping up after meals without being asked and then expanded on how well he was doing in school. Children assigned to sweep parts of the house should start first thing in the morning without prompting.

Sweeping is incorporated conceptually into an important category of child labor called *soma-soma* or running errands. This figures prominently in Asante definitions of a good child, as the visible expression of central moral qualities: obedience, reliability, and helpfulness. When Asante women discuss their own children, they freely comment on a wide range of good qualities and habits, as well as their faults. When pressed for a generic description of the good child, however, they revert abruptly to the child's willingness to run errands without repeated reminders and threats. Toddlers are sent on virtually useless errands, such as carrying a banana peel to the waste basket, as part of their moral training. Older children who go cheerfully and energetically on errands are also praised lavishly and rewarded to reinforce the good habit of obeying and helping their elders.

Dutiful young sweepers and errand-runners get material as well as moral benefits. A number of traders mentioned informal gifts and tips as their primary source of initial trading capital, however modest. Developing a reputation as a good child can be important to attracting a fair or greater share of parental resources. Asante mothers may love all of their children, but they do not always treat them equally. When scarce resources prevent them from meeting all of the childrens' needs completely, judgments as to an individual child's character can have a great influence. Parents express reluctance to commit to major expenses such as school fees and new clothing for children who seem careless or ungrateful. On the other hand, parents may make extra sacrifices for a child who seems serious and willing to help them in the future. Conspicuous good behavior may be especially necessary to attract the attention of a father who has children with several different mothers or in consolidating a relationship with a stepparent. These character factors feed directly into market trading opportunities by increasing a child's chances of being selected as a market assistant, given enough responsibility to learn business skills, or given enough capital or credit to start a more substantial business.

Child fostering also establishes reciprocities based on the child's labor. It can be arranged to provide for children with dead, destitute, or migrant parents, but just as often children move in to help the foster parent. Girls are requested especially often to provide cooking and childcare services for working mothers or aged kin. Depending on circumstances, the balance of gratitude may rest with the child, the donor parent, or the foster parent. When Asante children reside apart from their biological parents for a substantial proportion of their childhood, quasi-parental obligations of financial assistance and sponsorship build up over time. Market traders who can interlock these cycles of mutual assistance from and to subordinate kin successfully use the domestic labor they claim to build up the trading enterprise that enables them to reciprocate handsomely when this is needed. When other adults have provided some or virtually all of the financial support and sponsorship expected of parents, they gain quasi-parental authority and are entitled to respect and support in old age. In contrast to United States adoption practices, bonds with foster parents do not cancel out the obligations from biological parenthood, which remains publicly known and acknowledged by parent and child. Foster parenting here does not imply a previous breakdown in maternal competence or bonding, nor does it create such a breakdown.

Reciprocity with natural parents may be diluted by its equal extension to long-term foster parents, but it takes complete neglect and virtual loss of contact to decisively destroy the child's moral obligation. For example, international migration for long periods can be accepted as a valid economic strategy for either mothers or fathers. They have not abandoned their children as long as they make sure that the children are treated well by reliable kin, send money or clothes, and visit at intervals. Fathers who had divorced or never married the mother could maintain parental rights with surprisingly little in the way of visits and gifts, and co-residence in itself was no guarantee that children would not reject parents who neglected or abused them. The transfer of rights and claims is especially complete, however, in cases where the adult has no biological children or the child no biological parent. Several formerly fostered adults were concerned to prove this point, for example, when one stressed that his uncle had treated them exactly like his own children after his parents' death, even to the point of sending them just as far in school. Another elderly trader made the point by saying she and her children visited her childless foster mother first whenever returning from a trip to Accra, although she later conducted her birth mother's funeral with all the solemnity due.

Children's labor is what earns them benefits from fostering, since it is a conspicuous motive for fostering them with the senior relatives most likely to reciprocate with substantial material resources. Elderly people need foster grandchildren living with them because sweeping and going on trivial errands themselves would compromise their prestige as valued family elders. These physically active elders can still manage cooking for themselves, or eat with adult kin, and they are still in a good position to provide training, sponsorship, and financial backing. When frail elders need custodial care, it is delegated to young adult women rather than children because of the heavy physical work and complex judgment involved in nursing. These granddaughters may be those with the least promising career prospects, but they ideally should get some material compensation for their years of care—at least priority in inheritance.

Children themselves also initiate or promote errand-running relationships in order to establish relationships with neighbors, more distant kin, or influential adults such as schoolteachers that may prove beneficial in both the short and long term. Every errand should bring some reward, besides praise; for example, a child who runs to buy a loaf of bread or some cooked food should be given a share. Those who volunteer to help cook can often snack within reason, so children from resource-poor families can generate substantial amounts of extra food by regularly assisting more prosperous neighbors with shopping and cooking. They may also "hang around" attractive potential career sponsors such as schoolteachers with the hope of being sent on errands and thus coming to their notice. In theory, children should be willing to run errands for any adult known to them, but they can always claim a prior engagement (see also Schildkrout 1978b).

Children who consistently make themselves available should be given gifts at Christmas and other occasions in recognition of the relationship. These contributions can accumulate to a surprising proportion of the child's new clothing or startup capital. Sometimes such relations develop into fostering, payment of school fees, apprenticeships, and other substantial patronage. Contacts that remain informal may nonetheless become important later, when tapped for loans, credit references, job introductions, lodging, and other social resources. These are given partly in return for services rendered or expected and partly in recognition of the good character already shown.

Conclusion

Asante women's financial responsibilities toward children and other lineage kin shape the conflict between work and home in different directions than for Western, middle-class women. Asantes do not experience a direct conflict between income-generating work, on the one hand, and husband and family, on the other. Both survival and accumulation are contributions to the lineage, as well as to personal goals. The financial aspect of motherly and kinship responsibilities drives a woman to ensure a steady, high personal income rather than discouraging her participation in paid work. To some extent, this creates a conflict between motherhood and wifehood, in which personal services play a more central role.

Strategies and compromises actually employed in cooking and childcare reflect the strength of women's position in the kind of relations in which each is imbedded. Women have much less control within marriage and therefore much less room to maneuver in cooking. The strength of their lineage position primarily enables them to do without marriage, rather than modify relations within it. The compromises they negotiate with husbands over cooking therefore create more distance within marriage rather than entangling them deeper. Motherhood in this matrilineal society is identified with lineage loyalties rather than marriage. Practical conflicts between childcare and trading remain, even for unmarried mothers, but women have more unconditional support in mediating them. Extensive delegation to kin or older children, staying within the same lineage framework, bears little social cost. Intensive trading is seen as a sacrifice made for the children, not a betrayal of them.

The degree of interference between trading and domestic work depends as much on standards of timing, quality, and delegation of services as on the sheer quantity of labor involved. Values attached to cleaning, for example, allow women to involve a wide range of helpers using relationships in which they have considerable control. Changes which permit a woman to relax timing, compromise quality, use commercial sources, or delegate more can have a greater impact than changes which reduce cost or improve efficiency in the labor process.

Competition between trading and domestic work intensifies because peak demands in both areas come at nearly the same point in a woman's life (see table 9.4). At about age thirty, Asante women typically have four or five children, assuming two-year intervals. The oldest, if a girl, cannot yet take full charge of domestic work. Swelling financial demands as these children grow and progress in school make these women the most active traders. At the same time, they are trying to cement the relationship with their husbands by maintaining high cooking standards and frequently living with them, thus reducing access to their own kin (see table 9.5).

This domestic bottleneck halfway through the childbearing years defines a dual career path for Asante women traders. The two ideal types were well represented in life histories, although more traders fell somewhere in between. An ambitious young woman begins trading energetically as early as age ten or twelve. As a teenager, she takes advantage of her childlessness to accumulate experience and capital. By the time she marries and has her second or third child, she can afford to take in extra dependents to care for them. This enables her to intensify trading as her financial pressures mount and to send her own daughters to school. Women from wealthier families can use those resources to meet domestic needs and get farther in trading with less personal sacrifice. Less ambitious women have few immediate financial needs in young adulthood to force them to trade strenuously. They may get by with part-time work and gifts from boyfriends until the birth of their first or second child. The financial demands of motherhood then grow rapidly, so they can save little from their limited starting incomes. Without significant capital or domestic help, they must settle for small-scale retailing or home industries such as cooked-food sales. They depend more heavily on the contribution of their husbands, which personal domestic work may enhance. Women fortunate

Table 9.4 Age and Domestic Work: Percentage Reporting Doing Domestic Work at Home

0–14	15–24	25–34	35–44	45–54	over 54
83	84	77	59	47	38

SOURCE: 1979 Kumasi Central Market Survey

Table 9.5 Wives' Domestic Work by Residence of Husband

Residence	Domestic Work	No Work
Same House	74	20
Same Town	65	32
Elsewhere	68	26

SOURCE: 1979 Kumasi Central Market Survey

enough to find rich and reliable husbands may then reenter the higher path with resources saved from those contributions.

Women located in between these two stereotypes bridge potentially dangerous gaps in the developmental cycle or the daily routine by juggling cooked-food purchases, adult and fostered kin, or maids. Although surveys show low levels of use of these sources of domestic help, their existence yields a disproportionate benefit in preserving capital and permitting some accumulation because it allows an extra degree of flexibility. Resort to them, however brief or infrequent, keeps very low capital enterprises afloat through the short trouble periods or small emergencies that might otherwise bring total collapse. It also reduces the risk of brief but catastrophic domestic crises enough to justify the heavier investment in time and money needed to build up profitable larger enterprises. Successful management of these alternative strategies balances short- and long-term reciprocity so that neither present nor future financial and labor obligations overwhelm the trading enterprise.

Considering the multifaceted gender roles of women as mothers, sisters, daughters, and wives reveals the dynamic process through which gender and wealth rooted in the family affect women's trading position. Each of these roles has an intense but different gender content, each with its ideological and material basis, which is inflected differently for women at early and late points in the life cycle and for women with high and low access to capital, labor, and other social resources. The necessary articulation of these distinct identities, which depend on each other for complete fulfillment, creates conflict but also creates space within which individual women can maneuver. They attempt to manage the way in which all of these axes of domination interpenetrate, not simply to avoid conflict, but to accumulate power through using their position in one system to leverage dominance in another. Meanwhile, of course, their efforts dovetail with the equally energetic efforts of spouses and kin to manage back. These interminable, not always explicit, negotiations are the social process through which trading wealth builds independence in the domestic arena and vice versa. In the long run, they are as critical as market bargaining sessions to the growth and survival of women's market enterprises.

Unfortunately, it is the least favorable of these gendered identities, the marital relation, which is used as the paradigm in impersonal relations between traders and the general male public. The husband is the archetypal stranger, so every stranger is in some sense a potential husband or wife. The state, as government and bureaucracy, is as clearly male dominated as the marketplace is female dominated. Interactions as trivial as a quarrel between a female hawker and a male city tax ticket collector activate marital models. The woman was reproached by a nearby market leader for using insulting language because "he is someone's husband." Integrated into the national community as the wife, rather than as the mother of the nation, market women not only leave behind the considerable respect and authority mothers have in Asante culture, but bring in all the mutual ambivalence and distrust that characterize marriage.

10 THE MARKET UNDER ATTACK

The need to locate Asante women within the broader realms of kinship and marriage came as no surprise to me, given my British structural-functionalist training. Although readings in political economy had given me some sense of the importance of their relations to the state, the dramatic clashes between Ghanaian governments and market traders in the late 1970s and early 1980s soon made it clear to me that these were some of the most important relations Kumasi traders experienced. Within two months of my arrival, physical and verbal confrontations between market traders and police, soldiers and official publications over goods allocations, price controls, and other issues resumed their episodic cycle and built to a tempestuous climax in 1979. Trading survival clearly and immediately depended on access to protection from attack or on capacity for temporary withdrawal. These dual strategies intensified both the separation of many traders from all support or interaction with the state and the dependence of other traders on corrupt or manageable state relations. The intense antagonism also revealed fundamental contradictions within the state as its continuing needs for revenue and distributive service repeatedly led to compromise and periods of more indirect attack.

Traders, even those based in one marketplace, varied widely in their relations to the state. Cleavages based on gender, ethnicity, education, and wealth both create and are compounded by family relationships. The policeman's wife or sister operates from a very different position of constraints and resources than the poor rural widow, although both may sell rice. The state is likewise neither homogenous nor monolithic. Military and elected officials, party bosses, police, civil servants, and gazetted chiefs all have their own interests and interactions with traders and their own grudges against other state agents. Contradictions within and between parts of the state apparatus produce its own historical dynamic of change and provide traders with the leverage they need to defend and promote their interests within it.

Historical research later revealed that this mutual dependence and negotiation was characteristic of state/trader relations. Successive regimes in Ghana have been intimately involved in trade, stimulating and protecting it, while pushing it firmly and sometimes roughly into channels advantageous to state interests of the time, themselves often filled with contradictions. Gaps in the provision of goods and services by government agencies and officially recognized corporate activity very commonly provide the opportunities for the expansion or survival of market and street trading, either through toleration of their activities or incapacity of state agents to suppress or replace them (Hansen 1988). Individually well-placed traders show another kind of dependence on official resources or inaction, which provide their personal comparative advantage. They benefit from the removal of their competition through the coercive power of the state, although they very rarely invoked it directly for this purpose (see Ensminger 1990 for a Kenyan example of this invocation).

Despite a considerable degree of symbiosis, there is also a clear structural basis for hostility between the Ghanaian state and market traders. As in other parts of the continent, trading presents both material and symbolic resistance to state control of the economy. The establishment of industrial capitalism was "tied hand and foot" to such state intervention (Hart 1985). The promotion of wage labor in export production by colonial authorities seemed to require repressive regulation of urban residence and rural production to release labor for migration. This was most conspicuous in the mining districts of Central and Southern Africa, but conditioned family law and urban planning very widely (Wright 1982; Natrass 1987). Women living and trading in the cities contradicted these plans visibly and persistently (Parpart 1986; Mbilinyi 1985).

Traders also frustrated government attempts to channel commerce through large corporations and government agencies over which they had tighter control and which they could use for political support. Illegal trading could mean a considerable loss in taxes and customs revenues. In Ghana, markets in fact generated enormous tax revenues through rents and daily use fees, but these went largely to local rather than national governments. Smuggling was a more serious problem, since the government lost not only the customs duties but the pricing differentials and patronage from state monopolies, like the Cocoa Marketing Board, and comparable side benefits from import license allocations. The nature of the political coalition backing the state apparatus has a primary influence on the use of its interventions to shape trading patterns. Both colonial and independent governments had close ties to the large-scale formal sector, predominantly owned by foreigners but including some state enterprises. Licensing and zoning regulations were designed to enforce boundaries around their commercial territory within the cities by limiting where and how many small-scale traders could compete with them. Not only the high fees but the cumbersome and corrupt procedures of commercial licensing makes it prohibitive for small-scale traders in many parts of the world (De Soto 1989; Boissevain and Grotenberg 1989). Street clearance campaigns in Ghana, as elsewhere, appeal to sanitary and visual ideals of cleanliness and modernity that favor high-capital shops and stores in the Third World and in Western cities alike (Lessinger 1988; Spalter-Roth 1988). The coordination of mass arrests with international conferences indicates that these ideals, like the political pressures toward large-scale commerce, gain force from international acceptance and endorsement (Seidman 1990).

Like lineage and marital relations, the state anchors a distinct system of domination with its own historical dynamic, but one thoroughly intertwined with the history of power struggles within the marketplace system. The position of traders within this framework is not static or passive, since the process of mutual constitution involves influence in both directions, not usefully reduced to one-sided impacts or constraints. Traders go beyond simply resisting or circumventing the repeated efforts by the state to control, exploit, or destroy their commercial activities, although their efforts have been very frustrating to various state agencies. They also constantly accept, seek out, and manipulate relations with various parts of the state apparatus in order to gain access to the resources each part controls and to gain advantage over their trading rivals. Since hostile state policies and actions seriously limit accumulation and the expansion of individual enterprises or whole categories of traders, and even challenge their survival, such relations with the state provide or deny leverage to traders in their daily commercial struggles and define important cleavages within the marketplace system.

Historical Precedents

The centuries-long history of state commercial intervention in this region helped legitimize the increasingly harsh policies of the 1970s and 1980s in the eyes of Ghanaians. African and European governments grew up in the context of trade, continually promoting the often conflicting interests of their citizens and of specific state institutions such as the military. The level of pricing, the terms and conditions of negotiation, and the privileges extended to traders of different nations all affected the wellbeing of their constituents and thus were a major concern of government leaders. Individual traders were by no means passive in petitioning or circumventing their own or foreign governments, but they accepted the idea of official regulation.

The location and internal organization of precolonial African kingdoms underlines their relation to long-distance trade. The succession of Sahelian empires in present-day Senegal and Mali anchored the trans-Sahara caravan routes. Asante itself grew up around routes connecting these savannah networks to the Atlantic coast, and long-distance trade supplied important foodstuffs and state revenue. European traders relied heavily on the sponsorship of their own states through state-given and protected monopolies or companies, despite trying to circumvent this control in other ways. They lobbied a reluctant British colonial office to expand that protection through direct rule, while the Asante delegations championed free trade.

When the British held back from defending their coastal client states, some of the Africans met together to propose a Fante confederacy on the model of the Asante confederacy. The threat of an effective political unit to defend the coastal African merchant and chiefly classes finally induced the British to appropriate the territory of the Gold Coast Colony in 1830 so that such proposals could be termed treasonous retroactively. Colonial authorities maintained a close alliance with British trading firms, but their interests did not always coincide. Their political and financial interest in avoiding rebellion led them to revoke the Swanzy monopoly on Krobo palm oil when the company abused it, and they also compromised on leaving chiefs their royalties from mining concessions (Wolfson 1953; Hopkins 1965).

As colonial rule was established in each part of present-day Ghana, the colonial government made sponsorship of European export and import firms a high priority. European firms used their access to colonial authorities' police powers and to bank credit to bypass local magnates and begin buying and selling farther inland. Colonial officials consulted European merchants regularly on local policy, and their annual reports on economic conditions featured the progress and prospects of these firms (NAK1; NAK13). They enforced granting of mining concessions to European mining firms and put pressures on chiefs for mine labor recruitment, souring relations between chiefs and their subjects (Howard 1978). European firms were also favored in the allocation and pricing of transport on the newly built railways (NAK2). Price controls and import quotas instituted during the two World Wars responded to pressures from mining firms wanting to keep down wages and import firms wanting to keep their market shares.

Nationalist Interventions

Although the nationalists proposed different specific measures, their overall commercial goals echoed those of the British and of precolonial chiefs: to promote favorable prices and ease entry of their citizens into profitable commercial roles. Market traders were prominent as supporters of both leading political parties during the 1950s, Nkrumah's Convention People's Party (CPP) and Danquah's United Party (UP) and its successor, Busia's National Liberation Movement (NLM). Traders' contacts and patterns of travel between towns and regions made them effective organizers and propagandists (Manuh 1985). Similarly prominent roles for urban market women in political party formation and support before independence have been reported in Nigeria, Ivory Coast, Guinea, and Tanzania (Ogunsanwo 1988; Baker 1974; Lewis 1982; Schmidt 1992; Geiger 1987).

The market organizations which solidified in many Ghanaian towns at this time constituted important mobilization networks for fundraising, demonstrations, and eventually for elections, which began in 1951. Each party tried to get its members elected to market leadership vacancies as these occurred, and rival gangs of young men carried out beatings, arson, and other retaliations against targets that included market leaders affiliated with the opposition. The two gangs rioted in Kumasi Central Market in January 1955 (Allman 1993).

The alliance between traders and nationalist parties that had persisted from the cocoa boycott through independence in 1957 began to break down in the early 1960s over issues related to the terms and organization of trade. Personalistic favoritism in allocations increasingly bypassed the established traders who had contributed as propagandists and fundraisers to both of the parties active at independence. Public distribution through the Ghana National Trading Corporation, a nationalized expatriate firm, and through consumer and workers' cooperatives, posed a direct, if ineffective, challenge to marketplace distribution. Cut out of formal and informal political channels, traders began to ally with populist resistance to Nkrumah. After the release of an austerity budget in 1961, for example, Accra traders demonstrated massively. Those in Takoradi and other towns supported the subsequent railway strike by spreading the word and donating food for soup kitchens (Drake and Lacy 1966). Falling living standards through the 1960s generated popular backing for Nkrumah's overthrow and the subsequent election of Dr. Busia's Progress Party (PP) government (1969–72).

Kumasi traders had joined the Asante-identified PP in substantial numbers even before independence, but their efforts had brought little in representation or material benefit for market women. Busia did not stay in power long enough to implement his pricing and supply policies thoroughly, as part of his free market economic reorientation, obscuring their potential impact on the terms of trade. Although many regulations that had made ordinary trading more difficult were removed under IMF advice, his more elitist political coalition stopped even farther from including traders as central participants or constituents (Chazan 1983). Commissions and advisory bodies included professionals, businessmen, and civil servants, but not uneducated citizens like market traders. The decreasing capacity of more prestigious employment sectors to satisfy ambitious Ghanaians, with expectations raised by Africanization, created pressures diverted into ethnic scapegoating of the foreign traders expelled in 1969.

A devaluation proposal by Busia brought in another interventionist government, under General Acheampong, who led the National Redemption Council (1972–75) and the Supreme Military Council (1975–78). He renewed price, exchange, and import controls with an elaborate and personalized system of licensing that duplicated the worst of the previous CPP abuses (Chazan 1983). The sudden commercial success apparent among high officials' family members and romantic partners was resented and remembered by established market traders as well as by the general public in 1979. Civilian participation in decisions over pricing and allocations was extremely limited, except through individual concessions. The effect of official controls on real prices and distribution channels was uneven, modified by the patterns of massive corruption and diversion of goods.

The growing food and fiscal crisis in the mid-1970s drew Acheampong into more direct confrontation with market traders over prices and access to goods. Episodic enforcement of price controls on essential consumer imports was combined with crackdowns on smuggling and hoarding. Most notably, market women were forbidden to sell wax print cloth, the most profitable commodity within the marketplace system. Consumer cooperatives, storefront "designated supermarkets," and the Ghana Food Distribution Corporation all represented consistent but unsuccessful attempts to remove essential commodities and foodstuffs from the marketplace system to channels more easily controlled by the government. Distribution of local food crops was especially ineffectual, with large quantities of food grown under Operation Feed Yourself left rotting because of lack of transport or organization.

A symbiotic relationship between legal and illegal channels developed in the 1970s, since the government tacitly relied on illegal supplies to fill gaps in the legal system and illegal traders relied heavily on diverted legal supplies. The balance between the two networks as regards relative volume and pricing fluctuated with the strength of enforcement. Negative controls on access to illegal supplies were not combined with positive access to adequate legal supplies, due to foreign exchange shortages and frequent diversion of legal supplies. Consequently, illegal channels reasserted themselves as soon as the pressure lifted. Access to police or military protectors, to licenses, and to sources of legal, diverted, and smuggled goods became important commercial resources for both legitimate and illegal trading enterprises. Various state agencies appeared as chronic adversaries to traders as a whole, but also permitted or initiated high-profit transactions for a well-connected few.

The dual legal/illegal distribution channels, though intimately connected, created a dual or polarized pricing system in which the central question was who bought at what price. Access to legal supplies, at or near control prices, was best for civil servants and employees of large firms and their connections. Legal supplies went on sale to the public occasionally, most often at urban locations on very short notice. The self-employed, rural residents, and those too old or weak to stand in often violent lines had little chance to obtain them. Disruption in the formal sector creates problems for most traders but ironically reinforces the position of illegal intermediaries. Consumers cannot realistically patronize shops or large department stores because they cannot expect to find what they need. Those who urgently need a specific item, such as medical supplies, must endure an exhausting search through many stores, not always successful. Individuals prepare in advance by maintaining personal contacts with owners or employees in a few shops or firms, who may warn them of goods expected soon or allow them to purchase concealed reserves of scarce items, but they cannot expect steady supplies. Only the most important consumers could marshal this kind of influence for their personal purchases.

Illegal supplies required even tighter connections to well-placed official figures, sharpening the division between women imports traders with and without elite family backgrounds, which had previously been easier to bridge through market success. This cleavage has been richly documented in Zaire, where it is even more extreme (MacGaffey 1987; Schoepf and Engundu 1991). Family and marital connections to factory or store employees, political influence, previous commercial ties, and extra payments all helped in individual cases. Older women traders often stereotyped young intermediaries as trading on their sexuality, not their professional skills. They felt humiliated having to cultivate relationships with younger, less experienced traders whom they did not respect but who had more immediate power. One told me she would rather buy from a regular wholesale outlet at any price than spend so much time "begging" from these "girls."

The difficulty of obtaining supplies had created a more complex division of labor in controlled commodities, and a new set of intermediaries with these connections as their main commercial capital, even if they spent more hours retailing the goods. Traders who specialized in obtaining chits, sometimes called "chit men" or "chit women," could not also specialize tightly by commodity. They remained prepared to buy a range of items when in stock to keep their connection active. The gifts needed to maintain these relationships pushed up the total cost of the goods bought, even though the purchase price might conform to government price control regulations.

Widespread resentment over corruption was one factor leading to General Acheampong's overthrow in 1978. The reforms that followed aimed to enforce price control and other commercial regulations more strictly, rather than shifting to a new kind of government intervention. Lt. Col. Akuffo, the new head of state, arrested leading figures and ordered dramatic enforcement episodes soon after taking power in July 1978 and again in November. Although Akuffo removed many notoriously corrupt individuals from office, he had not insisted on fines or other punishments commensurate with the benefits they had accumulated. Standards of enforcement had already relaxed considerably by mid-1979, so the familiar intermittent pattern of post-coup and pre-Christmas raids and subsequent disinterest continued.

Akuffo's most dramatic intervention was the currency exchange exercise carried out in March 1979. On a Friday evening, the radio news announced that all paper money would have to be exchanged at banks within two weeks for new notes. Careful planning, aimed to eliminate the ill-gotten gains of corrupt officials and currency speculators by making their hoards of currency worthless, and the level of secrecy, while not absolute, was quite impressive. The banks had closed for the weekend, the land borders were closed, and even an airport closure had been scheduled "for repairs" in order to keep currency taken out of the country illegally from being brought back in for exchange. This nonviolent confiscation was also intended to catch illegal income kept within the country, since hoarders would fear revealing how much they had. Stories circulated for months about desperate measures taken by rich men caught outside of the country to send home keys to the deep freeze full of money, or having to tell relatives where money had been hidden from them. The complete and rapid demonetarization seemed bizarre to Ghanaians and foreigners at the time, but in fact Zaire and Nigeria followed suit not long after.

In Ghana, the currency exchange procedures merely reinforced the value of official and formal-sector connections. Formal sector workers were offered special exchange facilities through their companies or agencies and were more likely to use bank accounts, which were not affected. A better exchange rate for small amounts was meant to help the poor, but simply created employment for thousands who stood in line at banks with money for the wealthy. Those with the official contacts to accumulate illegal funds easily used the same connections to exchange large sums, while the life savings of cocoa farmers and rural traders were wiped out when they could not get to the exchange points in time.

Housecleaning

The June 1979 coup that installed Flight Lieutenant J. J. Rawlings in his first term of office was organized by junior officers who established the Armed Forces Revolutionary Council (AFRC). They argued that corruption was a matter of personal morality that could be cured by removing corrupt individuals permanently from positions of power and punishing them severely enough to deter imitation. Acheampong and other former heads of state and high officials were executed. The "housecleaning exercise" carried out from June to October 1979 attacked government officials, private formal sector enterprises, and market traders who had participated in the diversion of goods from official channels and the evasion of price and import regulations.

The AFRC attempted to shut down the unofficial channels completely and stop the recurring cycle of enforcement and relaxation. This required that price controls and other regulations be extended eventually well beyond the sector of consumer imports and manufactured goods to cover capital goods and eventually local foodstuffs and craft production. Under the dual channel system, unofficial channels had filled sizable gaps left by the official channels in the survival needs of the population. For example, the Ghana Food Distribution Corporation had notably failed to capture a significant proportion of the trade in local foodstuffs, due to its low producer prices and high spoilage rates. Under conditions of strict enforcement, the official distributive system fills all the recognized commodity needs of the population, or they go unfilled.

The AFRC began by punishing those who had offended against existing price and import controls on essential commodities. Although relatively brief, the campaign was thorough enough to demonstrate convincingly the dynamic thrust of the regulatory approach previously honored mainly in the breach. Official news releases in 1979 claimed that price controls targeted large wholesalers, not the ordinary retail trader, but confiscations, beatings, and market demolitions hit the ordinary traders hardest. The Makola #1 market in Accra was renowned as the premier marketplace in the country for wholesaling imported and manufactured items, especially cloth. This was their first target—looted the day of the coup, closed down, and eventually blown up with dynamite (Robertson 1983). Soldiers entered the central markets of all of the regional capitals, breaking open stalls containing imports and selling their contents on the spot or taking them away. Within a few days, police and soldiers had also seized all the major formal sector stores and began selling off their stocks. They arrested and beat managers of public stores and private store owners, especially Lebanese, and searched their homes and offices. Hoarded goods found were confiscated for sale through the government stores or seized private stores, or they were taken to the barracks.

In Kumasi, soldiers entered Kumasi Central Market the day after the coup to sell off at control prices the stocks of traders in the provisions section, where imported and packaged foods such as rice, flour, sugar, tomato paste, and sardines were sold. Sometimes the proceeds were given to the trader, sometimes they were kept for "government chest." Soldiers often did not know the legal prices but assumed all the asking prices were illegal and reduced them accordingly. Previous episodic price control enforcement had been largely in the hands of the local police, so they had a reputation for corruption but were also more likely to know control prices for items Akuffo had recently added to the controlled list or which the soldier had not bought recently.

The next day, soldiers broke open stalls in the adjacent cloth section and confiscated or sold the cloth found inside. Owners of confiscated goods could go to the barracks later to bargain about the price they would be paid, if they cared to risk a beating or trusted their high connections in the military or police. When the soldiers finished, the mob that had collected to buy cloth and watch the proceedings crossed the street to loot stalls at the main lorry park. Later that second day, soldiers took over the major department stores in downtown Kumasi, a few blocks from the Central Market, moving down each street in turn. When they moved to empty the large stores, the AFRC left legal price controls behind and began selling off items that had never had official prices, including expensive luxury items like freezers, mattresses, fans, and stereos. Soldiers set prices on the spot at one-fourth to one-tenth market value, indicating a sense of vengeance for unfair terms of trade as well as disrespect for regulations.

Price control sales in the market later extended beyond the legally listed "essential commodities," using similar rules of thumb. Obvious gender discrimination appeared at this point in the process of price-setting. The AFRC consulted organizations of craftsmen, such as butchers, shoemakers, adinkra cloth printers, car repair fitters, and truck drivers, about their cost levels before extending price controls to their products and services. Since many traders, as consumers, supported the idea of strict price controls, they offered to negotiate coordinated buying and selling prices, but the AFRC deliberately excluded them from cooperation.

For the first two or three weeks of the coup a Christmas atmosphere prevailed, with many scarce goods available to the general public in unusual quantities at windfall prices. Factories and smaller stores not already raided chose to sell out their stocks rapidly to avoid confiscation. I was in the market when the local soft drink bottling plant suspended its allocation system, long a focus of corruption, creating a brief glut and an impromptu party when we all bought each other tepid orange sodas and colas. The fruits of raids on hoards in garages and factory back rooms unpredictably replenished the exhausted stocks of legal goods in the pipeline. Long lines or queues formed even before the queuers knew what would be sold, and supplies often ran out before latecomers had their turn. Consequently, most goods were bought either by casual passersby or by youths who roamed the central business district during times of confiscations looking for lines to join. During peak periods, many salaried workers and some ordinary traders took time off to try their luck.

Enforcement personnel designed new sales procedures intended to prevent systematic commercial purchases and discourage resale. Shop managers or soldiers forced buyers to take a fixed selection of goods—in one instance two tins of sardines, two tins of milk, and a roll of toilet paper—reviving the conditional sales so unpopular after World War II. Neighbors swapped to get the items they wanted or sold to traders in order to buy what they really needed in the market. Government and factory workers had some access to confiscated supplies through union pressure. Very few such goods reached the rural areas, and their usual access to smuggled and diverted goods was effectively interrupted. Like legal supplies in the previous dual channel pattern, these legal goods went disproportionately to the young, idle, urban residents who could stand in line for hours and fight to reach the front before supplies ran out. Those fitting that description might then find themselves arrested as "queue contractors," because traders hired young men to stand in lines and purchase commodities with their money and otherwise unemployed persons made a living from buying such goods for resale (*Daily Graphic* [Accra], 17 July 1979; *Pioneer* [Kumasi], 28 August 1979).

A high level of public violence made taking advantage of these bargains dangerous. Turbulent crowds roamed the streets, carrying large sums of money for their chance at a freezer, ready to run for a place in line when a store suddenly began selling something. Pickpockets and thieves reportedly provoked stampedes with false reports. Standing in line could also bring injuries from the belts and nightsticks of the supervising soldiers or from the free-for-alls that erupted once sales began. Official and semi-official violence reached levels unknown since the months around national independence, when rival party thugs beat and burned out supporters of the two major electoral parties in Kumasi. Price control offenders and alleged hoarders were officially beaten, caned, and flogged naked in the lorry park. Unofficially, resisters were shaved with broken bottles, and one woman was shot. Traders who had taken previous episodic economic losses philosophically now seemed obsessed, repeating stories of violence and humiliation. Rumors circulated about women who had miscarried or who had babies beaten to death on their backs or crushed in stampedes.

These enforcement activities, though aimed at imported and manufactured items in the market, had an immediate negative impact on food sales. Villagers nervous about the general violence and theft stayed away from Kumasi with their local foodstuffs. Many foodstuffs traders, along with most other Kumasi residents with any money in their pockets, abandoned their work to search for lines to join. Shortages of staple foodstuffs like plantain and cassava led to long lines in those parts of the market, which also broke down into fights as supplies ran out. Rumors that soldiers would soon come to the produce sections of the market encouraged more traders to stay away if they could afford it.

It soon became clear that the military, as the leading active arm of government at the time, did have enough power over the marketplace system to disrupt it fairly completely, but not to control its response. Urban residents quickly saw that they were more dependent on the rural areas than vice versa. Serious food shortages developed in Kumasi and other major cities immediately after the 1979 coup. Large cities and institutions suffered the most, since they depended most on centrally purchased supplies. For more than a month, Kumasi households had trouble locating enough traditional foodstuffs for meals, regardless of price. Mothers among the traders told me of coming to market with money and crying because they could find nothing to buy for their children. Children and unemployed family members went to stay with rural relatives when possible, until urban food supplies improved, despite the risks and difficulties of travel. Newspapers considered the price and supply of food in different towns a major news item for the entire AFRC period. These issues affected the major AFRC political constituency among poorer urban workers and even among the barracks themselves as the stream of confiscations ran dry.

The AFRC moved very gingerly into food price controls, given the pressure of these urban food shortages. The timing and tactics of the first price control enforcement on local foodstuffs seemed intended to minimize panic and losses. First the national radio broadcast empty assurances of physical safety in the towns. Meanwhile, traders discussed rumors that food prices would be controlled, perhaps sparked by public calls for voluntary price restraint. The first raids began on the day of national elections, held as promised on June 18th. Most traders and customers alike had taken the day off to go to the polls, so few traders were present and their stocks were small.

The authorities even showed some gender sensitivity by sending in female police, not previously employed in price control work, instead of male soldiers. These women confronted traders politely, and traders were neither assaulted nor were their goods confiscated. The policewomen sold off small amounts of the yams, tomatoes, and plantains they found, allowing traders themselves to collect the money, and warned others to reduce their prices. Since no control prices had been announced yet, they simply reduced existing prices by half. To control the unruly lines that soon formed in the market, policewomen used the "female" method of throwing buckets of water rather than brandishing belts and nightsticks as male soldiers commonly did (although the policewomen wore both).

Despite this careful start, chaos reigned in the wholesale yards the next day. Arriving traders who had begun to unload their yams threw them back into the trucks and drove away when they heard the news. Villagers arriving at the lorry park likewise turned around and went home with their produce. Armed male soldiers began to patrol the wholesale yards daily, supervising forced sales from trucks and using the yards as a base for forays into the foodstuffs stalls. Drastic military action was highly effective in disrupting business as usual, but without achieving the desired result of low-cost urban food supplies. Urban food supplies dried up within days of the first confiscations. Enforcement efforts directed at traders could not release extra food, even temporarily, because limited space, poor facilities, and rapid spoilage prevent traders from storing significant amounts. Farmers, who could store, responded overwhelmingly by keeping their produce off the market as much as possible.

Irregularities in enforcement procedures undermined the credibility of food price controls even among urban traders who endorsed the stated goal of reducing food prices with enthusiasm. One wiry old lady refused to sell her yams or take any money, telling the policewoman bitterly to take them—she was stealing them, since the woman could not buy any more at that price. Her neighbors held her back and collected the money for her. Many traders now expressed the view that soldiers were mainly interested in getting food for their own consumption rather than enforcing low prices for consumers. It was well known that supplies at the barracks were short, and soldiers frequently took goods away without any compensation. One oil seller was told to come to the barracks in two weeks for her empty containers, with no mention of a control price. Even when soldiers sold goods from market stalls, they made their own purchases first, which often exhausted the available supplies. This pattern looked very familiar to me from episodic enforcement of price controls on imports, when soldiers could be seen buying cloth and other holiday items at the official prices early in the Christmas rush for their own use.

Traders also resented that they had not been breaking any law or regulation by selling local foodstuffs and craft products at market prices. The first price lists for local foodstuffs came out on June 23d, well after enforcement had begun, and these lists were not widely understood or applied. Without established legal prices, cooperation with the soldiers was impossible. If a trader tried to forestall confiscation by setting a low price to begin with, the soldier just halved it again. Possession of commercial quantities, at any price, was taken as evidence of hoarding. Ironically, food price control enforcement raised effective food prices well above their normal level. Absolute urban shortages were the most important factor, but movement of sales to clandestine locations also contributed. Information could not be safely gathered by either buyer or seller on supply, demand and comparative prices. Furtive, hurried sales meant little bargaining and high, irregular prices. The risk of miscalculation, added to the risk of arrest, pushed transaction margins higher to cushion against possible losses.

Traders' attitudes toward government intervention remained ambivalent when price controls were its major form. As consumers, they wanted lower prices for basic foodstuffs as well as for imports. Their commercial role as sellers of necessities to the lower and middle classes also gave them a stake in obtaining supplies at affordable prices. Most traders interviewed during the early AFRC period endorsed the basic idea of price control. They wanted it enforced more strictly on the managerial side and on farmers. Their complaints focused on the unfairness of holding retailers responsible for sales prices when they could not buy their supplies at legal price levels.

Setting official "control" prices for local foodstuffs presents immense practical problems because of the wide variations in size, quality, and condition characteristic of tropical foodstuffs. Price or quantity bargaining over individual units normally compensates for these variations in yams, plantains, dried fish, tomatoes, and the other most popular foodstuffs. Enforcement of uniform prices for plantain, for example, ensured that heavy, mature fingers stayed in the farmers' larders and only immature ones reached Kumasi. The same happened with chickens, since farmers had no incentive to keep feeding them until maturity. Even for a more standardized commodity like bags of corn (maize), insect infestation, dampness, and grain size affected the price. The first price lists published used units like kilos, not commonly used in retail sales, which made compliance impossible for traders who did not own scales. They also made no allowance for distance from the producing area or seasonal scarcity. With some commodities, like local pottery, soldiers admitted their inability to set a price and just took a percentage of the goods as a kind of tax. A pretense of cooperation could turn technical problems into some kind of indirect negotiation. Shea butter sellers gleefully told later how their huge filled calabashes broke scale after scale brought by the soldiers, who finally gave up in frustration.

In Kumasi, the Central Market *ahemmafuo* set up formal negotiations at the Ashanti Regional Offices under the sponsorship of the Regional Commissioner to bring order to the food price control situation. A month after the coup, they brought in samples of the major root and tuber staples (yams, cassava, cocoyam, and plantain) in different sizes and agreed on a price list with representatives of consumers, government buyers, and the military. In the next few days, however, soldiers in the market refused to recognize these prices or size grades and continued to set prices arbitrarily. The leaders then counseled traders to stop buying from farmers unless they could obtain low enough prices to allow for this.

The market disruptions and consequent food shortages that began in the major cities gradually spread out into the countryside, following the marketing channels in reverse. Without a financial incentive to bring their crops beyond the nearest town, farmers avoided the danger of confiscation that centered on the cities by suspending sales. They also found too little available to buy in rural markets to justify the risk. When foodstuffs stopped coming in to Kumasi and other large towns, soldiers expanded their activities to major village periodic markets. Soldiers stationed within driving distance would visit these markets on their market day, confiscating goods in the possession of villagers or traders for sale at reduced prices or for use at the barracks. Traders were conspicuous targets because they bought in wholesale quantities and transported goods on the roads, so Kumasi traders were afraid to visit their usual markets. The few who ventured out to rural markets in those weeks reported back that villagers were staying away, so it was not worth the effort. Villagers did not usually suffer the physical abuse traders did, but they often did find their goods purchased at control price by the military.

What commercial activity persisted moved out of the official markets and eventually dispersed away from any recognizable commercial location at the height of intervention. As hungry soldiers searched farther afield, farmers avoided even the informal sales locations found at farm trailheads or highway intersections. Those who wanted to sell would take a small quantity of goods and walk along the roadside. If questioned by soldiers, they could claim they were only carrying a load home for family consumption. In Kumasi itself, clandestine sales at back streets or dawn unloading points passed by word of mouth and became the rule for yams and plantains. Foodstuffs traders knew these techniques well from seeing them used for illegal sales of controlled imports, and I found complaints about them in the archives in records on wartime food price controls.

When even village markets largely emptied of goods, soldiers and other enforcement personnel began to "hijack" trucks entering the outskirts of town. Soldiers from more remote barracks had so far not benefitted from access to a major market. Now they lay in wait on the major highways leading to Kumasi to intercept trucks and confiscate whole truckloads of produce. They occasionally sold them retail at control prices on the spot, but more often they took them off to the barracks. They could link this practice only loosely to enforcement, since the goods had neither been offered for sale nor hoarded. Even a single bag or basket of produce was considered evidence of intent to resell and confiscated under threat of arrest. This subjective standard made mixed passenger/freight trucks fair game, as well as commercial freight trucks, bringing passenger traffic nearly to a halt throughout the region.

The AFRC justified its attacks on traders by emphasizing the economic advantages of direct sales from farmers to consumers. They had revived the old rhetoric of blaming falling terms of trade on market traders who conspired to prevent direct sales. These oligopolistic parasites thus forced the consumer to bear the cost of supporting useless intermediaries. This ideology had attracted considerable popular support before the AFRC; one letter-writer called market women "big cheats and nation wreckers" (*Daily Graphic,* 22 March 1979). During June 1979, Rawlings said Ghana was "at the mercy of selfish market women (*Daily Graphic,* 13 June 1979). National newspaper editorials called market women "greedy, get-rich-quick traders" (*Ghanaian Times,* 26 June 1979). I overheard conversations in lorry parks and on street corners that echoed this hostility; one young man said that all the women traders should be shot, since they always supported each other.

The hope that removing traders from the food distribution system would solve Ghana's food problems began to fade as one month of AFRC rule passed into two. The marketplace system had virtually ceased to function, but urban staple food supplies did not revive, let alone grow. Holding traders responsible for high prices or seasonal shortages lost credibility, as food farmers showed no inclination to sell directly to consumers at dramatically lower prices. Newspapers had accused traders of spreading rumors of violence to frighten away farmers or of offering high prices to tempt them (*Ghanaian Times,* 25 June 1979; *Daily Graphic,* 5 July 1979). Food price control quietly loosened to tacitly encourage resumption of trading. In Kumasi Central Market, the *Asantehene*'s own police occasionally made rounds to encourage low prices, but they approached the traders involved quietly and carried no arms or nightsticks.

As the October handover to civilian rule approached, the AFRC made one last effort to make a lasting mark on the nation's marketplace system. On September 5th, they demolished the Makola #1 market in Accra, a symbol of the powerful, entrenched market woman and a dominant location in the imports trade. Within a few days, markets in all of the regional capitals, including Kumasi, had been wholly or partly demolished. Divisions between different parts of the state apparatus were reaffirmed in the conduct of the Kumasi demolition, although open conflict was avoided. Local police and the *Asantehene*'s own police took no part in this action. Soldiers had not been seen in the Central Market for at least a month, until they appeared riding on the front of the bulldozers with their submachine guns. Rumors circulated afterwards that Kumasi City Council members narrowly managed to avert complete demolition of the Central Market by arguing that, unlike Accra, their city had no other wholesale market for food. The Market Manager claimed to have had no advance warning, and City

Council opposition may have reflected the heavy contribution of market revenues to the city budget.

Divisions between different categories of traders were utilized in the justifications as well as the implementation of the demolition. It began at dawn in an area of makeshift stalls at the rear of the market called the "French Line," where men from Northern Ghana and adjacent French-speaking countries sold shoes and other imported clothing and reportedly exchanged foreign currency. Their section was marginal, physically, organizationally and economically, to the rest of the market, which minimized initial resistance. Their foreign connections were publicized to justify clearing the land to uncover buried hoards of foreign currency, which were also rumored to have been found under stalls in Makola #1.

The bulldozers kept going, however, until everything outside of the old market walls had come down, including shade trees and several small mosques. Soldiers surrounded each area to prevent removal of property, while others searched stalls and confiscated goods. About one-third of the total contiguous area administered by the city as Kumasi Central Market was cleared within two days. Open areas where villagers sold their foodstuffs were emptied, storage and wholesale facilities were destroyed, and rows of stalls and kiosks selling used clothing, drugs, and craft goods were dismantled or burnt. Ironically, the cloth and provisions sections, most comparable to Accra's Makola #1 market, remained untouched because they lay within the old market walls. Traders there were violating not only price controls but a recent edict prohibiting women from selling nonperishable goods (*Daily Graphic*, 18 August 1979).

As with food price control, these demolitions had no apparent legal justification. These traders were in officially recognized market locations, visited by daily ticket collectors. Occupiers of stalls and kiosks were registered individually and paid rent to the city. They had erected their structures with city approval, and some had been given permission to expand or improve them only weeks before. Their capital investment was not necessarily lower than for traders within the market walls. Many businesses with valuable equipment—corn mills, chest freezers, and sewing machines—located outside of the walls to have more room for operating such equipment.

The flimsy rationalizations given out for the Kumasi demolition did little to disguise its punitive nature. Official announcements referred to it as a street clearance campaign, naming the goals of easy passage for pedestrians and supply trucks in the market precincts and tourist-oriented civic beautification. Long-dormant plans for a clinic and "superhighway" on one side of the market were briefly resurrected, although cement and money were then unavailable even for construction projects already begun. These arguments carried little weight with traders, who saw only token efforts to keep the empty areas cleared. Within a week, traders reoccupied the same locations, selling the same commodities, but without the meager comfort of roofing sheets and tables for themselves and their babies.

The Spiral Repeats

The early eighties brought repetition and intensification of first the episodic and then the strict enforcement patterns already established. Civilian rule by the People's National Party led by Dr. Limann began with a dramatic enforcement episode soon after they took power in October 1979. Its pre-Christmas timing was perhaps coincidental, but the subsequent relaxation of controls and rapid reestablishment of the dual legal/illegal distributive system for imports felt only too familiar. Many individuals from the Acheampong years had been disqualified from public office, but some reappeared there or behind the scenes, including the former CPP plantain *ohemma* in Kumasi Central Market.

Rawlings returned to office in a military-led coup on December 31, 1981, determined to change the distributive system permanently. Removing corrupt individuals had evidently not been enough to prevent corruption. In addition to strict enforcement of price controls, import restrictions, currency exchange, and other commercial regulations, the new Provisional National Defence Committee (PNDC) government made a serious attempt to set up alternative distribution networks and destroy the power of the marketplace system. While ultimately unsuccessful, this period had a deeper impact on traders than previous briefer episodes. The damage persisted after trade liberalization under IMF pressure reversed such policies after 1984.

Another series of attacks on major urban markets in 1982 marked the change of government, with looting on the first day, reportedly by civilians. Official confiscations and aggressive enforcement of price controls on the full range of imports and local foodstuffs quickly followed these unofficial attacks. No temporary propaganda gestures, they continued with little break throughout 1982. Local People's Defence Committees (PDCs) and semi-official militias supplemented the police and military in zealous patrolling of markets and investigation and punishment of economic offenders, with official encouragement. Their targets consistently included market women, singled out for both physical and ideological attack as presumed black marketeers.

The mobilization rhetoric criticized "capitalist profitmaking," justifying appropriation of even legal profits and property for public use. Populist fervor compounded considerable weakening of central coordination and led to violent abuses not easily distinguished from pure extortion by thieves impersonating officers or militia.

The relatively continuous strict enforcement during 1982 and 1983 caused more permanent damage to individual traders and to the marketing system as a whole than the briefer housecleaning exercise in 1979 or the repeated harassment episodes seen throughout the 1970s. This long siege of forced idleness or repeated losses exhausted capital reserves sufficient to carry a trader through many bad weeks of intermittent enforcement. After the losses of 1979, fewer traders even began at this normal level in 1982. Traders with medium levels of capital did not retain enough to keep trading at their 1978 scale. The accumulated capital losses forced traders to operate at less efficient levels, without even minimal economies of scale, making it almost impossible to save or accumulate. Any interruption in their meager income brought immediate hardship to their families, which forced them to venture out sooner under adverse conditions.

Unfortunate seasonal timing intensified the effects of the initial disruption of market channels in 1982 on food availability. The PNDC came in on New Year's Day, well after the main harvest period that had worked in favor of the AFRC. As the dry season progresses in the early months of the year, perishable vegetables usually become scarce. Only the promise of high off-season prices motivates Kumasi-based traders to scour the farming areas for the last few bags of vegetables, despite their low yields and slow turnarounds. In 1982 they didn't bother; marketed supplies fell off more quickly than usual and soon hit rock bottom and stayed there. As before, the unavailability of imported and manufactured consumer goods further reduced farmers' incentive to sell. Conspicuous enforcement of border and import controls, together with unpredictable vigilante action, brought smuggling and diversion of legal imports to a virtual halt. With inflation still running high and the memory of the currency exchange exercise relatively fresh, farmers were reluctant to trust that money payment would retain its value until goods became available again.

Hostile measures by important foreign governments complicated the economic problems faced by the PNDC. In 1979, Rawlings had honored the scheduled national election and openly prepared for handover to civilian rule, disarming external opposition. Without the immediate prospect now of a peaceful exit, his intensified anti-imperialist rhetoric and rapprochement with Libya alienated the

United States and other major donors and loan agencies. The resulting shortage of foreign exchange cramped supplies of consumer goods and production inputs. The Nigerian military government, looking nervously at the precedent of a young officers' coup, withdrew Ghana's extended credit facilities for oil imports. Extreme shortages of spare parts and gasoline built up to an unparalleled transport paralysis that crippled the capacity to move farm crops in from the rural areas. Such a long interruption in commercial traffic meant hardship for rural residents as well as city dwellers. Those who had committed themselves deeply to commercial food or export crop production depended on market purchases to supplement their own farm produce. Interregional trade softened annual seasonal shortages and relieved imbalances in protein and starchy foods. Families that needed cash for medical bills or school fees might face desperate choices about who to help or what to sell. These public services themselves were collapsing for lack of supplies—bandages and medications in the clinics, books and food in boarding schools.

The PNDC had aimed, in part, for this collapse of market channels, so they had set up additional public distributive channels intended to replace them. People's Defense Committees (PDCs) and their successors, the local Committees for the Defense of the Revolution (CDCs), set up community shops in rural as well as urban areas. Farmers could sell their produce on credit accounts to these groups and in exchange receive commodities such as cloth and soap when these could be obtained. These new institutions did give rural residents a legitimate framework for sending representatives off to negotiate for supplies of commodities, as had long been the practice among managers or union officials in government agencies and large industrial workplaces. This tacit hunting license gave a critical type of political or economic access, since such allocations now provided almost the only remaining source of consumer commodities, however irregular. Opportunities for rural exchange became more and more random or unpredictable. In the villages I visited during this period the community shops only occasionally had goods to sell. Consequently, farmers only brought them crops in small amounts, and only when an arrival of goods seemed imminent. Soldiers also went out in trucks to buy foodstuffs for provisioning their barracks. Farmers were quite willing to sell to soldiers, but only if they brought supplies of commodities to buy or offered to pay city prices. Traders with connections for scarce goods also brought trucks to the rural areas to buy food, and farmers remarked that they offered better terms or brought a better selection of consumer goods than official buyers.

Several changes taken together amounted to an economy on the verge of decommercialization. Farmers were increasingly reluctant to sell their produce without having the desired commodity in view. Buyer and seller still figured the transaction in cash terms, but when price control had already set the relative monetary values involved, as in government-sponsored transactions, only the barter aspect remained negotiable or variable. For example, cocoa farmers got a "package" from their marketing board that included cloth as well as agricultural inputs in return for marketing at least part of their crop officially.

Food Security

The danger and uncertainty of sales and purchases led farmers in some locations I visited to revert to a more diversified crop pattern that came closer to meeting their subsistence needs. In the long run, this made fewer crops regularly available for urban food supply. Farmers had specialized thoughtfully to take advantage of local climatic advantages and created economies of scale in transport and buying that made collection of foodstuffs from more remote districts worthwhile. Higher local self-sufficiency insulated farmers somewhat from the political disruption of trade they feared would recur without warning, but left them vulnerable to drought and other local crop failures no longer cushioned by interregional trade.

The intense drought during 1982 and 1983 cruelly revealed the inability of the contracting distribution and production systems to meet the challenge of food scarcity. At first, trading patterns responded to the drought as an extension of the dry season. When food supplies run low, traders normally intensify their search for supplies, spending more time in the rural areas and visiting more remote villages. Since the 1982 dry season had come in with the PNDC, this response had been muted by price controls and the danger of violent confrontations. Supplies had therefore been lower than usual after a normal harvest.

By the time it became apparent that the 1982 rains had failed, both urban and rural areas were seriously short of food. Search activities finally intensified, but they were less successful because the drought was widespread. The Northern and Upper Regions were facing nearly complete lack of rain, while rains in Asante and farther south were inadequate for the crops usually planted there. Traders could not bring food from neighboring areas with more favorable or at least differently timed rains because of continuing harassment on the roads. Prices skyrocketed out of control, but official tolerance became obvious too late in the season to stimulate production in less affected areas. Desperate consumers joined traders in scouring the countryside for the last scraps of an intensive harvest. Finally, the absolute lack of foodstuffs in the marketplace system pipeline caused many traders to abandon any attempt to work, simply eating what they bought.

Food supplies in the countryside were painfully inadequate, but apparently remained consistently higher than in the cities. Urban families sent or considered sending their children to stay with rural relatives to be fed in 1983, as they had in 1979. Without substantial debt burdens, Asante farmers could not be induced to sell off food actually needed for their subsistence, but they also did not have enough because most of the Asante region was also catastrophically dry. The expulsion of Ghanaian workers from Nigeria in February 1983, without advance warning, only added more mouths to feed, at a season when returnees could hardly be employed productively on the farm. Mikell reports inland rural villages half-emptied by malnutrition (Mikell 1989). When forest farmers tried to prepare fields for the next planting season, bush fires roared out of control, burning huge tracts of cocoa, plantain, and fallow land. Rural as well as urban communities reported deaths when desperate people ate inedible things such as coconut husks.

Net flows between the North and the relatively prosperous South were hard to determine, then or later. Millets and sorghums grown primarily in the North continued to be available in small quantities in Accra, even at the height of the famine. This suggests significant outflow from food-deficit areas, at least to wealthy Northerners living in the capital. On the other hand, rural Northerners interviewed later reported that typically southern foods such as gari appeared in Northern markets in quantity then for the first time, suggesting substantial backflow of this cheaper food. The destitute farmers, especially in the Upper Region, were those who found themselves with nothing to sell. Dry season strategies like labor migration and shea butter making were intensified and provided some relief, although the desperate situation in cities and southern farming districts curtailed labor opportunities.

In the need to deal with these unprecedented emergencies, the PNDC suspended hostilities against internal and external enemies. The expulsion crisis triggered an award-winning effort by Ghanaian and UN coordinators that successfully returned people to their hometowns without creating a long-term refugee problem. Relief eventually arrived in sufficient quantity not only to relieve immediate suffering but to rehabilitate the working population for the next farming season. The next season was fairly successful in terms of food production. The high corn prices of 1983, combined with the availability of burned-off cocoa acreages, led to a huge surplus of corn in the fall. Harvest prices fell below control prices and below cost. Other foodstuffs supplies rebounded less dramatically. Over the next several years, harvests remained average to good, effectively reversing the direct effects of drought. At the same time, Rawlings opened negotiations with the World Bank and International Monetary Fund (IMF), which would eventually lead to a dramatic reversal of PNDC commercial policies.

Deregulation and Adjustment

State policies may have performed an about face since 1984, but the framework of structural adjustment still involves massive state intervention in order to maintain fiscal discipline and open the economy fully to international investment and trade. Ghana has become a shining example of wholehearted adherence to World Bank guidelines and is frequently named as such in their overview documents. World Bank/IMF negotiators pressed for and got massive devaluation (to reduce prices of local exports), restraints on government expenditure (to balance the budget), and restraints on wages to assist both those goals. Other major policy thrusts aimed at encouraging externally oriented enterprises. Resources were transferred to sectors producing "tradeables" for the world market, products such as gold and cocoa that produce or save foreign exchange. The explicit policy goal of creating a favorable climate for foreign investment justified discriminatory tax, credit and foreign exchange regulations that made special concessions to expatriate and export-oriented firms. By pushing for more concentration on export production for revenue generation and reorienting the regulatory climate to make it easier for foreign firms to operate in Ghana, the policy priorities found under structural adjustment regimes strongly echo those of the early colonial period rather than marking a new direction.

Ghana's Structural Adjustment Programme (SAP) and its successor, the Economic Recovery Program (ERP) affected market traders by altering the balance of power between and within the large- and small-scale industrial sectors. Market trade had intimate links to both of these sectors, but of a very different kind to each. Since these policies aim at changing the balance between economic sectors, they involve the marketplace system through its mediating role between other formal and nonformal sectors of economic activity. The price incentives meant to reorient production implicitly rely on traders to transmit prices to the small farmers and manufacturers who currently perform most production and who sell almost entirely through the marketplace system. Effective stimulation of production also assumes that producer inputs and consumer goods will be readily available. Efforts at state-sponsored distribution of such items had not perceptibly displaced the marketplace system and were drastically cut back as relics of socialism.

The most obvious relation between SAP and market traders was their nonappearance in its provisions. Compared to the unwelcome and unremitting attention they had attracted in recent years, this omission came as a considerable relief. Traders could go about their business without fear of physical attack or sudden retroactive illegality. Price controls and other commercial regulations were lifted and foreign exchange could be bought readily, without resort to the black market. Borders were now open, although elaborate import and export licensing requirements and procedures effectively excluded small traders from legal status. Deregulation of transport and the phasing out of gasoline rations made freight and passenger transport more available, although lack of capital still prevented expansion of transport service to previous levels of service, since repairs and running costs were hard to finance.

Excluding market trading from the resources SAP allocated and the policy supports it offered was nothing new. In this respect, SAP continued another longstanding historical trend of increasing distance between market traders and the major centers of national and international resource control. The profitable new opportunities promised under the ERP arose only for those few individuals and groups with strong international connections and for a few daring entrepreneurs. Traders who traveled abroad to buy imports, for example, now obtained their passage and currency needs more easily. The parts of the economic structure most positively linked to most market traders were also becoming weaker and more distant from the centers of economic power. The weakened structural position of their customers and suppliers placed continuing and more effective restrictions on trading than state regulation ever had. The increased income polarization in rural and urban areas widens the gap between the rich and the poor, who buy most of the goods to meet their needs in the market. Waged workers in the public and formal private sector were the primary targets of demand restraints, which translated into reduced buying power. Amid shrinking demand, artisans and traders faced increasing competition from the entry into their ranks of masses of retrenched employees from the civil service and large enterprises.

Shifts in the structure of opportunity show up in detailed analysis of the GNP growth rates that enable Ghana's structural adjustment to be presented as a success, averaging 4.7 percent annually from 1984 through 1988 (Clark and Manuh 1990). In industry, mining and extractive industry and services have gained at others' expense. Considerable investment in the gold mines, timber industry, and railroads was financed by outside loans. These concentrated on upgrading capital equipment, which reduced the total number of employees needed. Investment in these centralized industries facilitated capture of the resulting GNP growth for debt repayment. In agriculture, cocoa production recovered by 37 percent between 1983 and 1988/89, while other crops stagnated. Higher producer prices for cocoa producers intensify rural income differentiation, since 32 percent of cocoa farmers earn 94 percent of cocoa income (ILO/JASPA 1989:16). Like gold and timber, cocoa exports do not pass through the marketplace system and can be easily taxed or priced to yield government revenues for debt repayment. Terms of trade for food farmers declined by half relative to cocoa and to nonfood consumer items, lowering real incomes for food farmers and food traders, both predominantly women. Road rehabilitation extended only to trunk roads in exporting regions and urban streets, confirming urban and export infrastructural biases (Clark and Manuh 1990).

The credit reductions essential to demand restraint affect traders indirectly even though very few market traders ever made use of formal sector credit themselves. When political events destroyed their capital stocks and macroeconomic policies restricted the capital supply of the nation as a whole, market traders appeared unable to replenish their capital by competing successfully for access to sources outside of the market, whether they were controlled by kinship or formal institutions. The informal loans from family and community members on which they used to rely were based on savings from employees' salaries and from larger enterprises which did benefit from official funding, not to mention outright diversion of funds. These financial resources shrank at the same time that demands on them increased from redeployees establishing their own small enterprises and from more influential family and community members squeezed out of the tight formal credit system. Individuals were able to enter trading with capital accumulated from other activities, but existing traders could not seem to draw in capital from other sectors on the strength of their trading relations.

Artisans and small farmers producing primarily for the internal market bought and sold in the marketplace system, so the crisis hit them from several directions at once. They were squeezed like wage workers by rising consumer prices and social service fees but lacked the wage protections and indirect subsidies provided to employees of larger formal enterprises. They could now buy raw materials and tools without danger, but demand restraints imposed on the clientele they shared with traders kept many artisans idle for lack of customers (confirmed by Steel and Webster 1990). Trade in secondhand clothing boomed, bought by a population too impoverished to afford new clothing or wax prints. Secondhand blouse and skirt sets sewn from "African" prints now appeared on the market, and the outdated blouse patterns revealed their origin in grandmothers' trunks, now opened to fund immediate consumption.

The hardships suffered under SAP by traders and other low-income groups should not be underestimated. Imports and manufactures they once could not find to buy, because of shortages, they now cannot buy because of price. Local foodstuffs prices lag behind imports, but they still rise fast enough that missed meals and painful nutritional choices remain part of everyday life. Fees for medical care, schooling, water, and electricity have been raised high enough that some traders' families I visited must shut off their water, forget about junior secondary school, and even pull sick children out of the hospital. As women, traders bear a disproportionate burden in compensating with their own labor for services and supplies cut back or foregone and for the falling real incomes of other family members. Belt tightening becomes a misleading phrase under such conditions; one must first own a belt in order to tighten it. Further reductions in consumption simply bring hunger, illness, and the exhaustion of human capital, lowering production levels rather than raising them.

Recognition of the negative effects of SAP on the most vulnerable social groups led to the formulation of the Programme of Action to Mitigate the Social Costs of Adjustment (PAMSCAD) in 1987. The modest US $85 billion allocation promised to provide for basic needs through community initiative projects, such as employment generation for redeployees (laid-off public and private sector workers) and women's programs for credit, skills, and management training. The "vulnerable groups" targeted included the rural poor, especially in Northern and Upper Regions, and underemployed and unemployed persons in the urban informal sector, but excluded traders. A credit program for small and medium enterprises advertised by PAMSCAD in 1988 explicitly disqualified trade and primary agriculture, although the needs assessment expected these sectors to absorb the bulk of the redeployees (ILO/JASPA 1989). Since these were by far the largest income-generating activities open to women nationally, redeployed women found especially little support. This suggests that the reduction in hostile actions toward traders represents a strategic retreat under outside pressure rather than a basic reevaluation of their contribution to the economy.

Political Openings

If the economic policies of the late 1980s confirmed trends of greater exclusion, political developments during the same years mitigated the absolute exclusion of traders from previous government decision-making processes. The local government elections held in 1989, choosing members of the new district and municipal assemblies by open nonpartisan votes, marked a turning point. These assemblies had considerable authority in determining local development priorities, and some were reported embarking energetically on local needs assessment and planning exercises, although financial constraints have restricted their implementation capacity so far.

Candidates for district assemblies came from a much wider range of local society than previous district councillors or commissioners, not least because the number of members went up tenfold. Deliberations in these assemblies must be conducted in local languages, so that effective representation no longer requires good command of English, evidenced by high levels of formal education. Pre-election publicity stressed this change, leading to the election of substantial numbers of illiterate or semiliterate members and a sharp rise in the proportion of women. With trading such a major female occupation across the country, reports of women traders among the newly elected members seem plausible. In Kumasi, the yam *ohemma* won a seat in the Kumasi Municipal Assembly, describing herself to me as the member for Kumasi Central Market.

Formal consultation with traders' organizations also began, showing a new degree of recognition and acceptance of their legitimacy. Traders had already been invited to participate in a few official planning or advisory commissions by 1989. All the specific cases I could trace involved Accra traders, who could more easily attend such national meetings, invariably held in Accra. Although this bias skewed the representation of traders' interests to the government, it made a welcome change from the days when market organization in itself was equated with conspiracy. The constituent assembly convened in 1991 to draw up a new constitution invited representatives from a national market traders' organization among other national interest groups, in addition to the delegates elected by district assemblies.

Closer alliances between traders and their governments have certainly proven workable in the past. Precolonial African traders had tight working relationships with their local and confederacy rulers to promote both elite and popular interests. They cooperated through organized groups of traders for the seventeenth-century Akani captaincies and through personal clientage and chiefly offices for nineteenth-century Asante caravan and market traders. British traders and trading firms also counted on enthusiastic government support before, during, and after colonial rule. After independence, Ghanaian traders found their government willing to champion their cause against those from other African or Middle Eastern countries, but not very willing to challenge control by European firms or restrict control by state agencies. In more recent incidents, noneconomic considerations about trading practices took precedence over issues of economic efficiency, equity, or development. The foreign exchange allocation system and import licensing requirements provided opportunities for patronage and favored large, formalized organizations who had or could cultivate state links. Price controls for essential commodities had propaganda value, but they subsidized private sales to influential persons more often than regular supplies to ordinary citizens.

This destructive dynamic showed even more clearly when the government used attacks on market women to satisfy or divert the aspirations of citizens in other economic positions. Attempts to bypass traders in the distribution of consumer goods and local foodstuffs not only failed, but did serious damage to the marketplace system. Despite impressive resilience at the individual and system levels, significant long-term losses of capital and structural flexibility have accumulated. The violence and uncertainty left a legacy of distrust on both sides and a lack of confidence in economic policy in general. Overt hostility no longer guides official policy, and the vitriolic rhetoric of its verbal expression has faded away, but it remains unclear whether this phase represents a change of heart, a capitulation to external pressure, or a pragmatic "breather" on the road to socialism (Robotham 1988).

If the tentative trend toward more inclusive government structures continues, it will help to reintegrate market traders and other economic groups which, though centrally important as employment and distribution sectors, had been marginalized from national decision-making processes. Traders (and the women and illiterates with whom they substantially overlap) will have to preserve their representation in the higher levels of political participation as these evolve through the constitution and other national institutions. The degree of autonomy which local assemblies can effectively exercise in policy initiatives has yet to be demonstrated. Autonomy of nongovernmental organizations from control by the PNDC also raises concern, particularly since all women's groups were asked to affiliate with the December 31st

Women's Movement, led by Rawlings' wife, Nana Agyeman, and closely affiliated with the PNDC.

Whether this inclusion will result in any significant reorientation of economic policies that continue to marginalize traders economically depends on external as well as internal factors. The conditionalities of World Bank lending policy enforce rigorous limits on local autonomy, especially on the economic and commercial issues that most directly concern traders as traders. Their quest for a rising standard of living may contradict state interests when the state depends on external legitimacy—when the endorsement of the World Bank is more vital than that of local citizens.

While the policy hegemony of World Bank analyses seems firmly established for the time being, it is neither absolute nor homogenous. The level of financial backing the World Bank is prepared to provide has clearly not been enough on its own to maintain political stability. Public unrest that erupted in several countries affected by structural adjustment has been taken seriously by World Bank analysts (Nelson 1989). At the same time, verification of the lack of appreciable increases in the general standard of living has generated some contradictory statements and analyses from within the cadre of World Bank/IMF experts and a noticeable public relations problem. The widening arena of public political participation in Ghana has the potential for providing a more stable consensus on the procedures, if not the outcomes, of political consultation. It may also create the basis for a more effective future negotiating position with the Bank and other international agencies and lead to eventual redirection of national economic priorities.

11 SURVIVING THE PEACE

How far will the resources and strategies that carried traders through the dramatic challenges of the decade from 1975 to 1985 serve them in the years of quiet desperation following structural adjustment? Trends emerging in the first decade after this transition indicate the answer to this key question. They suggest traders will be able to consolidate their position within their local and national communities while those communities continue to lose ground internationally. Traders' efforts to survive and accumulate lead them to keep using secondary and innovative trading channels that improve overall economic resilience and autonomy at the local and national levels. Flexibility has been critical to surviving the erratic fluctuations of past crises, and it preserves a greater range of viable choices for facing continuing and future crises.

Historical continuity in Asante marketplace trade paradoxically proves a key aspect of its current capacity for rapid change. Significant aspects of contemporary traders' economic and political position result from either inheriting positions established by very different categories of traders in the past or being evicted from others in favor of state or international control. Stability, diversity, and transformation in local commercial patterns signal and represent the results of intense but often implicit negotiation over control of material and cultural resources. Repeated government attacks confirm the need to understand traders' social location within broad social processes like state formation, as well as their exact places inside the marketplace system itself, in order to comprehend the issues they confront today.

During the same decades that commercial activity and the Ashanti regional market trading system expanded most rapidly, from 1920 to 1960, traders' relative power, both as traders and as Asante women, shrank with respect to the overall social formation. Through worsening terms of trade and more subordinate commercial relations, market traders lost ground with respect to the growing European and Lebanese import firms. They also lost ground consistently to state institutions, controlled largely by Asante and coastal men, and to international and multinational corporations, controlled by foreign men. Trends in marital and kinship relations show striking parallels, remaining powerful but more unequal. Recognized matrilineage obligations remained strong and women's access to resources through them remained appreciable, but women's access to lineage-based labor and capital assistance weakened, along with their claims on the brothers and uncles who had supplanted them. As wives, their rights to personal and child support similarly eroded, giving a bitter taste to their de facto autonomy within marriage.

The overwhelming trend of marginalization within each interlocking system of domination distances Asante market women from the major centers of power in the Ghanaian economy. Pointing out this marginalization is not enough without considering its causes and implications. Changes both within and outside of their own sections of the economy, kinship structure, or political configuration reduce their access to major resources. Fewer relations crosscut those boundaries, fewer resources pass across those boundaries, and more resources remain on the far side of those boundaries. They have less access to the largest incomes, whether in their own right or through husbands, uncles, brothers, or other women. With the dwindling role played by electoral politics and chiefly office, in which their participation was already a minority, women have even less access than before to the officially recognized channels which continue to become more dominant economically, even after structural adjustment and privatization. The prevalence of individually negotiated relations at home and between and within enterprises instead of communal or joint relations kept the erosion of their power less explicit as well as less absolute.

Robertson and Etienne and Leacock conclude from similar examples that this deepening cleavage between women and power is typical of women's colonial experience, although Guyer's Cameroonian study shows rapprochement is also possible (Robertson 1984; Etienne and Leacock 1980; Guyer 1984; Stone 1988). The question remains, under what conditions, colonial or postcolonial, do these cleavages deepen? The direction of historical change depends partly on women's and juniors' access to indigenous institutions, that is, how much they are shut out of power positions within their kin groups, marriages, and home communities, and partly on their access to power in the new institutions, such as monogamous marriage, elective or military office, and educated professions, including the civil service.

Traders' multiple strategies can be interpreted as trying to turn this marginality into autonomy, as much as is possible. The current autonomy they demonstrate, whether as traders or as wives, represents a consolidation of their positions internal to one or another system. In each context, autonomy was to some degree forced by de facto exclusion from major arenas controlling social legitimacy and resources, usually while maintaining the fiction of continued access. Hostile government strategies can also be interpreted as consistently aiming to convert this autonomy back into marginality.

Traders' efforts to preserve their own autonomy inevitably make a positive contribution to the autonomy of the communities and nations they help constitute. In Ghana, market women keep open diverse economic channels that work to preserve some local resources, such as farmland, by supporting production for local consumption that slows their absorption into the global economy. At a time when major international economic institutions seem to be losing interest in Africa, this delaying function may yield significant medium- or long-term benefits by earning benign neglect. As a basically conservative process, however, it does not in itself explicitly challenge the deterioration in Ghana's economic position or generate the resource base needed to do so. At best, it preserves the distributive capacity that would be needed to support any local productive initiatives that might begin.

The record of Asante market women's concrete social action shows continual feedback between systems of gender, commercial, and political relations involving them, which validates treating these as linked but autonomous interlocking systems. Asante women and men have gained access to specific trading positions through political institutions, for example, local chiefships, in which gender and ethnicity are critical intervening variables. Gender affects access to capital and labor directly, through inheritance, kinship status, and marital duties that vary with sex. It also controls access indirectly through affecting factors like chiefly office and, later, Western education and military recruitment, that offer direct access. Wealth and political connections conversely play a part in access to gender-linked resources and liabilities, for example, through marriage.

Combining distinct methods of analysis for each of these diverse systems of relations does not deny their interpenetration in constructing concrete relations in history and contemporary life. It comes closer to taking these multiple interpenetrations for granted by treating them as a central and integral characteristic of all of the categories or groups defined by each system. In the case of Asante market women, using differentiated frameworks to analyze their gender, commercial, and state relations ends up clarifying rather than confusing the interaction between those relations. By establishing a more precise picture of the dynamics of each set of relations, it permits a more exact, coherent account of their actual interactions, on both historical and daily time scales, that makes more sense of the concrete historical processes of balancing distinct sources of support, whether these conflict, compensate, or reinforce each other.

Close attention to the actual processes of strategic interaction between domestic, commercial, and state political relations confirms the central importance of resources, such as capital and labor, and the relations that give access to those resources in generating and resolving the practical dilemmas of everyday life. Traders discussed transfers and tradeoffs between domestic, commercial, and state priorities in terms of calling in claims to resources and establishing relations affecting future claims, and they negotiated over the fulfillment of these claims the most intensely and repeatedly. In these negotiations, traders and their situational adversaries invoked diverse ideological values and rules to support conflicting claims, showing significant ideological interpenetration, but ideological issues did not give rise to such persistent contests themselves. For example, many women traders seemed to accept marital and kin-based ideologies of deference and availability without much challenge, solving the potential conflict by compartmentalizing those norms as not applicable to their market trading. Only when men who entered market trading invoked these norms directly in the market did this contradiction feel problematic. By contrast, keeping separate their material trading resources—money, goods, and labor time—demanded constant effort and discipline from market women, and frequently required resort to deception or argument.

Kumasi market traders' experience of mobilizing to meet daily or occasional challenges encourages a new perspective on the cohesion of heterogenous groups and social categories. Kumasi Central Market is a highly differentiated location, and these distinct, sometimes contradictory systems of domination appear clearly as differentiating principles within it. Social action reveals that the tightest ongoing links do not necessarily unite groups or categories definable as homogenous in their relations to their most salient resources. The commodity groups incorporate members with different and opposing economic interests as retailers, wholesalers, and travelers. Their strongest claim on each others' loyalty arises because of this heterogeneity, not in spite of it. Categories based primarily on capital levels obscure the power of the resources of information, location, and personal reputation that traders share and exchange on the basis of commodity and locality to form a solid basis for coordinated action. Shares in these resources may not be equal, but they establish common interests in maintaining these resources that build coherent links between traders at very different levels of the distribution chain. Traders continue to use these same resources daily, even after business successes or reverses have pushed them up or down the volume scale.

Internal diversity clearly strengthens these groups for weathering economic reverses and transformations, since it enables either individuals or the whole group to expand or contract their scale of operations, relocate, or switch between other kinds of options without writing off their collective investment in group formation. Because heterogenous groups unite around a given center without necessarily sharing the same relation to it, the group can readily reconfigure itself, with different internal divisions, even different boundaries for different purposes. Analyzing these dynamic shifts seems a more productive direction than substituting less active homogenous categories or homogenizing existing groups to fit a model. This flexibility derived from heterogeneity also strengthens Asante matrilineal ties, which remain undeniable without implying full commonality of interest or entitlement, or coresidence. Lineage members can hope to fulfill a variety of imaginable needs within the kin network, from influence to capital to cheap labor, because urban and rural residents, rich and poor kin all remain recognized members. Similar dynamics may appear in many aspects of contemporary life as homogenous groups are becoming rarer.

The preceding chapters did separate these systems analytically, looking in turn at each major set of relations which involve Asante market women from Kumasi Central Market in contests over relative power and control of resources. A final stocktaking of the resources left available to the traders from the interlocking effect of all these relations makes a useful beginning to an assessment of their capacity for continued individual and group action, but it can only begin such a consideration of their future. Extrapolating beyond past experience requires more detailed matching of traders' strategies with current trends in the patterns of control over crucial resources likely to affect the success or implications of those strategies in future years. This goal suggests a brief review now of the major findings of the preceding chapters to identify the primary contested resources around which each set of relations is constructed, with special attention to those drawn upon or implicated in struggles within other systems of domination. Historical trends in the control of those resources, within the limits of the evidence available, indicate how each system is likely to affect the others by diminishing or safeguarding resources essential to them. This serves as the basis for a projection of these directions of change into the near future.

Competition for relative position within the marketplace system takes pride of place as traders' most constant concern. Privileged or differentiated access to sources of supply and control over the timing of buying and selling were essential for raising profit levels in each transaction and for attracting and keeping steady customers among buyers and sellers. These commercial controls implied both capital and labor control—control of one's own labor, to be able to buy or sell at favorable times, and control of enough capital so that buying and selling were not strictly dictated by immediate cash flow. Aspects of marriage and kinship relating to property rights and labor claims obviously conditioned this autonomy, but so did less personal gender relations in wage employment and law. A trader's capital position determined her direct access to trading patterns and purchasing patterns that were more profitable. Certain commodities such as cloth or yams required more capital for entry and rewarded it with higher rates of return.

The history of capital erosion from past confiscations and current inflation established a trend toward greater polarization and a more external focus that allows fewer and fewer traders within Kumasi Central Market to enjoy these advantages. During the late 1980s, self-financing traders in increasing numbers dropped down into dependent positions on slightly wealthier traders who could advance them enough capital to keep going after a catastrophic loss or when they slipped gradually below the minimum, pinched between inflation and low profits. These wealthier traders held their own, but I did not see them expanding much, due to the shrinking overall demand. The only few commodities booming provided cheap substitutes for the newly poor, notably imported secondhand clothes.

Recent trends in customer relations both reflect and reinforce the movement toward greater concentration and dependency of traders in more commodities. The revival of imports at the expense of local craft and manufactured products shifts more weight to distribution channels already relatively centralized around limited points of supply. Traders in these commodities had not formed groups since the demise of the passbook system and depended heavily upon their official contacts. Deregulation legalized these relations, stabilizing and intensifying their hierarchical aspects by making dependence on a single supplier and semipermanent credit extension practical. The capital squeeze in imports reached an extreme after a rapid sequence of currency devaluations in the middle 1980s. As among traders in local produce, rising capital demands created by higher prices and transport charges forced many independent traders to contract for extra capital. These dependent relations not only reduced individual traders' incomes from a given volume of trade, but reduced their freedom of operation in making pricing and buying decisions, commodity choices, and traveling. These trends consequently increase the overall rigidity of the distributive system and reduce food security.

Commodity-based organizations have also been important elements in survival and accumulation, intervening in relations inside and outside of the marketplace to establish a favorable climate for traders' commercial activity. Group members enjoy direct, daily services that stretch their personal resources. For example, supplier credit enabled traders to bridge seasonal or individual shortages of capital and to keep them operating efficiently. Buyers could establish it individually, outside of the group context, but the dispute settlement and recordkeeping services offered by groups encouraged suppliers to advance larger amounts more readily. Retail and wholesale traders have divergent interests, which the largest commodity groups acknowledge organizationally, but they primarily act in concert.

The strength of the commodity group organizational network protected market institutions that benefitted group members and nonmembers alike within the same market. The wholesale yards founded as part of the process of group formation in the 1930s and 1950s were crucial for maintaining the fast pace and intense level of commercial activity that made Kumasi Central Market so desirable a location, and they could only be managed through some sort of consensual authority. Collective decision making and negotiation processes within the commodity groups enabled the market wholesale yards to maintain this high degree of central function despite the political and economic crises they endured in the 1970s and 1980s. These crises served as litmus tests for solidarity, revealing that the commodity group network created nuclei that could effectively catalyze more broadly based temporary coalitions under the right conditions. In times of crisis, even traders normally working outside of the commodity-group framework fell in behind these leaders. Ties of location drew together traders across commodity lines, in smaller markets or in marginal parts of Kumasi Central Market, to send emergency delegations to local chiefs or to face daily problems like recalcitrant customers or funerals.

Continuing polarization of wealthier and poorer traders may eventually undermine the current commodity group structure, although no signs of this were visible by 1990. The middle-level, financially autonomous traders have historically been the most active in commodity groups, as leaders and as followers, because both the wealthiest and the poorest traders yielded to the pressure of work. Dwindling numbers of traders with capital autonomy could either weaken the commodity group structure or transform it into a patronage-based system run by the few remaining large traders, comparable with the association of cloth traders in Lome, Togo (Cordonnier 1982). Because commodity groups function as pivotal organizational nodes that reach far beyond their membership, such a transformation would have repercussions throughout the Ghanaian economy.

These patterns of social cohesion suggest that Western European concepts of class do not transfer directly to Ashanti Region with much explanatory power. Close replicas of proletarian workers and bourgeois capitalists can be found in Ghana, but the wage worker and employer remain a small minority in the national economy, without the privileges derived from location in the industrial core (Amin 1980). The bulk of the Ashanti Region population farm and trade on their own accounts, so their relations to the means of production take different forms. Still, calling these relations precapitalist seems almost insulting, given that their homeland has been involved in international trade as long as Europe, so it has intimately shaped their relations of production, kinship, and chiefship for centuries. There may be places where rural periodic markets primarily mediate exchanges between subsistence producers, but southern Ghana is not one of them. The distinction between merchant and industrial capital seems less patronizing now that postindustrial capital often consolidates control through finance rather than ownership.

Mode of production analyses generally divide market traders into several categories according to their level of capital. The simple or petty commodity mode of production welcomes traders with independent capital, while those who use borrowed or advanced capital, and those with sufficient capital to advance or lend to others, join the capitalist mode of production as capitalists or workers. Analysts who classify traders as a whole as incipient capitalists or proletarians tend to focus on either the borrower or lender categories, dismissing the independents as a negligible transitional level. For one thing, these divisions gloss over commodity differences that seriously compromise them, since an independent trader in cassava may operate at the same level of capital as a dependent hawker in dried fish. Debates over whether market traders are a "true" bourgeoisie or a "disguised proletariat" also tend to bog down, as authors defend traders' honor as members of either category rather than debating their conditions of work. Each of these modes of production inevitably disqualifies so many traders, since they span such a wide range of capital levels, that subsequent analyses can say only a limited amount about traders' broader-based oppositional or collaborative stances.

Neither domestic nor petty or simple commodity modes of production address the commodity divisions that underlay so much of the social actions Kumasi traders actually undertook, whether in organized groups or outside of them. The simple commodity mode could be construed to distinguish sellers of locally produced items to local consumers from those selling imports, although most authors using it do not make this distinction. But modes of production give no help in talking about the differences between selling cooked food and funeral cloth, or between selling tomatoes and onions—the differences in unit value, dispersal of supplies or customers, and perishability that are so central to entry or trading decisions. In fact, using an overarching ideal type implicitly denies the significance of such variations.

Both single and multiple modes of production models also skip over structural divides in gender, ethnic, and state relations that show up as significant factors determining the commercial options traders can actually use, on either an individual or group basis. For example, a domestic mode of production makes no distinction between childcare by mothers or by older girl relatives. Kumasi women traders move heaven and earth to achieve this distinction, which is essential to their access to urban and commercial privileges within the market itself. Even though both strategies rely on unpaid female labor, market traders can pass on some of the benefits and security of their marketplace work on to kin who stay at home. Robertson depicts a Ga communal mode of production at home and in trading that merges the interests of participating female kin to a degree Asantes seem to have never accepted and which rules out the conditionality and individual agency so central to Asante ideas of kinship and marriage (Robertson 1984). The assimilation of domestic labor and self-employment in trading and farming into a single category also seems to contradict Asante traders' strenuous efforts to maintain strict temporal and resource separation between these activities. Ethnic and national identities, and concrete relations invoking them, have received even wider recognition as key mediators of commercial access.

Historical materialism or political economy analysis seems to provide more adequate structural openings for consideration of these multiple systems of domination. With its close attention to the relations of production and of access to the means of production, their interpenetrations can be incorporated directly into more general formulations from the beginning. Considering that these interpenetrations are an integral part of each system, even viewed separately, this analytic procedure would reflect more accurately the dynamics of any single system, such as the marketplace trading system. This system may be as stratified as a factory in access to resources and income, but stratified through different distinctions rooted in its different interpenetrations. Compiling details of historical sequences in the labor process and finance within the market echoes Marx's fascination with the technical and financial details of factory work in *Capital,* reproducing his method more closely than formalistic arguments, as Young noted with respect to gender (Young 1980).

Theoretical efforts to integrate race, class, and gender have also recommended adopting nominally distinct theoretical frameworks for each system. Smith and Hooks imply that a somewhat eclectic approach would retain the specific insights based on historical experience of each form of oppression, without forestalling more thorough cross-fertilization in the future (Smith and Smith 1981; Hooks 1984). Their goal of eventual synthesis favors, as potential collaborators, authors who already combine and use more than one diverse body of theory, and especially those doing so out of some concern for social action. Collins's matrix model was developed, in response to this mandate, with the kind of flexibility called for by contemporary politics and economics. Modifications to accommodate the specifics of Asante market women's situation actually amplify rather than vitiate its explanatory power. The set of axes of oppression she uses are the trinity of race, class, and gender primary in the United States and much of Western society, but they would always undergo mutual redefinition in any case in the distinct process of social construction of these categories in other specific historical and geographical locations. The horizontal dimension in her model can easily accommodate diverse principles of domination, defined as slightly or radically different directions or axes. The three vertical levels she posits as individual, community, and system also depend on historically specific social construction processes, so the height and permeability of their boundaries need to adjust to local alterations in the definitions of these categories in order to better explain how domination actually passes between levels under local conditions.

The race and gender axes of Collins's trinity remain recognizable in the Ghanaian context, although they require some adjustment. The global system of black/white racism definitely has its direct impact in Ghana, visible even within the limits of marketplace transactions, but primarily as an international phenomenon. This differs from its expression in other former colonies such as Kenya or the United States, where interracial relations were dominated by large-scale white settlement and/or black slavery. The intermediate racial categories of Lebanese and mulatto were also historically important in Ghana and particularly relevant to trade. Interethnic relations between specific groups and between Asantes and the broader ethnic categories of coastal and Northern peoples take up some of the social space organized by race relations in the United States, entering into relations of occupation, residence, migration, and intermarriage.

The local concept of gender is thoroughly and mutually embedded in other systems that are both material and ideological. The femaleness of women traders does not make them any less professional, any more than the maleness of male state traders or cocoa brokers dilutes their economic identity. Indeed, Ghanaian commentators understand this better than we do when they treat the market traders' femaleness as an integral part of their commercial identity. Occupational categories like market traders are constructed with intrinsic gender and ethnic marking, just as part of the definition of gender and ethnicity is their occupational or economic content. The resulting gender categories are as historically and culturally specific as the class categories just discussed at some length.

Western European models of gender relations have considerable impact in Ghana through church, school, business, and governmental institutions but operate in a different way than in industrial countries. Not only are these models external, minority patterns here, but the models themselves and the institutions that impose them assign a very different position to poor women of African descent living in Third World countries than to the white, middle-class, industrial position they invoke as normal. Anthropologists as divergent as Douglas, Poewe, and Amadiume have cautioned against extending assumptions rooted in Western middle-class experience about the nature and extent of female subordination and family stability into matrilineal and African contexts and proposed alternative assumptions placing a positive value on maternal and sibling-focused units (Douglas 1969; Poewe 1981; Amadiume 1987).

Approaches to marketplace trading systems which already integrate ethnicity and gender to some extent are understandably privileged with reference to Collins's overarching framework of an interlocking matrix of domination. Fortunately, many of the classic studies of market trading do focus on the intimate relation between commercial dominance and subordination and gender or ethnic position. For example, migrant Hausa in Nigeria maintain a sharply defined economic base by controlling the cattle trade, which is reinforced by their religious organization (Cohen 1969). Migrant Yorubas in Ghana also developed a commercial identity, with distinct role stereotypes for Yoruba men and women (Sudarkasa 1975). In the Philippines and Indonesia, immigrant Chinese dominate intercity vegetable trading, while indigenous villagers retain control of the lower levels (Davis 1973; Dewey

1962). Minority Ladinos in Bolivia and Guatemala use their privileged access to wholesale and transport facilities to entrench their economic and political dominance over the Indian and mestizo populations (Buechler 1973; Smith 1975). Seligmann analyzes the historically continuing stereotype of Peruvian "cholas" as market traders and aggressive women, as they mediated first biologically and then culturally and economically between Indians and Hispanic mestizos (Seligmann 1989, 704).

Several studies of food security collected by Guyer show that gender and ethnic diversification contribute to the flexibility and consequent reliability of African regional trading systems (Guyer 1987). For Malawi, Vaughan and Pottier provide evidence of the central importance of women's access to commercial networks to local resilience in the face of drastic economic challenge—both negatively when restraining their access exacerbated famine and, positively, when women expanded trade to compensate for the loss of male income from labor migration (Vaughan 1987; Pottier 1986).

Traders have just as specific and heterogenous a relation to their ethnicity as to their gender or class status. High chiefly offices and community and lineage leadership positions reserved for Asante women gave important legitimation to the prestige and effective authority of commodity group leaders. Ethnic precedents for women's leaders (shared by many other ethnic communities in Ghana) cleared the way ideologically for acknowledgment of their standing by other traders, including men, and by other community leaders as representatives of women traders. Market leaders had invoked chiefly connections on rare occasions, for example, to defend their trading positions as local subjects from inroads by foreign Gao traders or traders from other towns in Ghana. They could not draw on the full protective authority of customary law because precolonial Asante had no true precedent for them in a specifically female market leader comparable with Yoruba or Igbo offices in Nigeria. Their ambiguous connection to Asante chiefship had advantages and disadvantages in public negotiations, leaving them vulnerable to government attack as upstarts but also partly insulated from the strong discipline still effective within the chiefly hierarchy. Open acknowledgment of market leaders by government revived slowly in the later 1980s after a deep trough in the previous ten years.

Asante ethnic identity also gives these market women fuller access to Kumasi and its corresponding urban/rural dominance. In their ethnic capital, Asantes have definite advantages in access to city resources such as market stalls and to local housing and jobs needed to maintain family residence there. Specific family connections brought disproportionate numbers of traders to live in Kumasi during their childhood years, either with their parents or fostered with other relatives. Growing up in Kumasi gave them familiarity with key urban institutions and personnel. Some traders had gained commercial connections to supply areas for agricultural crops or imported goods by growing up elsewhere, but these were directly useful only within commodity limits. Members of other ethnic groups originating to the south and north of Asante also lived and grew up in Kumasi, so they also could move into family-held housing, jobs, and market stalls but in fewer numbers and less desirable locations. The continuing multiethnic population in Kumasi now brings more non-Asantes to maturity with urban childhoods, although ethnic and family-based discrimination persist.

The economic dominance of urban over rural areas and of Kumasi over smaller towns in its surrounding hinterland makes the geographical centrality of Kumasi Central Market traders an important power base in the regional system. The largest Kumasi wholesalers, without rivals in smaller towns, reap disproportionate benefit from its central position, but even poorer retailers enjoy definite advantages over town and village market women of equivalent size. They have access to more complete information on regional supplies and demand, stable demand from urban consumers, extended seasonal supplies from a range of source areas, lower prices for distant or urban products, and better informal credit and other services. The external pressure of dominant international economic systems that penetrate Ghana mainly through urban contacts continually reinforces rural/urban power differentials.

The connection between concrete market locations and major trading relations or distributional tasks must be a flexible enough analytic link to accommodate historical transformations in which substantial continuity in both trading locations and trading tasks coexists with radical changes in the exact combinations found of locations with tasks and who performs them. Over time, the economic relations and institutions of trading appear much more stable than the spatial configuration, and stable precisely because their locational attachments can be shifted when the match is no longer appropriate. A repertoire of trading roles that includes some handed down with minor modifications over centuries has apparently been redistributed through a variety of central places and even reassigned to different ethnic and gender categories of traders without losing the storehouse of skill, experience, and contacts that enable their current practitioners to juggle them successfully. For example, the assembling of bulk quantities of farm produce for urban consumers has moved to different parts of Kumasi Central Market, to other city or village markets, and to nonmarket locations, responding to seasonal and historical shifts in the balance of power between the social categories involved in those relations. These include economic categories, like farmers and truck drivers, ethnic categories like Asantes, Northerners, or "French" immigrants, and men and women traders enmeshed in different contexts of family responsibilities and earning alternatives. This flexibility in no way undercuts the power of the connection between place and commercial function; changes are so hotly contested and so necessary precisely because the connection is powerful.

The layout and condition of national and regional transportation networks has been an important determinant of the strength of Kumasi's position within the national central place system. A twentieth-century cycle of expansion through the 1950s, degeneration through about 1985, and recent revival has confirmed and undermined Kumasi traders' regional dominance in a complex pattern. When transport improves, as now, Kumasi traders use it extend their range into more distant supply regions and to bypass local periodic markets in rural districts within their hinterland. During the same periods, however, traders from coastal cities (especially Accra) also begin to bypass Kumasi and buy directly from rural or small town sources within its hinterland and further north. Northern and small-town Asante traders can also travel south more easily through Kumasi to the Accra-Tema region to buy imports and local manufactures directly. Under the decentralizing trend when transport deteriorated, Kumasi traders reverted to gathering supplies from district and interregional periodic markets open to rural producers and traders, but this trend likewise protected Kumasi's intermediary position between the coastal cities and the North.

The recent road and rail rehabilitation intensifies the structural potential for dependency both between traders and between locations with its priority on trunk roads used for long-distance travel. The shift toward longer-distance, more direct farmgate buying can be expected to produce fewer, larger traders. Such segments of the distribution network currently and historically become concentrated in fewer hands, since the economics of truck transport favor traders that can fill one. Larger Kumasi traders will benefit, but smaller rural and Kumasi-based traders who rely on public and semi-public transport on periodic market days will be squeezed out. The transition from retailing to wholesaling through occasional traveling may come to require a stint as an agent or dependent of an established trader. In addition, by restoring only one North-South route, road repairs intensify the dominance of Accra over Kumasi and Kumasi over the North. Traffic from both Cape Coast and Takoradi must now pass east through Accra to reach Kumasi rather than going more directly north on separate trunk roads. Trade continuing farther north must follow one route through Kumasi via Sunyani, since the two alternatives are now impractical for commercial traffic.

Comparative studies associate this dendritic pattern with more rigid, hierarchical commercial relations and external dominance. Local transport conditions alone are unlikely to fundamentally change the size of the rural/urban gap, but they will probably reshape it to bring the extremes into greater contact. The farmer will face more powerful traders from more distant major cities in person at the farmgate. The alternative of selling in local markets where she can sell or observe herself or patronize relatives could dwindle away. By 1990, rural periodic markets were perceptibly losing their agricultural bulking functions and beginning to serve only for small consumer purchases. Fewer successive intermediaries may bring higher farm prices, however, at least in areas with good enough road access to provide competition.

Gender relations specific to traders' ethnic, state, marital, and lineage positions are also implicated in all of their accumulative processes by mediating their access to capital and skill resources that significantly affect their relative position within the market. It is impossible to participate in skill or wealth-based privileges except through gendered structures of inheritance and family resource allocation, which govern nonmaterial resources such as knowledge and education as well as money. Second- and third-generation educated families more often educated both boys and girls, raising their daughters with the literacy and other skills necessary to hold waged or salaried jobs. Elite kinship, marriage, and school networks more often included well-placed officials helpful as sources of supply for imports, allocations, licenses, and protection. Women's jobs generally paid less, however, than jobs their male relatives held, so their savings could not provide as substantial levels of commercial capital. More girls attend school now, but the shortage of semiskilled employment for them under current economic conditions leaves this gap intact. Nonelite families also hold knowledge and skills relevant to trading specific commodities and especially to craft production. Ethnically specific gender relations determined how much women participated in trade and learned from natal or marital family members.

The growing impoverishment of Asante men does not erase this presumption of favoritism. Men have been moving back into trading in larger numbers since the 1970s, although they still prefer to operate from store fronts rather than in the market itself, because of closure of higher-status options. Young men often operate market stalls while ostensibly saving capital for the equipment for entry into a more acceptably male occupation, such as auto repair or even tailoring. These gender boundaries, although blurred in individual cases, reconfirm the difference in capital status between acceptably male and female occupations. Although some female traders achieve or inherit ownership of stores or power machinery, or equivalent capital levels, the majority do not approach the levels considered minimally respectable for an Asante man.

The prosperity of Ashanti Region, compared with Ghana's other ethnic homelands, meant some Asante kin groups controlled substantial financial resources from cocoa farms and chiefly prerogatives that could benefit women members. Matriliny gives women a secure and partly independent position as lineage members. Ordinary women gain access to housing, land, and the labor of kin. Although mothers were expected to earn their own incomes and contribute to their children's upbringing, they also had recognized claims on senior kin and affines for subsistence support and sponsorship. Principles governing lineage loans and inheritance gave female kin legitimate but not guaranteed access to these lineage resources. Asante women are entitled under state-recognized customary law to control their own property and current incomes and to inherit from close female kin. Asante women share this financial autonomy, based on fiscal separation between spouses, with patrilineal women in West Africa (Sudarkasa 1973 [Marshall 1964]; Hill 1969).

Implementation of lineage and marital responsibilities creates more decided advantages for men. Capital loans and gifts reported by traders showed that more male traders had received such transfers from women kin than vice versa. Recent trends in inheritance practice seem also to increase the frequency of men inheriting both male and female lineal property. Although property rights for wives are increasing, at least in principle, fewer women reportedly establish legal marriages. In recent decades, women's claims on brothers and uncles have seriously weakened without compensatory increases in their effective claims on husbands and fathers.

Studies of market women elsewhere in West Africa and in Latin America draw a connection between independent trading by women and independence within the household (Sudarkasa 1973 [Marshall 1964]; Chinas 1973). Spending substantial amounts of time in the market implies more flexible household arrangements than average, and successful trading implies sufficient personal authority to allocate time and money without constant reference to others. Market trading also establishes social relations and income sources for a woman outside of the home, which clearly increases her capacity for autonomous social action. Whether this represents a positive or negative phenomenon has long been subject to argument. Nadel (1952) considers personal independence a negative side effect of trading. Katzin and Mintz consider Caribbean women's trading a positive adjustment to de facto financial independence resulting from family impoverishment and breakdown (Katzin 1959; Mintz 1971).

Women traders' unpaid domestic work responsibilities seriously compromise their control of their own labor. Cooking and childcare conflict directly with trading in this huge urban market, and the expansion of distant residential suburbs only separates home and market more completely. Domestic work can be embedded in either marital or lineal relations, depending on the woman's sexual and residential arrangements. Asantes have unusually complex domestic options, including duolocal marriage. This means that marital relations need not interrupt or replace those with adult kin or neighbors and gives women scope to manipulate household composition by supporting younger or poorer kin to substitute for them in domestic work.

More ambivalence and tension was currently expressed by Kumasi market women about marriage than parenthood. Marriage makes it more risky to relax cooking standards; on the other hand, conjugal coresidence and formal marriage reportedly increase the regularity of fathers' contributions, which leaves more money available to hire unrelated maids. Current declines in marriage rates may thus decrease domestic work pressures on women while increasing their financial pressures. The distinction between married and unmarried mothers may become more significant than was formerly the case in this matrilineal context, with reduced access for women to lineal and personal wealth. Asymmetry between marriage partners would then be likely to increase, along with co-residence and jointness. Cases from the market could not confirm such trends, but researchers studying such matters closely in other contexts report various indications of tighter marital relations and more sharing of spouses' resources (Mikell 1989; Tashjian 1991).

Deepening gender gaps in wealth and income are likely to make Asante women more dependent on male income as their access to that income becomes more precarious. After several decades when wages and salaries lost ground rapidly to business and self-employment incomes through inflation, structural adjustment policies have halted and partly reversed this trend. Restored salary and wage differentials especially benefit the professional classes, still overwhelmingly male. Stagnant real wages for minimum-wage workers reduce the capacity of the ordinary husband to fully support his wife and children, regardless of his inclination. Investment has buttressed the historically favored position of the mining, timber, and cocoa farming sectors, also male-dominated, compared with food farming and processing, predominantly female-dominated. This encourages families to give further precedence to the enterprises, jobs, and schooling of brothers and husbands, since those of women and girls now appear as bad investments.

Relations between women traders and the state constantly address both their gender and commercial identities. Explicit, impersonal gender norms affect interactional expectations and political representation directly, and the educational and professional qualifications required imply them indirectly. Relations between specific regimes and economic institutions they do not control directly, such as the marketplace system, have ranged from cordial and supportive to hostile and destructive over the years. Traders' intimacy with or estrangement from specific regimes makes the state willing to defend or attack their position. This alliance depends on gender as much as class, as the disparate treatment of traders and lorry drivers in 1979 showed. Official media condemned wealthy traders because they were insubordinate women insisting on earning as much as men, because they were uneducated people daring to earn as much as many professionals, and because they were lazy urbanites refusing to farm and contribute to national development in a less challenging way. Gender-based hostility featured prominently in the propaganda campaigns generating widespread public support for government attempts at price control and direct distribution from the 1960s through the 1980s.

Direct government actions failed to achieve much direct control of distribution, but they were much more effective in changing the ethnic division of labor in commerce. Largely by intent, colonial and national governments broke down barriers between ethnic groups now part of Ghana, succeeding except when those had strong commercial foundations. Successive governments have reserved commercial roles for their constituents: first for precolonial Asantes, then for expatriate British, and now for Ghanaian citizens. The government policies that most sharply affected the gender assignment of commercial roles were educational, industrial, and political policies which deepened and rigidified a gender division of labor in market and extra-market trade that was largely new to Asante. Market trade was not only feminized, but more subordinated and isolated within the national and international economy. When recent governments acted to intensify and enforce this gender isolation of women, fervent popular support suggested a substantial economic foundation for it.

Although popular, these polemics and policies had surprisingly little effect in terms of expelling women from the trading roles in question, as the government could not provide a viable alternative. Direct distribution of farm produce from farmers to consumers failed despite its popularity with urban consumers and with farmers when first promoted, because it could not provide a viable commercial network. State distribution personnel lacked the skills and resources to judge quality, estimate supplies, and price fresh produce, or to store and transport it without massive losses through spoilage and theft. Neither farmers or consumers could afford to rely on them, so both continued to patronize the marketplace system.

At present, two trends in public ideology seem to be canceling each other out: the typical trader and the typical official sound equally selfish and equally helpless to change the basic course of events. The legitimacy of market trading and of state commercial intervention both depend on their efficacy in securing urban food supplies and providing income for local citizens. Serious impairment of those functions undermines the economic credibility of either the state or the marketplace system. Food security in Ghana now depends as much on changes in the international economy as on actions by either local traders or the national government. Mergers and declining terms of trade affect the ability of workers to provision themselves at world prices and the ability of governments to pay for imports of staple foods and other perceived necessities. While some aspects of market trading mitigate the effects of this decline, they cannot reverse it enough to reemerge as saviors of the nation.

Current state policies, though no longer openly hostile to market trade, place the highest priority on opening the economy to international commerce and finance. The Structural Adjustment Programme of the mid-1980s was explicitly aimed at integrating the Ghanaian economy more tightly into the world market and has succeeded to a considerable extent. This privileges those sectors of production and commerce with international connections, which are distributed outside of the marketplace system through state agencies or corporate firms, mainly located in major cities. These same sectors of production and distribution are the most predominantly male, so gender balance also deteriorates. The renewed focus on cocoa and gold under SAP confirms the marginalization of the marketplace system along with other economic sectors aimed at an internal market. Major legal barriers between marketplace trade and other locally oriented sectors have been removed, but at the expense of a sharper dichotomy between all of them and the export-oriented sectors. The growing polarization between rich and poor populations also hurts the marketplace system by restricting the buying power of the lower- and middle-income groups that patronize it; the rich shop more often in department stores, boutiques, or abroad.

Political trends at the moment seem to offer market traders mixed blessings. Direct repression of trading activities and groups stopped abruptly with deregulation under IMF pressure, and state hostility has visibly moderated. Ideas about the parasitic nature of trading seem to persist to some extent, for example, in the explicit disqualification of trading from loans designed to ease the social impact of adjustment. Renewed support for the Ghana Food Distribution Corporation indicates that attracting rural suppliers and urban consumers away from market traders remains a long-term goal.

An ambitious program to decentralize responsibility for development planning and implementation has moved forward, although within the constraints of shrinking financial and policy autonomy at the national level. Local governments get the power to tax just as economic measures undermine the income generation potential of their constituents. Certainly market traders were among the sophisticated but uneducated citizens solicited to run in 1989 rural and urban local government elections. They participated freely as voters and as candidates, alongside farmers and others who accept them more as equals. It is not yet clear how much decisions taken at those levels will generate social resources valuable for trading. Accra market traders are occasionally included in consultations on national economic policy decisions. The incorporation of women's groups into the December 31st Women's Movement keeps tighter control on their actions and any outside funding but does promise some legitimacy, patronage, and an audience at the top. So far, market women's groups have not enlisted, although individual traders join as members of their other groups.

Contemporary trends in movement along the gender, state, and commercial axes show some commonalities that suggest patterns of coherent change. Tensions between internal and external orientations, between decentralization and concentration of control, between inclusion and autonomy recur on each axis but are played out in different ways. The polarization between rich and poor and between local and export production revives solidarity across local occupational boundaries, but potentially undermines solidarity within market commodity groups. The widening gender gap within each wealth and occupational category, another axis of polarization, seems to intensify both dependency and integration within marriages. With less segregation of traders from official national economic and political life comes renewed marginalization of marketplace trade itself and the nation at large. Centralization trends through international finance and in the national economy, including within the marketplace network, contradict political decentralization programs. In each context, integration at a microlevel accompanies more separation and steeper hierarchies on a broader basis. Does this mean that greater microlevel separation would reduce some of these broader hierarchies?

Thinking about the implications of these trends for the long-term capacity for social action of women traders from Kumasi Central Market immediately calls for finer distinctions than these rough dichotomies. At what point or under what conditions does autonomy become marginalization or exclusion? When does incorporation mean inclusion and integration, and when does it mean subordination and cooptation? When does increased access to resources bring crippling reciprocal claims on one's own? To some extent market women are constantly answering these questions for themselves in pursuing their various strategies in marital and kinship relations, commercial relations and state politics.

Looking at the actual course of historical transformation and contestation makes a convincing argument for stepping even farther away from dichotomous analyses. Remembering the structural potential of the multiple interlocking systems of domination helps to explain traders' complex and sometimes contradictory strategies as they manipulate and seek power within all of their relations. An institution offering protection against one kind of oppression often reinforces vulnerability to another, giving an ambiguous, double-edged quality to strategic decisions. Domestic substitution, which accommodates to women's subordination within marriage, makes more sense as a positive and valued choice in combination with its importance for commercial position and accumulation. The historical process of mutual construction or mutual constitution means that these different principles of power systems are mutually implicated at all locations, not just at key focal points of intersection. At some of these locations they may exert dominance in opposite directions, while at others they reinforce each other. In this model, the interlocking itself is central to the overall historical process, so the strong interference effect it generates becomes revealing rather than confusing.

Strategies of the dominant group show these interactive effects as clearly as do the resistance strategies of their situational subordinates.

Initiatives of resistance in terms of one identity can be effectively countered or repressed by invoking another, as when traders protesting antipopulist commercial regulations can be dismissed as unruly, selfish women. It is the gender attached to a class or racial identity that gives some women or men the authority to represent their class oppressively and the resources to represent it effectively. The question of whether gender, race, ethnicity, or economic position is the primary identity or the primary form of oppression dissolves into the question of when each aspect of identity or subordination is activated or invoked.

In the same way, the conflict between analyzing international or local levels of domination dissolves in light of their thorough interpenetration. International forces clearly participated in constructing the relative power of traders in imports and foodstuffs on the most local level. Local efforts in smuggling cocoa or evading price controls could also add up to enough leverage to affect international power equations. Different levels constantly interacted, as often reinforcing as contradicting each other. Most important, the specific social actions of contest that had significant impact at one level often were the same actions used to establish or contest control at a higher or lower level as well. For example, the national government enforced border controls in an attempt to retain access to foreign exchange transfers, among other goals. Kumasi traders who bought from smugglers supported those channels in order to have enough goods to stay in business, but their actions joined with others' to undermine the financial stability of the regime and its ability to insist on strict foreign exchange controls despite World Bank disapproval.

A focus on the actual forms and issues of contest also reframes the question of whether traders should be classified as fighting within or against the system. The gap between directly and indirectly controlled economic sectors is simultaneously shored up and bridged by the marketplace system, along with other unofficial avenues of exchange and production. Rather than having to choose between autonomy outside of or dependency within the international system, traders themselves were constantly struggling to be more autonomous within, not outside of, a capitalist profit framework. They tried to preserve the widest possible range of options in order to simultaneously gain more access to central resources and accept less central control.

The odds were against West African market women winning such contests in either absolute or relative terms. They and their communities were in fact falling further behind in an increasingly polarized economy. But winning or losing is not the only significant aspect of such contests. Equally important are the conditions that let some team members come out well ahead of others, either at the individual or at the international level. The political and economic forces that created and sustained diversity within the market affected all of the traders, winners and losers. Struggles over more and less direct control established levels of dependence between traders within the marketplace system while they were precisely the kind of marketing issues that historically have left traders in one country of Africa or one region of Guatemala more autonomous and in another more dependent, with significant implications for the position of their communities within the world system.

The same factors generating tension and transformation in the marketplace relations centered in Kumasi are at work in wider arenas. Strong parallels with Kumasi Central Market can be seen in many parts of the West African forest and coastal zones, and the broader issues of food security, commercial regulation, and economic growth are being debated in similar terms even on other continents. Traders' historically specific strategies and experiences are not presented as generalizable to these others or even to themselves today. These constitute only partly a voluntary strategy and partly an involuntary position, neither of which are strictly replicable. Readers working within other locations should consider rather whether similar factors and interlocking dynamics appear in their local context and what impact similar policies or actions are likely to have under their distinctive local conditions.

What view of power relations is given by the overarching historical trend identified above, of traders' increasing separation from male relatives and husbands, from Asante leaders and from state political centers? It seems clear that their isolation was not entirely voluntary, just as their subsequent and unstable partial reincorporation is not entirely voluntary. If recent indications of a turn toward economic and political reintegration in a context of increasing polarization prove accurate, what has that phase of separation won for traders as traders and in their other identities? Was it a dead end? an escape hatch?

As a temporary expedient, separation bought some benefits by buying time, helping to maintain community survival and resources through a period of intense economic and political pressure, until conditions stabilized somewhat. Market traders were able to accumulate some financial and organizational resources and preserve others by transforming them, but this was not tolerated indefinitely. The strategy of separation, never proof against the benefits of individual connections, also could not protect traders against overtly confrontational state initiatives. Eventually they and their resources were reintegrated forcibly to a limited extent as an alternative to virtual destruction.

Although their autonomy decreased at that point, the material and social resources market traders brought with them mitigated the terms of their reintegration. Far from atomized or destitute people, traders could maintain some individual and group effectiveness within the new framework of local government. Just as the new institution of rural work brigades for young men established a new basis for gender privilege in land access, market trading organizations might eventually be transformed into a new basis for gender or commercial resistance (Mikell 1989). Government leaders currently attempt to use both kinds of groups to establish tighter control of their members, while the members also are trying to use them to forestall direct control and gain greater access to official patronage and other resources.

Since recent political trends have this double-edged character, it is hard to judge their eventual impact on traders from this early stage of implementation. The now-growing importance of local governments compared to national government under decentralization measures certainly allows for more participation by individual traders in town and district assemblies. At the same time, greater integration into international economic networks under structural adjustment reduces the effective autonomy of national governments, making catching up with that level less significant. Some aspects of those international liberalization measures provide further weapons to less privileged economic actors. The free market ideology promulgated by international donor agencies to reduce the power of national authorities versus international firms also restricts the activity of states in directly interfering with the actions of lower levels of the economy, such as traders. Leading traders can invoke the rhetoric of entrepreneurship presently favored, even when external donors do not explicitly extend that rhetoric to cover small local businesses, let alone market stalls.

It remains to be seen whether traders can successfully use the space they may have gained from national governments to protect some autonomy of economic action in the face of international pressures, which would benefit the national economy as a whole. The accelerating loss of interest in African states and economies by Western industrial countries and corporations, as prospects in Asia and Eastern Europe take center stage, makes this paradoxically seem more likely. Their delaying tactics of separation may have preserved economic indigestion into a historical moment when their national assets are much less strenuously desired by international- and national-level actors. Participation by leading traders in nationally sponsored political institutions may therefore not carry the same degree of risk of either total cooptation of their organizations or violent repression now that traders perceived during the 1950s and 1960s.

International domination remains secure; the exclusion of market traders from access to major national financial and material resources shows no signs of receding from its high water mark. Within these rigid resource perimeters, subject to continued surplus extraction through worsening terms of trade, the deregulation of internal trading is unlikely to trigger miraculous economic growth. It is more likely to allow women and their dependents to stay alive, but this continued subsistence or survival capacity should not be taken for granted, considering the living standards typical of the current economic crisis. The efforts of market traders to preserve their livelihoods also keep alive for impoverished producers and consumers the option of producing for local consumption and purchasing at prices retaining some perceptible relationship to local buying power. It may be that continued survival for themselves, their families, and their communities is the most crucial as well as the most realistic contribution a resilient marketplace system can be expected to make.

APPENDIX: Survey Methodology

The survey of Kumasi Central Market was carried out on seven consecutive weekdays in July 1979. Interviewers were recruited from the sixth form of a secondary school and a teacher training college in Kumasi. They received three days of training by experienced interviewers Mr. Pappoe and Mr. Ndagu of the Department of Building and Planning, University of Science and Technology, Kumasi. The training and most of the interviews were conducted in Twi, but Ga, Ewe, and Hausa speakers were also available. Matching interviewers to respondents by gender or ethnicity proved effective in disarming suspicion. For example, a Hausa-speaking girl covered the sections where Northern men predominated, and the single boy interviewed Southern craftsmen. Interviewers worked in pairs, for security and ease of supervision, from 9 A.M. to 4 P.M. over seven working days. All completed questionnaires were reviewed the same day for omissions and inconsistencies, and mistakes were corrected the following day by the same interviewer.

The survey area covered the central portion of the market (about three-fourths of its surface area), the part with a stable enough daily population for reliable sampling. Based on a preliminary census, I decided on a sample of one in twenty traders, which yielded 618 responses. Craftsmen and women who had stalls there were included, since they sold as well as worked there. In the wholesale yards, where transient traders conduct their business and leave, and the squatter areas, where the character and population of the area changes several times daily, I considered that a one-time survey would not yield meaningful results. Hawkers without fixed market locations were also not included, for the same reason and because they had appeared only peripherally in the participant observation work which informed the survey questions. About two hundred distinct commodities were sold by those interviewed, including local food crops, packaged and prepared foods, and traditional and modern nonfood items, both imported and locally produced. The complete list is reproduced below.

The questionnaire was designed and tested to use traders' habitual terms and concepts in discussing the subjects of interest. The complete questionnaire is reproduced in my Ph.D. dissertation (Clark 1984). Sensitive and dangerous topics were avoided, because traders tended to either provide misleading information or break off the interview when these topics were introduced directly. Unfortunately, this made questions on current prices, debts, and income levels impossible. The logical flow of thought from one question to the next and the clear arrangement of questions and answers on the page proved important during pilot testing to the accuracy of responses to particular questions about training, partners, customers, etc. Forms also provided space for recording anecdotal material from the many respondents who volunteered more detailed and personal information than requested. Interviews averaged fifteen to twenty minutes, depending on the complexity of each respondent's personal and commercial life. Interviewers were instructed to allow the trader to continue selling as necessary during the interview.

The degree of traders' cooperation with the survey was remarkable considering the upheavals and tensions of the year in question. The survey week luckily fell in a lull between two periods of intense intervention by the Armed Forces Revolutionary Council (AFRC) government. One serious problem fortunately never materialized; public announcements that secondary students indistinguishable from my interviewers would be sent into the markets as price control enforcers never produced any action. According to visual evidence, the population of traders had returned virtually to normal that week; in fact, numbers turned out slightly higher than predicted from my preliminary count several months earlier, before the AFRC took power. Stocks and turnover remained below previous levels, but the accuracy of the survey did not depend on these directly. Interviewers reported refusals or hesitations to participate at once, which a visit from myself or an interviewer from their own ethnic group almost always resolved. Only three in the sample firmly refused, one because her child was ill; they were replaced by adjoining traders.

The same political crises that presented unusual research opportunities during most of the ten years I was returning to Ghana also placed practical and ethical restrictions on the topics and methods I could include. The undoubted presence of price control undercover agents in the market meant that any attempt on my part in 1979 to collect prices and calculate profit margins openly would have been fruitless and would most likely have scared off traders permanently. Even if successful, such work might have attracted undue government attention to my notes for use in possible prosecutions. This situation ruled out addressing some interesting questions about relative pricing and profit levels which required statistical treatment. As it was, ideas that I might be some sort of government agent took several months to dwindle away and occasional individual fears surfaced even during the survey. Fears of such connections about strangers were revived during renewed government attacks during the period from 1981 to 1984 and took years to die down. Only on the 1990 visit did it seem that public hostility had lapsed long enough that such statistical analyses might again be feasible.

So many distinct forms and degrees of government intervention appeared during the research periods that there was hardly a break between them. The survey week luckily fell during such a break, when the numbers of traders had recovered to approximately normal levels. Although business was still slow, the sample of traders still has considerable validity. If the survey had included questions on their levels of profit or even volume for that week, the answers would have been virtually useless.

The erratic nature and frequency of political and economic crises also would have undermined the general applicability of profit and price information collected during this period, making it even less worth the risk of collecting it. Pricing from month to month often did not follow normal seasonal levels, but reflected political as well as climatic fluctuations. Transport disruption due to gasoline shortages and military harassment influenced relative pricing between markets in irregular ways. It was consequently hard to tell what factor was responsible for recorded variations in profit levels and price differentials. Traders had to speculate, sometimes with little information, on the future level and kind of enforcement, so their pricing and search behavior did not always correspond either to actual or usual price differentials. Profit levels varied so erratically that one set of calculations could not be extrapolated plausibly to generate annual or seasonal profits for normal years, which were quite rare.

Commodities Represented in Survey Sample

Perishable Food

tomatoes	meat	yams
onions	crabs	plantain
pepper	eggs	fowls
fish	okra	palm nuts
shrimp	garden eggs	snails
corn dough	cassava	dried meat
cassava dough	kontomire	

Nonperishable Food

ginger	corn	egushi
oil	cassava flour	dry ground okra
salt	millet	corn flour
groundnut paste	gari	dried snails
shea butter	rice	cereals
beans	sorghum	pepre seeds
groundnuts	dry ground pepper	cattle
seeds for sauce	dry ground tomato	

Imported Food

baking powder	essence	maggi cubes
curry	vinegar	cloves
yeast	provisions	spices
nutmeg	coffee	

Craft Products

bags	chewing stick	wooden masher
kente cloths	bicycle repair	laundry starch
sandals and shoes	sews caps	corn husks
ice water	beads	bones
baskets	paper bags	sieves
mirrors	animal skin	lime
goldsmith	coalpot	calabashes
seamstress	adinkra cloth	fufu
handwoven cloth	native medicine	ampesie
hair plaiting	pots	bread
purses	hair dye	kenkey

Industrial Products

records
cassettes
materials
weaving thread
weaving machines
cloth
soap
towels
stationery
shoe materials
cosmetics
spare parts
drugs
bed sheets
mosquito coil
thread
combs
blue
cutlasses
carbide
wires
iron tools
plates
needles
blankets
enamelware
goggles
cotton wool
pencils
balloons
safety pins
animal products
jewelry
powder
plastic ware
locker cloth covers
plastic bags
cooking utensils
farming equipment
ribbons
calico cloth
hardware
chalk
envelopes
incense
hinge
hair thread
lamp shades
pins
bowls
ladles
aluminum products
ceramics
rope
zippers
hairnets
hair straightening cream
hair perming cream
boxes
brushes
drinks
yarns
sacks
saucepans
potash
sulfur
watch straps
steel wool
used bags
tobacco
variety

Clothing

brassieres
headkerchiefs
blouses
nightgowns
pants
dresses
children's dresses
school uniforms
underwear
shirts
t-shirts
singlets
vest
used clothing
trousers
shorts
belts
housecoats
tailor
clothes
hats
northern dress
veils
scarves

REFERENCES

Abu, Katherine Church
1983 "The Separateness of Spouses: Conjugal Resources in an Ashanti Town." In *Female and Male in West Africa,* edited by Christine Oppong. London: Allen and Unwin.

Addo, Alice
1980 Conversation with author, February.

Addo, Nelson O.
1969 "The Alien's Compliance Law of 1968." *Ghana Journal of Sociology,* vol. 1.

Aidoo, Ama Ata
1970 *No Sweetness Here.* London: Longmans.

Akoto, Baffour
1980 Interview with author, January.

Alexander, Jennifer
1987 *Trade, Traders and Trading in Rural Java.* New York: Oxford University Press.

Allman, Jean M.
1989 "Gender and Social Change in Colonial Asante; Reflections on 'Spinsters,' 'Concubines,' and 'Wicked Women.'" Paper presented at 32d Annual Meeting of African Studies Association in Atlanta.
1993 *The Quills of the Porcupine.* Madison: University of Wisconsin Press.

Amadiume, Ifi
1987 *Male Daughters, Female Husbands: Gender and Sex in African Society.* London: Zed Books.

Amin, Samir
1974 *Accumulation on a World Scale.* New York: Monthly Review Press.
1980 *Class and Nation.* New York: Monthly Review Press.
1990a *Delinking.* London: Zed Press.
1990b *Maldevelopment.* London: Zed Press.

Amonoo, E.
1974 "The Flow and Marketing of Agricultural Produce in the Central Region with Special Reference to Cape Coast." Cape Coast: University of Cape Coast Centre for Development Studies. Research Report Series no. 15.

van Appeldoorn, G. J.
1972 *Markets in Ghana: A Census and Some Comments;* Vol. 2: *Regions in the Southern Half of Ghana.* Technical Publication

Series no. 17; Institute of Statistical, Social and Economic Research: University of Ghana, Legon.

Aptheker, Bettina
1989 *Tapestries of Life: Women's Work, Women's Consciousness, and the Meaning of Daily Experience.* Amherst: University of Massachusetts Press.

Arhin, Kwame
1971 "Atebubu Markets: 1884–1930." In *The Development of Indigenous Trade and Markets in West Africa,* edited by C. Meillasoux. Oxford: Oxford University Press.
1975 "Some Asante Views on Colonial Rule as Seen in the Controversy Relating to Death Duties." *Transactions of the Historical Society of Ghana* 15 (1): 63–84.
1979 *West African Traders in the Nineteenth and Twentieth Centuries.* London: Longman.
1986 "A Note on the Asante Akonkofo: A Non-literate Sub-Elite, 1900–1930." *Africa* 56 (1): 25–31.
1988 "Trade and Accumulation in Asante in the Nineteenth Century." Paper given at African Studies Association meetings.

Arnould, Eric
1986 "Merchant Capital, Simple Reproduction and Underdevelopment: Peasant Traders in Zinder, Niger Republic." *Canadian Journal of African Studies* 20 (3).

Austin, Gareth
1988 "Class Struggle and Rural Capitalism in Asante History." Paper presented at African Studies Association meetings.

Awe, Bolanle
1977 "Reflections on the Conference on Women and Development: 1." *Signs* 3, no. 1: 314–16.

Babb, Florence
1987 "Marketers as Producers: The Labor Process and Proletarianization of Peruvian Market Women." In *Perspectives in U.S. Marxist Anthropology,* edited by David Hakken and Johanna Lessinger. Boulder: Westview Press.
1988 "'From the Field to the Cooking Pot': Economic Crisis and the Threat to Marketers in Peru." In Clark 1988.
1989 *Between Field and Cooking Pot.* Austin: University of Texas Press.

Baker, Pauline
1974 *Urbanization and Political Change: The Politics of Lagos.* Berkeley: University of California Press.

Barnes, Sandra
1986 *Patrons and Power: Creating a Political Community in Metropolitan Lagos.* Bloomington: Indiana University Press, in association with the International African Institute.

Barrett, Michelle, and Mary McIntosh
1979 *The Anti-Social Family.* London: Verso.

Bates, Robert H.
1981 *Markets and States in Tropical Africa.* Berkeley: University of California Press.

Bauer, P. T.
1954 *West African Trade.* Cambridge: Cambridge University Press.

Beals, R.
1975 *The Peasant Marketing System of Oaxaca, Mexico.* Berkeley: University of California Press.

Beckett, W.
1944 *Akokoaso: A Survey of a Gold Coast Village.* London: Percy, Lund, Humphries & Co.

Beckman, Bjorn
1985 "Neo-Colonialism, Capitalism and the State in Nigeria." In *Contradictions of Accumulation in Africa,* edited by Henry Bernstein and Bonnie Campbell. Beverly Hills: Sage.

Beecham, John
1968 *Ashanti and the Gold Coast.* London: Dawsons of Pall Mall. (Reprint of 1841 edition.)

Beechey, Veronica
1979 "On Patriarchy." *Feminist Review* 1: 66–82.

Bennholdt-Thomsen, Veronika
1981 "Subsistence Production and Extended Reproduction." In *Of Marriage and the Market,* edited by Kate Young, C. Wolkowitz, and R. McCullagh. London: CSE Books.
1984 "Towards a Theory of the Sexual Division of Labour." In *Households and the World Economy,* edited by Joan Smith, I. Wallerstein, and H.-D. Evers. Beverly Hills: Sage.

Berger, Iris
1986 "Sources of Class Consciousness: South African Women in Recent Labour Struggles." In *Women and Class in Africa,* edited by Berger and Claire Robertson. New York: Africana.

Bernstein, Henry
1986 "Capitalism and Petty Commodity Production." *Social Analysis* no. 20.

Bevin, H. J.
1956 "The Gold Coast Economy about 1880." *Transactions of the Gold Coast and Togoland Historical Society* 6:73.

Bleek, Wolf
1974 *Marriage, Inheritance and Witchcraft.* Leiden: Afrikastudiescentrum.
1976 "Sexual Relationships and Birth Control in Ghana: A Case Study of a Rural Town." Uitgave 10, Afdeling Culturele

Anthropologies, Antropologisch-Sociologisch Centrum, University of Amsterdam.

Bohannon, Paul, and George Dalton, eds.
1962 *Markets in Africa.* Evanston: Northwestern University Press.

Boissevain, Jeremy, and Hanneke Grotenberg
1989 "Entrepreneurs and the Law: Self-employed Surinamese in Amsterdam." In *History and Power in the Study of the Law,* edited by June Starr and Jane Collier. Ithaca, NY: Cornell University Press.

Boissevain, Jeremy, and J. Clyde Mitchell
1973 *Network Analysis in Human Interactions.* The Hague: Mouton.

Bromley, Ray J.
1974 *Periodic Markets, Daily Markets and Fairs: A Bibliography.* Monash Publications in Geography, no. 10. Melbourne, Australia.
1979 "Introduction." In Bromley and Gerry, eds. 1979.

Bromley, Ray, and Chris Gerry, eds.
1979 *Casual Work and Poverty.* New York: John Wiley.

Bromley, Ray, and Chris Gerry
1979 "Who Are the Casual Poor?" In Bromley and Gerry, eds. 1979.

Brown, Elsa Barkley
1989 "African-American Women's Quilting: A Framework for Conceptualizing and Teaching African American Women's History." *Signs* 14 (4): 921–29.

Brown, James W.
1972 "Kumasi 1898–1923: Urban Africa During the Early Colonial Period." Ph.D. diss., University of Wisconsin, Madison.

Brown, Judith K.
1970 "A Note on the Division of Labor by Sex." *American Anthropologist* 72: 1073.

Buechler, Hans, and Judith-Maria Buechler
1977 "Conduct and Code: An Analysis of Market Syndicates and Social Revolution in La Paz, Bolivia." In *Ideology and Social Change in Latin America,* edited by June Nash and Juan Corradi. New York: Gordon & Breach.

Buechler, Judith-Maria
1973 "Peasant Marketing and Social Revolution in the State of La Paz." Ph.D. diss., McGill University, Montreal.

Chayanov, A. V.
1966 *The Theory of Peasant Economy.* Homewood, IL: Irwin.

Chazan, Naomi
1983 *An Anatomy of Ghanaian Politics: Managing Political Recession 1969–1982.* Boulder, CO: Westview Press.

Chinas, Beverly
1973 *The Isthmus Zapotecs: Women's Roles in Cultural Context.* New York: Holt, Rinehart and Winston.
1976 "Zapotec Viajeras." In *Markets in Oaxaca,* edited by Scott Cook and Martin Diskin. Austin: University of Texas Press.

Christaller, Walter
1966 *Central Places in Southern Germany,* translated by C. W. Baskin. Englewood Cliffs, NJ: Prentice-Hall.

Clark, Gracia
1984 "The Position of Asante Market Women in Kumasi Central Market, Ghana." Ph.D. diss., University of Cambridge.
1988 (ed.) *Traders Versus the State: Anthropological Approaches to Unofficial Economies.* Boulder, CO: Westview Press.
1989a "Money, Sex and Cooking: Manipulation of the Paid/Unpaid Boundary by Asante Market Women." In *The Social Economy of Consumption,* edited by Benjamin Orlove and Henry Rutz. Lanham: University Press of America.
1989b "Food Traders and Food Security." In *The Political Economy of African Famine: The Class and Gender Basis of Hunger,* edited by R. E. Downs, D. O. Kerner, and S. P. Reyna. London: Gordon and Breach.

Clark, Gracia, and Takyiwaa Manuh
1991 "Women Traders in Ghana and the Structural Adjustment Programme." In *Structural Adjustment and African Women Farmers,* edited by Christina Gladwin. Gainesville: University of Florida Press.

Cohen, Abner
1969 *Custom and Politics in Urban Africa: A Study of Hausa Migrants in Yoruba Towns.* Berkeley: University of California Press.

Collins, Patricia Hill
1989 "The Social Construction of Black Feminist Thought." *Signs* 14 (4): 745–73.
1990 *Black Feminist Thought.* Boston: Unwin Hyman.

Comaroff, John
1980 "Brideswealth and the Control of Ambiguity in a Tswana Chiefdom." In *The Meaning of Marriage Payments.* London: Academic Press.

Combahee River Collective
1981 [1977] "A Black Feminist Statement." In *This Bridge Called My Back,* edited by Cherrie Moraga and Gloria Anzaldua. New York: Kitchen Table Press.

Coquery-Vidrovitch, Catherine
1976 "The Political Economy of the African Peasantry and Modes of Production." In *Political Economy of Contemporary Africa,*

edited by Peter Gutkind and Immanuel Wallerstein. Beverly Hills: Sage.

Cordonnier, Rita
1982 *Femmes Africaines et Commerce.* Paris: Orstom.

Curtin, Philip
1984 *Cross Cultural Trade in World History.* New York: Cambridge University Press.

Davis, William
1973 *Social Relations in a Philippine Market.* Berkeley: University of California Press.

de Lauretis, Teresa
1986 *Feminist Studies, Critical Studies.* Bloomington: Indiana University Press.

Delphy, Christine
1977 *The Main Enemy: A Materialist Analysis of Women's Oppression.* London: Women's Research and Resources Centre.

De Marees, Pieter
1985 [1602] *Chronicle of the Gold Coast of Guinea,* translated in 1985 by A. Van Dantzig and Adam Smith. Oxford: Oxford University Press.

De Soto, Hernando
1989 *The Other Path: The Invisible Revolution in the Third World.* New York: Harper and Row.

Dewey, Alice G.
1962 *Peasant Marketing in Java.* New York: Free Press of Glencoe.

di Leonardo, Michaela
1991 *Gender at the Crossroads of Knowledge: Feminist Anthropology in the Postmodern Era.* Berkeley: University of California Press.

Dill, Bonnie Thornton
1979 "The Dialectics of Black Womanhood." *Signs* 4: 543–55.

Douglas, Mary
1969 "Is Matrilineality Doomed?" In *Man in Africa,* edited by Mary Douglas and Phyllis M. Kaberry. London: Tavistock.

Drake, St. Clair, and Leslie Lacy
1966 "Government Versus the Unions: The Sekondi-Takoradi Strike, 1961." In *Politics in Africa: 7 Cases,* edited by Gwendolyn Carter. New York: Harcourt, Brace and World.

Dwyer, Daisy, and Judith Bruce, eds.
1988 *A Home Divided: Women and Income in the Third World.* Stanford: Stanford University Press.

Dzidzienyo, Stella
1978 "Housemaids." Paper presented at Conference on Women and Development, National Council on Women and Development, Accra, Ghana, September 4–8.

Eades, Jeremy
1979 "Kinship and Entrepreneurship among Yoruba in Northern Ghana." In Shack and Skinner 1979.
1983 *Transformation and Resiliency in Africa.* Washington: Howard University Press.

Eames, Elizabeth A.
1988 "Why Women Went to War: Women and Wealth in Ondo Town, Southern Nigeria." In Clark 1988.

Edholm, Felicity, Olivia Harris, and Kate Young
1977 "Conceptualizing Women." *Critique of Anthropology* 3 (9–10): 101–30.

Eisenstein, Zillah
1979 *Capitalist Patriarchy and the Case for Socialist Feminism.* New York: Monthly Review Press.

Ekejuiba, Felicia
1966 "Omu Okwei, the Merchant Queen of Ossomari." *Nigeria,* vol. 90.
1991 Conversation with author, November.

El Saadawi, Nawal, Fatima Mernissi, and Mallica Vajarathon
1978 "A Critical View of the Wellesley Conference." *Quest: A Feminist Quarterly* 4, no. 2 (Winter): 101–8.

Ensminger, Jean
1990 "Co-opting the Elders: The Political Economy of State Incorporation in Africa." *American Anthropologist* 92 (3).

Etienne, Mona, and Eleanor Leacock
1980 *Women and Colonization: Anthropological Perspectives.* New York: Praeger.

Ewusi, Kodwo
1984 "The Dimensions and Characteristics of Rural Poverty in Ghana." ISSER Technical Publication no. 43. Legon: ISSER.

Fortes, Meyer
1949 "Time and Social Structure: An Ashanti Case Study." In *Social Structure,* edited by Fred Eggan and Meyer Fortes. London: Oxford University Press.
1969 *Kinship and the Social Order.* London: Routledge and Kegan Paul.
1970 *Time and Social Structure.* London: Athlone Press.

Freeman, T. B.
1967 *Travels and Life in Ashanti and Jaman.* London: Cass.

Friedmann, Harriet
1980 "Household Production and the National Economy: Concepts for the Analysis of Agrarian Formations." *Journal of Peasant Studies* 7: 158–84.
1986 "Patriarchal Commodity Production." *Social Analysis* no. 20.

Gaisie, S. K., and K. T. de Graft-Johnson
1976 *The Population of Ghana.* United Nations: CICRED.

Geertz, Clifford
1963 *Peddlers and Princes.* University of Chicago Press.

Geertz, Clifford, Hildred Geertz, and Lawrence Rosen
1979 *Meaning and Order in Moroccan Society.* Cambridge: Cambridge University Press.

Geiger, Susan
1987 "Women in Nationalist Struggle: TANU Activists in Dar es Salaam." *International Journal of African Historical Studies* 20 (1): 1–26.

Gerry, Chris
1979 "Small-scale Manufacturing and Repairs in Dakar: A Survey of Market Relations Within the Urban Economy." In Bromley and Gerry, eds. 1979.

Ghana Census
1960 Statistical Office, Government of Ghana, Accra.
1970 Statistical Office, Government of Ghana, Accra.

Gore, Charles
1978 "Food Marketing and Rural Development: A Study of an Urban Supply System in Ghana." Ph.D. diss., Pennsylvania State.
1979 "Periodic Markets and Pricing Efficiency: The Case of Adawso Market and the 'Otwetiri Eleven.'" In *Market-Place Exchange—Spatial Analysis and Policy,* edited by Robert H. T. Smith and Erdmann Gormsen. Mainz: Geographisches Institut Der Johannes-Gutenberg-Universitat.

Granada Television International
1983 *Asante Market Women.* London: Granada. Television show/video in the *Disappearing World* series.

Green, Reginald
1981 "Magendo in the Political Economy of Uganda: Pathology, Parallel System or Dominant Sub-mode of Production?" IDS Discussion Paper #164. Brighton: University of Sussex.

Grier, Beverly
1989 "Pawns, Porters and Petty Traders: Women in the Transition to Export Agriculture in Ghana." Boston University African Studies Center Working Papers, no. 144.

Guyer, Jane I.
1984 *Family and Farm in Southern Cameroon.* Boston: Boston University, African Studies Center.
1987 (ed.) *Feeding African Cities.* Bloomington: Indiana University Press.

Handwerker, W. P.
1973 "Kinship, Friendship and Business Failure Among Market Sellers in Monrovia, Liberia, 1970." *Africa* 43: 288.

Hansen, Karen Tranberg
1988 "The Black Market and Women Traders in Lusaka, Zambia." In *Women and the State in Africa,* edited by Jane L. Parpart and Kathleen A. Staudt. Boulder, CO: Lynne Rienner.

Harrop, Sylvia
1964 "The Economy of the West African Coast in the 16th Century." *Economic Bulletin of Ghana* 8: 15.

Hart, Keith
1973 "Informal Income Opportunities and Urban Employment in Ghana." *Journal of Modern African Studies* 11: 61–89.
1982 *The Political Economy of West African Agriculture.* Cambridge: Cambridge University Press.
1985 "Some Contradictions in Postcolonial State Formation: The Case of West Africa." *Cambridge Anthropology* 10 (3).

Hill, Polly
1963 *Migrant Cocoa Farmers of Southern Ghana.* Cambridge: Cambridge University Press.
1966 "Landlords and Brokers." *Cahiers d'Etudes Africaines* 6: 349.
1969 "Hidden Trade in Hausaland." *Man,* vol. 4 (September).

Hodder, H. B., and U. I. Ukwu
1969 *Markets in West Africa: Studies of Markets and Trade among the Yoruba and Ibo.* Ibadan, Nigeria: Ibadan University Press.

Holy, Ladislav
1986 *Strategies and Norms in a Changing Matrilineal Society: Descent, Succession and Inheritance among the Toka of Zambia.* Cambridge: Cambridge University Press.

Hooks, Bell
1981 *Ain't I a Woman.* Boston: South End Press.
1984 *Feminist Theory from Margin to Center.* Boston: South End Press.
1989 *Talking Back: Thinking Feminist, Thinking Black.* Boston: South End Press.

Hopkins, Anthony G.
1965 "Economic Aspects of Political Movements in the Gold Coast and Nigeria, 1918–39." *Journal of African History* 7: 133.
1973 *An Economic History of West Africa.* New York: Columbia University Press.

Howard, Rhoda
1978 *Colonialism and Underdevelopment in Ghana.* London: Croom Helm.

Hull, Gloria T., Patricia Bell Scott, and Barbara Smith, eds.
1982 *All the Women Are White, All the Blacks Are Men, but Some of Us Are Brave: Black Women's Studies.* Old Westbury, NY: Feminist Press.

Hyden, Goran
1980 *Beyond Ujamaa in Tanzania: Underdevelopment and an*

Uncaptured Peasantry. Berkeley: University of California Press.

1988 "Preface." In *Approaches That Work in Rural Development,* edited by John Burbidge. Munich: K. G. Saur.

Hymer, Stephen

1970 "Economic Forms in Pre-Colonial Ghana." *Journal of Economic History* 30: 33.

(ILO/JASPA) International Labor Organization

1989 "From Redeployment to Sustained Employment Generation: Challenges for Ghana's Programme of Economic Recovery and Development." Addis Ababa: ILO.

Jain, Devaki

1978 "Can Feminism Be a Global Ideology?" *Quest: A Feminist Quarterly* 4, no. 2 (Winter): 9–15.

Jellinek, Lea

1974 "The Life of a Jakarta Street Trader." In *Third World Urbanization,* edited by Richard Hay, Jr., and Janet Abu-Lughod. Chicago: Mararoufa Press.

Johnson, Marion

1966 "The Ounce in 18th-Century West African Trade." *Journal of African History* 7: 197.

Johnson-Odim, Cheryl

1991 "Common Themes, Different Contexts: Third World Women and Feminism." In *Third World Women and the Politics of Feminism,* edited by C. T. Mohanty, A. Russo, and L. Torres. Bloomington: Indiana University Press.

Kahn, Joel

1980 *Minangkabau Social Formations.* Cambridge: Cambridge University Press.

Katzin, Margaret

1959 "The Jamaican Country Higgler." *Social and Economic Studies* 8: 421.

Kay, G. B.

1972 *The Political Economy of Colonialism in Ghana.* Cambridge: Cambridge University Press.

Kea, Ray

1982 *Settlements, Trade and Politics in the 17th-Century Gold Coast.* Baltimore: Johns Hopkins Press.

Kerner, Donna

1988 "'Hard Work' and Informal Sector Trade in Tanzania." In Clark 1988.

Kitching, Gavin

1980 *Class and Economic Change in Kenya: The Making of an African Petite-Bourgeoisie.* London: Methuen.

1985 "Politics, Method and Evidence in the 'Kenya Debate.'" In

Contradictions of Accumulation in Africa, edited by Henry Bernstein and Bonnie Campbell. Beverly Hills: Sage.

Laslett, Peter
1972 Edited and introduction by, for *Household and Family in Past Time.* Cambridge: Cambridge University Press.

Lawson, Rowena
1960 "Marketing Constraints in Traditional Economies." *British Journal of Marketing.*

Lessinger, Johanna
1988 "Trader vs. Developer: The Market Relocation Issue in an Indian City." In Clark 1988.

Lewin, Thomas
1974 "The Structure of Political Conflict in Asante, 1875–1900." Ph.D. diss., History, Northwestern University.
1978 *Asante Before the British.* Lawrence: Regents Press of Kansas.

Lewis, Barbara
1976 "The Limitations of Group Activity among Entrepreneurs: The Market Women of Abidjan, Ivory Coast." In *Women in Africa: Studies in Social and Economic Change,* edited by Nancy Hafkin and Edna Bay. Stanford, CA: Stanford University Press.
1982 "Fertility and Employment: An Assessment of Role Incompatibility among African Urban Women." In *Women and Work in Africa,* edited by Edna Bay. Boulder, CO: Westview Press.

Leys, Colin
1975 *Underdevelopment in Kenya: The Political Economy of Neo-Colonialism.* London: Heinemann.
1978 "Capital Accumulation, Class Formation and Dependency: The Significance of the Kenyan Case." *Socialist Register* 1978:241–66.

Little, Kenneth
1973 *African Women in Towns: An Aspect of Africa's Social Revolution.* Cambridge: Cambridge University Press.

Little, Peter
1989 "Traders, Brokers and Market 'Crisis' in Southern Somalia." Paper presented at American Anthropological Association Meeting, Washington, DC.

Lorde, Audre
1984 *Sister Outsider.* Trumansberg, NY: Crossing Press.

McCall, Daniel
1956 "The Effect on Family Structure of Changing Economic Activities of Women in a Gold Coast Town." Ph.D. diss., Columbia University.
1962 "The Koforidua Market." In Bohannon and Dalton, eds. 1962.

McCaskie, Tom
1980a "Office, Land and Subjects in the History of the Manwere Fekuo of Kumasi: An Essay in the Political Economy of the Asante State." *Journal of African History* 21.
1980b Conversation with author, August, Cambridge, UK.
1983 "Accumulation, Wealth and Belief in Asante History I: To the close of the Nineteenth Century." *Africa* 53 (1): 23–43.
1986 "Accumulation, Wealth and Belief in Asante History II: The Twentieth Century." *Africa* 56 (1): 3–23.

McCorkle, Constance
1988 "'You Can't Eat Cotton': Cash Crops and the Cereal Code of Honor in Burkina Faso." In *Production and Autonomy: Anthropological Studies and Critiques of Development,* edited by J. Bennett and J. Bowen. Monographs in Economic Anthropology, no. 5. Lanham, MD: University Press of America.

MacCormack, Carol P.
1982 "Control of Land, Labor and Capital in Rural Southern Sierra Leone." In *Women and Work in Africa,* edited by Edna Bay. Boulder, CO: Westview Press.

McDonough, Roisin, and Rachel Harrison
1978 "Patriarchy and Relations of Production." In *Feminism and Materialism,* edited by Annette Kuhn and Anne Marie Wolpe. London: Routledge and Kegan Paul.

MacGaffey, Janet
1986 "Women and Class Formation in a Dependent Economy: Kisangani Entrepreneurs." In Robertson and Berger, eds. 1986.
1987 *Entrepreneurs and Parasites: The Struggle for Indigenous Capitalism in Zaire.* Cambridge: Cambridge University Press.
1989 "Clientage in Trade: Predictability and Organization in Zaire's Crisis." Paper presented at African Studies Association annual meeting.
1991 *The Real Economy of Zaire: An Anthropological Study.* Philadelphia: University of Pennsylvania Press.

McGee, T. G.
1973 "Hawkers in Hong Kong." University of Hong Kong, Centre of Asian Studies, Occasional Papers and Monographs, #17.

Mackintosh, Maureen
1989 *Gender, Class and Rural Transition: Agribusiness and the Food Crisis in Senegal.* London: Zed Press.

Maier, Donna
1983 *Priests and Power.* Bloomington: Indiana University Press.

Manuh, Takyiwaa
1985 "Women and Their Organization During the Convention Peoples' Party Period in Ghana: 1951–1966." Unpublished ms.

1991 Conversation with author, November.
1992 Conversation with author, November.

Marshall, Gloria (now Niara Sudarkasa)
1962 "The Marketing of Staple Foods in Nigeria." Conference Proceedings, Nigerian Institute of Social and Economic Research.
1964 "Women, Trade and the Yoruba Family." Ph.D. diss., University of Michigan. Republished as Sudarkasa 1973.

Mbilinyi, Marjorie
1985 " 'City' and 'Countryside' in Colonial Tanganyika." *Economic and Political Weekly* 20 (43): WS-88.
1989 " 'This is an Unforgettable Business': Colonial State Intervention in Urban Tanzania." In *Women and the State in Africa,* edited by Jane Parpart and Kathleen Staudt. Boulder, CO: Lynne Rienner.

Meillasoux, Claude
1975 *Femmes, Greniers et Capitaux.* Paris: Maspero.

Mies, Maria
1982 *The Lace Makers of Narsapur: Indian Housewives Produce for the World Market.* London: Zed Press.
1986 *Patriarchy and Accumulation on a World Scale: Women and the International Division of Labour.* London: Zed Press.

Mies, Maria, Veronika Bennholdt-Thomsen, and Claudia von Werlhof
1988 *Women: The Last Colony.* London: Zed Press.

Mikell, Gwendolyn
1984 "Filiation, Economic Crisis and the Status of Women in Rural Ghana." *Canadian Journal of African Studies* 18:195–218.
1985 "Expansion and Contraction in Economic Access for Rural Women in Ghana." *Rural Africana* 21 (Winter).
1986 "Ghanaian Females, Rural Economy and National Stability." *African Studies Review* 29 (3).
1987 "Theory vs. Reality in Contemporary African Kinship Dynamics: The Akan of Ghana." Paper presented at African Studies Association meetings, Denver, Colorado, November.
1989 *Cocoa and Chaos in Ghana.* New York: Paragon House.

Mintz, Sidney
1957 "The Role of the Middleman in the Internal Distribution System of a Caribbean Peasant Economy." *Human Organization* 15 (no. 2): 18–23.
1961 "Pratik: Haitian Personal Economic Relations." In Proceedings of the 1961 Annual Spring Meeting of the American Ethnological Society in Seattle.
1971 "Men, Women and Trade." *Comparative Studies in Society and History* 13: 247.

Mintz, Sidney, and Eric Wolf
1950 "An Analysis of Ritual Co-Parenthood (Compadrazgo)." *Southwestern Journal of Anthropology* 6: 341–65.

Mitchell, J. Clyde
1956 "The Kalela Dance: Aspects of Social Relationships among Urban Africans in Northern Rhodesia." Rhodes-Livingston Papers, no. 27.

Mohanty, Chandra
1988 "Under Western Eyes: Feminist Scholarship and Colonial Discourses." *Feminist Review* 30.

Moore, Sally Falk
1986 *Social Facts and Fabrications: Customary Law on Kilamanjaro 1880–1980.* Cambridge: Cambridge University Press.

Moser, Caroline
1978 "Informal Sector or Petty Commodity Production: Dualism or Dependence in Urban Development?" *World Development* 6 (Sept/Oct.).
1980 "Why the Poor Remain Poor: The Experience of Bogota Market Traders in the 1970s." *Journal of Interamerican Studies and World Affairs* 22 (3): 365–87.

Muntemba, Maud Shimwaayi
1982 "Women and Agricultural Change in the Railway Region of Zambia: Dispossession and Counterstrategies." In *Women and Work in Africa,* edited by Edna Bay. Boulder, CO: Westview Press.

Nadel, S. F.
1952 "Witchcraft in Four African Societies." *American Anthropologist* 54: 18.

Nader, Laura
1988 "Post-Interpretive Anthropology." *Anthropological Quarterly* 61 (4): 149–53.

Natrass, Nicoli Jean
1987 "Street Trading in Transkei—A Struggle Against Poverty, Persecution and Prosecution." *World Development* 15 (7).

Nelson, Joan, ed.
1989 *Fragile Coalitions.* Oxford: Transaction Books.

Newbury, Catherine W.
1988 *The Cohesion of Oppression: Clientship and Oppression in Rwanda 1860–1960.* New York: Columbia University Press.

Ngole, Jean-Pierre
1986 "Social Relations and Group Identity among Women Fishsellers in the Congo." *Women's Studies International Forum* 9 (no. 3): 287–93.

Ogunsanwo, Adeyinka Theresa
1988 "The Development and Growth of Dugbe Market, 1910–1965." Master's thesis, University of Abidan.

Okali, Christine
1983 *Cocoa and Kinship in Ghana: The Matrilineal Akan of Ghana.* London: Kegan Paul International.

Okeyo, Achola Pala
1981 "Reflections on Development Myths." *Africa Report* (March/April): 7–10.

Ong, Aihwa
1987 *Spirits of Resistance and Capitalist Discipline: Factory Women in Malaysia.* Albany: State University of New York Press.
1988 "Colonialism and Modernity: Feminist Representations of Women in Non-Western Societies." *Inscriptions,* no. 3–4.

Oppong, Christine, ed.
1974 *Marriage among a Matrilineal Elite.* Cambridge: Cambridge University Press.
1983 *Female and Male in West Africa.* London: Allen and Unwin.

Osirim, Mary
1989 "Gender, Entrepreneurship and the Family: A Case Study of Southwestern Nigeria." Paper presented at African Studies Association annual meetings, Atlanta.

Owusu, Maxwell
1992 Conversation with author, May.

Parpart, Jane
1986 "Class and Gender on the Copperbelt: Women in Northern Rhodesian Copper Mining Communities, 1926–1964." In Robertson and Berger, eds. 1986.

Peattie, Lisa
1987 "Anthropological Perspectives on the Concepts of Dualism, the Informal Sector, and Marginality in Developing Countries." *International Regional Science Review* 5:1.

Pellow, Deborah, and Naomi Chazan
1986 *Ghana: Coping With Uncertainty.* Boulder, CO: Westview Press.

Poewe, Karla O.
1981 *Matrilineal Ideology: Male-Female Dynamics in Luapula, Zambia.* New York: Academic Press.

Polanyi, Karl
1957 "The Economy as Instituted Process." In *Trade and Markets in the Early Empires,* edited by Karl Polanyi, C. Arensburg, and H. Pearson. New York: Aldine.

Pottier, Johan
1986 *Migrants No More.* Bloomington: Indiana University Press.

Priestley, Margaret
1969 *West African Trade and Coastal Society.* Oxford: Oxford University Press.

Rattray, Robert Sutherland
1923 *Ashanti.* Oxford: Clarendon Press.
1927 *Religion and Art in Ashanti.* Oxford: Clarendon Press.
1929 *Ashanti Law and Constitution.* Oxford: Clarendon Press.

Ravallion, Martin
1987 *Markets and Famines.* New York: Oxford University Press.

Rey, Pierre-Philippe
1979 "Class Contradiction in Lineage Societies." *Critique of Anthropology* 13–14: 16.

Richards, Audrey
1940 *Land, Labour and Diet in Northern Rhodesia.* Oxford: Oxford University Press.

Robertson, A. F.
1976 "Rules, Strategies and the Development Committee." *Community Development Journal* 11: 185.

Robertson, Claire C.
1983 "The Death of Makola and Other Tragedies: Male Strategies Against a Female-Dominated System." *Canadian Journal of African Studies* 17 (3): 469–95.
1984 *Sharing the Same Bowl?: A Socioeconomic History of Women and Class in Accra, Ghana.* Bloomington: Indiana University Press.

Robertson, Claire C., and Iris Berger, eds.
1986 *Women and Class in Africa.* New York: Africana.

Rodney, Walter
1972 *How Europe Underdeveloped Africa.* London and Dar es Salaam: Bogle L'Ouverture and Tanzania Publishing House.

Roseberry, William
1983 *Coffee and Capitalism in the Venezuelan Andes.* Austin: University of Texas Press.
1986 "The Ideology of Domestic Production." *Labour, Capital and Society* 19: 70–93.
1988 "Political Economy." *Annual Review Anthropology* 17: 161–85.

Robotham, Don
1988 "The Ghana Problem." *Labour, Capital and Society* 12 (1): 12–35.

Russell, Diane
1989 "The Outlook of Liberalization in Zaire: Evidence from Kisangani's Rice Trade." Working Papers in African Studies, no. 139, Boston University.

Sacks, Karen
1989 "Toward a Unified Theory of Class, Race, and Gender." *American Ethnologist* 16 (3): 534–50.

Sahlins, Marshall
1972 *Stone Age Economics.* Chicago: Aldine-Atherton.

Sanday, Peggy
1973 "Towards a Theory of the Status of Women." *American Anthropologist* 75: 1682.

Sanjek, Roger
1990 "Maid Servants and Market Women's Apprentices in Adabraka." In *At Work in Homes: Household Workers in World Perspective,* edited by Sanjek and Shellee Colen. American Ethnological Society Monograph Series, no. 3. Washington, DC.

Sariri, Madhu
1979 "Urban Planning, Petty Trading, and Squatter Settlements in Chandigarh, India." In Bromley and Gerry, eds. 1979.

Saul, Mahir
1988 "The Efficiency of Private Channels in the Distribution of Cereals in Burkina Faso." In *Production and Autonomy: Anthropological Studies and Critiques of Development,* edited by J. Bennett and J. Bowen. Monographs in Economic Anthropology, no. 5. Lanham, MD: University Press of America.
1989 "The Organization of the West African Grain Market." *American Anthropologist* 89 (1): 74–95.

Savanne, Marie Angelique
1982 "Another Development with Women." *Development Dialogue* 1 (2): 8–16.

Schildkrout, Enid
1978a *People of the Zongo: The Transformation of Ethnic Identities in Ghana.* Cambridge: Cambridge University Press.
1978b "Roles of Children in Urban Kano." In *Sex and Age as Principles of Social Differentiation,* edited by Jean LaFontaine. ASA Monograph, no. 17. London: Academic Press.
1982 "Dependence and Autonomy: The Economic Activities of Secluded Hausa Women in Kano, Nigeria." In *Women and Work in Africa,* edited by Edna Bay. Boulder, CO: Westview Press.

Schoepf, Brooke, and Walu Engundu with Diane Russell and Claude Schoepf
1991 "Women and Structural Adjustment in Zaire." In *Structural Adjustment and African Women Farmers,* edited by Christina Gladwin. Gainesville: University of Florida Press.

Schmidt, Elizabeth
1992 "Women's Grassroots Organization and Mobilization in the Guinean Nationalist Movement: Some Preliminary Reflections." Paper presented to African Studies Association meetings.

Schwimmer, Brian
1976 "The Social Organization of Marketing in a Southern Ghanaian Town." Ph.D. diss., Stanford University.

Scott, Alison MacEwan

1979 "Who Are the Self-Employed?" In *Casual Work and Poverty,* edited by Ray Bromley and Chris Gerry. New York: John Wiley.

1986 "Towards a Rethinking of Petty Commodity Production." *Social Analysis,* no. 20: 93–105.

Seidman, Gay

1984 "Women in Zimbabwe: Postindependence Struggles." *Feminist Studies* 10 (3): 419–40.

Seligmann, Linda J.

1989 "To Be in Between: The Cholas as Market Women." *Comparative Studies in Society and History* 31: 694–721.

Sen, Amartya

1981 *Poverty and Famines: An Essay in Entitlement and Deprivation.* New York: Oxford University Press.

Shack, William, and Elliott Skinner

1979 *Strangers in African Societies.* Berkeley: University of California Press.

Sherman, Jacqueline

1984 "Grain Markets and the Marketing Behavior of Farmers: A Case Study of Manga, Upper Volta. Ph.D. diss. University of Michigan.

Skinner, G. William

1964 "Marketing and Social Structure in Rural China, Part I." *Journal of Asian Studies* 24: 3–43.

1965a "Marketing and Social Structure in Rural China, Part II." *Journal of Asian Studies* 24: 195–228.

1965b "Marketing and Social Structure in Rural China, Part III." *Journal of Asian Studies* 24: 363–99.

1985 "Rural Marketing in China: Revival and Reappraisal." In *Markets and Marketing,* edited by Stuart Plattner. Monographs in Economic Anthropology, no. 4. Lanham, MD: University Press of America.

Smart, Alan

1988 "Resistance to Relocation by Shopkeepers in a Hong Kong Squatter Area." In Clark 1988.

Smart, Josephine

1988 "How to Survive in Illegal Street Hawking in Hong Kong." In *Traders Versus the State: Anthropological Approaches to Unofficial Economies,* edited by Gracia Clark. Boulder, CO: Westview Press.

Smith, Barbara

1983 "Introduction." In *Homegirls: A Black Feminist Anthology.* New York: Kitchen Table Press.

Smith, Barbara, and Beverly Smith

1981 "Across the Kitchen Table: A Sister to Sister Dialogue." In *This*

Bridge Called My Back, edited by Cherrie Moraga and Gloria Anzaldua. New York: Kitchen Table Press.

Smith, Carol

1972 "Market Articulation and Social Stratification in Western Guatemala." *FRI Studies* 11: 203.

1975 "Examining Stratification Systems Through Peasant Marketing Arrangements: An Application of Some Models from Economic Geography." *Man* 10: 95.

1979 "Beyond Dependency Theory: National and Regional Patterns of Underdevelopment in Guatemala." *American Ethnologist* 5: 574–617.

1984a "Local History in Global Context: Social and Economic Transitions in Western Guatemala." *Comparative Studies in Society and History* 26: 193–228.

1984b "Forms of Production in Practice: Fresh Approaches to Simple Commodity Production." *Journal of Peasant Studies* 11: 201–21.

1986 "Reconstructing the Elements of Petty Commodity Production." *Social Analysis* 20.

Spalter-Roth, Roberta M.

1988 "The Sexual Political Economy of Street Vending in Washington, DC." In Clark 1988.

Spradley, James

1970 *"You Owe Yourself a Drunk": An Ethnography of Urban Nomads.* Boston: Little Brown and Co.

Steady, Filomena Chioma

1981 *The Black Woman Cross-Culturally.* Cambridge: Schenkman.

Steel, William F., and Leila Webster

1990 "Small Enterprises in Ghana: Responses to Adjustment." Industry Series Paper, no. 33. Washington, DC: World Bank.

Stone, M. Priscilla

1988 "Women Doing Well: A Restudy of the Nigerian Kofyar." In *Research in Economic Anthropology,* vol. 10, edited by Barry Isaac. Greenwich: JAI Press.

Sudarkasa, Niara

1973 *Where Women Work: A Study of Yoruba Women in the Marketplace and in the Home.* Ann Arbor: University of Michigan Press.

1974 "Commercial Migration in West Africa, with Special reference to the Yoruba in Ghana." *African Urban Notes,* series B, no. 1.

1975 "The Economic Status of the Yoruba in Ghana before 1970." *The Nigerian Journal of Economic and Social Studies* 17, no. 1 (March).

1979 "From Stranger to 'Alien': The Sociopolitical History of the Nigerian Yoruba in Ghana, 1900 to 1970." In Shack and Skinner 1979.

Swetnam, John
1988 "Women and Markets: A Problem on the Assessment of Sexual Inequality." *Ethnology* 27 (4).

Szanton, Maria Christina
1972 *A Right to Survive: Subsistence Marketing in a Lowland Philippine Town.* University Park: Pennsylvania State University Press.

Tackie, Ebenezer
1990 Conversation with author, Kumasi, January.
1991 "Kumasi Central Market Study Final Report." Government of Ghana Ministry of Works and Housing Technical Services Centre, Accra.

Tashjian, Victoria
1992 " 'It's Mine' and 'It's Ours' Are Not the Same Thing: Changing Economic Relations Between Spouses in Asante." Paper presented to African Studies Association meetings.

Terray, Emmanuel
1979 "On Exploitation: Elements of an Autocritique." *Critique of Anthropology* 13–14: 29.

Thompson, C. T., and M. J. Huies
1968 "Peasant and Bazaar Marketing Systems as Distinct Types." *Anthropological Quarterly* 41: 218.

Tordoff, William
1965 *Asante Under the Prempehs: 1888–1935.* London: Oxford University Press.

Trager, Lillian
1976 "Yoruba Markets and Trade: Analysis of Spatial Structure and Social Organization in the Ijesaland Marketing System." Ph.D. diss., University of Washington.
1981a "Yoruba Market Organization: A Regional Analysis." *African Urban Studies* 10: 43–58.
1981b "Customers and Creditors: Variations in Economic Personalism in a Nigerian Marketing System." *Ethnology* 20 (2): 133–46.
1985 "From Yams to Beer in a Nigendu City: Expansion and Change in Informal Sector Trade Activity." In *Markets and Marketing,* edited by Stuart Plattner. Monographs in Economic Anthropology #4, Society of Economic Anthropology. Lanham, MD: University Press of America.
1990 "Market Associations in Ilesa: Internal Regulation and Response to Crisis Situation." In *Traders and Traders' Associations in Southwest Nigeria,* edited by LaRay Denzer and Glenn Webb. Nigeria: University of Ibadan.
1991 Conversation with the author, November.

Tripp, Aili Mari
1990 "The Informal Economy and the State in Tanzania." In

Perspectives on the Informal Economy, edited by M. Estellie Smith. Monographs in Economic Anthropology, no. 8. Lanham, MD: University Press of America.

Uchendu, Victor
1964 "Some Principles of Haggling in Peasant Markets." *Economic Development and Social Change* 16 (1967): 1.
1967 *The Igbo of Southeast Nigeria.* New York: Holt, Reinhart & Winston.

Vaughan, Megan
1987 *The Story of an African Famine.* Cambridge: Cambridge University Press.

Van Allen, Judith
1972 "Sitting on a Man." *Canadian Journal of African Studies* 6: 165.

Vercruissje, Emile
1972 "The Dynamics of Fanti Domestic Organization." The Hague: Institute for Social Studies. Occasional Paper no. 20.
1984 *The Penetration of Capitalism.* London: Zed Books.

Wallerstein, Immanuel
1974 *The Modern World System.* New York: Academic Press.
1976 "The Three Stages of African Involvement in the World Economy." In *Political Economy of Contemporary Africa,* edited by Peter Gutkind and Immanuel Wallerstein. Beverly Hills: Sage.
1979 *The Capitalist World-Economy.* Cambridge: Cambridge University Press.

Watts, Michael
1983 *Silent Violence: Food, Famine and Peasantry in Northern Nigeria.* Berkeley: University of California Press.
1987 "Brittle Trade: A Political Economy of Food Supply in Kano." In *Feeding African Cities,* edited by Jane Guyer. Manchester: International African Institute.

Weiner, Annette
1976 *Women of Value, Men of Renown.* Austin: University of Texas Press.

White, E. Frances
1982 "Women, Work and Ethnicity: The Sierra Leone Case." In *Women and Work in Africa,* edited by Edna Bay. Boulder, CO: Westview Press.

Wilk, Richard, and Robert Netting
1984 "Households: Changing Forms and Functions." In *Households: Comparative and Historical Studies of the Domestic Group,* edited by Robert Netting, R. Wilk, and E. Arnould. Berkeley: University of California Press.

Wilks, Ivor
1975 *Asante in the Nineteenth Century: The Structure and*

Evolution of a Political Order. Cambridge: Cambridge University Press.
1978 "Land, Labour and Capital in the Forest Kingdom of Asante: A Model of Early Change." In *The Evolution of Social Systems,* edited by J. Friedman and M. Rowlands. London: Duckworth.
1979 "The Gold Stool and the Elephant Tail: An Essay on Wealth in Asante." In *Research in Economic Anthropology,* vol. II, edited by George Dalton, pp. 1–36. Greenwich: JAI Press.

Williams, Gavin
1976 "There is No Theory of Petty-Bourgeois Politics." *Review of African Political Economy* 6.

Woodford-Berger, Prudence
1981 *Women in Houses: The Organization of Residence and Work in Rural Ghana.* Stockholm: Social Anthropology Institute.

Wolfson, Freda
1953 "A Price Agreement on the Gold Coast—The Krobo Oil Boycott, 1858–1866." *Economic History Review* 6 (1): 68–77.

Wright, Marcia
1982 "Justice, Women and the Social Order in Abercorn, Northeastern Rhodesia, 1897–1903." In *African Women and the Law: Historical Perspectives,* edited by Wright and Margaret Jean Hay. Boston University African Studies Center.

Yanagisako, Sylvia
1979 "Family and Household: The Analysis of Domestic Groups." *Annual Review of Anthropology* 8: 161–205.

Young, Iris
1980 "Socialist Feminism and the Limits of Dual System Theory." *Marxist Perspectives* (Spring).

Young, Kate, C. Wolkowitz, and R. McCullagh, eds.
1981 *Of Marriage and the Market.* London: CSE Books

Archival Sources

Asantehene's Record Office, Manhyia, Kumasi

ARO1: File No. 1499/2/38, Market Rules "Palaver Held at the Central Market—Kumasi on Sunday the 13th October, 1946." Reported by Nana Yaw Kwanteng, Omantihene (Item no. 5746); "Sale of Yams in the Central Market," letter to Otumfuo, Asantehene from Yusifu Gao, Gao Headman, Kumasi (Item no. 90).

Ghana National Archives, Accra

NAA1: No. 437/35. "Delegation of Financial Responsibility to Native Authorities," Commissioner, Central Province, to Colonial Secretary, 15/10/35.
NAA3: No. 3677. Transport of Foodstuffs. J. K. Sedodo to Secretary for Social Service, 9/8/43.

NAA6: No. 0028 SF8. "Irregularities in Import Control," motion by Hon. Dr. J. B. Danquah, 26/3/47.

Ghana National Archives, Kumasi

NAK1: No. 179, item 18. "Western Province, Ashanti, Half-Yearly Report, 1st April 1926 to 30th September 1926."

NAK2: No. 487, Trade Statistics and Kola, item 24. "Kola Production in Ashanti." District Commissioner, Goaso to Commissioner, Western Province, Ashanti, 13/2/24.

NAK3: No. 1136, Foodstuffs and Meat Regulation, item 63. Director of Agriculture to Chief Agricultural Officer, Kumasi, 2/9/41.

NAK4: No. 1125, item 18. "Kumasi Public Health Board, minutes of meeting on Wednesday, September 24, 1930."

NAK5: No. 1253, item 3. Superintending Sanitary Engineer, Accra to Director of Public Works, 1/7/14.

NAK6: No. 1315, Kumasi Town Council. "Changes Proposed by Superintending Sanitary Engineer on Visit to Kumasi, July, 1914."

NAK7: No. 1315, Kumasi Town Council, item 44. "Minutes of a Meeting of the Obuasi Sanitary Board Held on 18th July 1941."

NAK8: No. 2866, Kumasi Town Planning. Hawkers' Controllers to President, Kumasi Town Council, 6/4/51.

NAK9: No. 2513, Kumasi Public Health Board minutes, 16/11/26.

NAK10: No. 2626, item 32. Bakers (5 women) to Chief Commissioner, Ashanti, 27/4/31.

NAK11: No. 2878. Kumasi District Annual Report, 1949–50.

NAK13: No. 124, item 18. "Report for the Period 1st April 1935–31st March 1936," Ashanti Division, Department of Agriculture, 27/4/36.

INDEX

Abirempon (the wealthy), 12, 13, 87–89, 92
Abusua (matrilineage), 95–102, 108; *abusua panin* (male elder), 98–100; *obaa panin* (female elder), 98–101
accounts, 145–48, 179, 188
Accra (Ghana), 37–38, 51–53, 57–59, 62, 166, 233, 318, 415; demolition of Makola #1 market, 381–82, 388–89; regional dominance, 59, 226; traders from, 48, 68, 150, 186, 204, 213, 234, 266, 399, 421
accumulation. *See* capital
Acheampong, General, 377–80
Ada (Ghana), 227–28, 234
add-ons. *See* bargaining
Africanization, 115, 323
age, 103, 275, 279, 284, 353, 368–69, 378; elder status, 102–3, 106, 342; social, 19–21, 291–95
agents, 209, 319; buying, 91, 117, 193, 236
ahemma (pl.). See *ohemma*
Akan (ethnic group), 62, 83, 85–86, 88–89, 93, 97, 108, 122, 290–91, 400. *See also* ethnic groups: Akani, Akuapem, Asante, Brong, Fante
Akuffo, Lt. Col. F.W.K., 379, 381
Aliens Compliance Order (1969), 120–21
allocations: of goods, 58–59, 80, 238, 392, 416; of land, 99–101
ancestors, 98, 103, 105
apprenticeship, 192, 198
Armed Forces Revolutionary Council (AFRC), 380–88, 391
Asafo market (Kumasi), 53–54, 254
Asante, 1, 27, 33, 74, 82, 85, 87, 111, 235–36, 251, 316, 325, 402; Confederacy, 89–95, 375, 399; formation, 61–63, 83–85, 89–95, 375; norms, 33, 253, 291–92, 361, 371
Asantehemma, 267, 270
Asantehene, 63, 92–93, 96, 102, 108, 116, 121, 251, 267, 388
Ashanti Region, 1, 34, 37, 41, 45, 47, 56, 65–66, 114–15, 145, 163, 209, 297, 330, 409
Asomfo (court officials), 96, 115
assistants, 15, 58, 191–200, 287, 302
autonomy, 32, 89; of children, 337; of commodity group leaders, 248, 282; of traders, 37, 75, 82, 122, 127, 236–37, 246–47, 400, 402–4, 407, 418, 422, 425; of wives, 105, 339, 403

Bantama market (Kumasi), 53–54, 221
bargaining, 32, 128–40, 169; add-on, 131–33; conventions, 128–40, 159–60; group, 160; language of, 132, 140; price, 93, 132–40; quantity, 129–35, 137–38, 144, 201; style of Asante, 135
barter, 139–40, 218
Bawku (Ghana), 163, 231
Black feminism. *See* feminism
black market, 119, 139, 168, 390
blood, 97–98, 104
bode. *See* wholesale yards
Bolgatanga (Ghana), 41, 143, 209, 227, 234, 278, 322
border controls: Asante, 92–93, 100, 114–15; contemporary, 59–60, 391, 396, 423
bread, 139, 156
British, 62–63, 90; colonial government, 6, 74, 108–21, 187, 251, 323, 373, 419; commercial firms, 108–11, 236, 375, 419
Brong (ethnic group), 62, 97
Brong-Ahafo Region (Ghana), 34, 41, 45, 47–48, 56, 68, 90, 114, 235, 297, 317, 330
budget: household, 340–42; national, 395
bulking, 9, 44–46, 70, 133, 221, 416
Burkina Faso, 242, 244, 320
Busia, Dr. Koji, 120, 376–77
butchers, 258, 287
buying locations, 8–11, 141, 169; access to, 34, 52, 85, 172, 302

Cape Coast (Ghana), 67, 75, 249, 318
capital, 82, 169, 195, 241, 301–3, 397, 416–17; access to, 29, 89, 95–96, 166,

capital (*continued*)
172, 283, 379, 403–5, 416; accumulation of, 3, 12–13, 25, 33–34, 37, 76, 79, 90, 114–16, 126, 159, 171, 218, 239–46, 330, 402, 408, 416; control of, 86–87, 230, 406; entry-level, 7–8, 55, 182–87, 284, 287, 288, 407; dependency on, 239–41; losses of, 391, 400, 407, 420; working, 146, 149, 159, 240
caravans, 61–62, 89, 92–95, 235, 320, 400; routes, 83–85
carriers, 12n, 83, 85, 88, 90, 93, 133, 151–52, 206–7, 265, 359; groups, 225, 266
cash: advances, 137, 162–63, 177–78, 237; payments, 139, 174–82
cassava, 42, 143, 155, 174–75, 243, 348–49, 383; *ohemma,* 253; traders, 160, 174–75; wholesalers, 159–62, 174; wholesale yard for, 273
central place theory, 36–41, 46, 52, 66–67, 71, 415
ceremonies, 268–71; funerals, 269–70; market, 270–71
cheating, 87, 148, 210, 231
chiefs, 85–89, 91–95, 100, 109–11, 116–17, 121–22, 187, 188, 237, 250–51, 256, 267, 325, 400. See also *Asantehemma; Asantehene*
childcare, 55, 125, 186, 333, 357–62, 410, 418
child labor, 189–90, 194–97, 332, 363–67; and school, 197; and childcare, 361; cooking, 351–54; running errands, 55, 365, 367; trading, 13, 15, 140, 189–91, 195, 295, 299, 337
child support, 343
China, 232, 296, 412; silk from, 86
chits, 58–59, 188, 379
chop bars, 347–48
chop money, 106, 342, 344–46
city-states, 87–90, 110
civil service, 115, 123, 323, 372, 378, 396, 403
class, 27–29, 74–79, 81, 121–24, 166, 285, 303, 326, 419
cleanliness, 365, 374
clientship, 86, 217–18, 232, 235, 237, 246, 400
cloth, 47, 51, 58, 62, 110, 117, 119, 151, 162, 165, 236, 381, 407; *adinkra* funeral, 297, 382; heirloom, 100; *kente,* 92; traders, 83, 252, 254, 328, 408; units of sale, 134, 142; wax print, 86, 165, 377, 398
clothing, 47, 86, 102, 146, 164, 270, 342; secondhand, 46, 52, 135, 155, 195, 256, 324–25, 398, 407; retailers, 46, 57, 134, 143, 155, 195, 287; wholesalers, 155
coastal trade, 65–66, 85–89, 139, 235–36, 325; and ports, 37; and women traders, 43, 62, 252, 321
cocoa, 65, 99, 110, 115–21, 127, 165, 236–37, 323, 395, 420; boycott (1937–38), 117–18; farm caretakers, 44, 117; farming, 6, 76, 82, 95–96, 115, 117, 125, 316, 324, 380, 393–94, 417, 419; Marketing Board (CMB), 118, 166, 236, 317, 373, 393. *See also* protests
cocoyam, 91, 179, 253
colleagues, 216–28, 235–36, 246, 248
Collins, Patricia Hill, 27–28, 411–13
Committees for the Defense of the Revolution (CDCs), 392
commodity group leaders, 116, 120–21, 223, 225, 248–81, 413; destooling of, 251, 271, 274; elections of, 251, 274–79; functions of, 14, 16, 206, 252–57, 259–74; origins of, 239, 250; succession of, 251, 274–79. *See also* ohemma; *under specific commodities*
commodity groups, 71, 184, 216, 246–48, 250, 405, 408; dues, 271; ethnicity of, 243–44, 248, 250, 256–57; gender of, 248, 250, 253–59, 286–87, 425; formal, 174, 219–28; informal, 115–16, 219–28, 248, 319, 398, 408; membership in, 12, 287
competition, 52, 244–45
concentration, spatial, 66–68, 128, 213, 407; and demand, 43, 166–69, 193; and supply, 34, 166–69, 193, 238, 287
confidentiality, 181–82, 205–6
confiscations, 13, 52, 87, 164–65, 261, 282, 380–90
conquest (British), 63, 110, 187, 237, 264, 316, 325–26
consumers, 70, 131, 134, 154, 164–65, 173, 247, 378; cooperatives, 120, 377; rural, 46–47, 56–57, 59, 68, 91; urban, 9, 11, 32, 48, 51, 54–55, 59, 91
containers, 130–33, 142–44, 152
Convention People's Party (CPP), 253, 277, 376

cooked food, 135, 155–56, 221, 348–50, 370; sellers of, 7–8, 13, 47–48, 54–55, 141, 143, 154–55, 231, 240, 356–57
cooking, 344–57, 418
cooking oil, 131, 156
cooperatives, 59, 120, 218, 377
co-residence, 331, 335, 355, 366
corn (maize), 243–44, 395
corruption, 5, 119, 149, 372, 374, 379, 381
court system, chiefly, 206, 262
crafts: associations, 253, 268, 287; products, 8, 50–51, 86, 91–92, 162, 380; workers, 54, 87, 142, 154, 192, 257, 296, 319. *See also* shoes; tailors
credit, 37, 62, 109, 122, 160, 173–82, 213, 219–23, 240–44, 246, 324; as cash loans, 137, 174–76, 180–81; as capital advances, 110, 174–77, 181–82, 417; default on, 138, 175, 179, 273–74; as goods advances, 174–76, 237, 240; and groups, 219–23, 239–42, 246, 260; supplier, 85–86, 137, 148, 174–82, 230, 408; and terms of payment, 137, 176; terminology, 178–80
currency, 131, 139; exchange, 88, 272, 291, 379–80, 391
customers, 129, 216–18, 228–34, 239, 246, 260, 274–75, 396, 407

Danquah, J. B., 119, 376
daughters, 98, 197, 277, 287, 353
debt, 122; national, 397; personal, 147, 174–81, 206, 241–44, 260
December 31st Women's Movement, 401, 421
delivery date, 136–37
demolitions, 17, 111, 381–82, 388–90
dendritic network, 39, 57, 59, 67, 416
deregulation: of imports, 68, 169, 396, 407; of transport, 67, 396
descent, 98, 277
devaluation, 127, 312, 377, 407
dispersion, 59, 127; demand, 166–69; supply, 50, 166–69, 212
display, 140, 153–56
dispute settlement, 248–49, 254, 259–64, 279, 281, 408
division of labor: and commodity categories, 36, 227, 379; and cooperation, 192–93, 290; ethnic, 1, 24, 29, 85, 90–91, 114–16, 152, 257; by gender, 1, 24, 29, 80, 85, 88, 90–91, 94, 105, 114–16, 152, 199, 210, 236, 255–58, 285–91, 300, 316–26, 419
divorce, 101, 103, 106, 295, 338, 342–43, 366
domestic work, 23, 105, 169, 196–97, 198, 368, 418; cooking, 105, 344–57; cleaning, 105, 363–67; done by men, 291; labor shortage, 350–55; laundry, 105, 363–65; and trading, 368–71
domination, 32, 123, 127, 129, 248, 285, 403–5, 410, 413–14, 422–23; chiefly, 34, 85–89, 237; class, 110, 115, 121, 423; ethnic, 34, 74, 89, 120; gender, 34, 74, 110, 115, 120; of Kumasi Central Market, 36–37, 51, 54–55, 148–49, 214–15, 299, 414; racial, 34, 74; and regional position, 37, 68–70, 124, 166, 415; state, 374
drought, 242–43, 246, 393
duolocal residence, 105–6, 339–40, 344. *See also* marriage
Dutch traders, 62, 108; and "Dutch goods," 86
dwadifo. *See* marketers
dyadic relations, 216, 222, 230–31, 234–35, 239

economy of scale, 167–69
education, 115, 188, 304–9, 317, 372, 399, 404, 416; and capital, 308
eggplant. *See* garden-eggs
Ejura (Ghana), 41, 43, 48, 63, 114, 242
elders (*mpanyinfuo*), 16, 98–100, 103–4, 116, 173, 250, 255, 257, 272. *See also* *specific commodities*
elite, 60, 92, 96, 124, 285, 319, 378, 416; alliances with traders, 109, 308, 400; values, 188
Elmina (Ghana), 62, 82, 86–87, 108
employees. *See* labor
enterprise, size of, 2, 7, 396–97
errands. *See* child labor
essential commodities, 164–66, 381–82, 400
ethnic groups: Akani, 88; Akuapem, 97; Dagomba, 93; Dioula, 83; Fulani, 83; Gonja, 62, 93; Igbo, 88, 256, 291; Krobo, 109, 375; Yaounde, 246. *See also* Brong; Fante; Ga; Gaos; Hausa; Mossi; Yoruba
ethnicity, 27–28, 73, 75, 81, 122–24, 295–99, 410, 413–14, 416; and

ethnicity (*continued*)
commercial roles, 74, 87, 90; and marketplace system, 39, 71–72, 91, 126; and trading boundaries, 82–83, 88, 295, 316, 326–29, 372, 419; and trading institutions, 69, 283
Europeans, 62, 83, 87, 402; early trade, 85–88, 108–10, 139, 235; goods, 86–87
expulsion, 120–21, 123, 394, 420

factories, 37, 57–61, 69, 120–21, 150, 168, 238, 287, 308
family. *See* kin
famine, 3, 25–26, 29, 246, 394
Fante (ethnic group), 48, 62–63, 87, 104, 110, 236, 251, 298, 322, 375; employment in Kumasi, 115, 317–18, 323; women traders, 8, 67, 156, 237, 264, 317–18, 321
farmers, 55, 66, 101, 114, 120, 133, 136–39, 159, 163, 211–12, 219, 263–64, 325, 384, 397; and credit, 137–38, 223–24, 392; direct sales to consumer, 9, 37, 42–43, 50, 55–56, 67, 116, 388; and regional trade, 37, 60, 246, 416. *See also* cocoa
farmgate buying, 114, 138, 160, 169, 211–12, 415
fatherhood, 93, 102–3, 336, 366; *asomfo* pattern of, 96–97; and child support, 102–3; and education, 102, 306–7; *ntoro,* 102, 336
feminism, 79–82; African, 28; Black, 26–29, 81–82, 123; Marxist, 79–80; materialist, 80–81; radical, 81
firms, 57–58, 119, 127, 169, 173; expatriate, 63, 108–9, 116–19, 237, 287, 317–18, 325, 375, 395, 400, 419; export, 117–19, 236, 395
fish, 91, 102, 110, 116, 173, 356; dried, 62, 69, 91, 143, 156, 264; frozen, 53, 120; *ohemma,* 253; smoked, 8, 15, 47–48, 62, 80, 89, 91, 120, 153, 155–56, 168; traders, 8, 67, 80, 91, 151, 156, 173, 226, 237, 251, 253, 264, 298, 318, 320. *See also* State Fishing Corporation (SFC)
flexibility, 3, 68, 71, 153, 214, 246–47, 402, 406, 411–15; of marriage, 106
flour mills, 58, 150, 156, 166
food farming, 90, 95–96, 105, 163
food processing, 60, 152–56, 240, 419
food security, 3, 242–43, 393–95, 407, 424
foodstuffs, 88, 102, 114, 118, 130, 143, 162–64, 214, 380, 398, 400; farm produce, 7–9, 11, 14, 24, 42–48, 53, 62, 90–91, 105, 131, 153–56, 160; imports, 47, 57, 88; market distortions, 243–44; manufactures, 11, 47, 57–59; Northern, 47, 50, 114, 327; retailers, 7, 11–12, 15–16, 48, 53, 62, 209, 219, 254, 297, 319, 321, 350, 387, 407; shortages of, 383–90, 391–95; travelers, 42–45, 47, 50, 88; wholesalers, 8–10, 14–16, 51, 214
foreign exchange, 119, 127, 165, 312, 395–96, 400, 423
formal sector, 120, 247, 324, 379, 395–96
fostering, 197, 335, 354–55, 362, 366, 414
"French" traders, 8, 51, 53, 389
fufu, 348–49, 351–53, 356
funerals, 99, 103–4, 107, 179, 255, 349; market, 269–70

Ga (ethnic group), 80, 104, 321, 347, 410
game meat, 91, 321
Gaos (ethnic group), 116, 152, 264, 320, 328
garden-eggs, 11, 42, 45, 116, 133, 136–37, 144, 265
gari, 143, 156, 162, 243, 356, 394
gasoline shortage, 25, 150, 207, 291, 392
gender, 27–29, 73, 79–81, 122–24, 126, 284–91, 404–5, 407, 410–14; boundaries, 88, 94–95, 316, 328, 372, 414–17; construction of, 28–29; ideals, 6, 80, 95–96, 105–7; and marketplace system, 284; relations, 34, 75, 416; segregation, 62, 285–87, 290–91; and trading institutions, 69, 71–72, 283
Ghana Assembly of Women, 256
Ghana Food Distribution Corporation (GFDC), 119–21, 323, 377, 380, 420
Ghana National Trading Corporation, 323, 376
gifts, 103, 106, 132, 137, 139, 179, 195, 269–71, 287, 417; premortem, 181, 302, 334
gold, 61, 83, 86, 90, 395, 397, 420
Gold Coast, 63, 86, 108–10, 119, 236, 375

government (Ghana), 74, 173; attacks, 5, 32, 380–90, 396, 400, 402, 419; buying, 56, 117–21; demolitions, 17, 381–82, 388–90; intervention in market trading, 61, 74, 114–21, 207, 323–24, 329, 372–74, 380–99, 419–20; relations, 17, 122–23, 372
grain, 153, 155, 162; trading networks, 242, 320, 394; wholesaling, 52, 116
Guatemala, 39, 78, 413

Hausa (ethnic group), 83, 412; bargaining style, 135–36; *magasia* (leadership), 258; Sarkin, 250, 256–57; traders, 83, 120, 232, 296, 328
hawkers, 7–8, 11–13, 15, 34, 52, 54–55, 63, 112–13, 141, 154, 164–65, 280, 314
holidays, 9, 163–64, 270–71, 367
home-based work, 52, 165
homes, 37, 104
hometown, 287, 296–98, 303, 335
horizontal relations, 224, 227
hostility toward traders: government, 6, 61, 121, 123, 182, 328, 373–74, 388, 398, 404, 419; public, 129, 182, 296, 328, 388, 419
housecleaning campaign, 5, 70, 380–91
household, 101–6, 331–71, 418; characteristics of traders, 291–95; division of labor, 331–33
husbands, 41, 93, 96, 101, 103–6, 124, 233, 339, 355, 403, 419; travel, 210–11; as partners, 199–200; and occupation, 305

Ibadan (Nigeria), 52, 145, 251, 296
identities, 3, 26, 34, 61, 69, 124, 290; construction of, 26–29; gendered, 370; KCM women traders, 61–63; multiple, 27–29, 95, 124, 283–84, 327, 370, 402–3, 410, 423; and power, 28, 423. *See also* occupational identities
Igbo (ethnic group), 88, 256, 291
illegal activities, 16, 52, 127, 170, 249, 380; sales, 165–66, 168, 187, 204–5; supplies, 57–59, 164, 168, 188, 238, 377–79, 387
imports, 52, 57, 85–87, 109–11, 135, 162, 164–65, 214, 298, 391, 398; diversion of, 57, 164–66; farm inputs, 181; large firms, 57–59, 169, 229, 237, 278, 378; legal supplies of, 57–58, 164–65, 168–69, 416
India, 52, 86, 173, 256, 285, 296
individuation, 107–8
inflation, 5, 55, 117, 201, 391, 393, 407, 418
informal sector, 77, 395
information, 42, 52–53, 200–207, 213, 219–22, 405; credit, 205–6, 235; price, 8, 44, 134, 201–2; sharing, 36, 135, 203–7, 230–32; supply, 8, 59, 83, 170, 202–3, 220, 230, 414; visual, 17, 132, 165
inheritance, 181; gender bias, 196–97, 200, 278, 287, 334, 337–38, 404, 416–17; matrilineal, 96–101, 302, 343, 417
institutional buyers, 9, 15, 43, 58, 60, 230–31, 244
International Monetary Fund (IMF), 377, 390, 395, 420
investment, 172–73
Islam, 83, 85, 228, 268, 327; and education, 83–85, 188; Muslim traders, 256, 297, 320; restrictions on women, 54, 85
Ivory Coast, 83, 376

Java, 229, 231–32, 241
joking, 20, 198, 290, 345

Kejetia (Kumasi). *See* lorry park
kenkey, 48, 156, 356
kin, 91, 95–108, 122–24, 180–83, 204, 299–305, 330–36, 402–7, 410; as assistants, 193–94, 355, 361; as customers, 133, 233; kin-based trading groups, 193, 226, 299; matrilineal, 96, 124
Koforidua (Ghana). *See* lorry park
kola, 62, 83, 85, 90, 93; traders, 53, 192, 237, 253, 256, 264, 297, 320; wholesaling, 135, 153, 205
Kumasi: City Council (KCC), 184–87, 277, 388; city government, 63–64, 399; City Manager, 186; market rents, 17; Public Health Board (KPHB), 111–12, 251
Kumasi Central Market: description of, 6–17, 183–87, 200–201; history, 111–17, 251; and housecleaning campaign, 381–90; location, 3, 6–7, 29, 32, 34–41, 50–61, 148, 183, 405, 408, 414;

Kumasi Central Market (*continued*)
size, 3, 51–55; trading institutions, 127–71; and urban planning, 63–64. *See also* commodity groups; market buildings; wholesale yards

labor, 90, 122–23, 169, 196–98, 230, 331; access to, 29, 95, 115–16, 172–73, 192–200, 283, 370, 403–6; farm, 105, 181, 290, 410; process, 80, 122, 126, 348; unpaid domestic, 332, 410, 418. *See also* division of labor
land: access to, 115, 125, 317, 335, 338, 404, 425; allocation, 99–101
landlords, 69, 85, 87, 106, 122, 204; system of clientage, 235–37
land tenure, 99–101
languages, 188–89, 327, 399; Ga, 189; Hausa, 189; Northern, 44, 188–89; Portuguese, 86; Twi, 24, 188–89, 198, 228
Latin America, 217, 232, 241, 413, 418
leadership, 95, 192, 248, 250–59, 326
Lebanese, 111, 119–21, 237, 296, 322, 325, 328, 402, 411
licensing, 69–70, 86, 113–14, 119, 166, 188, 237, 373–74, 378, 392, 396, 400, 416
life cycle, 54–55, 291–95
Limann, Dr. Hilla, 279, 390
lineage, 93–104, 107–8, 122–23, 285, 416; inheritance, 96–104, 108; leadership, 90, 95, 100; obligations, 97–98, 179, 331, 334, 402–3
literacy, 147, 188, 207, 306–7, 316, 399
livestock, 47, 53, 66, 245, 253, 256–57, 264, 297–98, 320
location, 34, 48, 182, 402, 405; geographical, 6–13, 29, 34–35, 45, 51–57, 61–64, 375; and identity, 35–36, 246, 250; power of, 32, 35–41, 68–72, 172–73, 213; and trader categories, 6–7, 41
lorry-chasers, 14, 280
lorry drivers. *See* truck drivers
lorry park, 34, 43, 149–52, 384; Kejetia (Kumasi), 11–12, 14, 53, 56, 208, 211, 221, 245, 265; Koforidua (Ghana), 55, 211, 234, 249

maidservants, 321, 332, 354, 359–60, 362, 370
male traders, 6, 62, 115–16, 135, 176, 286–91, 334, 381–82, 417; Fante, 115, 235, 316; Northerners, 115, 235, 256, 264, 297, 321–22, 327
Mankessim (Ghana), 48, 95
manufactured goods, 11, 47, 91, 109, 118–20, 143–44, 298; retailers, 11, 321; shortages of, 58–59, 164–66, 238, 391; wholesalers, 52, 306–7
market buildings, 48, 111–12, 157–59, 183–85; construction, 45, 54, 64, 111–12, 152
Market Manager, 16, 186, 251, 253, 265, 267, 388
marketers (*dwadifo*), 43, 46
marketing networks: for crops, 42–47, 242
marketplace system, 37–39, 68–72, 115–16, 126–28, 172–73, 215, 238, 299, 316, 374, 383, 390, 394–96, 402, 406–7, 420, 424–26; Asante, 91–92, 235; barriers within, 169, 247, 419–20; collapse of, 388, 400; and KCM traders, 73, 244
Markets (foodstuffs): Makola #2 market, 226, 228; Malata market, 51
marriage, 95–97, 101–6, 122, 234, 291–92, 330–33, 338–48, 355, 370–71, 403–5, 407, 416–18, 422; *asomfo* pattern, 96–97; avoidance of, 32; church, 106; customary, 103–4; duolocal, 104–5, 339–40; retirement, 106; status of KCM traders, 291–92
matrilineage, 29, 95–102, 123, 303, 330–31, 402, 406, 417. See also *abusua*
matrix model, 27–28
mbode. See wholesale yards
metal goods, 86, 92
methodology, 17–26; archival, 17, 24, 111; interviews, 21–22; fieldwork, 97; participant observations, 17; oral history, 24, 89, 194; and theory, 20, 28–29; work histories, 302, 269. *See also* survey of Kumasi Central Market
migration, 34, 44, 83, 99–100, 115, 287, 336–37, 366, 394, 412; child, 289; remittances, 346
mixed retail areas, 11–12, 54–55, 280
modes of production, 29, 77–80, 123, 409–10; articulation, 69, 77–80, 121; capitalist, 75–79, 409; petty commodity, 78–79, 122, 124, 409–10

moneylenders, 179–80
monopolies, 55, 62–63, 149, 298, 373, 375; state distribution, 328, 395–96
Mossi (ethnic group), 231, 242, 320, 328
mothers, 95, 101, 196, 277, 300, 335–36, 339, 362, 368–69, 371, 410; education of, 306–7; occupation of, 300

National Liberation Movement (NLM), 277, 376
nationalists, 119–21, 375–80
negotiations, 248, 264–68, 281, 370, 405, 408; ethnic, 61, 264; gender, 265; government, 122–23, 251, 267–68, 282; occupational, 16, 61–62, 138–39, 211, 249, 254, 265–67
neighborhood markets, 11, 53–55; in relation to KCM, 54, 112
neighbors: at home, 197, 260, 360; at market, 12, 15, 135, 139, 193, 205, 220, 262, 272, 281
Niger, 158, 244
Nigeria, 45, 52, 76, 110, 205, 232, 244, 249, 251, 256, 332, 376, 379, 392, 394
Nkrumah period, 54, 119–21, 186, 278, 376
nkwansofo. See travelers
Northern Region (Ghana), 34, 41, 47–48, 213, 287, 321–22; Kumasi traders from, 44, 48, 297–98, 320
ntoro. See fatherhood
nutrition, 47, 163, 243, 356, 341, 394, 398

oaths, 262–63
occupational identities, 35, 123–25, 246, 250, 309–16, 419, 421–22; reasons for shifts in, 61–63, 295, 302, 311–13; stability, 310–11, 328–29, 402
Ohemma, 92–95, 98, 116, 224, 250–80, 319, 386; and crisis management, 272–74, 386. *See also* commodity group leaders; *specific commodities*
Ohene, 94, 98, 250, 256–57
onions, 47, 130; *ohemma,* 273; traders, 163, 230–31, 273
oranges, 9, 53, 133, 156; commodity group, 223; hawkers, 231; *ohemma,* 191, 253, 260–61; traders, 163, 260; wholesalers, 148, 260; wholesale yards, 159
palm nuts, 44–45, 348
palm oil, 44, 58, 60, 62, 86, 99, 375; as export, 110, 115, 236
palm wine, 88, 90
partners, 58, 127, 192, 227, 234, 286–87; husbands as, 199–200
passbooks, 109–10, 115, 229, 236–38, 245, 318, 407
patronage, 217, 232, 400
pawns, 93–94, 123, 180, 354
People's Defence Committees (PDCs), 392
People's National Party, 278–79, 390
periodic markets, 12, 23, 43–48, 51, 60, 68, 91, 114, 213, 242, 387, 415–16; village rings, 43–44, 162; transport, 44, 65–66, 167–68, 212
perishability, 70, 127, 136, 159–62, 164, 167, 170, 192
personalized ties, 44, 59, 171, 216–19, 235, 237, 376
Peru, 132, 141, 147–48, 153–54, 239, 251, 256, 285, 413
planning: economic, 25, 63, 395–401, 320; market, 52–53, 389–90
plantain, 91, 348–49, 383, 386, 394; *ohemma,* 253, 278; retailers, 154, 278; wholesalers, 161, 180
police, 372, 378, 388; market, 113
political alliances, 75–76, 79, 116, 121, 123, 277, 376–77, 399
politics: party, 121; and traders, 32
polygamy, 104, 106, 338, 342, 344
Portuguese traders, 62, 86
poultry, 9, 192; traders, 168, 192, 256–57, 320; Upper Region (Ghana), 168, 189, 256, 298, 320
pregnancy, 97, 295
prestige, 116, 285, 307, 413
price control, 58, 60, 116–19, 123, 164–66, 253, 266–67, 378, 392, 396, 400, 423; gender discrimination, 285, 329. *See also* housecleaning campaign
price fixing, 132; by traders, 130, 216; by government, 116–19, 207
price formation, 56
price reductions, 15–16, 136–37, 146, 176, 205
processed foods, 86, 154–55
processing, 60, 152–56
protests, 118, 121, 322; of KCM market women, 116–17, 186

Provincial National Defence Committee (PNDC), 390–95, 400

quality, 30, 130
queens. *See* ohemma; *specific commodities*
queuing, 291, 382

race, 27–29, 61, 71, 73, 79, 81, 108–9, 122–24, 126, 283, 286, 411–12
railroads, 63, 65–66, 70, 111–12, 150–51, 397, 415; mixed retail areas near, 11; villages near, 151
Rawlings, Flight Lieutenant J. J., 380, 388, 390–91, 395
reciprocity, 103, 179, 235, 290, 335–36, 341, 366; displaced, 341; terminology, 232
records, 146–48; "checkers," 148. *See also* accounts
regional periodic markets, 23, 43, 48–51, 60, 91, 114, 213, 242, 415
regional position, 48–51; of Kumasi Central Market, 36, 41, 62, 69, 296, 415
regulation, 69; by chief, 87, 95, 258, 325; by leader, 271–74; by state, 32, 62–63, 112–13, 127, 328, 380–401
relatives. *See* kin
reputation, 135, 176, 206, 231, 235, 238, 260, 262, 405
residence, 96, 104, 418; childhood, 287, 297; co-residence, 331, 335, 355, 366
retailers, 14, 50–57, 143, 152–54, 160–61, 202, 229–30, 240–41, 405, 408, 415. *See also specific commodities*
retail trading, 47, 55, 62, 130–34, 140, 169, 174–75
retirement, 192, 302, 341, 346. *See also* old age
risk, 175, 180, 219, 221, 229, 234, 338
roads, 66–68, 70, 322; building, 66, 113–14; rehabilitation, 67, 397, 415; trunk, 114, 397, 415
rubber, 90, 115, 236–37
rural markets, 47, 55, 88, 211, 386, 415

Salaga (Ghana), 41, 83
salt, 11, 46, 62, 83, 89, 102, 139
sanitation, 64, 111–13, 154, 187, 374
savannah trade network, 83–85
savings, 147, 314, 397; clubs, 194
seasonal variations, 42, 57, 127, 136–37, 158–59, 162–64, 170, 391; shortages, 25, 41, 137, 153, 229, 240, 388, 392, 408; spatial divisions, 16, 45
secrecy, 165, 180, 204
sex ratio: children, 295; traders, 1, 37–38, 254–57, 285–87
sexuality, 290, 338, 344–48, 354, 356, 378, 418
shea butter, 62, 298, 320, 327, 394
ship captains, 86–87, 235
shoes, 8, 57, 135, 143, 164, 257
siblings, 98–99, 101, 103, 107, 124, 309, 335–36; and childcare, 361
slavery, 86, 89–90, 92–95, 110, 122, 236; and accumulation, 93, 123
smuggling, 57, 59, 162, 166–69, 238, 373, 377–78, 423
snails, 62, 90–91; *ohemma*, 253, 258
social action, 4, 26–27, 32, 81, 310, 404–5, 418
soldiers, 116, 165, 381–90, 392
sorting, 152–55
Southern Region, 34, 43, 114, 126, 235; Kumasi traders from, 48; produce from, 53
space. *See* location
specialization: commodity, 48, 50, 90, 155, 283, 287, 298; farming, 47, 70; farms, 192; location, 6–7, 46–47
specialized retail areas, 7–8, 9–12, 71, 280
spoilage, 51, 144, 153, 156–59, 164, 420
stalls, 7–8, 36–37, 157–58, 182–87; allocation of, 185–87, 287; rents for, 54, 111, 186–87; rights to, 34, 182–83, 187, 302, 413; sharing of, 16, 46, 335
state. *See* government
State Fishing Corporation (SFC), 53, 58, 119–20, 168, 323
storage, 157–59, 162, 183
storekeepers, 120–21, 316, 319, 381
stores, 58–60, 70, 119–21, 137, 316, 322, 417; community shops, 392; department, 378, 421; managers, 308
streetside traders, 34, 54, 63, 112, 146, 154
Structural Adjustment Program (SAP), 25, 31, 67, 281, 309, 312, 324, 329, 342, 395–99, 402–3, 418–22
subsistence, 341, 393–94

suppliers, 114, 188, 228–30, 239–40, 396; and credit, 85–86, 137, 148, 174–82, 230, 407–8; institutional, 244
supply districts, 68, 114, 204, 223
supplyfo. *See* institutional buyers
survey of Kumasi Central Market, 23–24, 36–37, 76, 201, 300, 304, 336, 345, 427–29
survival, 3, 25–26, 33, 52, 70–71, 81, 126, 159, 171, 228, 239, 330, 372, 402, 408, 425–26; rural capacity for, 243
Syrians. *See* Lebanese

tailors, 193, 287
Takoradi (Ghana), 48, 58, 62, 67, 151, 376
Tamale (Ghana), 41, 68, 116, 322
taxation, 69, 89, 111, 187, 251–52, 373, 397, 421
Techiman (Ghana), 41, 45, 48, 50–51, 68, 83, 210, 213, 242
Tema (Ghana), 57–59, 68, 166, 168
terms of trade, 214, 244, 397
theft, 149, 158, 231, 383, 391, 420
time cycles, 13, 172; annual, 16, 45, 165; daily, 6, 14–16, 141, 174, 201–2, 370, 404; historical, 16–17, 404; weekly, 6, 46, 50–51
tomatoes, 42, 45, 47, 60, 91, 159–60, 163; elder, 16; *ohemma*, 228, 253, 278, 322; retailers, 11, 51, 130, 144, 154; Upper Region (Ghana), 168, 227, 322; wholesalers, 209, 227, 234, 298, 322; wholesale yards, 14–15, 159, 228
trade liberalization, 57, 169, 425
traders' association, 256, 399. *See also specific commodities*
training, 189–92, 308–9
transportation, 53, 58, 64–68, 70, 113–14, 148–52, 173, 207–14, 415; buses, 44, 67, 150; charges, 137–38, 149–52; shortages, 149, 162, 209–11, 214, 392
travelers (*nkwansofo*), 9, 12n, 14, 42–43, 47–51, 68, 114, 133, 138–39, 142–45, 149–51, 160–62, 202–4, 254, 350; and credit, 174–82, 222–24, 230, 240–41; and transport, 208–14. *See also specific commodities*
truck drivers, 113, 150, 209–11, 266–67, 321, 347–48
trucks, 8, 44, 56, 66, 159, 209–12, 387, 415; freight, 12n, 150, 209, 230, 396; passenger, 12, 12n, 149–51, 209, 387, 396

uncle (*wofa*), 101, 403
unions, 256, 392
United States, 119, 285, 392, 411
units of sale, 130–36, 140–45, 169; number, 131–33, 138, 143–44, 147; volume, 133–36, 142–45; weight, 140, 145
Upper Region (Ghana), 41, 48, 60, 163, 213, 235, 245, 256–57, 287, 394
Urban/rural relations, 30, 34, 57, 69–70, 124, 126, 243, 283, 327, 383, 392, 394, 396–97, 406, 413–16

vegetables. *See* farmers; foodstuffs; *specific commodities*
vertical relations, 230, 416
village markets. *See* periodic markets; rural markets
village-based traders, 56, 212, 319
villagers, 14, 19, 55–57, 59, 68, 133, 144, 167; as sellers, 55–56, 68
violence, 6, 71, 86, 113, 207, 243, 277, 383, 391, 400
Volta Region (Ghana), 144, 163
Volta River, 50, 66–67, 91, 227

wages, 117, 314, 323, 375, 395, 418
wage work, 79–80, 178, 195, 243, 314, 317, 323–24, 354, 373, 396–97, 407
watchmen, 148, 158, 273
wax prints (*ntama*), 86, 165, 377, 398
wealth, 3, 89, 123, 167, 324, 372, 404
Western models, 412; economic, 120, 409; family, 102, 334, 344, 360, 366, 368; groups, 258–59
wholesalers, 8–11, 14, 37, 42, 50–54, 59, 75–76, 116, 133, 137–43, 160, 179, 214, 222, 228–30, 232, 239–45, 350, 380, 405, 408, 414–15; and credit, 175–81; and information, 201–4; and supply, 244–45. *See also specific commodities*
wholesale units, 133, 140–47, 156, 169; replacement cost of, 146–47
wholesale yards (*mbode*), 42, 45, 48, 51–53, 68–69, 71, 141–43, 148, 158, 162, 209, 213, 219, 279, 384, 408; KCM *mbode*, 8–11, 14–15, 52–53, 56, 60, 70, 133, 136, 169, 184–85, 201–4, 211,

wholesale yards (*mbode*) (*continued*) 222, 228, 239–45, 273, 350, 358–59; origins of, 112, 251
wives, 96, 103–6, 305, 403, 419
World Bank, 395, 401, 423
world systems theory, 30, 37, 69, 78, 121, 124, 215, 396, 411
World War I, 323; import quotas, 111, 375; price control, 6, 111, 116, 164, 243, 375
World War II, 66, 114–15, 323; import quotas, 111, 251, 375; price control, 6, 111, 116–19, 375

yafunu, 98–101. *See also* matrilineage
yams, 153, 243, 348–49, 407; bargaining, 161, 202; *bayerehemma*, 253–54, 258, 266–67, 269, 270, 277; commodity group, 148, 219–25; elders, 255, 263–64, 266, 270; *ohemma*, 112, 224, 252, 266, 399; traders, 7, 116, 136, 145, 151, 155, 177, 254, 258, 264–67, 269–70, 279, 298; travelers, 42–43, 48, 138–39, 167, 177, 222–24, 235, 263–64, 269–72, 314, 321–22; wholesalers, 140–43, 219, 222; wholesale yard, 14, 53, 133, 143, 148, 206, 208, 224, 228, 262, 269–70, 384
Yeiji (Ghana), 41, 83
Yoruba (ethnic group), 120–21, 231, 256, 350–51; Awe (Nigeria), 175, 204; traders, 136, 225–26, 249, 291, 296, 322, 328, 412

Zaire, 164–65, 167, 181, 217, 232, 238–39, 249, 378–79
zoning, 52, 69–70, 373